Yair Burn
Yair
River Tweed
Faldonside
Hareshaw
Three Brethern
Cribs
Sunderlandhall
Peat Law
Bridgeheugh
Linglie
Nettly Burn
Long Philip Burn
Linglie Burn
Boundary 1535-1541
Broadmeadows
Manor Hill
Greenhead
Harehead
Bell Hill
Clarilaw
River Yarrow
Selkirk
Philiphaugh
Haining
River Ettrick
Selkirk Hill
Whitmuir
Howden
Hartwoodburn
Friarshaw
Green Hill
Clerklands

0   1   2   3 Miles

North

SELKIRKSHIRE
and THE BORDERS

SELKIRKSHIRE
and THE BORDERS

A PERSONAL VIEW OF THE
ARCHAEOLOGY AND HISTORY
AS SEEN BY
WALTER ELLIOT

SELKIRKSHIRE, BOOK ONE
From the Beginning of Time to AD *1603*

DEERPARK PRESS
MMIX

First published in 2009 by
DEERPARK PRESS LTD
The Henhouse
Hartwoodburn
Selkirk
TD7 5EY

Text copyright © Walter Elliot 2009

The moral right of Walter Elliot to be identified as the
author of this work has been asserted by him in accordance
with the Copyright, Designs and Patents Act 1988

ISBN: 978-0-9562907-0-0

BRITISH LIBRARY CATALOGUING-IN-PUBLICATION DATA
A catalogue record for this book is available from the British Library

DESIGN AND LAYOUT: Mark Blackadder

PRINTED AND BOUND: Worldprint, Hong Kong, China

Contents

Acknowledgements

T his book was written at the suggestion and insistence of my friend, editor and publisher, Alistair Moffat, whose Deerpark Press took responsibility for all the tasks of publication. Thankfully.

To Helen Darling at the Borders Archive at St Mary's Mill, Selkirk, many thanks. She has provided me with help, ideas and assistance over the years and a wide variety of books from all ages for this publication.

I owe a deep debt to Fiona Colton of the Borders Council Museum Service, Ian Brown of the Trimontium Trust and Jamie McIntyre of the Borders College Library for keeping my information correct, spelling right and punctuation in the proper places.

To Richard Strathie for the double task of keeping my computer working and for providing Air Photographs of sites which I knew were there but could not get convincing ground evidence for.

To the many others who have expanded my horizons by giving me their views, ideas and finds, have accepted or questioned my conclusions and generally provided intellectual stimulation. Foremost amongst them are Ian Brown, Billy Butler, Kay Callander, Jack and Caroline Cruickshank, Roger Elliot, Dr John Gilbert, Valerie Gillies, Donald Gordon, Dr Fraser Hunter, Ian W. Landles, Teresa Maley, Bruce and Walter Mason, Debbie Playfair, Scott Sibald, Paul and Brenda Smith, Robert B.K. Stevenson and Dr Peter Symms.

To Liz Hanson for one of her many brilliant photographs as the cover and Gordon Lockie for making me look quite respectable. To Tim Douglas for allowing quotes from his poem 'The Conservationist'. To Jim Lewis for drawing good maps from indifferent instructions. To Mark Blackadder for designing the book and making it eye-sweet. To Kate Blackadder for picking out all the inconsistencies in the text.

Preface

When Alistair Moffat first hinted that it would be a good idea if I wrote a history of my native town of Selkirk, I managed to turn the conversation round to another subject. The next time it came up, I had given it a little more thought but pointed out that Selkirk has probably more written history than any other Border burgh. This is no criticism of our neighbouring towns but rather an acknowledgement that Selkirk had been a place of some importance since the time when the early kings of Scotland had come to hunt in Ettrick Forest; and there had been the fortunate accident of having a large number of early documents preserved for posterity, together with enough enthusiastic local historians who were prepared to spend the time and effort in investigating and publishing them.

The doyen of these was Thomas Craig-Brown, a Selkirk mill-owner, whose *History of Selkirkshire or The Chronicles of Ettrick Forest* published in 1886, is a masterpiece of Victorian scholarship, based on meticulous research of all the then-known documentary evidence. This was, and is, the basis of any investigation of the history of the shire and town, and is widely used. However, as most surviving documents are about land transfers and disputes or crimes of theft and violence, it gives a somewhat one-sided look at the history of the period.

Robert Hall's *History of Galashiels*, published in 1898, is largely the seventeenth, eighteenth and nineteenth century development of that town. This was brought up to date in 1983 with *Galashiels, a Modern History* edited by Adam S. Grant.

Not to be outdone, Selkirk Council brought out a 208-page book, *The Flower of the Forest* in 1985. This was the product of an over-subscribed evening class on local history, where people with that interest were invited to give talks on their own subjects.

So I put my arguments that Selkirk did not REALLY need a new history.

Alistair did not agree, quoting the huge collection of documents of the Walter Mason Trust papers, the work done on the Selkirk Court Books by Dr Peter Symms, Dr John Gilbert's book *Hunting and Hunting Reserves in Medieval Scotland*, which contains many references to Ettrick Forest and the number of small booklets on specialist subjects, written by knowledgeable Souters, the name given to the people of Selkirk which owes its origins to the large number of shoemakers in the medieval burgh.

Eventually, I agreed to Alistair's request that I would write an updated history of Selkirk and the valleys. However, he had broadened his horizons during my swithering period, and had extended his projection to include the whole of Selkirkshire. He suggested a book of about 400 pages or 200,000 words. This turned out to be an underestimate.

One reservation was that the book was to be a reading book, rather than a reference book, although I hope it will be both. I was born in Selkirk and raised in the Ettrick Valley. After two years' National Service with the KOSB, the next thirty-three were spent as a fencing contractor and woodcutter, working throughout the Borders. I was often working in high places and hidden places. Here I was collecting, by osmosis rather than by conscious effort, the ridges and ditches of archaeological and historical sites which were unrecorded, and unlikely ever to be visited by an archaeologist or historian. In the Borders, archaeologists are a rare and reclusive breed, seldom seen, who only communicate with others of the same species and, because of a missing gene, seem to be unable to reply to letters. Woodcutters and fencers receive a very low rating in the academic world.

However, I had the benefit of the oral traditions which had been passed down through many generations of my family, and from old friends. I have been lucky in that the people I met, and worked with, were often the tradition-bearers/storytellers, have willingly shared their knowledge with me. My family had been at the top of Ettrick for seven generations and four generations before in Eskdalemuir, so we spread over a wide area and time.

This book is a chance to record some of the historical and archaeological sites that I have noted during my travels, and which remain unwritten until now. I intend this book to be a history which is factual, but interesting enough to be readable by the general public. I have reviewed the facts and figures from previous publications (with suitable ascription) and used published sources, for we cannot change the past although we might have to reassess it in light of more recent thinking (and hope that this time, we get it right). Archaeology is a study of the past through its known remains and the emphasis must be on 'known'. New information or finds can change the 'accepted truths' of the archaeological world completely.

Even with written history and eyewitnesses, there has to be some questioning of the account because everybody has their own prejudices, and these can show through in the works of even the most exacting historian, while one misreading of an early source can be quoted at length until it becomes 'fact'.

With the above in mind, I will use some of my own and other peoples' thoughts where they seem feasible, and put forward deductions of which I am convinced, and able to prove that conviction. If I have made a wrong deduction, and this can be proven by contemporary documents or recent finds, I will concede that I am wrong.

Although this set out to be a book on Selkirkshire, it is written in two parts. Book One starts at the very beginning of the world, leading through the first human settlement in the Borders, the Bronze and Iron Ages, Romans, Dark Ages, Early Christianity, and so on up to the Union of the Crowns in 1603. In this part, Selkirkshire appears only where there is relevant information.

In Book Two, the situation is reversed with Selkirkshire being the main subject with the general Borders and rest of the world mentioned only when required.

I do not claim that this is the last word on the history of Selkirkshire. It is just the perceived history up to the present time and with the present knowledge; all mistakes are my own and I will do better next time.

WALTER ELLIOT, *October 2009*

SELKIRKSHIRE
in the Wider Context of
THE BORDERS

CHAPTER ONE
Description of the County

I t is unwise to look on Selkirkshire as an entity, a complete unit in its own right. It is an integral part of the River Tweed Basin catchment area and as such, Selkirkshire is part of the wider sphere of Borders geology, archaeology and history.

The area known as 'the Borders' is formed by the basin of the River Tweed which flows to the east from the great horseshoe shape of higher ground on the north, west and south, while the Liddell valley points an unruly finger in between Dumfriesshire and England and flows into the Solway.

There is a historical reason for this seeming aberration. In medieval times, both sides of the border were divided into three Marches, East, Middle and West, and a Warden was appointed to keep the peace in his March. This was not an easy task for anybody, and it was usually the roughest, most devious landowning ruffian with the greatest following who was selected to keep the reiving families in some semblance of order. On the Scots side of the Border, the West March was most often held by a Johnstone or Maxwell, the Middle March by a Scott or a Kerr, and the East March by a Ker or a Hume. With few exceptions the Wardens made the most of the near legitimacy of their office to pursue family feuds on both sides of the Border, help their friends and cast down their enemies.

Liddesdale was the territory of the Armstrongs and the Elliots whose followers included some minor named families, and the valley was so lawless that none of the Wardens would have it within their March. So a Keeper of Liddesdale was selected and his sole task was simply to keep the peace within that valley, a thankless and often impossible duty.

> This is the reason why Roxburghshire includes the Liddell Water that
> flows into the Solway Firth, and extends to Kershopefoot where the
> Warden of the Marches would meet on Days of Truce to try to settle differ-
> ences by peaceful means. Nearby is 'the Debatable Lands' which was
> claimed by Scotland and England as well as several families from both
> sides of the Border. Even today there is some doubt about the ownership.

Together the four shires of Berwickshire, Peeblesshire, Selkirkshire and
Roxburghshire form an entity within the barriers of hills and sea, so the
story of Selkirkshire relies on what was happening in the other three
shires for examples and elucidation. As the story unfolds, more information on Selkirkshire is available and reference to the three others
diminishes.

Selkirkshire is a comparatively small area of the country and
virtually at the centre of the part of Northern Britain that lies between
the two Roman Walls. The whole of the county is high-lying and much
of it is reckoned to be mountainous with the lowest point just below
Galashiels at 300ft and the highest, the top of the Broad Law, at 2,754ft
above sea level. Most of this is moorland pasture above 1,500ft, and there
is little arable land above 1,000ft.

Its total area at present is 173.006 acres or 270.3 square miles. It has
not always been this size because various landowners and local
government boundary commissions have added to and subtracted from
the County of Selkirkshire.

The medieval boundaries almost coincided with the boundary
lands of the Ettrick Forest together with the Selkirk Common Lands,
but since then bits have been chopped off and added on at will. The
1891 Boundary Commission sealed the county in its present shape,
taking away three portions of land from Peeblesshire, giving Meggetdale
back and two portions from Roxburghshire but returning Ashkirk
Parish back to Selkirkshire.

In the Report of the Royal Commission on the Ancient
Monuments of Selkirkshire published in 1957, the following opinion
was given. 'Selkirkshire is small in area and nature and history have
combined to render it poor in remains of ancient monuments. The

results of our survey have consequently been disappointing when compared with those obtained in the adjoining County of Roxburghshire, covered by our Fourteenth Report. Selkirkshire contains only one medieval building of any moment and its later architecture is undistinguished; the most interesting monuments are the Roman works at Oakwood whose existence was quite unsuspected before their discovery on an air-photograph by one of our officers, the Early Christian carving and inscription, and a series of small towers dating from about the early sixteenth century which reflect contemporary social change just as do the Georgian country-houses.'

In fairness to the Commissioners, it should be noted that their remit was to report on the 'contemporary culture, civilisation and conditions of life of the people of Scotland from the earliest times to the year 1707'. So their concentration was focused on the visible remains 'which seemed most worthy of preservation'.

Since the end of their remit period, there has been three hundred years of change and development in the Borders; since the publication of the Report fifty years ago, much new information has been added to the story of Selkirkshire through new discoveries by chance or design and the modern dating techniques like pollen analysis, dendrochronology and carbon14 sciences. Additionally, there has been more interest in the history and archaeology of the Borders and, equally important, a number of knowledgeable people who have had the time and expertise to devote themselves to study their particular interest.

It must be remembered that the Borders as we know it today, is basically a visual record of the changes made over these last three hundred years and more especially over the last hundred years. These are worth recording now while we still remember them or have heard them from our grannies. In fact, I am starting the history of Selkirkshire:

Fer back frae the stert o aa time,
There was naething at aa boot the place
Bit a jorum o slaister an slime
Whurlen around oot in space.

I intend to start the story with how geology affects the development of the natural history; how the plants and animals colonised the area, followed by the first humans; and thereafter how these humans developed and left traces of their occupation on the landscape. Geology affects our living places up to the present day and will continue to do so, in all future time.

To get a wider view of how Selkirkshire developed, the first part of the book takes a parallel look at what happened within the Tweed Valley basin since the dawn of time.

Chapter Two
The Man Who Defined Time

The concept of time has long been of importance to the human race. 'How old is the world?' 'How long is time?' are questions which must have been asked by thinkers from all periods and in every part of the globe.

It was a Berwickshire farmer who first put forward enough convincing proof that the world was many millions of years old, and had the courage of his convictions to prove and publish his theory.

James Hutton was born in Edinburgh in 1726, the son of a well-to-do merchant. He was one of those men who had an insatiable curiosity about the world around him.

As a boy, he went to the High School where he was fascinated with chemistry and then to Edinburgh University as a medical student, since medicine was the only profession in which chemistry played a major part. He spent two years in Paris studying chemistry and anatomy, returning to Edinburgh University for a further two years. He graduated in medicine but never practised as a doctor. In later life, he remarked that 'the more medical knowledge we acquire, the more we know how little efficacious that art is'.

During his student period, Hutton, together with a fellow student John Davie, experimented with the use of soot to produced salammoniac, a flux used in metallurgy to join two metals together. On the strength of this success, they established a chemical works that made both partners wealthy.

An unhappy love affair produced an illegitimate son and Hutton may have found it expedient to leave Edinburgh for some time. With no need to earn money and no desire to be a doctor, Hutton turned his far-ranging mind to agricultural improvement. He was already a small landowner, having inherited two farms in the Borders, Slighhouses, a

140-acre farm near Duns, and the hill farm of Nether Monynut on the edge of the Lammermuirs, both were suffering badly from neglect.

This was the period when the fashion for agricultural improvement was at its height. Many of the early 'improvers' were estate owners, anxious to increase the products of their estates for prestige as well as monetary reward and this 'respectability' encouraged smaller landowners and tenant farmers to increase the productivity of their land for more mundane commercial reasons.

Never one to do things by half, Hutton set about acquiring knowledge about his new interest. He spent the next two years travelling through England, especially the rich farmlands of East Anglia, observing improved methods of farming and journeying into parts of France and the Low Countries on the same quest. To amuse himself on his travels, he would study the surface of the earth 'looking with an anxious curiosity into every pit or ditch or bed of a river that fell in my way'.

During the two years that he travelled round England and the Continent, he had set out with the primary intention of studying farming methods, but at the same time almost unconsciously, was observing how the earth was formed in different parts of the country; in other words, 'geology', although that term would not come into use for some years later. At this period of his life, he looked on 'minerology' as an amusing hobby.

Returning to Scotland at the age of twenty-eight, Hutton ignored the fleshpots and possible embarrassments of Edinburgh, settling in the much-neglected farm of Slighhouses in 1754. He was to spend the next thirteen years there, restoring heart to the land by experimenting with ploughs and ploughing, changing crop rotations and studying plant diseases, types of fertiliser, the relationship between temperature and latitude, conditions of plant growth and diseases in trees. There seemed to be no variety of agricultural activity that did not take his active interest.

His handwritten account on 'The Elements of Agriculture' was started in the 1750s, and he was still adding to it when he died. It is nearly 1,100 pages and was obviously intended to be longer as the final chapter stops halfway through a discussion on potatoes.

His time at Slighhouses was spent in experiment, observation and study of the land and this was the basis of his achievements in modernising agriculture. At the same time, he was working on a theory that the world had to be much older than the Biblical conception of time.

Hutton was not simply a brilliant and innovative farmer, tied to his farms. He moved round the country and frequently travelled between Slighhouses and Edinburgh for the intellectual stimulation his active mind required. He eventually returned to live in the capital in 1767 and had his main residence there until his death in 1797.

This was a period when there was an intense intellectual and experimental activity in the central belt of Scotland. It was one of the most creative periods of Scottish history, a flowering of scientific, economic, philosophical new thinking and discoveries in science that was later to become known as 'the Scottish Enlightenment'.

Within the small and cramped Old Town of Edinburgh, Hutton could meet and converse with such influential original thinkers as Adam Smith, economist; David Hume, philosopher; Joseph Black, chemist; Robert and James Adam, architects James Watt, inventor; Adam Ferguson, sociologist; Hugh Blair, literary linguist; William Cullen, a specialist in clinical medicine, and others whose specialist skills and novel ideas which were to change many aspects of life throughout the world.

It was with but little exaggeration that Mr Amyat, the King's Chemist, 'a most sensible and agreeable English gentleman' who had spent two years in Edinburgh could observe 'Here I stand at what is called the Cross of Edinburgh and can, in a few minutes, take fifty men of genius and learning by the hand'.

By the early 1760s, Hutton had finished most of the hard physical work of turning his farm at Slighhouses into a model of excellence for the region and could utilise more of his spare time in the study of mineralogy (geology).

Over years of study, Hutton's curiosity was roused by the fact that many of the rocks he saw, had been formed from the debris from other older rocks, and this was eventually to give rise to his cyclic 'Theory of the Earth'. At Slighhouses, he first deduced that erosion was an important part of a cycle whereby the earth renewed itself. He knew that if soil was being continuously stripped from the land, within many centuries there would be none left on the surface of the earth – and soil was essential to sustain plant and animal life on earth.

In simple terms, Hutton's theory was that the earth was constantly restoring itself in a cycle lasting many millions of years. Through rains and wind, soil, itself the grains of eroded rock, was deposited as sediment on the sea floor and these, through time, were pressed into layers of rock; then movement in the central core of the world caused parts of the rock formation to rise above the surface of the sea. This formed new land masses which were in turn eroded by rain and other natural forces and thus completed the cycle.

Hutton hypothesised that this process could have happened twelve times over uncountable millions of years of the world's existence, and that 'the present continents are composed from waste of more ancient land, so from the destruction of them, future continents may be destined to rise'. He saw no conclusion to this cycle, 'We find no vestige of a beginning – no prospect of an end'.

It was on the 7th of March 1785 that Hutton was to address his intellectual peers, the Fellows of the Royal Society of Edinburgh, for although he had long discussed his theories with many, he had never published his conclusions. It was with great anticipation that at least fifty of the most learned men in the country assembled to hear the 'famous fossil collector' present his long-awaited 'Theory of the Earth'. Unfortunately Hutton was ill and not able to deliver his own conclusions on earth science. Instead, these were given by his friend, Professor Joseph Black, the most eminent experimental chemist of his day. On 4 April, Hutton was well enough to give the concluding part of his theory. It is recorded that he gave his lecture in a broad Scots accent– an obvious failure on the part of the High School which was intent on removing all 'Scotticisms' from its pupils' speech.

Hutton's Theory was greeted with much scepticism and his views were criticised on both scientific and religious grounds. Even his intellectual friends were sceptical. Although Hutton was well respected for his achievements in agriculture and mineralogy, he had never held a professorship or any post in academic life. Scots at this period, had a reverence of learning and Hutton was an amateur, although only an amateur in the true sense of the word, a lover of his subject. But nothing unites the professional classes so much as an amateur with convictions.

So his scientific conclusions were given the Scots verdict of 'Not Proven' even amongst those who respected him as a scientist and as a man.

PRE-HUTTON THINKING

Before looking at the mountain which Hutton had to climb to get his Theory even considered, let alone accepted, it is worth taking a short look at how religious thinking has shaped the world.

In primitive societies, the leader of the group was seldom the most powerful warrior but rather the person who had the most knowledge, the shaman or witchdoctor, and this person could be either male or female. In fact, the most powerful early deity was female, a Mother Goddess representing fertility and fecundity.

In time, the shaman became the priest of whatever god, goddess, spirit or object was worshipped and whose influence over the rest of the group was paramount, for they were seen as the interpreter of that god's wishes. This was the start of religion.

When the population of the earth increased, so did the number of believers in a variety of religions. As religions became more organised and powerful, so did the power of their priests who, as representatives of a heavenly or earthly god, were endowed with an influence super-seding that of temporal rulers. Competing religions and quarrelling sects within the same religion, made for uneasy neighbours and centuries of bloody battles ensued, as it does to this day. It is ironic that the followers of each god have to prove that their god is best by killing those whose faith is slightly different.

The advent of writing made it easier for religions to spread their message, for one man or body of men, could now send their thoughts or commands throughout the land without having to be there in person. It was an age when few could read or write, so the priests who could, formed a special elite, able to communicate directly with God through His Holy Word and interpret His wishes.

Each religion had its own Holy Book that was infallible, and had to be obeyed in every detail, and each had its own version of the creation of the earth.

For Christians of all denominations, that book was the Holy Bible. It was used by many generations as an exemplar on how to live a good life and be rewarded in heaven; live a bad life by being disobedient or unbelieving/questioning the Gospel, and you were condemned to spend an eternity in hell. The carrot of reward and the stick of punishment kept large numbers of believers under the control of an elite at the head of the Church. This is not unique to one religion but is common in most.

But the Christian Bible is not a single book but rather a compilation made from many different sources. The Old Testament is a history of the Jews in a compilation of Jewish sacred writings, originally in Hebrew, telling of the Jewish experience of their God. The New Testament comprises a diversity of literary forms from the early Christian period – letters from the Apostle Paul, historical chapters and the four books of the Apostles which are remembrances of the acts and sayings of Jesus, made to strengthen the faith of his followers. The New Testament was not given its complete form until *c.*382 AD.

During the Early Historic and medieval period, various gospels and parts of the Bible were transcribed into all the European languages. Learned medieval clerics had picked through the Bible and Hebrew prophesies to calculate that the Creation had happened around 5,500 years before.

The Bible was a comforting book, providing all the answers to the problems of mankind. There were some queries that it answered with ease. To explain the finding of sea shells in land hundreds of feet above sea level, the logical explanation was that when Noah's Flood receded, it let the land dry out and able to be resettled by human survivors. For in the Bible, God said 'Let waters under heaven be gathered together in one place and let dry land appear'; so it must be true and also fitted in with the accepted Creation dating quite well.

Reverence given to the Bible prevented any departure from the accepted truth. Any who questioned this were literally playing with fire, the real fire of a heretic's pyre as well as the fire of controversy.

When Nicolaus Copernicus, a Catholic priest living in Prussia, questioned St Thomas Aquinas' statement that the earth was the centre of the universe, he waited until he was on his deathbed before publishing his conclusions that the earth moved round the sun.

Ninety years after Copernicus' death, the Italian mathematician Galileo published an endorsement of his theory. For this, he was placed under house arrest by the Inquisition.

Although many scholars had developed hypotheses about the age of the earth, they never questioned the Biblical dating of around 4000 BC as given by the Church's teachings.

When Martin Luther launched the Protestant Reformation in 1517, he was vehement in his belief that the Bible was the Word of God and its contents had to be interpreted literally. He was the first reformer with access to a printing press, so his printed words were quickly distributed throughout Europe. Writing in 1541, he had calculated that the Creation had occurred in 3961 BC. Later chronologists would follow Luther's lead and set the beginning of the earth around 4000 BC.

Over a century later, James Ussher, Archbishop of Armagh, a distinguished scholar and biblical chronologist who had spent two decades studying all the evidence, came to the conclusion that the world was created on the 23rd of October 4004 BC at 'the sensible time of 9am'. Was he kidding? – probably not.

The Authorised Version of the Bible commissioned by King James VI and I in 1604, has the title '*The Holy Bible* containing the Old and New Testaments, Translated out of the original tongues: and with the former translations diligently compared and revised, by His Majesty's Special Command'. This commission required a panel of fifty-four scholars to produce the finished article in 1611. By its superior quality, it replaced all the many previous versions and for 250 years was the only one used.

Since Ussher's chronological conclusions were printed in the page margins of the Authorised Bibles, they were viewed as the same infallible truth as the Holy Writ and were accepted as truth for several generations. Despite being a noted historian in many other ways, Ussher is now remembered and ridiculed for his Creation dating.

Ussher's dating was accepted without question, not only by believers but also by men of science who conceded that the earth was young in comparative terms. Even Isaac Newton, the most famous scientist and thinker of his day, completed a formal calculation of the earth's age just before he died in 1727 and confirmed that the Biblical scholars were indeed right.

HUTTON'S PROOFS

Although Hutton's Theory was given some consideration by his learned compatriots before the verdict of 'Not Proven' was returned, on the religious side the verdict was unanimously 'Guilty'. He had denied the Biblical Creation, the account of the Flood and more importantly placed humans at the very end of the earth's existence rather than at the start of its being. He was challenging the truth of the Bible, and was condemned by all right-thinking shades of Christian belief – possibly the only time they had ever been united in a common cause before or since.

Although he was a deist, believing that there was a creator Deity, Hutton could not accept the Biblical version of Noah's Flood when the waters drained away to allow firm land to emerge. He believed that the opposite was true and instead of the water going down, the submerged land rose up. Hutton was one of the first to recognise that the fierce heat far below the surface of the earth which caused volcanoes, was also responsible for pushing long-submerged landmasses upwards. Additionally, these same elemental forces were responsible for the differences in the rock strata and the angles at which they could be seen to join together. But Hutton had to find incontrovertible proof that his Theory was correct.

In 1787 while on a visit to a friend near Jedburgh, Hutton made a dramatic discovery. At Allars Mill near the Abbey, he noticed an unusual formation in a cliff at the side of the Jed Water. There, a rock-face with horizontal layers of red sandstone was lying on top of vertical layers of the grey rock called greywacke, and between them was a layer of crushed rock conglomerate which had been derived from the top of the lower vertical layers.

Here was his proof. He worked it out that at some period, sand and mud had been compacted in rock-forming layers lying horizontally on the floor of the ocean; a powerful force had pushed the strata upwards until it stood vertically; erosion had ground down the tops of the vertical columns and then this had sunk below sea level again. Further erosion from land-based rocks deposited more layers, this time of red sandstone on the undersea vertical rocks; and finally the whole was raised above sea level again. It had taken more erosion, this time from the River Jed, to leave the cliff-face visible to prove Hutton's theory. As this did not fit into the usual rock strata, he gave it the name of an 'unconformity' because it did not conform to the more general rock patterns.

With the bit now firmly between his teeth, Hutton set about convincing his friendly sceptics. In the following year, he invited two of his half-convinced doubters to view the rock exposure on the battered cliffs on the Berwickshire coast. One was John Playfair, Professor of Mathematics at Edinburgh University and considered one of the cleverest men in Scotland; the other was Sir James Hall, a rich local landowner and accomplished scientific observer and experimenter in his own right.

They could have walked round the coastal path but decided to sail round so that they would be able to view the cliffs more easily. Sir James supplied the boat and crew.

At Siccar Point, they landed to view the unusual rock formation. Hutton was ecstatic, an 'unconformity' showing even better proof than that at Jedburgh; the situation was a classroom of geology. He explained that the now vertical layer of grey-coloured rock had once been laid down in horizontal deposits at the bottom of an ocean, but had been pushed into the vertical position by undersea forces of incredible power, and how other rock layers had been folded over, through and above, sealing the rock in the patterns which could be seen there. Playfair and Hall were totally convinced and thereafter supported Hutton's 'Theory of the Earth' up to and after his death.

Playfair would later recall the moment at Siccar Point. 'We felt ourselves carried back to the time when the schistus on which we stood was yet at the bottom of the sea, and when the sandstone before us was only beginning to be deposited in the shape of sand or mud, from the waters of a super-incumbent ocean. An epocha still more remote presented itself, when even the most ancient of the rocks instead of standing upright in vertical beds, lay in horizontal planes at the bottom of the sea, and was not yet disturbed by that immeasurable force which has burst asunder the solid pavement of the globe. Revolutions still more remote appeared in the distance of this extraordinary perspective. The mind seemed to grow giddy by looking so far into the abyss of time.'

After their Siccar Point conversions, Playfair and Hall became fierce supporters of the correctness of Hutton's 'Theory of The Earth' and defended it, often to the detriment of their own careers.

But this made little difference with the religious leaders and teachers who condemned Hutton as wrong and blasphemous while many men of science refuted his arguments, suggesting that he was totally wrong and probably mad.

Even with Black, Playfair and Hall arguing his corner it was a long time after his death that his 'Theory of the Earth' gradually became accepted by geologists who accepted the truth of it and expanded the theory by their own studies. Even at third hand, Hutton's theory was encouraging new ideas and discoveries.

In the 1788 publication of *The Theory of the Earth*, Hutton describes the Borders as 'the most important geological site in the world'. At his time and with his knowledge, this statement was correct. It was a lucky chance that a man who had the time, money, ability and determination to pursue a conviction, was living in a place where geological strata from ancient times were so visibly mixed in the rock formations.

In the post-Hutton period, much of the research into the sequence and aging of rocks has been worked out in the Borders. Early work on fossil beds by James Nichol of Traquair came from his discovery of graptolites, a primitive fossil grouping, at Grieston Quarry in the 1840s. Sir James Hall of Dunglass experimented with the Wrae limestones in the Broughton area.

Nor was the publication of new theories and ideas lagging behind.

In the 1840s, Robert Chambers of Peebles had written a book called *The Vestiges of the Natural History of Creation* suggesting that although there was a creative God, he worked through natural selection of the species over a long time to accomplish his designs.

Chambers was a partner of the publishing firm of W&R Chambers, a Fellow of the Royal Society of Edinburgh and a well-known figure in the city. Knowing that his conclusions would upset the 'hosts of the righteous in the city', he published the book anonymously. There may have been a commercial reason for this as the greatest print runs of the firm of W&R Chambers were for the Holy Bible.

For whatever reason, Robert Chambers took great care to keep his authorship secret.

He had the entire text copied by his wife in case anyone recognised his well-known handwriting. This copy was sent to Alexander Ireland in Manchester, who then sent the text to John Churchill in London. The proofs were returned by the same circuitous route and the corrected proofs sent back to London. *The Vestiges of the Natural History of Creation* was published in 1844 and was slated by all manner of critics up to Prince Albert himself. As Charles Darwin was later to remark to his publisher, John Murray, 'I suppose that abuse is as good as praise for selling a book'.

Vestiges went through four editions in six months, ten editions in ten years, sold 24,000 copies and was translated twice into German and once into Dutch. It was only in the twelfth edition in 1884, thirteen years after Robert Chambers' death, that his authorship was acknowledged.

The publication of *Vestiges* somewhat upset the plans of Charles Darwin who had been working on a similar proposition since 1842. It made him more cautious about rushing into print with his essay on 'Evolution by Natural Selection' and upsetting all and sundry. So he delayed publication of his theory and carefully checked his facts against all existing knowledge. He spent nearly twenty years collecting and marshalling evidence before publishing *Origin of the Species* in 1859.

The outcry and condemnation from theologians and academics was just as severe as that which had greeted Hutton and the anonymous Chambers.

But there was still much to be learned from the rocks of the Borders. In the 1870 and 80s Charles Lapworth, a Galashiels schoolteacher, pioneered the sequence of graptolites in the rock of Dob's Linn in Moffatdale, as the dating sequence for the Ordovician and Silurian rocks which covered a period of around one hundred million years. His work made the rocks of Dob's Linn a site of interest throughout the geological world.

A booklet by John Pringle of Selkirk told *The Story Of Boulder Clay*, proving the effects of glacial movement from the Ice Age deposits round his home town.

In the Victorian world, the Borders were temporary hotbeds of geological interest. In the manner of the times, Innerleithen and Selkirk both had their Alpine Clubs which combined a study of geology with mountaineering. The Innerleithen club was formed in 1889 and had a membership of eighty-nine in its first year. By unhappy coincidence its founder and first president was killed at Walkerburn Railway Station in 1891 and its first secretary was drowned in South Africa the following year. Selkirk Club was formed in 1890 but ceased to be in 1896.

As the world moves on, the study of geology has become more important. More and more of the world's natural resources are being demanded by an increasing population, and geology is often the key to the location of riches buried deep below the surface of the earth and more recently under the sea; oil is but a recent example.

Much has been built on Hutton's 'Theory of the Earth'. The man known as 'the Father of Modern Geology' would have been pleased to know that his theory was being accepted, expanded and utilised for the benefit of mankind.

CHAPTER THREE
Rambling Rocks and Story-telling Stones

T he structure of the earth is a very long and complicated story which I will try to condense into as few paragraphs as possible before showing 'how it has affected us, the human race'. At the present time (2009), there is much concern about global warming and the dire effects that human existence is having on the natural world. Although we are causing some harm during our short tenure of the earth, this is infinitesimal when compared with what happened before.

Earth's story can be told by using layers of rock as pages but, like any old notebook, not all the layers are in order; some are crumpled or torn, upside down and back to front and the story is a very, very long one. Occasionally a fragment of time can be seen in rock formations or erratic boulders deposited on the surface of the land.

So, before getting down to the nitty-gritty of the geology of the Borders in general and Selkirkshire in particular, we have to take a short look at the original formation of the earth; what made the rocks and how they took the shapes they now are; how the many ice ages scoured land and changed it and gave it the structure and grain it now has; and what determined the nature of the land to produce certain types of vegetation in specific places because plants, like humans, do best in the place that is right for them. All these factors formed the character of the people who have lived, and those who are still living, in the piece of earth we call 'the Borders'.

Two hundred years ago, Hutton's cyclic 'Theory of the Earth' was essentially correct for his time and with the limited knowledge then available. Since then, that has been augmented with new discoveries and new ideas from all over the globe, and by the advent of a scientific method of dating rocks by measuring the rate of their radioactive decay.

It has taken the work of many geologists, scientists and mathematicians to give us some idea of how the earth began to take its shape. There are different ideas about the timescale but most have agreed in general principle on how the planet was formed; there is still much more to discover and the proven fact of today might excite the ridicule of tomorrow.

Some thousands of million years ago, what we now call our world was a mass of matter spun from dust and accumulated through gravity. Thousands of meteorites battered into it, adding to its bulk. The oldest known datable rocks in the world are preserved in Western Australia and Greenland. These are 3,800 million years old and contain evidence that they were derived from even older rocks. So the earth had already been whirling around in the space of the universe for some considerable time. No one can guess how long it had been there but even a mistake of a hundred million years would be quite acceptable, given the timescale involved.

Over this long period, the mass gradually assumed its present shape and a relatively thin, hard crust was formed over the new planet that we call Earth. In shape and composition, it has been likened to an onion made up of concentric rings with a hard top crust, 30-60km thick over landmass continents but thinning to a mere 7-8km thick crust beneath the oceans.

Below this crust is a hard rocky layer called a 'lithosphere'. This is not a single solid layer but is split into segments called tectonic plates. These segments are large rigid plates that float on a softer layer below it and move about under the surface of the earth at the rate of up to 10cm per year. It is this relentless movement where the plates meet and grind together, that is responsible for volcanoes and tsunami disasters as well as for the fault lines in the earth's surface, and for the folding observed in rocks which were already there.

By progressing lower into the earth 'onion', we find a thick layer called the mantle which is solid, 2,900km thick and about 3,000°C. Further into the heart, an outer core of molten iron, 2,200km thick and about 4,000°C; then an inner core of solid iron 1200km thick and up to 5,000°C at the centre of the earth. It is this central radioactive 'heat engine' that has been, and still is responsible for most of the changes in the crust of the earth and the atmosphere around it.

THE GEOLOGICAL TIME CHART

It is speculated that the earth was formed in roughly its present shape, around five hundred and fifty million years ago. What follows is a brief look at the formation of the rocks of the Borders. Nobody claims that this is the whole story because many people are working on fresh discoveries and reassessing old theories. The table below gives the types of rock and its age in million-year multiples as it is presently understood. BP, in million-year units, stands for Before the Present Time.

The Rock-Formation History of the Borders

Period	Age	Main Rock Types
Ordovician	495–443BP	greywacke, siltstone, shale
Silurian	443–417BP	greywacke, siltstone, shale
Devonian	417–354BP	Old Red Sandstone conglomerate
Carboniferous	354–290BP	Sandstone, limestone, coal, lava

The Ordovician and Silurian Periods

Some time around 495,000,000 years ago, a landmass continent comprising the northern part of Scotland and Ulster was joined together with Greenland and North America to form what is known as the North American tectonic plate. Several hundreds of kilometres away to the south-east, another plate comprising England, Wales, Southern Ireland and Europe made up a European plate. Both lay south of the equator and it was to be many millions of years before they joined up and moved into the northern hemisphere.

Between the plates lay a large body of water, called the Iapetus Ocean by geologists. On the floor of this, millions of years of sediment had been deposited in layers and compacted into rock. There were three main types of rock, indicating three main eras of deposition: these are greywacke, a compact of gritty sandstone containing tiny pieces of rock, broken crystals and sand grains bound in a fine greenish mud; siltstone, a fine sand rock; and shale, a fine-grained rock rich in minerals. By studying the rock formations visible, it can be deduced that these rocks were laid down in cycles by currents that swept down the under-sea slopes of the Iapetus Ocean.

Evidence of the Iapetus Ocean can be found on the edges of the Southern Uplands at Romanno Bridge and Lamancha. This is in the form of 'pillow lava' which had been erupted from an undersea volcano. Associated with this lava is a hard flint-like rock known as chert, which was to become very important when the first humans came into the area many millions of years later.

In the ocean, life was starting to stir. Simple creatures called grapto-lites, and primitive fish, lived in shallow pools while some air-breathing amphibians were creeping on to the emerging land where plants had already taken root.

During this period, many layers of sediment were laid on the floor of the ocean and, in time, these had been compressed into thick horizontal layers of stratified rock within which the first primitive fossil remains were found.

Devonian

As the European and North American tectonic plates edged their way closer together, the sedimentary rock layers on the bed of the Iapetus Ocean were pushed upwards and complexly folded to eventually rise above the waters as the Ordovician/Silurian rocks of the Southern Uplands. The angles at which the two plates came together determined the south-west to north-east alignment of the Southern Uplands. The two plates joined with other plates to form a massive continent which geologists named 'Laurentia'.

In time the Southern Uplands became detached as off-shore islands. Britain was later to break off from Laurentia and drift across the increas-ingly widening Atlantic Ocean to join up with part of the European landmass.

As the plates ground together, under-sea volcanoes erupted and molten lava poured through cracks in the lithosphere to form dykes of coarse greywacke and chert.

The Southern Uplands belonged to the Caledonian mountain

chain that had been formed in Silurian times around 400 million years BP. At this period, the Caledonian chain must have been a red desert or semi-desert at least. This was subjected to massive erosion by rain, rivers and landslides with sediments washed down from the bare mountains to make up the Old Red Sandstone rock strata and, eventually, the red soil that can be seen in much of Berwickshire.

Throughout the Devonian period, volcanoes were particularly active in the eastern parts of the Borders, producing the lavas seen at St Abb's Head and the Cheviot Hills. The Great Cheviot is a granite intrusion forced through the base of the erupting lavas.

Carboniferous

The next phase of geological rock formation was when the red sandstones gave way to marine-formed limestone. The transition to the Carboniferous Age was a more sedate affair after the pyrotechnics at the end of the Old Red Sandstone period. There was a gradual land depression and flattening in the eastern part of the Borders as the red desert sandstones gave way to a tropical swampland with river deltas and coastal lagoons which were periodically flooded by rising seas.

During this period, the area was swamp with equatorial rain forests, full of insects and lizards. When the forests flourished, they produced many layers of decaying vegetation in thick peat bogs. As these were buried and compressed under overlaying sediment, they eventually fossilised to become coal.

There were periodic increases in volcanic activity in the area with lava being forced through gaps or vents in the older sedentary rocks. The Eildon Hills, the Black Hill of Earlston, Peniel Heugh, Ruberslaw and Minto Hills were formed in this manner.

From the end of the Carboniferous Period, there have been no geological finds of new rock formation within the Borders region, although to the west there are deposits of a bright red sandstone around Moffat and Annan. This is the New Red Sandstone of the Permian and Triassic periods (290–205 BP).

On the rocks of the Jurassic Period (205–142 BP) and Cretaceous Period (142–65 BP), we know virtually nothing except that the climate was variable. By 65 BP, the land of the Borders had edged its way upwards from being 15° south of the equator to being 48° north of it by around 65 BP.

The Permian, Triassic and Cretaceous Periods had all ended with some cataclysmic disasters which wiped out most of the animal and plant species then living on the earth. It is estimated that at end of the Permian around 248 BP 95 per cent of all living creatures were eliminated; at the Triassic, at least 65 per cent, and at the Cretaceous 77 per cent. The cause of such mass extinctions is still being fiercely debated by scientists and geologists.

In the Palaeogene Period (65–24 BP) and Neogene Period (24–2 BP) little is known about conditions in the Borders except that the climate was variable with intermittent spells of subtropical weather being interspersed with extreme Arctic conditions. However, almost all the evidence of this period has been swept away during the next two million years.

THE ICE AGE
(2 BP–11,000 BC)

The landscape

The two-million-year period known as the Ice Age was actually a series of cold phases lasting many thousands of years, interspersed with shorter warm intervals.

On several occasions during this period, ice sheets and glaciers have covered nearly one third of the earth's surface and portions of every continent exhibit the imprints of glacial movement.

Ice can modify the landscape in two different ways. Acting as a powerful scraper, a moving ice sheet can remove vast quantities of rock and sedimentary deposit; this eroded material is carried away, often for hundreds of miles, and laid down as a glacial deposit on the ground surface on, or near, the edges of ice as the glacier melts. This creates an entirely new landscape although, in some circumstances, the same glacial deposit can cover and preserve a more ancient landscape beneath the ice sheet.

The secondary effect of ice on the earth is that there was a vast amount of water locked up in the ice sheets and glaciers, causing sea levels to drop by as much as 120m, but the enormous weight of the ice had also depressed the land surface by almost the same amount. As sea levels fluctuated with changes in temperature, this could leave raised beaches and platforms around the seashores, but when the ice melted, sea levels rose up to, and above, the previous high-water mark. All round the coastlines of Berwickshire and East Lothian, there are examples of raised beaches and remnants of rock platforms, lying at 18m and 25m above the present sea level.

However, with the huge weight of ice being removed, the land also started to rise and this movement is continuing. The area around Dunbar is still rising at the rate of 52mm (just over two inches) per century. That may or may not preserve it from the predicted flooding to be expected by present-day global warming.

It is thought that there have been four major ice ages and several minor ones during the last two million years but nobody knows for sure because one ice age tends to obliterate the remains of the one before, and in turn, its deposited remains are wiped out by the next one. So in the Borders, we can only view the devastation and reconstruction of the land that the latest one has caused.

That Ice Age, the one of which we are sure, happened around 18,000 years ago when the whole area was covered in a layer of ice estimated to be at least 2km thick in places. This formed most of the landscape as we see it at present, and decided the character of the people who lived in the Borders even up to modern times.

The thickest local ice-dome of this Ice Age, was centred in the high ground at the headwaters of the Ettrick, Yarrow and Tweed rivers. As the temperature varied, the ice started to move in a north-eastwardly direction, then turned to the south-east over the broad plain of the Merse of Berwickshire. In doing so, it gouged out huge amounts of rock from the layers above the harder Ordovician and Silurian strata, scoring linear rock ridges on the hills of the upper valleys and carrying broken rocks and debris for varying distances over the landscape before dumping them as the ice melted. It moved very slowly but steadily, eroding the softer rocks of the Devonian and Carboniferous layers and depositing this crushed debris as sand, clays and small stones in sheltered places behind more durably prominent hills of the Borders. This is known as a 'crag and tail', a feature that can be seen in the land to the

north-east of volcanic intrusions such as the Eildons, Peniel Heugh and
Smailholm Crag.

The immense power of the glacial ice to erode and alter the
landscape, is evident at the top of the Yarrow Valley where a huge basin
had been scooped out of the hard rock, then deepened and now filled
with fresh water to become St Mary's Loch. Nearby, the whole of the
Moffat Water valley is a deep U-shaped trench originally cut by the
moving ice. The Ettrick and Yarrow valleys have been scooped out and
the valley bottoms have been refilled by deposited debris from the
melting ice at some later time.

The destruction of rock strata and the transportation and distribution by glacial ice, provides a simple explanation for the occurrence
of huge boulders that are thickly strewn across the South of Scotland.
These are the stones that tell the story of the Ice Age. The erratic
boulders have not been found at a greater height than 350m in the
Borders, so an assumption can be made that the last Ice Age only
reached that height. The geologist can trace the origins of the
wandering stones and decide from which rocks in which country they
had been torn. Scottish and Norwegian boulders have been found as far
away as Norfolk and Lincolnshire, a fitting testimony to the power and
range of moving ice.

Less impressive but equally interesting are the places throughout the
Borders where the moving rocks enclosed in the ice have deeply scored,
scratched and polished the static rock-faces which had defied glacial
movement. The west faces of these 'living' rocks are rounded and
polished showing that the glacial movement was from west to east and
it is worth noting that the western and south-western sides of hills are
always steeper and barer than those on the opposite side of the hill.

For obvious reasons Border quarries are most frequently found on
the west sides of the rocky hills; one notable exception to this is the
volcanic intrusion of The Dunion near Jedburgh which has been
quarried for its hard black/grey dolerite (whinstone) in recent times.

The Warming Climate

Somewhere around 12,500 BC, there was a sudden warming of the
climate and in the geologically short time of a few hundred years, the

ice had melted completely leaving behind a landscape dotted with signs of its passing. Huge quantities of boulders, pebbles and sand had been lifted and carried along in the glaciers before being redeposited on the ground surface as the ice melted.

Such sand and gravel deposits are common throughout the region, especially along the lower Tweed Valley. In the lower-lying ground of the Merse, some glacial deposits lie in long whale-backed ridges and are known by the old Scots word of 'drumlins', a word derived from the Scots Gaelic word 'druim' meaning a ridge. The word 'drumlin' has been adopted as a standard geological term for this type of glacial deposit.

One particularly impressive deposit is at Bedshiel near Greenlaw, where the ice sheet has been temporarily halted during the melt. Another is between Greenlaw and Duns where gravel deposits mark the edge of a melting glacier. This type of deposit is a 'kame' or 'kame-morraine'.

Large deposits of gravel, sand and clay could be laid down around a large block of detached ice. When the ice melted, a cup-shaped hollow was left in the surrounding ground; this is known as a 'kettle hole' or more often a 'pot' in the Borders and can be seen in many places, especially in the area around Eddleston and Happrew in Peeblesshire.

Geologically descriptive place-names like Minto Kames (Roxburghshire), Kettelshiel (Berwickshire) and Howdenpots (Selkirkshire) can be found throughout the Borders.

Most of the hill lochs have their origins at the time of glacial deposit. In fact, many are just larger versions of the kettle hole or pot in depressions in the boulder clay while others have been formed by the damming of a lateral valley with a drift deposit.

During the melt period, all the water that had been imprisoned in the ice fields and glaciers, was released to change the landscape again. Glacial melt water poured down the slopes, depositing its carried debris in thick layers of boulder clay in the valley bottoms. The steeper the slope, the greater the destructive power of the plunging flood-water. With outlet being blocked by the watersheds of the Southern Uplands on the north, the Cheviot Hills on the south and the Upper Tweeddale Hills on the west, the built-up body of water took the line of least resistance and drained eastwards along the path already cut by the glacier. This formed the Tweed Valley river system that we know today.

There is a pattern of the effects of melt-water that can be seen in the Tweed Valley catchment area. Large stones with ice or flood scoring are more likely to be found at the heads of the valleys. As the melted flood-water came to lower land, its strength diminished and consequently the size of the deposited stones become progressively smaller. In the flooded mid-valleys, the slower currents would remove only the silt, sand and pebbles, leaving some of the river haughs as stony as the beds of the rivers themselves. This soil was carried down to spread over the flatter lands of the Merse or carried on downstream to empty into the sea at Berwick where it became another sedimentary layer ready to be turned into rock over the next hundred million years.

As more and more water was released from the ice, the pressure of the floodwater cut its way into the clay deposits already lying in the valley bottoms. These boulder clays were in layers which could be up to 25m thick. In some places, the strength of the water cleared the layer completely away; in others, it cut its way down through the deposit to leave a steep cliff-like face. This 'scaur' frequently bears the traces of many layers of flood-water deposit.

But while the ceaseless destructive tools of Nature, the rain, frost, snow and winds worked away at redistributing the land surface of the Borders, a kindlier Nature was replacing what had been taken away. Nature abhors a vacuum.

Chapter Four
After the Ice

THE PLANTS

As the temperature rose and the covering ice sheets had melted, plants started to appear. First on the bare landscape were the mosses, lichens and dwarf alpine plants that could withstand the permafrost.

As the alpines spread, they allowed organic soil to develop on the glacial debris and crevasses in the bare rock. Later, plants of shingle and grasslands joined the early colonisers on the tundra-like landscape; these were grasses and then taller shrubs like juniper and willow that probably covered the land. Then trees followed; when birch became established in parts of eastern and southern Scotland, it took over the land, out-shading the shrubs and driving them into the higher hills to survive.

Following the plant colonisation, came the animals which fed on those plants and closely behind were the animals that fed on the grazing animals. There were human settlements on the edges of the ice sheet to the south and it is quite possible that humans were amongst the animal settlers, but no conclusive evidence has yet been found in Scotland for this assumption.

At this period, there was a land connection between what is now Britain and the rapidly warming Europe. Most of our colonising plants and animals came from the continent via the south or from the east across the low-lying plain that is now the North Sea.

About 10,500 BC, there was another dramatic change when the climate cooled and the ice returned. A large ice sheet covered most of the Grampians and, in the Borders, glaciers formed on the higher hills. On the lower levels, the landscape resembled the Arctic tundra, bitterly cold and empty save for herds of reindeer grazing on the surviving alpine plants and the carnivores which fed on them, bears, wolves and lynx. Animal numbers decreased as the plant food supply diminished. Organic soil was depleted and became scarce in nutrients, while species-poor grasslands, sedge tundra and crowberry heaths survived on what little there was in the soil. Birch, being unable to grow or scatter seed on the frozen ground, died out completely. Plant and animal life in the area came to an almost complete halt.

This climatic collapse lasted for around eight hundred years. It has been suggested that a tilt in the earth's axis was responsible for this change. Another equally believable explanation comes from the North American continent. During the preceding ice age, vast amounts of water were being stored in the ice sheets that covered parts of Manitoba, Ontario and Saskatchewan in Canada and Minnesota and North Dakota in the USA. This ice blocked any drainage down what is now the St Lawrence River valley. As the climate warmed, the blockage was removed and a colossal volume of cold fresh water poured into the Atlantic Ocean and down into the Gulf of Mexico. This fresh water deluge rode on top of the denser salty water of the Gulf Stream, effectively cutting off the Atlantic conveyor belt that had delivered warm water to the shores of Britain and Northern Europe during the warm interglacial.

Whatever reason, there was an abrupt cessation or redirection of the Gulf Stream taking its warm waters away from our coasts. This happened again in the period 6200 to 5800 BC and several times since then, and it is quite likely to happen at any time in the future, something we can do very little about.

However, the Gulf Stream re-diverted itself back to its previous course and the climate ameliorated around 9500 BC. The interglacial warm period happened very suddenly; modern reckoning suggests that it took the short space of fifteen years, to raise the temperature by 7°F. This gave Scotland a fresh start, as most of the ground which wasn't under ice had reverted to an open tundra of grassland, shrubs and only the toughest of trees.

A few alpine plants and shrubs had either survived the rigorous conditions of the Little Ice Age, or were quick to move into the vacant space when it melted but, for whatever reason, specimens of alpine plants like montane willow and Norwegian mugwort can still be found in the Whitlaw Mosses near Selkirk. The Whitlaw Mosses are five small basins which probably remained as small open lochs throughout pre-history but had become completely overgrown in historic times. The sediment layer is 7m deep of which only 3m have been investigated by pollen analysis.

The rapid rate of climate change was faster than the ecosystem could cope with, and it would take a thousand years and many adjustments before the woodland plants and animals could completely re-colonise the country.

All ecological groups are interdependent. The plant pioneers of lichens and moss made the initial moves, helping a new soil to develop. This richer soil was used by a new set of plants that flourished in the increasing warmth and rain. The newcomers were soon competing with the original colonisers, pushing them to the more marginal land that had just been released from the ice. Bigger and better plants followed, driving the second wave of immigrants to seek pastures new until they, in turn, were superseded by even bigger bullies, the trees. Somewhere around 9,000 BC, in the land we now call the Borders, trees appeared again and took over the place. Initially, these were mainly birch, but a cheeky and much smaller competitor in the shape of hazel was waiting in the wings to join the contest. During the time that this takeover battle was taking place, animals and humans were encroaching on the land to see what was there for the taking.

But before starting on trees, it is worth having a look at how plants had to struggle to get a roothold on the Borders in the first place.

It is Tough Being a Plant

Scotland had always presented barriers to plant, animal and, eventually, human colonisation. In the Borders, there were the Southern Upland hills on the north, the Cheviots on the south and the Upper Tweeddale hills on the west, making entry from these directions awkward, though not entirely impossible.

Height was a barrier to plant colonisation in that it changed ground temperature. James Hutton, in his experiments on the effect of altitude on temperature, concluded that there was a loss of $1\,^{\circ}$F for every 230ft climbed. On these calculations, the top of the Broad Law in Meggetdale at 2,754ft above sea level, is approximately 11° colder than the town of Berwick; that I can believe.

The sun is the dominant influence on annual temperatures and in Britain there is an average decrease in warmth of 1°F for every 116 linear miles travelled northwards. So altitude and latitude could slow or prevent plant colonisation in the Borders.

Rainfall was another variable factor and plants will thrive in the 'Goldilocks Zone' – not too much, not too little – but will struggle to adapt to other conditions. Most of the south of Scotland presently has an average rainfall of over 40in but this varies across the area. In the hills at the top of Yarrow, the average rainfall is 60in per year whereas at Jedburgh it is 30in and yet they are only thirty miles apart.

Within a pocket of hills, it was only the lower-lying Merse on the east that made for easy entry to plants and animals. Even there, things could be difficult for plant colonisation. Dispersal via wind, river or birds is a major factor in the rate of spread of seeds and this varied from one district to the next. Rivers and streams only flow downhill so that can be ruled out except for plants which are colonising from the west; winds can blow from any direction and birds fly to where they can find food or a place to nest. So that is another variable in the plant recolonisation of the Borders.

It could not have been easy to be an incoming plant species in the Borders at this time. First you had to work its way slowly up the East Coast of Northumberland and round the edge of the Cheviots, because they were too high for easy colonisation. Then around Berwick, you had to turn left and get your seeds to colonise up the banks of the Tweed; this was suitable ground into which to expand as the soil quality was good, another important factors in plant development. Soils develop at different rates in accordance with the geological contrasts within the area and the soil in the Merse is derived from the glacial and fluvial deposits washed from the upper valleys, thus making for a richer and thicker soil.

Plants usually like a rich soil, but they are remarkably resilient and can adjust to surviving on poor land, although this makes for different potentials of growth with some plants thriving in an area that discourages others.

To get back to the seed dispersal: with water being a non-starter, this was dependent on birds and winds, a chancy business at the best of times and it would probably take more than a thousand years for a plant species to make the journey from lower Berwickshire to upper Peeblesshire. On this journey, the plant species probably had to make some adjustments to cope with the changes in conditions. An interesting experiment would be to compare the generic composition of a plant at Berwick with its counterpart at Tweedsmuir.

Trees

After the lichens, grasses, heather and small Arctic shrubs, came the trees.

Trees have a very important part to play in the natural cycle of the land. When their leaves fall in autumn, they break down into mulch that releases nutrients to maintain the fertility of the soil. The following year, the tree absorbs the nutrients and ground water in its yearly growth. This annual cycle makes for a healthy forest floor and helps drain the soil because a big tree can soak up and release many gallons of water through its leaves. When the trees are cleared to make way for arable fields or grazing, this process stops and the fertile woodland soil breaks down into acid heaths and heather moorland. Heather is a very hardy plant and can exist on the poorest soils.

It is probable that no tree species managed to survive the last glaciation in the Borders although it has been hypothesised that juniper may have done so on the fringes of the glaciers. Certainly juniper together with willow and rowan were first to take advantage of the increasing warmth.

Like other plants, trees are highly competitive and in the effort to become 'top tree' in an area, the dominant species would often drive out others in the process. Some trees were more socially conscious and would happily co-exist with other trees and different types of vegetation.

When birch arrived from the east and south and out-shaded the shrubs, junipers were driven to higher altitudes to survive while, willow tended to retreat to boggy, wet ground. By 9000 BC, birch had covered most of the land with no check on its territorial claim, other than the distance that its seeds could spread.

Around 8000 BC, hazel had made its entrance from the west where it has been suggested that it survived on the edges of the glaciation that had affected most of southern Scotland. Finding all types of land condition suited its growth, hazel spread rapidly and was soon competing with the birch to be 'top tree'.

This would be a crucial factor in encouraging humans to investigate and eventually settle in the Borders. The carbonised shells of hazelnuts have been recovered from many Mesolithic sites in Britain, a convincing proof that they were an important food source for early human settlers. The nuts are rich in protein, oil, starch and sugar with vitamins B1 and C. They could easily be gathered in ready-packaged quantity and roasted, a simple process that preserves them as winter food when all other vegetation has died back. They then could be stored throughout the winter as long as they were kept in frost-free and vermin-proof conditions.

Hazel was not just an important food source for prehistoric people. It was also an important tree for construction and tool/weapon-making purposes. When coppiced ie cut down at ground level, the root quickly sprouts, making long straight shoots which do not break easily and which can be used for making wattles in wattle-and-daub walls for housing or interwoven fencing for stock enclosures. It was used until comparatively recent times for these purposes.

Hazel has some medicinal uses although the report by William Turner in 1551 'that ashes of burned nuts with hog's grease or bear's grease, laid upon the head from which the hair falleth off, it will restore the hair again' must be treated with some scepticism. If only it was so easy.

Hazelnut shells are invaluable to the archaeologist. Many empty shells are found on archaeological sites and since they had grown and were picked within a year, they made perfect information-carriers for carbon dating.

Pollen Analysis

How is it possible to know what happened thousands of years ago? How can we tell what was growing, and how it spread when there is nothing left to see?

The answer to these questions come in two parts, one partly

natural/partly scientific and one totally scientific. The first part of the answer is in pollen – the curse of everyone who suffers from hay-fever but of indispensable value to the modern archaeologist and archaeo-botanist.

In reconstructing the ancient landscape we have to look beneath our feet.

The natural history of the Borders is contained in tiny pollen grains that contain the record of plant migration and the development of woodlands across what had been a barren wasteland close to the ice sheets. That history can be found in the spores and seeds of colonising plants, carried on the winds and on the feet, feathers, faeces and fur of birds and animals.

From the earliest times, plants have supported life on earth and created much of our environment. As a plant dies, it decays naturally; if it lands or is blown into a waterlogged place, it sinks to the bottom where, in an airless environment, the normal process of decay is stopped. Further deposits form a layer of peat which preserves the plant in perfect condition and this includes the pollen grains that the plant had accumulated while it was a living organism.

Pollen grains are tiny and have to be viewed through a very powerful microscope for identification. Each has a shape which is individual to its own species and this allows the experts to identify which type of tree, shrub, grass or plant was established in a certain area.

To get a sample of the vegetation, a core sample is taken from peat deposits, or from the sediments built up in and around lochs. Using a microscope, it is then possible to identify the various pollen types within the sample, and by counting the numbers of specific pollen grains as a percentage of the total, the vegetation history within the area can be determined – which plants/trees were dominant and which were inferior.

Pollen analysis is in its infancy yet and has some way to go before it becomes a totally definitive method of reconstructing the ancient landscapes, but it is the most successful technique for looking into the history of plants that we have at present.

Pollen analysis reflects a much larger landscape than can be plotted by an archaeological excavation. The great advantage of pollen analysis, over historical and archaeological data, is that the records are continuous and specific, telling the prehistory and historic settlement with a record of landscape change in that one area. It has to be recognised that the same investigation a mile away might show a totally different picture.

One of the disadvantages, is that to do a scientific sampling, dating and identifying the pollen counts from even one site, is expensive and very time-consuming. In the Borders, we are lucky as there have already been a number of studies and research on local sites. These have shown how the environment in that immediate area has changed over the centuries.

Having discovered how to identify plants by their pollen, there now remained the question of how to date these very small grains. This was done by an even more advanced science.

Radiometric Dating

To date the layers in a core sample taken from peat and loch deposits, we have to turn to space-age science. The process of dating is complex beyond the comprehension of most people but I will try to give a condensed version of the process, as far so I can understand it.

The atmosphere is being constantly replenished by the action of cosmic rays. These bombard the earth's surface and are absorbed within the structure of living plants and rocks. Different elements decay at various rates, so they provide timescale clocks to measure the amount of radioactivity in rocks and thus determine their ages. The slowly decaying uranium isotope dates the oldest rocks on earth and, given enough millions of years, the radio-active uranium will eventually break down and become lead – a Philosopher's Stone in long-term reverse.

At the other end of the spectrum, the atmosphere contains three isotopes of carbon – Carbon 12, Carbon 13 and Carbon 14 and all living things are absorbing the carbon isotopes into their bodies at the same ratio as they exist in the atmosphere. When the plant or animal dies, the Carbon 14 isotope begins to decay while the other two remain the same. Using a mass spectrometer, an instrument which can measure down to part of an individual atom, and by measuring the ratio of Carbon 12 to Carbon 14 which has a half-life of a mere 5,730 years, the age of the object or grain of pollen can be calculated.

In order to be dated, the object must contain carbon which means that it must have been alive at some time. Rocks require different methods of dating.

The Combination

By combining the two sciences and taking the different layers of pollen from the peat sample, and subjecting them to the Carbon 14 dating technique, it is possible to tell what vegetation covered the landscape at any particular time. The core sample provides a look through time; different species may have colonised the area but lost ground when climatic conditions changed. This information is held in successive layers within the core sample, awaiting an expert with the skills to reveal it.

This technique is useful in collecting information from pits or ditches in archaeological excavations when only one or two core samples are required. To get a picture of the general landscape, core samples over a wider area must be taken.

The environmental evidence taken from peat deposits provide the storyline of prehistory in the Borders, revealing far more than the patterns of when and where new plants came in: how climate change affected the vegetation around the bog, whether early man started to burn portions of the forest to encourage wild animals to graze there for easy hunting, whether the ground was being cleared for cropping, and which crops were being grown. The list is educational, exciting and limited only by our own limitations.

THE PEOPLE

After many years of studying the ground and the finds of the Borders and weighing up the opinions of all those interested in both, my opinion is largely that the archaeology of the area is mainly guesswork and this changes with the decades. I am not inferring that the Victorian conclusions are necessarily all wrong while the modern theories are always right; rather that everything should be weighed up with an unbiased eye and a temporary judgement on what was likely as opposed to what is definitive.

What follows is an outline of the possibilities, mine and everybody else's, because nobody knows for certain.

Mesolithic Times c.8,000–4,000 BC

It has long been a matter of conjecture as to when the first humans came to the Borders to hunt and settle. From the evidence we have, it can be deduced that trees and humans came about the same time, although humans may have followed animals grazing on the open lands of the pre-Boreal times.

We do have evidence that there were bands of hunter-gatherers moving along the river networks of the Tweed basin, settling when food was readily available and moving on when it became scarce. Due to the enthusiasm of local fieldwalkers and collectors, Mesolithic material has been recovered from over a hundred sites in the valleys of the Tweed and its tributaries. These sites are recognised by the concentrations of flint, chert and stone tools found in situ. The majority are on a bank close to the river or burn but there are a number of sites beside the hill lochs, usually on the south-facing side.

These were the hunters who chased elk, wild cattle, red deer, aurochs (wild ox), wild pigs and smaller animals. They hunted in bands, driving the animals into traps where they could be killed. As tundra gave way to forest, they developed hunting techniques to compensate, finding that the bow and arrow tipped with a sharp sliver of flint was more effective for killing within the forested landscape and at a longer distance.

Fish were also an important part of the diet and large numbers of net sinker-stones are to be found in the fields beside the rivers, showing that netting was one method of capture; spearing and line fishing with a sliver of flint as a hook were alternatives.

The hunter-gatherers are regarded as having highly mobile lives, living on one spot for a short time and then moving to another to take advantage of seasonal abundance.

This may to true to some extent, but concentrations of flint tools and waste found on certain locations, suggest that they had a 'main camp' at river junctions and a network of small outlying camp sites.

This period of hunter-gathering is known as the Mesolithic or Middle Stone Age and lasted from 8000 BC to 4000 BC. Neither of these dates can be taken as factually correct as there is enough evidence in surface finds that humans could have been in the Borders before that date. Nor is it conceivable that itinerant hunters stopped hunting and started farming immediately around 4000 BC. Everything was gradual – early Mesolithic humans were erecting permanent houses around 8000 BC and the Neolithic or New Stone Age men may have grown crops but they also hunted the forests and fished the rivers for their food.

Fieldwalking

One day, in the middle 1950s, I was out working on the edge of a ploughed field when I saw a small shiny piece of stone that looked unusual. I picked it up and that night took it to Bruce Mason, a Selkirk baker, who had the reputation of being able to identify and date anything old. He told me that I had found a leaf-shaped arrowhead about 4,000 years old. He showed me some of a huge collection of objects which he had picked up while deliberately walking over ploughed fields after the rain had washed down the loose soil. I was fascinated and soon joined him in fieldwalking excursions.

Although in the 1950s and 60s, fieldwalkers were known disparagingly as 'magpie collectors' or 'scavengers' by many professional archaeologists and museum staff, fieldwalking is now a recognised key archaeological technique to locate sites and map patterns of human activity over large areas of landscape.

In the old days, any potentially interesting find was popped into a pocket, taken home and washed and, if it was important, taken up to the National Museum of Scotland in a matchbox or shoebox if it was large. Now that it is organised and official, the fieldwalkers are lined up in rows and walked slowly across the ploughed field. Any finds are not picked up but marked with a peg and the location is recorded with a surveying instrument. Then the finds are bagged and labelled before being washed and examined.

A few years ago, I gave up for study, a collection of 9,600 pieces of chert, flint, stone tools and waste flake/chips that I had picked up from the ploughed fields on a glacial terrace at The Rink farm, the site where the Tweed and Ettrick Rivers meet. I was only one of four fieldwalkers who regularly walked the site and their collections would be at least equal to mine. The tool types are almost totally Mesolithic and almost all are made from chert. There is a similarity between The Rink farm tools and those found under peat in Denmark dated to around 6000 BC. The theory is that when the area that is now the North Sea sank, the people who had lived on it retreated further and further inland along the river network until they found a place where they were safe from the encroaching sea.

The Rink was a good site, well-placed on the higher ground beside the rivers and had the added attraction that there were many natural chert nodules in the glacial deposit. Chert does not work as easily as flint but it was a good local substitute and was used for most of the tools and waste found here. With such attractions, it had been a well-used meeting place for a period of several thousand years to judge by the tool types found.

Considering that all organic material has long vanished and only flint and stone has survived, we can tell much from this assemblage of tools and waste flakes. In fact, the nodules of natural chert could provide a complete tool kit for their needs.

In the pre-Boreal days when the ground was open, a large animal had to be driven into a trap or a bog before it was killed. I have long considered that driving a big animal into a bog would be a great way of immobilising it and then it could be killed by flint-tipped spears or a stone-headed mallet that would be capable of smashing its skull with one blow.

Then the animal would be cut up with chert or flint flakes which still retain their sharpness thousands of years later. The hide would be dressed with rounded scrapers to clean any fat and offal from it. Gravers would score a bone to make a narrow strip that was bored by a pointed piece of flint to make an eye for a needle which was then used to sew the skin into garments, using some of the animal's tendons or intestines as thread.

As the tree cover extended, smaller hunting weapons were required. The Mesolithic hunters developed a more lethal hunting weapon – the bow and microlith-tipped arrow. Microliths, some as small as a centimetre in length, could be used as points and barbs for arrows, for fish spears, and conjoined to make composite tools like saws and sickles.

The bow was a tremendous advance on the spear as a hunting weapon, shooting a projectile at much greater speed with more accuracy than a spear thrower could achieve and having a range of up to 200m. The flint-tipped arrows were light and could be carried in bundles so that the hunter no longer had to rely on a single weapon. Additionally, the bow could be used from a hide in the forest without the hunter moving and could shoot birds on the wing or on water.

The new technology could be used on running animals and there was less dependency on driving herds into traps or bogs.

Other sites that I have fieldwalked, and that are equally prolific, are at Springwood Park, Kelso where the Teviot and Tweed Rivers meet, and at Kalemouth where the Kale Water joins the River Jed. There will be many others, we just haven't had time to find them yet.

From the concentrations of finds, these were well-established base camps and probably permanent sites for at least three thousand years of Mesolithic habitation, but despite three trial trenches at the sites mentioned no conclusive trace of hut foundations were found. So, although we have no concrete evidence of human habitation within the Borders area, we can look just outside its boundaries to make a well-educated guess at the living conditions of Mesolithic man.

The discovery of an important Mesolithic site near Howick, Northumberland, was made by two fieldworkers who spotted flint tools in an eroding cliff-face. During two seasons of excavation, in 2000 and 2002, there was evidence of a circular sunken-floored hut with post-holes for timbers that would have supported a conical roof. This was a permanent building, 6m in diameter, needing much effort to construct but sufficient to accommodate a family of six to eight people.

The site was well-chosen. On the coast there was easy access to fish, seabirds, seals, and seaweed as well as land-based food supplies. During the excavations, evidence was found that the inhabitants had eaten wild pig, grey seal, fox and a vast amount of hazelnuts. The remains of a dog or wolf was found during the excavations but there was no indication whether it was part of the food chain or a hunting companion; domesticated hunting dogs are known from the Mesolithic site of Star Carr in North Yorkshire.

Carbon dating put the original construction of the Howick site at around 7800 BC and well within the Mesolithic dating. Further excavation and carbon dating through the stratified layers show that the hut had been rebuilt several times over the next 150 years and was likely to have been home to five or six generations of the same family group.

Further to the north at East Barns Farm, near Dunbar, Blue Circle Cement decided to extend their limestone quarrying operations. Archaeologists were invited to dig a few test pits in the area to be quarried, to see if there were any archaeological remains worth recording.

Careful excavation revealed the sunken floor of an oval building measuring 5m by 5.8m. Discolorations round the edge of the floor were recognised as postholes. When cleaned out, the holes measured between 25cm and 55cm and most had been cut at an angle suggesting that the posts had been sloped inwards to form a conical roof – rather like a North American Indian tepee but on a much larger scale. This was obviously a permanent structure. To justify the time and effort to construct such a building, the builders must have intended to remain on that site for a long time.

Like Howick, this site is well placed near the sea with the Lammermuir Hills immediately behind them and a reliable burn of fresh water running past their hut.

Over 30,000 tools and waste chips of flint, chert, jasper and agate were found on the site and the usual fragments of hazelnuts provided a date of around 8000 BC.

So it is a reasonable conclusion that Mesolithic man was sufficiently well established to have a permanent residence along the coastline of Northumberland and Southern Scotland around 8000 BC. More of these huts are likely to turn up in time.

By 7000 BC, the temperature was improving and the battle for 'top tree' mastery was joined with the advent of two serious competitors from the south. Elm arrived in the Borders around 6500 BC and oak slightly later, although the pattern of colonisation is not regularly consistent

These two were the dominants, taking longer to colonise but once established soon out-shaded the softer birch and hazel, forcing them to seek pastures new. Being tall and with high foliage, they tolerated smaller shrubs and trees under their shade, forming an eco–system which was beneficial to plants, animals and humans.

By 6200 BC, the waters of the North Sea had been rising at a rate of 46mm annually for some time. This warm spell had been turning the ice-sheet in northern Canada into a huge meltwater accumulation held back by the remnants of the ice. At one point the ice-sheet broke releasing a massive flow of water into the North Atlantic and southwards towards the Gulf of Mexico. It was a repeat of what had happened 4,000 years before.

The ocean conveyor belt slowed, or even stopped entirely, for as much as four centuries. Colder and drier conditions descended on Europe. The influx of such a large quantity of water caused the sea to rise, enveloping huge tracts of land in the North Sea and Scandinavia and, at the same time, separating Britain from the Continent as the connecting land bridge was destroyed.

Around 5800 BC the Atlantic circulation was resumed, keeping the winter temperatures mild and the summer rainfall plentiful, resulting in a 'climatic optimum' that would last for another two thousand years.

It turned out that the rainfall was more than plentiful and in time undrained ground became saturated, resulting in the increase of blanket peat over the moors and raised bogs in places where water could not drain away or evaporate.

Peat is the decomposing remains of all the plants that grew in the area of the bog. Sphagnum moss and other wet-seeking plants congregated, making for increased water-logging and keeping the moisture from evaporating. As the bogs spread, the increasing acidity soured the soil and prevented the colonisation of the land by larger trees, usually the then-dominant Scots pine. These couldn't grow to seed-producing size partly because of the acidity and partly because their roots were being forced to the surface and unable to get a firm hold in the loose peat.

At this period, nearly all the major tree species were in places wherever they could find suitable conditions. Some grew in clumps but other species would be tolerated under the forest canopy or in the marginal ground on the forest edges: poplar, willow, ash, hawthorn, juniper and wild cherry have been recognised by radiocarbon-dated analyses. With the damp interiors of the woodlands providing shelter from strong winds and frost, many other species of plants survived and often prospered with fallen trees and leaf mould providing nutrients. The gaps in forest cover made by wind-blown or dying trees allowed more light to filter through the leafy closed canopy, helping many different species of plant and shrub to establish themselves within the forest ecosystem.

At this period, most if not all of the Borders was forested with the main trees being oak, elm and hazel in the lower ground and oak, birch and hazel on the higher slopes. Alder and willow occupied the river banks and other wet places.

Around 4500 BC the weather was much wetter, a condition which favoured alder and willow to spread and colonise. Alder had already been around some 1,500 years but had never been able to compete with larger existing trees to any great extent. In the wetter conditions, blanket peat growth expanded into ground that had previously been grass and woodland.

In a number of Mesolithic sites, palaeo-environmental evidence suggests that the hunters used fire to clear areas of the forest. Whether this was accidental or occurred naturally through lightning, this opened a space in the tree cover where grassland would entice grazing animals. Clearings by fire are recorded in Britain as far back as 6500 BC. This need not signal the arrival of new settlers with fresh ideas but rather attempts of the existing population to manage the landscape and its resources for their own benefit. It was a short step from capturing wild animals, to keeping trapped animals alive within an enclosure and breeding from the captive stock. Finds from Star Carr in Yorkshire show that red deer were herded there and a smaller breed of aurochs, the huge wild cattle, made its appearance during this period. Some Mesolithic sites show a high proportion of ivy pollen, and ivy has long been a traditional cattle food.

There are a number of sites in Britain which show that burning upland forests was practised at the end of the Mesolithic period, and it has been speculated that the increased food supply lead to a rising population which placed a greater demand on food resources. Burning off more upland forest cover made for easier hunting and more land available for cultivation, but was not a good long-term idea so far as the landscape was concerned as this contributed to the degradation and erosion of the now unprotected soils which, in turn, left the way open for further expansion of the upland blanket peat cover. Such peat expansion resulted in increasingly acidic soil, making the land unsuitable for plant/tree growth and human usage.

It was a vicious circle but, because it happened over a long period of time, the results would not be apparent to any one generation.

Climatic changes have happened over the centuries and will continue to do so despite all the well-intentioned measures to combat global warming. The climate has always varied and it is not solely a phenomenon brought about by greenhouse gases and holes in the ozone layer. Human devastation of a finite resource does not help either the world or its diverse inhabitants, but these are of minor importance when placed beside what the destructive forces of Nature can do on its own. To take a more recent example of the 'little ice age' which occurred in the Borders from AD 1350 to 1750. This was a period when the greenhouse gas effect would be nil and the ozone layer would have few holes produced by human activities. Yet the research shows that a climate-driven abandonment of many of the upland settlements occurred during this period.

Even a few degrees of temperature change can distort the whole ecological system of an area with a significant influence on the composition of vegetation/tree cover and make previously marginal land uninhabitable. This change does not need to be hot to cold; cool to heat can change the ecosystem as well.

The years 2006 and 2007 had early spring heat and there was evidence that birds, nesting earlier, were finding it difficult to find food for their young as the hatching of the brood no longer coincided with the peak numbers of insects available. Similarly, there were fewer bees and insects to pollinate early-flowering fruit trees and flowers which did not produce so well as they did in former years. Ecological communities can be very fragile and are dependent on each other, so it is important that plants and animals, especially humans, function in harmony. This harmony can be severely disrupted by natural climate change over which we have no control, but this does not mean that we should stop trying to live in harmony with our surroundings.

The Neolithic Period c.4000 BC–2000 BC

Somewhere in the period between 4000 BC and 3500 BC, life changed for the hunter-gatherers in the Borders when the first farmers are reckoned to have appeared on the scene. Hunting and picking was out ploughing and planting in – but it was not as simple as that.

As was shown above, the huts at Howick and East Barnes demonstrate that the Mesolithic hunters did have a permanent base, probably for the old, young, and pregnant mothers and for over-wintering. On the seashore, with seaweed and shellfish at hand, there would be little chance of starvation. But it would be unlikely that no animals were kept in the vicinity, nor that any edible plants were grown beside the camp. Food was important and the nearer it was the better the chances of survival, so it was likely that an early form of land management had evolved some time before the conjectured dating.

The transition from a mainly hunting and fishing economy into one that grew its food and bred its animals is likely to have been a gradual one. From evidence in other parts of Europe, Mesolithic communities who lived by what they could kill or find were choosy in selecting which elements of agriculture they wished to adopt but not necessarily taking every part of the package. At some period, the wetter climate had driven the hunters to the drier, better-drained but poorer land on the hilltops. The Neolithic settlers were looking for the deeper soil, rich in nutrients that could be found in the forest floors and valley bottoms, so the merging of cultures could have been quite peaceable; in fact the hunters could become farmers with a better control over the food supply.

As farming techniques and experience developed, the way that the population organised itself was changing. Only a small proportion of wild plants are edible to humans and by selecting these and growing them in concentrations, the early farmers were able to feed themselves and have some surplus to immediate requirements. It was equally important that they were able to store the surpluses for future use.

As well as domesticating plants, the farmers tamed wild animals for their own requirements. Sheep, goats, cattle and horses provided meat and milk as a source of protein in their diet and supplied manure for the fields. This increased the food supply still further. When cattle and horses were utilised as plough animals, this extended cultivation into heavier, more fertile soils and at the same time required less human physical labour. The bigger domesticated animals were used for land transport and, for the first time, it was possible to move bulk loads of heavy goods by means other than the backs of humans.

With more food available from store, an organised societal elite emerged: the king or chief to rule, priests or shamen to provide religious reasons for wars of conquest, and warriors to carry out the expansion of the kingdom. This did not include people who had more useful specialist skills like flint working, pottery making and leather or wood working. But the greater part of the population would still spend their lives growing or collecting food.

The settled life of plant and animal domestication yielded more food, leading to a denser human population. The land needed to sustain a hunter-gatherer family could now feed as many as a hundred people and this eventually gave the farming community a numerical advantage over the hunter-gatherers.

Additionally, the hunters moved camp frequently and the woman had to carry a child until it was four or five years old and able to keep up with the tribe while the settled life of the farming community meant other women close at hand, and able to child-mind if needed. It is reckoned that there was a two to three year space between farmers' children.

The farmers simply out-bred the hunters.

The same was true on Continental Europe where increasing populations were out-growing the available land, so it was inevitable that some would see the out-lying islands as a land of opportunity. They were at a slightly more advanced stage of evolution, with some different tool-forms and techniques. The incomers brought new forms of seed corns, some domesticated animals, and clay pots for storage and cooking. Studies of the pottery indicate that they came to Britain in seven groups over the space of several centuries. It is likely that most came to the Borders from the south although some could have come directly across the North Sea.

They are known as the Neolithic or New Stone Age people and, although they still used many of the tool-types of their Mesolithic predecessors, they had added new forms to their toolkit, the most easily recognisable of which are the leaf-shaped arrowhead and the stone axe.

To clear ground for planting, they had to fell the forest trees and for this they used a tool that is considered the hallmark of early farming societies, the stone axe. It is speculated that some axes were ceremonial or a symbol of power, being made of colourful semi-precious stone like agate, jasper, jadeite and greenstone. Two superb ceremonial axes made from rocks allied to jadeite were found at Cunzierton, Roxburghshire. But the more common tuff and mudstone axes which have been found all over Britain have the score marks of practical tools.

Stone axes are virtually indestructible and easily spotted in the plough soil, with the result that many have been picked up and recorded. Some time ago, I handed over my collection of forty-eight locally found stone axes or parts thereof to the National Museum of Scotland, for study and eventual possession. Some I had found myself while fieldwalking, some were given to me and the remainder were from the Mason Collection. The important thing was that they were all provenanced to where they were found. None were of local stone. Most were made of Langdale tuff from the Lake District, two were hornfels from Killin in Perthshire and one fragment of a light grey-green axe came from Shetland.

The spread of Langdale tuff axes suggests that the roughed-out axe blanks were traded across the country in their rough state and it was up to the customer to polish it into a working tool himself.

A few years later, I attended a lecture that used the evidence of the collection to prove a concentration of Neolithic agricultural activity in this part of the Borders. I was not too popular when I pointed out a more logical explanation was that the plotted spread of stone axes in Scotland tended to be a distribution map of the fieldwalkers' activities as much as proof of early farming settlements.

If axes had moved far from their location of origin, so had the arrow-heads. Although about a third of the locally found leaf-shaped arrow-heads are made from black, grey or olive green chert which is indigenous to the area, the remainder are made of a variety of flints from the south, jasper from East Lothian, agate from the Cheviots and one of pitchstone from Arran. The most far-travelled arrowhead that I know, is one that was found just outside Selkirk and which is made of Antrim Porcellanite from Northern Ireland. Early man travelled or traded over a wide area.

Taken together, the finds of axes and arrowheads show that there was a population movement in the country and well-established trading routes throughout the British Isles. In the Borders, the distribution plot shows that the early farming communities were using the riverbank lands for their permanent base and agricultural activities, but not neglecting the higher ground for grazing and hunting. With the work involved in preparing rough land for agricultural use, land itself became a possession rather than a resource and the population became more settled than migrant.

Lying on the 250m contour, pollen analysis taken from the Blackpool Moss on the farm of Nether Whitlaw show that the trees of the wildwood forest, oak, hazel, elm and birch, became less numerous around 4000 BC. This is thought to be due to humans clearing the forest for tilling and grazing.

In the 1920s and 30s, fieldwalkers were finding concentrated scatters of flint tools and waste material on the banks beside the Whitlaw Mosses, usually on the south-facing side. These finds fitted into the late Mesolithic/early Neolithic period. Here fieldwalking finds confirm the pollen analysis dating very well.

Another site is at the height of 500m where Loch Skeen in Moffatdale flows out into the Tail Burn before it drops spectacularly in The Grey Mare's Tail. Here a concentration of Neolithic flints, that had been washed out from under the peat layer, was found in the 1930s. This is more likely to be a hunting camp rather than a permanent settlement.

A more spectacular find was made nearby. In 1990, Dan Jones of Melrose was hillwalking at the aptly named Rotten Bottom in the Moffat/Tweedsmuir Hills, when he saw a thin stick protruding from a bank of peat. He pulled it out and used it as a walking stick until he got home where he put it in his garage. Some time later, it was identified as a flatbow, made of yew probably from trees grown in the northern

Lake District and carbon-dated to around 4000 BC. Originally, it was suggested that it was the relic of a failed hunting trip (the bow was broken at one end) into the bare hills but pollen analysis on the peat at Rotten Bottom reveals that birch, oak and hazel grew at this altitude of 600m above sea level, at the time when the bow was pushed into the peat.

One of the more dramatic changes happened around the time when the Neolithic settlers began to spread through Scotland. Pollen diagrams from sites throughout Britain, Ireland and Europe started to show a decrease of elm in the pollen count.

Simply known as 'the Elm Decline', this has been dated from many sites to 3800 BC. There are several competing theories as to why this happened. In the 1970s, Dutch Elm Disease decimated the elm trees in every part of Britain when a beetle-spread fungus moved swiftly across the country with dramatic results, and this was taken as an explanation of why elm had been wiped out six thousand years before. Climate change was another considered option but this did not show up so much on other trees and plants.

The Elm Decline coincided with the advent of new settlers who were clearing the forests for their grazing animals. Leaves of the wych elm that was the only species of elm in Scotland in the Neolithic period are rich, palatable food for animals during the summer. The same leaves can be collected and dried to provide winter fodder as they have been in Scandinavian countries to almost the present day.

Additionally, elm grows on better soils and may have been felled to clear the ground for tilling or pasture. It is also a hard durable wood when felled and dried, and is likely to have been used for building purposes. Eventually a compromise solution was agreed that the Elm Decline was probably the result of several actions.

Around 3100 BC, agricultural expansion appears to decline and evidence of forest regeneration can be detected in many of the pollen diagrams. This pattern has also been detected throughout the North of England and Scandinavia and is likely to be the result of climatic change. Clearings were still being made in certain parts of the area but no steady pattern of change can be observed in either lowlands or uplands until around 2400 BC, when there is solid evidence to suggest that the farmers were moving back into the uplands.

Housing

There are many sites in the Borders that produce Neolithic tool types, but we have to look as far north as Balbridie, Aberdeenshire, to see an example of Neolithic housing.

Aerial photography had revealed a very large rectangular wooden house or hall with bowed ends and this was identified as an Early Historic hall by its shape and size. It measured 24m by 12m which was a fairly standard size for such a hall.

However, on excavation, the building was dated to around 3350 BC and therefore was definitely Neolithic. Although no similar type of building has so far been discovered in Britain, there are others in France and the Netherlands with the same size, shape and dating.

The excavations at Balbridie proved to be an archaeobotanist's dream. Over 20,000 charred cereal grains were found, of which Emmer Wheat was the most abundant. Naked six-row barley, the rare hulled barley and some bread wheat that needs a rich soil to grow, was also found. The Neolithic people who lived in this building were living in a mixed farming economy as tillers of the soil as well as pastoralists.

It is very unlikely that the Balbridie building is unique in Scotland – we simply have not found any more as yet. There is a suspicion that the rectangular structure recorded as a cropmark at Sprouston in Roxburghshire could be a building similar to the one at Balbridie. Likewise the concentrations and tool-types of finds from Springwood Park and Kalemouth almost guarantee that there would be a Neolithic structure nearby.

The average one-family Neolithic house was a round structure of 7m to 9m in diameter, with a sloping roof covered with thatch, bark, turf or hide, or a mixture of all four. There must have been many such huts built over the Neolithic period but it is only in the hill ground that some scooped-platform sites have been tentatively dated as Neolithic; even this is by no means certain since this type of structure lasted without much change into medieval times.

There is evidence that some land had been cleared for cereal production as most sites produce quern stones used for grinding corn, but this could only have been on a very small scale and the inhabitants would rely on rearing animals and hunting for the bulk of their food.

One advance in living conditions was that the Neolithic people made rough pottery jars which facilitated food storage and cooking.

There is no reason why Neolithic houses could not be built on flat ground and most are likely to have been, but subsequent agriculture has destroyed all traces and we are left to guess where they were by the scatters of flint and pottery on the ploughed fields. This is where fieldwalking comes into its own as an intelligence-gatherer of site locations.

The Yarrow valley in Selkirkshire must have been a populous place in the late Neolithic/early Bronze Age time until the Early Historic period but this will be described in greater detail when I get to Selkirkshire.

Death and Ceremonial

If there have been few houses excavated that can be dated to the Neolithic period, the evidence for a large settled population is found in the cairns and cist burials which can be found in the Borders. The Neolithic people buried their dead and probably used the burial cairns to mark out their tribal territory.

Their burial structures come in varied forms and different sizes. Long cairns and chambered tombs gave way to low cairns of stone or clay and timber mortuary enclosures where the corpse was left to rot before burial. There have been many debates as to why such structures were built and what rituals were involved. The most common conclusion is that this was a form of ancestor worship and that such monuments were a constant reminder of the presence of friendly spirits from another world. Although this is a feasible suggestion, there is no way of knowing the beliefs and thoughts of the people who died so long ago.

The most impressive markers are the long cairns which were considered be communal burial places, but more recent thought is that they were religious monuments or more probably status symbols of a tribal grouping; in modern terms 'they made a statement'.

There are two long cairns to be found in Roxburghshire and one in Peeblesshire but the most notable is the huge cairn known as the Mutiny Stones in Berwickshire. It is situated in open moorland one mile NNW of Byrecleuch steading. It measures 82m in length and tapers from 27m in breadth and 2.5m in height at the eastern end to 9.8m by 0.9m at the western end. This huge monument would require a massive effort from a well-organised society over several generations. Although the monument was trenched in 1871 and again in 1924 when it was disturbed by the construction of a sheep stell, no vestige of original burial was found. With no graves, we resort to the much-used archaeological conclusion that it would be 'of ritual significance' and in this case, it almost certainly was.

Long cairns are thought to be late Neolithic, erected for one or several individuals of high status. This has to come under the 'not proven' verdict but it could indicate that an elite hierarchy was emerging to dictate how society would behave. Whether this was warrior- or priest- based is not known.

One of my more recent discoveries was a chambered cairn at NT 4495235556 on the Green Walk near Clovenfords. The possible capstone is roughly circular with hammer-dressing on one edge. It is 1.5m in diameter and around 0.3m thick. It overlies the remains of a chamber aligned N/S and comprising three stones set vertically on what would have been the east side of the chamber. There is no obvious trace of a covering cairn but the surrounding area has been disturbed by a nearby trackway and the insertion of quarry pits into the hillside. There are also a number of drystone dykes in the immediate vicinity that could explain the lost cairn.

This site was visited by an Inspector of Ancient Monuments from Historic Scotland and she agreed with my judgement.

CHAPTER FIVE
The Metal Ages

THE BRONZE AGES

The 'Bronze Age' is a handy label used by prehistorians to describe the period between approximately 2400 and 700 BC and is further divided into three parts, rather like Gaul, but, like 'omnis Gallia', no one is quite sure when it started, how long each phase lasted or when it ended; it is a loose description of the time rather than a hard and fast dating.

The earliest metal objects to be found in the Borders were made of copper. The only Border finds are a flat copper axe from Muirfield in Berwickshire and a copper pin from a grave at Springwood Park, Roxburghshire. Several other finds were reported in Victorian times but the artefacts have now been lost. Even then, it is doubtful whether these were from a 'Copper Age' or were of Early Bronze Age manufacture.

Malachite (copper-carbonate) occurs naturally in mineral-bearing rocks but can be released from the rock by battering with heavy mauls or by fire-cracking the rocks. The ore was heated up to $1,084\,^{\circ}C$ became molten and was then poured into a mould to cool, producing a finished object. Although there is an ancient copper mine at Elba in Berwickshire, there is no evidence that copper was worked there in early prehistoric times.

Like gold, copper itself is a soft malleable metal; but around 2500 BC, it was discovered that if 10 per cent of tin was added to 90 per cent of copper in the crucible, the resulting mixture made a much harder tool. This discovery was probably made by one of the new magicians of the age, the smith, in the vicinity of Cornwall where tin was plentiful. The new composite metal that we now call bronze was to be the precursor of a new age.

THE EARLY BRONZE AGE
2000 BC–1200 BC

Around 2000 BC, the Neolithic communal burial was replaced by single inhumations with a stone cairn covering the important people and a low earth mound covering the lesser mortals. One theory is that this change in burial practices coincided with the advent of another invasion of land-seekers who are now known as the Beaker People from their distinctive pottery types. It is assumed that they brought the first bronze objects with them in their quest for new land; this is yet another of the 'not proven' facts. Whatever the truth, it is likely that it would be some time after this that bronze weapons and tools arrived in the Borders.

To give some idea of the time scale involved, the following is a rough guide that is applicable (and disputed) in the south of England where there was a much greater population and concentration of evidence. Splitting the time scale into defined 'Ages' gives a false impression of an abrupt end and a new beginning starting immediately. This would never happen; one 'Age' would merge into the next over a long time span and would vary in different parts of the country.

In the south, the Early Bronze Age was reckoned to be from 2400 BC to 1500 BC; the Middle Bronze Age 1500 BC to 1000 BC and the Late Bronze Age 1000 BC to 650 BC.

With much of the Borders isolated by the surrounding hills, the Early Bronze Age here is more likely to date from c.1700 BC to c.1200 BC and the concentration of settlement and the spread of finds suggests that both colonisation and trade came via the East Coast and through the Biggar Gap on the West; these were the natural points of entry into the region.

It is noteworthy that the first metal objects to arrive in Britain were status symbols such as pins, dress-fasteners, earrings, flat daggers and flat axes. Evidently the possession of a bronze object carried considerable social kudos.

In the Borders, Early Bronze Age metal finds are rare: Roxburghshire six flat axes, Peeblesshire three flat axes and two daggers (now lost), Selkirkshire one flat axe and Berwickshire one flat axe. Even allowing for the fact that there may be much still to find and the realisation that many other finds may be unrecorded, this is not an impressive total. It could also be indicative of how few metal objects made their way into the Borders over the putative five hundred years of the Early Bronze Age.

For the bulk of the people living in the Borders from 1700 to 1200 BC, the coming of the Bronze Age would be a non-event, with little change in lifestyle if any was noted. For the commoners, flint, chert and stone continued to provide the cutting edge of the functional tools of everyday living but there were some developments and improvements in their lifestyle; the hunters' arrowheads changed from leaf-shaped to barbed and then barbed-and-tanged. It must be noted that the newer form of arrow and lance heads were not of chert but made with a finer flint, indicative of long-range, regular trading routes running through the country. Trade routes carried new ideas, new skills and new craftsmen as well as trade goods.

Around 2000 BC, the temperature started to rise and warmer weather made cultivation of the hill lands a feasible option. With increased food production, the population grew in size and more land had to be cultivated to supply an ever-growing demand.

With more people to feed, new ideas of crop-management and animal husbandry were introduced, either from outwith the area or by the native initiative. This produced a surplus of food and allowed enough non-food producers with specialist talents to develop as traders, craftsmen, warriors, priests and chiefs. With a settled life, differences in status would become more apparent, with a greater emphasis on social organisation and the rising importance of some individuals within the grouping. Society in its various strata was being formed and with it the idea of having recognised leaders and defined land holdings.

In the Bronze Age, the very possession of a bronze weapon or ornament would be the prerogative of the leaders, making them stand out in the community and, as such, the objects are likely to have been highly prized and treasured through several generations of the family.

For the elite of Early Bronze Age society, nothing but the best would do; the more unusual the object, the greater the status of its owner. From South Side Farm, on the boundary between Lanarkshire and Peeblesshire, two superb gold torcs known as lunulae and an armlet of spiralled gold were found in 1860. These can be dated to the Early

Bronze Age and the type originated in Ireland where over eighty have been found. The decoration is hammer-punched and is especially richly done at the terminals. There are thoughts that these types of object and ornamentation were associated with sun worship.

There is some doubt as to whether the three objects were found in Lanarkshire or Peeblesshire, as both counties claim their provenance. They were found on the farm of South Side that is now in Peeblesshire but were in the collection of Adam Smith of Coulter in Lanarkshire. Things are a bit more complicated as South Side Farm seems to formerly have been in the Parish of Coulter and in the estate of Adam Smith of Coulter.

Other items of gold and bronze have been found at Hillhouse, Lauder and Essenside, Ashkirk and probably many other places but most have vanished beyond ken or into a box somewhere.

Ground Evidence

If the object evidence of the period is scarce, the physical evidence on the ground is plentiful to see, if difficult to date precisely.

The remains of Neolithic/Early Bronze Age settlement are widespread in the Border hills, where they have survived above the limit of medieval and modern ploughing. On the ground, very little can be seen by the untutored eye but air photography has revealed the layout of the ancient farms showing the huts and fields of the early farmers.

Given the right light, soil conditions and angle of photograph, more sites are emerging in the hill country of the Border counties. This is one aspect of Border archaeology that, with a few honourable exceptions, has been neglected. The sites are there, I have seen them and could show them to any academic who could be persuaded to visit the Borders. In Northumberland, things are different and archaeology is a major and well-funded interest. So it is to that county that I must look to see if what is there can logically fit into the Borders landscape.

The remains on the Cheviot Hills form one of the best-preserved prehistoric landscapes in Europe. This is known because a great deal of work has been put into photographing, recording and analysing this vast site. In contrast to the bare hills of today, almost every part of the Cheviots were utilised in the Bronze Age period. Whether this is because the lower valley lands were already over-crowded or that the undrained flat land was sodden marsh, sour and unsuitable for stock-raising and cultivation, is a question that has long been a contentious issue among prehistorians. Perhaps the climate had changed, making the hill land more attractive for settlement and agriculture.

When land was taken into agriculture, trees were cut down to clear the land, and the timber was used to build houses with wooden walls, roofs and internal divisions; wood was also used to make animal enclosures. This use of wood is not wasteful if the trees are allowed to regenerate naturally, which they would do if kept free from grazing animals. This did not happen as pollen analysis from sites in the Cheviots show that the tree cover was vastly reduced as the land reverted to grass upland.

This was not beneficial to a long-term agricultural use. On the edge of Europe and influenced by the Atlantic Ocean, Scotland has a cool and windy climate with many wet days. Without the covering forest to replenish the nutrients in the land, the 'heart' was leached out of the soil by the rain and the spread of blanket peat.

For the original settlers in the Borders hills, location was the key. The land has to be reasonably level, on south-facing slopes if possible although east/west-facing ones were acceptable. A nearby source of water was essential. With time, patience and a lot of heavy labour, terraces capable of cultivation could be carved out of the hill slopes.

The fields were small, seldom more than half an acre in size, generally but wrongly known as 'Celtic' fields, and irregular in plan. The downside slope of the field is built up with clearance stones to prevent soil erosion thereby creating a series of terraces to bring more ground into cultivation, as and when required. This field pattern shows organised planning on a major scale together with a long-term understanding of the environmental needs of farming.

Such cultivation terraces can be found in most parts of the Borders but the concentration of terraces in the parishes of Yetholm, Hounam and Morebattle in eastern Roxburghshire indicates a large, well-organised community. There are similar groupings in the Roberton and

Teviothead parishes, in the Meldon area of Tweedsmuir and at the Biggar Gap in Peeblessshire and the Yarrow valley in Selkirkshire. There are bound to have been many other groupings on the lower lands but these have been destroyed by medieval and modern agriculture.

The houses can occur as single dwellings with an associated field system, but may also be found in loose groupings of six to ten houses with a much-extended agricultural pattern of fields. The houses being of wood and turf construction have decayed back into the ground, making the sites difficult to spot. In some, field-clearance stones have been piled up against the timber walls and give the impression that they were stone-built or built on a stone foundation.

It is not known what social groupings made and farmed the terraced land, whether it was family/community-based or individual plots. Certainly Early Bronze Age communities have been identified by grouped platform settlements with terracing on nearby hills indicating long periods of cultivation and permanent land clearance. These are likely to be extended family lands, held over several generations and well into the next Bronze Age.

Excavations in Northumberland reveal that the early farmers grew two types of barley, emer and spelt wheat, flax for cloth and oil, while also harvesting hazelnuts and wild fruit for food. It can be safely assumed that cattle, sheep, pigs and goats were raised on the unterraced hills.

Burial Places

The earliest Bronze Age burials used small cairns, barrows, cist graves and cinerary urns. The 'cist' burials were stone-lined graves covered with a capstone and a mound of stones or earth on top. Grave goods found with any remains of the body that has survived the acidic soil, are likely to be with a pottery vessel and of a type that gives the rough date of the inhumation.

We do not know if there was a form of organised religion in the Early Bronze Age but the presence of many types of pottery in the excavated graves suggests that there was a commonly held view of death and the rituals associated with it.

In the hill country where most of the cairn foundations can be found on the watersheds between valleys, they would stand out as markers of tribal boundaries in the prehistoric landscape. Of the 600 or so noted in archaeological records, most if not all have been used as convenient quarries to provide stone for new dykes in the eighteenth century agricultural enclosures.

As well as the more obvious single cairn or barrow remains, there are the clusters of cairns which have still to be investigated. These are known as cairnfields and I know of three that are quite obvious but, as yet, unrecorded.

Greenlaw Moor. NT 714 484. This is a huge area with many low-lying mounds up to 0.5m high and between 2m and 4m across. The mounds are of clay as there are very few stones on the ground surface of this peat moor. This type of cairnfield is common in Northumberland and is dated there to the Early Bronze Age.

The most remarkable feature of the site is a natural loch which seems to defy the laws of nature. Measuring about 400m by 150m, it lies on a flat piece of ground between two slopes, north and south. However, to the east and west of the loch, the ground falls away gently and it would seem easier for the water to run away than to stay where it is. This phenomenon would almost certainly account for its Anglian name of the Hule or Holy Moss.

There are also slightly smaller cairnfields at Turf Law, Oxton Parish, NT 471 556 and at Swinlaws, Kalewater, NT 770 159.

The Yarrow Valley was a populous place from the Mesolithic period up to the Early Historic and there are three cairnfields in the valley that will be noted in the Selkirkshire section below.

Ceremonial Sites and Rock Art

As the early farming community grew and multiplied, they met together and combined their labour to build ceremonial monuments for worship and as a symbol of their powers. We do not know what gods they worshipped although these are likely to have included a goddess of fertility and a god of the sun – both essential to a community which relied on what it could grow or rear for its food.

The most outstanding gathering place for the dispersed farming communities of the Borders is also the most striking – the Eildon Hills, to be precise the Eildon Hill North which is within a rampart 1.6km

(1 mile) in length and enclosing 39 acres in area. Inside the rampart are at least 290 house platforms still visible in air photographs and as many more would have occupied the flat land on the south side of the hill but later ploughing has destroyed all traces there. Excavations over a six-week period in 1986 showed that the site was occupied in the Late Bronze Age and there was a further occupation in the second century AD. It is a complex and interesting site and the excavations only scratched the surface (literally) as only a tiny proportion of the fort was excavated. Of the four platforms that were investigated, two were Late Bronze Age and at least one of the other two was Roman Iron Age. The amount of evidence suggests that there could have been a large gap between the two occupations. This may be explained by four centuries of extreme rainfall between 800 and 400 BC.

The excavation report was tentative in its conclusions stating that 'there is probably a Late Bronze Age hilltop settlement from the tenth or ninth centuries BC, which functioned as a local or regional centre; there is no certain evidence of pre-Roman Iron Age activity; there was probably a large-scale Roman Iron Age hilltop settlement'.

Victorian historians claimed that Eildon Hill North was one of the tribal capitals of the Selgovae in Roman times and this conclusion has been repeated until comparatively recent times. It is unlikely that the whole site was occupied on a permanent basis because of its exposed position and the lack of a convenient water supply. Current thinking points to the conclusion that Eildon Hill North was largely a ceremonial meeting place for the people who were farming the arable land of the surrounding countryside. If there were any permanent dwellers, they would probably be a few holy men to tend the holy place and supervise the worship involved.

Anthropological studies show that primitive societies are likely to come together at certain times of year to celebrate festivals, carry out rituals, trade goods, acquire partners, meet friends and share news. Eildon Hill North would fit all these criteria.

High places were thought to bring the worldly people nearer to the gods in the sky and there were three Eildons, three being a magic number in many prehistoric religions. Christianity followed that trend in having a tri-partite God in Father, Son and Holy Ghost. The mile long ramparts are too slight to be defensive structures and are more likely to be a barrier to keep the non-believers from the holy place on the top of the hill.

Another ceremonial enclosure can be found in Peeblesshire where the Lyne Water meets the Meldon Burn to form a raised promontory of around 20 acres. This is a natural meeting spot with access from every point of the compass. Across the neck of the promontory, a huge monumental stockade, 600m long, was built around 2200 BC. This was excavated in 1974–75 prior to the realignment of the road and produced cremation deposits and other 'ritual' features. Like Eildon Hill North, there are few signs of permanent occupation and the conclusion reached was that it must have been a place of worship. The site was deserted abruptly around 1700 BC, a date which may mark the advent of the Beaker People into the Border lands; or there again, it might just be a coincidence.

Pit alignments are curious monuments, hard to detect on the ground and difficult to understand once they are found, and requiring excavation before any conclusions can be reached. There are as many as thirteen 'pit-alignments' recorded in *Archaeological Sites and Monuments of Berwickshire District*, which was published in 1980. It is unlikely that all are ceremonial enclosures and may simply be substantial territorial markers or field enclosures.

These may or may not be associated with the 'Black Dykes of Berwickshire' which divided up the area at some period in the past, probably in the pre-Roman Iron Age or the immediately post-Roman Early Historic period or even in both.

Agricultural complexes are very difficult to date but, in regard to the dyke system, the current opinion is that these were large-scale territorial divisions between communities who wished to mark out their land. They did this, not by building a stone wall which is our modern version of a dyke, but by digging a trench or two trenches and mounding up the soil. This required a great deal of labour over a long time.

Herrit's Dyke is the best known and longest of the Berwickshire Black Dykes, originally running from Harefaulds Fort on the farm of Blythe near Lauder, to the south side of Paxton on the Whiteadder, a distance of twenty-three miles. Though now largely ploughed out by modern agriculture, the best part is a mile-long section across Greenlaw Moor. Here the mound is up to 11m wide and stands over 1m above the bottom of the trenchs which lie on either side of the mound. This would have been a formidable land marker at the period of its construction.

By using divining rods in their initial use, I was able to check that there were postholes at 2.5–3m intervals along the upcast mound. Further investigation showed smaller wattle fences running at right angles away from the Dyke, conclusive proof to my mind, that this indeed was a land division rather than a defensive structure.

Another ceremonial monument is the 'henge'. Henges were built in the Borders, not massive stone structures like Stonehenge but made from wood. Unlike the round forts which they resemble, the wood henges have the raised mound on the outside and the ditch on the inside. In the interior of the henge, there could be one or more circles of wooden posts. Hypothetically, the centre of the henge was the focal point for the performance of rituals.

Although we do not know what rituals were performed, analysis of residues surviving on pottery surfaces from the Balfarg henge in Fife, show that black henbane seeds had been part of the contents. As black henbane is a hallucinogenic as well as a medicinal plant, there may have been some suggestions of mind-bending.

Highly decorated Grooved Ware pottery has been found during several henge excavations. This pottery is decorated with triangles, lozenges and spirals and may be a special 'ritual' pot (no pun intended).

In the Borders, henges have been noted at Sprouston, Springwood Park, Mellerstain, Ancrum and Over Howden but all have been ploughed over until the only trace is a faint mark on air photographs.

Two stones on the edge of Dere Street near Pennymuir have scoring which I think is deliberate and man-made. The experts think that the scoring is natural, the results of ice-scoring, although they may never have seen the stones in situ.

Stone circles, of which there are several scattered through the hillier parts of the Borders, may be an extension of the henge monuments. They are classed as Neolithic/Bronze Age but are virtually undatable.

Also noted are standing stones which may range in dating from Neolithic monuments to medieval boundary stones.

More acceptable to the archaeological establishment are the cup-and-ring stones of which five are recorded from Peeblesshire, five from Roxburghshire, three from Berwickshire and two from Selkirkshire.

Since this list was made in the 1960s, a further four have been found: one at Ancrum, two in the rubble from the excavations at Soutra Aisle and one during ploughing in a field 200m to the west of the Aisle. All three were on moveable yellow sandstone blocks.

Quite what the abstract artwork symbols mean is a bit of a mystery. The rock sculptures had a long life covering a period from around 4000 BC to around 1700 BC (that date again). They appear from Northumberland to Argyll to Orkney in Britain and along the Atlantic seaboard of Spain and France as well as into the Mediterranean islands. Whatever message the symbols were meant to convey, it was obviously understood over a wide area and suggested a shared culture from Neolithic times onwards.

It is reckoned that the 'cup', a round hollow pecked out in the stone, represents the sun and the surrounding concentric circles are its rays. Found in burial cairns and in association with datable pottery, cup-and-ring marked stones still had 'ritual significance' in late Neolithic/early Bronze Age. Interestingly, if the capstone of a grave has cup-and-ring marks on it, these are always on the underside, facing the corpse.

Cup-and-ring marks first appear on exposed slabs of rock on high ground which led to the conclusion that they were tribal boundary markers; in other places they are deemed to mark a sacred site. By the time they appear in the Borders, they were on movable rocks.

The finding of three very similar cup-and-ring marked stones in the vicinity of Soutra Aisle, suggests that there must have been a ceremonial or sacred place on the hill. Soutra, originally named Soltre in a document dated AD 1153, has been given the derivation from Old Welsh, as 'the stead with wide view' which it is; but a more recent thought gives the derivation as 'the settlement of the sun'. Both would be equally apt and it takes but little imagination to postulate a temple for sun-worship on Soutra Hill where the medieval hospital once stood.

Neolithic/Bronze Age Saunas

When the Peeblesshire Archaeological Society decided to conduct a survey of the Manor Valley, they made some remarkable new discoveries. One of the most unusual was the investigation of the enigmatic 'burnt mounds'. These are horseshoe-shaped scatters of heat-shattered stones sitting on a bed of burnt soil and have only recently been recognised as having an archaeological function.

Excavations have suggested that they were places where large amounts of water was boiled. A stone or wood-lined pit was filled with water, stones were heated in the fire and then placed in the water. Experiments show that water can be boiled quickly in this manner. At first this was thought to be a place where food was prepared but the absence of burnt animal bones made that explanation unlikely.

Observing that the water pits seemed to be enclosed within a shelter, the suggestion that these were 'sweat houses' or saunas seems quite a plausible idea. The same idea is used in Scandinavia to this day and the North American Indians still do use 'smoke houses' to transport them to another world. Perhaps the Neolithic people of Manor Water combined the two functions.

Charcoal from the excavation indicates that what are bare hills today, were mixed woodland when the postulated sweat house was in operation around 2000 BC.

THE MIDDLE BRONZE AGE
*c.*1200 BC–900 BC

If trying to fix the initial date of the Early Bronze Age was difficult, to make a decision on when it ended is even more so. The best guess is probably around 1200 BC when the first of the next generation of bronze tools and weapons were traded into the Borders. This would not affect the lives of the people who were managing to scrape a living on the hills of the Borders. Their main preoccupation would be how to survive: how to grow and rear enough to feed a family through the winter and have some over to plant as seed the following spring: to try to understand the will of the gods and persuade them, through worship and offerings, to help in the future.

It has been surmised that the new objects were brought in by a new wave of settlers but an equally valid explanation was that more traders were coming into the area as the population expanded.

In the previous centuries, bronze had a scarcity value. Now it was being produced in quantity, and advances in metalworking technology meant that new types of weapons, tools and objects of personal adornment were becoming available. The Middle Bronze Age industry which flourished in Scotland was derived from raw materials of copper, tin and gold from outwith the area, probably Ireland as many of the completed articles exhibit a strong Irish influence. New objects like spearheads, daggers, rapiers and shields were being produced for use in war or simply as the status symbols of a ruling elite. That few specimens have been found in the Borders region, may indicate a peaceful and organised society or it may be that scarcity made them precious and kept safely.

The simple flat axe of the Early Bronze Age evolved through the palstave, winged and socketed forms of axe. Axes were probably the most made and most sought-after items; stone axes were clumsy and quickly dropped out of favour when the bronze ones became available. Bulk production would make the new axe affordable to working generations of people who farmed the land and, because of its fineness and sharpness of edge, this axe would make the felling and shaping of timber much easier. It was only one of a wide variety of bronze tools being made; chisels, hammers, gouges, knives, sickles and hooks were all practical working tools. By the Middle Bronze Age, the use of stone tools had practically ceased with the exception of flint arrowheads which were expendable and likely to be lost or broken when fired.

With the means of mass production and a reliable trading network, bronze had ceased to be a badge of the elite.

It has been suggested that hereditary military elites are likely to have controlled the lives of the community and, for the rulers, ostentation and the display of personal wealth was an indication of how important they were. The leaders of the hierarchical societies could strengthen their position by making gifts to their immediate followers, thus ensuring their allegiance. So there was still a demand for pins of various sizes and ornamentation for personal adornment, for torcs, finger rings and armlets. Whether this hereditary elite idea is applicable to the society that lived in the Borders at this time is open to doubt. The broken landscape of the Borders does not lend itself to large tribal groupings, but rather to small extended-family communities whose allegiance was to the local group leader.

Although the bulk of the population concentrated on food production, there is likely to have been enough surplus to allow for specialist craftsmen to develop their trade, the most important of these being smiths, the magicians who could make metal out of rock, and then make weapons and ornaments out of the metal.

Previously, in the Early Bronze Age, farms and settlements had been unenclosed but now this move towards enclosure defences, suggests a period of uncertainty and stress. The enclosures seem to have started around 800 BC and the tendency became more apparent in the Late Bronze and Iron Ages.

Out on the hills, things were changing and had been for some time. Around 1100 BC, the upland farms were being deserted, the cultivation of higher fields ceased and the people who remained moved into stock-rearing as a means of supporting life. Faced with little concrete evidence, we must fall back on uncertain speculation.

There is a valid suggestion that the bulk of the population moved from the hill ground into the valleys for the winter and returned with their flocks to spend the summer in the uplands. If the displaced upland populations had constructed unenclosed settlements similar to those they had left in the hills, this would put pressure on the people on the lower ground, to defend their own land. This may have caused turf wars (literally) and could explain the fluctuations in population.

Another speculation is that they had simply disappeared by emigrating to some other part of the country or died off through some plague or natural disaster. Although this depopulation has been acknowledged by archaeologists working in the area, why it happened is still debated with strength and vigour. Evidence from pollen analysis and excavation is patchy and a positive conclusion is still in the 'not proven' stage. Results from one site can be totally different from another a mere mile away and this confuses the overall picture.

Some archaeologists have tied the disappearance of upland settlement in the Cheviots to the volcanic eruption of Mount Hekla in

Iceland that happened in 1159 BC. This threw many thousands of tonnes of dust into the atmosphere, affecting areas from Scandinavia to Ireland and changing the weather patterns for many years. When the volcanic dust screened off the sun, temperatures dropped, the rain became more acidic and the growing seasons were not long enough for crops to grow and ripen to maturity. This failure of agriculture would cause famine and a decrease in population with a long-term effect on upland land-use of grazing animals superseding cultivated crops.

Others suggest that the deterioration of the upland habitat was spread over several centuries, the result of continuous heavy rainfall which had eroded the ploughed land on the hill slopes causing it to move downhill into the valley. There is evidence that woodland clearance had started or, at least, had accelerated the problem. When the trees were cut and the ground cultivated, the rich forest soil was opened up to the weather. This had been an on-going problem since Neolithic times, reaching its peak in the Middle Bronze Age.

Upland soil on acid rocks tends to be naturally thin and deficient in nutrients. In a wet climate, nutrients are lost as rainwater leaches through the soil, creating major changes in the soil and the vegetation it supports. Metal ions like iron are washed down into the soil and are deposited as a layer of 'iron pan' that does not allow water to percolate through it. This leads to water-logging and the death of growing trees which are replaced by bog plants which tolerate wet nutrient-poor conditions.

Whatever the reason, perhaps by cause and effect, there is a difference in the bronze objects found. Axes had previously been the most numerous find; now weapons were preferred: dirks, spearheads and swords. An axe is a tool that can be used as a weapon if required but spears, dirks and swords have their only purpose as weapons – dark times loomed.

THE LATE BRONZE AGE
*c.*900 BC–600 BC

The Late Bronze Age in the Borders is dated from around 900 BC to 600 BC, both dates dubiously provisional. Bronze objects and weapons were now appearing in quantity in the Borders. The two natural points of entry were still the Biggar Gap and the mouth of the Tweed. Either trading, raiding or colonisation could be responsible for the variety of bronze implements discovered by chance or excavation. Although poor in comparison with most parts of Britain, this was a period of conspicuous ostentation, especially in the votive offerings to the gods.

During this period, the Borders population seems to have recovered in number to what it had been several centuries before. With more people concentrated on a reduced area of tillable land in the low-lying valley-bottoms, it was inevitable that social and agricultural pressures would emerge. In the period 700–600 BC, the climate deteriorated again causing further demands on food production efforts.

For the last two or three centuries, fewer people had been living in the hill country and consequently the demand for timber was less, so the tree cover had re-established itself on the ground that had previously been cultivated. As in the Early Bronze Age, increasing demands on the lower-lying land was relieved by people moving back into the uplands. Pollen diagrams show some timber clearance in the hills and the resumption of grassland. Differences in grazing patterns must be taken into account; then as now, cattle required the longer and lusher grasses in the valley bottoms while the sheep and goats with different teeth and forage requirements were more suited to hill ground.

So the picture that emerges initially is that of a scattered population living in single huts and small settlements. The dispersed population gradually moved into village-sized units within a timber palisade wall. With up to twenty houses inside the enclosure, this settlement could be explained by several generations of one family living in one place with the palisade to keep out predatory animals and provide some defence in troubled times.

The dating of such settlements remains a problem, partly because little excavation has been done on them and partly because what little concrete evidence there is, suggests that this type of structure was in use from about 1000 BC until medieval times, but it should not be inferred that such occupation was continuous or uninterrupted in any one site.

Woodland Management

The very fact that village settlements were able to have one or more palisades and build their houses with wood, is a good indication that the hills had become reforested during the centuries of under-use and neglect. Building with timber is sure sign of a forested landscape; when timber is scarce, buildings tend to be of stone.

Wood is one of the resources that humans can replace. Woodlands had been managed for centuries during the Bronze Age but tree management became more imperative as the population grew.

Even with Bronze Age axes, big trees were hard to cut down and even harder to split into usable pieces. The most useful timber was small straight trees with a bole about 4–5m in length and 5–7cms in diameter at the base; but to cut down and split up this size of tree was wasteful, so they 'coppiced' their woodland instead.

When a hardwood tree is felled, it does not die but produces new shoots from the stump. As long as grazing animals can be kept away, these new shoots become trees in their own right, and after ten to fifteen years have grown sufficiently long and strong enough to be used for wattle frames in house building, roofing, fence posts or fuel.

If the tree is 'pollarded' ie cut above the reach of browsing animals, the new shoots sprout from there and can be harvested as required leaving the thick stem to produce another crop in a few years time. A pollarded tree has the treble benefit of having usable timber in the bole, long straight shoots for building etc beyond the reach of grazing teeth, and still leaving the ground below fit for grazing.

Wood pastures provided winter shelter and a longer grazing season for animals with a wide range of herbs and shrubs growing under the forest canopy. With the shelter provided by trees, grass shoots about a fortnight earlier in spring and lasts longer before the outset of winter, giving an extended grazing season. Sheep, cattle and goats could survive on the dry winter foliage. Sheep and goats can eat ivy and cattle munch away gingerly on green holly leaves. In the autumn, dry leaves from oak, elm, ash and holly were gathered for winter fodder – not very nutritious but enough to keep the animals alive. Acorns and bracken roots provided sustenance for pigs throughout the year. All in all, a sensible forest management policy was essential for the prehistoric upland farmer.

Population Spread

In this period, the Borders seem to have been carved into minor kingdoms, whose lands usually were marked by the natural divisions of river and hilltop. By linking the natural boundaries of hills and rivers with the roads that ran along the tops of the hills and the burial cairns beside the roads and together with the concentrations of finds and settlement traces, it is possible to speculate where the estate/kingdoms were located. As the estate boundaries often coincide with the Early Bronze Age find patterns, a further conclusion could be made that the bulk of the population had remained static while the new technology came to them by way of trade.

This speculation is not so ludicrous as it might first appear. Recent researches into DNA studies reveal that 80 per cent of the people in Britain can trace their ancestry to the hunter-gatherers who settled here after the last Ice Age. Most Borderers are not the descendants of the glamorised invaders, Romans, Vikings or Normans, but rather of the prehistoric hunters who first made there way up the river system and settled on its banks.

Nor is it feasible to say that the Yetholm/Hounam/Morebattle, Roberton/Teviothead and Meldon/Manor/Biggar Gap settlements definitely were the greatest centres of population throughout the Bronze Ages. They are simply the areas where the finds have been most prolific and the settlements most visible. It must be noted that these areas are mainly marginal hill lands where the ground has been undisturbed by subsequent agriculture. What had been found in earlier days and not been recorded, could change our conclusions of any previous ages.

No farmer from any age will settle on poor land if a better choice is available. So it is a sensible deduction that the lower and more productive river haughs were cultivated before land seekers moved into the hills. What has decayed or been destroyed in the lower land is unknown but it is likely to have been much more than what is now left visible on the hills.

It is worth repeating that archaeology is the study of the past through its *known surviving remains*, and from such small resources, the history of Border settlement must be written. New discoveries will change the concepts with existing evidence, thoughts and speculation requiring to be re-evaluated at periodic intervals.

Late Bronze Age Society

In southern England and the Continent, the Late Bronze Age society is known to have been organised on almost feudal lines with most of the people committed to food production. The king/leader/chief and his warrior aristocracy would be on top of the group, offering protection and refuge in return for a share of the farming produce; associated with them were the priests, specialist craftsmen and servants to carry out the king's commands and see that they were obeyed. Below them in social standing was the bulk of the population, the food producers, farmers and herdsmen; while really at the bottom were the slaves attached to the households of the king or aristocracy.

The group of warrior aristocracy would support the king or the ruling family and be the small core of the king's fighting force. This was a mutual bond, they being dependent on his bounty while he would have to rely on their loyalty.

This was not necessarily the way that the people of the Borders were organised. The large number and small size of hill forts surviving in the region would suggest a fragmentation of society into family or kinship groups within the natural boundaries of the land. The united tribal groupings recognised by the Roman historians do not fit into the Borders landscape and it would be more accurate to describe the population as a complex, disunited society of small tribal chiefs

This did not mean that they were inferior in their way of life. Despite the fact that there has been little modern excavation, the stray finds show that there were established trading routes for tangible goods and for new ideas. The magicians of the period, the smiths, may have had a home base in the larger settlements but certainly some travelled round the country collecting old or damaged bronze objects and recast them to suit the changing tastes. Several travelling smith's hoards of tools and scrap metal have been found in the Borders, deposited for safe keeping but never retrieved.

The only instance that bronze objects were made in the Borders is the find of a steatite mould for making bronze axes, that was found on the Eildons; this may have been a votive offering rather than part of a travelling smith's toolkit.

This period saw the introduction of a new bronze weapon – the sword. Bronze swords were known in parts of the Continent and southern Britain but it seems that it was in the Late Bronze Age that they first made their appearance in the Borders.

The possession of a sword not only demonstrated that its owner was one of the emerging warrior elite but also that he was rich enough to afford this new symbol of power. It was a slashing weapon compared with the previous Bronze Age rapier which was a stabbing weapon, and, combined with another innovation, the horse, could make the warrior practically invincible.

Horses had been in use in Scotland as riding and draught animals since around 1000 BC. Although small by today's standards, barely 13hh – pony size as the skeletons of prehistoric horses show – a warrior could ride one without difficulty although his feet would by near the ground. (Stirrups had not been invented yet; bridle bits had been developed by Continental horsemen at the start of the Bronze Age.)

The mounted warrior, even on a 13hh horse, had a considerable advantage over an opponent on foot. It is thought that the Celtic warriors of the time used the horse mainly as a person carrier to get him easily to the fight and equally quickly away if things went wrong. Yet the new bronze sword was clearly designed for slashing and could only be totally effective if it was used by a mounted warrior, giving him the advantage of height over a man on foot.

There is a magical aura about a sword that was felt even in the Bronze Age. In 1814, two bronze swords were discovered thrust vertically into the ground at Ewart Park, near Wooler. The obvious inference of the legend of Arthur drawing a sword from the stone comes to mind.

In 1864, a shepherd was crossing the sloping face of Horsehope Craig near the top of the Manor Water in Peeblesshire, when he saw something lying loose on the scree. He picked up several items and took them to the farmer. Together, they went back to see if there was anything else lying around and, underneath a massive rock, found a hoard of bronze objects. Twenty-eight items were recovered, two of them were socketed bronze axes and the remainder were bronze rings and other pieces of metal.

The axes are common but, when examined, the other objects were identified as chariot mountings and harness rings. Nothing like this had been found in Scotland and the nearest comparison is to Czechoslovakian or Alsatian carts, and dated to between 850 BC and 750 BC. The cart fittings are small-sized compared to their Continental counterparts and the suggestion was made that the Horsehope find was a cart-burial rather than the remains of a working chariot.

Swords have always been the symbols of power – even in modern times when the army is on parade, the officers carry swords while the NCOs and Other Ranks march with a rifle and bayonet.

This suggestion would fit in with the 'massive stone' under which some of the objects were found. What we have to consider is whether the remains and grave goods are from a chambered tomb or have been deposited as a votive offering.

In 1825, several urns containing human remains, nails and other articles 'resembling coffin mountings or handles' were found during the destruction of cairns at Hatton Knowe (NT 230460) near the village of Eddleston, Peeblesshire.

In the National Museum of Scotland in Edinburgh there is a big bronze cauldron which is almost intact. It is labelled as being from Darnhall, Peeblesshire, the mansion which is now the Black Barony Hotel, and is about 1km from the destroyed cairns.

It is tempting to put the two facts together and say that it is likely that the cauldron was found on the farm of Hatton Knowe and given to the estate owner who lived in Darnhall. Logical, tempting and most likely to be true.

Whatever the facts of the matter, the cauldron is from the earliest phase of the Late Bronze Age and fits into the same dating as the Horsehope Craig hoard.

In 1837 drain-digging in a marshy field about 600m north-east of the village of Yetholm, Roxburghshire, produced two round bronze shields which were found about a metre below the surface. The field, known as Yetholm Bog, had originally been part of a big loch but had been drained in 1830 as land-reclamation. Another almost identical shield was ploughed up in 1870. This was only 25cms deep but had to be part of the same deposited treasure.

The three shields are about 60cms in diameter, decorated by a simple design of concentric circles beaten out from the back of the shield with further punch-marks between the circles. With their concentric ribs and bosses, these are copies of the wooden targes with bronze studs that are known from Continental Europe from around 800 BC. But the Yetholm shields are not meant for battle; the metal is too thin and it is obvious that these were made for display, as status symbols or for votive offerings.

There are two other groups of shields that have been found in similar circumstances, one at Beith in Ayrshire and the other at Auchmaleddie in Aberdeenshire.

Of the three discoveries above, the Horsehope Craig was by fortuitious accident but the other two owe their discovery to the fact that, although the Agricultural Revolution in the Borders started around the 1750s, it took until the Napoleonic War period before it worked its way into the more marginal land in the hills. As in Bronze Age times, the need for more food production made estate owners and farmers look to new methods to develop areas which had hitherto been untouched. Lochs and bogs were drained and the land ploughed; fields were enclosed by dykes using convenient stones which could be easily obtained by knocking down old cairns. Many of the best finds made in the Borders are the by-product of the Agricultural Revolution.

This, together with the Victorian interest in the past, made country people more aware of what could be found in the ground. As the laird had first claim on the objects, many estates had their own small museum of objects found on their own land. Unfortunately, many such finds did not make it into the records, thus depriving interested people of valuable information.

I mentioned the possible chambered cairn that lies beside the Green Road near Clovenfords (see p.51). About 30m away, there is a disused quarry. In 1872, the quarrymen found a hoard of bronze and iron objects 'in the vicinity'. Four iron hammers, four iron spears, a bronze handled iron knife, a bronze enamelled brooch and several pieces of thin bronze plate, riveted together with bronze rivets were recorded. Local folklore tells that the 'best pieces' were sold for drink in the local hostelry.

It is tempting to put the two facts together and suggest that the iron finds were found in or near the chambered tomb. Reality makes it more likely that the hoard was the stock of a travelling Iron Age smith. What would make it really interesting would be to discover the exact findspot and the number and type of objects that were exchanged for beer.

THE IRON AGE
*c.*600 BC–AD 79

In 1690, Edward Lhuyd was appointed as keeper of the newly opened Ashmolean Museum at Oxford; a Welsh scholar, he had studied the languages of Cornwall and Brittany and found common ground amongst them. Requiring an inclusive term for the languages of Wales, Cornwall, Brittany, Scotland, the Isle of Man and Ireland, he invented the term 'Celtic'. In reality, its corporate use was to group together all languages that were used in the British Isles, other than English. By his invention, Lhuyd gave the non-English Britain the romantic images of legend – that of kings and warriors, bards, druids and princesses. This persists into the Hollywood images of King Arthur etc. That Arthur, the Welsh-speaking Christian warrior who fought against the heathen Angles, gets transposed into an English king, is only part of the mystique; people believe what they want to believe anyway.

In Greco-Roman writings, 'Celts' were the people of Gaul and Caesar regarded the Gauls and the Britons as ethnically different. The Romans saw differences between the various peoples of Brittania with the 'Britanni' in the south and the more derogatory 'Britonnes' in the north. Obviously the more civilised people in the south who accepted Roman rule deserved a Romanised name, and those in the north who didn't, didn't. From the Vindolanda letters, we find the natives described as 'Brittunculi' by the superior Romans. This can be translated as 'miserable little Britons'.

Before trying to make a reasonable case based on the slight artefactual evidence of the Iron Age in the Borders, it is wise to see what archaeologists and scholars have found south of the border.

In England

It is thought that iron was first brought into Britain by successive waves of settlers from the Continent, starting around 700 BC. In fact there were three major group/cultures and these have been used by archaeologists to delineate the specific tool and pottery types, to the peoples who used or made them.

Already known on the Continent from around 1000 BC, it was only a matter of time before Britain absorbed the new metal for tools and weapons. Iron was cheaper and more plentiful than bronze and, although requiring a higher temperature to work, its ores were more plentiful and needed no alloying with other metals to produce the finished article. Ultimately iron objects were within everybody's range. Initially, the tools and weapons were similar in shape and size to those of the Bronze Age but, being in the harder iron, were more durable. Bronze was still used for ornamentation and jewellery.

Over-population and land-hunger on the Continent made for a volatile situation. Tribal groupings, sometimes in the hundreds of thousands, moved to seek new land or to avoid the wars between the mobile Germanic confederations or the conquering might of Rome in the later stages of the age. Groups of immigrants from all parts of the Continent came in many waves and settled in different parts of England, causing pressure on the existing peoples to seek land elsewhere. This was usually found by moving northwards. It is not known whether any immigrants arrived in southern Scotland directly from the Continent but this would not be impossible.

Iron Age A was brought by a mass immigration of people from the French/Alps regions. Already iron-using, the Hallstatt culture was a continuation of the Late Bronze Age but with iron replacing bronze for their tools and weapons. They landed in the south and east coasts of England, spreading inland in search of land. Successive waves of immigration meant that they were the pre-eminent culture from 700 BC to 400 BC

Iron Age B came about when parts of tribes from the Seine-Marne areas of France emigrated en masse to the south east of England and eastern Yorkshire. After dealing with countless numbers of nameless peoples, we can now say that the cultural tribe that settled in Yorkshire were the Parisi and they spoke a language akin to early Welsh. They were more advanced than the Iron Age A people, being influenced by the Greek civilisation which was now spreading through Europe. This culture was generally known as La Tene and its main phase of influence lasted from *c.*400 BC to 100 BC.

When the La Tene peoples came to take over the lands of their predecessors, the Iron Age A people built hill-forts with banked and ditched enclosures into which they could take refuge in time of trouble.

The Parisi were reinforced by flows of refugees escaping from Caesar's Conquest of Gaul in the 60s and 50s BC. It was the Parisi of east Yorkshire who first made the flowing stylised animals in enamelled motifs on swords, shields and mirrors, the first examples of 'Celtic' art in Britain. This rich decorative art was cut short by the Roman invasion but survived in the 'barbarian' parts of Ireland and Scotland to return as part of the Scoto/Northumbrian culture when the Roman legions departed in the fifth century AD.

Iron Age C occurred with the advent of another tribal culture, the Belgae, a mixed nation of Celtic/Teutonic blood whose home lands were in central and north-east France.

They had started to settle in Kent around 100 BC. They were agriculturalists using the heavy plough that could turn the heavier soil of Kent and were thus able to plough land that was difficult to cultivate with the lighter ploughs of the previous inhabitants. By 50 BC, there was a strong Roman influence in southern England and a tribal currency economy based on Greek and Roman models.

Southern Britain under the Belgae produced a surplus of corn, slaves, hunting dogs, leather and other goods. So trade with the burgeoning Roman Empire built up to a high level. Caesar's expeditions in 55 and 54 BC, were because he had found out that Britannia was supplying reinforcements and support to the Gauls whom he was trying to control and perhaps to see if Britannia was worth conquering and bringing into the Roman Republic. Perhaps the fact that the Belgae had already been driven out of their original homeland by the Romans may have made them fight harder to defend their new lands. The eventual conquest in AD 43 was for political and economic reasons as well as to curb the potential threat posed to the Roman province of

Gaul by a nearby independent state that was willing to take in anti-Roman refugees.

It would be foolish to believe that the Continental settlers did not bring their customs, beliefs and language with them. Caesar wrote that the Druids' training was developed in Britannia and spread to Gaul but that diligent students of Druidism returned to Britannia to study it. It would be unlikely that the 'New Britons' of the Iron Age did not retain linguistic, trading and tribal links with their continental cousins.

Although the incomers introduced new methods and customs, the original inhabitants of the islands were still by far the most numerous, and their language and beliefs would survive to influence the newcomers.

In The Borders

'For much of the duration of the Iron Age in England we must in fact, regard Scotland as continuing the old traditions of the Bronze Age, while importing occasional trade-objects from the iron-using worlds.'
   Inventory of the Ancient and Historical Monuments of Roxburghshire, 1956

'The transition from the Late Bronze Age to the Early Iron Age is marked in SE Scotland by the appearance of dwelling-sites of varied plans, but essentially consisting of one or more round timber-framed huts enclosed within a single or double palisade … these can hardly be dated much, if at all, before the 1st century BC.'
   Inventory of the Ancient and Historical Monuments of Selkirkshire, 1957

'In Peeblesshire, as in the rest of northern Britain, the archaeological evidence for the Early Iron Age consists almost exclusively of the remains of habitations of different kinds, and the recording of these structures by the Commission provides virtually all the material upon which an evaluation of the local Early Iron Age can be based.'
   Inventory of the Ancient and Historical Monuments of Peeblesshire, 1967

Taking note of the above, we would have to reach the conclusion that there was very little that could be classified as Iron Age in the Borders until the first century BC and more realistically, that the Roman invasion of AD 79 would be the first time that many iron tools and weapons would come into the area. But these conclusions were based on work that had been done half a century ago and since then much has been found that has added fresh information to our knowledge of the period.

I find a gentle irony in the fact that a lot of the new discoveries have been made by people who were considered the scum of the earth by some archaeologists – the metal detectorists.

> In the 1980/90s, there were a few, very vocal academics who would have banned all metal detectors from the country and vilified those who pursued the hobby at every opportunity. I had never considered the responsible use of a detector as a menace to society and had never met one detectorist whose main object was 'how much is it worth?' But the public sniping soon caused resentment to such a degree that the two sides would not communicate with each other, being each in an entrenched position and lobbing insults at each other. This was to the detriment of archaeology.
>
> Being neither fish nor fowl, I maintained friendly relations with both sides of the heated debate. Eventually both sides found out that they were not always totally right and the other totally wrong, and they started to speak to each other (in some cases) and discovered that they had roughly the same aims, ie to add to the knowledge of the past with new discoveries and ideas. So all is well that ends well; but there is still a lot of liaising to do before we reach nirvana.

To get some idea of how the population lived, we have to look at the abundance of enclosures and hill-forts to see what information they can provide and add this to the recognisably pre-Roman iron artefacts which have been found since the Inventories were published. It is a jigsaw puzzle with a lot of pieces missing and some false clues can completely distort the whole dating sequence.

As an instance, one piece of Roman pottery found in an Iron Age context in the Borders can be taken to date the whole site as first century AD. This can be comforting datable evidence but can be totally wrong. One day while fieldwalking the Roman fort at Newstead, I

picked up a small silver coin inside the fort. This was eventually recognised as coming from a Greek island and dated to the third century BC
but no one ever suggested that the Greeks had settled there four
centuries before the Romans. The more prosaic explanation was that a
Roman soldier had lost his luck-piece while on his way back from the
wineshop in the east annexe. It is dangerous to build a story that is based
on one piece of evidence.

There used to be an inverted parochialism in Scottish archaeology
suggesting that most good ideas must have come from the south
because there have been more artefacts found there, more excavation
and more publications. This is a comfort zone for archaeologists and
historians but gives a southern Anglocentric view of archaeology in
general. This was particularly true from Victorian times up to the
Second World War, when even the published works of Scots, Irish and
Welsh academics looked to southern England for their comparisons and
superimposed a southern viewpoint on Scottish, Irish and Welsh
thinking.

This is not just my own Scottish nationalism showing through but
now is acknowledged as an accepted fact. Since the Second World War,
new breeds of archaeologists, many of them English, are looking at our
various cultures as entities in their own right. That said, many of the
'exotic' finds do come from the south.

It sometimes appears that the Iron Age in the Borders consisted of
nothing but hill-forts with at least one on the top of every hill. This is
wrong on two counts. Hardly any of the hundreds of hill-forts and
enclosures considered as possibly Iron Age have been proved by
excavation; and the life of a hill-fort could vary from the Late Bronze
Age until the Early Historic period, with some still being used as a
refuge during the troubled times of the late Middle Ages.

So for information on the period, we have to look at the few settlements that have been excavated, re-examine the findings and conclusions from there and project the results on to large numbers of hill-forts
that remain untouched. This will not necessarily give a totally correct
picture but it is the best we can do in the circumstances and until there
are more excavations to confirm or disprove the present deductions.

Hill-forts are the most easily recognised because they are most
easily seen, mainly on hills or ridges, and have often survived because

many were on ground not fit for subsequent cultivation. Consequently, they are the most numerous of all prehistoric monuments to be noted in the Borders. They vary in size from little more than enclosed hill-top farms to extensive multi-banked sites with large-scale earthwork defences and containing many houses of varying types. They were home to extended farming families numbering between thirty and a hundred people. Even the smallest could be enclosed by substantial earthworks which serve not only as a defence but also as a statement of prestige and power – 'Wha daur meddle wi me' is not the exclusive family motto of the Elliots.

On the theory that size does count, the largest of the forts built on commanding hill-tops are likely to have been centres where the leaders met and where people gathered for social contact, worship or trade. Eildon Hill North, Hownam Rings and Ruberslaw in Roxburghshire, White Meldon and Cademuir in Peeblesshire and Duns Law, Edin's Hall Fort and Blackchester in Berwickshire are examples of the larger hill-fort settlement. Selkirkshire has no known hill-fort large enough to be considered as the major focal point of a scattered community. The obvious deduction is that the marginal lands which comprise what is now Selkirkshire, were too poor to sustain a large population.

Hownam Rings was excavated in 1948, revealing several phases of occupation, each time with a reconstruction. The first settlement was enclosed by a single palisade, less defensive than for keeping out animals; then it was reconstructed in the same form; then a stone wall 3m thick was built around it; again remodelled with defences of three ramparts and three ditches. Finally the defences were abandoned and the site became an open sub-rectangular settlement with circular stone-walled houses.

This sequence was followed in whole or part, in the few excavated hill-forts in the Borders. As it repeated the patterns of southern England where single-rampart forts, definitely datable to the Iron Age A period, were frequently remodelled with multiple defences, it was assumed that this was the general pattern of construction throughout Britain.

It was known that there was fierce tribal warfare in the south of England from the first century BC which continued until the Roman invasion of AD 43. Many ruling families were driven from their kingdoms and had to seek new land elsewhere. The elements representative of the southern Iron Age cultures which did arrive from the south, seem largely to have been carried by refugee populations, numerically small but militarily competent, who established themselves as overlords in the Borders.

At Hownam, the changes in the defences were taken to reflect the ideas of the new leader and his followers. The tenure of the land could be of short duration as more refugees came from the south and the temporary owners of Hownam had to move on again. When the Romans came and introduced Pax Romana into certain parts of the Borders, there would be no obvious need for a defensive enclosure, so it was prudent and politic to dismantle the wall and fill the ditches.

This was a hypothesis that was well reasoned and fitted into the excavations at Hownam. The hypothesis became fact because it seemed a plausible explanation, so it was received uncritically and applied to similar sites, even although it was recognised that different parts of Scotland produced different results. This scenario was written into the archaeological papers of the time and some of these conclusions are still being used as the standard references for the period.

The appliance of modern science in the shape of radio-carbon dating, and the excavation of more sites, required a rethink on these previously accepted conclusions.

Chronological reassessment gives the first three phases at Hownam as spanning 600 to 700 years instead of the 200 to 300 years as originally thought. This would put the first phase of settlement to around 900 BC and into the Bronze Age. The three ramparts and ditches phase of Hownam occupation starts around 500 BC. This was a time when great social changes, ie invasion or threats of invasion from outside the area, made defensive structures necessary. Excavations at Broxmouth in East Lothian show that the main defensive systems started around the middle of the first millennium BC but falls into disrepair around 200 BC. This corresponds with the three rampart/ditch phase at Hownam.

It seems a logical conclusion that individual fortifications were not necessary because a strong central authority had taken command, ensuring a period of peace and security. So the ramparts would fall down into ditches and the people of the hills would resume their pastoral way of life. Inside the crumbling defences, the buildings previously thought to be Romano-British have now been proven to have originated in the pre-Roman Iron Age but were still occupied in AD 200. This explains why objects of Roman origin were found within the houses and added to the dating confusion of the excavators. The excavations at Hownam were right in execution but wrong in dating interpretation. What they do suggest is that the peasant community within the fort remained largely unchanged and in situ through the ages.

Reassess this new knowledge and if it is uniform throughout the area, a different picture of the pre-Roman Iron Age emerges.

From around 400 BC there is evidence of quite extensive forest clearance, dramatic in places where the whole pollen catchment areas have been denuded of timber within a fifteen-year period. This clearance varies from place to place but pollen from trees was being replaced by pollen from agriculture. It may have been because the climate was becoming warmer with a longer growing season but forest clearance indicates that an increasing population in both lowland and upland sites was involved in farming. Evidence from excavations in Northumberland has been sufficient to assert that many of the small earthworks and enclosures are associated with the removal of most of the forest timber. Buildings and field enclosures require a lot of timber and farming needs bare ground for cultivation, so the obvious conclusion is that these were farming villages, possibly with some defensive enclosure, rather than forts built for defence.

The chronological and territorial boundaries of settlement in the Iron Age Borders are almost impossible to define. Occasional field systems in the shape of cord rig cultivation can be seen beside some settlements but, like all fields systems, cord rig is tremendously difficult to date. It would certainly have its origins in the lower lying ground that is more suitable for tillage but medieval and modern farming there have destroyed all traces.

At Tamshiel Rig in Roxburghshire, there is the most extensive and best-preserved Iron Age fort and field system in Britain. Although it is dated into the Roman transition period in the Inventory of Roxburghshire, this was done on the assumption that the Hownam Rings dating sequence was correct. By updating the time scale to recent thinking, the Tamshiel Rig Fort is likely to be from around 500 BC with a later settlement superimposed around 300–200 BC and the fields are more likely to be contemporary with that settlement. How long it survived, we don't know because agricultural systems are never static – they expand and contract to fit the requirements of food production and vary with the size of the labour force, while weather and temperature can change the demands on the soil from grain to grazing or grazing to woodland.

So it is not possible to give a definitive plan of the various stages of the expanding field system. On visual evidence, the fields around Tamshiel Rig cover a total of 31½ acres. It has been extended three times with enclosure walls between 2m and 4m thick. The fields are long strips with at least one sub-divided into roughly rectangular plots about 15m each side. This indicates that the small fields were cultivated rather than grazed or perhaps as well as grazed. Stock could be herded on the outlying ground through the day and held safely overnight within the enclosures, at the same time manuring the fields for a subsequent crop.

Two unusual features are the D-shaped fields to the west of the fort. There is one long hollow between two walls on the north-west side of the fort which has all the appearances of an extended byre-shed for over-wintering breeding cattle.

Tamshiel Rig was a mixed agricultural farming system where tillage was as important as grazing. Dating might have to be reconsidered, but this would have to be done by excavation.

It has been suggested that the Tamshiel field system was introduced by pre-Roman Iron Age refugees from southern England. Certainly there was a stimulus for improved farming methods at this period. Previously the main thrust of farming had been towards sheep and cattle rearing with only enough grain production to satisfy the immediate family needs. Tamshiel Rig, with over 30 acres of arable fields, indicates that local corn-growing was being encouraged and improved.

Several iron ploughshares found in the south of Scotland demonstrate that plough-teams had replaced the hoe-cultivation of previous years, at least in some parts. It is worth noting that these ploughshares are of the Romano-Belgic type used by the Belgae, who had settled in Kent around 100 BC.

Smaller settlements with sufficient defences to qualify as forts in the various Inventories, come in two main categories, ridge forts and contour forts. To state the obvious, ridge forts are built on broad ridges as the land dictates, and are usually roughly rectangular. The greatest number of forts in the Borders are contour forts built as local conditions of terrain permit. Both types can have single or multiple defences, wooden palisades, sheer walls, ramparts of stone or clay and one or more ditches – or any combination of the above. In general terms, the larger hill-forts would fall into the category of defended village/farms with fields of 'cord rig' cultivation around, while the smaller ones are more likely to be the farmsteads of a single family unit.

Cord rig consists of narrow ridges of piled soil separated by shallow trenches, the distance between the centres of the ridges being about 1.5m. The higher ridging was designed to give a greater depth to the shallow soil of the hills while the hollows between drained away any excess water and prevented the soil from turning sour. This cord rig cultivation can be seen beside many of the hill-forts in the Borders hills and are often a clue to where a timber-built habitation once stood even although no other trace remains.

It is unsafe to assume that all hill-forts were simply the houses and storage huts of the farming community. Some might have been places where ritual ceremonial was performed.

The Romans were both fascinated and repelled by the Druids who they considered as religious leaders, healers, prophets, bards and magicians. The druids, who could be male or female, studied for twenty years in secret and sacred places, being fed and guarded by the local population. They were keepers of the oral traditions, passing their teachings through the generations by way of poetry and preserved their secrets by not writing anything down. So it is mainly through Roman writers that we know anything about the Druids and the Romans were definitely not pro-Druid.

It is pure speculation on my part that there were Druids in the Borders but there must have been some priestly class to carry out all the 'rituals' of a primitive society.

Some of the small hill-forts are likely to have been specialist production centres serving the immediate area. Two unfinished Roman-type brooches and a horse bit, still with the casting lumps, were found by a metal detectorist at the Falla Knowe fort, Middlesknowe in Roxburghshire, showing that some enterprising native smith was hoping to catch the Dere Street passing traffic in the first century AD.

Palisaded enclosures have had a long life in the Borders, being known from Bronze Age times until the post-Roman era. In Northumberland, the move towards enclosure is noted as starting around 800 BC and becomes more obvious in the Iron Age. It is unlikely that this trend did not spill over into the Borders.

The palisaded settlement at Harehope in Peeblesshire was excavated in 1960. On the surface it seemed a roughly rectangular, multivallate earthwork of uncertain age. On excavation it was found that it was two successive settlements with low banks and shallow ditches. The banks had traces of continuous palisades with a wooden tower at the entrance. In dating, the first settlement could be Late Bronze Age while the upper one fits into the pre-Roman Iron Age, and there seems to have been a continuous occupation.

Housing

In the excavation of pre-Roman sites in the Borders, the roundhouse dominated all other types of building. This was a basic ring of posts dug into the ground; these supported roof-poles that met in the middle like spokes in a wheel and the whole was covered with such wattle, straw, skins and turf as was available. In some, the roof-poles extended to the ground, in others, rested on the top of a wall of stone or wattle and mud. The fire was in the middle of the house unless there was a central pole, and there could be internal divisions made with wattle and daub if desired. Roundhouses had no windows and an open doorway was the only source of natural light. The central fire would provide heat, light and cooking facilities during the winter. In the better weather, cooking was done outside to lessen risk of fire.

Roundhouses were well-constructed family homes, established in the Bronze Age and lasting well into the post-Roman period. They were large and often spacious with a diameter of 10–11m. These used a lot of timber in their construction and this, together with the demands of agriculture and grazing animals, accounted for the decrease in forest cover. A pollen analysis of the turf-line beneath the Iron Age fort on Bonchester Hill reveals that grasses were the most numerous pollen type and that the locality was devoid of much 'woody vegetation' with only alder and hazel being represented.

A variant of the roundhouse was the ring-ditch house that appeared around 500 BC. This was a simple roundhouse, raised in the centre but immediately surrounded by a circular ditch, 2–3m wide and more than 1m deep. Although recognised as having some kind of archaeological use, the exact function of this type of building had puzzled archaeologists for some time. Recent thoughts have designated them as 'byre-houses' where milk cows, or those in calf, could be tethered at night or during the winter. This would protect the precious stock from predators as well as ensuring that they were kept warm and sufficiently fed to survive the hard winter months. An additional benefit was that manure was easier to collect and spread on the nearby field system which was being rested over the cold spell.

There is some dispute as to whether the central part of the building was used as a family home or as a fodder store for the animals. It is probable that both functions were considered. Up to two centuries ago, it was common in rural Scotland for cattle to share the same roof as humans, the heat from the animals being very welcome in the heights of winter; the smell was tolerated and accepted.

From the Peeblesshire *Inventory*, six ring-ditch stuctures were partly excavated with little result other than a few flint implements and a stone axehead. Only one of the six has a narrow entrance. It was still a pre-publication puzzle although the eighty-one recorded in Peeblesshire and numerous others in Roxburghshire and Northumberland, ruled out the idea that this was only a local phenomenon.

In 1962, an earthwork near Yarrowford in Selkirkshire was excavated by members of the Selkirkshire Antiquarian Society under the supervision of Dorothy N. Marshall. It was a flat-topped mound or platform 10m across with a surrounding ditch and external bank. There was an entrance on the north side.

It was a ring-ditch structure although this type of earthwork was not recognised at that date. Unlike the Peeblesshire ring-ditches, some datable objects were found during the excavation – a piece of Neolithic pottery outside the structure, half of a bronze ring and a whole bronze enamelled finger ring in the interior. The finger ring was dated to the Iron Age, possibly as late as the first century AD.

This gives a tentative dating of the ring-ditch structures to between

700 BC and AD 50 but more evidence is needed before accepting either date as an absolute.

Invaders or New Style Building Techniques?

At the end of the first century BC or the beginning of the first century AD, another type of construction came into the Borders. Previous ages had utilised a mixture of timber, earth and stone to build their forts and houses but this new method of construction was by dry-stone alone ie stone without any binding substance. Whether this technique was brought in by new settlers, or because the previously used timber resources had become scarce, is a matter of conjecture. Certainly this same construction is well-known on the west Atlantic coast of Scotland and in Ireland both of which had strong trading links with the Borders, so the most likely answer is 'a mixture of the two'.

The new constructions came in three classifications, the broch, the closely related dun and the large circular fort.

Of the three types, the most recognisable is the 'broch' which is most numerous on the north and west coasts of Scotland where about five hundred are known. The broch is a very special form of circular dwelling with a dating from the turn of the pre-Christian into early Christian periods. With a large stone base about 5m thick and an internal diameter of 9–12m, the broch was essentially a circular tower that dominated the shoreline or landscape. Judging from the relatively small amounts of debris found within the ruined structures, the broch could only have been 6–8m in height.

Of the lowland brochs, two are within the Borders Region at Edinshall in Berwickshire and at Torwoodlee in Selkirkshire (of which more later), with another just outside the regional border at Bow in Midlothian. The realisation that the lowland brochs fit into the Roman period and the fact that Roman artefacts have been found in their excavation, has produced some inspired guesswork to make their dating fit into the historical template of Roman occupation. On this, more later.

'Dun' is a Gaelic word meaning a fort or fortified dwelling and they come in all shapes and sizes but usually circular if the ground is suitable. Like the brochs, duns are most numerous on the north and west coasts of Scotland and in Ireland. As both brochs and duns have been used as convenient quarries during the dyke-building of eighteenth and nineteenth century agricultural enclosures, the wall-foundation remains of a smaller circular dun are very similar to that of the broch, making it very difficult to differentiate between the two.

Only one dun has been recognised in the Borders so far. This stands on a rocky promontory SSW of Stanhope farmhouse at the height of 305m (*Inventory of Peeblesshire* No. 338). The interior is roughly pear-shaped, 7.5m by 5.5m enclosed by a dry-stone wall 4m thick. When first investigated, the interior was 'heavily choked by the collapsed remains of the wall'.

In 1993, I was spending some time trying to trace the Roman road up the Tweed from the river crossing at Trimontium (Newstead). Things were going quite nicely and I managed to get a reasonable line up to the marching camp at Innerleithen. Knowing that there was bound to have been a series of signal stations connecting the one on Eildon Hill North with the Roman complex at Lynne, I thought that the summit of Lee Pen, just to the north of Innerleithen, would be an ideal location, in line of sight from the Eildons and still visible from the hills near Lynne. So I climbed the quite steep hill until I reached the flat below the summit of Lee Pen.

Sure enough there was a circular marking on the ground with enough definition to suggest a diameter of 8m – but there was no ditch to indicate a signal station. Instead, the original interior had been lower than the ground surface but this had been partly filled with field-collected stones. Outside the circle was enough rubble to convince me that a large broad wall had once stood here, and also enough to convince me that a plan of the site would come in handy some time.

So, at NT 326 380, there is a circular marking with an internal diameter of 8m surrounded by a wall base 4 to 5m wide. There is an entrance from the east, 1.5m at the outside of the wall reducing to 1m at the interior. This is likely to be a dun, in my opinion although others may be of a different mind. Near the entrance is a square marking a building 4m by 4m externally and 2.5m by 2m internally. About 30m to the south, is another circular ground-marking, 4m in diameter. This needs an unbiased eye to pronounce judgement.

The third group of dry-stone constructions are the hill-forts. The great majority of hill-forts in the Borders are defended by walls of earth and rubble cores or by ramparts made from the spoil of quarry ditches. These are to be found in large numbers in the rest of Northern Britain, Wales and parts of France.

Less common in the Borders are the forts enclosed by thick walls made entirely of dry-stone construction, with the thickness of the walls varing from 3.5m to 5m. As this type of structure is most numerous in Peeblesshire where at least six major and seven minor forts have been built using this technique, there can be little doubt that this was introduced from the west.

Selkirkshire has possibly two forts and two duns with dry-stone walls while Roxburghshire has several fort/settlements that come under the same category. The fort on Carby Hill in Castleton Parish, is a definite example of this drystone construction. Although extensively robbed for dyke-building stone, the remaining debris indicates an oval enclosure measuring 87m by 68m surrounded by a dry-stone wall at least 3m thick. The original builders probably came from along the Solway Coast or Ireland. If this theory is correct, it seems a logical conclusion that a considerable number of new settlers, land-grabbing or peaceful, came into the perimeters of the Borders in the immediate pre-Roman period.

Social Cohesion

With the large number of forts and settlements visible in the Borders hills, there must have been some kind of social cohesion binding the various groupings together. Each settlement or small fort is likely to have been based on the extended family, independent but in close contact with their neighbours with whom they would have shared blood ties. There is no convincing proof that there was one large unified tribal group as had become established in the south.

Although it is unwise to project the lives and mores of one age into another and expect complete similarity, it is tempting to view pre-Roman society in the Borders as fragmented in kinship groups, rather similar to the reivers of the sixteenth century whose first loyalty was to those of their own family name and the land that the family held.

Taking a look at the area involved, it is a logical conclusion that a loose confederation of tribes occupied the natural boundaries of the Tweed basin and, if we skip a century or two forward, they would be known as Otadini or Votadini by the invading Romans.

This knowledge comes from two sources, neither of which depends on first-hand information. Tacitus was the son-in-law of Julius Agricola who campaigned in what is now Scotland from AD 79–85. Tacitus wrote a book praising his father-in-law's campaigns; this was a strictly PR effort, a 'laudatio' for Agricola, and a prelude to his (Tacitus') own 'Annals' and 'Histories'. The book now known as 'Agricola' contains little history, seeming to be a self-justification of Agricola's actions combined with a paean of praise for the new Emperor, Trajan.

Tacitus would have heard a lot of 'old soldiers' tales' from his father-in-law and put them down in book form and old soldiers' tales are colourful but not necessarily very accurate.

The original book survived long enough to be copied into a manuscript in the mid ninth century and this in turn was the source material for three later medieval copies. Without these copies, there would have been little written knowledge of the Romans in Scotland. How much of it is a factual account is a matter of belief.

The second was a map in Ptolemy's 'Geography' that was based on stories collected from various sources by Marinus of Tyre. Ptolemy had never visited Britain but set about correcting and improving the information provided by Marinus. He seems to have been working with two lists – one with Roman forts and the other with tribal areas and names, but with no clear distinction of which was which.

His map suffers from one critical basic error as Britain north of the Tyne-Solway line is turned eastwards by ninety degrees. This has caused no end of problems for Roman historians trying to fit the names into their supposed locations. Trimontium is the one name that can be located with certainty; the 'three hills' could not be other than the Eildons. Ptolemy places this in the territory-list of the Selgovae but this seems to be a mistake. Taking the natural grain of the country and the watershed divisions as the most logical tribal locations into consideration, this would place the Votadini in the Lothians and in the Tweed basin; the Selgovae in the basins of the rivers Nith, Annan and Urr; the Novantae in Galloway, and the Damnoni in the Clyde Valley.

Taking this observation one step further, the absence of known Iron Age settlements in the Ettrick, Yarrow and Liddel Valleys and the top of Tweedsmuir on the east side of the Votadini/Selgovae watershed and a corresponding absence on the west side, suggests that the two were not the best of neighbours, or that neither group needed the marginal lands for agricultural exploitation.

Looking at the settlements and finds around the Biggar Gap which would be on the Votadini/Damnoni border, it seems that they enjoyed friendly trading relations and the later history of both the Votadini and the Damnoni suggests that neither were traditional enemies of Rome. This is pure speculation, of course.

Iron Age Finds

Apart from the settlements and hill-forts described above, the Borders have a number of isolated finds and three metalwork hoards, largely made up with iron objects. As the hoards are the most instructive, we will start with them and broaden the spectrum by adding a similar hoard from outwith the Borders area.

Blackburn Mill Hoard, Berwickshire
This was found by labourers cutting a drain in a haugh on Blackburn Mill. Sixty-five objects, whole and broken, were found in two bronze cauldrons, one of which was inverted on the other. The find was made before 1852 and some of the artefacts may have 'strayed' before being recorded.

Clovenfords Hoard, Selkirkshire
This is noted on p.51. Found by quarrymen in 1872, the 'best' objects were sold before they could be recorded.

Eckford Hoard, Roxburghshire
This was found by a workman digging in a little plot of land called Toddle (Toadhole) Rigs, on the farm of Easter Wooden, Eckford. Nineteen objects or fragments were recovered but the find 'appears to have been larger', nor was it sure that the finder recovered the whole deposit.

Carlingwark Hoard, Kirkcudbrightshire

This hoard was found by two fishermen in Carlingwark Loch in 1866. One hundred and three metal objects were found in a large bronze cauldron.

By lumping the information contained in these hoards together, it is possible to reach certain conclusions. No great difference in content can be detected between the hoards, with a mixture of military and higher status objects together with quantities of agricultural and craftsmen's tools in about equal quantities. Sword tips and chain mail represent a military component; horse harness and vehicle mountings are for carriages rather than carts and cauldrons; cauldron chains, tripods and gridiron, together with certain Roman items, suggest higher status depositors than the peasant shepherd.

A detailed examination suggests that some identifiable objects are from Iron Age cultures in the south and east of England, mainly from the Kent area where the Belgic influence was strongest.

A more exotic hoard was found at Netherurd on the Peeblesshire/ Lanarkshire county boundary in 1806. The hoard consisted of two identical loop terminal torques, one flat terminal torque, the single ring terminal of a multi-strand torque and 'upwards of 40' globular coins – all of gold alloy. The shepherd boy who discovered the hoard disposed of most of the items to 'some of the goldsmiths' in Edinburgh.

This hoard is a rare mixture. The two surviving coins of the forty originally recovered are from Belgic Gaul; known as 'globules a la croix', they resemble small gold-alloy hot cross buns. The penannular twisted torcs are from eastern England and the ring terminal is likely to be a product of an Icenian workshop from the area of Norfolk.

So the hoard seems to have Belgic-Gaul origins and arrived in Peeblesshire sometime around the mid first century BC.

In 1995, a metal detectorist found an unusual gold coin while detecting on the farm of Galadean in Lauderdale. It was identified as a South Ferriby stater of the first century BC and was out of circulation before the arrival of Roman coinage in the Borders. It was a coin of the Coritani who inhabited the northern part of Lincolnshire. A lone coin is not evidence of a currency economy operating in southern Scotland, so it may have been a curio brought up and lost during the Roman occupation.

As a fencing contractor, I used divining rods to find where the field drains were, in order to avoid breaking them while digging postholes. To hit and break a tile could take several hours baling out the water from the drain system in order to replace the tile with a new one. With two pieces of fencing wire turned at right angles, I could detect where the drain was and place the post somewhere else. The two divining rods were a practical labour-saving device.

This was fine and quite acceptable as water and drain divining, but when I used the same skills using the rods as archaeological search machines, this was totally unbelievable; yet there is little difference between finding a 0.3m wide drain and a Roman Fort outer ditch which was 7m wide and 3–4m deep. I have been, and still get 'leg-pulled' by friendly archaeologists over my use of divining rods – but they work for me, at least most of the time.

During the ten-year excavations at Trimontium, I was called in several times to find pits and ditches which Curle had already dug and mapped but which did not show up on the geophysics plotting. The Roman baths seemed to have disappeared between 1910 and 1990 and the great pit in the south annexe showed up nothing until the ground was dug. Divining rods found them no bother.

I know that divining rods are not infallible as I found out to my cost when an ideal Roman fortlet on a perfect site near Dere Street turned out to be nothing on trenching. This was after another diviner had found the same indications and the rods showed the same indications even after the JCB had proven that there was only natural earth there. Most peculiar. So I pass on my divining rod 'finds' as suggestions rather than proof positive.

'All truth passes through three stages. First, it is ridiculed. Second, it is violently opposed. Third, it is accepted as self-evident. Schopenhauer.'

I am midway between ridicule and violent opposition of sceptics whose belief in their own intellectual superiority has the unshakeable faith of an extreme fundamentalist.

In 1747, a bronze collar was found in a bog near Stichill, Roxburghshire. Obviously placed there as a votive offering, it is a piece of rare beauty and interest. It shows a combination of skills and regional styles that makes it unique: its hinged form shows links with south-western Britain: it has technical affinities to Irish metalwork of the same period: it makes a use of La Tene motifs without any trace of provincial Roman fashion and seems to be the masterpiece of a superb craftsman of the Hiberno-Scottish workshops of the first century AD.

In 1993, I was trying out the possibility that divining rods could find archaeological features that did not show on the ground surface. With my friends Jack and Caroline Cruickshank, I went to an earthwork on Ashkirkshiel, Selkirkshire where, with permission and using locations determined by divining rods, we dug two trial-pits, basically to see if there was anything there. In the *Inventory of Selkirkshire*, the earthwork was 'medieval or later'. Under what seemed to be a collapsed dyke, I found some very coarse pottery, a short iron blade and a bronze hilt-guard. On taking the finds to the National Museum of Scotland, I was told that, by the hilt-guard, the finds could be dated to around 50 BC but typology is at best a very fallible dating resource.

CONCLUSIONS

My conclusions on the pre-Roman Iron Age are largely based on the deductions of previous writers which, in turn, are based on previous writings and so on. So before stirring some of my own ideas into the muddy water of Border pre-history, I will give a full paragraph quote from a recent book by Professor D.W. Harding, *The Iron Age in Northern Britain*.

'Taphonomy, or the study of the nature of archaeological deposition and its interpretation, is crucial to any meaningful reconstruction of past societies. Unless interpretation, whether technological, economic, social or cognitive, is based upon a rigorous evaluation of the evidence and its content, it can never be more than creative fiction, an exercise in theoretical reconstruction divorced from the archaeological data-base. This is not to suppose that there is such a thing as objective archaeological 'fact' that is not in some measure prejudiced by the research strategy or subjective observation of the archaeologist. However accurately observed or recorded, what we observe or choose to record will inevitably be selective from the infinite data-resource, according to the questions that we bring to the investigation. Each generation of archaeologists has its own agenda of questions, and there need be no *a priori* assumption that a more recent agenda invalidates or supersedes an earlier one, though it might be expected to refine or qualify earlier agendas.'

Well said, sir; and the book is great too.

In a long life of amateur interest in the history, archaeology, literature and language of the Borders, I will add some caveats of my own to the above.

Air photography is a superb archaeological tool when it finds the right crop in the right field at the right time of year and soil condition, with the right light from the right angle of photograph on the right day. I have, on occasions, flown over the well-defined Roman fort complex at Newstead and absolutely nothing could be seen to suggest that the Romans were ever there.

Geophysics works well with large objects like ditches at 6m in width and walls the same; these are ideal. Small soil disturbance like graves are not so good although that technology might be improving.

Divining rods work for three out of four people; the bother is that there is no print-out as in geophysics and it takes a very experienced practitioner to make sense out of the shape being traced. It also leaves the practitioner with doubts of his own sanity and open to all manner of archaeological abuse. (See p.93)

Fieldwalking, formerly known as 'magpie collecting' or ' scavenging', is good for locating unknown sites. This is provided the farmer is amenable, has ploughed his field in the autumn and will sow it in the spring, and there has been a lot of frost and rain between. This is a wet weather hobby. Not so popular now as the era of autumn sowing of winter wheat reduces the walking period to around three weeks. Nevertheless it is a useful tool for pinpointing sites if there is a sufficient scatter of artefacts: single finds can be an object lost or thrown away, a scatter is likely to represent a settlement.

Metal detecting has suffered from a bad press. Detectorists have found much new evidence but it is good only for metal, ignoring pottery, glass and flint.

Pollen analysis/carbon dating determines the regional diversity of people, plants and climate although this can change from one location to another over the next hill. Still some doubts about the range and accuracy of dating but these are relatively new sciences with much to offer.

All the above are useful in collecting information, none perfect in their own right but each adding something towards the complete picture. Not that the picture will ever be complete without extensive excavations (expensive) and full co-operation between all interested parties – professionals, amateurs and metal detectorists (unlikely).

I have frequently found that the best way to collect evidence of the past is to observe the present, because the land can always provide clues to the past, either through finds made accidentally and deliberately, or simply by looking at the land surface. There is a modern veneer on the countryside that can be mentally stripped away layer by layer to reveal past land-holding or settlement enclosures, and even negative evidence can be valuable. The secret is in finding the right interpretation.

By looking at all the various sources of information on hill-forts, settlements, finds, climate changes, pollen counts through the centuries and fields systems, it is possible to get some idea of how the people lived, what their houses looked like, what they grew and made and some idea where the incomers came from. We are fairly certain that various waves of iron-using incomers imposed themselves on the Borders native population of Bronze Age cultures. By comparing types of habitation, tools and ornamentation, we can say with a bit of confidence that some came from the Iron Age peoples of the south; that trading was carried out with the Irish west and possibly people from there and the Scottish Atlantic coast came into the Borders. It is also possible that immigrants came directly from the Continent but we have little proof of that.

But for the rest, we have very little idea where the bulk of the native population was living when the Roman legions arrived in AD 79. This invasion was much to the relief of the archaeologists of the present and future, for without the reference point of Roman objects, the native cultures would be completely undatable.

Even with the influx of well-dated Roman pottery or coins, there is no certainty in dating material. A Roman coin of Hadrian found in the occupation layer of a native hut, only gives the assurance that someone lost or deposited that coin at some period of the hut's existence. The coin could be two or three hundred years old when it was lost and the hut could have been on a site that had been used for several hundred years before the coin was made. Conclusions made must be tentative rather than positive.

CHAPTER SIX
Selkirkshire: From Geological Times to the pre-Roman Iron Age

Archaeology is based on human activity – what objects humans lost or left (artefacts), what humans built (sites) and how human presence changed the landscape (environmental evidence). The most visible is the site evidence of forts of which there are many in the Borders but few in Selkirkshire; or at least few known, because what can still be seen may represent only a small portion of what was there originally. Stone forts and earthworks are durable; wooden palisades and houses are not. Artefacts are found by chance or actively searching for them. Environmental evidence is rare and expensive.

So to report on the prehistory of Selkirkshire, the most honest answer is: we know very little. In fact, even the written history of the county really starts with David I and his introduction of the abbeys, but this too is scarce and fragmentary. We only get a nearly complete view of life in the burgh and county in late medieval times, through the town records and the Walter Mason Trust papers that commence in the early 1500s.

Having painted a picture of as much as we presently know about the pre-Roman Borders as well as adding some speculative guesswork, it is now time to look at Selkirkshire specifically and see how the county fits into the perceived pattern of geology and the settlement by nature and animal that is postulated for the rest of the area.

Most history books are simply a reworking of the sites and knowledge already gleamed from previous writings. Certainly I will use what is already known but also add some of my own ideas and deductions to make a more rounded and probably controversial picture of the county. This may not suit current interpretation but hopefully, will encourage others to make a fresh appraisal of what is there.

I do have one advantage in researching the archaeology and history

of Selkirkshire in that I have worked on just about every farm in the
county, seeing the countryside from ground level, at first hand and in all
weathers. Looking at the ground surfaces, I found it interesting to work
out how successive generations adapted the land for their own use. To
quote a small portion of Tim Douglas's poem 'The Conservationist':

> The landscape has changed and its features arranged
> to suit every new generation,
> though most things remain through it all the same,
> evolution must follow creation.
> If the tractor and plough are masters just now,
> on the hilltops still grows the bog-cotton,
> and the roadsides will bloom with the glory of broom
> when we are all dead and forgotten.
>
> Since the landscape began to be fashioned by man
> he has practised his own conservation,
> and the view of the brae that we look on today
> we owe to a past generation.
> We are quickly surpassed if we dwell in the past
> the present won't wait for tomorrow.
> the future is fed by us looking ahead
> and by ploughing the new season's furrow.

In area, Selkirkshire is a miniature version of the Borders region, being
surrounded by hills on the north, west and south. These form the
natural frontiers of the territory and it is only the east, in the area
around Galashiels, that there would be easy access into the area in
prehistoric and historic times. The original county was largely the
Ettrick Forest, ie the valleys of the Ettrick, Yarrow and Caddon plus the
Common lands of the burgh of Selkirk and the monastic holdings of
Kelso Abbey, but the Boundary Commission of 1891 added two pieces
and removed four to give the county its present shape.

The early and medieval history of the county does not get a very
enthusiastic report even in its own *Inventory of the Ancient Monuments of
Selkirkshire*.

'Throughout the prehistoric period, and indeed well into historic times, Selkirkshire was, by virtue of its geographical position, poor soil and uncongenial climate, a remote and relatively unimportant backwater … under these circumstances, it is not surprising that structural remains earlier than the Middle Ages are comparatively few in number, and are mainly to be found in the more fertile uplands at the E. end of the county, where, in the absence of any physical barrier corresponding with the present administrative dividing-line, they form an integral part of the West Roxburghshire series.'

With such faint praise and acknowledging the fact that I have included much of the known information in previous chapters, I will try to place this in period and relationship within the county of Selkirk.

On geology, it has to be admitted that the rocks of Selkirkshire have now little of interest to offer. Before the ice ages, which started some two million years ago, Selkirkshire would probably have the full complement of rock strata, Ordovician, Silurian, Devonian, Carboniferous etc with a few igneous intrusions, but the upper layers were almost totally stripped away in one or more of the four major Glacial Periods which engulfed the Borders between two million years BC and around 11,000 years BC. The last of these happened around 18,000 years ago and it was this one that gave the countryside the shape we presently recognise.

That last ice age covered the whole of the Borders in a layer of ice estimated to be around 2km thick and deeper than that on the high ground at the tops of the Tweed, Ettrick, Yarrow and Moffat valleys. When the temperature rose, the ice-cap started to move slowly but inexorably in a north-easterly direction. In doing so, it removed almost every trace of the softer upper sedimentary rocks, exposing the harder Silurian and Ordovician rock strata. Further glacial pressure scooped out the valley floors and in the process, the glacier picked up and carried away millions of tons of ground-down sandstone rubble to be deposited in the lower Tweed basin and form the richer soil of The Merse.

Later ice and water pressure from the melting glaciers dug into the harder rocks, ground it down into boulders, stones, gravel, sand and clay before dumping it in the lower valley bottoms. This is known as boulder-clay deposits and can be seen in the eastern parts of the county, at the Linglie Todholes near Selkirk, The Rink, Lindean and Easter Langlee near Galashiels.

In the upper valleys, the grinding-up of the local Silurian greywacke produced a boulder clay which reflected the acidic quality of that rock and it is from this, that the county's agricultural soils are derived. This produced an acidic soil, lacking in the components required for high fertility, which influenced early farming settlers to keep away from the tops of the valleys.

To sum up the geological and natural features, it has to be recognised that the county's greatest natural resource was in its hill forest/pasture. This was as true in prehistoric times as it is today and is reflected in the sparse numbers of ancient monuments and finds in the western parts of the county.

With forest grassland, it would be an ideal habitat for grazing animals and the predators, animal and human, which pursued them. But even the human hunters left little recognisable trace of their passing other than the scatters of flint and stone tools that indicate temporary human settlements.

MESOLITHIC AND NEOLITHIC
Covering the period 8000–2000 BC

Selkirk has a long tradition of fieldwalking that dates back to the 1870s. Tom Scott, the water-colourist, was one of the 'starter' members; a keen antiquarian, he had a system of paying half-a-crown (12½p) to any farm-worker who brought him a reasonable flint arrowhead. As the ploughmen of that period tilled the land walking behind a horse plough, they were in the right place to keep a lookout for any flint objects lying about in the soil. Although their interest was pecuniary rather than intellectual, some ploughmen turned very knowledgeable in the tools of the Stone Age, and Scott's collection benefited accordingly.

Another 'starter' was Frank Roberts, one of the tweed-making family, who retired from work at the age of thirty-three to devote his time to fieldwalking. However, he did not drive so to get to known sites at a distance from his home, he was driven by his chauffeur who then got co-opted into walking the fields.

Since then, each generation has produced one or two people who have found pleasure in walking ploughed fields in the winter months.

This is not in pursuit of valuable treasure but rather the thrill of finding an artefact that was last used by a human being some hundreds or thousands of years ago. In this manner, the story of the county was, and is still being gathered.

Owing to the enthusiasm of a succession of local field-walkers, there are a vast number of Mesolithic and Neolithic flint and stone finds from Selkirkshire, largely unrecorded, sometimes deposited in museum stores, more often thrown out when the collector dies. The sheer mass of material has deterred all but a few archaeologists from making a serious study of it. Helen Mulholland's article 'The Microlithic Industries of the Tweed Valley' records over a hundred flint-producing sites in the Tweed valley, with fourteen major sites in Selkirkshire. The majority of sites are beside water, on raised riverbanks especially where two rivers or burns meet, or beside a loch. From experience I know that there is a good chance that worked flint can be found in the ploughed fields beside most streams.

As ploughed fields are essential for productive field-walking, the absence of sites on higher ground reflects the lack of agricultural ploughing in these areas. Since the 1960s when forestry took over many of the sheep farms, the larger forestry plough has revealed previously unknown flint sites at higher altitudes.

The most important site, or rather the most field-walked site in Selkirkshire, is at The Rink farm where the Tweed and Ettrick rivers meet. The site is ideally located at the river junction where there is glacial deposit that contains natural lumps of grey-green chert imbedded in the boulder clay. Although there is a concentration of mainly chert tools and waste products near the junction, the spread of worked implements extended over 1km along the north bank of the Tweed. I have noted that the Mesolithic implement concentrations are mainly to be found on the top of the glacial deposit while the Neolithic concentrations were on the sandy banks beside the river. This is likely to reflect the respective heights of the water in the different ages.

First noted in the 1920s, The Rink site has been diligently walked by five people, Bruce and Walter Mason, Jack Cruickshanks, George Ballantyne and myself. With a well-washed field and good light, it was possible to pick up to 200 pieces of man-struck stone, mostly grey, green or black chert, in a couple of hours; yellowish flint was present in some quantity with Bowmont Water agate and Arran pitchstone making an occasional appearance.

As no organic remains survived on site, the only other artefact-material was stone. Large round pebbles with an hour-glass perforation seem to be maceheads; a few small quartz pebbles with a highly polished perforation on one side are likely to be the upper stone of a bow drill; stones with opposed lateral notches making a figure '8' are sinker-stones for nets while much smaller ones with the same figure of '8' are presumed to be the weights from a throwing net or bolas.

One small excavation at The Rink produced over 800 pieces from the 25 square yards of the plough-disturbed soil investigated, 153 pieces amongst the stones and only six pieces below the stone layer. At the depth of 2–3ft, a fine-grained orange soil was empty of any man-struck stone but indicative of the glacial deposit of Red Sandstone from the top of the valley.

As The Rink site was conveniently near my home, I had picked up some 9,600 pieces before turning my boots towards the Roman-artefact-strewn fields at Newstead. The Rink finds were studied at Bradford University and then deposited in the National Museum of Scotland in Edinburgh.

Materials

Lacking any definitive dating of the tool forms, the material with which they are made can provide some evidence of their origins. The majority of the material used is locally occurring chert derived from glacial deposits, the chert being predominantly of the grey/green variety that is likely to have come from a volcanic intrusion in the upper Ettrick/Moffat sandstones.

The very distinctive agates are from the Bowmont Water and around the base of the Cheviots, while pitchstone is from Arran off the Ayrshire coast. Flint in a variety of colours has to be an import from Northern England. It is noticeable that the finer flint tools were of Neolithic type and design, leading to the conclusion that a trading route was well established in that period.

By the Neolithic period, stone axes of Langdale tuff from

Cumberland, were being brought into the region. It is noticeable that these are more to be found in the lower-lying ground that would be most suitable for early forest clearance but it could also mean that the lower ground has been more frequently ploughed in modern times. Some pieces of tuff, probably from a broken or worn-down axe, appear to have been reworked into smaller tools.

An Antrim Porcellanite leaf-shaped arrowhead from Northern Ireland, found during tree-planting at the Braw Gates near Selkirk, is a fine example of either trading routes or folk movement in the Middle and New Stone Ages.

The Mesolithic peoples have long been considered to be food collectors while the Neolithic people are classed as early farmers who hunted for part of their food. Selkirkshire has produced no proven habitation sites of either, other than the concentrations of flint working debris that must have been on, or near, shelter of some kind; but no certain proof can be tendered in the absence of excavation. In several places, there are some stonewalled hut-circles which may date from the Late Neolithic period but are more likely to be Early Bronze Age.

The only known sherd of Neolithic pottery was a stray unstratified find which was found 40cms below the turf outside the bank of the ring-ditch enclosure at Yarrowford.

To sum up the Stone Age in Selkirkshire, it would be fair to say that there were people going about the area in prehistory. Stone tools and waste debris can be found along the river banks and beside the small lochs in the hills, and arrowheads have been picked up from fields everywhere.

The Rotten Bottom bow found high up in the Moffat/ Tweedsmuir hills, demonstrates that hunters were prepared to follow their prey into the hill-country, but they left little trace of their passing. Their summer camps will be there but other than some flint tools found at the outlet of Loch Skeen in the Moffat Valley, none have been recorded.

As there are no impressive monuments like the Meldon Bridge enclosure, the Over Howden Henge or a long cairn like the Mutiny Stones, the Neolithic population of Selkirkshire must have lacked the numbers or direction to erect any large-scale structure.

THE BRONZE AGE

The Bronze Age in the Borders is reckoned to cover the period from around 1700 BC to around 600 BC. Both these dates are arbitrary, probably guessed at, and have been argued over by many over the years. However, I agree with the comment in the *Inventory of Selkirkshire* that the Iron Age probably did not come to the county much before the Romans; or rather we have very few positive proofs that there was a definite pre-Roman Iron Age in the county. So it might be more advisable to look on the Bronze Age in Selkirkshire as extending from around 1700–100 BC with a few iron tools coming in through trade in the next two centuries after that.

In this period of 1,600 years of the putative Bronze Age in the Borders, the recorded visible remains in Selkirkshire are scarce when compared with the neighbouring counties of Roxburghshire and Peeblesshire. To quote from the County *Inventory* again: 'Within the scope of this Inventory are three, or possibly four, short cists and eleven round cairns, all of which may be ascribed with certainty or probability to the earlier phases of the Bronze Age (*c.*1700–900 BC) A date within the same general limits would also be appropriate for the single standing stones Nos 171, 172 and 173, the stone setting of Bucht Rig (No. 203) and the unenclosed stone-walled hut circles at Kirkstead (No. 132), Dryhope (No. 133) and Cavers Hill (No. 134) if it was certain that the structures in question are prehistoric, but is at present undetermined … whereas unenclosed round huts are known to have been inhabited in the Early Bronze Age, this primitive type of dwelling had a long life and appears to have remained in use in SE. Scotland at least until the Middle Ages.'

This judgement is over cautious. Although the commissioners were men and women of learning and academic archaeological experience, there were some locations that they missed or which their remit did not cover. In some cases, local ground knowledge beats written expertise, especially if that knowledge is the accumulation of several generations.

Take the Yarrow valley as an instance. After long observation and careful thought, I am confident enough to say that the middle Yarrow was a major centre of population from the Bronze Age until the early Historic period. In the neighbouring farms of Whitehope/Whitefield,

Sundhope, Eldinhope and Dryhope, there are enough positive proofs of the claim in the number of burials in the vicinity – chambered cairns, long and round cairns and cist burials that can be seen by the discerning eye. Fieldwalking finds, divining rods (and only a little imagination) can confirm the statement.

Eldinhope

The farm of Eldinhope (formerly Altrieve Lake) is one such site that was probably a main settlement. Sitting on a knowe where the burn which is known as Altrieve Lake★ joins the Yarrow, it forms a raised peninsula between the two streams. Ideally situated with natural access from all points of the compass, it seemed to be a centre of population in the Bronze Age period. In the late nineteenth and early twentieth centuries, a large number of predominantly Neolithic/Bronze Age flint tools were found when the fields were ploughed. These are still being found but the land is now used for grazing and not so productive for fieldwalking.

On the observable antiquities on the farm, the following was noted by the Rev. Robert Russell, the minister of Yarrow before his death in 1847: 'There may still be seen, to the westward of Altrieve Lake, on rising knolls, five considerable tumuli. None of them has been opened but the surface of the largest exhibits a mixture of charcoal and ashes. Its top was surrounded by a circle of stones, thirty yards in circumference, with a small square of stones in the centre that were taken away to build dykes.' This was published in Russell's *Reminiscences of Yarrow*, a father and son account of the happenings and people in the Yarrow Valley for the period 1791 to 1883. The same information is repeated in the *New Statistical Account of Scotland* 1845 and again in the *Inventory of Selkirkshire*, 1957. The five tumuli appear on the 1863 map of the area and again on the 1896 one, so there is little doubt that the Rev. Russell's observations were correct. Since that account was written, the place has

---

★ For no apparent reason, this burn is known as Altrieve Lake whereas the Altrieve Burn flows past the farm of that name further up the valley. I can find no reasonable explanation other than to note that 'lake' is a fourteenth century Border term for a low-lying, marshy piece of ground and this must have transferred itself to the burn.

changed considerably but it must be noted that his description of the largest tumulus is what is now known as a chambered cairn.

I have worked on this farm several times over the years and knew that there was a lot more archaeology there still to be recorded. So, for this book, I went up Yarrow for two days with GPS and divining rods to map out what was actually there. By speaking to Walter Barrie, the observant farmer, I found out about more sites that I had previously missed.

Using divining rods, I did find five cairns or rather five shapes that suggested that cairns once stood there, and that some were nearly in the places indicated in the maps. In fact, I found similar shapes across other parts of the site. Taking the circular shapes as cairns, each had a passage leading into a central chamber; the passage was approximately 1m wide entering the cairn from the East and the chamber varied between 3m to 4m roughly square or rectangular. I took GPS locations and have noted them for possible future reference. All measurements are approximate.

1. Map Ref. – 812ft. NT 2995024373. Circular. 13m dia. Chamber 3m square.

2. Map Ref. – 828ft. NT 2996424372. Circular. 17m dia. Chamber 4m square.

3. Map Re.f – 812ft.NT 2983124407. Circular. 17m dia. Chamber 4m square.

4. Map Ref. – 805ft. NT 2976024381. Circular. 14m dia. Chamber 3m square.

5. Map Ref. – 806ft. NT 2970224350. Circular. 20m dia. Chamber 4m square.

This is the largest cairn in the group and is likely to be the one referred to by the Rev. Russell. There is the mark of a rectangular excavation in the middle of this cairn and in several other places on the site. Local oral tradition tells that Lady John Scott (poet and a very interested antiquarian) who was married to the younger brother of the Duke of Buccleuch, spent some time excavating on Eldinhope.

6. Map Ref. – 789ft. NT 2953824158. Circular. 17m dia. Chamber 4m square.

7. Map Ref. – 813ft NT 2944024167. Circular. 17m dia. Chamber 4m square.

8. Map Ref. – 839ft NT 29337 24125. Circular 11m dia. Chamber 3m square.

There were two long cairns on the same plateau of land.

9. Map Ref. – 78ft. NT 2954524231. This was approx 22m long by 10m wide and about 1m above the surrounding ground. Several small cairns were clustered round this cairn. These have been excavated and there are similar shallow rectangular holes in the surrounding ground.

10. Map Ref. – 816ft. NT 2953824158. This seems to be an undisturbed mound, 30m long and 9m at its greatest width.

Also on Eldinhope Farm, there is a visible settlement, approximately 220m by 100m.. This is at NT 2953123611 with the most visible wall-mound at NT 2958123532. There are a number of round shapes of 6m diameter within the wall.

I take these to be hut circles that could be any age from Neolithic to Medieval but the number of flint tools found in the vicinity would suggest Neolithic/Early Bronze dating, which would fit in with the chambered cairns.

Chapelhope,
NT 23000 18880

Halfway between Chapelhope Farm House and the Old School, a mound approximately 1.5m high stands enclosed by a square turf dyke. Divining rods say that this contains a burial, aligned east-west. The chapel which gives the area its name is about 40m to the west.

Dryhope

It was noted in *Reminiscences of Yarrow* that, 'On Dryhope Haugh there stood a large cairn called Herton's Hill, in the midst of which, when stones were removed about seventy years ago, to enclose fields, some urns were found, besides a coffin formed of slabs and containing ashes.' I found this at NT 28097 224343 at the height of 704ft. It was 17m in diameter and had a 3m square chamber which was entered from the east through a 1m wide passage. This shape is not so clear as the ones on Eldinhope as some of the stones have been built as a round sheep stell on the same site.

Whitehope / Whitfield

On what was once a barren moor between Whitfield (formerly Whitehope) and the Warrior's Rest Cottage, *Reminiscences of Yarrow* tell us that: 'On more than twenty different spots of this moor were large cairns, in many of them fine yellow dust and in one an old spear head was found. Two unhewn massive stones still stand, about 100 yards distant from each other, which are doubtless monuments of the dead. The real tradition simply states that here a deadly feud was settled by dint of arms; the upright stones mark the place where the two leaders fell, and the bodies of their followers were thrown into a marshy pool called "The Dead Lake", in the adjoining haugh.'

This 'real tradition' was an attempt by local storytellers to explain the reason for two large upright stones in bare fields and, like many of the legends of the Borders, is simply untrue; but still much quoted and believed.

In fact, one of the standing stones, the Glebe Stone, is at the inner end of a passage leading from the east into the chamber of a large cairn approximately 20m in diameter. This chamber is larger than usual, being 5m by 4m of which the longer side is sub-divided into three sections.

In my reckoning, there are more than twenty chambered cairns in this immediate area while to the east of this grouping there was another cluster of chambered cairns although these have been superseded by a number of east-west aligned stone cists which are characteristic of Early Christian burial.

Evidence of the presence of Neolithic/Bronze Age cairns in the area of the Warrior's Rest cottage, are the recorded finds of the fragment of a Food Vessel, an Early Bronze Age ring of cannel coal, a flint arrowhead and a stone hammer. Recorded in local folklore is a bronze axe which was found in the garden of the Warrior's Rest cottage in late Victorian times and used by the occupant to split kindling wood for his fire up to the time of the First World War. This is the axe which is recorded in the *Inventory* as being found at 'Whitehope'.

Taking the evidence of the Yarrow Stone and other east-west aligned graves, this remained as a burial area into the Early Historic period. This will be detailed below.

Ettrick

Only one large cairn that fits into this period has been discovered in Ettrick. This was on the Shaws Farm when, in 1864, material was required to built a march-dyke and a large amount of stone was available on a nearby mound called the Sleepy Knowe. About a sixth of this 'pile of stones' had been removed when a cist containing human remains was discovered. The dyke-building was stopped and the pile was excavated in 1868 and again in 1884. Described by T. Craig-Brown, the Selkirkshire historian, as: 'a rough honeycomb of small graves, the larger one in the centre being surrounded by others measuring about 24 by 20 inches'. Part of a Cinerary Urn, some sherds of a finer pottery, some cup-and-ring marked stones and the remains of a male skeleton were found in the excavations.

Elibank and Galashiels

In commenting on the Sleepy Knowe cairn, Craig-Brown notes that there was one, an exact counterpart of that at Shaws in size and shape, to be found several hundred yards to the back of Elibank Tower.

He also records that 'in June 1878, it became necessary to remove a mound in Gala Park known as the little Aiken Knock, situated close to the edge of the scaur above Botany Mill. Early in their progress, the workmen came upon a number of large stones standing upright in the gravely soil, arranged in a circle and at the top, in the centre, a great flat stone was struck, the removal of which disclosed a cist containing a quantity of mouldering bones.' No grave goods were recorded

The description of this cairn could fit with the one at Clovenfords described on p.51.

Ashkirk

While working on the site of the Blackcastle Hill earthwork, 1km south-east of Ashkirk, I found a cup-and-ring marked stone, a 'cup within a cup' to be precise. This is now in the Borders' Museum Service store in Selkirk. There are cultivation terraces beside the earthwork on Blackcastle Hill which are likely to be contemporary with the fort.

THE FINDS

The finds that can be safely placed in the Early Bronze Age are few in number. Pottery is represented by two pieces of Food Vessel from Galashiels and the Warrior's Rest respectively: an unknown number of cup-and-ring marked stones; a flat bronze axe from Greenhill; and a ground-flaked flint knife from Blackhaugh, make up the certain total although there is a flint dagger which is shaped like an Early Bronze Age dagger in the Halliwell House Museum in Selkirk but the provenance of this is dubious.

The Middle and Late Bronze Age artefacts are more numerous, perhaps because these were more highly prized and survive decay longer. Pottery has a single representative, an intrusion in the Sleepy Knowe cairn. Ten bronze axes from assorted sites, three looped spearheads, a socketed gouge, a dagger and a pennanular armlet make up the total.

Easter Essenside/Essenside

One intriguing question posed by the list of Bronze Age finds is that nearly half of them were found at Easter Essenside/Essenside in the upper Ale Water. The items known to have been found there are four socketed axes, a socketed gouge, a socketed knife and a penannular armlet. There is some confusion in the exact find-spots as some are given as 'Easter Essenside' and others simply 'Essenside'.

Two axes were found on the site given as: 'On the lower slopes of Gurnside Hill, south-west of Easter Essenside farm, Ashkirk parish, Selkirkshire; description of site – unknown; circumstance of finding – unknown'.

Information from the Berwickshire Naturalists' publication states that one axe 'was found during cultivation in a field on the farm of Easter Essenside, parish of Ashkirk in the spring of 1882 and the second turned up in the same field in February 1887'.

All these objects can be dated to around 7–800 BC and it was inferred that they were part of a larger hoard or number found.

Obviously a site that had produced so many artefacts of the same period had to be looked at. With permission from the owner Mrs Ursula Whitehead, I took divining rods and GPS to the field on the south-west of the Easter Essenside farm and there found six circular shapes, likely to be burial cairns. They were almost identical in size, being 9m in diameter, with a passage 1m leading to a chamber 1.5m by 2.5m. For reference they were at:

1. NT 45051 20269 at 713ft
2. NT 45034 20257 at 723ft
3. NT 45024 20244 at 721ft
4. NT 45006 20241 at 719ft
5. NT 44987 20226 at 718ft
6. NT 44971 20217 at 716ft

These potential cairns were in a rough line along the top of a slight ridge in the field and it is likely that this carried on into the next field which is on Wester Essenside. A reasonable deduction is that the ridge had been flattened during the yearly cultivation and this had exposed the grave goods from the chambers.

Further investigation on the farm revealed another group of graves on the west side of the farm buildings. Here the cairns were 6/7m in diameter with no entrance passage.

I plotted two that are at NT 45441 20543 and NT 45449 20526 respectively but there were several more.

Although this total of the tools of the Later Bronze Age is proportionally more numerous than those of the Early Bronze Age, this does not necessarily mean an increased population but rather the fact that the later implements were being manufactured in quantity and easier to obtain through trade.

Even although the positive proofs are scarce, it is obvious that there were people living in Selkirkshire in the Bronze Ages; it is just that we know very little of how and where they lived and how many they were, so we have to make deductions based on what we know and can see in or on the ground.

THE PRE-ROMAN IRON AGE

Despite some trepidation, I will note the sites that *may* be placed in the Iron Age and which *may* have come to the Borders in the first century

BC. Doubtless, iron tools or weapons could have been known in the Borders before this date but this is a grey period of archaeology and it is best to err on the side of caution.

The transition from the Bronze Age to the Early Iron Age has previously been calculated on the pattern of changes in the defensive structures with the 1948 Hownam excavations, thereby providing a regional model for the dating of Iron Age settlements. Recent fieldwork and excavations have questioned the deductions made there and radio-carbon analysis has made for a difference in dating the various strata. In typical Border fashion, hardly any of the excavations agreed with each other as their fortification patterns: palisades, single enclosure and multiple ramparts could be mixed to provide an enclosing or defensive structure. The differences in building techniques do not necessarily imply an immigrant population. It could equally mean that the successful people wanted better security – a very human reaction that is as relevant today as it was thousands of years ago.

But no relevant excavations have been conducted in Selkirkshire for the last fifty years, so we are left to transpose the findings from neighbouring counties in Scotland and England to see if they fit into our own county. This is not very satisfactory but it does allow us to re-examine previous convictions, and our deductions are just as likely to prove wrong.

Palisaded Settlements

For convenience, the builders would use the nearest available material if it suited the purpose. A palisade required a substantial amount of suitable timber with trees on the palisade wall having to be about 0.3m in diameter, and timber in the Early Iron Age was becoming scarcer. This type of structure could be built with fewer men and in a shorter time – a realisation made by the Norman settlers who built wooden motte-and-bailey strongholds on the extensive lands given by David I in the early twelfth century.

The oval earthwork at Huntly Burn (*Inventory of Selkirkshire* No. 142) is given as a dubious example of the only known Iron Age palisaded settlement in Selkirkshire. It has a substantial bank and ditch but is not classified as a fort as it is overlooked by rising ground on two sides. No traces of internal buildings have been noted as these would have been destroyed by subsequent cultivation and no finds have been recorded. In the absence of excavation, this must remain one of the sites that *may* be pre-Roman Iron Age.

At Broadmeadows Farm in the Yarrow Valley at NT 417 305, there is what I believe to be a palisaded settlement. Almost round and roughly 70m in diameter, the position on the top of a substantial hillock has enough encircling bank and ditch to indicate a fort. There are cultivation terraces on the south and west sides.

At Eldinhope as above mentioned, there is a settlement at NT 29531 23611 but this could be any age from Neolithic onwards.

Forts

From the *Inventory of Selkirkshire*, we learn that there were thirteen forts that were known or presumed to be of an early Iron Age dating and all these were in the more fertile eastern part of the county. This could infer that the inhabitants were more dependent on arable cultivation than a grazing economy. Ploughing needs a permanent occupation while the shepherd can move his flock to suitable available land as he wishes.

The Selkirkshire forts are ridge-built with rock outcrops used in the construction of heaped-rubble ramparts with an interlaced wattle structure on top. They were more labour intensive but the building material for the stone-faced, rubble-backed ramparts were quarried from the rocks on which the forts were situated.

I can add two certainties, and another nearly so, to the list.

1. The earthwork at Synton Mossend (in the *Inventory* as Ashkirkshiel, No. 137) was described there as 'the earthwork … is probably a medieval or later farmstead'. This is the one on which we did a trial pit dig to determine the usefulness of divining rods as an aide to archaeological surveying. In one of the metre-square trial pits under a collapsed wall, I found some thick grey pottery which I first thought was concrete; then an iron blade with a bronze hilt-guard. On taking it to a lecture in the National Museum of Scotland, I was told by Professor Stuart Piggot that he could date it to around 50 BC by type alone and the pottery was pre-Roman Iron Age. A certainty.

2. I was working on the hill above Fairnilee Farm on a windy and snowy day – not the best of conditions for archaeological observation. However, the wind had partly cleared the snow from the top of a nearby hill to reveal a shallow but beautiful hill-fort, complete with hut circles and a field system around it. This was quickly sketched before it vanished. The fort is at NT 460 337 at the height of 275m. It is about 80m long and 40m wide and is divided in two by a division wall. It contains 8–10 hut circles. A certainty.

3. The recent find of a first or second century AD brooch by a metal detectorist on the earthwork on Castle Hill, near Oakwood (*Inventory* No. 155), makes it likely that this may class as an Iron Age fort which survived into the Roman period. However an alternative suggestion is given in the following Roman section. A possible.

The 'Exotic' Forts

There are two more elaborate buildings that stand out from normal run of the hill/ridge forts of Selkirkshire. One is the broch at Torwoodlee and the other is the fort on The Rink hill. Both are of dry-stone construction, both are circular but with a great difference in size. Although the general principle of dry-stone wall construction is established above, both are sufficiently individual to be considered separately as an important part of the archaeology of the county. I would like to add two more to the tally and there are likely to be others still to be recognised beneath the vegetation cover in various forts.

Torwoodlee Broch and Fort
The broch of Torwoodlee and the fort in which it stands, lie on the 245m contour about 450m north-east of Torwoodlee Mains Farm. The scrub timber and weeds have recently been cleared off the site by a Manpower Services team, revealing the broch, or rather the remains of the broch which are left after extended stone-robbing over the last two centuries.

The fort, which has been severely mutilated by surface quarrying and cultivation, is oval in shape, measuring 140m by 105m and enclosed by two ramparts each with a ditch in front.

The broch is located within the west quarter of the fort, slightly protruding into the ditch of the fort. Excavations in 1891 and again in 1950, established that the circular shape and thick wall conforms to the Scottish pattern of brochs. The surviving wall-base is between 0.6 and 1m in height and 5.5m thickness. The entrance on the south-east is 1.8m wide with door-checks and a guard chamber and there is a rectangular cell in the wall measuring 4.5m by 4m.

The broch structure was surrounded by a V-shaped ditch, 1.5m deep and 3.6m wide. In clearing the boulders from this ditch, a cist containing the body of a woman of the local Iron Age stock was found.

During the two excavations, Iron Age pottery, a terret and a stud of Iron Age dating were found together with first century Roman pottery and glass. The verdict of the Commissioners was that 'it may be inferred that the fort was in all probability, built early in the 1st century AD or possibly a little earlier.

'The destruction of the broch so soon after it was built may be presumed to have been carried out at Roman military orders, possibly during a putative raid following their evacuation of the district in the early years of the second century ... the presence of so much Roman pottery and glass may well have been due to scavenging at the Roman fort at Newstead, six miles distant during the period of its temporary abandonment in the early years of the 2nd century AD.'

To explain the cist burial in the rubble of the ditch: 'It may, however, be commented that a Roman demolition-party is most unlikely to have disposed of a native so carefully and that the discovery would suggest an opportunity taken for burial while the work of demolition was being done by natives at Roman orders.'

I think that presumption is one too many. There is nothing to prove that the broch was built between the Roman incursions into the Borders; nor that it was demolished under Roman orders. To my mind, this is twisting facts to fit preconceptions.

It is equally feasible that the broch was functioning as a high status centre in the pre-Roman period and that the Roman artefacts were acquired through trade before or just after the legions appeared. The idea that high-status native chieftains would scavenge for scraps of Roman glass and pottery is more than unlikely.

The site is at NT 465 384. (Selkirk Inventory No. 118).

Crosslee, Bowland

On the farm of Crosslee on Bowland Estate, there is a small circular wood at NT 456 397. In this wood, there are markings very similar to those of Torwoodlee broch except that these are flat on the ground; although now overgrown with weeds and some dumped rubbish but when first seen, the outer stones of the broad circular wallbase were visible enough to dispel any doubt. Taking measurements, the internal diameter of the circle was about 8m and the wall 4.2m across; the entrance was from the south, tapering from 1.2m to 1m in the interior. There was a single-ditch enclosure in the fields to the east and south.

A broch or a dun? – could be either but this structure is almost equidistant from Bow Castle and Torwoodlee brochs and is visible to both.

Dun on The Rink Hill

On The Rink Hill at NT 484 331 and about 350m north-east of The Rink fort, there is a small oval fort measuring 42m by 30m and surrounded by a dry-stone wall, 4.5m thick and as much as 1m high in places. The interior has been used as a dumping ground for stones gathered from the fields. No known finds recorded. (Selkirk Inventory No. 121)

The Rink Hill Fort

The most massive of the dry-stone forts in Selkirkshire stands on a spur of The Rink hill about 400m north-east of The Rink farmhouse and, like the Torwoodlee Broch, stands within the bounds of an earlier enclosure. It is a strong defensive site with falling ground on the north, east and south and extended viewing up and down the Tweed and into the lower parts of Ettrick and Yarrow.

The fort is almost circular in plan, measuring 65m by 56m and with a wall width of 4.2m. The debris from the wall stands to a height of 1.8m above the level of the interior and from the base of the wall to the bottom of the ditch measures 2.7m. Divining rods suggest that there are both circular and rectangular buildings in the interior of the fort, and there are certainly visible rectangular foundations to the east of the gateway. From the great mass of debris tumbled into the ditch, it must be concluded that the wall was of considerable height. An outer rampart has been made from the spoil excavated from the ditch.

Recorded finds from the fort are Iron Age pottery, a whorl, two bronze brooches (one first and one second century).

The whole fort is in a wood and although this has preserved the general structure from predatory dyke-builders, it has made this monument almost unknown to the interested public. With the given situation and strength, there is little doubt that this stronghold would survive into the Early Historic period although there it no definite proof of this as yet.

Philological Note. The derivation of the name has long been taken to be from 'The Ring' because the fort is nearly circular. The earliest written record is 'Langrinck' at the beginning of the sixteenth century. My interpretation is that it derives for 'lann Giric – the settlement of Giric I' who was king of Scots from 878 to 889. Giric is believed to have extended Scots rule into parts of Bernicia which at that period, extended into the Scottish Borders. Near Smailholm, the farms of Girnick and Girrick commemorate the name.

NB 'Lann' is usually transcribed as 'church' but it can also be a settlement.

There is one site in the Ettrick Valley which has puzzled me for a long time and I include it in this section as its most likely home.

At the west end of Oakwoodmill hill, at the height of 580ft and map reference NT 42978 26441, there is a man-made mound, approximately 28m in diameter. With a rising slope 2m above the natural ground surface, it has an internal circular hollow, around 7m across with the ground falling sharply into the interior.

Divining rods say that there is a central post, posts round the bank top at 1m centres and an entrance from the east. It could be a variation of a dun but is unlikely to be a broch owing to the sloping sides and the lack of stone in quantity and is possibly a smaller version of a motte. Time and excavation may give the answer.

It was when I was revisiting and re-evaluating the forts of Selkirkshire that I had some thoughts that I now put forward for consideration.

On looking at the ring-ditch structure at Yarrowford and considering the very practical proposal that the ditch was a cattle shed rather than a defensive ditch or drain for keeping rainwater from the hut, I wondered if the same principle was being applied to the larger farm/homestead settlements within the county.

The Bell Hill Fort (*Inventory of Selkirk* No. 124) is one of the best examples of the 'ridge-top' forts in the Borders and defended by triple walls and ditches with an interior space of 70m by 28m. The walls are still massive in places. Walking between the walls, inner/medial and medial/outer, divining rods picked up rows of posts at around 3m spacing on the outer part of the inner wall and the inner part of the medial wall, and the same again between the other two.

Reading this as a wooden bulwark against soil spillage, I then had a look at the open ends of the walls and found the same line of posts there. Reasonable deduction was that there were a number of enclosures between the walls. It is my suggestion that the cow-byre of the ring-ditch huts was multiplied around the larger farmstead forts.

The housing area in the fort would contain an extended family with perhaps ten men. It is doubtful if they would expend labour on digging three deep ditches and piling the spoil up in three big walls just in case of attack. However, to build four cattle enclosures, two at least of which could be roofed, would be useful for the safety and over-wintering of valuable stock. The collected manure would be used as nutrient in the cord-rig cultivation that can be seen on a flat plateau, 80m east of the fort.

So my theory is that the outer wall of forts was used primarily as a cattle enclosure. It is only since the timber structure had rotted away that the defensive aspect has been put forward. This argument does not hold in every instance as some triple wall/ditches in Border forts are clearly defensive.

Linear Earthwork

The Inventory of Selkirkshire notes a linear earthwork which is mainly in Roxburghshire but has a visible stretch in Selkirkshire. Appearing on early maps as a 'Military Road', it is confidently regarded by the Commissioners as prehistoric: 'the fortified boundary of some communal or tribal territory, most probably that of which the great fort on Eildon Hill North was the capital. The construction of the work suggests that it may have been intended to act as an obstacle to chariots'.

The visible part of the earthwork in Selkirkshire shows a spread mounded bank in between two ditches; from bottom of ditch to bottom of ditch is around 8m. There is nothing to date the construction of the monument and although I would agree that it could be a land division, the theory that it is a chariot barrier requires some imagination.

Finds

Definite pre-Roman finds in Selkirkshire are few and most have been noted above.

The terret and stud from the Torwoodlee broch are from the pre-Roman Iron Age south: likewise the bronze ring from the ring-ditch hut at Yarrowford. Both are fairly certain, as is the hiltguard from Synton Mossend. The Clovenfords hoard could be pre- or post- Roman and the brooch from Oakwood is definitely Roman but could indicate a long-established settlement.

On Sundhope Farm in the Yarrow valley, there is a series of cultivation terraces (*Inventory of Selkirk* No. 88) and nearby are a number of visible hut circles. In one of these, a metal detectorist found a small iron ingot. Although this was found in one of the huts, this type of structure was plentiful from Neolithic to Medieval periods. As well as the more obvious huts, there are a few small circular stone piles which contain cist graves.

IN CONCLUSION

With the few excavations, comparatively few finds and the many deductions and assumptions, we have some idea of how the people of Selkirkshire and the Borders lived. We know a little more about the landscape because they changed the land to suit their own purposes and this happened through many generations, leaving marks on the ground that we can read today. We may not always read them correctly but to those interested, the land is a three-dimensional jigsaw puzzle with many pieces missing and some in the wrong places already. But we are learning to look into the past even although

> Time passes by in the wink of an eye
> and changes are many and varied.
> Changes are made and our memories fade
> and much of our past becomes buried.
>
> The earthwork is still on the top of the hill
> but what of the people who made it?
> The long vanished race who once mastered the place
> Their unwritten history faded.
>
> Tim Douglas, Rulewater

In AD 79 a major change took place when the Roman Legions marched over the Cheviot hills and made for the Place of the Three Hills which they called Trimontium.

CHAPTER SEVEN
The Romans AD 79–212

We know more about the short-term Roman occupation of the Borders than any other archaeological period and yet it is questionable if the area was under Roman military rule for more than seventy years in total. It was not a particularly successful episode in Roman history, either militarily or politically.

Unlike the previous section of this book, the Roman occupation of the Borders gives us some written evidence to join up the information that we get from the ground. Unfortunately, the written sources are all one-dimensional from the Roman point of view, who magnify their own successes and tend to ignore their failures.

After the Agricolan invasion and the alleged total destruction of the opposition at the Battle of Mons Graupius in AD 83, there were two major defensive walls built (Hadrian's and Antonine), several 'strategic withdrawals' and the tribes north of the line of Hadrian's Wall were 'conquered' on many occasions – and that only covers the period AD 79 to 212.

During this period, the fort of Trimontium was occasionally evacuated and consequently re-built on at least six occasions. This does not necessarily imply that the fort was taken and destroyed, but it does mean that the main Roman forces had left the area. So we have to muster as many facts as we can to determine what effect an intermittent military occupation had on the Borders and its people.

The Roman Army

When the Roman army first marched into what is now the Borders, they were pushing forward the frontier of an empire which already stretched from deserts of Africa and Arabia to the Atlantic Ocean and the North Sea. It had conquered all the nations and civilisations around the Mediterranean which they called Mare Nostrum, 'our sea', and merged them into the Roman Empire. As the Empire grew, it needed more soldiers for its army and these were recruited from the new provinces. In fact, by the end of the first century AD, very few of the serving troops who marched over the Cheviots would come from Rome itself, or even from Italy. The only true Romans were the higher-ranking officers from the patrician families of Rome, serving in the army to gain experience, fame and riches in order to climb the political ladder and enter the Senate of Rome.

The result of wholesale provincial recruitment meant that the Roman Army was one that served the Roman system, rather than being an army of Romans. It was a cosmopolitan force, trained, disciplined and equipped in a manner that had served the Roman Republic well in the previous two centuries. The troops were loyal to their commander firstly and to the Emperor secondly, because he provided their wages. They were professional soldiers, serving for twenty-five years before attaining the accolade of Roman citizenship on retirement.

The Emperor was usually a successful and open-handed military commander who was 'raised to the purple' by his legionaries. In reality, he was a military dictator with a supreme power based on army support, while the Senate and People of Rome made the speeches and took the benefits, thereby maintaining the appearance of democracy.

It was through the legions that the Roman Senate was able to maintain its proudest boast of Pax Romana or 'Roman Peace' making Rome the first-ever state to disarm its citizens and guarantee their protection by the state; this step had the added benefit, from the Senate's point of view, of making it harder for civilians to rise in revolt.

The First Steps

The Romans first came to Britain in 55 BC when Julius Caesar and his legions landed on a beach near Dover, and came back again in 54 BC. The historian Florus writing in AD 120 claimed that Caesar chased the Britons as far as the Caledonian Forest in the latter year. This is totally untrue.

In AD 43, the new Emperor, Claudius, needed military success to impress the Roman people, so he decided to invade Britannia. The landing was successful and his forces quickly conquered the south-eastern part of the island. After that, progress was slow and in AD 60-61 the Boudican rebellion nearly drove the Romans back to the Continent. The Roman Civil Wars of AD 68–69 saw four Emperors being acclaimed but, eventually, Vespasian won the battle to become Emperor. He had commanded part of the forces that had invaded Britain in AD 43 and, needing to expand the Empire to convince any doubters of his worth, he ordered that the remainder of the island be brought under Roman rule. After a struggle, northern England and Wales were overrun, clearing the way for an assault on the northern half of the island.

Between AD 71 and 74, Roman rule was established in Cumbria and parts of Northumberland with a number of forts eventually being built on the line between the Tyne and the Solway. These forts were linked by a road which became known as the Stanegate, the stone road, in early historic times.

This early road was on, or near, the line chosen for Hadrian's Wall about half a century later but in the AD 70s, the Roman Empire never thought to build massive linear fortifications to defend its extensive frontiers – the power of the army did that by periodically marching across any land outwith their provinces or where trouble was thought to be brewing.

For further conquest, the Romans had a good intelligence-gathering network built up from traders taking the highly prized Roman goods into barbarian territory, sounding out the native leaders and generally spying out the land. Using the information gained, this was followed by a reconnoitre in strength to impress/warn the native inhabitants of the might of Rome. Diplomatic gifts would be given to the appropriate leaders in a hearts- and minds- operation. It is not known for certain that this usual practice happened in the Borders between AD 71 and 74, but it is a reasonable guess that it did. There have been suggestions that the first permanent Roman fort built at Trimontium was on top of the earlier Roman temporary camp and I think that this is likely to have been the case – but it still has to be proved.

The Landscape in the Borders

Until the advent of carbon dating and pollen analysis, we had to rely on Roman writers for any description of Caledonia. These were complimentary neither to the landscape, which was either forest or marsh or both, nor to the Caledonians who were small, dirty and totally immoral. Tacitus, Cassius Dio and Herodian had brave Roman armies fighting their way through marshy forests from AD 80 to AD 305, before they could face and conquer the Caledonians.

We have to remember that Roman writers tended to be propagandists rather then unbiased observers and this makes it difficult to accept any of their writings unconditionally, even when we want to believe them. It is even more dangerous to pick out the facts that confirm our beliefs and ignore those that don't.

Imperial propaganda was extended to carved monuments where the Roman legionary or cavalryman is always portrayed as a superior being, twice as large as the naked, hairy Caledonians who cower under his raised sword or spear. An example of this 'superiority complex' is to be found on a Roman tombstone discovered near Inveresk in October 2007. Although much of the upper stone is missing, the motif is that of a cavalryman charging down a native Caledonian. The inscription shows that it was dedicated to the 'shades' of Crescens, a mounted bodyguard for the Imperial Governor who was in charge of the Roman-occupied parts of Britain.

To return to the landscape, using the evidence of carbon dating and pollen analysis, we know that Scotland had been a settled agricultural land for over 3,000 years before the Romans arrived.

In the lower and more fertile lands, the Late Bronze and Iron Ages had created a patchwork of small fields for cereal cultivation and animal husbandry. The population lived in small settlements and single houses linked by trackways. Woodland was tended, with coppiced and pollarded trees providing the long thin branches necessary for building, while still leaving the ground below fit for grazing animals.

There is no evidence for large concentrations of population in the shape of towns. The only location of a suitable size was on Eildon Hill North which encloses 39 acres within the rampart but the lack of a plentiful water supply rules this out as 'the largest pre-Roman hilltown in Scotland' as it had previously been claimed. The ramparts round the top of Eildon Hill North suggest that it was a seasonal meeting place with a good claim to be a religious centre for the neighbouring peoples.

The undulating and fragmented landscape of the Borders does not lend itself to large tribal groupings, as does the southern half of the island. The settlement pattern here is that of isolated communities, living as and where they could, at little above subsistence level. The distribution of small hill forts tends to confirm this hypothesis. Few of the known settlements would have been capable of holding more than a hundred people, and most would be the size to be suitable for an extended family. So the population in the pre-Roman period would be scattered with the greatest density in the Merse and lower Tweed valley and much sparser in the upper valleys.

If it was a Celtic warrior society, as has been frequently claimed, the men are likely to have been farmers or stock-raisers first and warriors only when necessary. The type of land would not be sufficiently fertile to support a large non-productive elite.

So when a Roman legion of 5,000 men, plus auxiliaries and supply units, marched into the Borders, they are likely to have been treated with a healthy respect, if not a welcome. For this, the natives, later to be given the group name of Uotidini or Votadini, were deemed to be friendly to Roman interests. In fact, nobody has looked for evidence of Roman settlement in the much better and more-cultivated lands of the Merse as far as I know.

Nor does anyone know how far the lands of the Votadini extended. There has been much learned debate on this question but my own un-learned suggestion is that the watersheds of the upper Tweed basin would provide a natural divider for tribal lands.

Trimontium

On crossing the present border from England into Scotland, you see an undulating landscape with the triple-peaked Eildon Hills as the most noticeable feature. Knowing that this was an important meeting place and religious centre, the Roman force headed for it and planted their first permanent fort at the foot of the northern hill and called it 'Trimontium', the place of the three hills.

The site was good, a natural mound overlooking the river and at a natural crossroads where any north–south traffic coming down the Leader intersected with the east–west movement along the banks of the Tweed.

It was unlikely that this choice of site was entirely accidental. The area would have been scouted well in advance and the site chosen deliberately. By placing their fort next to a native sacred place, they were demonstrating their strength to do as they wished when they wished to do it. Typical bully tactics but nobody can build an empire the size of the Roman one in the first century AD without breaking a few heads; and with 5,000 plus men in the invading force, there were few to say them nay.

At any rate, the Roman military surveyors who first selected the site chose well. A succession of seven phases of construction covering the period from AD 79 to around AD 185 have been determined by excavation and there is further proof that it was a gathering place for the army of Severus attempting yet another 'reconquering' of Caledonia in AD 211. These phases of occupation are detailed below.

Trimontium Lost

In each of the Roman forts that were known in Scotland in the eighteenth century, there were traces of embankments and ditches visible on the surface of the ground. At Newstead, the site of Trimontium, there was nothing showing on the ground and the earliest clue to its existence was in a short history of Melrose written in 1743 by the Rev. Adam Milne, the minister of the parish. Referring to the field called Red Abbey-stead which he thought might be an unknown abbey built with the red sandstone of the area, 'when the ground here is plowed or ditched, the foundations of several houses are discovered, a great deal of lead got, and some curious seals. At this place likewise there has been a famous bridge over the Tweed; the entrance to it on the south side is very evident, and a great deal of fine stones are dug out of the arches when the water is low'. This is at a point where the narrowing of the valley and the less precipitous river banks made it easier to bridge.

In 1761, General Roy, the military cartographer and antiquary, was searching for the Trimontium of Ptolemy's map and expecting to find it between Carlisle and the Antonine Wall. On seeing the three Eildon

Hills and observing that the track of 'Watling Street' headed directly towards them, he decided that 'the ancient Trimontium of the Romans was situated somewhere near these remarkable hills, at the village of Eildon, Old Melros or perhaps about Newstead where the Watling Street hath passed the Tweed'.

General Roy had a keen eye for the ground and his *Military Antiquities of the Romans in North Britain* gives illustrations of all their known forts. Yet even his experienced eye could detect no ground trace that would identify a Roman fort at Newstead. This is positive proof that all surface traces had been obliterated, the great ditches filled in, the ramparts levelled and the useful stone removed.

The first vital clue that there was something important lying just below the surface of the ground was made in 1783 when a Roman altar was ploughed up in the field to the east of Red Abbey-stead. It was dedicated to the Campestres, the goddesses of the Parade Ground by a decurian of the Ala of Vocontian Cavalry. That discovery was followed in 1830 by another altar being found in the field to the south-east of Red Abbey-stead. This one was dedicated to Silvanus by a centurion of the Twentieth Legion. The last find attracted the attention of Dr John Smith, the secretary of the Society of Antiquaries of Scotland, who observed the site and noted the finds.

It was the coming of the railway to the Borders that led to the re-discovery of the Roman Trimontium. In the winter of 1846, a cutting to take the railway track was made at the bottom of the field south of Red Abbey-stead and a series of well-like pits began to appear. Some were lined with stone, others simply dug out of the ground. They varied in depth from 2m downwards and had a variable diameter 1m to 1.8m. In one of them was the skeleton of a man, said to have been erect or nearly so, and reputedly holding an iron spear.

After an initial curiosity, no further investigation was initiated and for the next fifty years, the pits and the story of a Roman soldier standing upright with his spear, had passed into folklore.

Trimontium Rediscovered

In 1904, drainage operation in the Gutterflat, a field to the west of Red Abbey-stead, cut through the foundations of a large building, throwing up Roman tiles, mortar and pottery. The Council of the Society of Antiquaries of Scotland decided that the site would be worth investigating and appointed James Curle, a Melrose solicitor and a keen amateur archaeologist, to take charge of the excavations.

James Curle was already noted for his archaeological discoveries and publications on Scandinavian antiquities and his work on the broch at Torwoodlee. So it was fitting that he was given the task of overseeing the excavations at Red Abbey-stead field. The excavations began on 13 February 1905 and continued without interruption until May 1909. After a short space, work was recommenced on 22 December 1909 and concluded in September 1910.

During this time, Curle was working as a Melrose solicitor as well as serving on the Roxburgh County Council, Melrose Parish and Town Councils, the Royal Commission on Ancient Monuments of Scotland and as a Trustee of the National Library of Scotland. With such demands on his time, it was a wonder that he could write: 'During these periods of work, my residence within a mile of the site enabled me to make frequent, and often daily, visits to follow the progress of the digging and to carry home the smaller objects found, thus giving opportunities for study that would not have been possible had they been despatched at once to the National Museum of Scotland.'

Curle was very fortunate in having an experienced Clerk of Works in Alexander Mackie, who had already excavated several Roman sites in Scotland. The finds were numerous and staggering. Mackie's practical excavation skills combined with Curle's scholarly erudition produced the publication of *A Roman Frontier Post and its People* in 1911. This highly readable but scholarly tome provided a standard reference work fifty years ahead of its time, both in excavation techniques and swift publication – and a reminder to modern archaeologists that unless they publish their findings, the artefacts might as well be left undisturbed in the ground.

A Roman Frontier Post and its People was the most definitive work of its period and is still much quoted. It has the additional cachet of being a collector's piece.

In the post-Second World War period, a further excavation was carried out on the Trimontium site by Sir Ian Richmond with the labour being supplied by six German prisoners-of-war. His conclusions confirmed many of Curle's datings but some of his interpretations are highly speculative and have been subject to revision.

About the same period, Dr J.K. St Joseph was developing the use of air photography as an archaeological tool. Air photographs had been used to track enemy troops, fortifications and movements by both sides during the war; the same techniques could be adapted to trace the land disturbances from previous centuries. Former ditches held water and showed up as a denser vegetation while buried walls which do not retain so much moisture, showed up as lighter lines in the soil.

At Trimontium, a lot of over-flying showed a new complex of camps through cropmarks and at least nine new temporary camps discovered.

It was in 1955 that I was re-introduced to the Roman presence in the Borders.

In the spring of that year, I had picked up what was quite obviously an arrowhead made of a hard shiny stone, at the edge of a field in which I was working. A bit puzzled and wanting to know more about it, I was told to take it to Bruce Mason, a Selkirk baker who was the local identifier of all things ancient.

This I did and he explained that I had found a flint arrowhead that was about four thousand years old. Then he showed me some of the collection that he had found by deliberately walking the ploughed fields and looking for objects from earlier times.

I was hooked and it turned out to be a fortunate encounter for both of us.

Bruce had lost his only daughter two years previously and had never recovered from the loss. At the same time, illness had prevented him from walking the fields unless accompanied by someone. So we joined forces; he taught me the skills of fieldwalking and reading the ground to identify potential sites while I picked him up and drove him to the sites. Of course the greater part of his collection was from the Roman fort near Newstead.

Bruce died in 1963 and his brother Walter, an equally knowledgeable but more retiring man, took over my practical education. By now I was quite aware of the archaeological and historical potential of the countryside and my work as a fencing contractor took me all over the Borders. But I always returned to fieldwalk the fort at Trimontium.

Every Sunday afternoon from October to March, I could be found tramping the ploughed fields at Newstead, picking up a great deal of pottery, some bronze objects or an occasional coin and, on a golden day, a Roman sealstone.

By the mid 1970s, I realised that the *Roman Frontier Post and its People*, brilliant though it was, did not cover the whole story. So I started writing my own findings as papers for inclusion in *The Proceedings of the Society of Antiquaries of Scotland*.

I had found literally hundred-weights of pottery when I noticed that fragments of one particularly thick type of vessel, called a mortaria, had become misshaped in the kiln and were no use as pots. As faulty pots would not be brought into the fort, the obvious conclusion was that there was a pottery kiln on or near the site. Two types of pottery were stamped with the makers' names and I concluded that EMI and INVOM:ANDUS were potters working at Trimontium. While touting this theory around with little response, I had a stroke of luck.

This was that a student, Mark Gillings at the Department of Archaeo-logical Studies of Bradford University, was studying for a PhD and his subject was 'Roman pottery made in Scotland'. I had been bending the ear of Dr David Breeze on this very subject a short time before, so he sent the student down to examine my 'proofs'.

These turned out to be convincing enough to warrant further study but Mark was also very impressed with all my field-walking finds, so impressed that he told his tutor, Dr Ric Jones who came to see what I had been picking up. To cut a long story short, a five-year excavation was planned, permission to excavate was given and money raised. This first sod was cast in 1987 and was so successful that on completion a further five years was planned and carried out. Using modern methods, this added more information about the site. It is my regret that, after ten years of digging and ten years of waiting, this has not been made available in a published form.

When planned, the excavation programme was intended to explore the impact of the Roman garrison on the indigenous population. With this in mind, it was decided to dig one part of the Roman fort and a section of a nearby native settlement every year. This gave mixed results and no firm conclusions have been reached as yet.

A Trimontium Trust was formed in December 1988 to promote the study of the Roman occupation of southern Scotland and an exhibition, later to become a Museum, was opened in 1991. Thanks to an energetic secretary, Donald Gordon, and an enthusiastic bunch of Trustees and supporters, the Trust is in good health providing six celebrity lectures per year, a yearly publication called the *Trimontium Trumpet*, and manning (or more often womanning) the Museum in Melrose Market Place for seven months of the year.

I have gone on at length about the Trimontium Fort for the simple reason that it is the most investigated Roman monument in Scotland. From this site, we draw most of our knowledge and the dating sequence of the Roman occupation of the Borders. It gives us an established timescale for comparison with other Roman sites in Scotland. This may not be totally correct and opinions vary on some of the conclusions.

To unravel a disturbing complex of former walls and filled ditches, Dr Simon Clarke of Bradford University, who was in charge of the later stages of excavation, has drawn together information from the Curle and Richmond excavations together with the ten-year Bradford one, added geophysics and fieldwalking evidence to form a phased dating plan of the fort and surrounding camps. I have added the first 'temporary' camp of my own volition (and will take the blame if it is wrong).

NB All dates given below are provisional and may be altered at any time as and when new information is forthcoming.

Phase one. AD 72–79. This is my conjectural phase. With a line of forts established between the Tyne and Solway, it would be most unusual if no reconnaissance was made in strength to the north of line. The site at Newstead is at a convenient crossroads and ideal for an occasionally used temporary camp.

Unproven but likely; and see below.

Phase two. AD 80–87. The earliest permanent occupation was an irregular Agricolan fort. It had a cobbled-based rampart with two v-shaped ditches. Sill beam slots and masses of waterlogged timber debris show that this phase had permanent buildings rather than a tented enclosure. There was a west annexe, a double ditched defensive enclosure with a gateway on the west side, indicating that in this phase, the main approach road was from the west.

Phase three. AD 88–105. There was a reconstruction of the fort around AD 87 but whether this represents a short-term abandonment or simply a strengthening of the defences is not known. Certainly the cobbled wall-base was widened to 13.5m across, giving an estimated height to the rampart of 8.4m. Immediately in front of this was a single ditch 5 to 7m wide and 2 to 4m deep.

Settlement annexes were added to the south, east and probably north, giving a reasonable indication that a substantial civilian population was clustered round the fort. In the west annexe, a 'mansio' building and a bath-house were constructed, the mansio being either an inn for wealthy travellers or a trading post.

This phase of occupation seems to have ended in disaster. Trouble on the Dacian frontier meant that troops were withdrawn from the Caledonian frontier, leaving Trimontium without a regular army garrison. There is evidence to suggest that enemies had taken and burned the fort, leaving dead bodies and broken armour to be tidied up by returning legionaries or friendly natives.

*Phase four. c.*AD 105–137. There is no certain evidence that Trimontium was occupied during this period. It may have been scavenged for debris, especially iron which was a valuable commodity to the natives.

Around AD 117, there had been an incursion into the Roman province from the north of England and, although no details of this have been mentioned in written records, an inscription in Jarrow states that 'after the barbarians had been dispersed and the province of Britain had been recovered, he [the Emperor Hadrian] added a frontier line between either shore of the ocean for 80 miles'. We do not know how extensive this war was or even who the opponents were, but there was a coin with a Britannia reverse issued in AD 119. This is usually a public relations exercise to commemorate a victory and remind the people of Rome of what a successful soldier their Emperor was. In Rome, military success was lauded while military defeat was covered over (no change there).

Hadrian's Wall was commenced in AD 122, marking the limit of Roman military power in Britannia. What happened north of the Wall is unknown but it would be very unlikely that the northern natives would have been left undisturbed.

*Phase five. c.*AD 137–142. The re-occupation of the fort was supposed to have begun in AD 140 when the Emperor Antoninus Pius decided to complete the conquest of Caledonia but coin and other evidence suggest that this is likely to have happened a few years earlier.

This is only a minor revision of the chronology of the Roman settlement in Scotland but if this theory is correct, it shows that the Roman command were already planning to retake southern Scotland. Far from being a deserted fort, Trimontium had become a strong outpost of Hadrian's Wall – a promise of intent that the legions would return.

*Phase six. c.*AD 142–158. After a short period as a strong outlying post of Hadrian's Wall, Trimontium found itself at the rear of the Antonine Wall. Now it became a manufacturing, supply and distribution base for the Roman forces in the region. The fort area was reduced in size with part of the original defences cut by a third, by a reducing wall across the west side of the fort. This detached area became an industrial annexe involved in iron and lead working, presumably under military control, to supply the troops on and behind the wall.

In the south annexe, a tightly packed civilian population had their houses and workshops. A large number of pits were discovered in this area and, although these have been long considered to be wells, it is my opinion that many are more likely to have been tan-pits where leather was tanned. This involves digging a pit, water-proofing it with puddle clay and filling it with layers of raw hides and oak or willow bark alternately, before filling the pit with water. After some time, the skins are taken out, now tanned and useable.

During the Bradford excavations, a great number of horse heads were found in the ditches and pits, especially round the south annexe. The same was noted in the Curle excavations and the report on the horse remains was that 'as the majority of the horse skulls examined belong to aged animals, it may be inferred that the practice of eating horseflesh so common in Europe during the Early Stone Age was not followed during the earlier centuries of the Christian era'.

However, the Roman army did require vast quantities of leather and I have the idea that, after a lifetime of carrying a mounted auxiliary around, the skin of the poor old horse was turned into caligae (boots) for the legionary to march in, or a jerkin beneath his armour, or as part of a leather tent to keep him dry while out on campaign. What the

Roman cavalryman thought about Bucephala (cavalry mounts were mares or geldings) being turned into boots has never been recorded. Boots are the most likely use because horsehide makes the strongest type of leather.

The south annexe seems to have been home to another industry as it has produced evidence of at least one pottery kiln. Whether Emius or Invomandus worked it, we have yet to find out as the kiln was found on the edge of the excavation on the final days, and awaits further attention. The mortaria made by these potters are found at Trimontium and in the forts to the north along the Antonine Wall. An early study of Roman pottery in Scotland states that the work of these potters 'would not be inconsistent with production around Newstead'.

In the vicinity, there has been a Roman brickworks, probably in the field next to Oakendean House where 'clay pits' are noted in an early map★. This produced a variety of bricks, tiles and water pipes for use in the fort and its annexes. The kiln or kilns would be worked by the military for use in the adjacent fort and annexes. This brickworks may have been started in one of the earlier phases of occupation but was at its most productive in this phase.

The brickmakers of Trimontium must have been versatile as the finds from the site show the wide variety of their handiwork. The building bricks are in two sizes, nominally 30cms and 60cms square (pedales and bipedales): roofing tiles, one flat with raised edges (tegula) and the half-rounded covering tiles (imbrex); hollow box flue-tiles (tubulus) to carry hot air for heating the rooms; comb-scored tiles to hold plaster on the walls; and finally water-pipes, large, to take water into the fort and small, to distribute it in the south annexe.

After many years of fieldwalking, I was able to determine which areas of the fort had buildings with tile roofs but not built with bricks; and where brick-built houses with tiled roofs had once been, especially notable on the site of the granaries. Only the baths and the commandant's house had been stone and brick-built with tile roofs and

---

★ If not at Oakendean, the kiln was certainly situated in open ground where the moulded wet clay was laid out to dry before firing. In the bricks found fieldwalking, I have noted footprints of dogs of various sizes, sheep or goats, a pig and the footprints of a field-mouse seeking to extract a grain of barley from the wet clay.

central heating. The baths had been roofed with tufa, a light soft stone that prevented steam condensing on the tile roof and then dripping, coldly, on the customers beneath.

*Phase seven. c.*AD 158–163. There seems to have been a disruption somewhere to the north, on or near the line of the Antonine Wall which was abandoned in the early 160s. Inside the Trimontium fort, the reducing wall was demolished and what was previously an industrial area was rebuilt with long narrow buildings. These seem to have been put up quickly and represent a doubling of barrack facilities to house an increased garrison. This was a short phase, seemingly indicative of panic measures to meet a coming disaster, and it is tempting to view this construction as a measure to billet troops retreating from the Antonine Wall.

Although the period AD 158–184 has been split into two phases, this might be a false division and the differences in construction may have been made to suit the changing conditions. In deference to Dr Clarke's original, I will maintain his phasing.

Phase eight. AD 163–184?. This last phase must represent the period of occupation from the abandonment of the Antonine Wall until the withdrawal of a permanent Roman garrison in the south of Scotland. Trimontium had yet again been turned into a forward frontier post of Hadrian's Wall.

Outside the fort, there was a great reduction in the civilian population of the annexes; most of the buildings there were abandoned and the area returned to agricultural use. The people may have moved southwards in face of the perceived threat or retreated into the fort for protection.

Inside the fort, even more dramatic changes were taking place. This phase or the previous one saw the demolition of the principia building which was replaced by a larger 'exercise' hall. This was a roofed area to train and exercise cavalry horses during the winter when outside exercising was self-defeating but the horses still had to be kept fit. As this building must have been a priority, its construction suggests that a cavalry-based force was now the principal garrison of the fort.

The western part of the fort was cleared of the previously-built buildings and replaced by small structures, 3–4m by 4–5m standing clear of each other. These are reckoned to be 'chalets' to house the individual soldier and his family but could equally well be the billet/stable quarters for a cavalryman and his horse or two horses. In either case, this would represent a massive reduction in the military strength of the fort.

There are suggestions that this 'chalet' development happened when a fort was stripped of its permanent garrison, leaving only those retired veterans who elected to remain with their families in the area where they had served. In those circumstances, they were no longer paid or supplied by the central authority and had to rely on their farming or trading skills for survival. The latest coin to be recovered from the Trimontium site is dated AD 180 and this has been used as the probable date when the fort was finally abandoned by the Roman army. This is a reasonable supposition but to date such a major event on the evidence of one coin is unwise.

Even if the eastern part still retained the barrack blocks, now made into chalets, it is questionable if the garrison could number more than two or three hundred men. This would not be sufficient to control the area of the Borders unless it was garrisoned by a cavalry unit, mobile enough to quell minor local insurrections, yet able to give advance warning of threatening invasion to the Hadrian's Wall garrison and retreat to safety there if necessary. The lack of a regular infusion of fresh coinage into the fort would infer that its defenders, if there were any, were now citizen soldiers, perhaps the retired veterans who had settled beside the fort and were raising their families in Roman military ways and customs and spreading Romanitas to the native population. This was common beside many other forts in the Roman Empire.

In effect, Trimontium may have become the temporary base for a numerus (or unit) of 'exploratores', the frontier scouts who patrolled the area north of Hadrian's Wall, and gave a reassuring presence to the parts of the native population who were Romanised and reported any possible trouble coming from the north. The hypothesis of a Numerus Exploratorum Trimontanorum does not tax the imagination too far since another eleven numeri are known on Hadrian's Wall and in the forts to the north, in the early third century.

Incorporated in the fabric of Jedburgh Abbey are three Roman altar stones. One is indecipherable but the other two have third-century inscriptions. One is dedicated by 'the First Loyal Cohort of Vardulli, Roman citizens, part mounted' which was commanded by Gaius Quintus Severus. The other was dedicated by a detachment of Raetian spearmen under the command of Julius Severus. Clearly, there is an undiscovered fort of the third century somewhere near Jedburgh.

The idea of the former fort of Trimontium becoming the centre of a settlement of retired Roman veterans and their families has yet to be explored. I mention it as a possibility.

Phase nine. In the early third century between the years of AD 209 and 211, the Emperor Septimius Severus and his sons Caracalla and Geta embarked on a campaign to pacify the northern frontier. The main thrust of this seems to have been up the line of Dere Street (which appears below under Roman Roads) and eventually to Trimontium which one archaeologist suggested 'was perhaps the point where Septimius and his generals concentrated their forces for the big push into hostile territory'. Pottery sherds of the late second and early third centuries found on the site, have been seen as proof; as have the series of large marching camps which starts there.

More positive proof was made in 1988 when I was fieldwalking the ground just inside the north gate of the fort and picked up a red jasper intaglio with the engraved portrait of a youthful Caracalla. This could be dated to between AD 205 and 209 before he grew a beard. Such gems were given to supporters of the regime and were a major feature of Imperial gift-giving. Such 'loyalty tokens' would only be presented to influential army officers who supported the Emperor and his family, and this infers that whoever it belong to, must have been worth keeping sweet and was inside the fort of Trimontium when he lost it.

Further proofs of the assembling army are a coin of Severus and two of Julia Domna, his wife, which were found 500m to the west of the fort and within the likely extent of the ground needed as a camp site for the gathering force. One of the coins of Julia Domna was minted in Thessalonica in Macedonia which may indicate that a vexillation was drawn from Greece – although one coin does not make a conclusion.

The Severan campaign began in AD 209. The two literary accounts that survive tell of the hills being levelled, rivers bridged, forests cut and used to provide causeways through the marshes that the army had to cross before bringing the enemy to confrontation. The large Severan forts that have been identified indicate that the line of march was northwards along Dere Street.

No major battles are recorded as the Caledonians employed guerrilla tactics against the well-organised Romans. According to Cassius Dio, the Romans lost 50,000 men – a vastly exaggerated figure that would have meant the equivalent of ten legions being wiped out – a disaster that would make the three legions that Varus lost in Germania, look like a very minor incident.

Dio records that peace negotiations were conducted between the two assembled armies by the Emperor and the Caledonian chiefs. With this 'victory', Severus and Caracalla returned south and celebrated by adopting the title Britannicus. It is assumed that the Caledonians and Maeatae had conceded a large amount of territory of Strathmore and along the north-east coast.

In May 210 AD, Severus and Caracalla were in York when the Caledonians were invading again. Severus placed Caracalla in command of an army of vengeance with instructions to kill everyone they saw. This suited Caracalla whom later events proved to be a bloody-thirsty psychopath. While he was carrying out his orders with gusto, news came that Severus had died at York on the 4 February AD 211.

Caracalla now had other priorities. Making peace with the Caledonians by large bribes, he and his brother Geta rushed back to Rome to make sure that no one else was proclaimed Emperor in his absence. To make certain of the title, he had his brother Geta and many of the prominent and illustrious Roman citizens murdered in AD 212. After a short reign of extravagance and cruelty, Caracalla was murdered by his own Praetorian Guard in AD 217.

To Return to Trimontium

In the early 180s AD, the Roman frontier was stabilised at Hadrian's Wall with outposts of forts at Netherby, Bewcastle, Risingham and High Rochester being rebuilt and strengthened. These are not large forts but seem to have been the base camps for large, mobile forces from the 180s onwards. None were large enough to have billeted the individual garrisons of a 1,000 strong, part-mounted unit, a cohort and a unit of scouts, the 'exploratores'.

The above forts were the bases of outposted soldiers who had to maintain a long-range patrol through the area of southern Scotland, show the friendly natives that the hand of Rome was still there to help them in adversity, intimidate any troublemakers and give warning of any major attack from the north. Although the area was no longer part of the Roman province, it was a protected area, partly Romanised after a hundred years of intermittent occupation and a useful buffer zone between the Roman province of Britannia and the hostile native forces to the north of the Forth/Clyde line.

To maintain this presence, the area was patrolled in strength and in the course of time would have established routes along the lines of the Roman roads and have designated stopping places throughout the south of Scotland. Unquestionably, the stopping places would have a secure defensive structure although not necessarily within the structure of a standard Roman fort. A strong palisade with internal horse-lines would be more suitable if cavalry units were involved.

From altar dedications, it is known that Risingham and High Rochester, both on the line of Dere Street, were main bases for the exploratores' units. It has been suggested that the two Roman altars built into the fabric of Jedburgh Abbey had been robbed from the fort at Cappuck by medieval masons and therefore that Cappuck was another base camp for the numeri. This is unlikely as the fort is 5kms distant from Jedburgh and suitable building stone can be found beside the abbey. There is no evidence of a third century occupation at Cappuck.

These minor points do not invalidate the proposition that there was a permanent base in the region at Jedburgh, possibly on the site of the present town, where ninth century religious sculpture and Saxon coins have been found. If not there, at least somewhere between the town and Bonjedward or Mount Hooly Farm where Dere Street crosses the Jed and Teviot rivers. Topographically, this is a natural meeting place.

A Roman military entrenchment near Tweedmouth has produced third century pottery. On the south side of the Tweed, there are a line of temporary camps of unknown date leading up to Springwood Park near Kelso, where over three hundred Roman coins have been found by metal detectorists. These range from first century (a denarius of Mark Anthony and fourteen other coins) to fifth century (seven small bronze coins of Honorius, AD 394–403 and Arcadius, AD 395–408). The coins were mainly found in the King's Haugh where the putative Roman east/west road from Craik Cross to Tweedmouth crosses the river Teviot. This is not a scattered hoard or a modern collection but is spread over four fields on the Springwood Park farm. Immediately opposite is the medieval castle of Roxburgh and it would be surprising if there was not a third or fourth century fortress on this towering mound.

Take these separate facts together and they strengthen the proposition that Roman patrols policed the lower Tweed, Teviot and Jed valleys in the third, fourth and fifth centuries.

With consideration to the above, it is very likely that the site of Trimontium would also be a stopping place for patrolling units. After an intermittent hundred years of the benefits of Romanitas and the probability of several generations of military descendants in the vicinity, a base camp for the exploratores at Trimontium is not inconceivable.

This is a topic for debate; a test hypothesis that will need a lot more work to confirm, deny or develop, but absence of proof cannot be taken as non-existence.

Admittedly, there has been no recognisable evidence of third century building within the fort during any of the excavations so far reported. Yet the theory that Trimontium was a concentration gathering point for the Severan campaigns is based on circumstantial finds of a few sherds of pottery, three coins, one certain and one probable intaglio, and the fact that the first of the large 165-acre temporary camps has been located on ground next to the fort.

We have little idea of what life in the fort was like or any understanding of the local politics, whether there were pro- and anti-Roman groupings in the Borders. Roman objects have been found in various places and in different circumstances. These give us some indication of what was happening in the Borders and we can make an educated guess that the relationship between the native population and the people in the fort was generally friendly, based on mutual trading advantage.

Through the benefit of the Roman literacy, we know the names of five people who lived in or near the fort of Trimontium. All were Roman soldiers or suppliers: Gaius Arrius Domitianus, a centurion of the Twentieth Legion; L. Maximinius Gaetulicus a centurion; Aelius Marcus, a Decurion of the Ala Augusta of the Vocontii; and two potters, Emius and Invomandus. There were some names scratched on pottery sherds and bronze objects but these were simply named marks of personal possession.

Religion at Trimontium

Although we know little about living conditions in the fort, we have a much better idea of the gods and goddesses worshipped there. But before identifying the gods of Trimontium, it is worth having a simplified look at Roman deities and religious attitudes.

The Romans were heirs to the Greek traditions of deity ie they borrowed Greek gods and gave them Roman identities. Zeus, Hera and Athene became Jupiter, Juno and Minerva, retaining the same powers but now with Roman names: Ares became Mars, the god of war and so on down the line, for the Romans seemed to have gods for every purpose – they even had a goddess of sewers, Cloacina, and a separate one of bad smells, Mephitis – presumably the last two worked in partnership.

Added to this list were the number of heroes who were half-gods, Hercules etc, and a number of gods/goddesses of the countryside plus large numbers of satyrs, nymphs, maenads etc for all locations. On death, the emperors were deified; it is said that the last words of the Emperor Vespasian, were: 'I fear I am about to become a god'. Most cities had their own personalised goddesses, eg Roma, and there were plenty to go round.

Purely Roman gods could be, and frequently were, tacked on to native deities to make them more acceptable to the native tribes. The native cults were thus 'civilised' by conjoining them to a vaguely similar Roman god or goddess eg the relief of native goddess Brigantia, which was found at Birrens in Dumfriesshire is figured like Minerva and winged like Victory, with a mural crown which shows that she was a provincial goddess, the deity of northern Brigantes.

It was perfectly acceptable to worship a number of gods although 'worship' is not necessarily as we would know it in present day terms. Rather, bargains were made with the god – 'keep me safe for a year/make me rich/give me a son etc and I will worship at your shrine and/or dedicate an altar to you'.

Synopsis of gods/goddesses/beliefs at Trimontium

Deities	Altars	Intaglii	Terra-cotta	Bronze
Jupiter	I	4		
Apollo	I	I		
Diana	I			
Mars				I
Silvanus	I			
Campestres	I			
Juno		I		
Minerva		I	I	
Mercury		2		
Victory		I		
Fortuna		2		
Nemesis		I		
Luna		I		
Roma		I		
Cupids		3		
Bonus Eventus		2		
Satyrs		8		
Maenads		I		
Emperors		I		
Birds and animals		4		

If the bargain was fulfilled, then you had to keep your vow otherwise you would incur the wrath of the god, which was never a good idea.

With numerous finds from excavations and fieldwalking at Trimontium, it is possible to work out some of the beliefs of the inhabitants. As could be expected in a military site on a rough frontier, warlike deities were popular.

Evidence of religious preference has been found in the dedications of altars, one terracotta head and one bronze head, but by far the most infor-

mation is in the thirty-six ring-stones which have been found on the site
– only two have been recovered by excavation and thirty-four picked up
by fieldwalkers. The ring-stones were cut 'intaglio' into varieties of
chalcedony, cornelian, red jasper, two-layered onyx, paste and glass, and
mounted in an iron ring, but over the last 1,800 years the iron has rusted
away leaving the small carved stones to be found in the ground.

On this evidence, it must be concluded that the inhabitants of
Trimontium also looked on the sunny side of life, depending on good
luck (Bonus Eventus 2 and Fortuna 2) and liking a good time (cupids
3, satyrs 8 and maenads 1).

Gaius Arrius Domitianus, a centurion of the Twentieth Legion, is
likely to have been the commandant of the fort. He spread his religious
options, dedicating one altar to Jupiter as the best and greatest of the
gods, to Silvanus, the god of woods and hunting 'for his safety and that
of his household' and to Diana, the goddess of woods and hunting.
Obviously he liked to hunt and it is likely that his family were with him
in the fort.

Trimontium – The Future?

Before leaving the central subject of Trimontium, I would like to put
forward several of my own ideas on what is still to be discovered there.
The following are models for testing and debate rather than conclusions. I am convinced the reasoning and deductions are sound although
I expect that many will doubt that (and probably my sanity) but as an
interested amateur, I am at liberty to put forward suggestions without
any loss of professional reputation.

You would think that with all the excavation, air photography,
geophysics and field walking over the site of Trimontium, that there
would be nothing left to learn – but you would be wrong. There is still
much to be discovered and more questions to be answered.

Once we get the publication of the Bradford University Excavation
Reports, which were expected in AD 2000 and are still only a distant
speck on the horizon, it will open the way for further investigation of
the site.

As I have fieldwalked the site for fifty-two years, I know the ground
well, and with the distinct probability that I may not live to see the

Bradford Report, I am taking this opportunity to put down on paper, some observations for consideration by future inquirers.

As these largely rely on ground survey and divining rod evidence, I would ask the sceptics who doubt the efficacy of divining rods, to consider the conclusions before questioning the method. The results can only be proven by excavation anyway, but I am not foolish enough to put forward ideas of which I am not totally convinced.

Altars

In *A Roman Frontier Post and its People*, James Curle notes that 'the comparative absence of inscribed stones was a disappointing feature of the excavations'. In this book, Curle published the pictures of the six altars which had been found on the site, the first in 1783. Of the six, four were found in the southern part of the East Annexe.

As a fieldwalker, I walked this area many times but gradually ignored one part of it because there was little to be found on the surface there. It eventually dawned on me that this was the obvious place for the parade ground, beside the fort and reasonably flat. Now the parade ground was a sacred place to the Roman soldier, as indeed it was to the RSM of my youthful soldiering period, who would bellow at anyone walking casually across 'his' parade ground.

The Romans took their parade ground even more seriously, having animal sacrifices at the beginning of each year and, according to one theory, burying the previous year's altars round the edge of the parade ground; this latter is unproven although much repeated. My own theory, equally unproven, was that the altars were placed round the parade ground and left standing there to show that this was a sacred place, guarded against intruders by the Roman gods. This could be a Roman duplication of the 'head walls' set up to protect the Celtic forts and holy places. My idea is that the altars would only be buried when the fort was being evacuated or when one garrison unit was replaced with another. As I say, unproven but logical.

The first altar from the East Annexe was found in 1783 and was dedicated to the 'Campestres', the goddesses of the parade ground, by a cavalry decurion. Remembering that another three of the previously excavated altars were found on the same approximate line of ditch, to see if there were any others to be found, I walked the ditch of the East Annexe with divining rods. With divining rods, it is possible to look for specific objects or people – don't ask me how it works, there is no scientific explanation for it, but it does as I have managed to prove to even the most sceptical people on occasion.

One problem quickly emerged – Curle noted only a single ditch while air photographs clearly show a double ditch. Divining rods also indicate a double ditch and it is in the outer one that I got indications of altars, eighteen to be exact. With a GPS, I noted the locations where these are to be found and hope that some day, someone might believe my findings enough to conduct a trial excavation. Most of the altars are just over a metre below the surface.

Starting at the East Gate of the East Annexe, altars are located at:

1. NT 57336 34355	2. NT 57336 34339
3. NT 57342 34321	4. NT 57345 34308
5. NT 57347 34293	6. NT 57345 34279
7. NT 57339 34268	8. NT 57332 34255
9. NT 57308 34224	10. NT 57304 34213
11. NT 57299 34202	11. NT 57289 34203
13. NT 57277 34206	14. NT 57249 34211
15. NT 57163 34226	16. NT 57163 34226
17. NT 57153 34232	18. NT 57125 34273

All the altars are lying along the line of the ditch and in the middle of it except for No. 14 which is lying across the ditch. Excavation required to prove/disprove.

Gyrus? at NT 57309 34414

While looking at air photographs of the site, I have long noted a large circular mark in the middle of the East Annexe. It is not usual to get circular marks in a Roman camp complex and it seems to have been unseen or ignored. Divining rods suggest a solid circular palisade enclosing an area about 30m in diameter and another outer ring of posts set 2m from the first. This is almost identical to a similar structure at Lunt that was interpreted as a gyrus, a training pen for cavalry horses and recruits. I may be quite wrong but it would fit in with the altar of the decurion of the Ala Augusta of the Vocontii, a cavalry unit, which was found nearby. Horses were important in an outpost fort. More investigation required.

Water

I have never been convinced that the water at Trimontium was supplied from the hundred plus pits that have been found there. The fort and its annexes must have held at least a thousand humans and their water needs, plus the requirements for the baths, and this could not have been supplied by surface collection. Additionally, humans need clean, drinkable water to survive and stagnant water in storage pits would not remain potable during the summer.

The obvious source was from the foot of the Eildons where many natural springs are to be found. I traced a drainage line from there to what can only be a header tank measuring 11m by 7m at NT 56843 33898. From there the line went straight downhill towards the west side of the fort. To carry across the dip on the south of the fort, the water passed through sealed pipes. Before coming to the baths, a branch pipe diverted some of the water to the houses beside the first century road in the South Annexe.

'The water pipes were of two kinds – the larger fifteen and a half inches in length, with a diameter of three inches, neatly made with faucet joints having a diameter of one inch and three-quarters, the smaller without faucets and with a diameter of one inch. The latter probably served as branch pipes'. *A Roman Frontier Post and its People* p.102.

As a guess, some of the pits may have been wells but they were water storers rather than water collectors.

The Logistics of Supply

As far as I know, the logistics of supplying the fort of Trimontium has never been considered. Taking eight hundred men as an average garrison, add the civilian population in the annexes to those troops out-posted at the various permanent forts in the Borders and the passing units who would look to replenish their supplies as they marched along Dere Street, and the problem would be immense. It was not only food, the corn, wine and oil for rations that was required, but all the other supplies, iron, lead, leather etc needed to keep an army in the field.

From excavation and field finds, we know that wine, oil, garum (a vile and costly fish sauce), currants, dates etc, sealed in large pottery jars called amphorae, came to Trimontium from Germany, France, Spain, Portugal and Italy. Tableware pottery came from all the above and as far afield as the Eastern Mediterranean. Although Trimontium was on the edge of the Roman world, it enjoyed the benefits of the Empire. How these objects were transported there, is another matter.

Oxcarts were heavy, slow and ponderous, capable of ten or twelve miles a day on reasonable ground. Oxen need to be fed and grass was not sufficient to maintain their strength, so they had to pull their own fodder as well as any supplies being transported; and hilly ground presented problems both uphill and downhill.

This largely rules out Trimontium being bulk-supplied by oxcart from Corbridge (five days journey), Inveresk (four days) or even from Tweedmouth which would be three days over the flatter ground. The objection to Tweedmouth, where there must have been a Roman port, is that there are no obvious Roman roads between there and Trimontium.

Certainly the areas around the fort would be farmed to produce what they could, and the native population would have a ready market for any spare surpluses.

Much of the neighboring arable land was farmed to supply the cavalry mounts: it would require four acres to provide the yearly grain, hay and grass for each animal, so there would be little spare ground immediately available to food-farm. Supplies could be garnered from settlements some distance from the fort through trade or taxation. Recent excavations at a settlement at Lilliesleaf, nine miles from Newstead, found second century Roman pottery and coins in a rectangular house and it is likely that these would be for trade goods.

With obvious objections to overland supply, there is the question 'Did the Romans use the river Tweed to move around 30–40 tonnes of supplies into Trimontium every day?' and the answer has to be 'very probably'.

The Romans used water transport in every corner of the Empire where it was available. Experts have worked out that the power required to move one tonne on an oxcart on the road, could move fourteen tonnes on water. The Roman inland water barges were shallow flat-bottomed punt-like vessels that could float in 30cms of water, so draught was no problem. River skills were not a problem either, as there was a 'numerus Barcariorum Tigrisensium' (a unit of the bargemen of the River Tigris) stationed at South Shields at the mouth of the Tyne. The small boat (codicaria) capable of carrying ten tonnes was pulled by four bargemen on tow-ropes and carried one steersman.

So far, these are hypothetical arguments. More convincing is the oar found in Curle's Pit LXV. It was not a rowing oar, nor a paddle, but a steering oar. It was 1.65m long and, according to the expert who wrote the report: 'It must have been the steering oar of a small low-freeboard boat, one probably resembling the modern Nordland rowing boats and having a high sternpost such as would dictate a rudder at the side instead of the end'. Although it was found buried in a pit and might conceivably be a votive offering, it must have been a very religious seaman who carried it 40km upstream to make the offering. The obvious deduction was that it was a working tool and as such part of a river transport system.

Two boathooks were found during the excavations and while fieldwalking at Trimontium, I picked up a tiny gemstone with an engraved dolphin, a creature appropriate to Neptune. The gemstone stretches the argument a bit as dolphins have other attributes.

Potential Roman Temple on Eildon Mains at NT 57605 33683

While tracing the complex of Roman roads that lead to the fort and bridge site, I came across a square shape with another joined on to it. The first was 11m by 10.5m and the smaller was 6m square. Both walls were approximately 1m thick.

As this was the right size for a temple and just outside the fort complex, I got another divining practitioner to check the size and shape – and he got the same. I make no claims on this having been proved wrong by the false readings of a Roman fortlet, but this is a place to be kept under observation.

ROMAN PRESENCE IN THE
REST OF THE BORDERS

Using the much-studied fort of Trimontium as a dating sequence, it is worth seeing how the known Roman monuments in the rest of the Borders conform to this.

As the Roman army was very regimented and built their forts, camps and roads to standard patterns, this makes it easier to predict where their monuments are likely to be found. As the Romans were a very affluent, even 'throw-away' society when compared with the natives, a broken pot or a stray coin might be only nuisance value to the legionary or auxiliary cavalryman, but Samian sherds and Roman coins are valuable clues to later-day archaeologists in trying to made sense of the period.

While looking for evidence of Roman presence in the Borders, I would suggest that about half of the sites have been identidied. I have a few more and some bits of road to add to the total. These I will filter into the picture as and when required and there is no compulsion to believe them. I know where they are and hope that they will be discovered some day by more reputable means.

Taking the known sites, these are mainly roads and forts with the addition of some camps and signal stations. Forts are permanently garrisoned and can be of various sizes. Camps are temporary structures, giving shelter and safety to marching troops or road-building squads. Signal stations, of which few are known, are part of a network using beacons to pass information.

The sudden arrival of a large number of well-paid Roman soldiers, needing food and clothing especially leather, and other services, must have made a difference to the economy of the Borders. If the Roman army imposed peace of a kind on the Borders, it also brought other 'benefits' of civilisation like taxation, forced labour and slavery.

In looking for known Roman sites, there are no better references than the *Inventories* of Peeblesshire, Roxburghshire and Selkirkshire. Although these books were printed in 1967, 1956 and 1957 respectively, they do contain all the knowledge that was then available and most of this is visible. Some of the deductions may be considered wrong in the light of recent discoveries, but the solid knowledge of what could be seen, was sound. (*The Inventory of Roxburghshire* must make it into *Guinness World Records* in having four commas in five words –'Dimly, yet not, however, doubtfully,' – a classic.)

Berwickshire had an *Inventory of the Monuments of Berwickshire* printed in 1915 and an Archaeological Field Survey in 1980, but there is no mention of any Roman sites. I am sure they must be there but nobody has bothered to look for them. The Romans would not have ignored the most fertile part of the Borders.

To tie the rest of the Borders into the Trimontium dating, we have to look at the known remains, the most visible of which is the road system and the forts along it.

As these can be found in the above *Inventories*, I will give a brief synopsis and only add in other parts which I think/know are there.

Dere Street

The Romans made good roads. In the flatter south, they form the basis of the present-day road system and even here in the Borders, where the countryside does not lend itself to the grid system, we can drive over roads which were first laid down by Roman surveyors.

Dere Street, the main Roman road northwards, crosses Hadrian's Wall near Corbridge, passes by the Roman forts of Risingham and Bremenium, and reaches the border at Chew Green where there is a fortlet and a number of temporary camps. The signal station on Brownhart Law, 900m further on, gives a view right across the Borders.

Further along Dere Street is Woden Law, a native hill-fort with what is deemed to be a Roman practice siege-works surrounding it. The road descends to cross Kale Water at Pennymuir, where four temporary camps are largely visible. Divining rods suggest that there were a series of barrack buildings *c.*25m by 8m in the northern end of the largest camps. This may be a semi-permanent training camp or the quarters for a repair/escort detachment of troops.

Where Dere Street dips to cross the Oxnam Water, there is the small fort at Cappuck which has been excavated in 1886, 1911 and 1949. The occupation that corresponds to phase three at Trimontium, also ended by being burned. Both north and south of the Cappuck fort, a number of temporary camps or fields appear in air photographs.

From Cappuck, Dere Street runs in a straight line towards the Eildons, crossing the Jed and Teviot Rivers where they join at Jedfoot. Although it must have crossed the peninsula made by the two rivers, no visible remains have been noted. This is the obvious site for a Roman fort or fortlet to guard the dual crossings and has been the target for a series of air photographs but to no avail.

South of the river crossing there a good platform site which divining rods suggest is a temporary camp with corners at NT 66682, NT 67013 24022, NT 66923 24167 and NT 66774 24047. It had a single ditch and wall with three gateways on the north and south sides and two on the east and west. It measured *c.*320m by 240m and is certainly a marching camp with rubbish pits about 6m apart and in lines 9 or 10m apart.

This camp is very similar to a many-gated marching camp at Rey Cross, County Durham, which is reckoned to be dated to AD 71–74. If it can be proven by the acceptable means of air photograph, geophysics or excavation, it opens up the question of 'when did the Romans first invade Scotland and who commanded the army?' It may not have been Agricola who is credited with the invasion on the basis of his son-in-law's history, but rather Petillius Cerealis, one of his predecessors in office. It is now being considered that a similar site at Burnswark, Dumfriesshire, 'may be the first site in Scotland which we can identify as a scene of military activity preceding that of Agricola, a temporary base of the army of Petillius Cerialis campaigning against some northern part of the Brigantes.'

There is another temporary camp on the river haugh south of Jedfoot Station Bridge and there is likely to be more on the flat haughs to the east. A signal station of the usual Roman pattern, ie a squashed doughnut, with four posts in a 3.5m square, is at NT 66589 23384. From the slightly higher vantage point, both Eildon Hill North and Ruberslaw can be seen.

After crossing the Jed and Teviot Waters, Dere Street makes for the Eildons, crossing the Roman road from Craik to Tweedmouth at the present day crossroads at Wellrig before skirting Eildon Hill North on the east side.

The first century line of Dere Street passed the Trimontium fort on the west side before crossing the Tweed near the Eddy Pool and climbing the hill past Kittyfield Farm. This explains why the first phase of the fort had the main gate on the west side.

The second-century road line was on the east side of the fort, making entry from the south and east more understandable. The Rev. Adam Milne in his *Description of the Parish of Melrose* writes that 'At this place (Newstead) there has been a famous bridge over the Tweed; the entrance to it on the south side is very evident and a great deal of fine stones are dug out of the arches of the bridge when the water is low'. We don't know which branch of the road this bridge served but it is more logical that it was the 2nd century one. This has the easiest gradient on either side of the river, a fact made plain by the three present bridges there ('Tripontium').

After crossing the Tweed, the *Inventory* suggested that the road ran along a line to the present minor road past Clackmae and Kedslie until it reached Stonyford Bridge outside of Lauder.

The road then went to Stonyford Bridge, where Roman coins have

There is another road running in this direction which has a much better claim to be Dere Street and that is 'Malcolm's Road', variously mentioned in medieval charters as 'the road by which one goes to Lauder by the causeways', 'the Great Street', and 'the High Street'. It forms the medieval west boundaries of the lands of Blainslie, Herdesley and Kedslie.

This to my mind is Dere Street north of the Tweed. It has all the appearance of a Roman road, a central mound 7–9m wide, ditches on either side, culverts where required, quarry pits or quarry trenches in certain places. It is visible from NT546 379 to where it is on the line of the farm entrance road at Bluecairn NT 532 419. Of this stretch, 2.3km is in a straight line directly aimed to the hollow between Eildon Hill North and Eildon Hill West.

As a minor tarred road, it passes Fordswell before dropping down to pass close to Cheildhelles Chapel. The road can be seen in the next field as a crop-mark. I put a trench through this and found a flat, stone-covered mound, 8m wide with a kerbstone on the lower side and ditches on both sides. The 165-acre Roman temporary camp at St Leonard's lies beside this road line. (*Inventory of Roxburgh* No. 603) been found on the outskirts of Lauder, then passed the town on a line parallel to the High Street, and followed a line slightly above the track of the old railway. This part has been verified by air photographs.

From there on, it makes for Oxton and I agreed with the Roxburghshire *Inventory* route, p.470, past the village and on to Channelkirk where the road ran up a steep bank, passed the churchyard, traditionally 'through the Manse dining-room'. It did this for a reason – it was going to a Roman fort.

When the Roman fort at Oxton was discovered by air photography in the 1960s, I was working in that area. On publication of the excellent photograph, I was a little puzzled because I knew it was overlooked on two sides by immediate higher ground and was a most unlikely place for a Roman fort. And yet it was very obviously of Roman construction, a small fort with a large annexe and this was assumed to be a Flavian construction even although only Antonine pottery had been found on the site by fieldwalking. It has not been excavated as far as I know.

It took me some years to work out that there had to be a defensive fort in the vicinity. Looking at old maps, I found the words 'ROMAN CAMP (Site of)' beside the manse and graveyard of Channelkirk church. This had been noted but dismissed by several archaeologists but I felt it was worth investigating with divining rods.

On doing this, I found a nice, nearly square★ double-ditched fort with gateways in the middle of each side. There were roads into the fort and rectangular buildings inside. This was a Roman fort as had been originally noted by the early mapmakers.

A further temporary Roman camp together with a native settlement, has recently been found by air photography in this vicinity.

Leaving the Channelkirk Fort, the road is quite visible as a broad mound passing the known 165-acre Severan marching camp at NT 475 548. Though this camp is the right size and shaped rather like the one at St Leonard's, it is not well situated, being on an exposed hill and with no bulk water supply. In the strip of wood that bisects the camp, there is a shape which suggests a signal station. This is at NT 476 548.

★ Forts made by the Agricolan forces tend to have a nearly square shape.

My theory is that the Channelkirk Fort is of 1st century construction, an Agricolan or Flavian fort when a safe base was required, while the presently-known Oxton structure was Roman but from the Antonine era, (phases six and seven at Newstead AD 142 to 163), when defence was not a priority. The Oxton site is that of a guard post to escort travellers over the hilly ground with a large annexe to keep their goods safe if they decided to stop overnight before tackling the Dun Law. There is likely to be another such place on the other side at Soutra Mains Farm near the Dean Burn.

Moving on northwards on a well-defined road and passing the cairnfield on Turf Law, on the west side of the road at NT 467 558, there are two 2m deep parallel trenches which turn eastwards at a nearly right angle. In another place, I would have said that this was a definite Roman fort, except that the rest has been filled in. The ditches are on the map as an 'Aqueduct' which is one of the things they could not possibly be. Dere Street is visible and well documented from here on so I will turn to the line of the road up the Tweed Valley.

Trimontium to Lyne

The line of road westwards from Trimontium has been well documented in a paper 'Roman Communications in the Tweed Valley' by Graham and Richmond in *Proceedings of the Society of Antiquaries in Scotland* LXXXVII (1952). It is particularly good in the area around the Roman fort complex at Lynne and Easter Happrew but admits that the Trimontium to Peebles section 'remained a serious puzzle'. Despite this, they gave a convincing route relying on ground observation. Following their route with divining rods and an eye for the ground, I can give a more precise route for the lower sections.

The Tweed Valley road leaves Dere Street immediately after it crosses the Roman bridge at Trimontium. It proceeds on a straight line along the B6360, ignoring the drop down into Gattonside village, and joins up with the minor road leading past Gattonside Mains Farm, crossing the Elwyn Glen at NT 526 358, where a natural depression on the east side corresponds with a rising bank on the west side. It then veers slightly, passing south of Easter Langlee Farm where its line could be seen in the ploughed land.

In June 1965, the rounded hillocks of glacial deposit at Easter Langlee were being quarried for their sand and gravel content. While the bulldozer was slicing into the working face, the foundations of a small structure were uncovered, but the gravel shifted and the large red sandstone blocks tumbled into the pit below.

I heard about the 'muckle stanes' three or four days after they were uncovered and went down to see them that night, but by then they had been pushed into a heap away from the quarry face. The big dressed blocks, with a diamond broaching on the face and cramp dovetails on the top, had already been identified as Roman. Fifty stones in all, they would have formed a solid platform around 3.5m square. Various marks were cut in the stones and one had 'COH 1' chipped with a mason's punch. This referred to the First Cohort of a legion, the one that contained the skilled technicians of the unit, the smiths, masons and carpenters.

The purpose of the building was unclear with the most likely guess being a temple or the base of a commemorative statue. The problem was that no reason could be found for it being there. The answer is clear now – it was right beside a Roman road going westwards up the Tweed Valley.

I noted that there were the marks of three deep pockets in the sand-quarry face. These had been excavated holes, around 4m deep with a top diameter of 2m. They had only been opened a short time before being filled in again with clean sand. A discolouration 2m thick, lay in the bottom of each pocket but no artefacts were found there.

The following year, burnt marks in the vicinity were cleaned to reveal hut floors that held some Iron Age pottery amongst the stones.

From Easter Langlee, the road is likely to have run the ridge that is now the Melrose Road, High Buckholmside and the Edinburgh Road before crossing the Gala Water around NT 474 377. The road mound can be seen in front of Torwoodlee House, and from Torwoodlee Mains Farm a broad 'farm' road cut into the bank proceeds westwards until it crosses the Clovenfords to Bowland road and carries on across Whitebank Farm land. This section is 3km long.

On Torwoodlee Mains, the road is 7m wide with a divined ditch on the top side and culverted as required with broad flat stones. Some of these culverts are still running water from the land above.

The road crosses the fields of Laidlawstiel, appearing on an air photo to the east of the farm. A strip of 'massive stones' was noted during ploughing and this suggests a Roman road-foundation. From here on, I agree with the Graham/Richmond line with the following additions.

The marching camp at Innerleithen has a double-ditched fortlet in the south-east corner.

After leaving the marching camps at Eshiels, the road climbs the Venlaw hill to avoid the steep slope immediately to the east of Peebles town. It then crosses the Eddlestone Water north of Peebles, near Standalane where the road mound and several quarry pits were noted. Detectorist finds from the field in front of Chapelhill would suggest that a Roman fort/settlement was situated there. (See p.158)

Metal detecting and fieldwalking in the fields beside Easter Happrew fort has produced a large quantity of good quality Roman artefacts, none of which is later than the end of the first century. This is spread over an area that measures 400m by 250m, lying to the south and east of the fort. Given the number and quality of the finds, this could be an early vicus, the civilian settlement round or near a fort which became a centre of local marketing, and Romanitas, the spreading of Roman culture amongst the natives. The proposition that it was a trading centre is made more likely by the large number of Roman lead and bronze weights found throughout the detected area.

To establish this in a remarkably short time would suggest a population shift from the Romanised south into the wilder north – the Romans did this when it suited their needs. Such immigration had the double effect of introducing a Roman-friendly population who could act as a type of Home Guard if necessary, and who would also pay taxes and lessen the cost of maintaining an army of occupation.

The Easter Happrew fort was deserted by the end of the first century AD and this corresponds with the end of phase three at Trimontium.

Carbantorigum?

Peeblesshire has an acknowledged big gap in its Roman history. The Easter Happrew Fort had a short life span probably AD 80–85 but a great number of first century finds of high quality have been found there by metal detectorists, especially in the 1–10 Roman ounce weights in lead and bronze, suggests a trading centre. The finds area outside the fort covers 400m by 250m which would be a big vicus beside an early fort. The Lynne fort is late Antonine, say AD 160 at the earliest although an early Antonine dating has been postulated on the strength of one doubtful fragment of pottery. So this leaves a space of at least seventy years with no permanent Roman presence in the area – a supposition that I find hard to accept.

Over about two decades, I have driven up to Edinburgh Airport and looked across to a low mound on the farm of Chapelhill, remarking that 'that would be an ideal place for a Roman fort'. I said it so often that I have been banned from saying it again. In 1995, a metal detectorist brought in a bag of junk he had found, and amongst this was a fifth-century Anglo-Saxon stylus found on the Chapelhill field which I thought might have possibilities. It took until 2008 before I got round to doing something about it; in fact I was looking for proof of an early Christian chapel to fit in with the academically accepted theory that Peebles was a notable centre of worship in the early Christian period. Using divining rods, I didn't find evidence of a Christian chapel but did find shapes which suggested a double ditched enclosure 70m by 50m with gateways in the centre of each side. The inside corners of the fort are at A 24534 41902; B 24572 41902; C 24575 41843; D 24531 41841.

This is inside a larger enclosure which might originally have been a temporary camp but had been made into an annexe for the fort. A road leading out of the south gate has buildings on each side; these are 5 or 6m by 4m. There may be two separate occupations and the whole idea has still to be proved by air photographs at the Royal Commission or by putting two or three trial trenches across the ditches if the farmer is agreeable. If these can be proven 'beyond all reasonable doubt', as I am fairly sure they will be, this changes the concept of Roman Peeblesshire. What follows now is pure speculation and will be until I can provide irrefutable evidence.

Supposing that the Easter Happrew people were moved into the much better position at Chapelhill in one of the intervening periods or survived into the first Antonine period when only a smaller garrison was needed; and during this period, a settlement grew up in the vicinity. And this settlement survived into the post-Roman period to become a sizable Christian centre in the pre-Anglian days with the name of 'the place with the flimsy buildings' (ie wooden) – Pebyll in Cumbric, with an Anglian 's' to make them plural. The find of the Roman-type stylus shows that someone was still using wax-tablets for communication and were literate in the late Roman or Early Christian Period. The Old Town of Peebles with its Cross Kirk and its fifth-century Christian-inscribed stones, is about 1km from my potential Roman forts. Similarly, the Early Christian site of Old Melrose is about 1km from the Roman fort of Trimontium. Question – was Peebles founded by settlers who clustered round the Roman forts at Chapelhill and will Chapelhill turn out to be another Trimontium? Perhaps Ptolemy's Carbantorigum (or Carbantoritum) whose site is still to be identified?

Craik Cross to Tweedmouth

I was working in Eskdalemuir and up to Craik Cross in the mid 1950s. The Roman road from the Raeburnfoot fort was visible although much spread about by later traffic. It was a main thoroughfare in medieval times, 'the King's Great Rode from Annan to Rocesburgh' in the time of Robert the Bruce and still in use by sheep-drovers and cart traffic until the First World War. These later activities have worn away much of the original Roman road, and spread its deteriorated areas wider. Despite this, my father, who was brought up on Craik, always referred to it as 'the Roman road' and was able to point out various places of interest.

It was first officially identified as such by Dr Ian Richmond in 1945 and he published his detailed findings in *P.S.A.S. LXXX (1945)*. During heavy flooding in 1948, further evidence of Roman road-making was uncovered when a stone-built road-culvert was exposed at NT 342 077.

Although the Roman road has suffered considerably by the forest plantings and, more especially, the Forestry Commission's heavy machinery, there is still enough left to see the original line in places. While following it from the remains of the above-noted culvert, I crossed into a field where the road was quite apparent and found another culvert on the same line but this time grass-covered and presumably still there. Beside this was a Roman fort that I went over several times with divining rods to convince myself.

In fact, it was in a logical place to counter-balance the fort at Raeburnfoot, 13km away across the Craik Moor. At some period of the Roman occupations, there seemed to be the need for guard/patrol posts to provide escorts for travellers over wild moorland or hilly ground. In the Borders, this pattern can be seen on the Cheviots and with the Oxton fort on the south side of the Soutra hills.

The Craik fort is approximately 60m by 40m with its internal corners at NT 34853 08088, 34828 08061, 34777 08103 and 34819 08124. It is double-ditched on the east, west and north sides but single-ditched on the south side which faces the road. Each gateway has ten postholes, suggesting an arrangement similar to the gates at the Oak-wood fort. (See p.165)

An annexe on the north side is about 60m square and is single-ditch. On the west side of the fort a small annexe stretches from the gateway south to the line of rampart of the main fort. This is also single-ditched. Divining rods suggest that there are three Roman altars in this ditch but this might be stretching belief to breaking point.

Although this fort does not show on any of the few air photos, it would be quite easy to prove by putting one or two small trenches across one of the outer ditches.

As might be expected, there are two or more temporary camps in the flat haughs to the east of the fort. One that I measured was 100m by 80m and had the usual lines of rubbish pits 6m apart and 8m between the lines. The three corners which were available for plotting were at NT 35028 08283, 35062 08202 and 34991 08144.

On a dry year, this site would repay air photos.

Leaving the putative fort at Craik, the next potential line has been forestry disturbed but there is a bridge mound over a small burn where the road emerges from the forest at NT 385 104 and is seen on the Outerside Rig as a road mound at NT 385 108.

The road vanishes under cultivation until the east side of the Deanburnhaugh village but I picked it up again at Milsington NT 406 127 where it passes a deep marshy pool that had been drained sometime in the past. This is the most likely find spot for the Milsington leg, the life-size lower right leg of the seated figure from a gilded equestrian statue. Pure guesswork but likely.

It crosses the Milsington Burn at NT 406 130 and can be seen as a broad mound with a modern dyke built on top. Then it passes unseen through the Borthwickbrae policies to where an unusual mound at NT 410 137 may be a signal station. The Roman road curves round the south side of the minor road at NT 428 156, while on Borthwickshiels Horn there are a number of quarry pits – but no sign of the road.

The next visible remains are at Jubilee Wood NT 453 174 and eastwards to the ford at NT 460 177. On the open ground, the road mound is 7m across and the ditches are shallow and up to 3m across. This explains why most of this road line does not have quarry pits.

The next apparent line of road is at Hall Moss NT 490 197 where a series of rectangular raised platforms are beside a square enclosure with four post holes in a 3.5m square. The situation is such that it is likely to be a signal station.

From here on the next 5km are on the nearly straight line marked 'Drove Road' on the map. At Black Craig, NT 508 212, the rock shows signs of being ancient quarry ie the rock has been dug into and the debris carried out rather than being taken away by wheeled carts. About 200m further along, a line of quarry pits appear on the south side of the road. These are still 1m deep and one is a double pit.

After crossing the Lilliesleaf road, the Roman road proceeds for another 2km in a straight line to Netherraw, 1km of which is on the entrance road to the Firth Farm.

From then on it is totally divining rod inspired, until it crosses Dere Street at the modern Wellrig crossroads at NT 604 290. It carries on the same line, passing Maxton where air photographs show a temporary camp. In the area in and around Maxton, Roman artefacts and coins from the first to the fourth centuries AD have been found by metal detectorists, suggesting there was a permanent fort under west end of the village itself.

The finds of miniature and broken bronze objects from what would have been a boggy piece of ground beside the Roman road, give indications of ritual deposits.

On this last section of road, a number of signal stations/fortlets were placed near the road line but these are located only by divining rods as ploughing has removed any traces. I mention this for the future when advancing technology may prove what is there.

From Maxton, the divined road which follows the ridge above the Tweed on the south side, descends to the River Teviot on the west side of Roxburgh Castle NT 713 335. A line of natural rock across the river would provide a firm base for a bridge and, immediately opposite on the other side of the river at Springwood Park, several hundred Roman coins from the first to the fifth centuries have been found over a 1km square area. More of these later.

The road climbs to the ridge on the south and proceeds along the raised ground until it leaves Scotland at NT 797 375. From the line of marching camps, found and yet to find, the road must have gone to Tweedmouth where all agree there must have been a harbour/settlement.

Berwickshire

Berwickshire has the best agricultural land in the Borders and it is very unlikely that the Romans did not venture into it during the periods of occupation. This would be the most fertile area and have the greatest population, but because the focus has long been on Dere Street as the main through-route for traffic, and Berwickshire was within the area of the so-called 'Roman-friendly' Votadini, it has been assumed that there was no need for roads or camps in that county. Even if the Votadini were friendly, it would be unlikely that the Romans would not exploit them for men to serve in the army and for taxes or supplies for the use of nearby garrisons.

Certainly there was Roman influence in the county. Two hoards containing Roman artefacts have been found there, one from Blackburn Mill on the Eye Water near Cockburnspath, and one on Lamberton Moor. Both are on or near the line of a potential Roman road that ran through the county.

In the initial Roman invasion, it made more sense to move at least a portion of the army along a route near the coast while an accompanying naval support group could provide back-up if necessary and carry the vast amount of supplies required for an estimated thirty thousand men.

So it is likely that there is a Roman road somewhere along the coastal plain of Berwickshire. The ground of the plain favours road-making, being fairly flat with few deep gorges which need to be bypassed; but being good arable land it has been cultivated many times and nearly all traces of roadworks have been ploughed out.

The Roman road in Northumberland, known as the Devil's Causeway, left Corbridge, passed through Hartburn and Learchild where there are forts, and made directly towards Tweedmouth where there must have been an as yet unidentified harbour. It is unlikely that it stopped there.

If I had to guess, basing my judgement on old maps and studying the ground, I would say that the road crossed the Tweed almost on the site of the modern road bridge, then headed straight across the Lamberton Moor, reaching the Eye Water around Ayton where there is likely be a fort/camp. From there it went straight to Press Castle and over Coldingham Moor on or near the line of the Lang Latch. ('Latch' in this connection is a road for wheeled traffic and is a word from the early Anglians who came into the Borders around AD 450–500 – if they saw it as a road capable of bearing wheeled traffic, then it must have been constructed by Roman engineers, perhaps with help from the 'friendly' Votadini).

This is speculation based on the isolated finds of Roman material found along the coasts of Berwickshire and East Lothian and would need much more investigation before making definite pronouncements. I have noticed that along the line of Dere Street there is a concentration of Cumbric Welsh settlement place-names, 'tref', 'dun' and 'cair', as well as the number of early Christian churches that sprang up along its course. Perhaps it would be a useful exercise to identify these along the coast of Berwickshire and East Lothian to see if a similar pattern emerges to show a possible line of road.

I do not know the lands of Berwickshire very well, having done little fencing in the area during my working life. However, I did get a surprise when a friend showed me a picture that he used as a screen-saver on his computer.

Richard Strathie is a computer programmer but also flies a micro-light round the Borders for fun. When I suggested he take some photos of known and unknown sites for me, he was quite happy to do so. Over the years, he produced some valuable evidence for me and for the Royal Commission.

While flying over Greenlaw in 1998 he took a couple of photos of the known fort in Greenlaw Dean and they were so clear that he used one as a screensaver on his computer. It was while we were chatting years later that I noticed the straight sides and rounded corners of a potential Roman camp on the screen. For the rest of that year (2006), I spent spare time at Greenlawdean with divining rods and came across a number of interesting shapes in the ground, some visible, some not. On reporting them to the appropriate authorities then, I am still awaiting acknowledgements.

For the record: on Greenlawdean Farm, near where Herrit's Dyke crosses the Blackadder Water, there is a camp complex with at least two temporary camps and one permanent fort with an annexe at NT 694 479.

This complex has a large outer temporary camp with single rampart and ditch. Inside this, is a smaller temporary camp with double claviculae gateways, and inside that again is a double-ditched fort measuring around 120m by 80m and with a small annexe on the west side. This has buildings inside the fort and rectangular ones in the annexe.

To the north of this are two large enclosures approximately 250m by 280m, at NT 693 483. The wall mounds are 5m wide and still more than 1m high; there is a 1m deep ditch. Inside one enclosure is a (divined) large building approx 70m long and 7m wide with wings approximately 35m by 7m at right angles to the main body. Part of this shows on air photographs belonging to the Greenlawdean Estate.

If this shape was found in the south of England, there would no hesitation in pronouncing it was a 'villa farm'. Is there any reason why there should not be a Romano-British villa farm in Berwickshire?

On the other side of the Blackadder at NT 692 472, a recorded earthwork (Berwickshire No 340) is the size and shape of a Roman signal station. This appears on an early map as 'Station' and a 6m wide road runs through the field to the west of it.

In conclusion, I am sure that Berwickshire has a lot to offer and, if this is given attention, further discoveries will be made.

Selkirkshire

Selkirkshire did not have any known Roman remains until a fort and temporary camp were discovered at Oakwood in the Ettrick Valley in 1949, during an inspection of air photographs in advance of the publication of the *Inventory of Selkirkshire*.

The fort sits on the top of a small knoll lying on the south side of the road from Hartwoodmyres to Inner Huntly, which gives it a commanding view of the lower Ettrick and Yarrow valleys. The signal station on the top of Eildon Hill North, 15km distant, can be seen through a dip in the hill ridge. The siting of the fort would suggest that it was positioned as a 'glen-blocking fort' as has also been suggested for the line of forts at the mouths of various Highland glens. These were to acts as a barrier, keeping the tribesmen of the mountains back from the Roman-held territory. One slight objection to this explanation for Oakwood, is that there are no known native settlements in the upper Ettrick valley and only one possible in upper Eskdalemuir where there is another Roman fort at Raeburnfoot.

Excavations on the fort and temporary camp were carried out in 1951–2 and these showed that it had two structural phases in the Agricolan/Flavian period. These are similar to phase two at Newstead, AD 80–87 and phase three AD 88–105.

In the first phase at Oakwood, the fort covered 3.5 acres and was of the standard Agricolan square pattern with a gate in the middle of each rampart. The gateways were unusual in that they were set back 9m from the front of the rampart and had twin fighting platforms to protect the entrance. This size of fort could nominally provide accommodation for an infantry cohort of 500 men together with a mounted detachment but it is questionable whether the Oakwood fort ever had that number in its garrison.

In the next phase, the fort remained the same but the fort defences were re-conditioned and an annexe was added on the south side. This phase of occupation seems to have ended in disaster around AD 105. Charred oak posts were found in situ during the excavation of the west gateway and this would correspond with the destruction at the end of phase three at Trimontium.

Should anyone decide to excavate more of this site, I would suggest the south ditch at the south-east corner of the fort where I am fairly sure there are two altars.

The annexe is unusual in that it has its gateway in the south-west corner instead of the middle of the outer rampart but there is a reason for this. Recent air photographs and ground surveying show that the fort did not stand isolated. On the north side of the east gate a small enclosure contains a divined building and three rectangular buildings outside the enclosure, each of which stands on its own small terrace. To the west of the south-west corner of the annexe, a number of round markings on the ground suggest a native settlement.

The temporary camp lying 140m north of the fort is roughly rectangular in shape and measures 430m by 300m. The rampart is 4.5m thick and the ditch 2m wide. The gates have a double claviculae defence. The defences are more substantial than is normal, showing that it was intended to be used for some time, presumably for the labour force employed in the construction of the permanent fort. Temporary camps have the added function that when they are finished housing troops, they made a secure field for cavalry horses and other animals.

With a fort of this size and a lifetime of fifteen years, there must

In 1944, I was living at Inner Huntly when the shepherd next door, Jeck Watson, came in with the bottom of a flower pot and two black round things about the size of a sixpence. These he had found while burying a dead sheep behind a small wood on the inner hill. Eventually these were identified as Roman silver coins. This discovery had his grandson Tommy and me up on the hill digging small holes for the buried treasure we knew was there. Needless to say, we never found anything but this was my first encounter with the Romans. I did acquire one of the coins many years later. This was a denarius of Trajan struck in Rome between AD 103 and 111.

have been a road or trackway for troop movement and supplies. There is a potential line of road that stays on the higher ground going east and, by taking a combination of old roads, field and farm boundaries, a case could be made for the Oakwood Roman access joining Dere Street at or near St Boswells.

A much better case but one which relies greatly on divining rods, is one that leaves the Craik to Tweedmouth road at Gawndie's Knowe NT 447 174 where there is a likely signal station. Traces can be seen of a road construction in some places and a rectangular enclosure, c.80m by 55m is on the road-side at NT 440 182. It can only be seen in the best conditions of vegetation growth. I would have ignored it as a fail-dyke enclosure of the eighteenth century but there are eight rows of pits 8m apart, with the individual pits separated by 6m. I recognised this pattern from Roman temporary or marching camps and assigned this provisionally to a road-making squad.

When I found another two at NT 418 207 and NT 416 231 and a row of round cairns at NT432 187 along the side of my provisional road, I reckoned I had a Roman road linking the east-west road to the Oakwood fort. Following the road further, I found that the divined road ran into the Oakwood fort annexe through the gateway at the south-west corner.

These three very-temporary camps have a single ditch and rampart, both about 1.5m. To prove these structures would need an excavation on a number of the pits which are quite easy to locate or an advanced ground-penetrating radar that would show small pockets of soil-disturbance around 0.5m in depth.

The above are the known and the hypothesised Roman remains in Selkirkshire. From the native structures, there are the first century Roman pottery and glass from the excavations at the Torwoodlee broch and two Roman brooches from The Rink hill-fort, both detailed above. Such finds show that the structures were likely to have been in use during the Roman period. This dating is not absolute but is likely and the best we can do without further corroboration.

There are three artefacts which can be safely identified as Roman period manufacture.

The find of a first/second century AD ring during the excavations of the ring-ditch structure at Yarrowford, can be taken as evidence of a first/second century population which knew of the Roman presence in the Borders.

The more recent find of a first/second century brooch within the earthwork on the Castle Hill, Oakwood, could open up the possibility of an area of Romanised native settlement around the Oakwood fort. There are five earthworks and one palisaded settlement within 1.5km of the Oakwood fort. This represents 25 per cent of the minor earthworks and settlements of Selkirkshire. Coincidence or a local supply base for the Roman fort?

The third object is a much more spectacular find although how it got to the site is not so provable. By 1990, I had acquired the reputation of being able to identify anything that was found on the ground, so it was no surprise when a man produced an object from his pocket and asked 'What is that?'

But it was my turn to be surprised when he handed over a Roman gold ring with an engraved sealstone of Ceres, the goddess of agriculture. 'Where did you find it' – 'On a field at Philiphaugh with a metal detector.'

I had just finished a paper on 'Roman Gemstones from Trimontium', so I knew what I was talking about when I told him it could be dated from around the end of the first century AD to the beginning of the second. I could also tell him that it was only the second Roman gold ring to be found in Scotland and, as such, was definitely a national treasure, so he agreed to let me hand it over to the National Museum of Scotland for consideration as Treasure Trove.

I phoned the Museum late that afternoon and found two archaeologists arriving in Selkirk early the next morning – they are not usually so prompt in responding to my queries. However, all's well that ends well – the man got a reasonable sum for his find and the National Museum of Scotland got a unique ring (which still has to be written up).

The query is 'how did a child's ring of the first/second century get there?' There are no other Roman finds of coins or pottery which rather rules out the settlement theory, although air photographs show a remarkably Roman-like double ditch in the field on Philiphaugh where it was found. The rest of the photo shows an Anglian (ie Anglo-Saxon) field system with at least one Anglian hall and burial ground and the same field was the site of the bloody Battle of Philiphaugh. This is a field with a lot of archaeology and history.

So the ring could be lost when a Romanised family settled the area; or when an Anglian child from the hall took one of the family treasures out to play and lost it; or it was in the treasure chest of Montrose's army and got spilled out during the battle

There again, it might have been lost in more modern times which is even more unlikely. The best bet is the Anglian child, as Roman objects frequently turn up in Anglian excavations in the south.

CONCLUSIONS

There is still a lot more to discover about the Roman presence in the Borders; what they did when they were here and what they left behind when the legions left for the shelter of Hadrian's Wall.

CHAPTER EIGHT
Third to Fifth Century

The next two centuries of Border archaeology can be compared to a hundred-piece jigsaw puzzle with ninety-five of the pieces missing and the other five pieces having broken edges. We know very little of what was happening; even these few scraps are from the accounts of Roman writers and it is difficult to decide whether they are historians or simply propagandists. The written evidence is uneven as the Romans of Britain have left no written accounts of their history. All accounts are from Mediterranean writers who only mention Britannia and Caledonia when some important person visited the island, usually to quell a revolt or make war on the revolting northern natives. This happened intermittently as it was very important for Roman Emperors to add lustre to their reputation by military successes.

No war or any disturbance north of Hadrian's Wall appears in Roman records between the campaigns of Caracalla in 211 and those when Constantius Chlorus repulsed the 'Caledonians and other Picts' in 305–6. With such negative evidence, many have pondered this unusual situation and declared that the century of peace was the result of Caracalla's slaughter of the northern tribes, combined with generous bribery in silver coins for the remaining native leaders to keep the Pax Romana.

This theory explains why, until very recently, all the hoards of Roman silver coinage deposited in the twenty years after 211 have been found north of the Antonine Wall in the territory of the 'barbarians'. However, fresh evidence is being produced by metal detectorists who are turning up hoards in places as far apart as Birnie in Moray and Edston in Peeblesshire.

The Birnie hoards would fit in with a far-extended pattern of cross-frontier bribery but the Edston one doesn't unless the frontier is considered to be at Hadrian's Wall. The Edston hoard is unique in the south of Scotland so far. It comprises 290 silver denarii ranging in date from 32 BC to AD 222, and could have been a savings hoard or a sweetener to keep the Upper Tweeddale natives happy, or at least to make no aggressive moves. Other than this hoard, neither written record nor archaeological excavation has told us what was happening in the Borders in the third century. There were certainly people living in the area as I hope to show later.

So the bribery theory is feasible and does not conflict with excavated evidence. Thereafter, hard facts are less easy to obtain.

LITERARY SOURCES

The Venerable Bede (627–735) has long been given the accolade as the most reliable historian in post-Roman Britain and his *History of the English Church and People* is taken as gospel truth. It is gradually being realised that this is wrong; it is a mixture of fact, folklore and legend.

As a historian, Bede was quoting from earlier and unreliable sources which were often undated. His main source of late Roman history in Britain comes from a cleric called Gildas who lived from *c*.475–550 and whose tract, 'On the Ruin Of Britain' written around 540, outlines some of the history of the fourth to sixth centuries. Although this has a mainly religious theme on the divine judgement awaiting the evil rulers of his day, he begins by tracing the history of the island. He had almost no written sources on the history of Britain but was dependent on the memories of men who were old when he was young. Human memory is a fragile thing and only reasonably dependable for a period of 120 years – the time between the youth of a grandfather to the death of his grandson.

Nevertheless, Gildas should have been trustworthy while writing of his own time, say from 420 to 540, but he could only be certain of what was happening in his immediate area. The unfortunate part of Gildas' history was that he knew little of the Roman past history; he did not give dates to the events and seems never to have realised that there had once been a standing Roman army in Britain. His was the time of the citizen army defending the remains of the Empire from invading barbarians.

In *Ruin of Britain,* he made many provable mistakes, explaining that the two northern walls were built in the early fifth century by Roman expeditionary forces sent to drive back the barbarians from the north. In this confusion and lack of dating, he has managed to muddy the water for historians ancient and modern, who were unable to distinguish the false from the true. This is unfortunate as Gildas presents some interesting accounts of life in the fifth and sixth centuries. He was an intense Christian of the Romano-British church blaming all the woes of the world on the lack of faith and worship.

In a statement set down in his own lifetime, Gildas says that he was born beyond the Roman frontier, in the kingdom of the Clyde, but was brought south to be schooled in a fully Roman educational system. This shows in his writing which is that of a well-educated man with a sophisticated style and demonstrates that Romanitas was still flourishing in the former frontier regions of the Empire long after the official ties between Britain and Rome were officially broken in 410.

In the age of mass communication delivered almost instantly, it would be easy to devalue Gildas' writings as useless – they are not; they are the best that could be done within parameters of what was perceived to be correct at the time and even those statements now known to be clearly wrong, contain some hints of truth.

Bede was working under similar constraints. *The History of the English Church and People* was more an account of the Northumbrian Church and a points-scoring tally against the Scots, Picts and the Columban Church, whose monks had originally founded the Northumbrian one. That he copied the first part of his *History* from the undated Gildas and added further comments of his own, only muddied the waters further.

In reading Bede's *History*, it is wise to try to separate the wheat from the tares. For example in chapter 5, he writes that Severus was 'compelled to come to Britain by the desertion of nearly all the tribes allied to Rome, and after many and hard-fought battles, he decided to separate that portion of the island under his control from the remaining un-conquered people. He did this not, as some imagine with a wall, but with an earthwork, such as protects a camp from enemy attack, is constructed with sods cut from the earth and raised high above the ground level, fronted by a ditch and surmounted by a strong palisade of logs. Severus built a rampart and ditch of this type from sea to sea and fortified it by a series of towers.'

This is a description that fits the structure of the Antonine Wall between Forth and Clyde, which is sometimes called the Wall of Severus in early maps but no excavations on the Antonine Wall have found such refurbishment although a third century occupation at Cramond is known.

The 'tribes allied to Rome' may be true and could hardly be other than the Votadini, Novantae and Damnoni of southern Scotland. Whether they were Roman-friendly by desire or persuasion is not known.

Later, in chapter 12, Bede describes the location of the wall with the Scots on the northwest and the Picts on the north 'because their lands are sundered [separated] from that of the Britons; for two sea estuaries lay between, one of which runs broad and deep into the country from the sea to the east and the other from the west although they do not actually meet. In the middle of the eastern estuary stands the city of Guidi [reputedly the Isle of Inchkeith] while on the right bank of the western stands the city of Alcluith which in their language means "the rock of Cluit" [Dumbarton Rock], as it stands on the river of that name.' Again this is the location of what is now known as the Antonine Wall but the language is that of Bede's own lifetime. Was the Antonine Wall, sometimes known as the Wall of Severus and later the Wall of Theodosius, still looked on as a functional defence in the eighth century?

A third mention is a note that in the fifth century a Roman legion 'engaged the enemy, inflicting heavy losses on them and drove the survivors out of the territory of Rome's allies. Having freed the Britons from dire oppression, the Romans advised them to construct a protective wall across the island from sea to sea in order to keep their foes at bay'.

To make things even more confusing, some time after another barbarian invasion took place and another Roman legion came to the rescue. This time they built a stone wall 'between the towns which had been built as strongpoints, where Severus had built his earthwork'. As this wall is described as being 'twelve feet high and eight feet broad' this must have been Hadrian's Wall. Bede, a Northumbrian priest of Jarrow and Hexham, was familiar with the stone-built sections of Hadrian's Wall.

Obviously Bede/Gildas had been as confused as I am. Gildas had bothered with very few dates and Bede repeated the mistakes while trying to fit in others, usually wrongly, and the Anglo-Saxon Chronicle was written hundreds of years after the events. Archaeologists, taking the three sources as definitive, have tried to fit their discoveries into that time frame, with unfortunate results. In truth, for the fifth and sixth centuries we have to rely on inspired guesswork.

Archaeological and Roman Sources (with some speculation)

After the Roman troops had officially left southern Scotland, there was a reasonably secure northern frontier with the exploratores from Hadrian's Wall doing what they could to keep the peace. With a buffer zone over 100km wide and a relatively friendly native population, this would give a sound defence in depth, sufficient to turn back all but the most determined attack in strength, leaving the Roman province south of Hadrian's Wall in peace, other than local uprisings which would be unremarked by Mediterranean writers.

This strategy had not worked perfectly before, as at the end of the previous century 'the tribes in the island, having crossed the Wall separating them from the Roman garrisons and doing much harm, cut to pieces a general and his forces' in 184. It is not clear which Wall was breached; it could have been either.

In 197, the northern tribesmen raided southwards, destroying parts of Hadrian's Wall and burning as far as York. This was serious and the governor 'was forced to buy peace from the Maetae for a large sum'. It has been presumed that the lower right leg of a gilded equestrian statute found in a bog at Milsington in the Borthwick Water was part of the booty from that raid.

All Roman accounts are based on mass invasions from tribes north of the Antonine Wall line and there are no records of the tribes from southern Scotland taking part in any aggression. The remarkable resilience of the northern tribes is not in accord with Roman propaganda.

In 306, the Emperor Constantius Chlorus died at York after 'defeating' the Picts. His son, Constantine the Great, carried on the war in a further campaign against them, eventually 'defeating' the Picts and the Scots and claiming the title of Britannicus Maximus in 314. In 343, the Emperor Constans, son of Constantine the Great, came from Rome to deal with the Picts and the Scots again and signed a peace treaty with both. This was broken once more in 360 when the combined force of Picts and Scots raided south, laying waste to places near the wall, probably that of Hadrian.

Four years later, trouble threatened again when a combined force of Picts, Scots, Saxons and Attacotti made a concerted attack on the whole Roman province 'breaking in wherever they could, by land and sea, plundering and burning ruthlessly and killing all their prisoners'. These attacks were known as 'the Barbarian Conspiracy' when the four tribes above, were joined by the Franks who attacked the Channel coasts of England. This shows a sophistication of planning, logistics and execution in the days when communication was a matter of weeks rather than the present-day instant.

A Roman historian claimed that the frontier scouts had been bribed by the invaders to let them through without reporting to the Roman commanders. It may have been that some of the peoples of Southern Scotland had formed a common cause with the Picts and Scots to raid into the more prosperous province south of Hadrian's Wall. Whatever the cause, it did not bode well for the Romans with the Count of the Saxon Shore killed and Fullofaudes, the army commander, besieged by the barbarian hoards. The Emperor Valentinian sent Count Theodosius to rectify the situation and recover the whole province of Britannia before it was totally lost.

In 368, Theodosius, with a field army of four regiments and auxiliaries, rounded up and killed the raiders, recovered their booty and returned it to the original owners after taking a percentage for the army 'expenses'. He regrouped the garrisons by posting an immediate amnesty for deserters and hurried northwards to reinstate Hadrian's Wall and reclaim the area between the walls. He retook 'the place which owed allegiance to Rome and from that time onwards, this was called 'Valentia' in honour of the Emperor and his brother, Valens'. The phrase 'owed allegiance to Rome' would imply a protectorate rather than a

Roman province. To secure the frontier of this new dependency, he rebuilt the Antonine Wall which was then known as 'Theodosius's Wall'. This massacre of a Roman general and his troops and the response of Theodosius may be the folklore basis of Gildas' history.

As well as refurbishing the two walls, Theodosius established a new system of self-defence by placing Roman officers with small cavalry detachments in the territory of the Votadini, Damnonii and Novantae to co-ordinate defence and act as rulers in the Lowlands of Scotland. That these men were cavalrymen is without doubt, as an ala of horsemen would be a fast and effective peace-keeping unit to deal with small local uprisings and give warning of large-scale invasions from the north. That they were placed at strategic locations in the respective tribal areas is certain; that they and their descendants would eventually become kings is the logical conclusion. So it is to the early king lists that we must look for the names. The northern lists show that four dynasties were established north of Hadrian's Wall, two or three generations before the emergence of fifth century kingdoms south of the Wall.

Logical deduction can say that Catellius Decianus was given command of the northern Gododdin, the Welsh translation of the original Latin, Otadini/Votadini. They were based at or near the tribal centre of Traprain Law. South of the Lothians, the southern Gododdin were commanded by Paternus Pesrut and their base was at Merchidun (now Roxburgh Castle), near Kelso. Paternus Pesrut translates as 'the Man with the Red Cloak', a clear description of a Roman serving officer. Quintilius Clemens was placed amongst the Damnonii at Dumbarton Rock or near Dreghorn on the Ayrshire coast in Strathclyde, and Antonius Donatus in the territory of the Novantae at or near Dunragit in Wigtonshire. All the names are given in the official Roman style of nomen and cognomen, family and personal name, that was fashionable among the local nobility. These men were not native kings given Roman names in flattery but professional soldiers of Rome placed between the two Roman walls to prevent further invasion from the north. The reason why I chose to place the Romans in these places will become apparent in the next few pages.

Count Theodosius must have been pleased that his system worked because he used it again in 371 on the African frontier where he subdued the natives 'by a mixture of intimidation and bribery' and then 'put reliable praefectii in charge of the peoples he encountered'. This policy was approved by St Augustine of Hippo who wrote that 'a few years ago, a small number of barbarian peoples were pacified and attached to the Roman frontier, so that they no longer had their own kings but were ruled by prefects appointed by the Roman Empire'. St Augustine added that soon after this happened the people accepted Christianity as their religion.

With stability, did the forces of Theodosius also bring Christianity to the Borders? Unproven but possible, although there are many claims for early Christianity in Britain. Present knowledge can place Christianity in the Borders less than a hundred years after the reconquest. Further evidence, solid or by deduction has to be sought.

The dynasties established by Theodosius in the reign of Valentinian (364–375) were to be influential and long-lasting. Coroctius, the grandson of Quintilius Clemens, was told of by St Patrick that his followers were 'not citizens of the holy Romans, but of the devil, living in the enemy ways of the barbarians'. By this time, 441, Christianity had spread intermittently through the land and Roman ways and customs were linked with the religion, both having their base in the city of Rome. There is often doubt whether the Romanitas of the people meant looking back to the ancient Roman ways or were references to the new religion. However, the dynasty of Clemens survived in the Britons of Strathclyde until the Norman Conquest.

The dynasty of Paternus Pesrut transferred from the Scottish Borders to Wales when: 'Cunedag, ancestor of Mailcunus, came with his eight sons from the north, from the district called Manau Guotodin ... and expelled the Irish with enormous slaughter, so that they never came back to live there again.' Some of the sons founded their own dynasties in Wales and the main line of descent finished in the thirteenth century with the death of Prince Llywelyn.

South of Hadrian's Wall

It is very difficult to give a precise dating for anything that happened in the fifth century.

After the Roman military presence was withdrawn in or around 410, the local leaders struggled to ward off barbarian attacks. By now, there were few if any professional Roman soldiers to garrison Britain and no Imperial administration to run the affairs of the province, but this did not mean that the province was open for plunder to the barbarian hoards. In the southern half, the populous towns organised their own defences even although it still remained illegal, in Roman terms, for citizens to bear arms. Mercenaries were hired wherever possible and a local militia was formed. In the first few decades, life might have been uncertain but it carried on in an organised Roman fashion.

In 446 an attempt was made to secure military aid from Aetius, thrice consul, who was now in virtual control of the Western Roman Empire but this was rejected. The Romans in Britain now had no other option than to rely on their own resources for defence. For the next twenty or so years, the conflict was between the Romano-British defenders and the barbarian invaders who had now established themselves as permanent colonists along the east coasts of England.

In the period between 460 and 500, there was a new generation of British leaders waging war of attrition against the encroaching 'Englisc'.

However the centre of power had moved from the south-east of the island to the north, where the tribes in what is now the Borders of England and Scotland formed a loosely confederated block to preserve the Romanitas of the Empire. These men had borne arms for generations and were accustomed to use them in defence of their homes.

The legacy of Count Theodosius had produced a Celtic army based on Roman cavalry training, able to defend the area with enough reserves of manpower to be able to send reinforcements to help other hard-pressed 'Romans' in different parts of the former province.

NEW OBJECTS, NEW THINKING

We have very little idea of what was happening in the Borders during the third to fifth centuries. Much 'might-have-been' guesswork has gone into the various *Inventories* of the Border shires and this has been repeated and quoted until it has been accepted as proven fact. It isn't, but it is a good summation of what evidence was available at the time of writing.

In dealing with the period then known as the Dark Age or sub-Roman phase, the *Inventory of Roxburghshire* sums this up very well: 'The Dark Age means for our area less a recession in civilisation than a period in which the historian is without light. It is a convenient label, usually applied to the epoch between the close of Roman rule in Britain and the emergence of the Saxon Kingdoms. But in the Roxburghshire area it must be held to have both begun earlier and ended later. The withdrawal of the Roman patrols from the Cheviot zone in 369 marks the close of an epoch, although much of the picture was in fact already dark.'

Speculation on the dating of hill-forts is inconclusive. The few excavations carried out for the various *Inventories* have suggested that this type of earthwork could have been occupied from the Bronze Age until the Early Historic period and occasionally used as a safe gathering place into medieval times. With the exception of one glass bead found during the excavations of the Bonchester Hill fort, no known Dark Age relics had been found in Roxburghshire at the date of the printing of the *Inventory* in 1956.

Up to the 1950s, an interest in the archaeology and history of the Borders was largely confined to the professional and landowning strata of society but the advent of television widened the outlook of many, and others began to take an active interest in their history. This, in turn, provided a wider sphere of inquiry and an increased knowledge of the Borders past. This was a good thing which broadened the knowledge of the area although the keen amateur is often seen as an intruder by the stuffier members of the archaeological establishment.

NEW METHODS

There are several ways in which the interested amateur can add to the archaeological and historical information of the area, and the last fifty years have shown that there are men and women who were willing to put time and effort into collecting it. They were also willing to share it with others, either by writing it up themselves in book or paper form, or by passing on the information to those who could do so.

I have frequently mentioned fieldwalking, metal detecting and divining rods as sources of information and sites. The interested amateurs who practise those skills have added a great amount to the known past of the Borders and will continue to do so – as is gradually becoming acknowledged. This is a form of rural rescue archaeology and a method of pinpointing sites for future reference.

That these skills have their limitations I will cheerfully admit, but they can also be useful if encouraged by those whose professional life is a specialised study of the past. It has to be said that this encouragement is not always given, and the identification and recording methods of finds in England are much superior to the Treasure Trove laws of Scotland, where it can take as much as two years for the due processes of the law to provide a conclusion. This can be counter-effective as it makes the finders reluctant to hand in further finds for processing.

Of the amateur archaeological skills involved, fieldwalking used to be the most popular although only the exceptionally dedicated would spend their winter months plodding over ploughed fields in all conditions of weather. Fifty years ago, they were derided as 'scavengers' or 'magpie collectors'. Fortunately, these days are past now and fieldwalking finds are welcomed, and professional excavations usually commence by a day of fieldwalking over the site before a spade is lifted.

Unfortunately, agricultural methods have changed during the last half-century. It used to be that fields were ploughed in the late back-end of the year and got frozen, rained on and generally beaten down for a few months, until the soil was washed down, leaving stones and other hard objects on the surface. By the end of February, the fields were ripe for walking and retrieving the pottery, glass, flint and other archaeological objects that had been lost or thrown away over the previous centuries.

Modern agriculture does not favour the fieldwalker. Tractors are huge now and pulverise the formerly palm-sized pieces of pottery down to thumb-nail size. Even worse was the advent of winter wheat. This involves ploughing the field immediately after the crop had been harvested in August/September, then sowing a hardy form of wheat seed which sprouts in the back-end and by the onset of winter has covered the field in a blanket of green. This hides the soil and any interesting archaeological remains that may have emerged on the surface. It is not fair!

Metal detecting had its origins in the mine detectors of the Second World War which, if I remember correctly, were carried in a pack on the back, weighed a hundredweight, and a detecting head on jointed wooden rods that could extend to 15ft.

Modern detectors are compact and light, easy to use and require only patience, experience and a pre-study of the ground, to get results. Most detectors are functional up to 15cms below the ground surface for a single large coin. They have also been dismissed as 'Instruments of the Devil' by some archaeologists. This may be so in the hands of those who are only interested in finding treasure; in other hands, they are useful search tools.

The limitations of the above are that in fieldwalking over the ploughed and washed land, only items on the surface are presented to the searching eye; and metal detecting can only find metal, albeit under, as well as on the surface.

Both methods produce objects that cannot be denied, although they are sometimes queried as having been introduced from some other place. I have found that some archaeologists are suspicious of amateur finds – probably with reason in some cases, as there are a lot of 'eccentrics' in amateur archaeology.

On many occasions, I have had great difficulty in convincing a positive finder that a broken scythe blade was not a reiver's sword, the divider on a reaper blade was not a Roman dagger and a worn George II halfpenny was not valuable even although the date of 1742 could be seen on it.

My divining rods produce no objects or print-outs and are viewed with even more suspicion. They have always been useful for me in work and for my hobby. I put forward my 'findings' so that these can be considered and hopefully accepted at some future time. I make no claims to being a Merlin, Michael Scott or Thomas the Rhymer and I cannot explain how divining rods function either, but I know they do – and correctly in most cases.

Searching

To get back to the third to fifth centuries, the period formerly known as the Dark Age but now as the Early Historic Period.

Being an outdoor person, I have spent a reasonable amount of my scarce spare time, plodding over fields and up hills while looking for evidence of Roman roads. I thought that Roman roads should be easy to find as they are always straight, or so I was told. Not in the Borders they are not – they are only straight in small sections where the ground is suitable. Otherwise they sensibly go round the face of hills and avoid steep slopes wherever possible.

It was while I was on the course of Dere Street where it crossed the Jed/Teviot rivers at Jedfoot, that I thought that Jerdonfield on the peninsula was the most likely place for a guarding fort. So I recruited two friends, Roger Elliot and Scott Sibbald, to bring along their metal detectors to help in the search. It proved fruitless, but Roger produced some Roman coins that he had found on his own farm of Springwood Park near Kelso.

This was a surprise because, although the fields there are strewn with flint implements and waste from the Stone, Bronze and Iron Ages as well as medieval pottery and coins, there have only been a few finds which might have been from the Roman period. Even more of a surprise was that the coins that he produced were from the first and second centuries, which is what I would normally expect, but there were also three from the third and fourth centuries which shouldn't have been there. I knew from previous studies that there were no third and fourth century coins in use in the Borders and any that had appeared were either booty brought back by raiding parties from south of Hadrian's Wall or were souvenirs brought back by modern travellers, and then lost – everybody knew that.

When I went down to look at the site of the finds, Roger gave me a metal-detector and a lesson on how to use it. I found thirty-three third and fourth century coins in an hour and a half. Help from other detectorists has allowed me to hand in to the National Museum of Scotland 263 coins from four different sites on Springwood Park. There have been others found and handed in and, I suspect, more found but retained by the finders.

The Springwood Coins

I will give a short summary of the Springwood coins as I intend to use their pattern as dating material to compare them with other finds in the Borders, and as evidence for my theory that there was a currency economy operating here and in some other parts of southern Scotland in the third and fourth centuries. When I voiced this theory, it did my reputation as a normal, slightly dull person no good whatsoever.

Coins have a special place in the world of the archaeologist as they give good dating evidence that can be fitted into any sequence being studied. Knowing that this was an unusual find, I paid particular attention to where in the field the different dates of coin was being found.

The bulk of the Springwood coins came from the King's Haugh, a flat field opposite the impressive mound of Roxburgh Castle. I had traced the east-west Roman road which came from Craik, eastwards until it crosses the River Teviot where a series of natural rock formations on the river bed would have provided a sound base for a bridge.

The Roman coins found on the King's Haugh were segregated within the field. Those of the first and second centuries are found in an area of around 80m by 60m, in front of the Victorian Mausoleum; there are no traces of a fort but it is likely to have been a trading settlement at the bridge crossing. No Roman pottery or glass has been found on the site despite much searching. It is likely that the Roxburgh Castle mound would be the fort of a Votadinian chief who was 'approved of' by the occupying Romans ie Romanitas at work.

The later Roman coins were spread along the side of the road that ran for about 200m along the bottom of the bank before turning to mount the higher ridge to the south. Curiously, no first and second coins were found in the third and fourth century findspots and vice-versa.

The coins which I know for certain, came from the King's Haugh and were submitted to the National Museum of Scotland on 6 June 1995, are:

First and second centuries

Silver	M Antonius, Trajan, Nerva and one unidentifiable
Bronze	Vespasian, Hadrian, Domitian, Sabina, Antoninus Pius, M Aurelius and four uncertain

With the exception of the denarius of M Antonius which had a long circulation, the others are within the period given for the Trimontium occupation, AD 79 to 180 and it is quite reasonable that this range could be found in a settlement in any part of the Borders. It is equally reasonable to suppose that the removal of the troops ended the supply of new coinage coming into the area. What is not known is how long the coins already in native hands were being used as means of trading.

No coins dating between AD 180 and 253 have been found at Springwood.

There are forty-eight late third century bronze radiates from Gallienus (253–268) to Carausius (287–293), with twenty of these being Tetricus I (271–3) and eight barbarous radiates which are the products of unofficial mints imitating the official coinage. The bulk of the coins are products of the Gallic Empire period (259–273) when the provinces and armies of Germany, Gaul, Spain and Britain broke away and formed an independent Empire with its own Emperors.

One hundred and sixty-two fourth and maybe fifth century coins show a concentration of seventy-two of Constantine, his family and House of Constantine and forty-nine from the house of Valentinian and six of Arcadius (394–408).

Further investigations have discovered another four separate sites spread over a square kilometre on the farm and these have produced more third and fourth century coins but none from the first or second century. Site A – sixteen, Site D – scattered four, Site D1 – three and Site D2 – six.

These coins were handed in to the National Museum of Scotland on 25 July 1997.

The dating range is very similar to that of the King's Haugh, starting with Tetricus I and only slightly extending the timescale by one coin of Honorius (394–403).

In addition to the above, one coin of Licinius and one of Constantine had been previously noted as being found 'in the Kelso area'.

In reviewing the sum of the Springwood Park coins, there are three obvious bulge points in the currency supply: at the time of the beginning and during the Gallic Empire; at the time when the Constantine family were in serious dispute with the Picts and the Scots;

and when Count Theodosius was regaining and restoring order to the province of Britannia, and eventually Valentia. This is not coincidental and numismatists are looking to produce a study of later Roman coins found in Scotland.

To me, the obvious conclusion is that the third and fourth century coins found at Springwood were the small change of commerce; the site was good, beside a large mound which would certainly have been fortified, at the river crossing of a main road and in the middle of good agricultural land.

My explanation was deemed to be too simple because there was no currency economy in southern Scotland during that period – as everybody knew. So, these small, pitifully thin and worn copper coins were said to be booty or bribery to keep the peace, somebody's coin, collection which had been thrown out as of no value or, even more, ridiculously, had been bought in the south where they are plentiful and scattered over a wide area so that we could find them. (That last suggestion may have been a leg-pull – although I am not totally convinced.)

Nor am I convinced that because Roman coins are found in the same field as those from different times or cultures, that they should be ignored as being compromised. During fieldwalking at Trimontium, within the fort I have found a third century BC Greek silver coin, a George VI penny which had been flattened by a train and a cut halfpenny of Henry II of England in the south annexe. I do not think that these finds compromise the authenticity of the twenty-plus first and second century Roman coins which I have picked up on the site. So I am treating any third and fourth century coins that are found within the area as genuine losses until they are proved otherwise.

OTHER MAJOR COIN CONCENTRATIONS IN SOUTHERN SCOTLAND

For comparison, I checked the list of coins found in secure circum-stances during the excavations at Traprain Law. There were sixty-three identifiable coins and these fell into the same datable patterns as the Springwood finds. There were twenty-three coins from first century BC to AD 161. This was followed by a blank gap from 161 to 250.

In the next phase, there were fifteen from the third century Gallic Empire and the Carausian Revolt. In the fourth century, the Constantine family provided eleven and the Valentinian family five. The remainder of the identifiable coins were made up with Arcadius six and Honorius two.

At the Piltanton Burn, near Dunragit in Wigtonshire, a metal detectorist has found 1,000 plus coins which fit into the patterns of Springwood and Traprain Law. With the exception of a silver denarius of Severus Alexander dated AD 226, the remainder are all copper with the bulk being barbarous radiates or barbarous copies of late third century and fourth century.

Dunragit is from Dun Rheged, 'the fortress of Rheged', and although the name Rheged reflects a territory rather than a people, this was a kingdom of the Celtic people which emerged from the disturbed politics of the late third and fourth centuries and who were originally named as 'Novantae' by Roman writers.

Wigtonshire has been a particularly good area for finding later Roman coins. The Balgreggan hoard found near Stoneykirk consisted of 125 coins, 119 of which are available for study. Of those recognisable, Constantius II had eighteen, Constans twenty-two and Magentius fifty-five. Indeterminate coins which could be either Constantius or Constans were fifteen and all had been struck between 324 and 354.

During the Second World War, a soldier digging a drain in a camp near Stranraer found 'about fifty' coins, the only one of which he kept was of Constantine I.

A case can be put for this concentration being brought from across the Solway from the Roman province, but for what use other than trade?

In 1897, a group of thirty-six coins 'in fair to poor condition' was found at Dreghorn in Ayrshire. These comprised thirteen of the Gallic Empire period, ten of the Constantine family and three of the Valentinian family plus ten of uncertain fourth century dating.

Although I would like some further evidence to prove the theory, I am reasonably certain that these finds represent some of the trading capital of the kingdoms of the people of the districts who were formerly called the Votadini, Novantae and Damnonii.

This is not totally one of my mad ideas. Others who are knowledgeable in numismatic studies have been close to putting forward the same idea.

Dr Anne Robertson, who assiduously recorded all the known Roman coins found in Scotland, wrote in her 1971–1982 report in *P.S.A.S. CXIII* (1983), 'The majority, however, of post-Severan coin finds from Scotland remain an enigma and a challenge. Some may have been lost in Roman or ancient times, others may have been brought back to Scotland by modern travellers to foreign lands. In the latter case why were so many subsequently lost, when they had presumably been acquired out of interest. It is often just as difficult to explain the modern loss of an ancient coin, as it is to explain its ancient loss.'

Although this is an open statement, it has been taken to mean that any coin that does not fit into the accepted pattern, must be a modern loss. Or it might mean that the system must be re-examined with an open mind.

In an interesting study of 'The Roman Coins From Traprain Law', M.F. Sekulla has a comment on the period AD 250–400, 'All except one, of the coins are of base rather than precious metal and their obvious lack of intrinsic worth militates against them having comprised either booty or part of subsidy payments from a Roman source. Attested large scale military activity in Scotland which might have provided a context for coins to change hands after the early 3rd century as they had done earlier, is almost totally lacking. Indeed, the evidence derived from sources other than the literary record would seem to point to a running down of the military establishment in the North, possibly during a long period of peace. This renders it much more probable that the coins were obtained as a result of peaceful encounters with the southern provinces rather than through hostile contact.' Exactly!

It is worth noting that during the Roman Empire, the coinage which had started as tri-metallic, ie gold, silver and bronze, finished its last century as a shaky bi-metallic one with the gold solidus and its division being used to pay the army and for the personal use of the Emperor and his court, while the rest of the Empire had to get along as best it could with various sized copper coins lightly washed with silver or tin.

This hindered trade because, at its most basic level, the coin is an easily portable token for a real object – it is easier to travel with a coin in your pocket than a sheep.

There is one explanation why the later Roman coins found in the Borders are of thin copper – a gold coin was worth looking for if it was lost while a small copper one was not.

RETURNING TO THE BORDERS

The success of collecting the Springwood coins depended on the six or seven metal detectorists who were willing to spend time searching for them and handing them over for official recording. That they continued to share the knowledge of finds from other sites, is their recognition that the finding of an interesting object is only part of the process which is only completed by having it officially recorded.

I return to my original thought that the pattern of any archaeological finds is more often a distribution of the people who are looking, rather than the density of the finds in any particular area. This is especially true of the small, late-Roman copper coins which are almost impossible to find by fieldwalking and require the use of a metal-detector. To find such coins in concentrations is an indication of where people were living and trading at that period. Even blank spaces in the pattern does not necessarily mean that there is nothing there; it could equally mean that nobody has looked at the site.

In plotting out all the known find spots of the third and fourth century coins throughout the Borders region, I was struck by the fact that they are mainly on or near the projected Roman road system which is given above. This is equally true of the first and second century finds, so it is not a coincidence.

So I will follow the roads and fit in what coin finds are known to have been made on, or near, the line of road. I will not mark the first and second coins unless the site has also produced later coins. If first to fourth century finds occur, this is likely to be a long-term settlement even if nothing shows on the ground surface.

Sprouston

The late David Welsh, who farmed at Sprouston on the banks of the Tweed 5km east from Springwood Park, used to pick up items of interest as he went about his daily business, and some of these were coins. He picked up seventeen Roman coins without specifically going out to look for them.

Metal detectorists have previously found three coins on the farm, a denarius of Mark Antony, a dupondius of Antoninus Pius and one uncertain sestertius. David Welsh's fieldwalking produced another denarius of Mark Antony and one of Nero. The third and fourth centuries were represented by two coins of Claudius II, two Gallic Empire, seven Constantine family period, two barbarous copies and two Valentinian.

This is a very good fieldwalking collection and it is unfortunate that we are deprived of knowledge of the findspots by the recent death of David Welsh.

This site is near the line of the east-west Roman road from Springwood to the mouth of the Tweed.

Maxton

Maxton village is probably on the site of a Roman fort, or was a settlement in Roman times. The east-west Roman road passes on the immediate south of the village and Dere Street is 1km to the west. Air photographs show the outline of a temporary camp or a Roman field-system, to the east of the village. Several miniature or broken bronze weapons in a site to the south of the village would suggest votive offering. Coins recovered are two Hadrian, one Antoninus Pius, one Marcus Aurelius and one Constantius. Several other coins were recovered from the site but not recorded.

Laretburn

(now known as Kellyburn) one Vespasian and one Valens. This site is 1km west of Maxton and 0.5km from Dere Steet.

Borthwickbrae

Beside the east-west Roman road as it passes towards the summit at Craik Cross, three late third or fourth century copper coins were found.

This is a hilly area that tends to get ignored by metal detectorists.

Newstead

Leaving aside all the first and second century coins which are associated with the Fort complex and its garrison, the following coins have been discovered 0.5km to the west of the fort: one Victorianus, one Tetricus, one Probus, one Carausius, four Constantine, one Gratian and two Theodosius, covering the date spread of 265–395. Further coins of this period were found by a Mr Dalgetty of Melrose but as they were mixed in with various other currencies, they were deemed to be contaminated.

In 1998, the Trimontium Trust had an interesting donation of a coin mould which had been found by a Mr Keith Allison who, as a boy in the 1940s, had been fieldwalking around the fort of Trimontium. Although now living in Australia, he had read about the Trimontium Trust and wanted to donate this unusual 'object' that he had carried around the world with him for nearly fifty years. Recognising that it was a very rare find, we accepted with pleasure and passed on the information to the National Museum of Scotland where it was definitely identified as a mould for making counterfeit coins★. It was only the third one to be found in Scotland and it caused some problems in trying to fit it into the accepted numismatic theories of the period.

It was part of a composite mould whereby several coins could be made with one pouring of metal. On one side was the impression of a denarius of Caracalla, of which the original coin was minted in 199–200 while the impression on the other face is an antoninius of Aurelian whose original was minted in Milan in the period 270–275.

This meant that any counterfeit coins from this mould could not have been made before 270 and the unusual combination of impressions would be unlikely to fool anyone who had ever seen and handled genuine Roman coins of either period. That rules out a forger on this side of Hadrian's Wall making counterfeit coinage to circulate on the other side.

★ Since then another coin mould from the site has been found. This adds further credence to my theory.

My theory is that the forged coins were intended to circulate in the immediate vicinity. This is a feasible suggestion as a community that had traded with a currency economy was unlikely to wish to return to the barter system. Although no new coins from official sources seem to have been brought into the Borders in the 180–250 period, very worn coins of the previous Roman occupation have been found on many sites. Some of these have 'been accepted as modern losses' and, with the absence of Samian pottery, were put forward as convincing proof that there was no Roman influence in the area. I believe that this reasoning is wrong and that the Trimontium coin mould, which was found to the south of the fort, is evidence that the Romanitas of previous generations was being continued in the shape of a Roman coin-like currency.

When official coinage is scarce, privately struck tokens take their place. In the late eighteenth/early nineteenth centuries, the government mint could not strike enough small denomination coins to meet demand, so tradesmen, craftsmen, shopkeepers and mills struck their own to keep the economy running.

Jedburgh

It is acknowledged that there must have been a Roman presence in the vicinity of Jedburgh in the third century: see Roman altars in Jedburgh Abbey. So one would have expected to have found some coins of the period in the area but only two have been found 'in the Jedburgh area'. One of these is a copper coin of Maximianus which fits into the Constantine period.

The other is more intriguing, a gold solidus of Valens which would fit into the Valentinian period. This was found on the banks of the Jed somewhere around 1970 and was eventually reported in 1999 after the finder had died, thus the exact provenance cannot be determined. Cautiously recorded as 'possibly mounted and lost in comparatively recent times' and claimed as Treasure Trove, it is an interesting find.

Jedburgh is 2km from Dere Street but is the conjunction of several natural roads that run down the Jed and Rule Waters.

A silver coin of Gordian (238) was found in Rulewater; it is known that Numerus Exploratorum Bremeniensium were stationed at the fort of High Rochester at this time, and it is likely that Rulewater was one of the regular routes of the patrol.

Two copper coins of Maximinus I or II, which were found in Rule Water, show some Romanitas in the area, while recent detecting in the area has produced Roman horseshoes and a second century brooch from one of the settlements previously thought to be medieval.

Lauder

The following coins have been found in the field directly to the south of the burgh: one of Marcus Aurelius, one of Constantine I, two of Valens and one of Honorius. Dere Street runs about 100m to the west of, and parallel to the Main Street in Lauder.

Away from any proven road, the site of a native settlement at Lilliesleaf, Roxburghshire, has produced one coin of Domitian, one of Vespasian, one of Postumus and several uncertain small bronzes of the late third and fourth century.

Listed in the *Inventories of Roxburghshire and Selkirkshire* are several coins with no known provenance: three Constantine, one Constantius, one Valentinian and one Valens.

By adding all the coin evidence together, the logical conclusion must be that these are not all 'modern losses'. This leaves the next logical conclusion that there must have been a coinage economy at least in those parts of the Borders which were still being served by the Roman road system.

It is regrettable that we have little other evidence to produce and must rely on speculation to round up the story. However, speculations combine to breed other speculations, so it might be wise to leave this period until we get some more definite and provable information about it.

IMPACT

Before leaving the Roman period entirely, it is worth looking at what impact the Romans had on the Borders after a century of intermittent occupation and more than two centuries of external influence. The evidence is scanty and varied. It is only a classical conception that the Romans introduced 'civilisation' into the barbarian world; this was the view of the Roman writers – and they would say that, wouldn't they?

In the lower-lying and more populous land, the intermittent Roman occupation would have introduced a newer and more material lifestyle and, almost certainly, a refreshment to the human and animal gene pool. In the less populated hill country, life would probably have remained in Bronze Age traditions. At Lilliesleaf, the second century round huts gave way to rectangular buildings, probably as a copy of Roman building techniques, but round huts continued to be constructed and, in each case, wood remained the material of choice.

There may have been an attempt to plant a Romanised population at Easter Happrew where a fully integrated fort and settlement was placed and removed within a decade or two. This is beside an important east-west road and river junction, and a good place to dominate passing traffic. At Oakwood, the fort and annexe with several buildings outside the ramparts and another five settlements within a kilometre and a half, may have been the beginnings of a permanent settlement. Both ideas are entirely speculative.

From the much-excavated fort at Trimontium, we have a good idea of what life was like there. The Romans built with brick and stone, used pottery for tableware/food storage and coins for trade. Glazed pottery was perhaps the most important introduction for although there was some coarse native pottery it was rough-grained and must have retained bacteria after being used. Roman tableware pottery was glazed, making it easier to clean and so more hygienic. To my mind, the glazed Samian ware that is found in native settlements was for hygiene and not as a status symbol as is commonly supposed. The fine Roman pottery of the first two centuries almost ceased to enter the Borders when the main customer base, the in-fort troops, withdrew from the area.

The most visual Roman relics are the roads which criss-cross the countryside. The Roman 'trunk road' of Dere Street was one of the main highways into Scotland in the Early Historic period when Cumbric/Welsh settlement names can be found scattered along it like beads in a necklace. In the fourteenth century, Edward II of England took a twenty-mile-long baggage train to Bannockburn in 1314, which is fairly convincing proof that the Roman road system was still in good condition over a thousand years after it was built. The road remained as a major route through the Borders to Edinburgh in the eighteenth century and is under the A68 at St Boswells.

The east-west road over Craik Moor was the 'Kinge's Great Rode' from Annan to Rocesburgh' at the time of Robert the Bruce and was still in use as a Drove Road at the start of the twentieth century. This road can only be seen in places and a lot of surveying is required to give it archaeological provenance.

The same is true for the other east-west road that leads from Leaderfoot to Lyne and goes on to join another Roman trunk road leading from Carlisle through Annandale to Upper Clydesdale.

I am sure that there are small land-holdings of a standard pattern, laid out along the sides of some parts of the road system but these are difficult to prove to everyone's satisfaction.

It is possible that Christianity was introduced into the Borders in the later Roman period. In the fourth century, almost nothing is known about Christianity in Britain other than it existed. To find positive proof that it existed in the Borders, we have to look into the next century.

In the *Inventory of Selkirkshire*, the impact of Roman occupation has left few traces of life-change other than a first century fort with a possible ring of supply settlements. For the second, third and fourth centuries, we know nothing and can only present the vaguest of speculations which are likely to be wrong anyway.

But they did leave a population who were used to warfare, trained in Roman traditions and prepared to stand up for themselves against all comers.

CHAPTER NINE
The Dark Ages AD 400–1100

The centuries between 400 and 1100 are what used to be called the Dark Ages, not that there was nothing happening in the Borders, but because we know so little about it. For that reason, it was ignored by earlier historians who preferred to work on the visible buildings and objects of the Roman Empire or on the written parchments of medieval times.

Coins, pottery and stone buildings are the lifeblood of archaeologists, giving a datable sequence to their finds and theories, while medieval historians require written evidence on parchment, paper or stone to prove their points. In the earliest part of the Dark Ages there was little of either and in the later part, only a fraction more.

And yet the Dark Ages, or Early Historic Times to give them the modern nomenclature, was a period of great change and, although much of the change is unknowable, this was the gestation period of the lands we call the Borders and formed the character of the people we call Borderers.

As noted in the previous chapter, the Romano-Britons still considered themselves as Romans in 446 when they appealed to Flavius Aetius, thrice Consul, for help to resist 'the barbarians who push us back to the sea, the sea pushes us back to the barbarians. Between these two types of death we are either slaughtered or drowned'. This was the plight of the former Roman provinces south of Hadrian's Wall where the sense of having shared the Romanitas of the Empire allowed help to be requested when required.

In the Borders, Romanitas was physical rather than intellectual. In the first and second centuries AD, the south of Scotland had been the buffer zone between the northern Roman province and the barbarian Caledonians and Picts. In the next two centuries the sub-Roman period saw the emergence of three autonomous tribal confederations ruled by local kings. The lands of the Votadini (later Gododdin) shared a boundary with the lands of Rheged and the Britons of Strathclyde. Trained in Roman methods and battered into shape by frequent wars, they, individually and in conjunction, held back the Scots in the west and the Picts in the north. That they raided into the neighbouring kingdoms is known, but seldom recorded unless it was a big battle or a slain monarch.

The people who lived within the bounds of the former Roman Empire still regarded themselves as citizens of a single state. They fought as 'cumbrogi' or fellow-citizens, sharing a joint language and as Christians against pagans. Their bonds were strong and their cause was just. They were so confident in their military strength that when the Romano-Welsh Cumbrogi appealed for help as they were being driven from their lands by invaders from Ireland, the Manua-Gododdin, whose area was around Stirling, could send an expeditionary force of mounted warriors to their aid. Under their prince Cunedda whose name means 'Good Leader', they drove out the Irish and many stayed to establish their own kingdoms within Wales. The only reasonable explanation of why these men rode 500kms to rescue the Romano-Welsh was their common language and shared Romanitas, and possibly, their Christian faith.

In the area of what is now Borders Region, it is reckoned that there were three minor kingdoms within the lands of the Southern Gododdin – Goddeu (the land of trees) in upper Tweeddale; east of that was the lordship of Calchvyndd, certainly based at Merchidun (Roxburgh Castle); and further to the east and south was Bernicia (parts of Berwickshire and Northumberland).

The collapse of the Roman state meant that the responsibility for law and order had passed down to family and kinship groups with the result that the leaders of local communities assumed command and society regrouped around them. The greatest households gravitated towards the most easily defended places, often those which had previously been Bronze or Iron Age strongholds.

So it is a reasonable speculation that the principal residence of the lords of Goddeu was at Tinnis Castle in Peeblesshire, that there were lords of Calchvyndd at Roxburgh Castle and lords of Bernicia at Din Guauroy (Bamburgh Castle).

It is less of a speculation that there were Romano-British Christian monasteries at Peebles, Old Melrose and Lindisfarne. This has been somewhat obscured by Bede's mention that the monastery at Old Melrose was founded by St Aidan, monk of Iona and bishop of Lindisfarne between 635 and 650, and thus was a Northumbrian foundation. This will be examined in detail below.

In looking to literary sources for information of what was happening in the Tweed Valley in the fifth and sixth centuries, we have to be guided by Gildas (475–550) and from Bede (672–735) using Gildas almost word for word. Although both have been quoted almost as Holy Scripture, academics can never quite agreed on their reliability and definitely not their dating. Both were clerics and their written language was Latin. Both probably spoke Latin as their official language though it is likely that Gildas, as a native of Strathclyde, spoke Cumbric as his native tongue, while Bede who was an Anglian would speak 'Englisc' as his.

In the Borders, the most commonly spoken language was Cumbric. One of the best-known of the earliest 'Scottish' poems was written in Cumbric or Old Welsh in Edinburgh around AD 600. It involved a battle at Catterick and the disaster suffered by the Cumbric warriors was to be an omen of things to come.

It is unlikely that new documentary evidence of the Early Historic period in the Borders will come to light, so we have to look to other sources for further information. There are several sites of the period which would repay extensive excavation but this is unlikely as it would be prohibitively expensive and Historic Scotland keeps the known sites inviolate and in a bulldog grip.

However, there are two other lines of enquiry which can add to our knowledge of the period. One is in the various languages which named the area, for this preserves in a hidden form, the people who founded the settlement and can occasionally give a description of the land as it was at the time. The past, like the poor, is always with us except that the past requires considerably more effort to find.

A variant of the above is to trace the introduction and, eventually, spread of Christianity in the region through the ecclesiastical place-names. In fact, the two lines of enquiry are mutually dependent as the earliest and most informative form of place-names are preserved by happenstance in the writings of the men who preached the Christian faith.

The saints, monks and priests were literate and although their accounts of their own branch of the church may not be totally unbiased, they give an insight into the events in the world outside their religious sphere. Memoirs of the life of a saint may have been written to boost a cult worship but they also give an insight to the story of his time. As the acceptance of Christianity often depended on the goodwill of the local king, the religious writings could also tell who he was and proclaim his worth or condemn the apostasy and unworthiness of his enemies.

Amongst the list of place-names are some which indicate early Christian settlement eg 'eccles' a church and 'cil/kil' the cell of a religious hermit who sought a solitary place to worship God. This will be examined in greater detail below.

LANGUAGE AND PLACE-NAMES

All spoken languages have to keep evolving otherwise they die. In this they mirror the changes taking place in life, and borrow words and word constructions from other sources. Invaders, settlers and traders bring in different languages and cultures.

This is particularly true in the Borders for the area has been literally a border where different cultures met, and often fought over, for the last two thousand years.

As each group of settlers or invaders came into the area, they re-named the settlements and many of the natural features in their own language, sometimes using or adding bits to the previous name. The distribution of place-names and their dating shows how people named the landscape as they saw it and the natural features and wildlife that were there. In this, they provide us with information which is unavailable from other sources.

As the tide of settlement and conquest moved backwards and forwards through the area, many languages met and mingled in the dialect that we call Border Scots. But this is not consistent throughout the Borders and although the influences of radio, television, English teachers and snobbery have gone some way to iron out the differences,

Border Scots in its many varieties can be heard throughout the area.

Since the Early Historic period, the languages which have been spoken here to a greater or less degree are, in order, Cumbric (a form of early Welsh), Anglian (a variation of early German), Scots Gaelic, Scandinavian, Norman French, and Flemish. Late Latin may have been spoken as well as written but we have no proof of that, although in 731 Bede records that 'At the present time there are in Britain, in harmony with five books of the divine law, five languages and four nations – English, British, Scots and Picts. Each of these have their own language; but all are united in their study of God's truth by the fifth – Latin – which has become a common medium through the study of the scriptures'. With so many different languages making their own contributions, the study of the place-names of the Borders resembles the layered cake which has to be stripped layer by layer to determine the story.

My initial burst of curiosity about the place-names of the Borders came when I was working on a fence at the Fairnielee Estate, near Galashiels, where the Catrail, an ancient linear line of demarcation, crossed the Tweed. On the estate map, the pool nearby was called the 'Rae Weil' which I knew was Anglian for a mossy or slow-running pool in the river. The haugh above was known as the Green Inch and 'inis' is Scots Gaelic for a riverside meadow. What puzzled me was a large stone in the middle of the river, marked on the map as 'The Riding Stane'. Being blessed or cursed with an abounding curiosity about the countryside, I eventually discovered that 'rhyd' was Old Welsh for a ford or river crossing and it was on the spot where the Catrail crossed the river. So within a stone's throw, there were three places, each named in a different language. Since then, I have gone about the countryside looking at the names of places in a new light while trying to identify which linguistic group gave them their names. This was not so easy as it might sound because naming languages have overlapped and merged into each other over the centuries.

A fascinating study and valuable evidence of the history of the Borders though it is, place-names only tell us a part of the story. Names can give false clues as spellings in early documents can vary so much; this is especially true when knowledge comes solely from extensive documentary research but without knowing the ground and, more importantly, the local pronunciation of the long-resident population.

But place-names do give an indication of the ebb and flow of history that has left traces in the place-names of the Borders. It can also be very confusing when one language group adds their own description on to that of its predecessor. Not knowing what a word meant in the previous naming, they would add their own description to it. Thus we get duplication – 'The Loch o the Lowes' in Yarrow is the 'lake of the lakes' in Gaelic and Cumbrian; 'Farne Islands' is 'island islands' and 'Peniel Heugh' is 'hill-hill hill'. It is a long and involved story with little common agreement.

I am no linguist or philologist but I will try to give a few examples of each, while putting them into their archaeological or historical context. The languages of the Borders fall into two main divisions, the Celtic and the Teutonic. Throughout the years, academics have used their own terms to distinguish the various nations and tribal confederacies who have left traces of their passing in the place-names. As these terms have changed from age to age, from scholar to scholar and from ancient meaning to modern meaning, this has caused confusion amongst all otherwise normal people.

For ease of understanding, I intend to give them my own standardisation as follows – the language of the people who lived in the whole of Southern Scotland from the post-Roman period to the seventh century have been known variously 'P-Celtic', 'British', 'Brythonic', 'Old Welsh' and 'Cumbric or Cumbrian'. It is a descendant from the Celtic root-language through P-Celtic, Old British, Romano-British to the more commonly used Cumbric. Its modern associated languages are Welsh and Breton. This will be known as *Cumbric* and the people as *Cumbrians*.

The immigrant Teutonic races from the northern regions of Germany and the Low Countries were known as 'Angli' by Latin writers before the middle of the sixth century but they collectively referred to themselves as 'Engle' or 'Englisc' or, in the northern territories, as 'Angli'. Here, I intend to call the Angli of Northumbria, *Anglians* and their language as *Englisc* to prevent confusion with the modern English. I will use *Anglicised* in its modern usage.

Around 470, a number of 'Scots' sailed from Ulster and settled in the peninsula of Dal Riada, now Argyll, and probably along the Solway coastal region. This brought another Celtic language known as Q-Celtic into the country. They maintained a close relationship with their original homelands in Ireland and for most of the Early Historic period the terms 'Scots' and 'Irish' remained interchangeable. As the Scots grew in strength and conquest, they came in conflict with the Picts whose language was thought to be another form of Q-Celtic. By the ninth century, the king of the Scots also became king of the Picts, joining their languages in Gaelic. Two centuries later, Gaelic was spoken throughout Scotland except for the extreme north which was Scandinavian and the Borders which was Englisc. For my purpose, *Scots from Scotland*, *Irish and Picts* all speak *Gaelic*.

Scandinavian place-names tend to be clustered in the south-western part of the Borders, suggesting that this influence came from the Norse settlements around Dublin via Dumfriesshire and Norman-French names came in with David I in the early twelfth century.

Ecclesiastical names, I will leave to the next chapter.

Before the Romans

It is generally true that river names are the most durable of names for several reasons. The river makes a natural line of division between peoples of different race and culture. Rivers provide water and are a source of food, a means of transport either by boat or foot, can be a meeting place or a defensive barrier against invaders. So it is no surprise that the derivation of the Tweed, the most important feature in the Borders landscape, has never been satisfactorily explained as we have no idea of its origin. References in Bede's *History* (731) give the Latinised version as Tuidus or Twidus and is written as Tweoda in 970.

Likewise the river Ettrick has no satisfactory root word and remains equally obscure. These linguistic fossils are thought to be Indo-European names given by a people whose identity is unknown to us. There are several other rivers of doubtful origin which I will not consider lest it bring the wrath of experts on my unsuspecting head.

Even in modern speech, the rivers of the Borders have different definitives: Yarrow is a Valley; Gala and Jed are Waters; Teviot, Megget and Lauder have Dales, and the rest are Rivers, Burns or Streams.

The Roman and Immediate Post-Roman Period

It is accepted without too much debate that the language of the Borders in this period was Cumbric. There may have been small pockets of others but they seem to have made no discernible impression.

Amongst the most easily recognisable indicators of Cumbrian settlement in the Borders are 'cair', a fort, a farm or manor house. This can be found in Carfrae near Lauder, a farm on the hill. Caerlanrig in Roxburghshire has been given the derivation as from 'caer-lanerch', the fort in the hollow. This is obviously wrong as the fort stands on a ridge overlooking the right bank of the River Teviot; its ramparts are still 1m high with an external ditch, and a gold coin to the Emperor Vespasian was found in the garden of the farm cottage. My suggestion is that it was made by two Cumbric words 'caer' and 'lann', an enclosure (sometimes a church), plus Englisc 'hrycg' meaning ridge. This derivation makes sense; I could be wrong though.

Another Cumbrian settlement word is 'tref', meaning a farm or a small village, often the centre of a 'maenor' estate. Traquair 'trefquair' is the village on the Quair burn in Peeblesshire and in Lauderdale, Trabrown 'tref yr bryn' is the farm on the hill. Also in Lauderdale, I think that the name of the Threeburnford Farm beside the Mean (Cumbrian – Stony) Burn is an Anglicised version of 'tref bryn forde' the road to the hill farm – but I could be wrong again.

Another settlement name is 'dun' which is found in Eildon, the old fort and Earlston, which before being Anglicised was Erciledun. The most important 'dun' was where the rivers Tweed and Teviot meet, and this was Merchidun, the cavalry fort which we now know as Roxburgh Castle. As this will play a part in the story, I will leave the explanation to a later page.

The top or head of a hill was 'pen' as in Ettrick Pen, Penchrise, Penmanscaur, while 'pren' was a tree as at Pirn, Pirnie, Primside and even Primrose, 'pren y ros', the tree on the moor. Some trees seem to be special and noted, as if they held some religious significance in the pre-Christian era.

The Cumbrian word for stone is 'maen'. From this comes 'maenor', the stone-built residence for the chief of a district which in turn comes to mean the estate of the great man. The 'maenor' estate consisted of seven trefs or villages in fertile lands and thirteen in the hill country. In Peeblesshire, the Manor Valley is a Cumbrian maenor preserved in almost perfect detail, although there are only twelve farm village at the present time; in the 1800s two had been amalgamated into one.

These maenors are likely to have covered the countryside from the late Roman period until the Englisc takeover which must have happened around AD 600. It is possible to detect where these Cumbric estates lay by stripping the layers of language from the place-names, especially in the hill country where change has always been slower.

Examples of Cumbric place-names could be extended for some time. They are worth further study but we must pass on to the next linguistic stage.

THE ANGLIAN PERIOD

We are not quite sure when the people of northern Germany first settled in the area now known as Northumberland. Certainly there were Teutonic troops guarding Hadrian's Wall and the surrounding countryside in the third and fourth centuries but they had not then attained the critical mass required to leave a discernible linguistic mark on the country. At this period, we are dealing with a great deal of uncertainty, possibility rather than probability; legend as opposed to provable fact.

The Northumbrian priest and historian, Bede, writing in 731, tells how a great plague swept across Britain, killing off the largest part of the 'British' (ie Cumbric) population, and that the Picts and Irish/Scots pirates were sweeping through the countryside destroying and plundering as they went.

'A terrible plague struck this corrupt people and in a short while destroyed so large a number that the living could not bury the dead. But not even the death of their friends or the fear of their own death was sufficient to recall the survivors from the spiritual death to which their crimes had doomed them. So it was that, not long afterwards an even

more terrible retribution overtook this wicked nation. For they
consulted how they might obtain help to avoid and repel the frequent
fierce attacks of their northern neighbours, and all agreed with the
advice of their king, Vortigern, to call on the assistance of the Saxon
peoples across the sea. This decision, as its results were to show, seems to
have been ordained by God as a punishment on their wickedness.'

It is known that Bede copied most of his pre-600 history from
Gildas who did not date his sources. This plague may have happened in
the 450s as is reported but there was a severe plague in the 540s which
was about the time Gildas' *Ruin of Britain* was written and this may have
coloured his writing.

The 'even more terrible retribution' came in the shape of a new
immigration from the Teutonic tribes on the Baltic regions of the
Continent.

Bede records that Vortigern, the High King or Leader, invited three
longships of Teutonic warriors to protect the country in AD 449, giving
them land on the east coast for their services. They were pagans,
worshipping strange gods, and this did not fit well with the now mainly
Christian, Cumbric-speaking population. More recent analysis place
this, if it happened as told, at AD 424.

Land pressure on the Continent saw ever more longships bringing
fresh immigrants of Angles, Saxons, Jutes, Frisians, Franks and Swedes
who settled in enclaves along the east coast of what is now England.
They were not there by invitation but held the land by right of conquest.
At the northern end of the settlements were the Angles who came from
Angeln, on the Baltic coast. Their new lands were in the Cumbrian
kingdom of Bernicia; it is not known whether the first Anglian settlements extended as far as the Berwickshire coast but it is likely.

About a hundred years after their official invitation, enough
Anglians had emigrated from the Continent to be sufficiently
numerous to take over the kingdom: 'In the year 547, Ida began his
reign which lasted for twelve years. From him the royal family of the
Northumbrians derives their origin'. The wording of the sentence
suggests that Ida may have become king by invitation rather than by
conquest. This may be true, especially if the earlier date of 424 is
accepted as the first landings; but one sentence is too slender a thread
on which to hang a theory.

It has been suggested that when Ida seized the rock fortress of Din Guauroy, he was leading a small band of Anglian pirates. This could be an unlikely story put about by sore losers. To take and hold such a vast kingdom as Northumbria became, would seem to require a large number of warriors under capable leaders, but this was not necessarily the case. The Anglo-Saxon Chronicle defines an 'army' as more than thirty men, between thirty and seven is a 'war-band' while less than seven were reckoned to be robbers. The same phenomenon can be observed in the Anglo-Norman settlement of Scotland in the 12th century when a small number of well-armed lesser nobility of England were given vast estates in Scotland and held them without much dispute from the local population.

One reason why the Anglians were able to seize so much land in what is now northern England and southern Scotland, was a bubonic plague which devastated much of the known world over a ten-year period beginning around 540. Starting in the Eastern Mediterranean in 541–2, it killed half a million people in Constantinople in 543 and worked its way through Europe until 550.

The plague killed off about 70 per cent of the Irish/Scots in Ireland and the Cumbrians in Scotland but not the Anglians on the east coast of the former Roman province of Brittania and the reason is because the Irish/Scots and Cumbrians had converted to Christianity some centuries before while the Anglians were still pagans. This was not Divine Retribution as suggested by Gildas, who may have seen the results at first hand, but a series of unlucky coincidences.

This unlikely story starts when the 530s saw a catastrophic deterioration in the world's weather. This was caused by a series of meteoric impacts wiping out most species of animal life. Deadly germs from the decaying bodies spread into colonies of African gerbils which were immune to the disease but passed it on to the black rats or ship rats. Another and probably more believable explanation was that a massive volcanic eruption in Alaska threw huge quantities of dust into the atmosphere, veiling the sun for two or three years and producing an acid, crop-destroying rain worldwide.

The monks of the early Celtic Church followed the examples of the 'Desert Fathers' in the eastern Mediterranean seeking isolated places to seek communion with their God and the Irish/Scots monks travelled there to study and learn. So there was much ship-board commerce between there and the monasteries of Ireland and western Scotland. The claims that some of the saints floated there on leaves or stones can be cheerfully countered by the numbers who are recorded as having paid for ship passage.

Archaeology can confirm the documentary evidence as excavations on monastic and royal residences of the period often reveal pottery imported from Egypt and wine from southern Gaul; the ships that carried trade goods also brought rats and, through them, the plague. The disease spread rapidly amongst the gregarious Celts, the warriors in the halls and the priests in monasteries, for infection is more likely to spread in places where men slept, ate and shared a cup in common. Less affected were the scattered population of the countryside.

Evidence from Irish, Cumbric and Englisc documents show that the Christian Celts would have no communication with the pagan Anglians. This lack of contact could not have been total, but what evidence we have shows that the plague did not affect the main body of the Anglians to such an extent. This left more men to take over the lands of their Celtic opponents who did not give up without a struggle.

In the Borders, facts about the battles between the invading Anglians and the defending Cumbrians are scarce and very secondhand. The few reliable sources tend to concentrate on what was happening in southern Britain where the conflicts between the surviving Romano-British and the assorted Teutonic invaders ended with the Romano-Brit forces accepting defeat around 460 and many migrating to what is now Britanny.

In the north and west, things were different with the Romano-Cumbric kingdoms in Wales, Cornwall and southern Scotland opposing Anglian settlement for generations. It is ironic that the people who most fiercely resisted initial Roman culture, were those who fought most strongly to retain it.

The best known leaders of the British in the struggles were Vortigern, Ambrosius Aurelianus and the legendary Arthur, who was not a king but a war-leader. The most famous of these is Arthur, the subject of many books, being made a king in French medieval romances, TV programmes and Hollywood epics; and, ironically, he is also the one of whom we have least positive knowledge.

Most historians agree that there must have been an Arthur-like British commander who inflicted many defeats on various enemies but most notably the heathen Anglians. They even accept that Gildas' account of a famous victory at Mount Badon, which might have happened *c*.495, is probably correct but nobody has been able to locate the site. Nor is much known about the historical Arthur and he remains a shadowy figure whose legend as a great warrior was passed down through the years. In 'Y Gododdin', a poem written in Edinburgh in Cumbric-Welsh just after the defeat at Catterick, a powerful warrior is praised for his valour 'though he were not Arthur'. Here Arthur was being remembered as a doughty fighter eighty years after his death and in the later sixth century, many rulers gave their sons the name of Arthur.

Although many have claimed Arthur as their own, the Gododdin poem puts him in southern Scotland. In his book *Arthur and the Lost Kingdoms*, Alistair Moffat makes a sound case for the historical Arthur being based at Merchidun, the horse-fort at the junction of the Tweed and Teviot rivers near Kelso. It is not unlikely that the historic war-leader was the lord of Calchvyndd. Centrally placed in the Cumbric kingdoms, he was able to sally forth to fight the Anglians in the south and the Scots and Picts in the north and west. With nine of the thirteen of his battles being able to be convincingly placed in the south of Scotland and north of England, the suggestion that Arthur was a Kelso man, stands up to interrogation as many historians have now admitted (quietly) that they 'always knew that Arthur was a northern figure'.

To Return to Anglian Progress in the Borders

There is little doubt that the Anglian warrior bands expanded during Ida's reign and those of his short-lived successors, six of whom ruled from 559 to 592. These early kings left no letters and any inferences from their few recorded deeds tend to make us forget that most of what they did was not recorded at all. For kings had to expand their kingdoms by fighting battles and usually ended by being killed. So the first seven pagan kings of Bernicia left little trace of their conquests; as far as we can make out, they were not very concerned about acquiring more territory but concentrated on raiding in warbands gathered for the occasion. They were warrior kings, warlords in an age when men lived by the sword. In this they resembled the Border Reivers a thousand years later.

We know more about Aethelfrith, grandson of Ida, who had built up his kingdom until it was strong enough to beat the Christian Gododdin at Catterick in 600 and the Christian Scots of Dalriada at Degsastan,★ which is either Dawston in Liddesdale or more likely Addinston in Lauderdale, in 603. Thereafter, he 'acquired' Deira to the south, creating the Kingdom of Northumbria. There is little doubt that Aethelfrith ruled from the fortress of Din Guauroy which he renamed 'Bebbanburch' in honour of his wife Bebba, and which we now know as Bamburgh.

It is interesting to note that after the battle of Degsastan, there are no further mentions of any battles being fought between Bamburgh and the Firth of Forth. It may be that both sides had fought themselves to a standstill and needed time to build up their strength again but whereas the Anglians were able to ship in new warriors from the Continent, the Scots and Cumbrians had no such reserves of immediate manpower and had to wait for the next generation to reach maturity.

For whatever reason, there is no reference as to when the Borders came into Englisc hands. Perhaps the defeats at Catterick and Degsastan were turning points in the battle for possession of the eastern Borders and, if the battles had gone the other way, we would probably still be speaking Welsh.

It is equally significant that nearly all the provincial place-names of early Anglian Northumbria remain Cumbric in origin and although this is not proof positive, it is a good indication that a high percentage of the population survived the trauma of war and occupation.

However, the pagan Anglians did convert to Christianity in 627 under Edwin of Deira. Their next ruler, Oswald, besieged and captured the fortress of Edinburgh in 638, occupying and settling the Lothians while his brother Oswy acquired the Cumbrian Kingdom of Rheged

---

★ Bede was in no doubt that the Christian Cumbrians and Scots deserved to be beaten by pagan victors because it was their own fault – they had never preached Christianity to the Anglians and had refused to accept the authority of Rome in the observance of the Passion and Resurrection.

by marriage, leaving Strathclyde as the only survivor of the three
Cumbrian kingdoms. By the mid-seventh century, the kingdom of
Northumbria was extended to cover most of southern Scotland and
northern England.

As far as the Borders are concerned, English literary and historical
sources for this Early Historic period are scarce and often inaccurate, so
we have had to rely on peripheral mentions in the Anglo-Saxon
Chronicle, Gildas, Bede and other early religious tracts and Lives. This,
changed for the better when the area became part of the Kingdom of
Northumbria in the early seventh century.

Ironically, it was that collapse of the Gododdin and Rheged
kingdoms and the takeover by the Anglians that was to preserve for
posterity the best records of what life was like in that era. As their
Christian world disintegrated, refugees from the two kingdoms poured
into Strathclyde and northern Wales, taking with them their poets and
written poems. As these poems were found in Wales and written in
Cumbric/Old Welsh, it has long been assumed that they referred to
events in post-Roman Wales. In fact, we have to thank Taliesin for
recording the struggles of Urien, king of the Britons of Rheged against
the Anglians and Aneurin for his eye-account of the Battle of Catterick
where he was (reputedly) one of three survivors of three hundred
Cumbrians who rode from the Lothians and Borders to fight against
the pagan Englisc. His poem 'Y Gododdin' gives superb descriptions of
what the life of a warrior was like in peace and war.

To present more than the briefest outline of the shifting frontiers
given above would require more academic erudition than I possess and
the original purpose of this book was to present the history of
Selkirkshire, which I will get round to in due course.

From the ground, we could learn more. We know that there are a
number of Anglian sites on the banks of the Tweed especially where the
river wash had left a steep bank and air photographs show marks of
triple palisade enclosures. This type of settlement can be found near
Hawick and above Selkirk in the Yarrow Valley. They are likely to be
initial Anglian intrusions but no excavation has been attempted on these
sites, so this has to be filed as 'likely but unproven'.

It is difficult to determine when the Borders ceased to be part of
the Cumbric-speaking Romano-Celtic kingdom of the southern

Gododdin and became the Englisc-speaking one of Northumbria, but it must have been a fait accompli after the capture of Edinburgh in 638. Once the Anglians were in nominal charge of the area, we don't know if the pattern of settlement was a sweeping invasion or a creeping advancement. Place-name evidence would suggest that the advance was gradual and could even have been quite peaceful. By studying the evolving Englisc names up the banks of the Tweed and its tributaries, it is possible to say with some conviction that it took around two hundred years, from 550 to 750, for the settlements to work their way up the valleys to just above Hawick, Selkirk and Peebles. This is not the blitzkrieg tactics of an invading army but rather the creeping advance of a more productive agricultural system; the plough was beating the sword. There is good reason to suppose that Cumbric was the language of the upper valleys until the twelfth century.

It seems likely that there was no major massacre of the original population when the Anglian settlements moved up-country as Cumbrian place-names were still retained in major settlements and especially in religious sites, a subject to which I will return. I question if the takeover of land resulted in much disruption amongst the native population, the people who actually worked the land. Fighting in defence or in conquest was the province of the warriors and their immediate entourage.

A new lord taking over the estate by legal or other means, still

Professor Bryan Sykes mapped DNA profiles of the peoples of Britain, going back many thousands of years, and came to conclusions that no amount of archaeological excavation or historical research could have revealed.

The genes of our ancestors are passed down through many generations until they form our being and this can be interpreted from our DNA. The conclusions are that 80 per cent of us are the direct descendants of the people who came here after the last ice age melted. Only a small elite have left their DNA in the population, just enough to confirm the beliefs of those who are convinced that they are the descendants of Roman generals, Celtic kings, Viking warriors and Norman-French nobles.

required the same services, so it was not in his interests to kill or drive out the indigenous supporting workers unless he had an equally large number of servile followers to farm the land. Linguistically, this meant that although the new lord and his immediate retinue spoke Englisc, the bulk of the population retained their Cumbric language and place-names. In one generation, they would be bi-lingual and several generations later would speak Englisc as their first language. This was the basis of what we now know as Border Scots. Although the language of the peasant population may have changed, recent genetic discoveries have proved that the Anglian takeover was unlikely to transform the existing gene pool to any major degree.

Shires, Estates and Land Use

Around 650, Anglian 'scirs' appeared, supplanting the Cumbric 'maenors' and frequently using the same land boundaries. These shires were basically a grouping of 'vills' (villages) into an administrative unit for the purpose of supplying services to a manorial lord or thane. This unit was based on a 'dominium' or central place, the probable site of a mother church or the habitation of a 'manorial lord', together with a number of dependent 'vills' at some distance from the shire centre. The early Anglian estates of Berwickshire, Coldinghamshire, Norhamshire and Islandshire have been mapped out by Professor Barrow in *The Kingdom of the Scots* where he also presented convincing proof of a Yetholmshire, encompassing land on both sides of the present border between Scotland and England. I intend to postulate a Melroseshire based on later land-grants from Selkirk and Melrose Abbey records

The Anglians newcomers brought in different methods of agriculture to the Borders. Cumbrians were basically stock-raisers who ploughed a little ground for their corn requirements. The Anglians were tillers of the soil, raising stock as a necessary but subsidiary crop. The Cumbrian peoples spread out over the countryside in single farmsteads or small communities; Anglians lived in larger villages or townships which were organised in a social hierarchy with recognised strata and rules. Land was held from a 'manorial lord' who received food-rents in produce and kind or labour services for the use of the ground.

In theory, all land belonged to the king and he would keep some estates (*villae regis*) for his own use and would reward his trusted followers by granting them certain manors within his kingdom for their lifetime. In return, the manorial lord would guarantee to supply the royal household a stated amount of food-rent and certain services. For these, the king also expected loyalty and support in wars of conquest or defence.

When a manorial lord died, his heirs would hand the land back into the king's hands and hope that he would give it back again for their lifetime. Soon the land grants were being recorded in writing to prevent any misunderstanding, rather than being made verbally before witnesses. Eventually, noblemen requested that land grants be made permanent to be passed down their families on a hereditary basis.

As his part of the bargain, the king used his wise judgement to protect his kingdom and its people and interceded with the pagan gods on their behalf.

> The coming of the Christian Church broke this principle of landholding. Communication with God was made by the priest and the land grants, which may have been made to an abbot or bishop, were looked on as being given to the Church which was everlasting and so did not hand back the lands to the original donor. This meant an ever-decreasing pool of land available to be given out by the king for his disposal and, in time, this made the Church more influential with terrestial as well as perceived celestial powers.

Below the king, the lord lived in a 'dominium' as the centre of his estate that could be a 'scir' (a rule or province, later shire). His main residence would be a large timber hall in which he held court, gave feasts and entertained guests. The Great Hall could be as much as 30m long and 15m in width. From air photographs, we know that there are Anglian halls at Sprouston and Philiphaugh in the Borders but no excavation has been done to prove them, a project I would like to see considered.

In concentric rings outside the hall were the houses of the retainers and servants. These were much smaller in size and usually had a hollowed-out rectangular pit beneath them; this could be used as a workshop or for storage or more probably for animals, whose heat would be most welcome during the winter months. They are known by their German name of 'grubenhauser'.

As both halls and retainers' housing were made from timber and thatch, they leave little trace on the ground other than can be detected by a fortunate air photograph taken at the right time, place, crop and angle. With little pottery and no coinage, especially in the early Anglian days, only a lucky find would allow fieldwalkers to pin-point a site.

Spread through the 'scir' were twelve 'vill' or townships. These were agricultural villages whose inhabitants farmed the land, providing food-rents to sustain the lord's retinue and, indirectly, the king. They also had to contribute a certain amount of labour to work the lord's land during the peak demand times of ploughing, sowing and harvesting.

The village was centred on an open piece of ground that was big enough to provide a market place where people could meet to sell or exchange produce. Houses clustered round this central point and behind the houses were long yards or gardens that could be owned or permanently leased by a family. The land surrounding the village was held in common by the community although they did not own it. The individual fields were balloted for annually, the number of fields leased depending on the individual's status within the community. With no certainty of getting the same field in successive years, there was little incentive to improve the fertility of the land by manuring, and this could lead to ground exhaustion and poorer crops.

This village/field pattern can be seen in many of the older villages in the Borders such as Midlem, Bowden and Lilliesleaf. Lauder had a similar pattern of village development and field system but grew in size and importance by reason of being on the route of Roman and medieval Dere Street.

As the Anglian settlements prospered, new land that had previously been forest pasture was cleared of trees and brought into cultivation. Cropping produced more food than grazing and soon they required more land to feed their increasing population. This also meant that the new communities that were springing up on the flat lands of the Merse and Roxburghshire were named in Englisc, and this is noticeable in the names of the village communities of the present-day Borders. The new settlers developed the land, naming the topographical features of the countryside in their own language, where there were deer or pigs, where the springs and woods were etc; as houses were built on the sites, these became descriptive settlement names in their own right, Oakwood, Springhill, Hummelknowes (hummel is a bumble bee).

While the Anglian place-names gradually worked their way up the valleys, they pushed the mainly pastoralist Cumbrians into the higher and less fertile ground.

There is no proof one way or the other that the takeover was antagonistic, as arable and pastoral products were mutually tradeable.

More Place-names

The earliest provable Englisc name is the one derived from 'inga' originally meaning 'the descendant of' and later 'the settlement of or at'. There was the Cumbrian fort on St Abbs Head in Berwickshire, called 'Caer Colud' meaning 'the fort of Colud'. When the Anglians took over the area, they retained the original meaning but renamed it in their own language 'Coludesburh'. A settlement developed in the vicinity of the fort, which for convenience was known as 'Coldingaham', the settlement near Colud's fort.

This is the only provable 'inga' name in the Borders although Whittingham and Tyningham in East Lothian have similar ancestry.

Next in the chronological progression up the river system is the Anglian 'ham' which can mean an estate, settlement or village. Berwickshire and the eastern part of Roxburghshire are covered with 'ham' names – Ednam is Edenham, the village on the river Eden; Birgham is the village at the bridge; Oxnam is Oxenham, the oxen village; Smailholm is Smallham, the small village; and Midlem is Middleham, the middle village.

At about the same time as the 'ham' affix was being added to a descriptive root, another was being added to personal names; this was 'ingtun' meaning the farm belonging to. Thus Mersington is the farm belonging to Mersige, Renton is Regna's farm and Edington is Edda's farm.

Neither 'ham' or 'ingatun' names are known to appear in documents before AD 1050 but this could be because only a few early documents have survived. For most of the place-names, we have to rely on the charter books of the four Border Abbeys, which were founded in the first half of the twelfth century.

In the next step in Anglian linguistic evolution, we get 'tun' which means an enclosed farm/village or homestead and is usually used as an affix to a personal name or location description. Paxton is 'Pacca's farm; Maxton is Maccus' farm/village; and Aschechyrctun in Selkirkshire was named by an Anglian, turned into Scots as Eshkirktoon and re-Anglicised as Ashkirktown in modern maps.

'Tun' appears as 'ton' in later documents and maps and it has been remarked that few are to be found in the upper Selkirkshire and Roxburghshire valleys; this can be explained by poor soil quality which could only support a sparse population. There simply were not enough people to make a 'tun' or 'ton'.

The same does not apply to parts of Peeblesshire where a clutch of 'tons' are to be found around Eddleston.

A fortified habitation with wide lands or with surrounding settlements can be a 'burh', 'worth' or 'wic'. When an Anglian warlord captured the Cumbrian fortress of Merchidun at the confluence of the Tweed and Teviot, he renamed it as his own 'Hroc's burh' (the Rook's burgh) and it has been Roxburgh ever since.

The old Border town that stands on the Jed Water, had as its first known name Gedwearde or Gedwirth. This was changed to Jedburgh around 1300 but Borderers, an ever stubborn race, still refer to it as Jethart.

Cessford is another 'worth' name, written as Cesseworthe in 1296; the name may mean the fortress of Cessa or it could be derived from 'cess' a spear. Polwarth, the enclosure by the pool, is the only 'worth' which retains the name in its original form.

'Wic' is well spread throughout the Borders from Berwick, the barley farm, to Hawick, the farm surrounded by a hedge. There is also Borthwick which has been taken to mean ' the home farm' or principal farm on the estate but it could also be a personal name ' Bortha's farm'. Darnick is 'derne wic', the hidden farm possibly amongst the trees.

So far I have concentrated on settlement names. The topographical names of the landscape are equally instructive and most have their derivations in Englisc: 'lie or lee', a clearing in woodland; 'law' was a height or hill; 'feld' open country; 'slaid' a hollow, to give a few examples.

Animals and birds take their place in names – 'Nowt Lair' is where cattle rested for the night while Ern Cleuch, Pyat Shaw, Gowk Moss and Gledswood were the favoured places of eagles, magpies, cuckoos and kites respectively. The list is not endless but could take up a great deal of time without adding much to our knowledge of the Borders at that time.

Having established the two main linguistic groups who were in the Borders in the sixth and seventh centuries, this does not necessarily mean that there were no other races involved.

Scandinavian settlers appear in the area introducing names with 'bie' a farm or hamlet; 'gil' a ravine; 'grain' a fork or branch; usually in a burn; 'fell' a hill. Clusters of Scandinavian personal names appear in some areas of southern Scotland but in the Borders the ground-naming examples given above tend to be in the western parts of the region, suggesting that the settlers came in from Dumfriesshire and were originally from the Scandinavian settlements around Dublin.

Around 950, there seems to have been an influx of Scots Gaelic speakers into the Borders with 'bun' a river-mouth, as in Bonjedward; 'ceap' a lump or mound, appears as kipps in several places while 'creag' and 'glean' come into Scots as craig and glen.

There is evidence that Gaelic came into the Borders from Dumfriesshire and Lanarkshire. Bedrule in Roxburghshire was originally Bethoc's Rule (Bethoc's Estate); Bethoc was the wife of Ranulf of Stranit (Nithsdale) who was alive in 1140.

Giric I, king of the Scots from 878 to 889, is believed to have extended Scots rule in Bernicia for the first time since 603. This gives us a reasonably accurate dating for the farms of Girrick and Girnick in Berwickshire and Lann Giric (The Rink) in Selkirkshire.

With Cumbric and Scots Gaelic being cousin languages, there is difficulty in deciding which was the naming language.

The farms of Deloraine in Ettrick could have its name starting with Cumbric 'dol' or Gaelic 'dail' both meaning a haugh or meadow. However, there is no doubt about its origin when hearing a Ettrick man or woman pronounce it 'Doloran' with stress on the first syllable; it is 'Dol Urien' the meadow of Urien, king of Rheged who was assassinated at the siege of Medcaut (Lindisfarne) in 590 and therefore the name has Cumbric origins.

There is a story that Kenneth III, king of Scots from 997 to 1005, was hunting in Ettrick Forest when he was cornered in a cleuch (ravine) by a large stag and rescued by a Galloway huntsman. Being grateful, the king gave him all the land that the hunt had covered that day and forever after, was known as 'John le Scott of Buck Cleuch'. The Scott name might be true as a Gaelic speaker coming into an Englisc-speaking community would be called 'the Scot'; a Briton from Strathclyde would be 'the Welshman' or Wallace/Welch and an Anglian in Strathclyde as ' Englisc or Inglis'

In fact, the name Buccleuch, pronounced by Ettrick people as Bacloo, is from two Gaelic words: 'bal' meaning a settlement, and 'cliabh' pronounced 'cloo' meaning a basket or hollow shape. The name 'the settlement in the hollow' describes the location perfectly although it does little for the romantic tale.

As shown above, kings' names are useful in dating settlements. The township at Edibertshiels, the sheilings of Edbert later known as Auld Wark, in the Yarrow Valley, commemorates Edbert, the last expansionist king of Northumbria, so the dating must be around 750 when he added Kyle to his kingdom. This expanded kingdom didn't last long because the Northumbrians got soundly thrashed by the Britons of Strathclyde in 756. The name Edibertshiels became Cathermach, meaning the fort of ? in Scots Gaelic and was afterwards Anglified into Carterhaugh.

The study of place-names can be a guessing game. From the village we now know as Eddleston in Peeblesshire, we have positive evidence of just how variable place-names can be.

It first appears in documents as 'Penteiacob', a Welsh name meaning the promontory of James's House; a new owner, a Gaelic speaker, re-named it 'Gillmorestun', the tun (Anglian ending) of Gille Moire (Gaelic – St Mary's Lad); the next change was when the land was granted to Edulf, son of Utred, an Anglian, and he called it 'Edulfstun' sometime before 1189. These three changes in three languages took place within eighty years.

The area around Eddleston seems to have been home to a multi-national or at least a multi-lingual, population. From the Register of the

Bishopric of Glasgow, we find that within Peebles itself, around 1200, there are a number of Gaelic names: Gille-Micheil (the servant of St Michael) twice; Gille-Crist (servant of Christ) twice; Gille-Moire (servant of Mary) twice; Cristein (twice); Padruig (twice); Gille-Caluim, Padinus, Bridoe (Bride); together with the Cumbrian names of Queschutbrit (St Cuthbert's servant); Cospatricius (St Patrick's servant); Cosmungho (St Mungo or Kentigern's servant); and Cosouold (St Osuald's servant). There are also Englisc names, Adam, son of Edolf, Randulf of Megget, Mihhyn Brunberd and Mihhyn son of Edred.

As most of the above have Christian connections, this reinforces the belief that Peebles must have been a noted place of Christian worship probably from the sub-Roman period. To which I will now turn.

CHRISTIANITY

The lands of the eastern Mediterranean have been the cradle of three of the major religions of the world, Judaism, Christianity and Islam. All have certain beliefs which link with each other, and some borrowed from previous civilisations. All became successful in gathering millions of followers but, like many enterprises with strongly held opinions, soon split up into various factions who fought each other and are continuing to do so. This is a long and complicated affair in which I do not wish to get involved, as it is not relevant to the history of Selkirkshire.

Christianity was the only one to come into Scotland in ancient times, so I will examine how a religion which came from so far away, influenced the way we have lived and, to some extent, are still living.

The Beginnings of Christianity

In the Roman province of Judea, there were many holy men of the Jewish faith who went into the desert to contemplate the relationship between God and man. Some lived communally in monasteries while others preferred the solitary life by going into the desert to live as hermits. All lived under the Judaic Laws but were split into different cults or sects.

Around 2,000 years ago, a child was born in the obscure town of Nazareth. On reaching manhood, he retired to the desert to contemplate, and returned to preach to an ever-increasing following. To many Jews, he seemed to fulfil most of the ancient prophecies that he was the one chosen to set them free from their Roman rulers. He was called Messiah in Hebrew and Christos in Greek although he probably spoke Aramaic.

The Roman authorities, fearing his abilities to inspire a large portion of the people, promptly executed him in the most humiliating way possible. However, his preaching had inspired others to carry his message of love, peace, forgiveness and the promise of a better future life, to various parts of the Roman Empire.

As the majority of the citizens of the Roman Empire passed their short lives in wretched conditions of poverty with little hope of betterment, this new religion promised future rewards to compensate for the pretty terrible existence of their present. It was to the poorest and most down-trodden members of society, the slaves and women, that Christianity was most appealing.

Christianity struggled to spread through the Empire although it took root in pockets inside and outwith the Roman frontiers. After Constantine declared Christianity to be the official religion of the Empire in 313, it became popular in some sections of Roman society, but most Romans continued to worship their old gods. To many, Christians were seen as a minor Jewish sect who were irritating and intensely disliked even by the orthodox Jewish community within Rome. Now free from persecution, the Christians were able to expand their faith throughout the Roman Empire and beyond.

In Britain

Since Victorian times, the history in the British Isles tends to be Anglo-centric, how circumstances affected the English way of life. So although there are Christian martyrs known to have been within the Roman province of Britannia in the earlier centuries, the Christian church in England is usually acknowledged to have been founded when Pope Gregory sent Augustine to the pagan Anglo-Saxon kingdom of Kent in 597. This ignores the Romano-British and Celtic Christian Churches which had been in Britain and Ireland for at least two centuries before that.

It is worth bearing in mind that history is always kind to the victors and Christendom is no exception; what follows is, at best, a collection of stories written from the early Christian point of view and usually many years after the event had taken place. It is difficult to make an unbiased report as only one side of the story is given in writing, no matter how sparsely. The story of Christianity in southern Scotland and northern England is based on few concrete (or rather inscribed stone) facts, accounts which have been written and rewritten several times over the centuries; and a lot of speculation Fortunately, the speculators have qualified their statements with a lot of 'seems likely', 'could have been', 'is possible that' and this allows for further consideration and speculation. I intend to follow their example, taking what seems feasible while allowing for flagrant mistakes. Dates are given more in hope than belief.

Christianity at the Wall and Beyond

Christianity was in the Borders from an early date, introduced by the Celtic Church and then taken over in parts by the Roman Church after 627 when Edwin, king of Northumbria converted to Christianity to cement a marriage settlement with the daughter of Eadwald of Kent, then the only Christian king in England.

It should be borne in mind that the Northumbrian church was started by Celtic monks from Iona or Ireland, and that Lindisfarne, as an offshoot from Iona, was originally subject to the authority of the Columban Christian confederacy. With such close ties, it is difficult to distinguish between the two very similar forms of Christianity in the absence of absolute evidence, and there is much debate amongst academics.

When the Roman army left southern Scotland around 180, there is no positive evidence of Christianity in the region between the Walls of Hadrian and Antonine. One first or second century bronze vessel from the Curle excavations at Trimontium has markings which have been tentatively identified as Christian, but are more likely to be accidental scraping rather than a positive marking.

There are speculative but quite compelling reasons to suggest the Christianity came to the lands around Hadrian's Wall and the south of Scotland in the third and fourth centuries.

The historian Tertullian, writing in Carthage around 200, claimed that 'parts of Britain beyond Roman rule had been subdued by the Church'. Tertullian was a far from unbiased reporter but this is unlikely to be a fictional tale. It is possible that Christianity was being spread by the mainly Greek sea-borne merchants from the Eastern Mediterranean when they were trading round the coasts of Cornwall, Wales, Ireland and Scotland. From objects found in these locations, it is certain that such trade was taking place.

Were there established trading posts as has been found as far away as south India during the Roman period, and if so, did they bring Christianity with them? This is not unlikely. Were these the first links in the long-standing connection that developed between the Celtic Church and Eastern Mediterranean Christianity? Serious questions but no discernible answers.

The Early Saints

The saints of the early Celtic Church closely followed the examples of the 'desert fathers' who sought out isolated places to live a hermit's life of prayer and contemplation. In Ireland and Scotland there were no deserts but there were remote places to which the holy man could retire. These became known as 'diserts', an Irish borrow-word derived from the Latin 'desertum', a desert, which are scattered through Ireland and can be seen in the stone-built cells of the monks, preserved on the rocky West Coast of Ireland. They survived by being stone-built – stone was easily available while wood was scarce and would have decayed or been blown away.

In Scotland, 'Kil' followed by a saint's name often indicates where a monk had his solitary cell. Although there are a few 'kil' names in the Borders, there are no known stone-built cells.

Celtic monasteries were established on promontories into the sea or, if inland, on high banks where rivers met or where a river turned almost round on itself to form a peninsula. The site chosen was always one that could be easily cut off from the secular society by a wall or ditch across the narrowest part of the peninsula. Although known as monasteries, they were not large buildings like the later abbeys but rather groupings of individually standing single-room cells where each monk could retire to pray in solitude.

It is now largely accepted that there were pockets of Christianity along the line of Hadrian's Wall in the final years of the Roman Empire. When considering the presence of a late Romano-British/Celtic Church, it is best to look at the non-portable symbols of Christianity. Rings, jars and plates with Christian symbols can be brought in but large inscribed stones and buildings are static.

At Housesteads, Vindolanda and Birdoswald, there are buildings whose ground plans resemble the shapes of early churches – small and rectangular with a round apse. At Maryport, there was a plaque with a Chi-Rho, an early Christian monogram although this is now lost, and at Carlisle, the tombstone of Flavius Antigonus Papias, a Greek, is inscribed with a formula recognisably Christian. Several Greek names have been recognised in the Vindolanda documents. Were they Christians? Nobody can say for certain.

From the tentative evidence collected, we are able to deduce that the area in and around Carlisle had a substantial Christian community in place during the period of the late Roman occupation. As the Roman 'Luguvalium', it was the provincial capital, responsible for the smooth running and services of the region and, given the evidence from other late Roman towns in Britain, it is more than probable that Carlisle was the centre of a Christian bishopric in the late Roman period.

The city had survived as an administrative centre after the departure of the Roman army and continued to be a viable civic entity for centuries to come. In 685, when St Cuthbert was being given a conducted tour of the city by its proud Northumbrian governor, he was shown a working fountain, which implies piped water, and was taken on a circuit of the stone-built walls which were intact from the Roman days.

The grant of Carlisle, including a fifteen-miles radius of the surrounding area, to St Cuthbert and the Lindisfarne See is a good indication of a long-established Christian community within the town.

By the time the Roman Empire collapsed in the fifth century there were Christian communities established outwith the imperial frontiers. In northern Britannia they were members of the Celtic church; they would speak in Cumbric and some would speak and read Latin, and their commemorative inscriptions were carved in a truncated form of Latin.

Under the sub-Roman kings, monastic foundations seem to have played a vital part in the spread of Christianity through southern Scotland. There is positive proof of the spread around the Solway coasts, in the shape of inscribed stones which are irrefutable, and the written lives of a few of the men who made it happen, which are not quite so reliable.

There are many saints of the Celtic church commemorated with 'kil' before their names. One book on place-names of Scotland notes 15 Brendans, 15 Brigids, 16 Faolons, 30 Cronans and 218 Colmans and we must come to the conclusion that it was the founder men and women who were remembered, rather than the church. Not all were recorded in writing but two who were most influential are given below.

St Ninian

Ninian, or more correctly Nynia, was the Apostle of the Solway coasts. Bede tells us that Nynia was a Romano-Briton, probably born at the beginning of the fifth century. The name is British ie Cumbrian, which was written as Niniavus in Latin and this has been misread as Ninianus, 'v' and 'n' being indistinguishable in script, and from there became Ninian in later times.

We know little of the man himself other than histories written after his death. What we are told is that he established an ecclesiastical foundation at Whithorn and built a stone church there. This was called Candida Casa, the White House, notably built in stone in contrast to the other Celtic Christian churches which were wood and wattle.

This is an interesting comment. It is supposed that Nynia spent his youth in or around Carlisle and would be quite familiar with the stone buildings of the late Roman period. One version of his life suggests that he was sent by a bishop of Carlisle to convert the inhabitants along the Solway coast. Another train of thought maintains that there were settlements of Irish Christians already established in several locations before he arrived.

Although much of Ninian's life is deductive reasoning and guesswork based on later writings, there are a number of inscribed stones found in the vicinity of his foundation.

The oldest Christian record from Whithorn is a tombstone

commemorating Latinus aged thirty-five, and his unnamed daughter aged four. This was erected by his grandson, Barrovadus. The inscription starts with 'Te Dominum laudumus' – We praise thee Lord. Latinus was obviously a Christian and the Latin inscription has been dated to no later than 450. So working backwards, here are three generations of Christians in the area dating back to a period when Roman troops still garrisoned Hadrian's Wall. This poses the question: 'Was this before or after Ninian came to Whithorn?' This is a question that cannot be answered as humans move around, and where they died does not necessarily mean they lived there.

There is a related site 40kms to the west at Kirkmadrine where four inscribed stones have been found. Two commemorate 'holy and outstanding bishops' named as Viventius and Mavorius. The third has the Christian Chi-Rho symbol and an inscription 'Initium et Finis', the beginning and the end, while the fourth lost stone is said to have borne the name Ventidius with the description 'diaconus'- deacon.

From this, we can deduce that the Novantae of Galloway who lived outside the Roman Frontier could have been converted to Christianity in the fourth century.

St Patrick

The man who is generally known as St Patrick, was born around 410 at a 'villula', a small estate, near the western end of Hadrian's Wall. We are reasonably certain of this because he wrote his life story in 'Confession', in which he gave some autobiographical details. His original name was Sucat. His father was Calpurnius who held office in the church as a deacon, and his grandfather was Potitius who had been ordained as a priest. Three generations of Christian worship, places Christianity in the area around, or more likely in, Carlisle back to the mid-fourth century. It also suggests that the church was strong enough to have a bishop who was able to confirm new priests.

At the age of fifteen, Sucat was captured in a slaving raid 'along with the male and female servants of my father's house' and taken to Northern Ireland. He escaped six years later, made his way to France where he is said to have come under the influence of the teachings of St Martin of Tours who died in 397. Sucat returned to Britain and trained for the priesthood 'having been regularly instructed in the mysteries of the Christian faith in Rome'. This wording does not necessarily mean that he was in the city of Rome but could indicate that he was trained in Roman rituals. Other versions suggest that his training was at Carlisle where the thriving Celtic church could train and confirm priests.

While his priesthood training was taking place, Sucat's father died, leaving him a town house in Carlisle and the estate. These he sold and used the money to finance a mission to Ulster where he had been enslaved. He is credited with introducing Christianity to Ireland as well as driving out the snakes. Actually he did neither as there had never been snakes in Ireland and there were groups of Christians in Ireland since 431 when Palladius was sent by Pope Celestinus to convert the pagans there. There is a conviction that there were a number of Christian establishments in Southern Ireland before either Sucat or Palladius.

However, Sucat was very successful in his mission and took, or was given, the name 'Patricius' which means the Patrician, the Father or the Noble One. Time enlarged his fame while his name got Anglicised to Patrick and he became the patron saint of Ireland.

To look for ecclesiastical foundations, we have to consider the large number of 'eccles', 'kill' and 'kirk' place-names along the Solway coast. This is a big task and does not come within the scope of Selkirkshire, so I will avoid the traps contained there.

Nor is it possible to decide whether a site is Celtic or Northumbrian or even a Northumbrian church overlying a Celtic one. Recent excavations at the known Northumbrian monastery at Hoddom have postulated that on the evidence of sculpture and the use of Roman stone within the structure that it was a centre of Christianity during the sub-Roman period and could have been the principal diocesan Celtic church within the Kingdom of Rheged and was later a Northumbrian one. This supposition is given credence by the Kentigern association and the number of ecclesiastical place-names in the vicinity.

With the story of Christianity placed into a time scale, it is now important to examine how it fitted into the history of the Borders in general and Selkirkshire in particular.

Early Christianity in the Borders

Christianity can be placed in the Borders from the mid-fifth century but proof is scarce and speculation plentiful. The case for its introduction rests on five inscribed stones (one lost around 1261), several place-names with 'eccles' and 'kil', Bede's writings which present a fair but Northumbrian-centred view, a well-reasoned argument that there were at least two diocese centres in the upper and middle Tweed valley at Peebles and Old Melrose, and others which I am about to add. The likely takes the place of the positive when firm evidence is lacking.

There are some sites that are worthy of consideration as early Christian locations that would require excavation to literally dig up the knowledge, but until that happens we must make do with what we have.

Christianity came into the Borders in three phases.

Phase one happened when St Ninian left his base at Whithorn, and is said to have led the first Christian mission into the lands of the southern Picts early in the fifth century. Southern Pictland was the general name of the lands between the walls of Hadrian and Antonine. So Christianity seems to have first filtered into the Borders from the south-west.

This is a reasonable projection as four of the five inscribed stones found in the region come from the upper stretches of the Liddel, Ettrick, Yarrow and Manor Waters. From the roughly executed and truncated Latin inscriptions, they have been dated to the period between AD 450 and 550. The inscriptions, datings and find-spots of two of the stones fit in with holy men seeking 'diserts' to spend their lives in prayer and contemplation. The veneration of the Desert Fathers had a strong influence on the sub-Roman church of St Ninian.

The other two stones are commemorative. One is a memorial to a woman Coninie who was a member of the Christian church in Manor Valley, while the other comes from the Yarrow Valley and is a memorial for two princes; this stone stands in the middle of a large Dark Age cemetery.

Phase two of Christianity also came from the west, but if the Christianity expounded by Ninian was represented by individual monks in lonely places, the next phase was definitely community based.

Columba was an Irishman of aristocratic birth who founded the monastery of Iona in 563 or 565 depending on who is writing. He had previously founded monasteries at Derry in 550 and possibly Durrow and Kells, but for his part in the battle of Cul Drebene in 561 he was exiled, or sought exile/safety, in the Irish colony of Dalriada, where King Conall gave him the island of Iona to found a monastery there.

In the early centuries, the Irish church was organised on a monastic basis, a closed community dedicated to the worship of God, but it was the custom for Irish monks to go into voluntary exile from the monastery, wandering the countryside preaching the gospel as they went. They evangelised through Britain and went across western and central Europe and, from the seventh century onwards, monasteries of exclusively Irish monks were founded on the continent. Schottenkirken or the equivalent name can still be found in European cities.

The Irish were known as 'Scoti' up to the eleventh century and this led to the idea that these foundations were made by Scots from Scotland. This misconception was used to bolster the myth that the origins of The Auld Alliance between Scotland and France dated back to the time of Charlemagne.

On Iona, Columba established a monastery in the Irish traditions. At that time, Irish society was tribal in organisation and gregarious in life. As the monastic element became dominant in society, Irish monasteries formed confederations which took no account of boundaries of tribal kingdoms. So Iona became the centre of the Columban 'paruchia' which spread across northern Britain.

Bede was to write about Iona: 'This island always has an abbot for its ruler who is a priest, to whose authority the whole province, including even bishops, have to be subject'. So the followers of Columba gave their allegiance, not to a king or noble, but to their abbot and ultimately to the Abbot of Iona.

In contrast to the priests of Ninian, those of the Columban Church lived in closed communities but in an area which had easy access to a much greater population for conversion and support. They did not live separate from humanity; in fact they moved about the country so much that they had to be restrained by ecclesiastical legislation which was imposed 'by popular demand' because the wandering priests expected to be welcomed, fed and housed by the outside community.

In the Borders there are three sites likely to have originally been Columban foundations, at St Abb's Head, Old Melrose and Peebles; there are others, hypothesised but not proven yet. At a later date, the sites were taken over or re-colonised by the Northumbrian Church, which itself was an offshoot of the Columban Church. This may be because of the religious prestige attached to the site but it is worth noting that each location was conveniently placed for access.

St Abbs Head was on the coast and it was easier to travel by ship rather than overland. Old Melrose was on a fine peninsula where the river Tweed swings round in a sharp bend and, additionally, was at the crossroads where the main Roman road of Dere Street was crossed by the largely unexplored east-west Roman road up the Tweed Valley. Peebles was beside the Roman road up the Tweed Valley and at a natural junction of roads and rivers. These are places where you would expect to find a Columban monastery, where people would naturally congregate and settle.

Monasteries are people-gatherers for religious and commercial reasons and soon the isolated monastery became the hub of a thriving secular population, a subject to which I will return below.

Life in a monastic establishment was not all praying and chanting. Within the monks, there had to be a body of workers, the smiths and carpenters, bakers and brewers and all the support services required for the smooth running of the community. Praising God was important but so were teaching, reading and copying manuscripts into book form. Men expressed their devotion to God by the use of whatever skills they had.

To see what the churches of the Columban foundations could have been like, we have to look at examples excavated in Ireland. Modern expectations would imagine large stone buildings with bustling monks and large numbers gathered to listen. This is totally wrong because as late as the seventh century, although some churches were built of stone, the vast majority were of wood and wattle, straw thatch and sod, and could be distressingly small, as little as 3m by 2m. A building this small was known as an oratory and used for individual and private worship.

So far, none have been positively identified in the Borders but there is a stone foundation on the shoulder of Lee Pen in Peeblesshire which might fit the specifications. A romantic imagination would place St Ronan here.

Larger church buildings for congregational use were known by the Latin term 'ecclesia' which can mean a church or a Christian congregation, depending on the usage, and from this we get the place-name 'eccles'.

There is little question that all structures of churches, and the housing for monks and the secular population outside the enclosed area, were made of wood and wattle with four corner posts and intermediate uprights at the door and in the longer walls if required. With thatch and sod, they would be ecologically sound, probably warm in the winter and cool in the summer, but totally useless for the modern archaeologist who likes stone walls and deep ditches for geophysics. All that would remain of such wooden structures would be a series of postholes revealed during a careful excavation which so far has not materialised in the Borders.

In 1999, Richard Strathie of the Trimontium Trust was flying his microlight over the site of Old Melrose to see if there were any signs of Roman occupation visible in the ground. The peninsula is a kilometre from the fort of Trimontium and its surrounding annexes, so it was unlikely that such a convenient area would not have been utilised at some period. His air photographs show several hundred small rectangles in rows on the peninsula leading into the Old Melrose site. Thinking that it might have been a temporary or marching camp, I investigated further. Fieldwalking produced no coin or pottery evidence to give a Roman or even medieval dating to this pattern. Metal detecting outside the scheduled area produced nothing but Georgian/Victorian debris and few samples of those.

Divining rods give credence to rows of totally degraded wooden houses, each measuring approximately 6m by 3.5m, with a doorway in the middle of the longer wall facing east. I put these down to the wooden housing outside a Columban monastery but only careful excavation outside Historic Scotland's preserves can prove or disprove this theory.

Under the auspices of the Trimontium Trust and with the permission of Col Younger, the owner of the ground, two geophysical surveys were commissioned by the Trimontium Trust on the three areas which seemed to show most promise. These produced very little in the way of anything; in fact the absence of any finds in the ploughed lands was noted on both reports. A third 'desk-top' survey was equally barren.

More positive but also more ephemeral proof of a concentration of wooden buildings, can be found in the place-name of the town of Peebles which derives from the Cumbric word 'pebyll' with an Anglian plural added. This is usually translated as a tent or pavilion. I suggest that 'wood and wattle building' would be more factually correct.

Both Old Melrose and Peebles kept their original Cumbric names despite later Anglian foundations, certainly at Old Melrose and likely in Peebles. This can be taken to mean that both sites were of importance as sub-Roman Christian localities whose prestige as known holy places were worth retaining. It is tempting to suppose that Peebles was the diocesan centre of the upper Tweed Goddeu while Old Melrose held the same position of the middle Tweed Calchvyndd. But that is supposition with only a smidgeon of likelihood of acceptable proof; we live in hope.

Phase three of Christianity came from the south and was actually an offshoot of the Columban Church. At the end of the sixth century, the area we now know as Northumberland, was occupied by the pagan Anglians. There would have been pockets of Christians within the area, converts by Columban and Ninianic monks and hermits, but the rulers were pagan.

It was a time of strife as kings sought to enhance their power and prestige by taking over other kingdoms through conquest or marriage. I will try to condense a long and bloody story into a short and relevant one.

Aethelfrith, king of Bernicia 592–604, king of Northumbria 604–617, was definitely a pagan. Bede tells us that, before a battle against the Christian Romano-British, Aethelfrith saw about 1,200 monks praying for his defeat; so he attacked them first, killing all but fifty who had the sense to run away. However, Bede excuses this slaughter of Christians by a pagan by explaining that the Christians were of the

British Church and did not obey the instructions of St Augustine to keep Easter at the same time as his Catholic (Roman) one, and for this they were killed. As I mentioned before, Bede was perhaps mistaken in some of his information and was a propagandist for the Northumbrian Church rather than the English Church.

When it was Aethelfrith's turn to be killed in battle in 617, his family had to flee. His sons Oswald, Eanfrith, Oswy and daughter Aebba went north where they 'lived in exile among the Irish or Picts and were there instructed in the teaching of the Irish church and received the grace of baptism'. We are not told where they went but Oswald is known to have been on Iona at some period of the exile.

Meanwhile in Northumberland, the conquering king, Edwin, ruled for seventeen years, as a pagan for eleven and converting to Christianity for the last six. Then he was killed in 633 by the army of Cadwallon, king of Gywnedd, who carried out whole-scale massacres as if he meant to exterminate the whole population (allegedly).

He in turn was killed by Oswald who was king of Northumbria from 634 until 642, when he died at the battle of Maserfield.

From Bede's point of view, Oswald's most important act was to send for Irish priests to establish, or more probably re-establish, the church in Northumbria. They were led by a monk from Iona called Aidan, who founded his monastery on the island of Lindisfarne, close to the chief royal residence of Bamburgh. Bede tells us that Aidan could speak very little Englisc and King Oswald, who had learnt Gaelic during his exile, often acted as his interpreter. It is noteworthy that the first three bishops were Scots/Irish – Aidan, Finan and Colman – and the next two Anglians were trained in the traditions of the Celtic Church – Tuda and Eata.

More importantly for my purposes is the fact that Aidan brought Old Melrose into the sphere of the Lindisfarne See. This meant that Bede's *Ecclesiastical History of the English People* contains the first written accounts of Old Melrose and Coldingham as part of the Northumbrian Church. That Bede never mentions Peebles may indicate that the presumed monastery there remained within the Columban sphere of Christianity during his lifetime.

Nobody can state catagegorically whether it was a new foundation at Old Melrose or there was a Columban monastery already there. My own inclinations would suggest that the latter is more likely as the site retained its Cumbric place-name, possibly on its reputation as a well-established Christian settlement.

Further Clues

In looking for further information, the 'eccles' names provide further evidence of a centre of Cumbric Christianity established in or before the late sixth century. Eccles in Berwickshire remained a religious establishment with a nunnery surviving until the mid sixteenth century. Ecclaw near Duns and Eccles Cairn in Roxburghshire are said to represent Celtic Christian enclaves in an early settlement of Anglians while they were still pagans.

'Kil' from Scots Gaelic 'ceall', and derived from Latin 'cella', has the meaning of church or cell and is usually followed by the name of a saint. There are only three possible 'kil' names in the Borders – Kilpallet could be the church of Palladius, the fifth century missionary. The names Killyminshaw and Kilochyet I am not going to even make a guess at in order to avoid embarrassment.

However 'kil' can be disguised as 'kiln' and there are many 'kiln' names in the Borders. In Selkirk 'Kiln Croft' never had a kiln of any kind but appears on early documents as 'Kilcroft'. Similarly 'Kilnknowe' in Galashiels was spelt as 'Kilknowe' until Victorian map-makers changed it to make the name more socially acceptable.

The now-vanished farm of Mount Common in the upper Ettrick Valley was written as Mountcolman in 1458. This may be a reference to Colman, the Irish monk of Iona who became Bishop of Northumbria but could not agree with the Northumbrian dating of Easter and left after the Synod of Whitby in 664; or may commemorate one of the other 217 St Colmans known.

East-west oriented graves in regular lines are taken to indicate Christian burial. These can be found in many parts of the Borders, usually with a small rectangular building in their midst. Given good conditions, such graveyards can be picked out on air photographs, but are much more easily found by divining rods though not so easily proven.

Churches bearing the names of saints Ebba or Abb, Aidan, Bathan or Bothan, Bede, Boisil or Boswell, Bride or Bryde, Cuthbert, Ethelrede, Gordian or Gorgon, Mungo or Kentigern and Ninian can be examined to see if the sites could fit in with an early Christian foundation. Some comparatively modern churches within old towns are probably on early Christian sites. The kirks at Channelkirk and Stobo have quite justifiable claims to have an early dating.

I have mentioned Kilcroft and Kilknowe above — both are on high banks near a river or at the point where two burns join. I always look at the site of St Mary's Kirk in Hawick and think that this fits the criteria to be an early Christian chapel or cell and there must be others; or maybe I have an over-active imagination.

Most of the possible locations only come into documentary recording in the twelfth century but the remains of a chapel at Abbey St Bathans was found to measure 11.6m by 4.7m and had 'a small chancel' at the east end, which does suggest an early Christian church.

Evidence Sought

Archaeological evidence for major early Christian centres within the area of the Borders is scarce and will continue to remain so until excavations are made on one or more of the possible sites. Old Melrose, Peebles and Coldingham are recognised as likely to have been centres and of these the most convenient for investigation is Old Melrose.

Old Melrose

'The site of Old Melrose is one of great importance on account of its association with famous names of the very distant past.' (*Inventory of Roxburghshire*).

The location of the site has never been in doubt but, like the nearby Roman fort of Trimontium, there is very little visible above the ground. For this reason, little is known about the monastery other than what can be gleaned from ancient records. Historians quote Bede and leave it at that; archaeologists have left the site strictly alone.

All that visibly survives of the monastery of Old Melrose is the double-ditched vallum which can be traced across the peninsula at its narrowest point. Within the enclosed area would be the church and graveyard. Divining rods evidence points to the location of the church being to the east of the mansion building and situated in the middle of a group of graves on east-west alignment. Three graves have been found in this location but I have been unable to find out exactly where, when and by whom.

Without excavation, it is not possible to say what happened on this site. Bede gives the impression that it was a daughter foundation from Lindisfarne, interesting enough but not particularly important. Book-copying is one of the likely occupations of the monks; bookbinding certainly was. The original cover of the Lindisfarne Gospels was made by a man who lived and worked at Old Melrose. He was Ethelwald, Abbot of Melrose and 'he impressed it [the Gospel] on the outside and covered it as well he knew how to do'. To some this has been taken to mean that the Lindisfarne Gospels may have been written at Old Melrose.

For documentary evidence of Old Melrose and Coldingham we have to rely on the writings of Bede.

The Old Melrose monastery is recorded as being founded about AD 636 by Oswald, king of Northumbria who sent for Irish (ie Celtic) monks to establish the church in Northumbria. Aidan, the monk from Iona, had established himself at Lindisfarne and trained twelve Anglian boys in the ways of the Columban Church. This fixed Christianity in Northumbria in the Columban or Celtic rites.

At Old Melrose, the first recorded abbot was Eata, who was one of the Northumbrian monks trained by St Aidan at Lindisfarne. During his rule the monastery was at its peak as a centre for religious excellence. Amongst its early notables were St Boisil its first prior, now recalled by the village of St Boswells nearby; St Bothan whose name can be found in Bothendeanham, now Bowden; and St Bathan recalled in the Berwickshire village; but the best remembered is St Cuthbert.

Cuthbert was born in 634. His name is Anglian and he was raised in the Englisc-named village of Hruringaham, now vanished but the site was near Smailholm. When he was sixteen he rode to Old Melrose, a distance of about 5km, handed over his horse and spear to an attendant and sought training as a monk in the Columban tradition. Cuthbert was in the Old Melrose monastery during his novitiate and then went round the Borders, preaching and teaching. Cuthbert is credited with many miracles and his good deeds and philosophy were recorded by Bede. He became a prior, first at Old Melrose and then at Lindisfarne, reluctantly becoming bishop of part of Northumbria in 685.

He died in 687 and his cult was promoted until it became a strong political force. A book of the miracles which Cuthbert performed runs to three hundred pages and, although many are beyond modern belief, these accounts provide an accidental but valuable source of information about everyday life of that period.

But times were changing and politics were making inroads into religion. There had been an increasing schism amongst the Christians of Northumbria, and the Celtic Church of Columba was coming under threat from the Catholic Church of Rome. Like most divisions, the prizes were more temporal than spiritual, but the ostensible debate was about the date of Easter and what style of tonsure the monks should adopt. At the Synod of Whitby in 664, King Oswy of Northumbria decided that the Church of St Peter in Rome was more likely to hold the keys to the after-life than that of St Columba in Iona; a theoretical decision that was to affect the lives of millions for many centuries to come. Oswy was to find out six years later.

This did not mean an end to the Celtic Church. Anglian Christians did not suddenly spurn the Celtic traditions. Anglian students still went to Iona and Ireland to study and the peak of Northumbrian artwork shows continuing links between the Anglian and Celtic cultures. In church matters, a monk trained in the Celtic church was just as likely to become a bishop in the Northumbrian Church as an Anglian was. When convenient, the ruling made at the Synod of Whitby seems to have been ignored.

Bede uses his *Ecclesiastical History* to tell parables to illustrate how people should live their lives and what would happen if they didn't. The following is a parable of example which I have shortened.

Drythhelm

Around AD 700 there was a merchant called Drythelm who lived in Cunningham (Coldingham?) in the country of the Northumbrians. He was a good and worthy man but one night he took ill and died, to the loud lamentations of his family. However, at daybreak the next day he sat up and said that he had indeed died but had been restored to life again though now must lead a different life to that he had known. So he divided his worldly goods into three parts, with one for his wife, one for his children and the third to be given to the poor.

Then he left his home and went to the monastery of Mailros which was on a peninsula formed by a loop in the Tweed. There he sought admission and entered on such a life of prayer, penance and mortification of the body, that he was soon given a distant cell of his own.

Gradually he told of his experiences of the night he had died. 'A handsome man in a white robe lead me along a path; one side was fiery flames and on the other, raging hail and snow. Both sides were filled with men's souls; these wretches jumped from one side to the other to get relief from the burning flames and the bitter cold but this was to no avail.

Then I was left in a terrible darkness while shrieking devils dragged human souls and threw then down into a burning pit. These dark spirits rushed at me with glowing eyes and foul flames coming from their mouths and nostrils. With red-hot tongs, they tried to drag me to the pit but my guide saved me and led me to a high wall which stretched in all directions. When we got over the wall, there was a bright meadow with crowds of young, happy people and I thought that this was the Kingdom of Heaven.

My guide then told me that the horrible valley was the place where souls were tried and punished; that the fiery pit was indeed the mouth of Hell and the bright meadow was where the souls of the good people of the world waited until Judgement Day when they would enter the Kingdom of Heaven.

He then told me that I must return to earth to live a life of virtue and simplicity.'

For the rest of his life, Drythelm prayed, fasted and endured extreme physical penance. He would stand up to this neck in the Tweed during the coldest winter day reciting prayers. On emerging, he would not dry himself but let his wet habit dry on his body.

When asked how he could bear this extreme cold, he gave a typically Border answer 'Ah hae kent it caulder'; and about the fasting and abuse to which he subjected his body, he replied 'Ah've seen greater sufferin'.

For more than a century after this, Northumbria was one of the main centres of European culture. Its monasteries produced brilliant illuminated manuscripts and standing stone crosses; its craftsmen made superb jewellery of gold and semi-precious stones and its poems continue to be viewed as prime. One eminent scholar has pointed out that the entire culture was invigorated by the impact of books and the desire to learn for the sake of learning. Alcuin, a Northumbrian noble and advisor to Charlesmagne, was the foremost thinker of his day (735–804) and his advice was that you should 'never give up the study of letters but have such young men with you as are always learning and who rejoice more in learning than in being drunk'.

The Demise of Mailros

After Bede's death, Old Melrose as a religious centre disappears from surviving records, which does not mean that it was deserted – we just don't know. An incidental mention in the 'Historia Regum of Symeon' is that in 761, the second son of Eadbert of Northumbria, Oswin 'a noble aetheling', was killed in a severe battle which was fought for three days beside Eldunum near Mailros (Eildon near Melrose).

So both Eildunum and Mailros were recognisable settlements, both being on or near Dere Street and presumably worth fighting for. By implication, Mailros was the more important of the two.

The victor of the Battle of Eildon was Ethelwald 'who was also called Moll' but little is known of this self-appointed king who reigned until 765 when he was 'deprived' of the kingdom. However, it is quite possible that he settled in the Bowmont Valley where his name survived to appear many times in the Kelso Abbey records and in the present farm of Mowhaugh.

The monastery of Mailros, which was still the property of Lindisfarne, was destroyed by the Scots under Kenneth MacAlpin in 849. It was evidently rebuilt by 875 when it was said to serve as a resting-place for the remains of St Cuthbert, then being carried round the country to avoid desecration by Viking marauding bands.

It was deserted and ruinous in 1073 although some monks found shelter there in 1075. Shortly after this, a chapel dedicated to St Cuthbert was erected by the monks of Durham on the site of the monastery. Judging by the red sandstone gargoyle in the Melrose Abbey Museum, this must have been a stone building but no trace of this has ever been found.

In 1119 David the Earl, afterwards David I, in the foundation charter of Selkirk Abbey, gives the new abbey 'the vills of Middelham (Midlem), Bothendeanam (Bowden) and Aldona [Eildon] just as I posses them in lands, waters, wood and cleared ground and my whole lordship of Malros, by the middle street and middle well as far as the fosse and as the fosse marches falling into Tweed. [et totum dominium meum de Malros per medium vicum at per medium fontem usque ad fossam; et sicut fossa dividit, cadens in Twoda].'

For Earl David to call it a 'dominium' meant that Mailros was the centre of his estate or scir, and obviously a place of some substance if it had a middle well and middle street. Around 1133, David exchanged the church of St Mary at Berwick for the chapel of St Cuthbert at Mailros, which he gave to the Cistercians whom he brought from Rievaulx to the site of the present-day Melrose Abbey.

The chapel was burnt by the English in 1321 but restored when the Bishop of Galloway granted indulgences to those who made a pilgrimage to the chapel and contributed to the cost of rebuilding. A similar indulgence was granted by the Pope in 1437.

From Milne's *History of the Parish* written in 1743, we learn 'the convent is inclosed with a stone wall reaching from the south corner of the Tweed to the West corner of it, where the neck of land is narrow; the foundations of the wall are still to be seen. At the entrance to the convent, about the middle of this wall, there has been a house, built likely for their porters called yet "the Redhouse". The place where the chapel stood, is still called The Chapel-knowe'.

The building and then reconstruction of the mansion house and walled garden at the end of the peninsula in the eighteenth and nineteenth centuries have eradicated any traces of buildings and the double-ditched 'vallum monasterii' is the only visible remains of what was an important place in the early Christian story of the Borders.

St Aebbe's Monastery and Coldingham

Bede twice refers to a monastery 'which they call Coludi's Urbs' while two other sources refer to a monastery at Colodesbyrig and Colodaesburg. Bede gives a picture of Urbs Coludi as having lofty buildings, cells and sleeping places and oratories for prayers and reading.

This monastery may the foundation of Aebbe, sister of Oswald and Oswy, both kings of Northumbria who had converted to Christianity when the family sought refuge amongst the Scots/Irish. On her return, she may have founded the monastery which bore her name, on the cliffs at St Abb's Head in the 650s, but we are not specifically told that she did found the monastery but rather it was 'monasterium Aebbe abbatissae', the monastery in which Aebbe was abbess.

Two sites have been traditionally given as the location for the monastery, St Abb's Nunnery and St Abb's Kirk, both on promontories and both within earlier fortifications. Excavations in the 1980s settled on the headland known as St Abb's Kirk, now known as the Kirk Hill, as the site of the monastery. This was an ideal site for a monastery, a wild and desolate headland with a turf and clay rampart vallum monasterii to keep out the secular world.

The monastery was a double-house for men and women, with Aebbe as abbess, but this was not a success according to St Adomnan who complained that 'the cells that were built for prayer and reading have become haunts of feasting, drinking, gossip and other delights; even the virgins who are dedicated to God … spend their time weaving elaborate garments with which they adorn themselves as if brides, thus imperilling their virginity, or else make friends with strange men'.

The dating of St Aebbe's death and the destruction of her monastery is uncertain but both seem to have occurred between 680 and 686.

There is nothing known about St Aebbe from the time of Bede until the eleventh century when the beginning of a cult first started to appear. The most important development of her cult was the foundation of a priory by the monks of Durham at Coldingham, 3km from the original site of St Aebe's monastery on Kirk Hill. There is no known connection between the two foundations but the monks of Coldingham would have known of the local saint through Bede's works. The distance between the site of St Aebbe's monastery and the Priory of Coldingham can be compared with the distance between the twelfth century Cistercian Abbey at Melrose and the Columban/ Anglian foundation at Old Melrose.

There must have been an earlier settlement on the site of Coldingham priory as a bronze Saxon belt latch was found by grave-diggers around 1900.

Peebles

The case for Peebles being the centre of a early Christian diocese, or paruchia, rests on more solid evidence than that of Old Melrose and less on documentary sources because there are none known.

I have already given the explanation that 'Peebles' gives the derivation as the place of the flimsy buildings and that, around 1200, there were a number of Gaelic and Cumbric personal names suggesting a concentration of Christian belief. These are used only as incidental pointers to more positive proofs.

Professor Charles Thomas in his book on *Christianity in Roman Britain to AD 500*, uses a number of carved stones to suggest that there had to be an early Christian diocese based in Peebles, which served the Upper and Middle Tweed basin. These are inscribed 'locus sancti Nicolia episcopi' (the place of St Nicholas the bishop) and 'Neitano sacerdos' (Neitan the priest or bishop).

The first was reputedly found in 1261 on the site of the Cross Kirk but the stone has long since disappeared and no illustration is known. This is unfortunate as the lettering of the inscription could have dated it. If this stone is genuine, it would certainly place Peebles as an important centre for Christianity in the fifth century and there is similar use of 'locus' in the 'Petrus' stone at Whithorn.

This conclusion must be treated with some caution as 'Nicolas' does not come into religious popularity until the eleventh century. There are three possibilities: firstly that the reading is right and the stone is genuine, see the St Gorgian (a fourth century Christian martyr) dedication in Manor Valley; the reading could be wrong in which case the stone may be genuine; or the stone was a medieval invention intended to draw in pilgrims to the monastery.

In the thirteenth century there were a surprising number of relics of saints and kings uncovered, the most noteworthy of which was when the monks of Glastonbury just happened to find the bones of both Arthur and Guinevere, complete with name plate, in the abbey. This 'discovery' flattered Edward I of England as the saviour of his country and the Welsh because Arthur was a Welsh folk hero.

It also increased the numbers of pilgrims who came to fill the abbey's coffers; and still does to this day.

On surer ground is the kite-shaped stone which was removed from a wall in the Old Town district of Peebles in 1967. The shape of the stone (48cm long by 22cm at the top and 5–9cm in width) and a carved cross on both sides, shows that it was made to stand upright and be viewed from either side. On what is obviously the front is a Latin Cross with barred terminals and a reading 'Neitano Sacerdos'. The name is easy, Neitan is the Cumbric equivalent of Nechtan; but 'sacerdos' which could mean 'bishop' in the fifth century, had changed to 'priest' by the beginning of the seventh century. By its lettering, this stone is thought to date late seventh century/early eighth century. Either way it demonstrates that Peebles continued as a place of Columban Christian worship into the period of Anglian expansion.

This fits into the period when Irish/Scots monks were taking Christianity into Anglian territories with their monasteries at Lindisfarne, Old Melrose and Coldingham. I have the impression that Peebles must have remained with the Columban Church until 731 otherwise Bede would have made some reference to it in his *History*.

To return to Professor Thomas's postulation that a possible sub-Roman Christian diocese was based in Peebles. Certainly one stone and a suggestive place-name does not constitute proof but the area around the town has produced several objects which strengthen the theory.

The Manor Valley requires further investigation. Firstly, it has retained a Cumbric 'Maenor' in its name, a sign of longevity in the out-of-the-way valley. Secondly, there are two items of evidence which would give clear indications of an early Christian community in the upper valley.

Near the top of the valley, where the Newholm Hope Burn runs into the Manor Water, a number of building foundations can be seen. Amongst these are the reputed remains of the chapel of St Gorgian. This unique dedication was so unlikely to be preserved in an desolate upland valley in the Borders that the ascription was viewed with grave suspicion. However, in 1890 an early memorial stone with a comparative dating was found in a cairn 200m west of the enclosure.

The stone was a memorial to a woman called Coninia. The inscription and the remains of the cross-patty carved in front of the legend, tells us that she was a member of an early Christian community. Taken together, they might explain why the much later parish church of Manor is dedicated to the obscure Christian martyr.

As noted on p.158, a Roman-type stylus was found in a field at Chapelhill, just north of Peebles. Knowing it was a good find on an unusual site, I took it in to the National Museum of Scotland where it was identified as a fifth-century copper-alloy stylus of an Anglo-Saxon type.

Being found near the site of a chapel and of an early date, it is reasonable to suppose that the chapel could also have been there in the fifth century when writing and the means of writing would be an essential part of religious life. The stylus may also show that the Roman method of communication by wax writing tablet was still in use in the sub-Roman period.

There will be other unrecognised places of worship in the surrounding countryside, such as Stobo, the main structure of which dates from around 1120, but tradition has it that it stands on the site of an earlier church which was founded by St Kentigern in the sixth century. This may be true. Religions are very conservative by nature and Stobo was an important 'mother church' in early medieval times with outlying chapels at Tweedsmuir, Daywick, Drumelzier and Broughton.

Other Sites

Early ecclesiastical sites are not necessarily monastery-based and there will be some still waiting to be found by casual happenstance.

Not all inscribed stones of the early Christian period bear distinctly

Christian symbols and, this lacking, we have to rely on the wording and type of lettering of the inscription to identify Christian burials.

The Liddesdale Stone

In 1933 part of the dyke standing where the Ralston Burn joins the Liddel Water at NY 491 889, was washed away by a flood, leaving the stones in the bed of the river. Amongst these was a large stone with an inscription cut longitudinally in three lines. These read 'hic iacit/caranti fili/cvpitiani' (here lies Carantus, son of Cupitianus). The lettering is a mixture of Roman/Celtic traditions and is similar to stones of the fifth /early sixth centuries while the names Carantus and Cupetianus occur on similarly dated monuments in Merionethshire.

April 2008. Investigation with divining rods on this area shows that the reported location of the stone was within a double palisaded enclosure with closely packed graves on an east–west alignment. The walls of the palisade were 3m apart. In the middle of these is a building measuring 7m by 4m, with a narrow wall-base and postholes. As the river is washing away the bank, there is the possibility of further finds.

Early Christianity in Selkirkshire

Despite being the smallest and poorest county in terms of ancient monuments, Selkirkshire has produced the most evidence of early Christianity in the Borders. Perhaps this is because Selkirkshire, with its poor soil and colder, wetter climate, was last to be agriculturally developed and this happened at a period when the country people were more aware of their past.

There is also the fact that many of the early Christian holy men preferred to spend their final days in the solitude of wild places and some place-names in Selkirkshire give indications of early Christian hermits. In total, Selkirkshire has two inscribed stones, two cist cemeteries of early Christian dating, one proven Anglian Christian cemetery and three still to prove, three place-names with early Christian 'hermetic church' site names, and several other locations where later Christian chapels and kirks could be on the sites of earlier foundations.

But leaving the speculative, we will take the obvious first.

The Over Kirkhope Stone

In the mid 1850s Walter Elliot, shepherd in Over Kirkhope near the top of the Ettrick Valley, decided to enclose a portion of the hill next to the farmhouse to make an in-bye field.

With help from his son Jim, he ploughed the rough ground, dug some drains and used the stones turned up by plough and spade to build an enclosing dyke. While they were doing this, they noticed that some of the larger stones had rude figures carved on one side. The best one was kept and built into the dyke at the end of the house while the others were broken in two to serve as convenient thru-stanes for the field dyke and, presumably, are still there.

This story was passed down to my father from his grandfather, Jim Elliot, who was the original finder. Jim Elliot died in 1922 when my father was twenty-one, so I have no reason to doubt the story. Unfortunately, my father never discovered exactly where the stone was found.

The stone was recognised as being of some importance and was exhibited to the Society of Antiquaries of Scotland in 1885 and 'temporarily placed' in the Museum of Antiquities in Edinburgh; it can be seen in the Museum of Scotland in Chambers Street.

The Over Kirkhope stone is a slab of the local greywacke, 1.22m in length by 33cm in width and 10cm thick. It is carved on one face with a figure about 40cm high. The head is over-large with the features roughly drawn in full face, and curly hair is indicated. The hands are raised to shoulder height with the palms turned outwards. The body is clad in a tunic which reaches to the knees and the feet are bare and turned to the right. There is a small cross on the breast and two circles with dots in the middle which are supposed to represent candlesticks. These are all made by pocked technique.

Further marking made on the stone by a nail or knife, in contrast to the original pocked method, are a small cross by the head of the figure, a panel with the initials PP, and a natural flaw in the stone being made to resemble a phallus by some additional scratching.

The top of the stone has been hollowed into an oblong cavity, 18cms in length, 5cms in width and 2.5cms in depth. This hollow has been un-noted in written reports.

It is very unlikely that the unremarked hollow is natural and my suggestion is that it performed a similar function to the saucer-shaped hollows on the tops of Roman altars – to hold liquid for some form of religious ceremony.

The Over Kirkhope stone is the type of early Christian memorial stone known as orants or orantes. The standing figure with uplifted arms and palms to the front represents the early Christian gesture of submissive prayer and, although known in Romano-British Christian art, is unique north of Hadrian's Wall. The few known orantes in Britain are generally dated to the fourth century but the Over Kirkhope stone has been estimated to the early sixth century. This may be correct, in which case it must represent an ancient form of Christian belief surviving in the upper Ettrick valley.

The visible foundation mounds of five rectangular buildings are 500m to the north-west of the farmhouse. These are taken to represent the chapel and village which grew around it. (See *Inventory of Selkirkshire* No. 77.) However, it must be noted that traces of alluvial gold have been found in the vicinity recently and the houses are as likely to have sheltered gold prospectors.

Kirkhope Farm, near Ettrickbridgend

With one kirk hope in the valley referred to as Upper Kirkhope, by deduction there must be another somewhere down the valley known as Lower Kirkhope. There is one but it is simply Kirkhope, inferring that it was there first and did not need a descriptive placing.

In Craig-Brown's *History of Selkirkshire*, we read: 'Although the name is ancient and indicates the existence of a church at a very early period … the absolute silence of ancient and modern records in regard to Lower Kirkhope suggests, on the other hand, a church that had disappeared before the time of even the oldest charters'.

The first recorded church in the parish was built at Ettrick-bridgend in 1852.

I went to primary school at Ettrickbridgend and often played in the fields around the village. Yet it was only as a man in the extremely dry year of 1959, that I noticed a number of circles, lines and oblong/square shapes appearing in the parched grass in the fields in the aptly named

Midge Cleuch. The lines and circles were thin whereas the oblong/square shapes were bigger and greener, holding the moisture longer to the delight of a family of moles who left their mark in a series of square patterns across the fields. Moles are useful indicators of soil disturbance.

I have gone back to the site several times over the years. With divining rods, I am reasonably certain that there was a small church with a surrounding graveyard within a double palisaded enclosure, a number of grubenhauser and perhaps two larger timber halls. The grubenhauser would suggest a dating of eighth century or later, which rather destroys the reasoning that this Kirkhope is the earlier of the two.

The Yarrow Stone, Whitefield

The area between the Whitefield Cottage, NT 346 274 and the Warrior's Rest Cottage, NT 354 277 is a fluvio-glacial deposit measuring approximately 800m by 200m. In a previous chapter, I noted the twenty or more large cairns which were removed from this area: in this chapter, I aver that there is evidence of two Early Christian cemeteries and one slightly later though less well defined. This area seems to have been a burial place over two thousand years – could it be a Selkirkshire version of the 'Valley of the Kings'? That is not a facetious suggestion.

The area was known as Annan Street and this puzzles me. Taken at its face value, it certainly could be on the road to Annan, but no other part of the road up the valley bears the name so it is fairly safe to disregard that explanation. As a long-term burial place, it might come under the annaid/annat/annet umbrella of church/religious ground but the 'street' part has me puzzled.

In the eighteenth century, Annan Street was 'a barren moor, covered with stunted heather and a few peat mosses'. The farmer at the neighbouring farm of Whitehope and the minister of Yarrow had the privilege of casting peats and sods for firing and roofing while the minister could also graze his cow on any suitable grass. Both took so much out of the land that there was soon 'not a turf to be had'.

When this happened, the factor to the Duke of Buccleuch gave permission to utilise the ground for whatever was possible. Although the farmer tried to break up the ground, it was so hard and stony that the plough could only scratch the surface so the attempt was given up in despair. However, the minister, anxious for a few acres to graze his cow, set his servant, 'a man not burdened with work and a horse with more bones than blood', to the task of subduing the stubborn 'soil'. During the course of the labour in 1803, a large flat stone of unhewn greywacke bearing a rude Latin inscription was unearthed and 'bones and ashes lay beneath it and on every side, the surface presented verdant patches of green'. At the time of its discovery it was lying horizontally and buried to a depth of 20cms. A later note by the Rev. James Russell clarifies that statement to 'on a spot presenting many verdant green patches'. The fact that the inscribed stone was thin and flat made a contrast to the two other rounded standing stones in the area.

The stone was conveyed to Bowhill House where it was examined by Duke Henry, Sir Walter Scott, John Leyden, Mungo Park and others 'of antiquarian lore' before being returned to be placed upright beside the road leading up to Whitefield, where it can still be seen. It is by no means certain that it is in its original position as several contemporary writers reckoned that it was found about 200m to the east.

However, my divining rods say that its present placing is in the middle of seventy or eighty grave-like shapes on an east-west alignment and these were surrounded by a wooden, double palisade. There was no indication of a building within the enclosure.

The inscription on the stone is in six vertical lines reading downwards and the text has been the subject of great discussion amongst academics since it was first discovered. The most likely reading is:

HIC MEMORIA PE[RP]ETV[A]
[I[N LOCO INSIGNISIMI PRINCI
PES NUDI
DUMNOGENI ' HIC IACENT
IN TVMVLO DVO FILII
LIBERALI

The Latin is of the type known as Vulgar which doesn't adhere to the rules of grammar and the carver was careless or couldn't read in the first place, so there many different opinions on the exact meaning: the most likely translation is 'This is an everlasting memorial. In this place lie the most famous princes Nudus and Dumnogenus. In this tomb lie the two sons of Liberalis.'

The general consensus of opinion is that the Yarrow stone was set up to mark the grave of two British (or Pictish) Christian chieftans and dates from the early sixth century. Whether Nudus and Dumnogenus were the two sons of Liberalis is another strongly debated point, as is the fact that the two princes seem to have been Damnonians of the royal house of Strathclyde.

Sir Walter Scott, with his usual flair and imagination, stated that Annan Street was the scene of terrible slaughter during a great battle and that the leaders were buried where they fell. This explained the amount of human bones strewn about the fields and this explanation was accepted as fact, as it still is by many. Who could doubt Sir Walter?

Warrior's Rest Cottage

On the eastern end of the Annan Street plateau, there is a standing stone at the south-east corner of the cottage known as the Warrior's Rest. While this cottage was being built in 1858, the workmen digging the foundations and levelling the ground to the south came across quantities of human bones and eight stone-lined cists aligned east-west. The cist stones were so large that straw ropes had to be wrapped round the iron wheel of the barrow to prevent it sinking into the ground while the stones were being moved from the site.

With no grave goods, these were obviously Christian burials. However, fragments of a Food Vessel pot, an Early Bronze Age ring of channel coal, a flint arrowhead and a broken hammer-stone were also found amongst the graves. The conclusion was that the site had been used for Bronze Age and Early Christian cemeteries.

With this in mind, I took divining rods to the field to the west of the cottage garden and found three lines of grave-shapes with two small rectangular buildings approximately 8m by 4m with a wall-base about 0.5m wide. These were of timber construction with post-holes every metre. Both buildings were within a double-palisaded enclosure. This fits the pattern of an early Christian church with surrounding graveyard.

The standing stone at the cottage is 1.60m in height, 1.75m round the base and 1.22m round the shoulder. There are no obvious markings on the stone and this may be a relic marking the religious site of a pagan age. There are no references to a standing stone on this site before the construction of the cottage, so it is more likely to have been a capstones from one of the cist graves.

A Later Cemetery

In the field immediately to the east of the Yarrow Stone, there is a rectangular cemetery with the closely-packed graves laid out in ten rows, aligned approximately east–west and enclosed by a double palisade. The foundations of a stone-based building measuring 9m by 5m internally with an apse-end on the east side, lies to the west of the cemetery at NT 35002 27546.

This type of cemetery is known at Yeavering and at Sprouston, Kirkhope (Ettrick) and Philiphaugh near Selkirk. Those in the Borders can be tentatively identified as seventh or eighth century but require extensive excavation or very clear air photographs before confirmation.

Additional Comments

While mapping out the grave positions in the Annan Street plateau, I did notice that they were all spread along the side of the present road, which is probably an early track up the valley. The eighteenth century graded road can be seen on the south side of the river.

On the bank on the north side of the Annan Street plateau, above the Whitehope Burn, there are three large buildings surrounded by a cluster of the 8m by 4m shapes that would suggest minor dwellings. By pinpointing the postholes, I can say with some confidence that these large buildings are Anglian halls, one 30m by 15m which has two internal rows of posts, and two 20m by 10m which have a single rows of posts in the middle; one of the halls has been further extended by 10m.

As these are all speculative and deduced by divining rods, I note them in passing rather than in hopes of belief. Perhaps another generation of humans and more sensitive machines will be able to confirm my findings.

With what is known about the piece of land called Annan Street and what is surmised, this is an area of great potential.

Philiphaugh near Selkirk NT 456 283

In 1980 I was putting up a new fence between the Cricket Club pitch and the most easterly of the fields on Philiphaugh farm. I was using divining rods to find the positions of the field drains when I found a number of shapes about 2m by 1m. They were in several rows, so I put them down to graves, probably from the Battle of Philiphaugh, the main part of which took place in that field. Amongst the grave shapes was a building about 8m by 4m at NT 456 285.

In July 1989, a series of air photographs of the same field revealed three rectangular buildings defined by continuous walltrenches and several rectangular patches of the same size suggesting the sunken-floored buildings known as grubenhauser.

In the north-east corner of the field is part of a substantial square, double-palisaded enclosure, of which parts of the south and west boundaries are visible and joined by a rounded right-angled corner. The shape is reminiscent of a Roman camp or fort but was overlooked on the north side by a steep bank and nothing Roman has ever been found on the site.

To the south of this, a cemetery with tightly packed graves aligned east-west appeared on the air photographs. This was what I had discovered by accident nine years before.

A number of continuous wall-trenches marked out a field system of Anglian appearance, which is similar to that of the tentative phase three revealed by air photographs at Sprouston.

It is noted that Sprouston is denoted by an Anglian name 'Sprow his ton'; as is Selkirk Seleskirke, 'the hall-kirk' or 'the church beside the hall'. So an Anglian settlement with a dating of seventh to eighth century is probable and this could correspond with the description of an 'old town' which lay near the river in David I's foundation charter of Selkirk Abbey in 1119. The 'old town' was distinct from the 'King's Selkirk' and the 'Abbot's Selkirk', making three distinct settlements called Selkirk in the twelfth century.

In 1991, the Roman gold ring which I described in a previous chapter, was brought to me by a metal detectorist. He told me that he found it at the west end of the same field at NT 455 284. On fieldwalking with divining rods, I found three rows of posts in a shape that suggests an Anglian hall, around 20m by 9m with a row of posts up the middle with doorways in the middle of both the long sides and one at the south end. This does not show in the present air photographs but I record it for future reference.

Chapels and Kirks

The place-name evidence of two 'kil' sites and a Mount Colman, I have given above, but it is always worth looking at the places which are known to have been early chapels or kirks and even fields which have these in their place-names. If the site compares with other known early Christian sites, these must be considered as possibles, and I commend the following for consideration.

Chapelhope is at the head of the Loch of the Lowes and derives its name from a chapel which measures 7.5m by 4.2m on an east-west alignment. It is apse-ended on the narrow east end and has a door in the middle of the south side. This lies within a circular enclosure 15m in diameter, within another wide-banked circle 40m in diameter. A series of closely-packed graves were in the space between the two circular walls.

Other wall-traces nearer the river show that it has been a considerable village at some period, but this is likely to have been from 1436 when James I erected the Melrose Abbey holdings in the Ettrick Forest into a 'free regality' where the baillies of Rodono dispensed justice on behalf of the Abbot of Melrose. These justice courts were held on an artificial mound known as the 'Standard Knowe'.

St Mary's Chapel, Yarrow, first came into recorded history in 1292 when Edward I of England appointed 'Adam de Letham' to the Church of the blessed Mary of Farmainishope. It was probably around this time that the lochs became St Mary's; previously they had been known as 'lwch' (which sounds like lowes but is Cumbric for a lake).

Buccleuch Kirk in Rankilburn survives only as grass-grown wall-mounds but would be an ideal site of an early hermetic church, but no evidence of this has come to light. Local legend has it that a gold cup and a silver basin were buried nearby at the time of the Reformation but even Sir Walter Scott and James Hogg together failed to find either.

There are certainly others at which I have not quite had time to look.

EARLY HISTORIC SELKIRKSHIRE. SEVENTH TO ELEVENTH CENTURY

If the early ecclesiastical history of Selkirkshire is convincingly rich for such an agriculturally poor county, in other remains it is surprisingly poor. Not that the area was deserted, as the Christian monuments and names suggest that it was populated enough to sustain both a religious and a ruling elite but, as usual, definite proof is lacking. In fact we have only one linear monument which can be attributed to this period and we have to rely on the study of place-names to fill in the spaces in our knowledge.

The Catrail or Picts' Work Dyke

In his book *Itinerarium Septentrionale*, 1728, Gordon, an eighteenth-century antiquary, claimed a continuous 'limes' extending from Gala Water to the Peel Fell in Liddesdale, a distance of fifty miles, but this was a wish-fulfilment to back his claims of a Romano-Caledonian frontier after Caracalla had made peace with the northern natives by bribery.

Victorian historians tended to go along with the limes suggestion and several confirmed many of the man-made earthworks. In more modern times, the archaeologists and historians who reported in the Ancient Monuments Counties surveys of Roxburgh and Selkirkshire were dubious that it was a fifty-mile continuous boundary but conceded that several parts of the linear earthwork may be worth study and that 'it would be reasonable to ask whether a corresponding kernel of truth can be extracted from the statements made by Gordon and those who followed him about the Selkirkshire components of the discredited fifty-mile work.'

Translated, this means that there may have been something in Gordon's original theory even although the given line of the Catrail comprises shorter sections of ditch and bank which may, together with burns and ridgeway roads, make up a recognised boundary; a line of demarcation rather than a defensive barrier to keep people out or in. In several places, it is a ditch and mound construction with the mound changing sides for no apparent reason and this cancels out the defensive structure theory.

I have explained that my interest in the language of the placenames of the Borders was kick-started at the Riding Stane where the Catrail crosses the Tweed. This intrigued me to take the interest further and when I looked at the settlement names along the line of the Victorian version of the Catrail, I found that the early Anglian names were on the better agricultural land while the Cumbric names tended to be hillier ground.

So it is a reasonable suggestion that, at some period, the Catrail, visible, projected or imagined, did constitute a recognised boundary between the ploughing Anglians and the grazing Cumbrians. Within the enclosed area are Selkirk, Galashiels, Ashkirk, Howden, Oakwood, Helmburn etc, and Sunderland is the ground sundered or divided by the line of the Catrail, while Sundhope Burn is the 'hope' that the Catrail uses to cross into Ettrick.

As far as dating goes, the site known as Auld Wark in Yarrow was formerly Edibredshiels which is likely to commemorate Eadbert, the king of Northumbria who was expanding his kingdom in the 750s. Auld Wark seems to have been the centre of a group of Anglian names like Lewinshope (Leofwine's hope) and Fastheugh (the defensible hill) and could have been an early Anglian scir. On the other hand, the site also appears as 'Cathermauch' or a variation thereof, which could be Cumbric or Gaelic for a fort or a seat/established headquarters or even a fairy knoll. Auld Wark was the centre of the court of the Forest until the New Wark was built in 1406. In the Exchequer Rolls of 1497–1501, the two forest settlements of Catkermach are on the sites of Auld Wark and Carterhaugh and it was at Carterhaugh that the ballad of Young Tamlane is placed. I think that this ballad is the most Gaelic in content of all the Border ballads but this could be a coincidence.

With a Catkerwood further up the valley, these might be traces of an earlier Cumbric maenor but that is only conjectural.

At the top of the Yarrow Valley, there are a number of places with distinctly Cumbric names to suggest that there was a maenor there until

David I included the area in his Forest of Ettrick in the twelfth century. The centre could have been where the three stedes of Fayrmaenhope suggest a stony farm; the Loch of the Lowes combines Scots Gaelic and Cumbric as 'the lake of the lakes'; Berrybush is 'bar-y-bwlch' the top of the pass; Eltrefe is a 'tref' settlement name, and other names in the Megget and upper Yarrow are convincing enough to encourage a philologist to take this study further, with the caution that an interested amateur has bother in deciding whether a place-name is Gaelic or Cumbric.

There is a similar concentration to the top of Ettrick and the Tima valleys, where Ettrick Pen is the top of Ettrick; Mighop in 1455 is now more realistically named Midgehope; the Dalglieshes were 'dal or dol glais'; the green meadow and Mount Common was 'mont Colman'; the hill of the Columban priest, Colman. More study is required before any convincing conclusions can be reached.

As the Borders has a long history of linguistic immigration with people coming from all sides, it is important to note what they brought with them and what is left behind. Even negative evidence is valuable. Distribution maps of Scots Gaelic names in Scotland show that Gaelic was never the language of everybody south of the Forth-Clyde line, but there has been a Gaelic-speaking elite who left their mark on the place-names of the Borders.

I have previously told the totally fictional tale of how Scotts of Buccleuch first acquired land in the Borders and how the local pronunciation of Bacloo was actually from two Gaelic words 'bal' and 'cliabh' meaning the settlement in the hollow. The vanished stede of Bellendaine is reckoned to be the Gaelic 'house of the Dean', a linguistic relic from the days when the Abbot of Melrose held the lands and had a dean in residence to care for it.

In the Ale Water, Salenside (sailin, a spur of land) and Essenside (easen, a small rapid) are descriptive of the respective locations.

IN CONCLUSION

To sum up the history of Selkirkshire for the four hundred years between the seventh and eleventh centuries, we have to admit that we know very little for sure. This is not because there was nothing happening here but rather that it was not important enough for someone to write down and preserve.

Christianity was strong enough to leave tangible evidence in the county and place-names provide clues to suggest that we probably all spoke Cumbric at the time of Urien of Rheged c.580. Some on the eastern corner of the county would speak Englisc from around 750 thanks to Eadbert of Northumbria and a few of the upper strata of society would converse in Scots Gaelic owing to the efforts of Giric I, the king of Scots from 878 to 889.

None of these variants would result in mass elocution lessons for the bulk of the population who would continue speaking as they always did, but each wave of linguistic settlers brought a fresh vigour to the dialect we know as Border Scots.

Gradually the Englisc of the Anglian settlers became the dominant speech of eastern Selkirkshire while the hillier western regions are thought to have retained Cumbric/Early Welsh until the twelfth or thirteenth centuries.

The linguistic dividing line is the Catrail, real or imagined, and there are enough Cumbric place-names at the top of Yarrow and Ettrick/Tima to put a tentative claim for two 'maenor' estates there.

At the eastern end of the county there is a good claim for the centre of 'Seleskirke scir' based at Philiphaugh which shows Anglian halls and a field system, or at Edibertshiels which, as Auld Wark, survived as a centre of the forest courts until the fourteenth century. Another may have had its centre at The Rink, the 'lann Giric', named after Giric II the king of Scots who ruled from 997 to 1005.

Leaving the suppositions of Selkirkshire, we are on firmer ground when looking at what happened in the rest of Scotland, at least as far as the kings and battles are concerned.

Kenneth Mac Alpin was the king of the Scots of Dal Riata in 840 and in 842 or 3 became 'king of the Picts' probably because the two kingdoms were suffering from heavy Viking raids and needed mutual protection. For this, he is known as the first king of 'Scotia' and the founding father of Scotland.

In fact, Kenneth only ruled the middle Highlands. In the north, Orkney, Shetland, Sutherland and Caithness were under Norse rule. In southern Scotland, the surviving British kingdom of Strathclyde stretched down the west coast and down into Cumbria, while the lands of Lothian and the Borders were largely in Anglian hands.

But it was a start. Kenneth Mac Alpin died in 858 and no less than fourteen of his male MacAlpin descendants ruled in succession until the death of Malcolm II in 1034.

By skilful diplomacy through a system of temporary alliances, some convenient deaths and a few successful battles, the MacAlpin kings established a strong Gaelic power base but the dynasty hit the buffers on the death of Malcolm II. Three men claimed the throne: Duncan, Malcolm's grandson, MacBeth of Moray, Malcolm's nephew, and Lulach of Moray, MacBeth's stepson. This was a period in history when the minor kings and major nobles were notably interbred and ruthlessly ambitious, changing alliances almost yearly. Consequently, the lineal descents of the kings and the battles in which they usually died are hard to separate.

Duncan won the first round of the dynastic battle, reigning from 1034 to 1040 and was killed in battle 'at an immature age' by MacBeth, earl or king of Moray (the man much maligned by William Shakespeare) who then ruled from 1040 to 1057. Macbeth was confident enough in his kingdom to be the only king of Scots to visit Rome, where 'he scattered money like seed to the poor'. Despite the defeat at Dunsinnan in 1054, he was finally killed in 1057 by Duncan's son, Malcolm Canmore. This is not an unusual story in medieval dynasties.

Macbeth was the first king of Scots to welcome Norman exiles from the English court in 1052, thereby initiating a trend that would change the cultural and ethnic landscape of Scotland for all times.

CHAPTER TEN
The Normans

The ninth, tenth and eleventh centuries were dominated by the peoples of Denmark, Norway and Sweden, now known collectively as Vikings. Why these Scandinavians should have such an influence over an area which stretched from North America to the Black Sea has never been satisfactorily explained. Climatic changes and an increasing population could have meant that there was no longer enough arable land to sustain each new generation and a proportion of them had to seek fresh pastures, figuratively and literally. Improvement in ship design and navigation made it easier for the seafaring peoples to get about the world whether as marauders or as traders and settlers, and soon the Vikings were carving out kingdoms and earldoms in all parts of Europe.

At the beginning of the tenth century, the king of the west Franks granted a substantial amount of land around Rouen to a Viking chief named Rollo. For defence of the kingdom of Frankia, further grants were made to Rollo and his descendants until the area became a separate political entity towards the end of the tenth century. These 'Northmen' or Normans quickly assimilated into the Frankish population, marrying local women, speaking a form of French and accepting Christianity but still retaining political and economic ties with Scandinavia and the Scandinavian settlers in Britain and Ireland. All the Vikings who did not wish to return to their families in Scandinavia were given a 'man's share' of land in Frankia and it is reckoned that five thousand men took up this offer, thereby becoming a ruling class; marriage to a wealthy heiress was an optional extra.

By the eleventh century, Normandy was the centre of an extensive movement of colonisation into Britain, Northern Europe and round into the Mediterranean. In demand as warriors, they soon had extensive lands and influence, becoming kings of England and Dublin and earls of Orkney and the Western Isles of Scotland. In fact, they were the spearhead of a new aggressive aristocracy that would create major changes in England, Scotland, Wales and Ireland. When Macbeth welcomed two Norman-French knights into his court, he was following the example of many other kings, seeing them as part of his military strategy for the protection of his kingdom. In fact the Normans were superior mercenaries who would fight for whoever gave them the best deal.

IN ENGLAND

Being nearest to Normandy, England received more than its fair share of Viking settlers in the tenth century. Although recognising the authority of the English kings, they also continued to follow their traditional laws in the land they controlled. This area was known as the 'Danelaw'.

In 1012 the English king, Aethelred, introduced an annual land tax to pay for the Norman mercenaries who had been recruited to protect his kingdom. The tax, Danegeld or Dane money, continued under Cnut, the Danish king of England and his sons, to pay for their own armies, before being abolished by Edward the Confessor in 1051.

Edward the Confessor was king of England from 1042 to 1066. He was Anglo-Norman, his mother being a daughter of Richard, count of Normandy and he was raised in Normandy. During his reign, he brought in Norman clerics to run the English church and built Westminster Abbey in the Norman style of architecture. At court, there was a constant battle between the Anglo-Norman favourites of the king and the Anglo-Danish party whose leader was Harold Godwinson, the Earl of Wessex.

When Edward died on the 5 of January 1066, Harold Godwinson claimed the throne as Harold II and had his coronation the next day, but there were three other claimants for the vacant throne – William the Bastard of Normandy, Sweyn II, king of Denmark and Harold Hardrada, king of Norway. It must be remarked that all four were Vikings or were of Viking descent, which makes nonsense of the belief that the eventual Battle of Hastings was a contest between the English and the French. In fact it was a scramble to see which branch of the Viking dynasties could claim most of England.

Harold Hardrada (the Ruthless) was first to make his move. He was a flamboyant character who had been in the Varangian Guard in Byzantium, had fought in Africa and Sicily, been to Jerusalem and married a princess of Kiev. Harold set sail as soon as he heard of the death of the Confessor, sailing by way of Orkney, collecting men and ships as he went and perhaps recruiting Malcolm III, king of Scots with promises of Northumbria. Harold moved south of the Tyne and entered the Humber, with his fleet, joining up with Tostig, Harold II's rebellious brother, then marching through the former Scandinavian kingdom of York until he met up with Harold II of England's forces at Stamford Bridge. The Norsemen were clobbered and both Hardrada and Tostig were slain.

Three days after the battle, William of Normandy landed his forces near Hastings, so Harold II turned his tired men southwards to confront the new invaders and made an epic forced march, covering two hundred and fifty miles in twelve days. This was an exceptional speed to move a medieval army; even the well-organised Romans reckoned that a legion could make a daily march of ten or twelve miles before making camp.

On the crest of Senlac Hill, Harold formed up his men in a shield wall and awaited the charge of the feudal knights of Normandy. Wave after wave of Norman cavalry could not breech the line of shields and battleaxes until the Normans were ordered to pretend to retreat. This drew the English shield wall out their position and into broken formation where they were more vulnerable to mounted horsemen. Harold was killed by an arrow piercing his eye, his huscarls (bodyguard) fought to the last man and Guillaume le Batard became Guillaume le Conquerant and William I, king of England.

William crowned himself in Westminster Abbey on Christmas Day 1066 and proceeded to terrorise the southern half of Britain over the next three years, erecting wooden temporary castles called 'motte and bailey' while forcing the people into submission to his rule. In 1069, William launched an attack on his Norse rivals in York but Sweyn of Denmark had a large fleet hovering along the coast to prevent just such an eventuality and which was available to seize the kingdom while the Norman forces were over-extended. Northumbria remained uncon-quered and was the focus of several envious eyes, principally from the north.

IN SCOTLAND

In Scotland, the son of Duncan I, Malcolm Canmore ('great leader' or 'big head') sought to avenge his father's death and retrieve his kingdom. With help from Siward, the Anglo-Danish Earl of Northumberland, who was probably his cousin, he defeated MacBeth at Dunsinnan in 1054 and again in 1057 where MacBeth was killed.

However, the kingship was awarded to Lulach, MacBeth's stepson, but Lulach was killed 'by treachery' after eighteen weeks on the throne, leaving Malcolm to claim the crown as Malcolm III.

At the period of his accession, Cumbria was still in Scottish hands and Northumbria was in turmoil. Seeing vacant possession available, Malcolm invaded Northumbria on five separate occasions – in 1061, 1070, 1079, 1091 and 1093, to reclaim what had been part of the kingdom of Bernicia. This stirred the hornets' nest every time and provoked an English counter-invasion. In 1072, the Conqueror himself marched his army as far as Tay and forced Malcolm 'to be his man', a vow that Malcolm had no intention of keeping if a suitable opportunity offered itself.

Recognising that the Scots would always be an irritation, the Normans decided to make a northern frontier by building a line of stone castles roughly along the route of Hadrian's Wall and anchored by the New Castle (1080) and Carlisle (1091) in the vicinity of where the Roman forts of Arbeia and Luguvalium had once stood. The lands on each side of this line were granted to Norman, French and Breton adventurers on the basis of 'we grant you these lands in the King's name, hold them if you can and pay man-service to the King'. Thus, Cumbria and parts of Northumbria were planted with Norman landowners and a sizable Norman population who were placed to repel invaders from the north.

Despite this, Malcolm III on his final incursion into Northumbria in 1093, found time to lay the foundation stone at Durham Cathedral. This was to be one of his final acts before he and his eldest son Edward, were killed in an ambush near Alnwick.

His death caused much dynastic confusion. Malcolm had been married twice, once to Ingibiorg of Orkney by whom he had a son, Duncan, and then to Margaret, sister of the exiled English prince Edgar the Aethling. Margaret produced six sons and two daughters. That marriage opened up the way for many external influences to pour into Scotland, most especially in religious faith and ecclesiastical organisation.

Queen Margaret is credited or blamed for introducing English ways and people into the rough Scottish court of Malcolm. This had been resented by the Gaelic establishment of Scotland who elected Donald Bane, Malcolm's brother, to reign as Donald III, king of Scots. Queen Margaret died within days of hearing the news of her husband's death and the 'Englisc' influences were driven out of Scotland by the new king and his Celtic supporters. These refugees included the remaining sons of Malcolm.

Donald reigned for a year before he, in turn, was driven out by Duncan, the son of Malcolm and Ingibiorg. Duncan was a Celt who had been brought up as a Norman knight and he attained the throne thanks to an Anglo-Norman army provided by William Rufus (William II of England). Duncan's reign was short – winning his throne in May 1094, he was killed in November of the same year and Donald III reigned again until 1097.

Edgar, King of Scots 1097–1107

Next in line was Edgar, Queen Margaret's third son who reigned for ten years. He had been placed on the throne of Scotland thanks to the Anglo-Norman forces of William Rufus and additionally he held lands in England, so from then on Scotland took a more pro-Anglo/Norman stance. The centre of Scotland's political life had moved from the Gaeldom of Malcolm Canmore and into the Lowlands. Power now rested in the hands of the native Lowland aristocracy with a leavening of Anglo-Norman-French-Breton knights who had continental connections in lands and trade. This brought fresh influences and ideas into what was an often inward-looking society.

The reign of Edgar was a period of reconciliation and repairing fences. The Norman kings of England, William Rufus and then Henry I (1100–1135), were having serious trouble on the Welsh Marches as well as in their French possessions, and consequently, were quite happy to have a quiescent northern frontier. By inference, it is likely that the lands of the Borders had been so devastated by Malcolm III's savage raids into Northumbria and Anglo-Norman counter-invasions, that there would be areas of total devastation with few people living on fewer resources.

To re-inhabit the part of the Borders that had suffered most, Edgar granted estates to those of his trusted followers who would have the strength of will and arm to hold them. That such men were English and Anglo-Norman is evident in the place-names of the lower Tweed. The fact that Norman society preferred to have their land grants recorded in writing, is appreciated by later historians.

Although surviving written evidence is scarce, two preserved letters show that sometime in Edgar's reign, Thor Longus had been granted the lands of Ednamshire when it was 'waste'. However by 1105, the new thane was proudly writing that he had built a church at Ednam at his own expense and that the king had endowed it with a ploughgate (104 acres) of land for its upkeep.

To the west of Ednamshire was the more important Hrock's burh (Roxburgh) on the peninsula at the joining of the Tweed and Teviot. It is a natural gathering point and the first place on the lower Tweed where it then was feasible to build bridges across the rivers, so it became a conurbation with the highest population in Scotland at the time. As well as the castle and burgh on the peninsula, there were three other vills in the immediate vicinity – Maccus Vill now Maxwellhaugh, Easter Kelso where the present town and abbey stands and Wester Kelso, the site of which lies under the entrance to Floors Castle. A further ring of vills lay around the central location with Old Roxburgh, Heiton, Sprouston, Ednam, Nenthorn, Stichill and Makerston making up the original Hrocksburh scir (Roxburghshire). How many of these were held on thane's/knight's service is not known.

What is known is that there was a sheriff of Roxburgh in the early twelfth century. This royal officer, a 'scir-gerefa', literally a shire steward or shire officer who would had the responsibility to the king for the taxes and man-service of the vills within his shire. The first known sheriff of Roxburgh was Cospatrick, son of Uhtred, son of Ulfkil whose pedigree traces back three generations of Border history. Grandfather Ulfkil left his name in Oxton, originally Ulfkil's toun; father Uhtred served two bishops of Durham as thane of Hexhamshire in Northumberland; Cospatrick who served David the Earl, later David I, as sheriff of Roxburgh, and was important enough to be a witness to the foundation charter of Selkirk Abbey. (See p.273)

Amongst the names of the 'new' men who were thanes in the Borders or, at least, had incorporated their names in their estates there, were the Orms, Eadulfs, Sweins and Liulfs. The name of Maccus stands out, for not only was he founder or owner of the vill near Roxburgh but also Maxton, the toun of Maccus and possibly Longformacus, the shieling of Maccus. A pool in the river Tweed near Kelso is known as Maxwheel – this is the 'weil' (a deep/slow running pool) of Maccus – perhaps he liked fishing as well.

It is interesting that the names show a linguistic mixture of the various races where the basic Celtic/Germanic stock of Cumbric and Anglian origin is joined by the Scots Gaelic and Scandinavian later arrivals. This cannot be a definitive study as only the landowners and those 'of a lesser rank of nobility' are included. The bulk of the population, probably 99 per cent, remain unrecorded and thus unknown.

The reign of Edgar was not plentiful in documentary evidence of the Borders; this may be because no news is good news or even that few happenings were worth writing about, but one important survivor is the document whereby Edgar granted a charter for the lands of Coldinghamshire to the monks of St Cuthbert at Durham in 1095. This was issued by Edgar in the churchyard at Norham on the English side of the Tweed and witnessed by his brothers Alexander and David. In the document Edgar was described as 'son of Mael Colium king of Scots, possessing the whole of Lothian and kingship of Scotland by gift of my lord William, king of England and by paternal heritage'. The wording makes it clear that Edgar was recognised as king of Scots by William and also gives a clear reminder to whom he owed his kingdom.

The document gives us the extent and structure of Coldingham-

shire at a period when the small individual scirs were being enlarged
into the shires under royal officers. The dominium or centre would have
been at Coldingham and the supporting vills of Lumsdaine, Renton,
Swinewood, two Aytons (another likely candidate for the dominium),
Prenderguest, Renton and (?)Ferney were feeder communities,
supplying the lord with supplies of food and manpower when required.
The unlocated 'Crammesmuthe' could be at Eyemouth or less probably
at Burnmouth.

Edgar relied on his Anglo-Norman allies for the security of his
throne. In 1098, he came to terms with Magnus, king of Norway that
he would not dispute the claims of Norway to the Western Islands. This
was to bring a measure of peace to the long-ravished western seaboard
and allow Edgar to concentrate his energy and resources on lowland
Scotland.

Meanwhile in England, William II, a man not known for his tact or
diplomacy, was 'accidentally' killed while out hunting in his New Forest
in 1100 and his youngest brother, Henry, took the opportunity to have
himself crowned king of England before his older brother, Robert,
could return from the First Crusade to claim the throne.

Henry moved quickly to consolidate his coup, marrying Matilda,
the daughter of Malcom Canmore of Scotland and niece of Edgar the
Atheling, thereby creating a dynastic link with the old English royal
family and an alliance with the kingdom of the Scots at the same time.
Marriages amongst the nobility were made to secure useful allies and
Henry had a number of illegitimate daughters whom he parcelled out
to the minor kings and great nobles in Britain and Europe. His legitimate marriage was to have profound effects on the future of Scotland
and the Borders. With Matilda as his wife and her three brothers, Edgar,
Alexander and David, having been brought up in his court as Norman
knights, Henry was relatively secure in his northern frontier.

During his lifetime, Edgar had allowed his next brother Alexander
to rule most of the country between the Forth and Solway. This system
was called appanage, a device whereby a portion of the royal lands was
assigned to the younger son or heir to maintain his following and
perhaps to give him experience in maximising the use of people and
land. That Edgar made this grant is an indication that he considered
Alexander to be his heir. No such provision was made for David, the

youngest son of Malcom Canmore and Queen Margaret, who was being raised as a poor Norman knight but now had the added prestige of being 'brother to the Queen'. This rise in status was to prove very beneficial to his future prospects.

Alexander I, King of Scots 1107–24

When Edgar died childless in 1107, Alexander became king of Scots as Alexander I, ruling from 1107 to 1124.

Under the law/custom of appanage and by Edgar's bequest, Alexander was to be king and rule from the Forth/Clyde line northwards in the old Gaelic kingdom while David, his younger brother, would govern Strathclyde and Lothian in his brother's name. This power-sharing did not please Alexander; for while he ruled the larger share of the kingdom, it was also the poorest and most troublesome. Meanwhile in southern Scotland, David would be able to enjoy the benefits of the more prosperous better land and the support of Henry I of England who provided him with estates in England through marriage to a wealthy widow. Additionally, most of Cumbria and Northumbria had been planted with Norman settlers who would come to his aid if required.

If Alexander was prepared to accept this division during Edgar's life, he was not willing to keep his promises once he was king. David only received his inheritance with assistance from his Norman friends as they continued to remind him even thirty years later. At the Battle of the Standard in 1138, Robert Bruce is reputed to have said 'You, yourself, O King, when you demanded from your brother Alexander, the part of the kingdom which at his death your brother [Edgar] bequeathed to you, obtained without bloodshed all that you wanted through fear of us'. The inference is that Alexander only gave up the southern part of Scotland on the threat of military intervention. When David did secure his inheritance is unknown but, six years after Edgar's death, he was in enough control of the area to found an Abbey near Selkirk.

Perhaps as a gesture of conciliation, King Alexander in his role of an English landowner led one of the divisions of Henry's army in an invasion into Gwynedd in 1114 and is credited in the *Welsh Chronicle* with making peace between Gruffudd ap Cynan and Henry.

Alexander further cemented friendly relations with his powerful brother-in-law in the same year, by marrying one of Henry's illegitimate daughters, Sybilla, who was recorded as having neither 'modesty nor refinement'. Perhaps for this reason, Alexander had no legitimate heirs although it is known that he had at least one son.

However, Sybilla died 1122 without having produced an heir to the Scottish throne, so unless Alexander remarried quickly and his new wife produced one or more sons, Henry's plans for Anglo-Norman domination of the British Isles would be disrupted.

If Alexander died without heir, William, son of Duncan II, had the best claim to the throne of Scotland with David, the youngest son of Malcolm Canmore being second in line.

In the early 1120s, Alexander seems to have regarded William fitzDuncan as his potential heir and he appears in royal Scottish acts as 'the king's nephew' or 'my nephew'. William had strong connections with his mother's kinsmen in Cumberland, then a stronghold of the Anglo-Normans from the base of Carlisle and he appears to have been in Alexander's court in the early 1120s.

Despite the possible rivalry between the two claimants, it seems that William was supportive of Alexander, and then David, until his death in 1147 or 8.

Alexander was a moderniser although his efforts have been largely ignored by contemporary and modern historians and his achievements overshadowed by those of his brother David, whose reign was nearly twice as long. David had the benefit of a glowing account of life in his court written by Ailred of Hexham, afterwards Abbot of the Cistercian monastery of Rievaulx in Yorkshire, who had began his priestly duties in David's household.

Alexander continued the reforming practices of his brother Edgar and his mother Queen Margaret by giving Augustinian canons the ancient church of Scone which had been a Scoto-Pictish religious and political centre for some considerable time. At the same time, he had a further three centres planned at Inchcolm, Loch Tay and St Andrews but these had not been founded at the time of his death. Establishing new religious practices in sympathy with Continental norms and placing Englishmen in the new bishoprics was not popular, as the native clergy were largely hostile to foreigners in any form. For this reason, Alexander was careful to preserve the independence of the Scottish Church.

In April 1124, Alexander died and David became king of Scots. Abbot Ailred of Rievaulx claims that Alexander 'had not sought the Kingship but abhorred it and had only accepted because there was no other acceptable alternative'.

David MacMalcolm

David was born *c.*1085 and, as sixth son of Malcolm III and Queen Margaret, had little expectation of improving his personal position.

Malcolm and his oldest son and heir, Edward, were killed at Alnwick on the 12th of November 1093 and Queen Margaret died four days later after being informed of the tragedy by her son Edgar. This removed the three people who provided the leadership and stability to the kingdom and it became a matter of urgency for the remaining sons to get out of the country. If they had not fled with 'the Englisc', it is unlikely that they would have survived. As their two sisters were already in their aunt's care in England, they fled southwards and arrived at the court of William Rufus in early 1094. William recognised the opportunity to secure his northern borders by accepting the boys for training as knights and as pawns in the continuing game of political kingsmanship.

In 1098, David was a peripheral figure in the English court. Third remaining son of a banished royalty whose older brothers were healthy young adults, the young prince, landless, penniless and without influence had little prospects of betterment. He had, however, found a place amongst the younger sons of nobles who clustered round William's court in the hope that they would achieve notice and personal fortune through service to the crown.

However, on 2 August 1100 the 'stray' arrow that ended the life of William Rufus, also opened an indirect window of opportunity for the young prince. The marriage of King Henry 1 to his sister had greatly improved David's prospects for, as 'brother to the queen', doors previously closed to him now stood open. He now had more immediate access to Henry I who seemed to take an interest in his young brother-in-law. Henry was establishing a new nobility by promoting men of ability to counterbalance the older and more settled Anglo-Norman and Norman-French magnates. This was a political move as the 'new men' depended on Henry's goodwill and support for their continuing prosperity.

This period formed David's character. His later life shows that he was a young man of talent and ambition, willing to watch and learn. It is thought that he would have been admitted to the king's inner circle of advisors and officials at an early age, learning at first hand the methods of royal government, administration and law.

This was to stand him in good stead when his brother Edgar, king of Scots, died in 1107. Now Alexander was king of Scots and, in accordance with Edgar's wishes, David had responsibility for the province of Lothian from Forth to Tweed and the whole of the kingdom of Strathclyde except for Galloway.

David the Earl

It is thought that David was unable to claim the whole of his inheritance from Edgar for several years although he seems to have control over parts of Tweeddale and Teviotdale. The dispute over this was only settled when Henry travelled north to York in July 1113 to persuade Alexander to hand over the southern half of his kingdom, and when this threat of invasion was successful, David ruled the vast area as a vassal of his brother Alexander with the clear connivance of Henry who wanted a man he could trust in control of the whole the Anglo-Scottish border line.

As lord of the territory, the recording clerks gave him the title of Prince of the Cumbrian Region or Prince of the Cumbrians but were careful to add 'he was not in truth lord of the Cumbrian kingdom'. There are only fragmentary hints that he was actually in the area during this time. These three provinces of southern Scotland still looked on themselves as separate entities rather than as part of a united kingdom; in this they reflected the Early Historic kingdoms of Strathclyde, Bernicia and Cumbria.

During the formative years when the kingdom of Scotland was taking shape, its border with England was formed by the Cheviot hills. This was an inhospitable barrier of wilderness which meant the English conquest of southern Scotland had to go as far as the Forth before it could find a defensible frontier while the Scots needed to advance as far as the Tyne for the same security. The early Norman kings of England were too busy protecting their gains on the Continent and Wales to make any serious bid to extend its frontier northwards. The kings of Scots had no such qualms, casting greedy eyes and armed raids into Northumbria, usually with unfortunate results on both sides.

David had spent most of his early life in the Anglo-Norman courts and in France where he acquired a culture that was rare in his native land. While moving through the Continent as a member of the Anglo-Norman court or as part of Henry's army, he was learning his trade as a knight and leader of men while seeing the innovations which were taking place there. This was a time of renewal as well as destruction.

There is negative but convincing evidence that David was campaigning in France with his brother-in-law Henry and participating in the 'pacification' of Normandy from 1106 to 1113. As part of the spoils of war, David received part of the Cotentin peninsula where Robert Bruce, the lord of Brix was one of his vassal tenants.

It was in 1113 when the Anglo-Norman followers of Henry had sufficiently trounced the Norman-French followers of his brother Robert, Duke of Normandy, that King Henry and his court could return to take care of some business at home.

The year 1113 was a good one for David, with control over the south of Scotland and north of England, either as a tenant/vassal of his brother Alexander or his brother-in-law Henry, as well as having lands there which were his by right. There is little surviving documentation that either king interfered much in his running of the principalities.

His good fortune did not end there. When Henry was holding his Christmas court at Windsor, he granted David the hand in marriage of Matilda de Senlis, the widowed, Countess of Huntingdon and Northampton. This was a political union showing how high he stood in Henry's esteem and made David one of the great magnates of England. Matilda was a countess in her own right being the daughter of Judith, niece of William the Conqueror and Waltheof, the former Earl of Northumbria. Through her father, she could claim the Earldom of Northumbria which had formerly extended into the Lothians, Tweeddale and Teviotdale. On the monetary side, her extensive properties in the eastern Midlands provided a substantial income.

By now, David was leading a very mobile existence round his estates in Scotland, England and France as well as being a trusted right-hand man and magnate of Henry.

We can only trace his movements by the surviving documents in which he was a principal mover or witness and these show that he spent most of his time in England and France.

It would be during this period that David first became aware of the monastic reforms sweeping Europe in the early twelfth century. One of the new foundations was that of St Bernard at Tiron in the Forest of Perche not far from Charters. Although divisions in religious orders tend to fight like wet cats in a bag, St Bernard of Tiron received some good reviews. William of Malmesbury records that 'The other (Bernard), a noted admirer of poverty, leaving a most opulent monastery, retired with a few followers into a wooded and sequestered place and there he founded a monastery, more celebrated for piety and the number of monks than for the splendour and extent of its riches', while Orderic Vitalis notes that the monks of Tiron were 'joiners and blacksmiths, sculptors and goldsmiths, painters and masons'. This type of craftsmen-monks would appeal to the young earl as ideal settlers to subdue the rough lands in what is now the Borders.

When David first had the idea of transplanting them from the warm land of France to the rugged Borders is not known, but Gaufridus Grossus, a monk of Tiron who, around 1135, wrote the life of St Bernard, records that: 'About this time [1108] David afterwards king of Scotland, came to hear by report of the signal merits of our most blessed father then still living. By dint of strenuous embassies he obtained no small number of disciples from the congregation; and in Lothian he built them a house on a pleasant site near the river Tweed, which he sufficiently endowed with rents and wide possessions.

'After he had done this, desiring ardently to see the man of God, he set out from his northern home and passing the bounds of many adjacent regions, braving the terrors of the British Sea and crossing the provinces of Normandy, he arrived at Tiron. But he could not behold what he desired for the holy father had already departed to heaven. Yet, lest he might appear ungrateful or careless of so great a man, he laid aside his royal dignity and, on his bended knees, presented himself before the tomb with becoming reverence. The monastery which he had already founded, he endowed with wider territory and revenues. And taking with him twelve monks with an Abbot of the Order, in addition to those he already had, at length reached his own kingdom.'

This is a very important eyewitness account and is a primary document in the study of Selkirkshire even although it demolishes some of the preconceived ideas of the period. If Gaufridus the Fat is correct in his dating, it would seem that David the Earl had acquired 'no small number of disciples' in the year before the wooden church at Tiron was consecrated to celebrate the first mass at Easter 1109.

For David to bring them to 'the pleasant site near the river Tweed' and build them a house with wide possessions, meant that he was in control of the Tweedside area before 1113 and the pleasant site could be almost anywhere along the Tweed although later documents would place it on the site of Selkirk Abbey.

Fortunately, the document of the foundation of Selkirk Abbey still exists and is the cornerstone of the beginning of the history of Selkirkshire. I will leave out the original Latin wording (except when I need it to back up my arguments) and will return to Gaufridus later.

THE CHARTER OF FOUNDATION
OF SELKIRK ABBEY

David the Earl, son of Malcolm, King of Scots. To all his friends, French, English and Scots, and to all the sons of Holy Mother Church of God, lasting salvation.

Be it known to all present and to come, that I have founded a certain monastery in Selkirk, that is to say at the Abbey in honour of St Mary and St John the Evangelist, for the weal of my soul, of the souls of my father and mother, brothers and sisters and of all my ancestors.

To the monks of the which church I have given in alms perpetually the land of Selkirk from where a rivulet descending from the hills runs into the Yarrow, as far as to that rivulet coming down from Crossinmara, flows into the Tweed; and beyond the said rivulet which falls into the Yarrow, a certain particle of land between the road which leads from the Castle to the Abbey and Yarrow, that is towards the 'veterem villam' [which must be the Anglian settlement in the haugh of Philiphaugh]. And all these I have so given them in wood, in cleared ground and in waters. And the vill of Middelham [Midlem] and of Bothendeanham

[Bowden] and Aldona (Eildon), just as I possess them in lands, waters, wood and cleared ground, and my whole lordship [totum dominium meum] of Malros by the middle street and middle well, as far as the fosse, and as the fosse marches, falling into Tweed, in like manner in lands, waters, wood and plain. And in Sprostona [Sprouston] a ploughgate and ten acres and one maisure [house] belonging to the ploughgate. And in Berwick, one ploughgate and one maisure, below the church as far as the Tweed; and half of one fishing and the seventh part of the mill and forty 'solidos' [shillings?] of the burgh revenue every year. And in the burgh of Roxburgh, one maisure, and the seventh part of the mill and forty 'solidos' of rent and the seventh part of the fishing and a tenth part of the kain cheeses [kain is rent paid in produce] of Galloway. And the half of the skins of my kitchen and half of all the cuttings of which I have the other part; and a like share of the suet and tallow and of hides and all skins of sheep and lambs and a tenth of all the hides which my huntsmen shall capture; and my waters about Selkirk shall be common to be fished by their own fishermen as by mine; and my pastures common to their men and mine; and my wood to be used for building and fuel as by me. And in England, in Hardingstrop, twenty-four acres of land in lordship, that is to say with the meadows belonging to that lordship and one maisure belonging to the same; and two oxgates, to wit each having ten acres; and besides, six and a half roods of land and six maisures near the bridge of Norhamtune and a certain island meadow next to the bridge; and the mill of the said vill.

And all these have I confirmed to the monks of the aforesaid monastery to be freely possessed and peacefully by right for ever; in such sort that none of those succeeding me shall presume to exact anything whatever but prayers only for the weal of his soul.

This was done with Henry reigning in England; Alexander King in Scotland; John, Bishop in the Church at Glasgow; Herbert Abbot in the said Abbey; these being Witnesses – the foresaid John the bishop; Matilda the countess; Henry, son of the Earl; Gualthine, Osbert and Alwyn, chaplains; William nephew of the Earl; Robert de Bruis; Robert of Umphraville; Walter of Bolbec; Robert of Painton; Cospatric, brother of Dalsin; Hugh of Moreville; Pagan of Braios; Robert Corbet; Reginald of Muscamp; Walter of Lyndsay; Robert of Burnetville; Cospatrick the Sheriff; Cospatrick son of Aldene; Uchtred son of Scot; Macchus; Colbanus; Gillmichel; Ordard sheriff of Babenburch; Lyulf son of Uchtred; Ralf Inglis; Aimer Welch; Roger of Lerecester; Adam the chamberlain.

POINTS TO PONDER

The river below the meeting of the waters of Yarrow and Ettrick to where it joins the Tweed was formerly called the Yarrow, whereas now it is known as the Ettrick. This causes a great deal of confusion while trying to work out the location.

The land grant can still be traced. The stream descending from the hills which runs into Yarrow (Ettrick) is known locally as the Batts Burn, derived from Selkirk Abbatis, while the rivulet coming down from Crossinmara is the one running out of Faldonside Loch. It is accepted that the site of the Abbey is the ruined church of Lindean which is the only ecclesiastical location within the given area.

To this substantial land grant are added the vills of Middelham, Bothendeanham and Aldona as well as the particle of land lying towards the 'veterum villam' which have appeared previously. How much country the three vills encompassed is not known but taken together, they form a broad band round the south and east of the Eildon hills.

David added more land, houses and other useful perks from Sprouston, Berwick, Roxburgh and Galloway with the right to fish in the waters around Selkirk and to graze animals on common land there.

From his estates in England, David gave land, houses and a mill. These were particularly welcome as the rents would be paid in coin. At the time, Scotland did not have a monetary economy, having to rely on England and the rest of the Continent for currency. It would be around 1135 with the discovery of silver mines in Cumbria, then in David's possession, that the first Scottish coins would be struck.

Why choose Selkirk to site an abbey when there was much better land available in the lower Tweed? We don't know but it could be that the better land was already in other hands.

There were already established churches of the older forms of Irish/Scots Christianity in the Tweed Valley and it was the faith of many, if not all of the population. The placing of a new monastic order at the Abbot's Selkirk is likely to have been resented, especially with the gift of wide lands, but there was a convenient earl's castle in the King's Selkirk if the anti-innovators resorted to physical violence against the newcomers.

The countryside in the Forest of Selkirk would be very similar to that in the Forest of Perche and this might be what attracted the Tironensian monks to seek a solitude where they could worship far from worldly distractions. Perhaps David was testing the new order to see how able they were to cope with rough land and possibly wild people.

In fact, why did David bring them to Selkirk in the first place when he had better lands and an established church in many parts of his domain? Two reasons seem obvious. David saw how the settlement of reformed Benedictine agriculturalists would benefit the people who lived on and worked the land. The Order of St Bernard of Tiron was noted for its emphasis on physical work and each monk was required to have one or more manual skills. This was originally seen as a device to prevent idle hands from seeking mischief.

Then there was church politics. In 1119 Thurstan, the new Archbishop of York, was intent on acquiring Scotland as part of his see to strengthen his hand in countering Canterbury's claim to primacy, while David was determined to maintain Scotland as an independent entity within the Roman Church. If the Scots church was subject to English control, then the king of Scots could be looked on as a vassal of the king of England. Much was at stake and John, Bishop of Glasgow in whose presence the foundation charter of Selkirk Abbey was enacted, had to journey to Rome to state the case for that independence.

The fact that the Selkirk Abbey charter was put into writing six years after the abbey had been founded is likely to have been a positive step to assert that freedom. It is never wise to interfere in any argument about religion and this happened nine hundred years ago, so I will leave the subject for academia to debate.

That the foundation document was important is evident from the number and ranks of the witnesses: David the Earl, his wife Matilda and their son Henry who must have been a very young boy at the time, David's nephew, William fitzDuncan, John the Bishop of Glasgow and an assortment of Norman knights and local landowners, many of whom would take a leading part in the fledgling country of Scotland. Robert de Brus, Robert de Umfraville, Hugo de Moreville and Robert Corbert had received or were about to receive lands in the South of Scotland: all were Normans, new to the area and all French-speaking.

Additionally there was Uchtred, son of Scot, Aimer the Welshman and Ralph the Englishman. Cospatrick the sheriff, formerly Earl of Northumbria, was by now governor of Roxburgh Castle and David's representative in his absence. This was an eclectic grouping chosen with care to represent all shades of opinion.

The Foundation charter cannot be dated until around 1119. It was done when Herbert was Abbot of Selkirk Abbey and Prince Henry was old enough to be a witness.

It gives us the first historical insight into what was happening in the Borders in the early twelfth century. That the villages or vills of Bowden, Midlem, Sprouston and part of his dominium of Malros were worth mentioning, indicates existing communities, while his grants of land and monies from the revenues of burghs of Roxburgh and Berwick show that these must have been thriving towns with a sizable merchant population with access to a currency economy.

The Short-lived Selkirk Abbey

Selkirk Abbey was the first of the reformed Benedictine orders to be settled in Britain. It was to have only fourteen years in its original location, but by gathering what information is available from the various sources, it is possible to work out a time-scale for the beginning, lifetime and demise of Selkirk Abbey.

Founded a mere four years after its mother house at Tiron, the 'abbey' was likely to have been a wooden church surrounded by a few wooden buildings housing the monks. The myth that the carved stones from Selkirk Abbey were barged down the Tweed to build Kelso owes its origins to overactive imagination in Victorian times.

Phase one. David, travelling through Normandy, meets St Bernard and persuades an Abbot and twelve monks to return with him in 1113 when he returns from Henry I's pacification of the area. David gives the monks lands beside the Ettrick where they build a wooden church on the site of Lindean Kirk. The first Abbot was called Ralph and he ruled Selkirk Abbey from 1113 to 1116 when he returned to Tiron to succeed St Bernard who had died on 25 April 1116.

Phase two. It is likely that David travelled with Ralph to Tiron where he collected more monks and a new Abbot called William who became the second Abbot of Selkirk. William ruled until 1118, returning to Tiron to become Abbot there.

Both Ralph and William are likely to have been Normans.

Phase three. The third Abbot of Selkirk was called Herbert, who seems to have been a monk of Selkirk. Perhaps the Foundation charter was penned and presented to mark his induction. It was in his term of office that Selkirk Abbey was relocated to a new site in the church of St Mary at Easter Kelso, across the Tweed and slightly downriver from the royal castle and burgh of Roxburgh. The explanation given was that Selkirk 'was not suitable for an abbey'. Although the abbey had been removed, the original land grants were retained by Kelso Abbey and subsequently added to; this fact was to prove very beneficial to later historians as it kept the lands of Selkirkshire within the written records of Kelso Abbey. The move from Selkirk to Kelso was started in 1126 and completed when the New Abbey of Kelso was consecrated on 3 May, 1128.

A more probable reason for the move was that David, now king of Scots, used Roxburgh Castle as one of his main residences and the burgh of Roxburgh was the most prosperous in the kingdom while the main seaport of Scotland was at Berwick, a few miles away.

David the King

In April 1124 David had been crowned king of Scots at Scone but, although a son of Malcolm III and Scottish by birth, he was never to be popular with the Gaelic elite in the north of Scotland. He was virtually a foreigner, an Anglo-Norman by upbringing and training, who relied on the military might of his Anglo-Norman friends to keep him in power. The very fact that he was an innovator, bringing in new rules and forms of government would count against him. However, although he would destroy some individuals like the earls of Ross and Moray, he made no attempt to replace the native aristocracy as a class. Ten provincial earldoms which existed at the time of his birth were still in the hands of the same native families at the time of his death.

Although himself a supporter and noted benefactor of the Roman Church, he paid reverence to the native saints of his own kingdom, St Mungo of Glasgow, St Cuthbert of Melrose and St Columba of Iona.

David was a man torn between two worlds. He was conscious that his own roots lay far back in the various kingdoms of Scotland and in this he was a traditionalist. But he had been educated and trained in the household of Henry Beauclerk (later Henry I of England) and was aware that an explosion of new ideas of government and policies were sweeping through England and the Continent. It would take a strong and determined king, with formidable military backing, to introduce such measures into a backward-looking Scotland. He had seen how the concept of 'feudalism' and reformation within the church, had improved the lot of the people as well as the wealth of the royal exchequer. He had already put into practice some of these innovations in a small way, as in the Foundation of Selkirk Abbey. Now he had the opportunity to work on a larger scale.

With a view to stability, David chose the chief seat of government to be at Roxburgh which was central to the areas of his main interest, southern Scotland and northern England. What Roxburgh provided was security where his closest friends and supporters were most numerous. From here he hoped to bind the diversely separate components of his country into a prosperous one that could take its place in the then modern world.

Even southern Scotland, which had been under his authority for over a decade, there was an unusual mixture of languages and cultures. The Lothians and Tweeddale had been part of the kingdom of Bernicia and spoke Englisc while Strathclyde and Cumbria would speak Cumbric, and Galloway was Scots-Gaelic speaking.

How many of them considered themselves as 'Scots' is open to question. Yet David's charter to Selkirk Abbey gave greetings to all his friends 'Francis, Anglis et Scottis', the French being the Normans and Anglo-Normans whom David had introduced into his new domain. In order to weld these diverse cultures together into one whole, David was to draw on his experience from the Continent and England where the law structure was basically a Norman feudal one. To do this, he needed help from men who knew the system and whom he could trust.

David started his reign with a statement of intent. While his brothers Edgar and Alexander had introduced a few Normans into the kingdom, David granted Robert de Brus, one of the most senior

Normans in his entourage, the whole 200,000 acres of Annandale. From his estates of Huntingdon, Bedford and Northampton, he recruited many of the younger sons of his tenants to come north and settle permanently in Scotland. The prospect of advancement to positions of power and wealth in Scotland was one that attracted the young Norman and Breton hopefuls who could not achieve the same in England or France, and it was unlikely that they would refuse their feudal lord.

In this way, he populated the south of Scotland with an aristocracy used to the feudal society and whose loyalty was to their benefactor. To assist in the management of the kingdom, David introduced new offices of state, filling them with foreigners who knew the rules. Walter, son of Alan, was a Breton who was his steward and eventually the ancestor of the Stewart dynasty who became kings of Scots. (The origins of this office was from 'sti-wards' or pig-keepers, an important position in Anglian society.)

The Norman Hugo de Moreville was the first hereditary Constable of Scotland and held the lands of Lauderdale. But David also kept in place important Englisc/Gaelic-speaking servants such as the 'door wards' or door-keepers, the Durwards, as royal bodyguards.

With these and other appointments, David was now able to make Scotland into a composite kingdom. In short, he was intent on reproducing in his own realm the pattern of tenure that worked well in his large English estates and in the rest of Norman England.

Once established, David's inner circle of advisers at Roxburgh was an amalgam of Anglo-Norman knights from his lands in England and France and clerical servants from his new religious foundations, mixed into the older aristocracy of the region. From such varying shades of opinion and experience, David drew copiously, making laws for the governance of the country by joining up the disjointed parts of earlier kingdoms into one which would be principally Scots.

David was basically a law-maker making laws to ensure peace and justice for all, if that was possible: laws for the conduct and encouragement of trade for the benefit of the people and the exchequer, and forest laws mainly for the benefit of the hunting aristocracy. That the new feudal laws had to fit in with the existing rules of behaviour required patience and diplomacy.

FEUDALISM

It was Victorian historians who put forward the idea that what they called 'feudalism', was brought to England by William the Conqueror and spread to Scotland, Wales and Ireland over the next centuries, an idea that was a product of their time, class and thinking.

The Victorians were living at a period when Britannia ruled the waves and about a third of the known world. As rulers of 'the Mightiest Empire in the World', the mainly English historians and archaeologists viewed previous civilisations from their own perspective. Successful empires of the past were looked on with the 'one of us' appreciation that a lady politician of the immediate past used as a mark of approval. Victorian historians were often from the land-owning aristocracy who, in their early days, had served in the British army during the conquest of the 'lesser lands beyond the sea' and who could empathise with previous lord conquerors, the Romans and the Normans – upper strata, of course.

Consequently, the idea of a ruling elite who brought the idea of a society with layers of power and responsibility appealed to the Victorians. It was an added bonus that both the Romans and the Normans left their records in the written word.

Writing is possibly the greatest invention of the last five thousand years. As a form of information technology, it has transmitted knowledge with great accuracy, quantity and detail through the centuries. However, the written record can reflect the views of the writer and the art of 'spin doctoring', is by no means a modern phenomonen, so the historian must *caveat scriptor,* remembering that history is always on the side of the winner.

Far from being an introduction by the Normans, a form of feudalism has existed since the time when humans first grouped together for support or protection. In any organised society there are those who lead and those who follow, those who order, those who obey and those who question the orders. It is a human trait that the people on the top of the pile wish to remain there while those at the bottom or middle seek to climb in status and wealth. As the concept of an individual being able to own land as a commodity evolved, so did the fact that some would have more land than they needed and some less.

By mutual agreement those who needed land or more land, agreed to do work in exchange for the use of the spare land, so tenancies were agreed. This gave two or more layers in society and eventually became a multi-layered and mutually interdependent society.

Anglian Feudalism

In the pre-Norman Borders, there was a perfectly good Anglian pattern of estate-holding which can still be discerned with a little thoughtful imagination. Some of the Cumbric maenors can be traced through the surviving Cumbric settlement names and, as human beings are tremendously conservative, the Anglian 'scir' often followed the same natural land boundaries.

Of the people who held the land, the highest below the king was the old nobility of the eorlas or earls. Below them were the theyns or thanes who were high-status tenants, landowning but dependent on the wishes of their immediate superior and the king. Below the theyns were the lower-status tenants, the drengs who fetched, carried, ploughed and harvested so many days in exchange for the use of their land; these were later to be called husbandmen. The next stage downwards in social standing were the cottars who had a small piece of land which could vary between one and ten acres, and who depended on their labour for survival. Lowest still were the nativi who were nominally free men, but together with their families were tied to the estate of their birth and could be transferred with the property if it was sold or donated to the church. Recorded evidence of this period is scant and known conditions of the underdogs obviously decline the further down the social ladder you descend.

At this period, about 97 per cent of the people of the Borders depended on agriculture for their livelihood, cultivating arable land where possible and grazing the rest. In the flatter areas of the present Berwickshire and most of eastern Roxburghshire, there was a pattern of nucleated villages surrounded by an area of open fields which were ploughed in rotation. The modern term 'nucleated village' is a settlement of houses which has grown round a central point, a lord's tower or a parish church. The arable land lies in unfenced tracts round the village with intermittently cropped land: surrounding these were the outfields which were mainly grazing and for haymaking. Outside that and often at some distance away, was the summer hill-grazing and woodland.

Beyond the central village, a number of outlying settlements (vills) could be linked to the estate centre (dominium) to form a scir which was held by or came under the supervision of a theyn acting on behalf of the earl or king. The Anglian scirs were basically the estate of a nobleman or sometimes a parish, and were much smaller than the later Norman shire. Several can be traced through early documents and in some cases by likelihood and place names.

By combining the information from the 1095 charter of King Edgar of Scotland to Durham See and the contemporary writings of Bede, it is possible to delineate the bounds of Coldinghamscir, Bunklescir, an early Berwickscir, Ecclesscir and Haddingtonscir in Scotland with Norhamscir, Hexhamscir and Islandscir in England. The lands of a reconstructed Yetholmscir lie on both sides of the present Scottish/English Border line, giving a conclusive deduction that this Anglian pattern of vill development was in place long before the border line was recognised as a division.

The name Tinnis is sometimes taken to mean 'a theyn's place' and by others as a derivation of 'dinas' a fort. There are three places called Tinnis in the Borders: two are forts but the Tinnes in Yarrow has no trace of fortifications. However, there is no reason why a theyn should not live in a fort. An interesting speculation.

For the good governance of the area, the theyn had the rights of 'sake, soke, toll, infangthief, pit and gallows' to punish the wrongdoer and tax the just. In other words he could do just about what he liked. He was aided in his exercise of civil law by the dempster (a judge), and a dewar or relic-keeper. One of the theyn's duties was to see that everybody paid their teind to the church promptly. Failure to do so resulted in a hefty fine: a theyn would have to pay eight cows to the king while a dreng would lose one cow and one sheep. This was serious money for the subsistence farmer.

As part of his service to the king, the theyn had to organise the military service at scir level, the scir being the unit assessing the requirement for service in the 'common or Scottish army'. When the scirs were royal, the theyns provided the king and his attendants with lodgings or prepared for his coming if he had a royal residence there.

In the Anglian system of feudalism, the power in the land lay immediately in the hands of the thanes and to a greater degree in the earl's court.

It is questionable if the feudalisation of the Anglian scirs made much difference to the peasant working the land but, fortunately for the historian, the Normans liked to have their deeds and contracts in writing, so we know more about them.

Norman Feudalism in Theory and in the Borders

In Norman feudalism, the king was in control and only delegated power to those he trusted. In Scotland, David had the problem of grafting the Norman system of government into the existing Anglian one while still retaining the support of both. In England, the Normans had imposed their ways by military might whereas in southern Scotland, it had to be adopted gradually and by persuasion.

To achieve this end, David used different methods in each strata of society.

To rule the kingdom, he needed the support of the aristocratic landowners who already knew the system and had benefited from Norman feudalism in England and France. To them, he gave land which he could claim back if they did not support him. This gave him an army if required, and at little cost to himself.

Visualise the kingdom as a layered pyramid with the king at the top. As he could not utilise all the land himself, he let some large parts of it out to his friends and great lords in return for the service of so many knights, sergeants, archers etc to fight in his wars of offence or defence; and so much food and or labour on his own land to support his retainers at court.

In the Borders, this layer of great nobles is represented by the lordships of Annandale, Liddesdale, Eskdale, and Lauderdale. These were surviving pre-feudal Anglian estates of earls and may previously have been Cumbric maenors. They were brought into the Norman feudalisation when David gave Robert Brus the whole of Annandale; Ranalf de Sules got Liddesdale; Robert Avenel got Eskdale; Hugo de Morville got Lauderdale and so on.

For his 200,000 acres of land in Annandale, Robert Brus had to supply ten knights to David's service when called upon. As tenant-in-chief, he did this by keeping some of the land for his own needs and 'enfeoffing' or subcontracting the rest to his friends and supporters in return for their knight's service to him and indirectly the king, whenever they were called upon. This third layer of knights were lesser landowners who held the land, sometimes vills, sometimes parishes, in fee. They owed their allegiance directly to the great lord and were in effect, his own private army. By careful management of acquisition, alliance and marriage, a great lord could be strong enough to present a threat to the king.

Additionally, in this third layer of landowners were knights who held their land directly from the king. These grants were for less extensive territories and many of the recipients came from David's lands in Northamptonshire. It is likely that they were the younger sons of nobles with poor prospects at home but this did not prevent them from rising in status in their new home. Gervaise de Ryedale got part of the lands on the north side of Lilliesleaf which is now the Riddell Estate and rose to become the sheriff of Roxburgh and Teviotdale. By the end of the twelfth century, Roxburghshire was mainly Norman in lordship although William the Frenchman was in Longnewton and Thomas of Lothian held Lessudden.

The 'king's knights' with much smaller estates, probably only owed one knight's service for the use of the land. We cannot tell what acreage is involved even when the places can be identified on a modern map, but the extent of the estates must have varied with the productive capacity of the land. In early Norman England, the amount of land regarded as sufficient to maintain a knight was a five-hide unit which worked out as between three hundred and five hundred acres depending on the fertility of the soil. Ideally, this would be in a solid economic unit but it was also quite common for unconnected vills to pay for the portion of a knight's service.

In the fertile lands of the Merse, it might only require two or three vills to support a knight's fee while on poorer land it could take the production of ten vills to maintain a his household in the appropriate manner. The taxes on each vill were based on a proportion of their products, and it was not uncommon for the fractional fees to come from different parts of the country.

It is possible to make an informed guess at where these knights were located, even with no documentary evidence. Look for the name 'Mains' and this is usually a sign that this is the main farm the infeft knight kept for himself as his 'demesne' or manor house with the adjacent lands not let out to tenants. If there is an East Mains and a West Mains, it could mean that two knights of the same family, possibly father and son or brothers, each had their own manor house within the family estate.

If there is only one Mains but a cluster of names with the same derivation, this is likely to mark the extent of the knight's land. This might take the form of the original name with the addition of north, south, east, west, hill, mill, park etc.

In Roxburghshire, the block of land round the village of Nisbet contains East Nisbet, West Nisbet, Nisbet Mill, Nisbet Hillhead and Upper Nisbet Moor. This is an ancient settlement as the vill of Nisbet was granted to Durham by Earl Cospatrick II before 1138, but its earlier history is not recorded.

In Selkirkshire there is a sweep of the Ale Water just below Ashkirk. Within this piece of ground, Synton Mains overlooks the river while the outlying lands of Synton Parkhead, Synton Mossend, Synton Mill and on the other side of the river North Synton, form an estate which would be seven square kilometres in extent. The site of the former Georgian mansion known simply as Synton, may have been the original settlement where the unknown 'Syn' established his 'ton'. This is another ancient settlement likely to have been established in Anglian times or before.

In both cases, these are examples of the vill system with its associated features of feu-ferme and obligations of seasonal work on the lord's land during the agricultural bottle-necks of ploughing sowing, hay and harvest-times. There would be some time demanded for peat and wood cutting, some transporting and tribute in a portion of the produce of the land involved.

On the knight's land, the lower strata in the social scale would have progressively less land to farm until the bottom layer would be depending on their labours alone rather than the fruits of the land. As the lower orders are only coincidently mentioned in early documents, I will defer this subject as the church records note the taxes and labour dues imposed on their tenants in much greater detail.

Temporary Accommodation

When the Norman settlers first came to the Borders, they had no knowledge of how they would be received so, as a temporary expedient, the immigrants set up motte-and bailey wooden castles on natural or man-made mounds. These could be quickly built and were easily maintainable to provide safety for the family and retainers. The motte is usually looked on as a personal family castle as opposed to the early twelfth century royal castles of Berwick, Roxburgh, Jedburgh, Peebles and Selkirk.

It has been thought that motte-and-bailey structures of wood were only temporary constructions until stronger stone-built castles could be completed but this is not necessarily so. The fortress of the Bruce family in Annan was a wooden construction when Robert the Bruce became king of Scots in the early fourteenth century and the Selkirk Castle of the same date was similarly built.

In the Borders there are very few motte-and-bailey sites known, especially when compared with the western half of southern Scotland, the Strathclyde and Galloway regions. This may be because the incoming settlers had a blanket coverage of the area and did not need any temporary stronghold for defence. Only the motte at Hawick has been excavated and the datable evidence, a coin of Henry II, suggests a twelfth century occupation when Hawick was held by the Lovell family.

Where known, as in Selkirk and Hawick, the motte-and-bailey was placed near an already established community but once there, it acted as a focal point drawing people for the security it provided and as a marketplace for the growing population.

The best example of this is at the burgh of Selkirk where an early motte was built on a mound near the Haining Loch. The inhabitants of the original Selekirke, an agricultural vill near the river, moved up to live beside the castle, thereby enlarging Selekirke Regis, or the 'King's Selkirk'. Its location on the edge of Ettrick/Selkirk Forest was ideally placed to be the base of royal hunting parties and the early kings of Scotland were frequent visitors, enlarging the burgh and giving its inhabitants the opportunity to provide the necessary services.

Selkirk was a place of intermittent importance from the time of David until the Wars of Independence, when possession of Selkirk

Castle was fiercely contested. The English wanted to retain it as a stronghold while the Scots under Wallace tried to prevent this from happening. This is a story to be told later.

During this period, Selkirk became the capital of a shire and the base of a sheriff who had the uneasy task of maintaining the king's laws in the Forest of Ettrick.

The King's Burghs

To bring the country up to European standards, David knew that it would have to develop economically. There was a demand for raw materials to supply the growing populations of Europe and in the Borders there were areas of land which were relatively unused. With plenty of available land to graze sheep, and wool becoming the growth industry of its day, it made sense to take full commercial advantage of this bounty, so David encouraged the growth of burgh settlements with privileged commercial opportunities to make the most of what was available. The purpose of the burghs was to expand trade and enrich the king and the nobles who had much to gain from a thriving economy.

Most of the early burghs of Scotland were on land belonging to the king and enjoyed trading concession under royal protection. With few exceptions, they were already centres of population although the number of inhabitants was probably fairly small.

The burgh was placed a short distance from the king's castle as a matter of convenience; the castle needed supplies and services that the burgh could provide, while the burgh had the immediate protection of the castle. A vaguely modern analogy would be the siting of groups of superstores on the edge of a city.

The word 'burg' is a Germanic one to define a settlement of merchants and tradesmen which was larger than a vill and probably took over the role of the 'dominium' or central location which was established in the Anglian scirs.

During his reign, David granted the status of 'king's or royal burgh' to Roxburgh, Berwick, Jedburgh and Peebles in the Borders. Selkirk probably had a similar status but documentary proof is absent. However, Selkirk had the use of an immense area of common land of 22,000 acres which was still being claimed by the inhabitants of Selkirk in the seventeent century, and the only period when such a large area was likely to have been available would be the early twelfth century.

Meanwhile, the relative peace and royal control was having a beneficial effect on the Borders. The burgh of Roxburgh and its surrounding vills were becoming a major commercial centre where the wool crop from forest pastures in the Tweed Valley was collected for onward transmission through the ever-growing port of Berwick. Wool was a major cash crop and in great demand in the expanding cities in the Low Countries and Northern Italy. With merchants and wool buyers from the Continent and Italian bankers, Roxburgh became an international trading centre.

The trade was not all one way. In general terms, raw materials were passing out through Berwick but the more sophisticated finished products were coming in.

As well as goods, there were people coming in from the heavily populated and industrialised regions of Europe. Flemish craftsmen and merchants were being attracted to settle in Berwick and Roxburgh by the royal offers of cheap tenements of land. These seemed to have formed the bulk of the settlers but this might be because the Low Countries immigrants were more likely to have their holdings recorded in written documents that have survived the centuries. Another immigrant block came from David's extensive land-holdings in England; they brought their commercial expertise and the English language to reinforce the Anglian language base which was already in place in the Borders. Although all European languages would have been heard in the market, the burghs had become places of English speech while French remained the language of the aristocracy.

The smaller inland burghs of Jedburgh, Selkirk, Peebles and Lauder benefited by acting as gathering points and as local market centres. The scale of trade in these markets would probably be quite small but its effect would stimulate production and improve the living standards of those who owned and worked the land. For the poor, this could be the difference between subsistence and surplus; for the landowner, it could put money in his pouch, supply him with necessities and luxuries and give him the incentive to make his land produce more.

As David's income was from the animals and produce of his estates, he and the market traders had a mutual interest in the ecouragement of specialist communities beside the royal castles and halls and, by creating burghs with favoured trading concessions, the king was able to divert some of the profits into his own treasury through market tolls and harbour dues.

For the privileges conferred by the king, the burgesses of the king's burgh paid rents directly into the royal exchequer and they had to supply 'watch and ward' services when the king required men for his army. This gave David another reservoir of men who did not have any feudal commitment other than to the king himself. As well as building up the economic strength of the kingdom, a strong merchant community helped to counterbalance the military strength of the nobles.

To encourage this entrepreneurial endeavour, the burghs were given an independent status within the laws of the land and were able to make their own regulations for trading and acceptable behaviour. To be a king's burgess was a privilege not to be bought by simply paying a fee or rent as there was a system of burgh laws which had to be obeyed. These were established in the twelfth century Leges Burgorum which set out the regulations and conditions for burgesses of Berwick, Roxburgh, Edinburgh and Stirling, the four most important burghs in Scotland. They were largely market and behavioural regulations: who was allowed to become a burgess and the conditions of receiving the privilege; setting the standards for the goods to be sold in the market and the penalties if these were broken; how disputes were to be settled between burgesses. In short, the Leges Burgorum were long and complex enough to cover every eventuality. They set the standards for all burghs within the kingdom and were valid until the seventeenth century.

Equally importantly, the burghs were often the focal point of the new shires and the establishment of sheriffs throughout the Borders. The sheriffs were royal law officers with the power to supervise the setting up and running of the new shires, the collecting of taxes and the general maintenance of the realm. They reported directly to the king, were dependent on his goodwill and were usually wealthy landowners in their own right, so it was in their own best interests that the rule of law should be obeyed by all.

The new shires were sizable groups of what were formerly scirs and nucleated village groupings, placed under one central authority, a sheriff. The shires and sheriffdoms set up by David I were Berwickshire, Roxburghshire, Selkirkshire and Peeblesshire, all of which remained in existence until regionalisation in 1975.

The planting and encouragement of burgh communities were part of David's plans for the economic development of his kingdom. The rapidly growing trading links with the Continent made him realise that barter was not an option. The silver coins from England, Ireland and the Continent made trading easier within Scotland but national pride required a separate Scottish coinage. This became a reality in 1135 or 6 when David moved south in support of his niece, the Empress Matilda. The Scots captured Carlisle with its mint and there, the first sterlings of the coinage of Scotland were struck. Soon Scottish coins were being produced in Roxburgh, Berwick, St Andrews, Perth and Aberdeen in David's name, and at Carlisle, Corbridge and Bamburgh in the name of Prince Henry. This Scottish coinage lasted until 1708 when the last coins were struck in the royal mint in Edinburgh.

The burghs survived a long time after their foundation by David I and were finally voted out of existence by the Local Government (Scotland) Act of 1973, having been part of Scottish history for eight and a half centuries.

THE CHURCH OF ROME

When David became King of Scots in 1124, there was a vibrant Gaelic church in the north as well as a native Christian Anglian one in the south of his kingdom. The introduction of the Church of Rome had been encouraged by his mother, Queen Margaret, and both his brothers had continued in the same innovative tradition. If there was a conflict between the already established churches of Scotland and that of Rome, it was a difference in form rather than of belief, but this did not prevent the newcomers from conducting a propaganda war against the native churches.

The new monks considered themselves much superior in religious practice, technology and culture to the native church who were 'wont to celebrate mass contrary to the custom of the whole church'. Similar divisions in religions can be observed today.

In David's eyes the various branches of the imported Christianity were just as important to the cultural regeneration of Scotland as the introduction of Anglo-Norman knights with their retainers and the establishment of new burghs. They represented a tradition in which he had been raised and thought of as a civilised norm; in fact they were the religious face of feudalism with the same method of a structured society.

As a young man, David would have seen benefits of royal patronage to religious orders and observed the effects of religious politics. As seen above, his first essay at the planned foundation of an abbey was at Selkirk on the edge of Ettrick Forest. Although this site may have suited the reformed order's preference for solitude, David found it convenient to bring his new foundation to Kelso, near his castle and burgh of Roxburgh in the belief that it gave him spiritual benefits through their prayers and masses.

David had selected monks from the order of Tironensians and brought them from France so that the See of St Cuthbert in Durham could have no claim on their allegiance. Durham had long laid religious claim to Jedburgh, Teviotdale and parts of the Tweed valley. Soon after being crowned in 1124, David revived the bishopric of Glasgow, the ancient and prestigious see of St Kentigern, and installed his Chaplain, John Achaius, as bishop there. This was part of a plan to retain the independence of the Scottish Church, a theme which appears several times in the early ecclesiastical history of the Borders.

I do not intend going deeply into the history of monasteries/abbeys and churches in the Borders as many books and papers have already been written on the subject but, as there is only a limited amount of evidence available, the conclusions and presentations are very similar. So I will give a brief synopsis of the various functions of the early monastic settlements here.

The terms monastery and abbey are frequently taken to be synonymous but it is generally accepted that the monastery was principally a community of monks who lived within the abbey, a complex of buildings. This included the abbey itself, the show-piece part in which the main prayers were said and, as such, was available to the secular population.

In a monastery, the monks lived within an enclosed society withdrawn from the world and devoting their religious time to praying, studying, copying texts for wider distributions. They did not go out to evangelise, pray, preach or conduct services outwith their closed precincts. On the business side, the monks had to supervise their extensive commercial holdings.

The abbey building was looked on as a religious centre where the privileged could be nearer to God, thanks to the prayers of the monks, and where He was more likely to intercede on their behalf. Donations, usually of land, were always welcome for the upkeep of the abbey/monastery and in a brief period of time, the monasteries grew very rich since land, once donated, was permanently church property. As well as being a spiritual insurance policy, such donations earned the king's approval.

From the monastery or abbey, individual priests could be called to serve the king with advice, spiritual or secular, and these chosen men could rise to exalted positions in court. As bishops and abbots, they were influential in the Roman church which had become a multi-national concern with business and religious connections but was also a superb news-gathering network keeping up to date with what was happening over the known world. This intelligence-gathering network was unsurpassed until the time of the Second World War.

Below the cloistered monks were the canons who were looked on as being inferior in spiritual status but they were much more involved in the real world outside the monastic settlement. The canons were communities of priests who lived within the monastery but moved through the countryside to serve as preachers to the laity, as parish priests if called upon; they would also administer to the sick in the abbey's infirmaries and outlying leper hospitals. Both monks and canons had their different skills that they used for the benefit of communities inside and outside the monastery walls.

These were the front line troops in the battle against evil, but to provide the monastic communities with the services required a large number of 'support workers' were needed. The Foundation Charter of Selkirk shows that the initial cost of founding an abbey was colossal and Selkirk Abbey was likely to have only the minimal requirement of an abbot and twelve monks. As the wealth-producer was the land, it took a number of men, women and children to work it. Chief of these were the lay brothers or conversi who had the task of clearing the land and running the outlying granges. These were farm settlements with a small chapel and living quarters attached. The aim for such developments was an economic one; the monasteries needed to be self-sufficient enough to be independent of the outside world.

The move from Selkirk to Kelso was beneficial to the Tironensian foundation in prestige and wealth. Being near the generous king and within a concentration of important royal and noble estates, Kelso Abbey quickly became the recipient of more land, donations and supplies in lieu. It seems facetious to say that the monks became very rich by selling prayers but that is what happened – 'I bequeath so many ploughgates of land etc for prayers for the good of my soul'.

Soon Kelso Abbey became one of the largest and the second wealthiest of the religious houses in Scotland, and they made very good use of their expanding estates. The monks were agricultural innovators, introducing new techniques and management practices for the profitable exploitation of the land. Monastic estates were well organised and, with little chance of losing their estates, were able to plan for the long-term future. Soon the great landowners, the Anglo-Norman-French elite, were copying their examples for the benefit of themselves, their own people and the country in general.

In the early days of monastic settlement in the Borders, abbey lands were free from the attentions of aggressive warlords or passing armies seeking plunder; this attitude was to change as the Scottish/English differences became wars of attrition.

The monasteries were also major players in the trading life of the new kingdom, being active in the countries round the North Sea. David's improvements were turning Scotland from being largely a subsistence economy into a market place with surpluses to sell. Goods to sell meant that commodities which Scotland was not able to produce could be brought into the country and, with links to the commercial world of Europe, the monasteries were able to keep an eye on changing trends.

It is clear that monastic settlement was an integral part of David's plan for the economic development of his kingdom. With the successful experiment of the Selkirk/Kelso Abbey foundation, David probably decided to have more of the same for their economic input as much as their religious strengths. The monks were wealth–producers.

Kelso Abbey and Selkirk Lands

It is known that Selkirk Abbey had been relocated in Kelso by 1128 but the document which authorises this dates between 1136 and 1152. It could be that the original charter had not survived and that this Charter of Removal was re-subscribed and witnessed by Prince Henry, David's son, at a later date.

In this charter, David renews the grant of Selkirk Abattis, Midlem and Bowden including the same 'particle of land beyond the stream with falls into Yarrow and between the road which leads to the castle and falls into the river above the old abbey, and Yarrow'. In place of Melrose and Eildon, David gives thirty acres of land of the territory of Lilliesleaf and a tenth share of the profits of the mill in the vill of Lilliesleaf, and Whitlaw with its proper marches.

Absent from this grant is the dominium of Melrose and the vill of Eildon as these had been conveyed to the new Cistercian abbey of Melrose which had been founded in 1136.

By combining the two foundation charters and the Charter of Removal and using the land grants involved, it is possible to reconstruct an Anglian 'Melrosshire' or 'Eildonshire'. This would have its centre in the dominium of Malros with the supporting vills of Selkirk Abbatis, Midlem, Bowden, Eildon, Gattonside, Darnick and Fordel. It is also worth noting that although Selkirk, Midlem and Darnick are Anglian place-names, Melrose and Eildon are Cumbric, and two Celtic saints are commemorated in Bowden (Bothendeanham) and St Boswells (Boisil) where there was a church of St Mary at Lessedewyn before 1153.

So maybe there is a Cumbric maenor beneath the Anglian scir which became the estate which David gave the abbeys of Kelso and Melrose. This is speculation and it will require a more erudite person to take up the case.

Melrose Abbey

Melrose Abbey was founded in 1136 with monks brought from the Cistercian Abbey of Rievaulx in Yorkshire. Although the Cistercians were devoted to poverty and Christian worship in a remote 'desert' region far from the temptations of worldly men, David settled them in flat and fertile lands at Little Fordel about 2kms west of the famed Celtic/Anglian Christian monastery of Malros which was on the end of the peninsula now known as Old Melrose. In keeping the name, Melrose, the Cistercians were probably capitalising on the reputation of the Old Melrose establishment although movement of place-names is by no means uncommon.

It has been suggested that Bishop John of Glasgow, who had been Chaplain and close friend to the young Earl David, had rejected the site of Old Melrose because, if a new Cistercian abbey was built on the site of a shrine of St Cuthbert, it would come under the influence of Durham where the saint's body lay, and which was the focus of his increasingly powerful cult. The politics of the church were fought with as much fervour as the battles between kings.

David gave the new foundation a generous land grant, taking his 'dominium' of Mailros and the vill of Aldona from Selkirk/Kelso Abbey and giving it to the new foundation, as well as adding the vill of Dernwic (Darnick) and Gattonside Haugh (ad incrementu Galtuneshalch) on the north side of the Tweed. This made a compact estate of flat land which was welcomed by the Cistercians who were noted for their ability as agricultural entrepreneurs.

They were also great water engineers and diverted the river Tweed, which meandered through the haughs to the east of Melrose Abbey, into its present course some time after the Abbey foundation. In the dry year of 2003, it was possible to see large adze-squared oak beams held in place with impressive red sandstone blocks, keeping the Tweed in the course originally planned by the Cistercians. The road running from the Abbey to Newstead bisects the flat haughs making two arable blocks about 200m in length and this is the measurement of a furlong or furrow-long, the distance that an ox-plough could till before the oxen needed a rest. If this is a coincidence, at least it is a happy one.

In the initial grant, Melrose owned around 5,000 acres in arable ground and leased 17,000 acres of forest pasture in which the lay brothers tended flocks of sheep. This made the Abbey financially self-sufficient with a huge surplus to sell. They also had tenements in several burghs, peat mosses, fisheries and salt marshes with other divisions and portions from various places. The Cistercian principles of poverty, hard work and devotion in isolated places had turned into a very profitable capitalist business.

Certainly Ailred of Rievaulx's account of his early life was somewhat different. 'Our food is scanty, our garments rough; our drink is from the stream and our sleep is often upon our book. Under our tired limbs, there is but a hard mat; when sleep is sweetest we must rise at a bell's bidding. Self will has no place; there is no moment for idleness or dissipation … Everywhere peace, everywhere serenity and a marvellous freedom from the tumult of the world'.

Economic development over the centuries was to change this until the time when a medieval poet could write 'The Monks of Melrose: made guid kaill. On Friday when they fastit'.

Jedburgh Abbey

The present Jedburgh Abbey was originally founded as a priory by David in 1138 and then colonised by Augustinian monks from St Quentin near Beauvais to become an abbey in 1154, but it had been a place of Christian worship for around three hundred years before that.

As early as 854, Bishop Ecgred of Lindisfarne had formed two settlements on the Jed Water, calling them both Gedwearde and there is a series of carved stone in the Abbey Museum which dates to around this period. The early church or churches, must have still been in existence when it became the temporary burial place of Eadulph Rus who was the alleged murderer of Bishop Walcher of Durham in 1080.

The body of Eadulph was exhumed on the orders of Turgot, Archdeacon of Durham some time before 1107 and thrown out of the consecrated ground. Fairly recent excavations of a drain in the abbey grounds found fragments of a human body and an exquisite comb in walrus ivory. It is tempting and feasible to put the two together and suggest that Eadulph used this comb to remove the fleas from his beard.

On more practical terms, the fact that Turgot was able to issue such orders is an example of how far-reaching the powers of the See of St Cuthbert was. By the twelfth century, the bishops of Durham had become Prince-Bishops with total power over all levels of society. One Prince-Bishop was said to like his meals served by 'ladies in tight-fitting bodices' but that might a rumour from the tabloid press of the day.

John, the Bishop of Glasgow and David's friend and advisor, must have had some influence on the siting and foundation of the abbey because he was laid to rest in Jedburgh rather than his own see at Glasgow, in 1147 or 8.

Dryburgh Abbey

Dryburgh, like Kelso, has a much earlier precedent claim to Christianity. In the calender of Scottish Christian saints, the sixth-century St Modan is described as 'Abbot of Dryburgh' and there is also, on site, an early Northumbrian cross socket which would tie in with that period. Although no remains can be traced because the buildings are likely to have been of wood, the probable location would have been where the Tweed makes a horseshoe bend. This is similar to the placement of Old Melrose and Kelso abbeys.

There is some debate about who was the founder of Dryburgh Abbey as King David gave 'certain territories' in his great Charter, but *Chronicle of Melrose*, the records of Melrose Abbey, notes Hugo de Moreville, the Lord of Lauderdale and Constable of Scotland, as the founder.

In 1140, the site was selected by Canons of the Premonstratensian Order to be their first home in Scotland, the parent house of the White Canons being at Alnwick in Northumbria. By 1150, the building must have been progressed enough for the Canons to move in and the official foundation was in December 1152.

If not the founder, the Constable, de Morville, was a generous benefactor to the Abbey, giving the churches and lands of Channelkirk and Saltoun and a ploughgate of land in Newton stretching from the west of Dere Street to the lands of Thirlstane. The king gifted the Churches of Lanark, Pettinain and Caddisleya with their lands, and Lessudden, now St Boswells, was granted to Dryburgh by an unknown donor.

Like other early religious foundations, Dryburgh soon gathered enough property and concessions to become a major factor in the regeneration of the Borders.

The religious orders also financed various hospitals and leper hospitals for the care of the old, infirm and poor, and provided hospitality inns for pilgrims passing through the Borders.

As well as their religious and wealth-making roles, it was clear that the new monastic orders had political attractions for the king. Their dependence on his benevolence was equally balanced with their independence from the Prince-Bishops of Durham who had been trying to claim Jedburgh, Teviotdale and the upper Tweed as part of the Durham See. The abbeys of Selkirk/Kelso, Melrose, Jedburgh and Dryburgh together with the nunneries at Eccles, Coldstream, St Bathans and Berwick made a substantial block which changed the political boundaries of the Borders.

THE RESULTS

David I is rightly hailed as the king who made Scotland and was proclaimed a legend in his own lifetime, but his proclaimers were his own scholarly priests and Anglo-Norman chroniclers. Living legends are never overly popular with their contemporaries, but it is fair to say that he left Scotland in a far better condition than he received it.

Certainly he transformed the backward-looking country into one that could take its place in the Europe of the time, but the speed at which that transformation was accomplished has been exaggerated by some historians. Many of the changes begun by David would take another half century or more to reach fruition.

David had laid the foundations for a modernised country and we have to assess his innovations by the reasoning of his time and not judge them by ours. Despite this there have been some detractors, of whom Selkirk's Andrew Lang takes a Victorian romantic's view that: 'With Alexander, Celtic domination ends; with David, Anglo-Norman and English dominance is established'. This is almost a guilt trip about the noble Celtic savages being replaced by ruthless English overlords – and this at a time when the 'British' Empire was conquering and often pillaging the 'lesser lands beyond the seas' for the enrichment of the Mother Country.

David was an astute politician. Unlike the blitzkrieg Normanisation of England by William the Conquerer and his son William Rufus, he pursued a policy of skilful manipulation by making the best use of men and resources. His gradual changes were accomplished through the use of royal patronage to both church and state, the empowerment to the landowning and merchant classes without being seen to favour either unduly, and the Norman feudalisation of society which was accomplished without antagonising most of the old nobility.

David was fortunate to be living at the time he did and with the opportunities he had. This was almost a Golden Age when Europe was thriving with new deeds, production and thinking. More importantly from the late tenth century to the end of the twelfth century, Europe experienced hot dry summers and colder winters with accumulating benefits to food supplies, resulting in population growth. The standards of living were rising and, although the bulk of the people would still be living on the land on a near subsistence level, demand for goods was increasing. David's innovations meant that Scotland had the capacity to supply some of the needs of a burgeoning Low Countries populations.

In Scotland, the average temperature in the 1140s was 1°C higher than in 1900 to 1950. With this slight but vital rise, farming could be extended to higher levels on the hillsides and the growing season was increased by two to three weeks in the lower arable lands.

This warm period with its good harvests was the period when the new monasteries were introducing sheep farms into the Border hills and the feudal estates were copying their example. As the population increased, more woodland was cleared for farming and to supply timber for housing. This was a period of some prosperity when the rich became richer and the poor got fed.

It is true that all was not sweetness and light and some of David's judgements were flawed. He had to contend with four dynastic rebellions in his lifetime. In 1138, he led what was probably the largest Scottish army ever assembled into England, ostensibly in support of his niece, the Empress Matilda, in her claim for the throne of England, but in reality to re-acquire Northumbria and consolidate Cumbria for the Scottish Crown. The defeat at the Battle of the Standard cost him dearly in manpower and prestige.

But the greatest disaster came in 1152 with the death of Prince Henry, his only surviving child, leaving the aged and ailing monarch with an eleven-year-old grandson, Malcolm, as his heir while the other grandson, William, was the nine-year-old Earl of Northumberland.

The ailing monarch knew that the accession of a young boy to the throne was likely to be challenged, so he sought to minimise the risk by presenting Malcolm to his future subjects as the acknowledged heir. David sent the young prince on a tour of the northern part of the kingdom under the guardianship of the Earl of Fife, the most senior of the Gaelic nobility.

As Malcolm, the king-designate, travelled north, David escorted his second grandson William through Northumberland to Newcastle and presented the nine-year-old boy to the nobility of the earldom as their future lord. To bind their oaths of loyalty, he also took hostages from the Northumbrians.

In the spring of 1153, David's health deteriorated badly, so 'he made his peace with God and prepared for death'. On the morning of 29 May 1153 he was found dead in his bed in the chamber of the great tower at Carlisle. His body was carried to Dunfermline and he was buried in the abbey there beside the bodies of his father, mother and brothers.

The long period of stability during his reign was at an end and, within four years, Northumberland and Cumbria had returned to England, leaving the border settled on the line of the Tweed and Solway.

CHAPTER ELEVEN
1153 to 1500

Until now we have been concentrating on the early beginnings of the Borders and the areas around, with Selkirkshire appearing only where there is enough known or postulated, to justify the mention.

In this chapter, the written and ground evidence of the county becomes slightly more plentiful and Selkirkshire takes its place in the history of the Borders. That said, Selkirkshire was still a pocket of poor agricultural ground enclosed by hills, with no abbey or great castle to make a focal point and no through roads with large amounts of passing traffic; so it is only when something important was happening in the area that written records are more plentiful.

During the wars to retain Scottish independence, Selkirk and Selkirk Forest appear frequently as English military reports in the *Calendar of Documents Relating To Scotland* (see p.310). Various Abbey cartularies note their holdings within the county. The lands of Selkirk/Ettrick Forest are recorded in some detail only after the fall of the House of Douglas in 1455 when the lands reverted to the Crown to be noted in the Exchequer Rolls of Scotland. The name of the forest changed from Selkirk to Ettrick Forest or variants, over the centuries but for more on the forest, see p.361.

Monastic cartularies provide a source of information between 1150 and 1560 and as a result our knowledge of rural development is largely based on the monastic surveys of Kelso and Coldingham around 1300. These are biased towards monastic estates and the condition therefore cannot be safely transposed to the non-monastic agricultural settlements throughout the Borders. In more recent writings, there is also the fear that modern assumptions have been made to fit into medieval farming methods.

Field-walking finds and archaeological excavations together with the work of archaeobotanists have been able to add more information about the people and conditions of life in this period. But even within Selkirkshire, there were distinct divisions: the lands of the Forest with rough grazing with areas of timber and scrub; the semi-cultivated eastern part of the county ran by and for the Church; and the town of Selkirk between the two, relying on and supplying both.

At the time of the death of David I in 1153, Selkirkshire was held almost totally by the Crown or the Church and by far the largest portion was taken up with the royal hunting reserve known as Selkirk/Ettrick Forest.

The village that became the burgh of Selkirk was a royal vill with the right to use part of a common land of 4,532 hectares, most of which lay within the modern county boundaries. The Forest drew the various kings of Scotland to hunt there and their attendant courts would help Selkirk to grow in size but also prevented any other large settlement within the forest boundaries.

Church holdings within the county were comparatively smaller but more scattered. Selkirk Abbatis, a land block of a similar size to the common, was the land given to Selkirk Abbey and now belonged to Kelso Abbey. Melrose Abbey held the 'waste land' in the Upper Ettrick Valley and Little Yarrow above St Mary's Loch. The Bishop of Glasgow was in possession of the lands of Ashkirk (Aschechyre) as early as 1116 and had a 'Palace' at The Woll.

It sometimes seems that the written story of the Borders consisted wholly of kings, nobles and reivers together with the battles they fought. In fact they represent the superficial and glamorised story of less than 0.01 per cent of the people who lived and worked here in the four and a half centuries between the time that David I left his imprint on the land until James VI rode through to become James I of Great Britain.

I will be using some of these already-recorded people, facts and figures because this is what appears in documents but I will also try to identify the lesser mortals who are seldom recognised but are equally important in the history of the Borders.

Contemporary descriptions on the lot of the commoner are rare, since most medieval records surviving are charters for the holding or transference of property. Charters may detail land boundaries with rights of grazing on common lands, access to forest etc but can include snippets of human interest.

Fortunately these charters are preserved in cartularies of the Border abbeys and provide the main source of information for the period 1150 to 1500. They are written in a shorthand version of monk Latin which is a barrier to all but the most determined medieval historians. Even then, the word contractions used which are meant to save paper/parchment, can cause some differences in academic opinion.

We are on safer ground in the later part of the medieval period which, in addition to the previously quoted sources, is covered by the much under-used Walter Mason Trust collection, a vast store of documents saved from destruction by Selkirk bakers Walter and Bruce Mason in 1940.

SELKIRK – THE TOWN AND CASTLE

The first mention of Selkirk is in the foundation charter of Selkirk Abbey 'a certain particle of land which leads from the Castle to the Abbey and the Yarrow, that is towards the old town (veterem villam)' This tells us that there was both an old town and a Castle in the immediate vicinity but in different places. It has been established above that the 'old town' is the Anglian settlement on the flat fields at Philiphaugh while the 'particle of land' is at Kilcroft, now Kilncroft.

This leaves the castle situated in the present burgh with the only feasible site on a raised mound known as Peel Hill, now within the Haining House policies at the end of Castle Street, formerly known as Peel Gait. The names give a convincing clue and there is no other defensible site near the town.

On the north of the site, a steep slope reaches round to the burn known as the Clockie – a survival of the Norman-French 'cloaque' meaning a drain. The south and west sides were protected by the Haining Loch, then more extensive than it is now, leaving only the ridge of Castle Street as a means of access from the east. This entry was protected by a deep ditch cut across the ridge. In area, the enclosed space must have measured around six hundred square metres. It has been suggested that the castle in the Foundation Charter must have been built by David I when he was still David the Earl.

It is evident that Selkirk was an important gathering place for the number of peers and prelates who attended and witnessed the decrees and judgements enacted by the various kings of Scots who used the castle as headquarters when they came to hunt in Selkirk Forest.

In the 1159 charter of Malcolm IV, 'the church of the other Selkirk', ie the 'king's Selkirk' as opposed to the 'abbot's Selkirk', was conveyed to Kelso Abbey. From this we know that the vill of Selkirk possessed its own place of worship in 1159. The two Selkirks are recorded in a privilegium of Pope Innocent IV (1243–54), who confirmed possession of the Monks-Selkirk and the King's Selkirk.

This church would be erected on the outskirts of the housing round the castle; so it is possible to say that, by the mid-twelfth century, the king's Selkirk had extended as far as the site of the Auld Kirk in the Kirk Wynd.

William the Lion was a frequent inhabitant of the castle and issued at least twenty-seven charters from there and refers to 'my town of Selkirk'. Alexander II appears in the Melrose cartulary giving deeds 'apud Seleskirk' and in 1223 he sat 'in plena curia apud Seleskirk' to settle a dispute between the monks of Newbattle and the canons of Holyrood. (Most of the references recorded within the cartularies of Kelso and Melrose are land disputes between the various religious establishments.)

The most interesting of Alexander II's Selkirk Acts was in 1234, when he granted the lands on both sides of the river Ettrick, then held by Richard son of Edwin, to the monks of Kelso for the perpetual maintenance of the bridge of 'Ecctrick'. This charter was signed at Selechirche on the 7th of June in the nineteenth year of his reign before a number of nobles and church dignitaries.

The bridge became a noted gathering place and the Abbots of Kelso with a powerful retinue, would travel there to hold ecclesiastical court 'apud pontem de Selcrig'.

Although the bridge could not be of long duration despite the deeds of perpetual maintenance, wooden piles driven into the river-bed can occasionally be seen when the river is low and a large red sandstone block on the north bank shows that the site of the bridge was exactly where the mounted cavalcade crosses the Ettrick on Common Riding Day. The bridge may be long gone but is still remembered in the name of the estate on the south side of the river, the Bridgelands.

It is not known if an Anglian hall with surrounding housing had preceded the wooden tower of David but it seems likely. When the Castle was built and became the centre of the royal court during the hunting season, this must have created a huge demand for food and services in the area. Traders and craftsmen would settle beside the castle to supply such needs.

For defensive purposes, castles were kept apart from the supply settlement by an open space. In the case of Selkirk, it is certain that the supply cottages would extend along the ridge which is now Castle Street and Back Row; this was the main road which ran between the castle and the Abbey which lay at Lindean. The early market place is likely to have been where Kirk Wynd crosses the Back Row and exits through the South Port. There was an open space there, which was still being used as a wood market as late as the sixteenth century.

When this central area of the town was demolished in the mid 1960s, some unglazed pottery that could have dated from the twelfth or thirteenth centuries, was picked up from the debris but no discernible house foundations from the period were recognised. The reason for this may be that only perishable and degradeable material like timber, turf and clay was used in the construction, and medieval buildings had only stone foundations.

In the mid 1980s, the Border Burghs Archaeological Group carried out an excavation at Springwood Park, Kelso, where fieldwalkers had picked up a vast amount of medieval pottery. (The Elliot family staggered up to the National Museum of Scotland with four large boxes of Springwood pottery in the late 1970s.)

With the Springwood buildings in mind, it is a feasible suggestion that the Selkirk houses were much the same size and construction. They varied from 8m to 12m long and 3.5 to 4.5m broad internally with a stone foundation nearly a metre thick and at least two courses of stone high. The walls were heightened by alternated layers of stone and turf or by a woven wattle covered in a thick layer of water-impervious clay. The roofs were likely to have been supported by cruck-trusses with pairs of wooden rafters held by a cross-piece near the top. Bound to these, were interwoven wattle panels covered with a thick layer of straw thatch and the whole was covered with turf. The floors were often made with hard-packed puddle clay or clay and flat stones.

The most important feature was the fire. In the more basic houses, the fire occupied a central hearth and the smoke filtered its way through the straw and turf roof. Everyone sat, ate and slept round the fire, especially after a hard day's work in the fields. There is a hypnotic effect of sitting staring into a flickering fire on a dark winter's night. One problem there was the supply of fuel. Wood was becoming scarce through the implementation of Forest Laws; gorse, broom and heather were needed for other building purposes while the workable peat mosses were becoming further and further away.

Although these small houses seem very primitive in modern terms, they were snug and waterproof dwellings as long as they were well maintained and if they were blown or burned down they could be easily replaced.

The People of Selkirk 1153–1286

We have no written record of what the inhabitants of the town were like in this period but it is likely that they would be the same mixture as could be found in any medieval burgh of inland Scotland. All would be largely dependent on the product of their rigs of land outside the town and the tradesmen would rely on the surrounding countryside for raw material. Standing on the edge of Ettrick Forest, Selkirk benefited from the proximity of the forest pastures. The mixture of merchants, tradesmen and craftsmen would be similar to the variety who founded the Incorporations in the seventeenth century.

The fleshers or butchers would buy an animal in the burgh market place, kill it, keeping the meat for sale. The skin would be sold on to the cordiners or leather workers who would tan it in the tan-pits which still appear during construction in the town. The tanned leather was then made into jerkins, horse-harness, buckets and, principally, shoes. (It is not for nothing that the people of Selkirk are still referred to as 'souters', a derogatory name derived from the Latin 'sutor' a shoemaker.) Wool from sheep grazing in the forest would provide raw material for the weavers who would spin and weave it into cloth for sale to the tailors who would make clothing to order for their fellow burgesses and for the nobles who came to hunt in the Forest. With everyone busy at their trades and tilling their outlying rigs of land outside the town, specialist builders, smiths, coopers and joiners would be called on to provide new housing and repair the old. In time, these would form the Hammermen's Incorporation.

Around the town lay the burgh and common lands, the use of which had been granted to the townfolk to be shared by the 'homines meis'(my men) of David I and the monks and tenants of the Abbey. The common lands were common in the sense that several communities had the rights of grazing over them and the common was controlled by whoever held the land; in the case of Selkirk, this was the sheriff in the name of the king. This common land must have been huge in the time of David I and despite numerous land-grabs, the Selkirk Common was 11,200 acres or 4,550 hectares, in the sixteenth century. There is no documentary evidence to back up Selkirk's possession of this common but the only time when enough land was available on the royal demesne was in the time of David I.

Alexander III, in his reign of thirty-seven years, is recorded in being at Selkirk Castle on several occasions. From Selkirk on 16th June 1275 he gave a charter of free warren and free forest to the Priory of Coldingham, also granting a Fair to be held at Coldingham on St Cuthbert's day in Lent or St Ebba's the Virgin's day (25 August) for fifteen days or eight days and permission to hold a market every Wednesday.

From Selkirk on 25 May 1279, he wrote to Edward I of England asking for a favourable audience to his (Scots) ambassadors and not permit his liberties to be violated.

It may be that the castle was no longer a suitable royal residence as he was more frequently at Traquair, and maybe Alexander was not a keen huntsman. Selkirk would continue to be a place of importance being the centre of local government and the venue for sheriff courts. As such, it would continue to grow in size and importance until the death of Alexander in 1286 brought an end to a 'golden period' of Scottish history. I would suspect that the golden period was only known as such when compared with the twenty-eight years which followed.

THE WARS TO RETAIN
SCOTTISH INDEPENDENCE

On the death of Alexander III, Scotland was left with the Maid of Norway as the only heir to the throne but she died before reaching her new kingdom. A dozen claimants put themselves forward. Edward I of England was suggested as an unbiased judge to decide who should be king of Scots but first he made each one swear to accept him as Overlord of Scotland. John Balliol was quite legitimately chosen as king of Scots in 1292. That same year, Edward sent a notice to John le Tailleur, the tenant of Selkirk Mill, that the rent of £28 which he owed in arrears was to be sent to the executors of the will of Master Robert of Dumfries, lately Chancellor of OUR kingdom of Scotland.

I did find it slightly ironic that the first Selkirk man to be identified appears on an English document as the debtor to an English king but this was to be a pattern of things to come. Most of our knowledge of early Selkirk come from from surviving English records and naturally are somewhat biased. Originally in Norman-French and medieval Latin, they have been collected, translated and published in a four-volume set *The Calendar of Documents Relating To Scotland*. This is fortunate as my medieval Latin is not too bad but my Norman-French is a mixture of hope and guess-work.

Once in command Edward was very generous, with 138 stags and 64 oak trees from Selkirk Forest being given to magnates and potential supporters. To Robert Wishart, Bishop of Glasgow, he gave twenty stags together with sixty oak trees to repair the spire of St Mungo's Church in Glasgow, but it is said that the Bishop had them converted into mangonels and catapults to batter down Kirkintilloch Castle, then in English hands, before putting them to the use for which they were intended. Bishop Wishart was keen to preserve the independence of the Scottish Church.

By June 1294, the Mayor, burgh officers and community of Berwick, a Scottish burgh, were buttering Edward up by addressing letters to Edward which started 'as King ruling by Divine Providence, the three realms of England, Scotland and Ireland'. Ironically King John of Scotland was also complaining to Edward 'on behalf of the burgesses of Berwick'.

Edward was making ever-increasing demands for more taxation from all, and greater military service from the nobles, this to be served in France. Aware that his actions were unpopular in Scotland, Edward struck a pre-emptive blow in October 1295, ordering the lands of all Scotsmen living in England to be confiscated and, in December, issued writs for an armed muster at Newcastle on 1 March 1296.

Balliol would have heard about this and decided to be prepared for all eventualities, mustering an army at Caddonlee, near Clovenfords, the traditional gathering point for an invasion of England, on 11 March 1296. Balliol has received a poor press for his actions during his four-year reign but this is perhaps because the known original sources are either pro-English or pro-Bruce/Stewart, who were hostile to Balliol. The Bruce faction did not turn out at the Caddonlee muster as their hopes for the throne of Scotland were still very much alive.

Although Edward had a large army waiting at Newcastle, he waited until the Scots had captured Wark Castle and another Scots army had devastated the countryside around Carlisle before making his move. The English forces, estimated at 1,000 men-at-arms, 60,000 infantry and an unknown number of knights, were veteran professional soldiers, paid to fight, and vastly experienced through service in Edward's campaigns in France and Wales. In fact, the bulk of the English army were not English but a composite force from the Continent, Ireland and Wales.

On 30 March 1296 the English army came to Berwick-upon-Tweed. Although it was Scotland's most important and prosperous burgh, it was defended only by a wooden palisade which was quickly overthrown. The castle commander surrendered but this did not save the inhabitants of the burgh who were slaughtered in their thousands. The report came from a Scottish source and has become accepted fact through much repetition, but is unlikely because Edward would have wanted a working port and population to add taxes to his exchequer.

The Scots army who were attacking the north of England returned home and seized the castle of Dunbar as a stronghold against the approaching English who were commanded by Balliol's brother-in-law, the Earl of Surrey. The Scots rushed into action too soon and were soundly defeated. Thereafter, Scots resistance collapsed and Edward made a triumphal procession round the east coast of Scotland as far as Elgin and Banff. During this expedition, Edward made a point of exacting an oath of fealty from every person of note. Among those professing loyalty to Edward on the infamous Ragman's Roll, were 174 names from the county of Roxburgh, forty from the country of Peebles and nine from the county of Selkirk. The reason for the small number of worthy men in Selkirkshire was that the main part of the county was a forest in the royal demesne and as such had few notables within its bounds.

Edward removed the records and relics of the conquered Scots to destroy the reminders of national identity. Amongst those removed 'as a sign of the resignation and conquest of Scotland' were the Stone of Destiny, the Black Rood of St Margaret, and any documents relation to the independent kingdom.

But if Edward found it easy to conquer Scotland with his superior numbers, he found it less easy to hold. Like the Romans before him, Edward found that English forces could control parts of the Borders by garrisoning the castles of Roxburgh, Cavers, Selkirk and Jedburgh, but these were isolated strongholds which required food and supplies. As well as a supply train to convey these to the outlying castles, there had to be a guarding force to prevent the supplies from being stolen en route. Only Berwick, as a port, town and castle could be easily supplied by ship; but the natives were restless and Edward was finding that maintaining an army of occupation was an expensive business.

Wallace

In April 1296, Sir Robert Clifford was collecting hostages from the Selkirk Forest to ensure their good behaviour; this proved to be futile as the Scots simply retreated deeper into the Forest, which the English horsemen were reluctant to enter. The Forest became a gathering place for the disaffected rebels and they had a charismatic leader in the shape of William Wallace. On 23 July 1297, a letter written at Berwick by the English general, Sir Hugh de Cressingham urges an attack 'upon William Wallace who lay with a large company (and still does) in the Forest of Selkirk, like one who holds himself against your peace'.

How many Borderers joined Wallace in the Forest is unknown but

it is unlikely that Sir Nichol de Ruthirfurd was the only one. Sir Nichol
had already been forced to sign allegiance to Edward but this did not
prevent him joining Wallace.

> Gud Ruthirfurd, that euir trew has beyn
> In Atryk wode again the sotheroun keyn
> Bydyn he had, and dome them mikell der
> Saxte he led of nobil men in wer.

Meanwhile, in the north-east of Scotland, Sir Andrew Murray was
leading another uprising and, hearing that Wallace had left the security
of Selkirk Forest and was besieging the English-held castle of Dundee,
marched south to join forces. The conjoined force was a 'common
army' of around eight thousand foot and thirty-six horse, most of
whom would have come with Murray, the nobleman.

On 11 September 1297, the Scots common army scored a
spectacular victory at Stirling Bridge. The Scots cause lost a noted leader
when Sir Andrew Murray died a few months after the battle from
wounds received there – an unsung hero of the wars to retain Scottish
independence.

After the battle, Wallace, as representative of King John and 'the
Community of the Realm of Scotland', went on the offensive, moving
southwards to besiege Roxburgh castle and Berwick, whose town was
captured by forces led by Sir Henry de Haliburton. Sir Henry held lands
in Upper Lamberton on the outskirts of the burgh. Roxburgh castle
was besieged but not taken. Jedburgh town and castle were taken and a
Scots garrison installed. At the same time raiding into the north of
England caused panic stations at Carlisle and Newcastle, seriously
damaging the economy of the area as the Exchequer Rolls show.

During late 1297 and early 1298, it is likely that Wallace had
returned to Selkirk Forest as a secure base. Whether he was there in
person is not known but it is unlikely that he would not be present at
the siege of Roxburgh and Berwick, the two principal burghs and
castles in Scotland. It was only through the intervention of a relieving
English army that the siege of Roxburgh was lifted on 12 February
1298 and that of Berwick three days later.

It is not certain when Wallace was first acclaimed as a Guardian of

Scotland but in a charter given to Alexander Scrymgeour at Torphichen
on 29 March 1298, he was first described as 'Custos Regni at ductor
exercituum ejusdem' in the name of Lord John, king of Scots and by
consent of the community. If this happened between 15 February and
29 March, the most likely scenario for his knighting and being
proclaimed Guardian would have been in Selkirkshire, either in Selkirk
Forest or more probably at Selkirk itself which was the administrative
centre of the Forest, the location of previous parliamentary precedents
and had buildings capable of sheltering a gathering of nobles and
leaders. In Blind Harry's epic poem *Wallace,* written between 1476 and
1478, we read that:

> At a consail iii dayis sojornyt thar
> At Forest Kyrk a meeing ordand he
> Thai chesd Wallace Scottis Warband to be.

It seems a logical conclusion that Selkirk was the most probable venue
for the council although positive documentary evidence is lacking. As
one historian pointed out it could have happened anywhere in
southern Scotland. Another states quite happily that 'Wallace was
dubbed by Bruce and made guardian in March 1298 in the forest of
Selkirk'.

It is unlikely that we will ever know for certain but I choose to
believe that Selkirk was the location and will continue to do so until
someone can find sufficient contemporary evidence to convince me
otherwise.

Fact or fiction? There is a murky division between fact and fiction
that provides the historians of this period with an everlasting battleground. For contemporary comment we have to rely almost totally on
the English records which were mainly military reports sent to London
by the various English field commanders in Scotland. These war analysts
are unlikely to have written critical reports unless the situation was
really desperate and they needed more troops or, more frequently,
money to pay those already here. For the Scottish perspective, we have
to rely on Barbour's *Bruce* and Blind Harry's *Wallace.* Both are based on
fact but what they represent is a propaganda war conducted by King
Robert the Bruce against his predecessor, John Balliol and his

supporters, notably the traditional Bruce enemies the Comyns. Exchequer Rolls and Treasurer's Accounts provide some additional facts and learned historians have added their own interpretations.

In fact, it is very difficult to separate the factual Wallace from the fictional Wallace, who has become an impossibly inspirational figure over the centuries. Folk legend provides where documentary evidence fails. A large stone on Meigle Hill is known as Wallace's Putting Stone and a sixteenth-century pele tower near Roxburgh is cheerfully claimed as 'Wallace's Tower'. In Peeblesshire, there is a Wallace's hill behind Cardrona, and in Selkirkshire a linear earthwork cutting the Minchmoor track from Yarrowford to Traquair called Wallace's Trench, is accepted as the camp where the rebel forces took shelter before the victory at Stirling Bridge. The fact that it is a straight single ditch and on the worst possible place for a camp, makes little difference to the legend. I think it was the 'trench of the Welsh' as a cluster of Cumbric (Welsh) names appear on one side and a number of Anglian names on the other but it also provides a dividing line between the Yarrow and Ettrick Wards of the Forest.

The results of Stirling Bridge encouraged several Scots nobles to leave Edward and join the rebellion but, in general terms, the Scottish nobility were not yet ready to come out in open revolt; that they changed their coats two or three times before finally taking sides was a sign of the times. It must have been difficult to decide which side to support when you held lands in England, Ireland, Normandy and Scotland.

It must be admitted that the Battle of Stirling Bridge was lost by English incompetence rather than Scots' brilliance and the weakness of Scots in formal battle was to be revealed at Falkirk the following year.

After the Battle of Stirling, the English administration was now taking the situation very seriously. Edward was in trouble in Flanders, the Scots were raiding through the northern counties of England, Scotland north of the Forth was lost and even the castles still held in the south-east Borders were short of provisions and the garrisons had not been paid for some time. By mid February 1298 the English noblemen still on campaign or holding castles in Scotland, informed Surrey that they were not able to remain there any longer unless the foot-soldiers were paid for without wages they could not buy food.

On 14 April 1298, Edward returned from Flanders and set about re-taking Scotland. Writs had gone out for a summer campaign on 8 April. The exchequer accounts show that 12,779 Welsh, 4,047 men from Ireland, Shropshire and Staffordshire, 2,057 from various English counties and 1,027 from the Berwick garrison were initially recruited, but the numbers increased until 25,781 foot-soldiers were paid their wages 20 July 1298.

The logistics of feeding and otherwise supplying this number must have been a nightmare. Sticking to the coast, the English army could be fed from supply ships coming from the gathering point at Berwick but contrary winds had prevented this for nearly a month. The retreating Scots carried out a burnt earth policy to prevent the English from living off the land and they had been in Scotland since 3 July.

News that the English forces were starving and rumours that Edward had received broken ribs when his horse stood on him during the night, heartened the Scots. This led to Wallace's decision to risk all in an effort to expel the English from Scotland permanently. Wallace chose his ground well, on a low hill near Falkirk which had a wet peat-bog in front of it. His spearmen were placed in four schiltroms, a hedgehog formation with archers between and cavalry behind.

The battle started well for the Scots with two English cavalry divisions floundering in the soft peat, but when another cavalry force got behind the Scots army, the Scots cavalry led by Sir John Comyn fled the field, leaving the Scots archers to be slaughtered by the mail-clad knights. Then the spearmen in the schiltroms stood helplessly while the English archers rained down their deadly volleys of arrows. The schiltroms were weakened until their formation could be broken by mounted knights and footmen. It was a disaster for the common people who made up the bulk of Wallace's army.

Although Edward had achieved a resounding victory at Falkirk, his army also suffered. Drawing on payroll accounts, there were three thousand fewer English foot-soldiers to be paid after the battle than two days before and these, together with the loss of about a tenth of his own paid cavalry, made him unable to secure the complete subjugation of Scotland. In September 1298, Edward had to leave owing to unrest in the north of England and he would not return to Scotland until July 1301. This gave the battered Scots time to retrench and regroup.

Military tacticians have agreed that it was unlikely that Wallace had intended to fight a formal battle when another two days would have reduced his enemy to helplessness by starvation.

Much has been made of the Scots cavalry fleeing the field without striking a blow. This had happened previously at Dunbar and accusations of treachery or cowardice were made. In Edward's army the English and Welsh long-bowmen and Genoese cross-bowmen could only be dispersed by cavalry and, by leaving the field, the departing Scots cavalry deprived Wallace of the only counter, and this was to prove a decisive factor. There was a large number of the Scottish nobility who were actively and passively against Wallace and more particularly against his assumption of the Guardianship. His success at Stirling Bridge and invasion of northern England only deepened their dislike.

Not all the Scots noblemen fled the field, some fought on foot in the schiltrons. Sir John Stewart of Jedburgh, the brother of James the Stewart, fought and died with the bowmen of Selkirk Forest. Hemingford records that: 'The Steward of Scotland's brother, while giving orders to the Archers of Selkyrke Forest, fell by accident from his horse and was slain in their midst. For the archers crowded round him and with him perished many men of lithe form and unusual stature.' This is the first recorded instance of the 'Flowers o the Forest being aa wede awa' – it would happen again many times in the succeeding centuries.

After the battle, Wallace resigned from the Guardianship. He must have known that the quarrelling nobility would never accept his leadership or join together to secure independence. As the remnants of the independence-minded Scots regrouped in the Selkirk Forest, Wallace realised that future freedom for Scotland lay in diplomatic rather than military activity.

He must have been totally disillusioned with the inability of the Scots nobles to work together to achieve the common goal and was realistic enough to know that the numerically superior English forces could not be defeated in open conflict by a divided Scottish nation. Wallace thought that, by political pressure, some form of self-determination might be available by the restoration of Balliol, even under Edward's sovereignty. Wallace never veered from his loyalty to King John Balliol and it would be seven hundred years later that this form of devolution would be acceptable to the people of Scotland.

Wallace was not the romantic outlaw of modern fiction. He was a warleader when required but also an astute politician when war failed. So he travelled abroad selling the cause of Scotland as an independent country and possibly as a thorn in the flesh of the belligerent Edward. We are fairly certain that he travelled to Norway first, where he received the safe-conduct issued by Hakon V that was in his possession when he was captured in 1305. Moving through France and Italy, he gained some support from the king of France and the most powerful organisation in Europe, the Catholic Church. In this he was greatly aided by William Lamberton, whose election as Bishop of St Andrews had been largely due to Wallace's influence.

Confronted with the possibility of having to fight in France and Scotland, along with unrest in Wales and Ireland and the enmity of the Pope and Church, Edward put his ideas of total conquest of Scotland on hold. It would be 1303 before he was free from other distractions and free to pursue his ambitions for a final subjugation of Scotland.

In Selkirk Forest

Back in the Selkirk Forest, the remnants of the national party were beaten but unbowed and their continued resistance was causing trouble to the English commanders in that vicinity. With the connivance of Sir Simon Fraser, the English-installed forester, the Scots were reforming. The Constable of Edinburgh Castle was warning the Lord Treasurer of England that Fraser was not to be trusted as he had allowed the fragmented Scots into the Forest without warning the English garrisons who could have dealt with them piecemeal.

This information must have been passed to Edward who wrote to the commanders of Roxburgh and Jedburgh Castles that: 'they must on their part make some good expeditions upon the Forest of Selkirk and elsewhere, where they perceive it will be good and that they exert themselves to do this so well that the king may thereof have some good news'.

These expeditions into the forest were led by Sir William Latimer, captain of the eastern garrisons, who had some successes but not without cost. In a list of horses killed up to September 1298 is a white horse valued at twelve merks 'in a sally towards the Forest of Selkirk'.

Within a year, much of the Forest was in English hands but the Scots were fighting back to retain their safe refuge. At the beginning of August 1299, the Scottish leaders had a meeting in the safety of Selkirk Forest to plan an attack on Roxburgh but, owing to the strength of the town's defences, decided that 'they could make no exploit without great loss of their troops'.

They met again later to discuss further plans. In a letter to Edward dated 20 August 1299, a spy for Robert Hastings, the English Constable of Roxburgh, reported that a meeting of Scottish nobles was held at Peebles on 8 August. Amongst those present were the Bishop of St Andrews; Robert Bruce, Earl of Carrick; the Earls of Buchan and Menteith; the Stewart of Scotland; and the young Sir John Comyn.

Their avowed intention was to further discuss plans to attack Roxburgh but the protagonists soon followed their own agendas. Sir David Graham (a Comyn follower) demanded the lands of Sir William Wallace because he had left the kingdom without the permission of the Guardians. Sir Malcolm Wallace (brother to William and a Bruce follower) said that the lands were protected as William was leaving in the kingdom's service. The two knights 'gave each other the lie' and drew their knives. Sir John Comyn took Bruce by the throat and the Earl of Buchan (another Comyn) seized the Bishop of St Andrews (a Wallace/Bruce supporter). It took the Steward to restore calm if not peace.

Eventually it was decided that Bishop Lamberton should have the nominal custody of the castles in Scots hands, Bruce and Comyn to be Guardians, Sir Ingram de Umfraville be Sheriff of Roxburgh and Sir Robert Keith be Warden of Selkirk Forest with a hundred barbed horses and fifteen hundred foot who, together with the foresters, would make raids on the English march.

Selkirkshire, and especially Selkirk Forest, was a battlefield with English forays into the Forest being countered by Scots raids on English-held castles outwith the forest. We have little evidence of the Scots successes other than number of lost horses claimed in the English expense accounts.

When Edward granted a truce from 30 October 1300 to 21 May 1301, there must have been a collective sigh of relief although two

English knights lost a ferrand horse and a roughard horse that had 'died in Selkirk Forest' during the period of truce.

The truce, however loosely interpreted, gave both sides a period of recuperation. Sir Aymer de Valence had time to replenish the supplies at the castle of Sellechirche after notice of the truce had been given to the suspect Sir Simon Fraser, the English-appointed Warden of Ettrick Forest.

It is doubtful if Edward intended to renew the truce since he was already issuing orders for mustering two armies by the end of March; one at Berwick to serve under his own command and another at Carlisle under his son, Edward, Prince of Wales.

Having mustered at Berwick in July, Edward's army moved up the Tweed to Roxburgh. Leaving there to make for Selkirk, he reviewed his forces at Midlem on the 25 July 1301 and moved on to Selkirk where he paid the 6,800 men of his army. Included in this number were ten Selkirk foresters, a minor contribution that would suggest that the English hold on the Forest was not totally secure. From Selkirk, Edward went up the Yarrow Valley, crossed the Minchmoor to Traquair and on to Peebles, where he remained two weeks before arriving at Glasgow on 21 August.

This progression was no leisurely stroll but a slow reconnaissance in strength through the Selkirk Forest to daunt and pursue the rebels sheltering there. Despite the number of troops involved, the column seems to have been harassed along the journey.

Edward must have been impressed with the potential of the forest as he placed Sir Hugh de Audeley with fifty men-at-arms and 120 foot-soldiers to maintain his hold there. The wages for the two knights and twenty-two men-at-arms who were left in the Forest of Selkirk was 26s per day.

At this period the wages paid to the English forces were 8 shillings per day for a magnate, a banneret 4s, a knight 2s, a sergeant or man-at-arms 1s and a common soldier 2d.

Selkirk Castle

Selkirk Castle is first mentioned in the foundation charter of Selkirk Abbey in 1119 and was used frequently by the kings of Scots when they hunted in the Forest, issuing charters and holding court within the two-acre site. As a centre of government and venue of the Sheriff and Forest courts, the castle and town grew in importance. Little is known about the size and shape of the castle or town during this period but during the wars to retain Scottish independence the castle became a focal point for control of the Selkirk Forest.

It must have been during Edward's 1301 visit to the area and his progression through the Forest that he realised the potential of what had been previously thought of as a small castle. Edward spent the winter of 1301–02 at Linlithgow while the Scots continued their tactics of harassment. The Scots knew that they could never match the numbers and ability of the English (mainly Welsh) army in open battle but could tie down large numbers with hit and run raids. This was hitting Edward where it hurt – in his pocket. He was constantly in need of money to continue his programme of conquest and his constant raising of taxes made him almost as much hated in his own domains as he was in Scotland. The barons and commons of England were proving as troublesome opponents as the Scottish rebels. In fact it was only the war in Scotland that unified the English in their counties to pay the necessary taxes to pursue that conflict.

Lack of money and the expense of keeping an army in Scotland during the winter season forced Edward to concede a truce of nine months on 26 January 1302.

This did not mean that the English left Scotland but rather that each side kept to its own territory and did not infringe on the other's rights and privileges.

On the assumption that the English held Selkirk Forest on 12 February 1302, Sir Alexander Balliol of Cavers made a bargain with Edward to guard the Forest with thirty men-at-arms at his own expense and also to find 600 foot-soldiers at four days' warning and 1,000 at eight days' warning 'as often as the warden saw fit for the defence of the forest'.

Edward and his Council at Roxburgh had been assessing the site of the old pele of Selkirk as a defensive focal point from which his forces could attack the Scots in Selkirk Forest. The other was to be in Peebles at the north-west side of the Forest so that the rebel forces could be attacked in a pincer movement from both sides.

On 14 February 1202 Edward authorised work to start.

Sir Alexander Balliol, the pro-English Constable of Selkirk Castle and Sir Robert Hastangs, the Sheriff and Constable of Roxburgh, were appointed to be surveyors of the works devised by the king for erecting the castle of Selkirk. William de Rue, the king's clerk, was to pay the workmen and other expenses incurred but Balliol and Hastangs were each to have a clerk present at every payday to ensure honesty. Master Renaud the Engineer, who had supervised the defences at Berwick, and Master Stephen of Northampton who had fortified Jedburgh, were to superintend the carpentry. The Sheriff of Northumberland was commanded by a letter under the Privy Seal to send sufficient carpenters, masons and diggers for the work as well as carriages for the materials; other workmen and carriages were to come from the bailliaries of Balliol and Hastangs themselves.

Work on the new Castle of Selkirk was so rapid that by 14 September 1302 it was reported that: 'The tower of the fortress of Selkirk is finished except for the roof from the shortage of plunk (planks) And a postern is made out of the tower to the west where there is stone facing, a drawbridge and a portcullis together with a good brestasche (gallery) above. And the stone work of this same drawbrige is half-finished. And 14 perches of the pele (in this case, an enclosing fence made from wood) are made from one part of the tower and from the other. And there are 43 perches yet to make. And the stone work of the chief gate of the fortress is raised above the level of the ground to the drawbridge.'

We have no descriptions of the internal buildings at Selkirk although later accounts of the Edinburgh and Stirling Castles in 1335–7 would suggest that the buildings in Selkirk would be no better and probably a great deal worse.

In Edinburgh, 'the houses for the garrison were evidently of timber and the walls covered or built of turf for warmth. The roofs of these houses were covered with straw or heath fastened in the usual manner with 'wattelyngs of twigs in considerable quantity. The hall, pantry, kitchen and other houses especially named also [had] straw, wekir and tempil for their roofs. Much timber was used on the great chapel which was converted into a granary'.

At Stirling: 'the partitions and ceilings were daubed with mortar and the roofs were of turf. The new pele erected in the inner bailey on the north side of the castle was entirely of timber and daubed with mortar as a precaution against fire'.

> When the trees were clear-felled from the castle site in the late 1960s, I
> went there with Jack and Caroline Cruickshank one day in winter and
> tramped out the lines of the divined buildings in the snow. We were able
> to mark the location of the motte, the outer bailey wall, the gateways to
> north and west and several buildings within the enclosure. The most
> prominent of these was a large L-shaped building whose arms were about
> 25m long and 4 to 5m across. It would be nice to have a trial dig in the
> motte but this is unlikely to ever happen. Digs cost a lot of money to do
> properly.

In the Wardrobe Accounts of 1303–4, the cost and details of building the castle are itemised: ' For pennies paid by William Rue to clerk assigned to pay the wages of the workers round the pele of Selkirk, to several carpenters, masons, surveyors barrow-makers, furnace stokers, fellers of trees in Selkirk Forest, sawyers, diggers, weighers of machines (?), to several men drawing branches and timber in the foresaid forest and for women carrying hods of lime and charcoal for the foresaid work and for several other workers from 28 March to 2 December 1302 and for the wages of the supervisors £1,061:0s:5d.

For pennies paid for iron bought for making several iron works in the said pele, for sea coal bought for these works and for canvas bought for making grain stores in the pele and … for expenses of burning lime £57:6s:1d.

For 9 crowbars at 3d each, 4 mallets at 7d each, 24 pick axes at 3d each, 34 chisels at 1.5d each, 24 spades at 2.5d each, 63 shovels at 1.5d each, 3 crossbows at 6s 8d each, 3 pairs of hand mills with bread and ale delivered to Roger Daylmer Constable of Selkirk pele. 109s 7.5d'. (I took the liberty of converting the silver half penny into decimal coinage because my computer does not do the halfpennies of yesteryear.)

The total cost for the erection of the castle was £1372:13s:10d which represents 329,446 silver pennies of the day. With this total to build one comparatively small castle in mind, it is no surprise that the metal detectorists in the Borders turn up so many.

This was not the end of the expense incurred; both the workmen and the incoming supplies had to be guarded. Sir Simon Fraser, the English-appointed Keeper of the Forest, had changed sides and on 13 August 1302, Sir Hugh de Audley was ordered to remain as Warden of Selkirk Forest with twenty men-at-arms and two hundred foot-soldiers. This was changed when Sir Alexander Balliol became Warden with 30 men-at-arms from his own retinue for a period from 1 September 1302 to Christmas day. For this he was paid £50, another 12,000 silver pennies. Towards the end of 1302, the Scots were gaining in strength and Sir Alexander was suspected of being about to change sides. To make sure that such an important castle remained in English hands, Edward had him arrested, and only when he delivered his son to be held hostage at Berchamstede Castle, was he released. His son Alexander was not to be held in irons and was allowed 4d (pence) per day for his sustenance and his warder was to be paid 2d for his trouble.

This great influx of money coming into the burgh must have caused inflation in the local market place and the area around Selkirk was not able to supply all the food required for the workmen building the castle. On 5 September 1302, 60 quarters of wheat, 10 casks of wine, 120 quarters of malt, 160 quarters of salt, 20 quarters of beans and peas and 60 quarters of sea coal were sent from Berwick (a 'quarter' is a quarter of a hundredweight ie 28lbs). Also included in the consignment were 20 crossbows and 5,000 quarrels (crossbow bolts) which must have been in preparation for the recommencement of hostilities when the truce ended. The end of the truce saw the English-held garrisons being strengthened in numbers and structure 'against the coming of the Scottish army'.

In spite of the precautions, the Scots emerged from the Forest to capture Selkirk Castle in January 1303. It is likely that much of the structure was destroyed to deny the English the full benefit of the castle as a base. Edward was not best pleased that his expensive castle had been taken and issued orders for the arrest of Sir Alexander Balliol on 3 February, but he could not be found in Kent where he had been inspecting his English estates. He must have been located and imprisoned as records show that he was released on 14 March after renewing his promises to Edward, but Thomas, another son, was to remain in English hands. Edward's memory was long and it took until March 1305 before he forgave Sir Alexander for the loss of the pele at Selkirk and restored his lands in Scotland and England.

The taking and destruction of Selkirk Castle had all the hallmarks of a Wallace plan to harass the enemy but he had not yet returned from his diplomatic tour of Europe and the national party in southern Scotland was being led by Sir John Comyn and Sir Simon Fraser. By now the Scots had accepted that they were never going to be able to counter the massive English superiority of heavy cavalry in open battle. They countered this advantage by exploiting its weaknesses. The Scots used hit-and-run tactics with a retreat into Selkirk Forest and other remote regions where heavy cavalry were unwieldy and had to operate without the infantry support on which they depended. The English forces and their Scottish allies could retain the isolated garrison castles while their supplies and money lasted, but as long as the Scots could hold the forests and keep sniping away at the supply trains, there was always going to be a stalemate.

Towards the end of the truce (1 November 1302), the stalemate continued. The Scots could not get King John back as their sovereign by diplomatic means but, on the plus side, there had been no English forces north of the Forth/Clyde line for the last five years. South of the line, the English military gains were held despite a continuing drain on resources and the supply line to the various garrisons was shakier than ever. The problem of sustaining a continuing war must have hit the Scots exchequer with fewer resources, even harder.

Worse from the Scots point of view was that the people of lowland Scotland were becoming increasingly sick of the struggle and were beginning to tolerate Edward's rule if it meant peace. Building on this feeling, Edward had been making plans and had decided to lead an expedition into Scotland to suppress rebellion once and forever.

On 7 November 1302, the first notices of summons went out for a campaign to start on 26 May 1303. This was made more urgent when the newly constructed castle at Selkirk was taken by the Scots and destroyed in January 1303 and a Scots army of about seven thousand ambushed a small English force of perhaps one thousand at Roslin on 24 February 1303. Amongst the English dead was Sir Ralph Manton,

Edward's cofferer (tax gatherer) in Scotland. The skirmish boosted Scots morale and left the English even more moneyless and dispirited.

The expected English muster at Berwick was changed to Roxburgh where only 7,500 had arrived by June 1303. For the first time, levies were called from Scotland itself. Around four thousand Scots were called to serve but there is no record of how many actually appeared. The English army went along the coast where it could be supplied by ships from Berwick, until it reached Linlithgow.

On learning the proposed route, the national army took advantage of this and 'entered Annandale and Liddesdale and elsewhere within the marches in the county of Cumberland with a great multitude of armed men'. This 1303 June raid was led by Sir John Comyn, Sir Simon Fraser and Sir William Wallace who had returned from his embassy abroad.

Other than the minor hiccup at Roslin, Edward's main invasion of 1303 met with little opposition. This English invasion made no difference to Selkirkshire other than Sir Alexander Balliol, as Warden of Selkirk Forest, had to contribute men to escort the queen of England from Berwick to Dirleton Castle.

Edward's main invasion forces spent the winter at Dunfermline and were sending out raiding parties, one of which defeated a Scots army led by Wallace and Fraser on Fraser's own land at Happrew in Peeblesshire in February 1304. (Comyn and eleven associates deserted the Scots side and had surrendered to Edward on 9 February 1304.)

Now all Edward's efforts were concentrated on taking the greatest centre of resistance, Stirling Castle. It took three months to capture Stirling. Commanded by Sir William Oliphant, the garrison of about two hundred men held out while being battered by thirteen siege machines, the most advanced technology of the age. The garrison was allowed to surrender after the castle had been used as a day's demonstration of 'Warwolf', Edward's favourite weapon. This happened on 20 July 1304.

On his way back to England, Edward passed through Selkirkshire, was in Eddlestone on 19 August, Traquair on the 20th and at Jedburgh from the 21st to the 23rd. It must have been during this passing visit that Edward ordained 'a pele with a stone gateway at Selkirk'.

By April 1305, the English hold on southern Scotland was secure enough for Edward to make grants of fifty oaks from the Forest of

Selkirk and Maudslie to the Bishop of Glasgow and for his tax collectors in Scotland to be gathering fines and rents from Selkirk Forest – 'From John de Moffette, from the ward of the Forest on the east side of Tweed, of a fine 17 merks. From Roger de Aylmer, from the ward of Trequair in the said Forest, £17:13:4d. From Walter le Corour on behalf of the same, for the ward of Selkirk in the said Forest £20'. These would be English appointees as subordinate foresters who guarded their own ward of Selkirk Forest. Roger de Aylmer had signed the Ragman's Roll in 1292 and 'corour' is the trade name for a watcher or ranger in the forest.

By the summer of 1305 there was little activity against Edward's all-conquering forces except a few pockets of resistance in remote places. The Scots nobles had accepted English terms and came 'within the king's peace'. The resistance was dealt a further blow when Wallace was betrayed by a Scot and captured by Sir John Menteith, the Keeper of Dumbarton, on 3 August 1305. Twenty days later he was given a mock trial at Smithfield and condemned to be hanged, drawn and quartered. The gruesome manner in which Wallace was executed was not a unique event. Edward had executed a Welsh prince by the same method in 1283 and Sir Simon Fraser and several other Scots nobles would go to their deaths in similar manner in the following years.

Resistance did not cease on the death of Wallace. The gift/bribe of fifty oaks to Bishop Wishart of Glasgow had been of little avail because, a year later, Edward was writing to Sir Aymer de Valence on 18 June 1306 that he was very much pleased that the Bishop had been taken for he had 'done him [Edward] all the mischief in his power, for though chief of the Guardians of Scotland appointed by him [Edward] he had joined his enemies'.

From 3 April to 27 April 1306, the garrison at Selkirk Castle was four knights, twenty-seven squires, eight hobelars (horsemen with light armour), thirty balisters to fire catapults and four archers. This was obviously a defensive force for the protection of the castle.

Things were going well for Sir Aymer personally. On 4th October 1306 he and his heirs were granted: '*the castle of Selkirk, the manors and desmesne lands of Selkirk and Traquayr, the burgh and mills of Peebles and the Forest of Selkirk with power to disforest and impark the same, or lease to tenants at his pleasure. To be held of the King and his heirs as a knight's fee and for the*

payment of £130 annually at Pentecost and Martinmas; provided that Aymer
and his heirs shall annually pay the following alms conferred by former Kings of
Scotland, viz 113s from Traquayr, 65s from Selkirk, 50s from Peebles, and 19s:4d
from the mills of Selkirk. He and his heirs to be heritable sheriff of the counties
of Peebles and Selkirk.'

This charter was sealed with the Great Seal of England.

As well as the above, the king granted Sir Aymer the lands forfeited
by the rebels who held the castle and others. This charter was sealed
with the Great Seal of the Government of Scotland. From the wording
of this charter, it would seem that the Scots were still holding Selkirk
Castle in October 1306.

Around the same time, Edward was writing to Aymer de Valence
that he was: 'well pleased that he had burned Sir Simon Fraser's lands in
Selkirk Forest. Commands him to do the same to all enemies on his
march including those who turned against him in this war of the Earl of
Carrick … and in like manner to inform the King's foresters of Selkirk
how they have loyally and painfully served the king and done well.'

However, all was not well in the whole of Edward's realm of
Scotland. Unexpectedly, on 25 March 1306, Robert Bruce, the Earl of
Carrick had been crowned as king of Scots at Scone. Bruce was a
grandson of Robert Bruce who competed for the crown in 1291, and
whose claim to the throne was almost as good as John Balliol's. Bruce
the Earl was a cunning end-game player who changed sides when the
circumstances seemed right. He had been making secret pacts with
those Scots who had opposed Edward. Edward was now an old man
and was supposedly close to death when Bruce struck. Despite his age,
Edward was not to be thwarted.

On 5 April 1306, Aymer de Valence was appointed to put down the
rebellion of Robert de Brus, now formerly Earl of Carrick, who had
betrayed Edward's confidence and had murdered his liege, John Comyn
of Badenagh. De Valence was also given permission to receive those
'middling men', who had risen in insurrection, into the king's peace but
with the exception of those who had taken part in the murder.

De Valence quickly gathered his forces, meeting and defeating the
new king of Scots at Methven on 19 June 1306. Bruce fled; his brother
Neil was later taken prisoner and hanged at Berwick. Further orders
were issued for the capture of the Countesses of Carrick and Buchan,

Marie and Christine the sisters, and Margerie the daughter, of Robert de Brus, and other Scottish prisoners. Three of the ladies were to be kept in 'kages'. Legend has it that these cages were to be hung on the walls of Berwick Castle where all could see them.

Edward's fury knew no bounds. On 4 August, fifteen Scotsmen and one Englishman, who had been taken prisoner at Methven, were put to death without trial and without being able to answer the charges – on the king's express command.

One of these was Peebleshire landowner, Bernard de Mohaut who had also slain Edward's valet Roget de Tany in Selkirk Forest on his way to join the king in his Scottish war.

De Valence spent the next year trying to catch up with Bruce and his supporters. The account of De Valence with his cavalry force and John of Lorne with eight hundred foot tracking the fleeing Bruce with a bloodhound which once belonged to him, is borne out, but not proved by a surviving letter written by De Valence written at Dalmolin near Ayr on 19 July.

However, when De Valence did meet up with Bruce, it was at Loudon Hill on the borders between Ayrshire and Lanarkshire on 10 May 1307. This time Bruce won the battle and Edward was much enraged that the Guardian (De Valence) and his force had retreated before 'King Hobbe'. The writer of this anonymous account records that 'James of Douglas sent and begged to be received but when he saw the King's forces retreat, he drew back'. This was to be a wise decision as later events would show.

The action at Loudon Hill was not decisive and English operations were continued a few days afterwards. De Valence was mounting forays in pursuit of Bruce but without success. The death of Edward at Burgh-on-Sands when he was intent on leading yet another expedition into Scotland on 7 July 1307, was to be the turning point in the fight to retain Scottish sovereignty.

Edward II, a different man from his domineering father, ascended the throne at the age of twenty-two. After accompanying his father's body southwards for several days, he retraced his steps and joined up with his father's intended army by the middle of July. He marched northwards as far as Cumnock before he turned round and retreated into England and safety.

As the English retreated, the new king of Scots left the hill country around Glentrool Forest and went to punish the MacDowals, whose chief had given up his brothers to be hanged at Carlisle by the late king of England's command. In 1308, King Robert spent his time in the northern part of his kingdom, settling a few scores there while his brother Edward Bruce was subduing Galloway and expelling English garrisons and punishing English sympathisers with the MacDowals being specifically targeted.

Meanwhile, on 12 December 1307. Edward II had replaced Aymer de Valence with the Earl of Richmond as Warden of Scotland and his first task was 'to restore to Aymer de Valence earl of Pembroke his lands in the counties of Selkirk and Tweeddale and the forest of Selkirk which has been seized on account of the men and tenants there having traitorously joined Robert de Brus'. Neither the burgh nor castle of Selkirk is mentioned, so there is a good chance that it had been reoccupied by the Scots.

By 1309, Selkirk castle must have been retaken by the English as De Valence was ordered to provision the castle with men and victuals against the king's enemies and rebels.

The following year Edward II returned to Scotland to direct the war in person. On 25 June he was at Berwick-upon-Tweed, sending letters under the Privy Seal to the constables of the Pele of Selkirk and the castles of Jedworth, Cavers, Lochmaben, Bothwell, Dalswyntoun and Dumfries. (NB Selkirk had a 'pele' while the rest had castles.) Edward made Selkirk Pele his headquarters for several days on his way back to England. A writ was tested at Selkirk on 13 September 1310 and further letters of protection were written there on the 23, 27 and 28 of the same month. Obviously Selkirk had not lost its status as a place of importance although that might be because of its position on the edge of the Forest rather than the strength of its pele.

Knowing that nobody was winning the battle for hearts and minds, peace feelers were going out from both sides. In an anonymous letter in the Calendar of Documents, there a note that: 'Sir Robert de Clifford and Sir Robert fitz Pain had, by the King's [Edward II] leave, been at Selkirk 8 days before Christmas [1310], to speak with Robert de Brus and since then the Earls of Gloucester and Cornwall were to have parleyed with him at a place near Melros but it is said he had been warned by some that he would be taken'. This was dated 19 February 1311.

Obviously Selkirk was a safer place than Melrose for the new king of Scots.

About the same period, Sir Alexander Balliol of Cavers, a man much associated with Selkirk castle and Selkirk Forest, disappears from the scene. He was unusual in that era, having remained a consistent Scottish supporter of the English interests. Perhaps the fact that he had estates in England and that Edward I kept his son as a hostage may have had something to do with his constant allegiance.

In the roll of castles and sheriffdoms held in the English interests in the fifth year of the reign of Edward II (1311–12), only eight castles were English garrisoned; of these only Berwick and Roxburgh castles and shires being in the Borders. Interestingly, neither Selkirk nor Peebles castles/shires are mentioned, so perhaps they were in Scots hands. Within two years only Berwick was English-held.

There are detailed accounts of the numbers of men within the castles and fighting in the English interest. From the names and titles of those 'of the better sort', it must be admitted that a large number of Scots were hostile to the new king of Scots. Whether this was family antagonism, heart-felt or forced upon them through circumstance, is not known, but after the victory at Bannockburn, many would return to their national allegiance and their own interest.

Of the 'pitaille' or commoners, nothing is mentioned, but there is a long list of all the horses belonging to the various nobles in the English garrisons with a description of the animals and a valuation of their worth. If one was killed in the line of duty, the equivalent cost could be reclaimed from the English exchequer.

From Edward II's expedition of 1310–11 until the Battle of Bannockburn, Selkirk and Selkirkshire seem to have vanished from the written records. Bannockburn is an iconic battle for all Scots, being fought so often in imaginary writings. In fact, it was a victory which Bruce should not have won, and would not have won but for the incompetence of the English commanders. Ignoring the Scots writers, estimates of 100,000 men in the English army, the most reasonable calculations are that there would not be more than 50,000. Using the same deductions, the poor and thinly populated country of Scotland, devastated by a long war, could not have provided more than 16,000 for Bruce's army. It is reckoned that two-thirds of the English army left the battlefield without engaging the Scots.

The English records are uniquely reticent about Bannockburn. *The Calendar of Documents of Scotland*, which are mainly the English records, has items like 'the Chancellor discharged the King's [Edward II] sergeant who has care of the cart harness of his baggage horses and other things and lost his roll at the battle of Stirling in the 7th year [of his reign] and can render no account of his intromissions up till 24th June that year'. It was recorded that the English baggage train, moving slowly northwards along the Roman Dere Street, was twenty miles long. During the return journey, it was shorter and moved a great deal faster.

Another knight complains that he was made prisoner at the 'descomfiture' at Stirling where he lost horses and armour worth 200 marks, was imprisoned for two years and was now 'brought very low'.

The only mention of Selkirk men being at the battle appears in Craig-Brown's *History of Selkirkshire*: 'when the king's division, carried too far by their ardour, began to waver under the terrible hail of English arrows, the archers were soon routed by Edward Bruce who attacked them in the rear with Selkirk spearmen'. I have not been able to confirm this anywhere else. Barbour has Sir Robert Keith dispersing the English archers with spearmen but no mention of Selkirk.

To add to the speculation, Sir Robert Keith had been appointed by the Scots Guardians to be Warden of Selkirk Forest at the meeting held in Peebles in 1299. With 100 barbed horses and 1500 footmen besides the foresters, he was charged to make raids on the English March. So it would make logical sense that he was still commanding 'Selkirk spearmen' at Bannockburn.

Selkirkshire gets no further mention until King Robert I bestows the forests of Selkirk, Ettrick and Traquair on Sir James Douglas in 1321. This was confirmed when the three forests were erected in free barony in 1324. These were the lands that had previously been granted to Sir Aymer de Valence by Edward I of England.

With his grant of Selkirk Forest, Sir James Douglas moved the forest court to Edibredshiels, which stood of a mound about a kilometre south-east of the New Wark in the Yarrow valley, thereby depriving Selkirk of its power centre.

On St Nicholas Day 1321, Sir James Douglas was issuing a safe-conduct for Richard de Topcliff and a companion, with their servants, to come to Jedburgh. This was written at Etlebredehelys – spelling was not consistent in medieval documents.

About the same time, Turnbull of Philiphaugh was appointed to be Constable of Selkirk with all the perks that had been associated with that office in the time of Alexander III. This demonstrates that the burgh of Selkirk, the king's vill, had not yet been joined to the Douglas-owned Forest of Selkirk to become the County of Selkirkshire.

In the Exchequer Roll of 1368, the only one to survive of that period, the burgh of Selkirk paid 4s:8d out of the shire's total contribution of £14:14s and a half pence.

Such wealth as was available, was in the landward area and not the burgh.

King Robert's policy of rewarding his followers with lands and honours was a sound one. They expected a reward for their efforts and Bruce had not only to win a kingdom but also had to retain it. Lands throughout the Borders were given to the brothers, Sir James and Sir Archibald Douglas, and Sir Thomas Randolph, none of whom had been great landowners before the wars. The Douglases were mainly in the central and western Borders which included the royal Forest of Selkirk. Randolph received Annandale, formerly Bruce's own lordship, and Nithsdale with other lands in the eastern Borders, making a solid block of Bruce supporters on the border with England. This strategy was effective when an English invasion of 10,000 men was defeated at Linthaughlee near Jedburgh in 1326.

In 1328, negotiations of a treaty of perpetual peace were concluded at Holyrood, Edinburgh, between the two warring nations and then ratified by the English Parliament at Northampton in May. Edward III of England, or rather his mother Isabella, recognised the complete independence of Scotland and Robert Bruce as King Robert I. To seal the Treaty a marriage was arranged between Robert's young son David and Johanna, daughter of Edward II. In return for this and for the damage caused by invading Scots on the northern regions of England, the Scots were to pay a 'Contribution For Peace'. The county of Peebles paid £130, the county of Lanark £376, the county of Berwick £200:3s:4d and the county of Selkirk £10. Selkirkshire has never been a wealthy county and this goes right back to geology and location.

The king of Scots was not present at the marriage of his son David to the English princess at Berwick on 12 July 1328. His long struggle and a wasting disease, sometimes thought to be leprosy, were taking their toll.

Robert the Bruce had a long campaign to achieve the kingdom of Scotland but he was lucky in one respect. For most of the time, his opponent was the weak and vacillating Edward II rather than his aggressive father, Edward I. In the next round of engagements between the kingdoms, the situation would be reversed with Edward III, a chip off the old block that was his grandfather, against a hapless and pleasure-loving David II of Scotland.

In his latter years, King Robert had expressed his intention to go on a crusade against the infidel. (The infidels were actually a much more cultured civilisation than that of the Christians who sought to replace them – but that is another story.)

He died on 7 June 1329 and, by his wish, his heart was removed from his body and placed in a silver casket for Sir James Douglas to take to the Holy Land. Sailing from Berwick, Douglas never made it to the Holy Land because he stopped to fight the infidels more conveniently placed in Spain.

According to ever-expanding legend, the hard-pressed Scots were surrounded by Moors when Douglas took the silver casket containing Bruce's heart and flung it into the battle saying 'Onward brave heart, Douglas will follow thee or die', both of which he did, thereby inspiring Mel Gibson and Hollywood to rewrite Scottish history.

After the battle, the heart of Bruce returned to Scotland where it was buried in Melrose Abbey according to his wishes. In 1999 it was dug up again and reburied with pomp and circumstance. One curious circumstance was that in the speech of celebration of the life and achievements of Robert the Bruce given by Donald Dewar, the First Minister of the newly devolved Scotland, the word 'independence' was never mentioned.

In real life, the Treaty of Perpetual Peace was unravelled the next year by the death of King Robert and the coronation of his son, David, only five years old at the time. Sir Thomas Randolph, the last of the Bruce's great captains, took over the government of Scotland.

It took five years before the temptation proved too much for Edward III of England who declared that the Treaty of Edinburgh was void because he was under age when he signed it and that he was forced to do so by an illegal government, his mother Isabella. Therefore, all bets were off and the two countries lined up for another conflict with the Borders in the middle as usual.

There were many Scottish nobles who had opposed Robert I, living in exile in England, and were now were anxious to regain their lands in Scotland. To this aim they had been planning to invade the country with which England was nominally at peace. Using Edward Balliol, the son of John Balliol, as a claimant to the throne, they decided to bypass the Bruce-supporting south of Scotland and sail into the Firth of Forth. Edward III must have known about the proposed expedition as he warned the knights of his northern counties to prepare to repulse an invasion.

While the invasion fleet was still at sea, the Regent Randolph died in suspicious circumstances at Musselburgh, with poison being a distinct possibility. The Scots Parliament chose Donald of Mar to be his successor. This was an unhappy choice as Mar had lived the last two decades of his life in England and knew little about his fellow Scots. At Dupplin Moor outside Perth, the Scots met the army of Edward Balliol and was soundly defeated, Mar losing his life in the process.

Edward Balliol was crowned at Scone on 24 September 1332. Now styled King Edward I of Scotland, his army left Perth for Galloway and went to Roxburgh. Near Jedburgh, Sir Archibald Douglas was lying in wait for them but was discovered before the ambush could be sprung.

Balliol lodged at Kelso, probably in the Abbey, while his army was at Roxburgh. Fearing that a rising Tweed might cut him off from his forces, he moved to Roxburgh. The Scottish Regent, Sir Andrew Moray attacked the bridge with the object of isolating and capturing Balliol but, in the melee, a detachment of English horsemen swam their horses across the flooded river and captured Moray instead.

The situation was nearly reversed and Balliol had a lucky escape when Sir Archibald Douglas attacked his camp near Annan on 16 December. One hundred of Balliol's supporters, including some Scots, were killed and he escaped with difficulty to Carlisle. Balliol showed little interest in his titular kingdom but proceeded to parcel out land

and titles to his followers. As many of these lands were still held by the supporter of the Scots government of David II, this made for some ill-feeling between the kingdoms.

Even more peculiar was that, as King Edward I of Scotland, he laid siege to Berwick which was being held by the Scots government of King David II. In this action, he was joined by the person and forces of Edward III of England. On 2 June 1333, Edward of England was writing that he had heard that the Scots would certainly attack him in force before midsummer to raise the siege and was looking for reinforcements. This document was written at the 'Siege of Berwick'.

Sir Archibald Douglas had been chosen as Scots Regent on the captivity of Sir Andrew Moray. With a force reckoned to be around 15,000 men marching to relieve the Scots garrison of Berwick, which was surrounded by a Scots/English besieging force, he gave battle to the English army at Halidon Hill near Berwick on 19th July 1333 and was totally routed. Douglas, five earls and 'many barons of eminent rank' were killed. The Earl of March, one of the defenders of Berwick, seeing little prospect of victory, decided to join the English monarch and nine days after the battle, he was rewarded by a grant of £100 of land. However, he had reverted to his original loyalty by 1 February 1334 and forfeited the land that was then given to Sir Henry Percy.

The fact that Edward Balliol, king of Scotland, commanded one wing of the English army at Halidon Hill, showed where his loyalties lay.

In May 1334, the young King David and his queen were despatched to France and safety while his adherents continued to battle for his kingdom and their own estates.

On 12 June 1334, Edward, king of Scotland granted to Edward (III), king of England 2000 librates* of land in the Marches of Scotland, conceding the castles, towns and counties of Berwick-upon-Tweed and Roxburgh, the town, castle and forest of Jeddeworthe, the town and county of Selkirk and the forests of Selkirk and Etryk, the town, castle and county of Edenburgh with the constabularies of Hadyngton and Lynliscou, the town and county of Peebles and the town, castle and county of Dumfries. This huge area, which covered much of southern

-----

*A librate is a piece of land whose yearly rental value was £1.

Scotland, was 'to be held separately from the Crown of Scotland and annexed to and incorporated with the Crown of England for ever'. He also did homage for the remainder of the country.

This was done at Newcastle-upon-Tyne in the second year of his reign.

It is interesting to note that in Selkirk and Peebles no castle is mentioned and it is possible, even probable, that both counties were not under English control.

After spending Christmas 1334 at Roxburgh, Edward III decided to mop up any remnants of resistance, making a fruitless expedition into the Ettrick Forest but the foes that he had expected to find there had retreated 'under the hospitable covert of the wilderness'. The foes were likely to have been the retainers of the Douglases who had, in theory, been deprived of their holdings there.

As was customary, Edward III broke up the area of southern Scotland to reward his followers. In 1334, Robert de Maners was Sheriff of Selkirk and Warden of the Forests of Selkirk and Ettrick. In 1335, Edward granted the Forest of Selkyrk and Etrik together with the town and shire of Selkyrk to William Montacuto 'for unwearied labours rendered to us and our kingdom, not without great expense'.

William de Coucy received a huge amount of real estate which he handed over to his son, also William de Coucy, on 5 June 1335: included amongst these were the 'fraunks hoghtelx' of Haldecambhouse (Old Cambus), Selkyrk and Trequayr.

(I don't know what that means either; but I have heard the word 'hoghtel' used in Border Scots to mean a mixture, but it may have something to do with the forests there.)

It is not known whether the English grantees ever lived in the area but, if they did, it must have been of short duration as Sir William Douglas had raced round southern Scotland reclaiming his own and expelling the English from much of the Border countryside and most of the castles.

The Scots must have recovered from the rout at Halidon Hill and were now carrying the war into England. In July 1335, Edward III again invaded Scotland through Carlisle. This time he had the assistance of the Count of Namur and a contingent of French knights 'who had come to the King's aid against the Scots'.

For the next three years, Edward and the English army, which included many dispossessed Scots, ranged across the country pursuing a burnt earth policy on whoever favoured the national party and reclaiming the lands of those who favoured the English interest.

Edward III was abroad in 1339 and 1340, concluding a truce with France and this helped the national cause. During this period, the Scots had been picking off the English-held castles one by one, helped in some cases by the English Council neglecting to supply provisions for their men.

In 1897, a most unusual hoard of silver coins was found at Cleuchhead in Roxburghshire. Unlike most hoards of the period, it did not contain any English, Scots or Irish coins but was totally composed of 138 Continental deniers from Flanders, Hainaut, Namur, Brabant, Cambrai Herstal and Looz. The hoard was found on the farm of Cleuchhead 'about six inches below the surface in the Hill End Field at a spot 17 yards from the Hill End Plantation and 100 yards from the Old Roman Road'.

The dating range of the coins was between 1307 and 1312 with deposition somewhat later. These could be a Continental merchant's working capital or from the pay chest of a band of Templar knights who were escaping persecution.

This was the period when King Philip IV of France was carrying out a campaign against the Knights Templar through accusations of heresy; in fact he was after their rich treasury to bail out his empty exchequer. Eventually he succeeded in getting the Order suppressed and many Templars were executed but, when Philip got to the Templars' Treasure House, the cupboard was bare. Being excommunicated, no country would accept any Templars fleeing the persecutions – except Scotland where Robert the Bruce welcomed them.

It appeals to my romantic nature to put the Cleuchhead hoard forward as part of the Templars' treasure that has never been recovered. Surely it cannot be a coincidence that there is a farm called Templehall nearby.

With most of the country now being under Scots control, it was thought safe for David to return from France. In June 1341, he was back home and is said to have taken part in forays made into Cumberland and Northumberland several times. By 1342, only Berwick and Lochmaben were held in the English interest.

Stirred by martial ardour plus the fact that Edward had again declared war against France and was engaged in the siege of Calais, David decided to invade the north of England in strength. On the fourth mission his luck ran out. On 17 October 1346, he had reached Durham to be opposed by local English forces led by the Archbishop of York. Through bad judgement and worse luck, the Scots were soundly defeated and David was wounded and captured, remaining a prisoner of the English until 1357. Shortly after the battle, a truce was arranged while Edward held secret negotiations with David and Sir William Douglas who had also been captured at the battle. David was to surrender the independence of Scotland and pay homage to Edward but this he refused to do.

Sir William Douglas, the Scottish patriot who had won so many battles in the Scottish cause that he was known as 'the Flower of Chivalry', was to bind himself to serve the English king in war, except against his own nation. In 1352, Douglas accepted the terms and received the territory of Liddesdale with Hermitage Castle and part of Moffatdale from Edward. He did not live long enough to enjoy the fruits of his betrayal. In August 1353, he was hunting in Ettrick Forest in defiance of the Warden, another Lord William Douglas, when he was shot by a 'stray' arrow on the heights above The Peel at a spot now marked as William's Cross on early maps. His body lay in Lindean church overnight and was carried to Melrose Abbey where it was laid in the family tomb.

The fact that the other Lord William Douglas, as well as being the Warden of Selkirk Forest, was also nominally Lord of Liddesdale and Keeper of Hermitage Castle on behalf of King David of Scotland, might have caused some suspicions about the accident.

The following year, William, Lord Douglas was confirmed by the charter of David II, in the 'Forests of Etrick, Selkirk, Yarrowe and Tweed with their ancient meiths and marches' together with other lands and pertinents while, south of the Border, Edward III granted his squire, John de Coupland the Keepership of the Forests of Selkirk, Peebles and Ettrick.

This time, Edward tried to play the truce differently by offering security of life and property to any who would swear fealty to him. The Borderers on both sides were sick of near-constant war and the prospect of a chance to rebuild their lives must have been very tempting. Many of the nobles who had lost their lands in the previous conflicts, regained them. The Lovels were back in the barony of Hawick and Branxholm; if Paris was worth a mass to a later king of France, Hawick was worth kneeling and giving your word to support an English king. You could always change your mind later if the circumstances warranted it. In fact the Lovels had been consistent in their loyalty to the English monarchs.

For the next eleven years the Borders was not a peaceful place. Edward III had turned his attentions to uprisings in other parts of his realms, having left his Scottish conquests in other hands. This allowed marauding Scots with a free hand to commit all manners of mischief, thereby provoking a responding riposte from the English.

Sir Thomas Gray of Heton witnessed the period and gives his account in a document called 'The Scalacronica', Writing about the period after the debacle at Durham, he says: 'in the meane whyle that King Davy was prisoner, the lords of Scotland, by a little and a little, wan al that they had lost at the bataille of Duresme; and there was much envy among them who might be hyest; for every one ruled yn hys owne cuntery; and King Edward was so distressed with his afferes beyond the se, that he toke little regard to the Scottisch matiers.'

In 1355, there was a fracas at Nisbet in Roxburghshire where Sir Thomas Gray, the Constable of Norham and the above-named author of the Scalacronica, was captured. Shortly afterwards the town of Berwick was taken by the Scots. The threat that the castle would also fall brought Edward III swiftly to the scene and the town was surrendered to him shortly afterwards. After that, the English army swept through the Merse and Lothians, burning and plundering and in the process totally destroying Haddington, the seat of learning known as the Lamp of the Lothians.

Edward (Balliol) the other king of Scots must have been on the expedition because in a series of instruments executed at Roxburgh and Bamburgh between the 20th and 27th of January 1356, he made formal resignation of his kingdom of Scotland and all its appurtment rights both in England and Galloway to Edward III, king of England. In return for this he received a pension of £2,000 per year, assistance in payment of his debts and other matters. This may have been a wise move for Balliol as 'the Scots wer ful of rebellion; he had no heyre nor any very nere of his linage; and he could not tell better wher to bestow his title and corone of Scotland than on him.'

Although Edward III could now claim to be king of Scotland as an almost legal right, he was getting tired of combating the troublesome Scots who would never accept that they were beaten. To solve this problem and replenish his exchequer, for lack of money was a constant problem for medieval kings, he decided to sell their king back to the Scots on a hire purchase basis.

David, the captive king of Scots was being held in an 'open prison' at Odiham Castle in Hampshire where he seemed to be enjoying life. After long negotiations his release was secured in October 1357 by the Scottish nation paying a ransom of 100,000 marks in ten yearly instalments during a ten-year truce and with the agreement to send other hostages to England in his place. Reading between the lines, it would seem that David was reluctant to leave his feather-bedded captivity and resume the arduous duties of a king of Scots. Within a few months of his release, he was requesting and receiving permission to revisit England and year after year made long and expensive visits to the English Court.

On his return from captivity, David rewarded Lord William Douglas, 'valiant leader of the men of Selkirk to the dignity of Earl' – the first of the Earls of Douglas. For the remaining years of David's reign, the English hold on the castles of Berwick, Roxburgh and Dumfries as well as most of their shires, remained firm. David was in the uncomfortable position of being unable to pay 10,000 marks as his yearly share of the ransom. On 21 January 1358 or 9, Queen Johanna had to ask her brother Edward for a respite of the sum due until Martinmas (11 November). The queen died in 1362 and David married his longtime 'belle amie', Margaret Drummond or Logie, in the early part of 1363. This was probably in the hope of providing a male heir for the throne but as this did not happen, he divorced her in 1370 and intended to marry Agnes of Dunbar but he died unexpectedly early in 1371.

In November 1363, David had concluded a secret arrangement with Edward that 'in default of male issue of the King of Scotland, it was agreed that the King of England should succeed to the kingdom of Scotland'.

This was amended in a later document to 'if the present King of Scotland die without an heir begotten of his body in matrimony, one of the sons of the King of England other than the heir to the Crown shall succeed to the Crown of Scotland'. There was also a treaty of peace for 1,000 years and the English king would hand over all the castles, towns, fortresses occupied by the late King Robert (the Bruce) when he died. Each king would assist against each others enemies and the king and lords of Scotland would assist in the English war in Flanders and all the English supporters who had lost their lands there would have them restored.

There was a codicil added to this agreement that 'in the case of no treaty following, all things shall revert to their former state'. It did not happen and the Borders reverted to a familiar state of anarchy. There were several short-term truces agreed and broken with impunity on both sides over the next forty years. There were so many fluctuations of fortune that only the major battles and raids were noteworthy and the captures and ransoms of the great were recognised.

Selkirkshire and Selkirk, being out of the way and enclosed in a pocket in the hills, are seldom mentioned other than being doled out as a reward to the victors of whatever nation was winning at the time. Looking at the *Calender of Documents Relating to Scotland*, it must have been a dangerous but exciting time to live and die in so I will try to give only the highlights and only those of relevance to the Borders.

David II died in 1371 and was succeeded by his nephew Robert, the High Stewart, who had reached the mature age of fifty-five. Robert II was the grandson of Robert the Bruce and had acted as Guardian of Scotland during David II's captivity. Though skilled in ruling an unruly nation, he was too old to take the field himself, so he used his younger nobles to carry the war to the English. This was a double-edged weapon as it provoked counter-raids into the Borders, reaching as far as Edinburgh.

Edward III died in 1377 and was succeeded by his grandson Richard II who was only nine years old when he became king. With a child on the throne and the English nobility at war with each other, this was the time for Border Scots to make mayhem.

Much of Roxburghshire and Berwickshire were still English-held and ambiguous in their loyalty to either realm.

In July 1377, the town of Roxburgh was taken, plundered and burned during a Fair Day and in reprisal the Earl of Northumberland ravaged the Scots March for three days. The English-held castle and town of Berwick was taken by the Scots on 25 November 1378 and again in December 1384 but were quickly retrieved by the English with reports that all the Scots were killed★. Except for a period from 1461 to 1482, the important castle, town and port was to remain in English hands but, by the early 1380s, most of the lands of Berwickshire, Roxburghshire and Dumfriesshire were again under Scottish control.

In 1382, a new phase of Border warfare emerged when the 'gunnes' made by John Phelipotte of London were provided for the protection of Roxburgh Castle and 100 pounds of gunpowder (pulveris de gunnes) at 2s:6d per pound were supplied to Berwick. By 1384, three brass guns were cast at Carlisle. This new weapon was to revolutionise warfare and eventually make the armour of the knights obsolete, but guns were initially used as a static weapon of defence.

In 1384, William Earl of Douglas captured Lochmaben castle and in the same year the Earl of Gaunt with an innumerable army camped within three leagues of Edinburgh but held back to allow the Scottish husbandmen to transport their goods over the Forth. When the English took the city they found it empty and the straw roofs of the houses burned. It was so cold that 500 horses died but no number was given for the men.

In 1385, Richard II arrived in person with 1,100 French knights and men-at-arms. After burning Melrose, Dryburgh, Newbattle and the town of Edinburgh, he returned to England 'without loss'. This was because the Scots under James, Earl of Douglas and Sir Archibald Douglas were raiding in Cumberland, capturing Carlisle and extorting £200 from the Abbey of Holmcotran.

About this time, Richard had made an indenture which contained a clause that any forces supplied by the English Border families had to be two-thirds strangers to the Marches. This is the first mention of the

---

★The inference is that those Scots who had captured the castle were of 'the inferior sort' as any knights or landowners taken alive would be kept for ransom.

belief that Borderers were not inclined to seriously fight each other in battle but only in pursuit of their own private feuds.

In 1388, James, Earl of Douglas and his brother the Earl of Moray invaded Northumberland with 3000 men while the Earls of Fife and Strathearn attacked Carlisle and Cumberland. James Douglas had advanced as far as Newcastle and in a skirmish before the walls of the town had beaten Henry (Hotspur) Percy in single combat taking his personal pennant as a trophy. Douglas taunted Hotspur and said that he would plant it in front of his castle of Dalkeith. On the way back to Scotland with their booty, the Scottish army camped at Otterburn. Meanwhile Hotspur had gathered an army and made a night attack on the Scots. In the melee, James Douglas received three mortal wounds and instructed that his body be buried 'by the bracken bush, beneath the blooming brier' so that the Scots would not be disheartened by the death of their leader. When the morning came, the victory belonged to the Scots.

This is a good story and subject of a brilliant ballad called 'The Battle of Otterbourne'. Douglas was killed at the battle and Henry Hotspur and his brother were both captured. Hotspur was ransomed for the sum of £1,000, £500 of which was as a gift from Richard II.

Also captured was Hotspur's esquire, Aleyn Horsle who had been given the lands of Maxwelle and Softlawe in the land of Tevydale but the official bookwork (letters patent) had not been filed so the lands were forfeited 'by the rebellion of the inhabitants of Tevydale'.

Following the battle a ten-year truce was arranged but this did not interrupt the continued antagonism between the Scottish Douglases and the Northumbrian Percys which lasted for many years longer. As the Douglases held the lands of Selkirk/Ettrick Forest, they would certainly count on the men of the Forest for their support.

In 1389, Richard II was having second thoughts about having burned Melrose Abbey and on 15 October issued letters 'allowing the Abbot and convent of Melrose an abatement of 2s a saak on the custom of wool of Scotch growth sent by them to Berwick-upon-Tweed to the number of 1000 saaks as an alms from the King for the destruction and burning sustained by the abbey when he was there with his army'. A saak or sack would be more like a bale as an English sea-pack weighting 364 or 365lbs (164 kgs).

Three days later, he sent further letters of protection, 'allowing a three years truce for the Abbot and convent of Melrose, their converses to the number of 12 on horseback, to sell their beasts and chattels in Northumberland and Cumberland and buy victuals, wine and other lawful merchandise'.

This was a strange time when both nationalities were allowed into the other realm if they had a safe-conduct pass 'while the truce holds' or 'if war does not break out meanwhile'. It was usual in those days of chivalry for knights to challenge each other to mortal combat, so in 1390 Sir David Lyndsaye was allowed to bring twenty-nine unarmed retainers to 'do feats of arms in England with John de Welle whom he has challenged and to bring fitting armour'.

Sir David must have won his jousting as he returned to Scotland with £100 and a silver cup and ewer with gilt covers worth £6:16s:8d given by the king's command. Several other knights returned with equal trophies. Scotland four, England?

These contests seem to be an almost yearly occurrence as long as a truce had been arranged, or not, in which case the contest was in earnest.

In 1390, Robert II died and was succeeded by his son John, the Earl of Carrick, who for reasons of diplomacy changed his regnal name to Robert and reigned as Robert III, king of Scots. (John was not a favoured name for Scottish kings since the disaster of John Balliol, though much of his unpopularity can be placed on later Bruce/Stewart propaganda.)

According to the fifteenth-century historian Walter Bower, Robert II had been a successful ruler, with peace and prosperity at home and Scotland almost totally free from English control. This view cannot be held in the Borders where individual lands could be won and lost within a year.

Robert II had been legally married twice with numerous progeny who were to cause trouble in Scotland for the next two and a half centuries. Through Robert II, the direct line of Scottish kings was unbroken for nine generations, from his grandfather Robert the Bruce 1306–1329, to James VI and I, 1567–1625, and then onwards through the kings and queens of Great Britain.

In 1391, Richard II instructed his Collector of Customs in Berwick that, because of the losses and 'depauperisation' of the town and the falling off in the population and also for the benefit of his lieges in Scotland, he has granted the mayor and burgesses leave to export wool, hides etc at these rates of customs.

1. For each sack of wool grown between the Tweed and the Coket – 26s:8d; for 240 lambskins of the same growth 26s:8d and for each last of hides, 4 marks.

2. For wool, lambskins and hides of Tevydale and other parts of Scotland at his allegiance, one half of these rates.

3. For wool, lambskins and hides from the king of Scotland's subjects, one-fourth of the above rates.

This caused some consternation to the customs officer who set up a jury of men from Berwick, Roxburgh, Norham and Jedworthe to prevent the king's leiges in Northumberland from carrying clothes, wool, skins, hides etc across the Border of Scotland by sea or land in order to receive the lower rates.

In 1397, Richard II ordered a proclamation throughout his kingdom that Scottish money should be reckoned at half its nominal value: a groat at 2d, a half-groat at 1d etc. This was in recognition that the Scottish coinage had gradually deteriorated over the years. In 1150, twenty-one Scottish pennies had been coined from an ounce of silver, whereas in 1393, the ounce of silver was alloyed with other metals to make forty-four Scottish pennies.

In February 1399, proceedings were taken against Robert Karlisle for transferring English money viz, groats, half-groats and sterlings of full weight into Scotland and bringing back Scottish groats, of false alloy weighing a penny less than the English coins, thus defrauding the lieges.

At around the same period an undated letter from the people of Tevydale, both cleres and lay, to the king (of England) said that after the battle of Durham, they had surrendered the castle of Roxburgh to the lords Percy and Neville and had accepted the rule of the king's grandfather who guaranteed their enjoyment of the laws, usages and customs of the county in the days of Alexander (III) king of Scotland. But now their sufferings and losses are daily getting worse and worse through the Warden of the March, in 'ruberys, larcenies and slaughters not only by the Scots but also by some of the king's own lieges, as they could easily show the wardens but scarcely dare leave their houses for fear of their lives'.

Richard II of England did not have an easy life what with Peasant Revolts, Poll Taxes and enemies in Parliament. In May 1399 he led an expedition to Ireland, which was a serious mistake as Henry Bolingbroke, John of Gaunt's son, returning from ordered exile, had invaded England in the king's absence. When Richard returned from Ireland, he was taken prisoner in north Wales and agreed to abdicate. Henry had only intended to recover his inheritance which had been seized by Richard but, with the throne now vacant, he claimed it as well.

Henry IV had big ideas – he invaded Scotland in the summer of 1400. By 7 August, he was writing to the dukes, earls and other peers of Scotland to induce their king to do him homage and fealty in person at Edinburgh on Monday 23rd of the same month, or which failing to do it themselves. He had the same order published in Kelso, Dryburgh, Jeddeworthe, Melros, Edinburgh and elsewhere in Scotland where they thought fitting. The king, peers and commons of Scotland did not think much of the idea.

It was probably at this period when there was a hotly contested skirmish at 'Fulhope Law' which is reckoned to be Philiphaugh in Selkirkshire. Amongst the captives were Sir Richard Rutherford and John Turnebull known as 'out wyth sword' who may have been one of the Turnbulls of Philiphaugh. He certainly held two parts of the barony of Minto in 1380; his captors, the Percys of Northumberland were forbidden to ransom him in 1400, and in 1401 he was released, setting out for the English king's service in Scotland.

In May 1402, Henry learned that the Duke of Albany and the Earl of Douglas were mustering forces to attack his lieges on the Scottish border, and the Sheriffs of Nottingham, Derby, Lincoln, York, Northumberland, Cumberland and Westmoreland were commanded to send their array to resist the threatened invasion.

In June, he ordered the Sheriff of Kent to arrest and imprison all persons who were spreading the rumour that the late King Richard was still alive in Scotland.

In September, Henry got news of the victory over the Scots and their French allies at 'Homeldon near Wollore' (Homildon near Wooler) and forbade the Earl of Northumberland or Henry Percy (Hotspur), his son, from freeing or ransoming prisoners taken. This did not please the

Percys because they had a good crop of ransomable prisoners whom they were not allowed to turn into cash. However Henry did reward the Earl with 'the lordship of Selkeryk and the Forest of Etryk with everything that to the forest pertained; and all lordships, camps, peels, fortalices, manors, towns, hamlets, sheilings and lands which the first three Earls of Douglas had held, or Archibald that is now or Joan his mother enjoyed when the Earl was taken at Homildon Hill'.

This generous gesture of lands not under English control was because Douglas had been taken prisoner in the battle but only after he had lost an eye and received five wounds. He was so well entertained by his captors, the Percys, that he joined in their rebellion against the English king, allegedly because of his no-ransom policy.

King Henry had heard of the potential rebellion and he commanded the sheriffs of London to prohibit any publication of any sinister news from the Marches of Wales, to which he was setting out in person to put down a rebellion because Henry Percy was 'threatening to invade England with the Welsh rebels and some Scots in his company.'

Henry Hotspur had been making for Wales to join up with Owen Glendower when King Henry's army met and beat them at Shrewsbury. In the battle, Hotspur was killed and the Earl of Douglas was severely wounded, and again taken prisoner. However, his feats of strength and courage in the battle had earned him the praise of his opponents and he remained as a favoured captive in England from 1403 to 1407.

Two defeats, and an eye and several other bits missing, had not lessened Earl Archibald's appetite for the fray. After returning home, he was the dominant force in southern Scotland and was part of the triumvirate who ruled Scotland during the captivity of James I. Crossing to the Continent to aid Charles VII of France in his fight against the English, he took many Border Scots in his train. Douglas was created Lieutenant-General of the French Army and Duke of Touraine but was killed in battle at Verneuil in August 1424. Amongst those Scots who fell with their leader was his shield-bearer, Robert Hoppringle of the forest stedes of Galashiels and Mossilee. How many other Borderers lost their lives there is not recorded.

For his participation on being on the losing side of the battles of Homildon, Shrewsbury and Verneuil, Archibald Douglas, 4th Earl of

Douglas, Lord of Galloway and Annandale and Duke of Touraine was given the nickname 'the Tyneman' (the Loser).

Robert III suffered ill health most of his life. His first son Robert died young and his second son David, the Duke of Rothesay, ran the country between 1399 and 1402 when he was arrested by his uncle, the Duke of Albany. David of Rothesay died in suspicious circumstances within three weeks and his youngest son James, aged seven, was the sole surviving male member of the family and the heir to the throne.

The country was racked by anarchy and civil war with the Robert III loyalists ranged up against the Albany/Douglas faction. Early in 1406, James was placed on the Bass Rock for safety and then took ship for France. But news of the flight had been leaked and he was captured at sea in total disregard of the existing truce and handed over to Henry IV of England. Less than two weeks later, King Robert III died and James became king of Scots, as yet uncrowned and now in English hands.

While a captive and learning the ways of the highly centralised English government, James was also keeping up with what was happening in Scotland. In a surviving letter written when he was eighteen, he grants the lands of Drumlanrig, Hawick and Selkirk to the Red Douglas of Angus instead of the Black Douglas of Ettrick and Teviotdale. This letter is particularly interesting in that it is written in his own hand and in the Lowland Scots of an educated person.

'Jamis, throu the grace of God, Kynge of Scottis. Til all that this letter heris or seis sendis gretynge. Wit ze that we haue grauntit and be this presentis letters grauntis a special confirmacium in the mast forme, til oure traiste and wele belofit Cosyng sir William Douglas of drumlangrig of all the landis of drumlangrig of Hawyyk and of Selekirke, etc …whilkis this presentis letters we wrate with oure proper hande vndir the signet vsit in seling of oure letters as now at Croidoune the last dai of Nouember the zere of oure lorde (1412)'.

'The lands of Selkirk' would mean the lands around the burgh of Selkirk as well the lands of Selkirk/Ettrick Forest held by the earls of Douglas.

In 1418 the town of Selkirk was burned by Sir Robert de Umfraville, the governor of Berwick, in retaliation for Scots raiding into England and the English-held Merse. We have no information about the severity of the attack.

James I spent eighteen years in captivity before returning to his kingdom in 1424 with English ways and an English wife who provided him with twin sons and a plethora of daughters, whose dynastic marriages were to benefit Scotland. During his captivity he had taken part in England's wars in France, often against his fellow countrymen.

On his return, James set about the families who had delayed his homecoming for as long as they could. By making pre-emptive strikes against his own nobility, he could redress old enmities made while he was held captive in England and at the same time increase his own authority and resources.

The Duke of Albany, his two sons, and the Earl of Lennox were executed in 1425. Archibald Douglas had escaped the king's vengeance by being killed at Verneuil the previous year but his son, also Archibald, managed to maintain a reasonably friendly relationship with the king despite being briefly imprisoned in 1431. George, the Earl of March had his lands forfeited and given a safe conduct to England in May 1435.

Ultimately, James was a victim of his own methods. Already unpopular and feared by the nobility, his failure at the siege of Roxburgh Castle in 1436 led to rumours of an assassination plot and there was an attempt to arrest him at a General Council meeting. Another assassination attempt was made at Perth in February 1437 – this time successful. His son, James II was six years old when he was crowned in March 1437.

In the Exchequer Rolls of Scotland, James I is mentioned in connection with Selkirkshire in an entry where six barrels of tar★ worth £4 is bought and delivered to Sir William Myddilmast for the king's sheep pastured in the Yarrow Ward of Selkirk Forest. This means that he not only had flocks of his own grazing in Selkirk Forest but also that he was likely to be exporting his wool to Flanders.

Peace between the two countries prevailed during the reign of James I with transfers of hostages, safe conducts to traders and march meetings being the bulk of business done. There was also the matter of truces being signed at frequent intervals but the truces were between

---

★ This must mean Stockholm or Swedish tar which was mixed with butter to make a water-proof coating where the sheep's fleece divides along its back.

kings and kingdoms and not necessarily binding on the people who lived on the Borders. The Border nobles were always ready to take the law into their own hands at the slightest provocation and would invade England with a force that for a time was irresistible. When the English Border nobles gathered their forces together, reprisals would follow as a matter of course.

Roxburgh Castle was a focal point in the possession of the fertile lands of the Merse and was held, besieged and lost by both nations in turn. It was more often in English hands than Scottish and this turns out to be a good thing for later historians, because the English commanders were sending reports to their king in London and these have been preserved in the Public Records Office there.

An account of the castle in 1416 paints a dire picture of decay and neglect. The following year it was besieged by the Scots but was saved by a hasty reinforcement of men and weapons. By 1419 repairs had been made on orders from King Henry V.

Gunpowder had gone down in price with 300 pounds now costing £10, about a quarter of the previous price, and 'gunnes' were an integral part of the defences of a castle.

Although James I seemed to be on friendly terms with Henrys IV, V and VI, there were always tensions running through the Border counties. In June 1436, Henry VI was warning the sheriffs of Cumberland, Westmoreland, Northumberland and York that there was a threatened invasion of the Scots and to have their county arrays prepared. At this period, the English held the castles of Berwick and Roxburgh and were replenishing their arsenals in preparation. Almost all of Berwickshire and eastern Roxburghshire was English-held although the hold was often tenuous. The Prior of Coldingham wrote to King Henry V in 1437, that from their situation on the Marches, they were so exposed to constant deprecations from the king's forces invading Scotland and the Scots making reprisals, that they had neither meat nor drink and could he please issue a special protection for them, their servants, farmers and possessions for a year.

When James II came to the throne in 1437, he was a young boy controlled by the remaining members of his father's supporters, headed by his mother the queen. The forfeitures and executions during his father's reign meant that there were very few of the top layer of nobility left, the earls. This political imbalance meant that power was concentrated in the line of the Black Douglas but there was a growing tension between the Royal party and the increasing power of the Douglas family.

James was ten years old when his guardians Livingston and Crichton invited the young Earl of Douglas and his brother to the 'Black Dinner' at Edinburgh Castle. When the head of a black bull was placed on the table, the two young noblemen were seized and killed. Their French estates reverted to the crown and the Scottish estates were divided between their sister, the Fair Maid of Galloway, and their old uncle, known as James the Fat, now the seventh Earl of Douglas. James the Fat died in 1443 and his son William, the eighth earl, divorced his wife and married his cousin, the Fair Maid of Galloway, thereby uniting all the Douglas lands.

This made the family stronger than ever and when William became lieutenant-general in 1444, together with his brothers James, Archibald, Hugh and John, they were the effective rulers of Scotland and used their influence to acquire earldoms, lands and honours for themselves and their brothers, allies and friends.

Now the Douglas family held all the royal lands of Ettrick Forest as well as a large slice which had been granted to Melrose Abbey by Alexander II. The increasing power of the Douglas family in Ettrick Forest was causing grave anxiety to the Scottish king.

An entry in the Exchequer Roll of 1442 records the payment of £5 Scots to Master Nicholas, carpenter, for removing a great bombard, a large gun for throwing bombs, from the 'dominium Regis versus Galoway Schelis in Foresta'. Was this the king's party taking the precaution of moving a new and powerful weapon from the lands of a potential enemy?

Which raises the question of why a great bombard should have been in the king's dominium in the vicinity of Galashiels in the first place. The answer might lie in the place-name, the Gun Knowe, which is opposite Galashiels on the other side of the River Tweed at Galafoot and now under the new town of Tweedbank. In the low ground beside the knowe, there are large deposits of fine puddle clay which would be ideal for metal casting. So the possibility that cannon were being cast in this vicinity cannot be ruled out.

The gun connection with Galashiels did not end with the king's death. In 1476, David Wricht in Galwayschelis was supplying spades and shovels for the king's artillery and in 1486, Pringle of Galashiels, the ranger of the Tweed Ward, sent poles and ropes for the bombards in Edinburgh Castle.

William, the eighth Earl of Douglas, now the most powerful man in Scotland, travelled through Europe, meeting with kings and the Pope on an equal footing, while in Scotland James was gathering his forces for a struggle for supremacy. During one of the earl's absences abroad, the now adult James plundered Douglas lands in Selkirk Forest. The tower of Craig of Douglas in the Yarrow Valley was taken and burned down by the king's supporters in 1450. (Craig-Brown has this happening in 1460.) As it was a wooden tower, there are few visible remains of its existence but there is a sculpted mound beside the Douglas Burn about 300m north of Craig Douglas Farm, which must be the location. This is also likely to be the site of the Border ballad, 'The Douglas Tragedy'.

In 1452, William returned from Rome with a great train of nobles and knights. These included Humes, Hoppringles (Pringles), Bells, Grahams and Kers from his lands in the Borders. A meeting was held between the king and Douglas in Stirling for which Douglas was given a promise of safe conduct; but during a confrontation, the king took out his dagger and killed Douglas with his own hand.

The murdered man's brother nailed a notice on the door of Parliament House declaring the king a perjured man and a murderer. Civil war followed.

In April 1453, James, the ninth Earl of Douglas and brother of the murdered earl, was representing King James in conducting a truce agreement with England. James Douglas withdrew his allegiance to the king in the same year after the Douglas army was defeated in battle at Arkinholm where one of the ninth Earl's brothers was killed, and another captured and beheaded. Taking the hint, James Douglas fled to England and the Douglas lands were forfeited in 1455. With this Act of Attainment 'the lordschip of Ettrik Forest with all boundis pertyning thairto' were annexed to the Crown after having been in the hands of the Douglas family for a hundred and thirty years.

With the Douglas family successfully exiled to England, James II appears to have been more peacefully disposed towards that country despite its assistance in Douglas attempts to recover their Scottish lands. A four-year truce was ratified between the two countries on 31 December 1457, the same year in which James received a huge cannon called 'Mons Meg' as a gift from Philip of Burgundy. The king's fondness of artillery pieces is shown in the frequent entries of expenditure for bringing in bombards, repairing bombard, drying gunpowder for bombards etc.

In May 1459, James sent the Abbot of Melrose on a friendly embassy to England and the Borders were peaceful (a relative term). However, a revolution in England had removed Henry VI from the throne and installed Edward IV on 4 March 1460.

James II saw this as an opportunity to recover Berwick and Roxburgh which had been in English possession for over a hundred years. The truce had been made with Henry VI of Lancaster and James no longer considered it binding now that Henry was in the hands of his enemies. His recent military preparations allowed James to field a well-equipped army in a very short time and this included his siege guns.

Word of the forthcoming invasion leaked to the English Court and a letter was sent to Lord Dacre that the king of Scots with all his power was expected to lay siege to Berwick 'eftsones'. But James diverted and laid siege to the Castle of Roxburgh instead. On Sunday 3 August, 'King James haueng sik plesure in discharging gret gunis past til a place far fra the armie to recreat him selfe in schuiting gret pieces, quhairof he was verie expert, bot the peice appeiringlie, with ouer sair a chairge, flies in flinderis with a part of quhilk strukne in the hench or he was war, quhairof (allace) he dies.'

On hearing the news, his queen, Mary of Gueldres, brought the eight-year-old Prince James to Kelso Abbey where he was crowned James III, king of Scots, after the castle had been taken and demolished to prevent it being refortified by the English. The Scots may have lost a king but they had regained control of what had been a frontier stronghold of England.

Like his father, James III was a child at his accession and the years of his minority were largely guided by his mother, Mary of Gueldres. Through her intercession, the Scots regained Berwick which Henry VI, now exiled in the Scottish Court, agreed to in 1461 and a fifteen-year truce was concluded in 1463. Edward favoured a peaceful solution to the problems between the countries and encouraged Scotsmen to settle in England and become English citizens through letters of denization (naturalisation).

Scotland in general and the Borders in particular, benefited from the political upheaval and instability in England as the houses of Lancaster and York competed for the throne in what is usually known as the 'War of the Roses', although the actual phrase does not occur until the nineteenth century. The battle for dominance in northern England between the Percies and the Nevilles meant that the Scottish Borders were spared while the English northern barons fought amongst themselves.

The wars between York and Lancaster saw an almost political change of rulers in England. When James III became king of Scots, the Lancastrian Henry VI was on the throne having been crowned king of England in 1429 and king of France in 1431 (He eventually lost both kingdoms but that is another story.)

Henry was deposed by the Yorkist Edward IV on 4 March 1461. Edward reigned until 9 October 1470 when Lancastrian exiles invaded and deposed him, reinstating Henry VI on the throne. He ruled for six months before being replaced by Edward IV for the second time.

James III began his personal reign in 1469, the same year as his marriage to Margaret, the daughter of Christian I, king of Denmark and Norway, thereby ending a two-hundred-year dispute over the payment of the annual tribute for the Western Isles. It also included handing over all the lands and rights which the Danish-Norwegian crown held over Orkney and Shetland until her dowry was paid. This was never paid in full and the earldom of Orkney and then the lordship of Shetland were annexed to Scotland in 1472.

The queen bore her husband three sons, James (IV), James (Duke of Ross) and John (Earl of Mar). An Italian biographer wrote that Queen Margaret had more skill in running a kingdom than her husband – a true summation as time would tell.

James III was by nature a man of peace; disliking war, he preferred to deal amicably with the English threat on the Borders. On the other hand, Edward IV of England was ambitious to extend his kingdom northwards, protecting and paying the exiled James, Earl of Douglas as a valuable pawn for interfering in Scottish affairs. Edward was having trouble with his foreign policy on the Continent so a forty-five year peace was concluded in Edinburgh in 1474. This extended to mutual trading between Scotland and England and again Scots were encouraged to live in England and receive English citizenship.

In 1474 a marriage was arranged between the infant prince of Scotland (later James IV) and Princess Cecilia, daughter of Edward IV with a dowry of 20,000 marks. This was paid in instalments and in 1479 James was writing to Edward thanking him for paying in English rather than Scots money. By this time one English penny was worth three Scots pennies.

Edward lost patience with the lack of progress and demanded the delivery of the young prince, the surrender of parts of southern Scotland, the restoration of the Earl of Douglas, and the homage of Scotland; otherwise he would invade Scotland and take everything by force.

James was having trouble with his parliaments, avoided speaking to his nobles unless absolutely necessary, kept trying to make peace treaties with an irate English king and had the Douglases hovering in exile in England. Yet his worst enemies were within his own family. James III had two legitimate younger brothers, Alexander and John as well as three Stewart half-uncles.

Things came to a head in 1479 when Alexander vocally disagreed with James' policy of appeasement towards England. Alexander was arrested but escaped and fled to France. The other brother, John, Earl of Mar, was accused of treason and witchcraft, arrested and died in prison in dubious circumstances in the winter of 1479–80.

James III reneged on the marriage bond after 7,000 marks had been paid and in 1482, the Provost of Edinburgh and 'the hale fellowscip of merchandis, burgesses and communite of the same toune' promised to repay all sums paid by Edward if the bargain fell through.

This did not appease Edward who instigated a major English invasion of southern Scotland, led by James, Earl of Douglas, and

Alexander, the king's brother, who had returned from his retreat in France. Edward had promised to assist Alexander to gain the throne of Scotland as Alexander IV and even offered Princess Cecilia as his consort if he could get free of his wife.

Meanwhile the family conspiracy against James, which seemed to have involved his queen, was taking shape. James was seized by a group of his nobles led by his three half-uncles at Lauder. He was returned to Edinburgh to be lodged as a prisoner in the Castle while his close friends and advisors were hanged over Lauder Bridge. The English army advanced to Edinburgh and laid siege to the Castle. The prospect of Alexander as king of Scots did not appeal to anyone except himself and the conspiracy imploded. The English withdrew and James was released to reign as before but now with the conspirators fighting amongst themselves for a share of the cake. However, the invasion had cost the country dearly in humiliation and land with the permanent loss of Berwick, the main port of southern Scotland.

In 1483, Alexander was involved in another conspiracy with England and thereafter his life was a series of unsuccessful attempts to gain the Crown of Scotland. In 1485, he was killed by the splinter from a broken lance while competing at a tournament in Paris.

James had not learned by his mistakes and his fondness of the artistic, rather than the military and civil, had alienated him from the magnates of his kingdom. A group of the greater nobles played on the estrangement between James III and his fifteen-year-old heir Prince James, and were planning a coup to place the father in custody and install a regency with Prince James as ruler, under their wise guidance, of course. This was to be a demonstration to show that they were not happy with the way the country was being run, rather than the regicide as it turned out to be.

The prince's army gathered near Bannockburn, having managed to enlist most of the higher nobles of Scotland to their cause. King James, armed with the sword of Robert the Bruce, marched out of Edinburgh and engaged his son's forces at a place which was called Sauchieburn a hundred and fifty years later. The prince's supporters came from the south and west of the kingdom while the king's were from the north and east. In the clash on 11 June 1488, the king's party were routed and King James 'happinit to be slane'. Despite a parliamentary inquiry and a reward of 100 merks of land for the name of the perpetrator, nobody could be found to take the blame although Hume of Godscroft was strongly suspected of striking the killing blow.

The reign of James IV started with a projected truce between the two countries while Henry VII the new Tudor king of England was planning with several Scottish exiles to kidnap James. More seriously, Archibald, the Earl of Angus, was bargaining to deliver the Castle of Hermitage to Henry and join in the war against his own king.

James must have received information about the proposed betrayal so he deprived Angus of Hermitage Castle and Liddesdale on 6 March 1492. However, Angus seems to have been one of James's ambassadors to England later in the same year and it appears that all must have been forgiven, or at least Angus was being kept where he could be seen.

James IV had observed many revolutions against his father's rule and took steps to spread his own influence over a wider range of the population. In contrast to James III, he took pains to include the great magnates of the country in the royal council and courted their opinions. This made for more debate and fewer revolutions. He was a ceaseless traveller round his kingdom, holding justice eyres, soothing minor feuds before they became major offences and generally showing himself to the people. This was in stark contrast to James III who hardly every left Edinburgh.

James put himself about in more ways than one as George Burnet the Victorian Lyon king-at-arms who edited the Exchequer Rolls, disapprovingly acknowledges: 'It is to be regretted that the Scottish king was not equally conspicuous for his abstinence from excess of another kind; for though the story regarding his precocity in vice founded on supposed allusions to Margaret Drummond will not bear investigation, he was by no means an example to his age in continency as in temperance. Several daughters and other near relatives of the Scottish nobility were the mothers of illegitimate children of whom the king is the acknowledged father.' The Exchequer Rolls show that the king took care of results of this early interest in personal relationships.

The same noble families were well aware that a nubile daughter was a distinct asset when a young king came calling. It was ever thus that some families rose to positions of prestige and power on the bodies of their womenfolk rather than the strength of their sword arms.

In his official capacity, James was a Renaissance king with a cosmo-politan court that kept up to date with current intellectual thought and European fashions. He spoke six languages including Gaelic, yet took part in jousting and tournaments and cultivated his image as an intel-lectual warrior king. Added to this, was a diplomatic effort to secure recognition for himself and the country in the wider courts of Europe. The perceived image was as important to medieval kings as it is to modern politicians.

James was a builder of ships and palaces. The Palace of Holyrood and the great Hall of Stirling Castle cost vast sums money and he spent over £100,000 Scots on the Scottish Navy. In the first two decades of the 16th century, there was a naval supremacy race between Scotland and England. The Scottish *Margaret* was followed by the English *Mary Rose*, both about 700 tons burden but both were surpassed by James's *Great Michael* which was 240ft in length and of 1,000 tons burden.

His interest in the sea was not solely a warlike one. His Acts of 1493 and 1505 directed that ships of 20 tons burden were to be built in all seaport towns and had to be manned by any idle able-bodied men who were to be found. This was for the development of the export trade of salmon, cod and herring.

Despite vast expenditure on ships and buildings, James kept an eye on government and personal spending. Realising that his father's methods of raising money by forfeiture of estates, debasement of the coinage, and increasing taxes were self-defeating, James IV leased out the bulk of royal lands and encouraged national and international trading (and thus taxation), with acts of revocation (taking away and re-granting certain privileges) for his main fund-gathering. Thus he trebled his income from £13,000 Scots in 1490 to £40,000 in 1513.

The relations between James and Henry VII of England were always going to be thorny. Both employed spies to discover the plans and intentions of the other and welcomed refugees as exiles from the other's court. The diplomatic relations between the two had always been conducted from positions of mutual distrust, despite frequent negotiations for peace and truce. Equally important were the marriage settlements to cement relations between the kingdoms.

In 1496, Henry made an offer to James of the hand of his daughter Margaret, then a very young girl. Negotiations broke down when James welcomed Perkin Warbeck, a pretender to the throne of England as 'Prince Richard of England' and gave him Lady Katherine Gordon, a daughter of the Earl of Huntly, as a bride. James had made a bargain with Warbeck that he would support him on condition that if he (Warbeck) won the throne of England, Berwick would be returned to Scotland and a payment of 50,000 marks be paid to cover the cost of the proposed invasion. By way of supporting Warbeck's claim, the Scots did enter England and looted their way through Northumberland in 1496.

Henry immediately ordered all Scotsmen expelled from his realm and ordered the Sheriffs of northern England and as far south as Derby to put all fencible men from sixteen to sixty on an hour's warning to serve against the 'auncient ennemyes' the Scots.

The invasion failed and a further attempt was made by Warbeck to seize the English throne but this time from Cornwall and the West Country of England. That invasion lasted one day before he was captured and eventually hanged in 1499. Despite this, Lady Katherine was made very welcome at Henry's court, receiving from the royal exchequer many yards of black and crimson velvet, black satin gowns lined with mink, much linen and cotton cloth, black kersey for 'hosyn' and many other items suitable for a lady of fashion. Although no portraits of her are available, it must be deduced that she was a very attractive lady; she made a further three marriages.

The following year the Scots were again in England, this time besieging Norham Castle. This lasted a week before the Earl of Surrey appeared with a superior force and James withdrew.

On 30 September 1497 a truce was concluded at Ayton mainly through the good offices of the Spanish Ambassador. With peace restored, the marriage contacts were reopened as well as a further treaty binding the kings to peace during their lifetimes and for a year after the death of the survivor.

On 24 January 1501, the treaty was signed for the marriage of the king of Scots to the Princess Margaret, the daughter of Henry VII and sister of the future King Henry VIII. By agreement 'The Princess to be brought to Lamberton Kirk by the 1st September 1503 and the marriage to be solemnised fifteen days after. Her husband to endow her for life as a marriage gift by 1st July the same year with lands etc yielding £2000 sterling per annum, equivalent to £6000 Scottish money. Twenty-four of her attendants to be English. The Princess to have £1000 Scots or 500 marks sterling yearly at her own disposal. The king of England to pay her dowry 30,000 gold English nobles on the marriage day and the remainder two years after.'

James's aggression was yielding diplomatic rewards. It is recorded that the Earl of Surrey was guest of honour at the wedding but that he had little time for his royal host. Their next encounter ten years later was to have a more dramatic outcome.

Two separate treaties were signed on the same day. The town and castle of Berwick was not to be attacked by Scots and the Berwick garrison not to attack the king of Scots or his vassals; and the extradition of murderers, robbers etc had to be certified in ten days if within a 100 miles of either march and in twenty days if outside the 100 miles limit.

On 1 June 1503, sasine, the legal possession of property, was given by John Murray, Sheriff of Selkirk to Queen Margaret's attorneys, of the lordship and Forest of Ettrick and the tower of Newerk. This was done at the 'tugurium' and manor of Galloscheilles in the said lordship in the presence of Walter Scott of Bukcleuch and David Hoppringil of Smalehame, Nicholas Ridley of Willemontswyke and Edward Par, esquires of England, William Ker, Master James Murraye, rector of Wiltone, William Hoppringill, Sir Thomas Tyndyne, rector of Wyle and Henry Broune, Englishman.

('Tugurium' is correctly translated as a shepherd's hut or cottage but, as will be shown later, it was the tower or hall erected around 1460.)

With this grant it might be a good time to leave the historical aspect of Scotland and the Borders and look to particular aspects of Ettrick Forest and Selkirkshire in general.

THE SELKIRK/ETTRICK FOREST

With the Forest back in Crown possession, the administrative paperwork can be found in the Exchequer Rolls of each period and we can look at the reasons why most of the county was taken up by the Forest.

Hunting in the forest had been practised since the first humans wandered up the valleys in pursuit of the animals living there, but it would take the Normans to formulate the idea of an area of land being set aside as an exclusive hunting reserve, first to England and then to Scotland.

Before 1066, a series of hunting reserves were well established in Normandy. These were not necessarily forests as we know them with lines of regimented trees grown for the wood they produced. The Norman 'foresta' was principally a hunting playground, the preserve of the royal and baronial families: if the chase provided meat for the table and skins for parchment and leather making, then that was a bonus.

The Norman invasion brought the forest system into England in the eleventh century when William II and Henry I established hunting reserves with a recognised code of forest laws in many parts of the country. Hunting was a recognised sport of the nobility because only the wealthy could afford the servants, horses and dogs to maintain the sport, but it also was excellent training for war. The horsemanship and weapon-skills needed in hunting were the same ones required in fighting.

One large hunting reserve had been established by Henry I on the earldom of Huntingdon which David, the youngest son of Malcolm III, held through his marriage to Matilda, the great-niece of William the Conquerer. There, David saw forest laws in practice as his lands were tenanted by Norman-French families who were well used to the concept of hunting reserves. When David became king of Scotland in 1124, he brought the younger Anglo-Norman Bruces, Morvilles, St Clairs and de Soules from Huntingdon and settled them in southern Scotland.

It is not known when the first hunting reserve was established in Scotland but it would have been done by David I. This might have happened while he was still Earl David but it was certainly in place by the 1130s when he was King David. By turning the area of royal demesne in the Ettrick and Yarrow Valleys into a hunting reserve or forest, he created a place where no one could hunt or use the land without his specific permission.

In the foundation charter to Selkirk Abbey given in 1119, David the Earl shows that he is controlling the use of timber from his woods and also that he employed huntsmen to provide: 'half the skins of my kitchen and all the skins of sheep and lambs and a tenth of the hides of stags and hinds which my huntsmen [veltarii or greyhound keepers] may capture. And my waters about Selkirk shall be common to be fished by their own fishermen as by mine; and my pastures common to their men and mine; and my wood to be used for building and fuel as by me.'

David was commercialising the products of the forest but there is no written evidence formalising a royal hunting reserve at this period. This was forest control *de facto* even if it was not known to be *de jure*.

The forest as a hunting reserve could be created by the king or by a baron with the king's permission, provided it was on his own land and he had complete control of all that was in, on or above the ground, but the king's authority was necessary. Access to the forest was strictly controlled by the owner, who could exploit its resources for his own benefit. He could allow others to hunt in his forest, graze their animals there and cut wood at his discretion and usually on payment of a rent or toll. The laws of 'vert' and 'venison' were strictly enforced: vert meant all the herbage growing in the forest as this was essential for harbouring and grazing the animals there; the laws of venison referred to the greater game animals, red deer and wild boar. Smaller animals like fox, wild-cat, hares and martens were also covered by this law and hawking and fishing were similarly regulated. This would apply to rabbits which were introduced in the twelfth century and were so reluctant to breed that special rabbit enclosures or warrens had to be made. These took the form of long narrow mounds of turf with a tunnel built inside; none have been recognised within Selkirk/Ettrick Forest.

Tolls or rents were charged for grazing other animals, usually sheep or cattle in the forest pastures, and 'pannage', allowing pigs to dig for roots and acorns in the forest.

The forest laws are complex and far beyond my remit and under-standing, but the most erudite and well-researched book on the subject is *Hunting and Hunting Reserves in Medieval Scotland* by Dr John M. Gilbert, who was history teacher at Selkirk High School in the 1970s. There the Selkirk/Ettrick Forest gets prominent mention.

The historical references to Selkirk/Ettrick Forest are complicated by its expansions and contractions with varying names given to different sections. The whole area was known as ' the Forest of Selkirk' in early documents; sometimes as 'the Forest of Selkirk, Ettrick and

Traquair' or simply as 'the Forest'. Eventually it became known as 'Ettrick Forest', an unspecified area of land somewhere from the lands of the burgh of Selkirk to the tops of the Ettrick and Yarrow Valleys. We have little idea what the Forest was like at that period. Certainly clumps of naturally grown matured trees grew there as various kings gave numbers of oak trees to religious houses and favoured supporters for building purposes. The remainder of the area was likely to be scrub timber and forest pasture under the taller trees, with the hill tops being marginal grazing without tree cover. This was poor agricultural land.

The story of the Forest is further complicated by the fact that southern Scotland was frequently in English hands with English-appointed Keepers in Ettrick and Jedburgh Forests, and many of the earliest mentions are in English documents. When the forests were in the possession of Edward III of England, he placed them under the chamberlain and chancellor of Scotland who tried to collect more revenue from them. This was a forlorn hope as forty years of skirmishing there had reduced many of the forest stedes to piles of ashes. In 1335 William de Montague held the forest and sheriffdom of Selkirk for a rent of £30 while in 1336, the town and sheriffdom of Jedburgh was valued at 50 merks (£33:6s:8d). This was not really a time for property speculators.

The Douglases and the Percys continued to dispute possession of the forests of Selkirk and Jedburgh for most of the fourteenth century. Even although Henry IV of England granted Henry Percy the lordship and forest of Selkirk in 1402, it was the Douglas family and their vassals who controlled the actual forest.

Around the beginning of the fifteenth century, probably as early as 1406, Archibald, the fourth Earl of Douglas moved his principal residence in Selkirk Forest from Edibertshiels to a prominence a kilometre to the west. This became known as the New Wark while the old site of Edibertshiels decayed and became known as the Auld Wark.

It is probable that Newark castle was originally built as a wooden motte but, by this time, good oak trees were scarce in the Forest and stone buildings were built of necessity rather than by choice. There are few stone towers or peels in Selkirkshire that can be securely dated before 1500.

The largest oak trees were jealously guarded from the earliest times and not included in grants of forest pastures. This may be because the high trees were valued as the nesting places of hawks and falcons rather than for their timber content. In the fourteenth century, the gift of an oak from Ettrick Forest was rarer than the present of a stag and no one, noble or abbot, could take an oak tree from there without the king's special permission.

The records of the Forest Court up to the time of Flodden show that a strict account was kept of all the large trees growing within the Forest. Those trees felled for the erection of Newark Castle or to repair Melrose and Kelso Abbeys after an English invasion were strictly noted in the ranger's accounts.

The Douglas removal to Newark meant that the Forest Courts were held there and, twice yearly, at the festivals of Beltane and All Hallows (1 May and 1 November), justice was served by the king's forester or baillie who, in the early fifteenth century, was one of the Douglas earls. The early Forest Courts mainly dealt with crimes against the hunting regulations such as deer poaching, illegal hawking and hunting without leave, but as the century progressed, and especially after 1455, the cases became increasing financial – the regulation of leases of the forest stedes, the illegal enclosure of land and the theft or destruction of wood, in particular cutting green wood.

By this time, the Forest as a wood producer was under severe pressure. With so many sheep grazing in the Forest pastures, young seedling trees were being cropped by ovine teeth and had no chance of growing into mature timber. Sheep literally ate the future of Ettrick Forest.

Charters of David I refer to the Forests of 'Seleschirche et de Trauequair' and later kings granted certain liberties therein, but the Forest remained a Crown possession until 1324 when it was given to Sir James Douglas in free barony. It remained in Douglas hands until 1455 when it returned to royal possession to become the dower lands of the queens of Scotland, Margaret of Denmark, wife of James III and later Margaret Tudor of England, wife of James IV.

In 1455 the accounts of Ettrick Forest appear in the Exchequer Rolls in detail for the first time. These show that the forest lands were split into three wards of Ettrick, Yarrow and Tweed and within these wards the forest stedes were let out. As the three wards were a conjoined unit of Crown lands, the head of administration was a 'forester' or 'baillie' who was appointed by the king to look after his interests. The baillie was usually a noble who held lands in the vicinity. Under the baillie, who had nominal charge of the Forest, were the hands-on officers with the responsibilities of controlling their own area.

Each ward was under the supervision of a master-ranger or head forester with a 'currour' or under-forester who seems to have been in charge of the financial administration and the collecting of rents/fines and acted as a messenger/policeman to see that everyone obeyed the forest laws – which they didn't if they could get away with it. For their labours, the officials were given land commensurate with their status and this was held rent-free. Some of these lands can be traced in the place-names with Baillielees, (the meadows of the baillie) and Wardlaw, (the hill of the warden), still remaining in Ettrick Valley.

In 1456, remission of rent for one steading each was granted to Thomas Cranstoune of that Ilk as baillie; Sir Walter Scott (of Buccleuch) as master ranger of Ettrick with Atkin Scott as ranger of Ettrick; Sir William Myddilmast as master ranger of Yarrow with Robert Ledale as ranger of Yarrow; George Pringill as master ranger of Tweed and David Pringill as ranger of Tweed. These offices were a sure means of acquiring further lands. As in a natural forest where the smaller trees get room to grow when a mighty tree falls, so the downfall to the Douglas family allowed the minor nobility to expand their lands and influence.

Amongst the most acquisitive in the Tweed Valley were the Kers/Kerrs, Scotts, Humes, Murrays and Pringles with a number of other families, the Turnbulls, Olivers, Rutherfords, Beatties, Littles and others, who rose and fell in prestige and property. Liddesdale was the territory of the Elliots and Armstrongs along with the lesser families of Nixons and Crosiers and a smattering of Robsons, Turnbulls and Hendersons – some known to fame but more to infamy.

Within the Forest Area

In Selkirk/Ettrick Forest, the principal risers in prestige and power were the Scotts who became extensive landholders in the Ettrick and Tima valleys, spreading out from their original base at Buccleuch in Rankleburn and eventually into Teviotdale and the Yarrow Valley.

With a notably acquisitive nature, the family of Scott held the Ettrick and Yarrow Valleys above the joining of the two rivers by the mid sixteenth century and, as a family grouping they had a great influence on the history of Selkirkshire. The stedes of Annelshope, Bowhill, Broadmeadows, Buccleuch, Carterhaugh, Catslack, Deephope, Delorraine, Deuchar, Dryhope, Gamescleuch, Gilmanscleuch, Haining, Huntly, Hartwoodmyres, Kirkhope, Ladhope, Middlestead, Newburgh, Oakwood, Sinton, Whitehillbrae, Whitehope, Whitslade, Winterburgh and The Woll were all occupied by Scotts at one time or another. But gradually the lands of the lesser Scotts were subsumed by the Scotts of Harden and more often the Scotts of Buccleuch, who were, and remain the greatest landowners in Scotland.

The Pringles, originally Hoppringles, were vassals of the Douglases but on the fall of that family, quickly transferred their allegiance directly to the king. They held most of Gala Water and soon acquired the lease of some forest stedes around what is now Galashiels. One branch of the Pringles received the forest stedes of Galashiels and Mosilee while another got Torwoodlee and Caddonlee in the early sixteenth century. The Pringles were not quite so successful as the Scotts in acquiring and holding on to their lands.

Families Outwith the Forest

Below the joining of the Ettrick and Yarrow, the names of Barber, Turnbull and Murray held portions of the lands of Philiphaugh. John Murray of Falahill was granted part of the lands of Philiphaugh in 1461 and soon acquired leases of several stedes in the lower Yarrow Valley. The Peeblesshire family of Hays of Hayston held the Megget Valley from early medieval times. The Kers of Cessford had acquired most of the Kelso Abbey lands on the north and east of the county, Lindean, Greenhead, Sunderland Hall, Whitmuir and Whitlaw.

In Selkirkshire, the named family possession of certain lands was never certain. The Wars of Independence began a long period of English invasion and control with much of the area claimed by two contenders, one Scots and one English. Although harryings of Henry VIII's armies during the Rough Wooing in the 1540s were the last committed attempt by the English Crown to annexe Scotland,

Selkirkshire was near enough to the Border for the violence to spill into the county.

Family feuds and reiving forays made life uncertain for many of the Forest dwellers while the town of Selkirk could muster enough armed men to deter even the strongest band of casual reivers and was only vulnerable to English armies.

The Ettrick Forest Stedes

In looking at the Forest stedes on the Exchequer Rolls of 1456, it is possible to draw a comprehensive map of the 'forest stedes' in the area. The stedes are the agricultural holdings within the forest and, unsurprisingly, most of the present-day farms occupy the same sites and bear the same names. In a few cases, where a set of new farm buildings are relocated away from the original site, the name goes to the new site; in others, they appear as the 'Old' and the 'New' even although the 'new' may be four or five hundred years old.

In the two volumes of Craig-Brown's *History of Selkirkshire*, the history of the owners of each stede has been comprehensively researched and meticulously recorded in 441 pages. All known information about that stede up to 1886 is available there and as there is little I can add to the sum of knowledge, I can only direct the inquiring reader to that source. Another, more concise, version can be found in the 1957 *Inventory of the Ancient and Historical Monuments of Selkirkshire*.

Most of our knowledge of the Ettrick Forest comes from the Exchequer Rolls which show the profit and loss account of the Crown holdings there. These show that the three wards of Ettrick, Yarrow and Tweed were further divided into 'forest stedes', each paying a yearly rent of £6 as well as a quota of sheep and cattle as rent in kind. There were 45 stedes in the Ettrick Ward, 23⅓ in the Yarrow Ward, and 17 in the Tweed Ward. Additionally there were two smaller holdings called 'hamilots' which paid 30s in rent but were exempt from rent in kind, and 'boundelsoure' the pasture land of a labourer which was rented at 13s 4d.

The total rents of the Forest stedes came to £519:13s:4d which had to be paid on 1 November and 1 August, presumably in equal parts. From the rents, money had to be found to cover the expenses for the

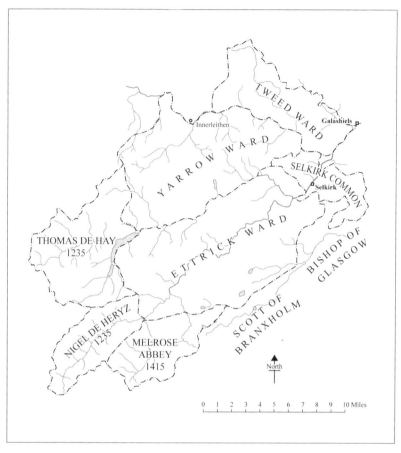

forest officers, repairs to buildings on stedes held by the king and sundry 'expenses of the king's household etc'. The Exchequer Rolls show that sundry expenses include such diverse items as shoeing the king's horses and 12 bolls of oatmeal (1,680lbs or nearly a ton) for a celebration called 'Scotis Silvestribus' to be held while the king was in the forest with his followers. In 1457, a further 35 bolls at 10s each were required when the celebration was held at Melrose.

Not all the entries were for expenses and payments made for services. There was the sum of £252 remitted to twenty-one stedes situated beyond the water of Ettrick in consideration of their destruction in time of war. This is a frequent entry.

The Exchequer Rolls make fascinating reading, telling who owned or was living in each place; what they were doing, especially if they were known to be breaking the Laws of the Forest or enforcing them; whether they were being robbed and murdered, or were themselves robbers and murderers.

Any encroachment on the privileges of the Royal Forest of Ettrick was punishable.

To take timber from the Forest without permission was a fineable offence; pasture rights of herbage and foggage were restricted lest the hunting reserves be ruined; pigs and goats were illegal for the same reason; and, more especially, clearing Forest lands for arable agriculture was forbidden except by royal grant. Illegal enclosure, ploughing and sowing could lead to the forfeiture of the tenant's holding or the confiscation of his crops. Any industrial activity that would prevent the movement of game was forbidden: this included bark-peeling, tanning, charcoal-burning, carpentry and arrow-making. Trespassers were prosecuted by a fine, prison or the seizure of goods. In theory, the king controlled everything in the Royal Forest but, in practice, this was not possible.

Recorded in the Exchequer Rolls are the fines for offences against forest law. In 1467, George Davisone was charged £60 for cutting six oaks trees but this was remitted, probably because he would not have been able to pay such a large sum anyway. This type of remission occurs frequently in the Exchequer Rolls: 'Remission of 136s due to fifteen

The Ward of Ettrick

Brademedow	Middlisted of Fauwside
Harehede	Hanyng
Estemeststede of Hartwod	Mydstede of Hartwod
Akewod	Huntlee
Mydmeststede of Warmwod	Westmeststede of Warmwod
Estmeststede of Langhop	2 Westmeststedis of Langhop
Estmeststede of Gildhouse	Mydstede of Gildhouse
Westmeststede of Gildhouse	3 Stedis of Redefurde
Dalloryane	Aldanhop
Moncomane	Torschelaw

Wyntyrburgh	Half stede of Berybus
Stede and half of Fauhopeschele	
and Fauhopgranys	Gilmyiscluche
Singil	Stede and half Ernhuche
Kirkhop	Faulishop
2 Stedes Catkermach	Half stede of Fasthauch
Half stede of Craghop	Kershop
Ladhop	Sundhop
Stede and half Eldanehop	Eltrefe
Bourhop	Half stede Corsecleuch

The stedes of Hartwood are Hartwoodburn, Middlestead and Hartwood-myres. Mydmestestede of Warmwood is Hutlerburn and the Westmeste-stede is the now vanished settlement of Whitehillbrae. The Langhops are Langhope, Todrig and Howford. The Redefurdes are Redfordgreen, Dodhead and Hyndhope. Aldanhope is Annelshope. Moncomane is Deephope. Wyntyrburgh is Newburgh. Erncleuch is a vanished settlement between Singlie and Kirkhope. The two stedes of Catkermach are Carterhaugh and Auld Wark.

The stede and a half of Fauhopschele and Fauhopgranys is likely to be Crosslee and one of the settlements up the line of the Crosslee burn.

persons fined at the Boundecourte, and having neither goods nor pledges, one of them James Walkare being dead before the court was held'.

Sheep and cattle could be grazed in the wood pastures but no building could be erected to house the shepherds without permission from the forest warden or the king, and such privileges had to be paid for. Temporary buildings called sheilings were allowed for brief periods of occupation during the summer grazing time; 'shiels' were permanent houses.

'1478. James Hoppringill credits himself with £9 for 2 cottages called "scheillis" in Caldanele and another in Galwayschelis because the said stedes have been granted to our lady the Queen with liberty to have sheilings'.

The Ward of Tweed

---

2 Places and 1 hamlet of	Holewelle
Gatehop and Presthop	
Thorniele	Caldanhede
3 Places of Wynndiduris	Creglath
2 and a half places in Corsle	Torwartlee
Blyndle	Galowaschelis
Mosylee	1 and a half places in Farnyle

The three places of Gatehop and Presthop lie outside the present Selkirkshire boundary on Gatehopeknowe Burn and Priesthope Burn. The places of Wyndiduris are Windydoors, Blackhaugh and the vanished settlement at Trinlieknowes, opposite Laidlawstiel. The two and a half places at Croslee are Crosslee, Old Reidhead and Whytbank

With the Forest now being run as an increasingly commercial proposition, the Rolls have entries like: 'Easter and Wester Montbergeries, Blakgrane and Catslack still occupied with the king's own flocks and let in steilbow to David Crichton for 340 merks yearly'.

'Steilbow' is a system where the landowner, in this case the king, provides the land and the sheep to stock it. The man who looks after the animals either gets all the lambs, as in this case where he pays a rent for the land and breeding animals, or he gets half of the lambs with the other half going to the land-owner but pays no rent in cash. In either case, the land and the same number of sheep had to be returned at the end of the lease.

The same steilbow bargain could be made on arable land where the landowner provided ploughs, harrows and seed to enable the tenant to cultivate the ground and harvest the crop. Again the tenant had to return the same items as he received.

The £6 Scots rent for a forest stede in 1455 was raised to £9 Scots the following year and to £20 Scots in 1479. This may be partly exploitation and partly monetary depreciation. A steady depreciation of the Scottish coinage now meant that in 1455, ninety-six pennies were

The Ward of Yarrow

3 Places in Fayrmanhop	Garlacleuch and Blakhous
Douglascrag	2 Places in Mountbergeris
Catslak	Blakgrane
Quhithop	Duchar
Tynnes	Lweynnishop
Hangandschaw	2 Places of Yare
Williamehop	Hayrtherne
Eschesteile	Alyburne
Ploro	Glengabir
Half stede at Helvenel	Glenpoyte
Glensax	

The three places of Fayrmanhop are Dryhop, Kirkstead and St Mary's Kirk settlement or possibly Cappercleuch. Garlawclewch is between Craig Douglas and Blackhouse. Blackgrane is probably Whitefield or a settlement further up the Whitehope Burn. The two places of Yare are The Yair and The Peel. Hayrtherne is a deserted site near Willamhope. Aylburne is Elibank. Helvenal is likely to be Hannel, a deserted site near Glengaber.

being struck from an ounce of silver, the monetary difference then being less than half that of the English, ie two pennies Scots was equal to one penny English. By 1483 the coinage was debased further with 140 pennies being struck from an ounce of silver and a corresponding devaluation of the Scottish exchange rate. In documents, the difference is quoted by giving the value with Scots behind ie '£6 Scots.'

Forest Justice

The Forest officers were diligent in carrying out the duties of their respective posts. So much so that in 1480, James III had to issue an order under the Great Seal: 'considering the hardships endured by the burgesses and indwellers of the royal burgh of Peebles, who had frequently and recently been summoned, arrested and attached by officers of the Forest of Ettrick, and compelled to appear and answer in the Forest Courts, for the singular favour he bore towards the said burgesses, relieved them for ever from all citations and attendance at the courts of the said Forest of Ettrick. And if it should happen that the burgesses or any of them transgressed by destroying green trees or taking deer, cattle, wild beasts and game from the said forest, the king wished that the transgressors should be punished and corrected and fines levied on them by assize in the royal circuit court of justiciary at Peebles and not in any court outside the liberties of the burgh.'

To get an idea of any time and place, there is no better method than to examine the cases brought before the Courts of Justice and the findings thereof.

From the forty-nine charges placed before the Lords Drummond, Glammys and Lile at the Justiciary Court of Selkirk from 4 to 7 March 1494, I have picked two cases, by no means the worst, with the defendants from two reasonably peaceable families of Rutherfords who lived across the river from each other in the Ettrick Valley. (This is a personal choice because I spent the first ten years of my life on Oakwood and the next five on Fauldshope.)

'*Walter Rutherford in Fawlishope, to compear for the theft of 6 sheep from Robert Nichol out of Hartwood; of 22 sheep from Robert Scott of Haining; of 5 sheep from John Scott son of Robert; a cow from Robert Turnbull, a cow from James Dickson, an ox from the house of Robert Atkyn in Minto; 2 horses from Robert Scott and a chaplain; 65 geese out of Fairnington; 100 thraves of oats out of Fairnington* [a thrave was 12 sheaves]; *14 sheep from Robert Turnbull of Howdenbrae; 2 sheep from Thomas Robison of Carterhaugh and for common pikary* [pilfering] *and common theft.*'

Pledges for his appearance in court were John Rutherford of Edgarston and Laurence Rutherford. But the next hearing was:

'*Laurence Rutherford in Aikwod presents remission for art and part of theft of 3 cows from Thomas Stoddart; 3 cows from Mathew Gibson out of Innerleithen; a cow from the vicar of Ancrum; 3 sheep from John Stonys; 30 sheep from William Ker of Yair; a mare out of Ancrum Law; 4 horses and mares from Mosshouses; 28 sheep from Ninian Murray of Kershop; 7 oxen and cows from William Wod of Haythorne; burning out William White Turnbull in Hartwood; 40 sheep from Ninian Murray and his tenants; 5 cows and a red waistcoat and the whole goods and utensils from Marion Dickson, widow-wife of the late William Dickson in Baillielee.'*

Pledged to satisfy the parties – John Rutherford of Edgarston.

But two cases down was: '*John Rutherford of Edgarston called to enter Walter Rutherford, son of Walter Rutherford in Fawlishope to underlie the law and not compearing, is fined £40.'* The law was, if one man guaranteed that another would be in attendance at court and he failed to turn up to be tried, the man who stood surety had to pay the fine.

Amongst the more interesting charges in this session was bringing in thieves from Liddesdale or 'intercommuning with the English in treasonable manner' (fairly common); the theft of the iron windows, doors and crooks from Howpaslot Tower; several murders including that of women and children (thereby disproving the legend that women were never molested by reivers); and the intriguing 'theft of a haystack'. This last was an improvement on Wat o Harden's excuse that he could not take a haystack because it had no legs and was therefore unstealable.

In looking through this session of the circuit justiciary court records, several speculations and deductions come to mind.

At this period of history, I had always assumed that the Ettrick Valley was relatively peaceful because it was about 50kms from the border line, but this may be that nothing about it appeared in the popular writings. Everyone who is interested in Border history knows about the reivers, who were rough but romantic heroes if you believe the writings of Sir Walter Scott, or men who stole because they were desperate and had no other way to feed their families, or were bloodthirsty evil ruffians who deserved to be hanged, and often were.

For the Rutherfords above, the second option is the most likely. They were not a particularly noted 'reiving' family like the Elliots and Armstrongs from Liddesdale, to the Scotts and Kerrs from everywhere else, and the smaller family names whose claims to fame can be found in Pitcairn's *Criminal Trials of Scotland*. Nor could they claim a celebrity ruffian like Johnie Armstrong, Nebless Clem Crosier, several Walter Scotts, Dand Kerr, Willie 'Kang' Irvine and little Jock Elliot of the Park.

So it must have been need rather than greed which caused them to venture up to 25kms to steal the 65 geese and 1,200 sheaves of corn from Fairnington. Even if this was done 'on divers occasions', it shows their desperation and/or ingenuity.

The Fauldshope and Oakwood Rutherfords did not stand out from their neighbours, most of whom appear in the same court records. As many of the thefts were done in the immediate vicinity of their farms, it must have been very difficult to prevent the neighbour from recognising his own sheep/cattle/horse grazing in the field.

Rousing and dangerous times for a quiet place like Ettrick.

ASSART ENCLOSURE AT OLD TINNES

We know little about the archaeology of the farming communities in the lands of Selkirkshire, other than incidental information in documents. In the uncultivated uplands, grassy foundations of deserted buildings give indications of vanished settlements but these are impossible to date by outline alone. In the late medieval period, the number of people in the burgh of Selkirk could not have been more than 500 and Selkirk was the only major settlement in the shire. So about 95 per cent of the population lived, or rather survived, on the land, but we know little about them other than the information which can be teased out of justiciary and Exchequer Rolls.

But there is also a lot of information held in the ground that could be released given the time and finance to do so.

In the fifteenth century the population of Selkirkshire was growing and needed to bring more land into cultivation. The Forest lands were less being kept as a hunting reserve and used more as a commercial proposition, so it made more sense to bring some of that land into food production by means of a grant of 'assart'. This is an official permission which allows a small part of the forest to be cleared of trees with the right to 'plough and build, make hedges and enclosures' within the area round a permanent habitation. Outside that enclosed land, the Forest Laws still applied and the new tillers of the soil were not to let their animals enter the forest, especially in the close season. But they were allowed certain privileges such as autumn 'pannage' when pigs were allowed into the forest to eat the acorns which fell from oak trees, and they could have blown or dead timber for building and fuel with specific permission from the forester.

As most of the medieval landscape has been obliterated by the improvers of the eighteenth and nineteenth centuries and the heavy tractors of the present day, little evidence of the stedes of Ettrick Forest survives except as grassy foundations on marginal uplands.

The best survival I know is at Old Tinnes in the Yarrow Valley where the ground is not particularly suitable for arable agriculture. The foundations of fifteen to twenty buildings can be seen in the turf. There is a mini-village with two lines of four or five houses, each with a garden behind, and the indications of a larger building about 7m by 6m internally, with thick walls that would suggest a fortified farmhouse or pele. Small fields cluster round the village with larger strip cultivation sweeping along the glen to the north. The whole is enclosed by an impressive assart dyke. This is basically a large ditch with the spoil forming a bank on the field side. There would be a wattle fence on the top of the bank to prevent wild animals from jumping in to eat the crops.

The first mention of 'Tynnes' was in 1455 when the Forest lands returned to the Crown but the indications are that there was already an established community on the site.

The site of Old Tinnes was surveyed by the Border Burghs Archaeological Project who mapped the field system. That information is good to pass on to future generations who might be tempted to carry out an excavation there.

SELKIRKSHIRE: THE CONDITIONS OF LIFE

It is difficult to imagine the lives of the common people of Selkirkshire during the tempestuous years of the early medieval period. From the few written records which are mainly from the English viewpoint, we can tell that some fought on the Scots side at the Battle of Falkirk in 1298, some joined with Sir Robert Keith in 1299 in harrying the English marches, and some supported Bruce in 1306. On the other hand, ten Selkirk foresters were paid at Selkirk by Edward I on 25 July 1301 and thanked by the same king in 1306 for having burnt Sir Simon Fraser's lands in Selkirk Forest in 1306.

There is no indication of how the inhabitants of the Selkirk burgh and Forest felt during this time. National loyalty, if any, would be secondary to survival and Borderers on both sides were often indifferent to which nationality they took. Logic would suggest that the people of the burgh would deal with and tolerate the English when they held the castle, while those in the Forest would have greater freedom of choice but also a greater chance of being killed/burnt out by either side. Briefly, the people of the burgh were most likely to lean towards the English/Welsh garrison while the Forest dwellers would favour the Scots.

On the profit and loss account, the burgh was far from prosperous and unable to pay rent to the king on many occasions. There were some glimmers of hope though.

With a permanent garrison of English troops being paid in silver pennies, this must have benefited the burgh to some extent. As a token of the burgh's slowly increasing prosperity, the meal mill which was let separately from the town, brought in a rent of 19s:4d to Edward I in 1306 while in 1329 it paid £1:6s:8d.for Robert I. The burgh must have benefited from the growing demand for skins and wool from the Forest pastures and the trade was not confined to the immediate locality.

During the time when the south of Scotland was deemed to be the northern part of England, Borders merchants were given safe conducts through England and all was ostensibly well on the border but, despite this, Scots merchants were frequently arrested in England on the premise that they were Scots and thus likely to be rogues.

English merchants were arrested for secretly carrying wool and lambskins into Scotland where the cheaper export taxes defrauded the king of England's customs.

However, the Forest pastures were producing ever-larger quantities of wool and skins for the increasing populations on the Continent and trade was good.

Much of this trade went through the port of Berwick, as did the wool crop from the north of England. This caused a lot of legal wrangling as there was a variation between the sacks of Scottish wool which weighed 20lbs more than the English ones. Lambskins, 'fotfell' and 'shorling', were not subject to the 'coket' (official harbour stamp) by Scottish customs but were charged when going through English ports.

Disputes also arose when Continental ships loaded at Berwick and paid their harbour dues there, but were then arrested if they put in at an English port and had to pay another set of harbour dues.

Trade seemed to go on despite wars between the countries. Thomas Kene of Selkyrk complained to Edward III that, when on the highway between Dankastre and Wynbrigge with his merchandise, John of Montkyl and John Parker and their company attacked him on Tuesday next before the Nativity of our Lady, in the fields near Wynbrigge, robbed him of his horse, money, 6 gold buckles and everything but his shirt, to the value of 60 merks (£40) and because he refused to forswear his remedy at law, John of Montkyl, his wife and Rauf and Thomas his sons, imprisoned him in their house to force him to a fine. He prays remedy as the king's 'lel valet' (true servant). Although there is no date on this document, it is between 1335 and 1346. Kene was quite a common name in Selkirk but it is likely that Thomas was a merchant who had long departed the burgh rather than an in-dwelling burgess.

In 1360, John Turnbull was Sheriff of Selkirk (burgh) and acknowledging a receipt of £11:15s:10d for all the goods, corn, chattels etc pertaining to the taxes of the town. This amount he paid to the High Chamberlain of Scotland except for 5s:6d 'for his own labour'. He was confirmed as deputy of the Sheriff of Selkirk in 1364. In 1366, Selkirk was revalued to help pay for the king's ransom which remained largely unpaid at his death in 1370.

As a burgh of the royal demesne, Selkirk had to pay a rent directly to the king and there is no record of any other revenue being paid into the exchequer until 1455. This suggests that Selkirk was not a prosperous place in which to live, a fact that could be explained by the Douglases owning the Forest while the castles of Berwick and Roxburgh, with most of their shires, were in English hands. This did not make for a peaceful existence.

In the early years of the fourteenth century, the climate began to deteriorate and would continue to do so with environmental variations over the next four centuries. This became known as the 'Little Ice Age', a time of cold winters and bad summers, heavy rains and gale force winds. A pattern of heavy rain resulted in crops being unable to ripen in the arable lands of the Borders and a lack of fodder to enable animals to survive the hard winter in the pastoral areas. Consequently, this led to a reduction in the numbers of the animals grazing in the wood pastures of Ettrick Forest, making life on the marginal land at the tops of the valleys very precarious and some sites are likely to have been deserted. Hill lands that had been rig-ploughed in the warmer climate between 1000 and 1300 were now deserted or given over to sheep grazing.

The second half of the fourteenth century was an intermingled period of war, disturbance and bloodshed with occasional truces to allow a breathing space for recovery. With two kings granting the same lands and two nations competing for supremacy, there were few winners and many losers. The conditions of life must have been horrendous with the constant dread of having homes burnt, cattle and sheep stolen, and crops destroyed. Almost as bad was the prospect of being summoned to do the same to an equally poor English Borderer with the prospect of being killed while doing so. Men had the possibility of retaliation to redress their injuries; women and children didn't and flight was their only hope. Plumes of smoke advancing up the valley were notices to gather up anything portable and make for the hills, driving your cattle and sheep if you had any, into the most remote glen you could find.

Added to the starvation and deprivation which was widespread in the Borders during the fourteenth century, was the advent of the pestilence known as the Black Death. This had struck the south of England in the summer of 1348 and within a year had swept its way through the country and into southern Scotland. Here it was known as 'the foul death of England' or 'the English Pestilence' and although English figures show that between a third and a half of the population perished, in the Borders it may not have been so severe. No death-rate figures are known but the population was more widely spread and thus less prone to pick up infection. But as labour became scarcer, the Exchequer Rolls show a decline in wool production and rents fell. For those left, there was allegedly 'an abundance of provisions in the kingdom'.

There were further outbreaks of plague in 1361 and 2, 1379, 1392, 1401 to 3, 1430, 1439 and 1499. The Four Horsemen of War, Famine, Pestilence and Death were devastating the country. It is questionable if the population of the Borders rose over that century; in fact it is surprising that there were any Borderers left.

The Kelso Abbey Lands in Selkirkshire

When David I founded Selkirk Abbey, the lands around it were marked by natural features 'from where a burn descending from the hills falls into Yarrow' etc. These descriptions are vague but discernible.

Around 1300, an entry in the Kelso Abbey Cartulary gives a graphic description of the duties and rents of the people of Selkirk-Abbatis, the Abbot's Selkirk. Although not quite a census of the population, it gives an indication of how many lived, worked and paid rent on the Abbey land. There would certainly be others who did not come within the rent or tax brackets of the Abbey and are thus remain unrecorded.

Selkirk-Abbatis

'They have the said town of Abbots-Selkirk. One ploughgate and a half which used to yield 10 merks yearly. Fifteen husbandlands, each containing an oxgang (13 acres) rented at 4 shillings. All the husbandmen have to give the Abbot ten days work in autumn; two to furnish a cart for carrying peats from the moss to the Abbey. They have to give the same service as the Bowden husbandmen – to plough every year an acre and a half in the grange at Newtown; to harrow one day with a horse; to find a man to assist in washing and another in shearing the sheep; to carry corn with a cart one day in autumn; to carry the Abbot's wool from the barony to the Abbey and to find their own carriage beyond the muir towards Lesmahago. Besides the husband-lands, there are 16 cottages in Selkirk-Abbatis with ten acres of land between them; 15 rented at 12 pence and one at 2 shillings with nine days harvest work and assistance with the sheep-shearing. Three breweries each pay 6s:8d per annum; and one corn-mill at five merks.

Beyond the lordships they have 30 acres yielding 5s besides four acres called 'Richard Cute's land' yielding 6s yearly.'

This is the tally of a large agricultural estate spread over the lands of Lindean, Faldonside, Whitlaw, Greenhead and Bridgelands. Mentions of ploughing and harrowing show that cereals were grown, with corn ground for eating and making the nutritious (but weak) beer; sheep were kept for wool; peat was cast and dried before being taken to the Abbey. The mention of carts is an indication that there were roads able to take wheeled traffic.

A few terms must be explained.

A 'ploughgate' was 104 Scots acres of land 'where plough and scythe may gang' – that is arable land fit to plough, sow and harvest. The ploughgate was originally the amount of land that a plough team could deal with in one year and a Scots acre was about 25 per cent larger than the standard English acre.

A 'husbandman' was a crofter who farmed 26 Scots acres of land or the quarter of a ploughgate. This included an oxgang of 13 acres which was the grazing land for oxen and cattle. He usually kept two oxen as his contribution to the motive power of the plough-team. With fifteen husbandlands in the area, this meant that sixty men were working the land there.

For a new husbandman, Kelso Abbey provided two plough oxen, a horse, three chalders of oats, six bolls of barley and three bolls of wheat to get him started on his farming career. This is the arable version of the steilbow bargain.

The 'cottagers or cottars' had little land to cultivate but this does not necessarily mean poverty. A cottar shoemaker at Drummelzier paid sixpence a year for a house, brewhouse, garden and two acres of land, one of ploughland and one of grassland. Additionally he had the right to pasture a number of plough-oxen, cows with calves and sheep with lambs on the common grazing. It is rare to find an example of the rights of the medieval common man. Cottars tended to be labourers or craftsmen who had a garden for growing food rather than crofters depending on the land for their sustenance.

The third layer of working population was the 'nativi', serfs or carles who were indentured servants. They were not recognised as slaves but men who, through hunger or fear, had placed themselves and their families under the care of the Church or a great lord, and as such could be transferred in ownership with the land they worked.

In one record of 1290, Waldev, Earl of Dunbar gives a whole family to the Abbot of Kelso: 'I give and confirm to the Abbot and the monks of Kelso, Halden and his brother William and all their children and all their descendants'.

In parts of the country, the nativi, serfs or carles were not free to leave the estate of their birth but equally could not be evicted from it unless they wished to be. This may be the explanation why Halden could be transferred with the property.

The nativi did not figure in many records of possession of Kelso Abbey simply because they did not pay any rent into the Abbey coffers.

To return to the document itself.

For me this is tremendously interesting as I spent six years of my youth living near the site of Selkirk Abbatis and a further fifty intermittently fieldwalking the various sites there.

First point to note is that, unlike the Forest produce of wood, hides and wool, this is an arable area that was ploughable in places if not particularly fertile, but it also contained enough pastureland to make for a mixed agricultural economy.

The reason that I know where ploughing took place are the finds of white quartz pebbles with one or more striated faces which can be picked up during fieldwalking. The ploughs of the period were made of oak with only an iron share-tip to break the soil. To prevent wear through soil-drag, white quartz pebbles were studded into the wooden mould board. Through time and use, the pebbles became striated on one side but were eventually torn from the wood, leaving proof that this land had been cultivated in medieval times even though later ploughing had wiped out most surface trace of the fields themselves. Medieval field systems can be seen in several parts of the Borders: Midlem, Bowden and Lilliesleaf have once had strip field systems for about a kilometre around them but modern agricultural methods have demolished the hedge rows which defined the fields because tractor ploughs work best in large square or rectangular fields.

The cumbersome oak plough of medieval times required three or four pairs of draught oxen to pull it through heavy soil; so oxen and plough combined to measure over 12m in length. This made turning difficult at the beginning and end of each furrow. Consequently the fields are long and narrow with a sweeping curve at both ends and this elongated 'S' shaped is seen in places where conditions are suitable.

Although the ox-plough could produce a deeper cut, it did not turn the sod over. This was done by a following band of women and children who turned the grassy side down and pulverised any clods to prepare a tilth ready for sowing.

Some places in the Selkirk Abbatis document are easily identified. The corn-mill is obviously the Lindean Mill whose old mill-lade can be seen as a broad ditch along the bank beside the river. Situated on the riverbank with no great fall of water, the mill would have had an undershot wheel that was turned with the action of water flowing under it. This was the earliest, simplest and cheapest type of mill to construct and needed only a small head of water to work efficiently. About 200m upstream from the mill site an elongated island effectively splits the river and at the bottom of the island the remains of a rough barrier of stones could once be seen.

The Abbey mill at Lindean is likely to have been built in the middle to end of the twelfth century and there was still a working mill on the same site until the mid twentieth century. The mill was an important part of agricultural life in medieval times as its produce was the chief source of food for most people; and this was true in Scotland until early Victorian times.

The Abbey tenants, the husbandmen and cottars who grew cereal crops were thirled to the mill, meaning that all grain produced had to be ground at the Abbot's mill, giving the abbey further income. In the Selkirk Abbatis document, while the husbandmen paid 4s plus some services for their land, the miller paid 5 merks (£3:6s:8d) for his mill. Obviously this was a thriving commercial business with a number of tied customers.

The area round the ruined church is known as 'the Batts' which is a contracted version of Abbatis. The fields around the church have produced early medieval pottery, some white quartz plough-pebbles and a black jet bead tentatively identified as a rosary bead. Divining rods suggest a cluster of buildings, each about 10m by 4m internally, and a road which passes the graveyard site on the south, rising to run along the bank. This road carries on past Bankend houses and Lindean Hall. Along this line several other house foundations were traced and fieldwalking produced pottery and coins of Edward I or II. This was the medieval road between Selkirk and Melrose.

A branch from the road over Minchmoor comes past Ovenclose on the line which demarks the boundary of Selkirk North Common (and is still ridden as the boundary at Selkirk Common Riding). It crosses the Ettrick where the Selkirk Bridge (1234) stood, then passes on the west of the Abbey site and up the Green Path on the way to Jedburgh. This places Selkirk Abbey site at a crossroads but whether the

Abbey preceded the crossroads or vice versa is a matter of conjecture.

As well as the central village round the former Abbey site, the monastery had three out-lying granges at Faldonside, Whitlaw and Whitmuir. These were farm villages away from the immediate vicinity of the Abbey and supervised by a lay brother who lived in the main house of the estate. All the cattle, sheep and implements required for working the land were kept there, together with a work-force of nativi housed in the vicinity. These are the closest in structure to the farms of yesteryear where numbers of workers lived on and cultivated a certain piece of land.

There is documentary evidence that sheep were kept on the high ground at the grange of Whitlaw and on summer pastureland at Minchmoor; there was a brewhouse at Whitlaw as well. Field-walking evidence of plough-pebbles show that some of the south-facing fields were tilled.

In the fields to the south-west of the present Whitmuir Farm, there are a number of quite deep wells and enough visible foundations to suggest a reasonably substantial village. In the Abbey records, the 'villa de Witemer' has ten husbandlands each of whom paid a rent of 6s. This meant that about forty husbandmen worked the land there. Additionally, seven cottars paid rents varying from 5s to 1s:4d. Another cottar who had no land paid 6d, presumably for his house. The agricultural duties on the Abbot's lands were similar to those of Bowden.

In 1494, two Elliots and five Armstrongs raided Whitmuir driving away a hundred cattle and oxen as well as taking the household goods of the tenants. This is the plunder from quite a large establishment.

To the east of this, the 'grange of Wittemere' (now Whitmuirhall) had two husbandlands valued at 10 merks yearly.

At the grange of Faldonside no husbandmen are mentioned but twenty-one cottars pay a rent of £6 Scots. The remainder of the population of the grange would be nativi who paid no rent. The whole produce of this grange probably went straight to Kelso Abbey.

In the document of Selkirk-Abbatis the phrase that 'they had to give the same service as the Bowden husbandmen' could be open to interpretation. Bowden was smaller in agricultural size but with better ground. Twenty-two husbandlands and six cottars had much the same services to perform for the Abbot but their village had to contribute thirty archers to the common army when called upon. This was organised by a man-at-arms who was paid with the rent of specific ploughgate of land. This military responsibility does not seem to have been placed on the husbandmen of Selkirk-Abbatis unless it is covered by the phrase 'the same service as the Bowden husbandmen'.

Looking forward to the 1567 Rental of the Abbey of Kelso, this record confirms their property of Lindean with its church, Whitmuir and Whitmuir Hall, Faldonside, Whitlaw, Cauldshiels, Ovensclose and Greenhead within the original grant; of these Faldonside, Whitmuir and Whitelaw were granges.

Farming the Abbey Lands

What we know about farming the lands comes from the cartulary records of the Border abbeys but even then the knowledge is deduced rather than described and this changed as the ground fertility varied. The cartulary records tend to note rental receipts and conventual changes, rather than rural agricultural life. The Kelso Abbey book covers an area from the rich Berwickshire lands to the marginal sheep-breeding hills of the Bowmont Valley. Added to the written records are the excavations which have taken place at Springwood Park, Kelso and Eyemouth.

Medieval farming in the Abbey lands of Selkirkshire was a mixture of cultivation and stock-rearing as it is at the present day, because this mixed economy suits the soil, location, climate and temperature. Cultivation could produce the main staples of oats, rye, barley and bread-wheat while sheep and cattle gave wool, milk, cheese and manure when alive and meat and skins when killed.

Pigs were allowed to dig for acorns and roots in the woods of the forest, provided 'pannage' was paid but in general terms, pigs were not farmed animals kept in a sty, as they required food which humans could eat and there was seldom much of that to spare. The name Swinewood appears in the Coldinghamshire charter of Edgar, and 'Muckra' in the Yarrow Valley is the place of the pigs in Gaelic-speaking times. Hens were kept for eggs and eating. A castrated cockerel, called a capon, was a useful means of paying a minor rent. The Capon Tree near Jedburgh is where the tenants of Jedburgh Abbey gathered to pay their rents and the Caponlands near Midlem were held on the yearly payment of one of these unfortunate birds. (It is now erroneously called Capelands.)

Oats were milled at the Abbot's mill (at a price) to make oatmeal and barley was malted, ie steeped in water and allowed to sprout, then dried in a kiln to make malt which is an essential ingredient in brewing ale. Medieval ale was as much food as drink and was the drink of choice, especially in towns where the well-water was often disastrously contaminated.

The importance of the corn-mill in a rural or urban society cannot be under-estimated as the mill was the supplier of practically every mouthful of food eaten in the community. Cereals provided the bulk of the Scottish diet with added variations depending on circumstance and season, so a working corn mill was a necessity of life.

We have a better idea of what could be produced on the farm by looking at the inventory of the Priory of Coldingham in 1374. This list is mainly the contents of the chapel, storerooms, cellars and kitchens etc but it also gives the farm equipment and produce together with the animals kept on the home farm. As it was a rich Priory, the home farm would have better tools and livestock than an outlying grange, but would be required to keep a greater supply of food readily available for its people and visitors.

In the Coldingham Priory Farm byre and pastures there were: 7 bulls, 42 cows, 17 three-year-old bullocks, 9 two-year-old bullocks and 13 calves. In the fields were 2,214 sheep and there was a stable containing one riding horse for the Prior's use and a packhorse.

In the farm buildings there were: 3 draught horses, 34 oxen for ploughs and wagons, 3 wagons with all the necessary equipment of which 2 are shod with iron (presumably iron-rimmed wheels), a pair of new wheels for the wagons, 2 ploughs with equipment, a pair of plough irons, 6 harrows, 2 sledges, forks, flails, rakes and a pair of weeding tongs and 'other tools necessary for husbandry'. Also included in this list is a heifer, 5 sows and a boar, 7 boxes of tar for sheep and 52 acres of alfalfa sown with the wheat.

In the Priory larder there were stored: 25 salted beef and 8 salted cow carcasses, 24 salted salmon, 2 boxes of dried white herring, 16 vats of soused herring, 42 dried cod/ling and 12 magre (boxes?), each 500, of 'red herring' (kippers?).

In the granary where the flour and meal was kept, there were 4 quarters of wheat of home growth, 2 chalders and 1 boll of barley, 10 chalders of oats apart from sheaves of fodder given to the horses of guests and also to the Prior's horses, and the plough-oxen employed in cultivation, 2 beef cattle being fattened for the kitchen and 2 boxes of wheat-flour were kept in store.

In the pantry there was 20st of cheese (280lbs) and in the cellar a pipe of wine and a half pipe of Gascony wine.

This was not subsistence farming but an agricultural estate run as a shrewd commercial proposition to have Priory lands worked 'for the Glory of God' with minimum cost to the Prior. In food terms, the monks of Coldingham had the potential to enjoy a standard of living equal to that of the higher levels of medieval society, but it is unlikely that they did, and even more unlikely that the workers on the land would have anything as good as the monks.

Before commenting on the amounts and types of food stored at Coldingham, it is worth looking at the types of measurement involved.

A quarter or firlot was a fourth of a bushel which is a dry measure of 8 gallons and used for grain. In Scotland, 6 bushels make a boll which had a weight of 140lbs (63.5kg). In England this varied from 2 to 6 bushels to make a boll.

A chalder is 16 bolls − 2,240lbs (1,016kg). This is also the standard Imperial ton which is 20 hundred weights of 112lbs each.

From the inventory it is plain that oats and barley were the main crops. Oats could be ground into oatmeal for making porridge or fired to make bannocks and oatcakes, and could be bruised as fodder for the Prior's riding horse and draught animals which needed more strength than grass or hay could provide.

Barley was used mainly for malting and the brewing of beer which, in a later quote 'is sometimes strong enough to arm 'em against the coldness of the climate'. This brew would likely be from bere, an indigenous form of barley which produced better crops on poorer ground and also provided the food of the poor. Bere, peas and beans were milled together to give a diet of 'bere porridge morning and night and whole barley with whatever kale plants and other greens boiled together for the mid-day meal'. From other sources it is known that almost anything edible could be added to the mid-day soup-pot. On the rare occasions when meat was available, it was added to the pot to be cooked, then taken out to be eaten separately. The mid-day soup-pot was largely dependent on colewart from the kitchen garden which gave the broth its usual name of 'kail', in my youth a generic term for soup.

Nettles make an equally nutritious vegetable soup and have the benefit of being easier to acquire. Nettles tend to grow most abundantly where human or animal refuse has been dumped and also in graveyards – a thought which I will pursue no further except to say the nettle plant has a high phosphate content.

Bread wheat at Coldingham was grown in small amounts presumably for the Prior and his special visitors. Wheat grains have greater nutritive value than most other cereals, containing some starch and a quantity of protein. The pipes of wine would likely be for the same people.

The 52 acres of alfalfa (lucerne) meant that corn and alfalfa seeds were sown together, drawing each other up as they grew. When the corn was cut, the alfalfa left valuable forage for the winter grazing of cattle and a good base for the next year's grass.

From other records it is known that peas and beans were grown for food and to improve the nitrogen content of the soil. Both peas and beans were staple foods of the poor and, as such, do not appear in the Inventory.

Hemp was cultivated in fourteenth century Coldinghamshire for making nets, sacks, ropes and canvas while flax was grown to make linen for the priests' robes, altar clothes and shrouds.

In all, the Priory of Coldingham was a largely self-sufficient unit providing most of its needs from within its land boundaries. As the barter of the previous ages had long been replaced by a currency economy, any surplus products could be shipped to the thriving port of Berwick and turned into the silver coinage of England and Scotland for saving against hard times or used to purchase goods which could not be produced on Priory lands.

Selkirkshire: the Rural Economy

The relatively good life of Coldingham cannot be safely transposed into the Abbey lands of Selkirkshire. The soils and climates are different with Selkirkshire having poorer soil and a colder climate; and whereas

Coldingham had easy access to markets and trading options for agricultural surplus, the Abbey lands of Selkirkshire could only sell in Selkirk or take its produce down to the markets of Kelso or Roxburgh. Additionally, the Abbey granges were scattered over a wider area with only the roughest of roadways between. In consequence, the people of Selkirkshire with fewer economic opportunities, were likely to have been poorer.

The idea of a rich aristocracy enjoying the life of plenty with deer, cattle and sheep from the forest, salmon from the rivers and imported luxuries contrasting with the permanent near-starvation of the peasants, is a matter of whose interpretation you believe. I would suspect that truth lies somewhere between the two.

Certainly the later fourteenth century had periods of relative peace with economic growth, expanding towns and greater money supply. We do not have sufficient evidence to make categorical conclusions on how this affected the Borders. Berwick was a prosperous international port while Roxburgh drew in Flemish merchants and Italian bankers. How much of this prosperity filtered down to the people of Selkirk, the peasant labourer on the lands of Selkirk Abbatis and the stock-raiser/woodman in the stedes of Selkirk Forest can only be guessed at.

The war to retain Scottish independence and the Black Death together had contrived to lower the population, making more land available for leasing and at lower rents. The growing economy is demonstrated by the number and size of the coin hoards found in the Borders. These have been identified as army pay chests or merchants hoards but this is not necessarily correct. The 6,000 silver pennies and silver brooches found at the hill farm of Langhope near Ashkirk could equally be the savings of a successful sheep farmer, while the number of single silver coins of the Edwards I, II and III which are being found by metal detectorists through the countryside, suggest that money was the medium of exchange amongst the peasantry

Looking at the economy of Selkirkshire, it is the countryside where the wealth was created. As already quoted, in 1368 the shire paid taxes of £14:14s and a halfpenny into the royal exchequer of which 4s:8d came from the town. Selkirk was not a wealthy town. So the lands around Selkirk, the Abbey lands of Selkirk-Abbatis and the Forest must have provided the bulk of the taxes.

In the fourteenth century, wealth was provided by the rural economy. It has been reckoned that at the height of the export trade to England and the Continent, the clip of 2,000,000 sheep and the hides of 50,000 cattle were shipped each year through the Scottish ports; how much of this came from Selkirkshire is not known but there must have been some. Flocks of sheep had been established by James I when Ettrick Forest was in the hands of the Douglas family and sheep were still there when the land reverted to the Crown in 1455. Where the king led, others were sure to follow especially when there was money to be made.

The Borders were well suited for the production of wool, the great money-maker of the thirteenth and fourteenth centuries. Kelso Abbey is recorded as having extensive areas in the Cheviots and Lammermuirs with grazing for 7,000 sheep. Melrose Abbey had between 12,000 and 15,000 sheep, many of them running in the Tima Valley at the top of Ettrick. Being part of a great international agency, the Abbeys were also international traders. As well as their own wool, they bought from lesser producers for sorting, packing and shipping to their outlets on the Continent and Italy.

The development of the wool exports to Flanders and the Low Countries transformed the suffering Scottish economy and boosted urban development on the east coast ports. Berwick was the largest wool-exporting port in Scotland with English, Italian and Flemish merchants having permanent bases there.

By the late fifteenth century, the profligate spending of James IV on his buildings and ships meant that the royal exchequer was empty. This resulted in economic pressure on the Crown lands to produce more revenue, and in Ettrick Forest this could only be done by releasing more of the hunting reserve land for agriculture. Previously, certain tenants were allowed to graze sheep within the Forest but by 1473 sheep were officially allowed to graze nine of the stedes, five in Tweed, two in Ettrick and two in Yarrow. Another three were added by 1479 together with the right to erect 'sheilings' for the shepherds. The land originally set aside for hunting was now having to co-exist with grazing and ploughing.

This led to the degradation of the Forest as a timber producer with the reservoir of naturally grown timber diminishing as the sheep nibbled the young tree shoots and prevented natural regeneration. Consequently, timber for building and fuel was scarce. This shows up in the circuit justiciary courts held in Selkirk in March 1494, November 1502 and December 1510.

The 1494 Court tended to deal with thefts of stock, killing of stags, a few murders and general rebellion. The 1510 Court has a number of the same cases but the greater part of the proceedings are long lists of men, including forest officers, who were convicted of 'the destruction of the woods of Ettrick Forest'.

This destruction had been noted with concern for some time. As early as 1424 an Act of Parliament was passed to punish 'the stealers of green-wood and destroyers of trees' and a later law called upon all freeholders to get their tenants to 'plant wood and trees, make hedges and to sow broom★' according to the size of their holding.

By 1503, the woods of Scotland were deemed to be utterly decayed and the penalty for burning greenwood was fixed at £5 per offence. Every landowner was ordered to make 'parks for deer, dowcats (dovecotes), orchards etc and plant at least one acre of wood where there is no great forest'.

The diminishing returns of timber meant that there was less bark available for the tanners and leatherworkers. Bark was a very lucrative by-product of the forest because it was light, easily transportable and very necessary for tanning hides into leather. The sale of a suitable tree always included the 'hale bark and bough' both of which could be sold separately. With less of the preferred oak bark available, the cordiners (leatherworkers) of Selkirk were being forced to use willow and alder bark or to get oak bark from further afield.

After a century of intensive grazing, the forest became 'decayed' and a policy of active tree management was pursued outwith the forest lands. This was done where the monasteries had secure tenancy of their land. On Bowden Moor there are a number of 'woodbanks' which are thought to have been constructed around 1500 by Melrose Abbey. These take the form of a broad mound 8–10m across with a ditch on

---

★ Broom was very useful as thatch or fuel and was a quick and persistent grower.

either side. Hedges were planted on the edges of the mound and the middle filled with trees. With a 60cm ditch and a 60cm turf wall behind it, this made a field barrier of 1.2m, quite ample to deter all but the most active animal jumpers. So this one construction made fields for animals, a shelter to protect them from the worst of the climate, and internal trees to be coppiced every ten to fifteen years.

Between 1486 and 1490, there was a very high turnover of tenants of the Forest with 56 stedes changing hands. This has to be connected with the change of government when James III was killed at Sauchieburn in 1488 and James IV became king. It seems that the tenants of the Royal Forest sided with the reigning monarch but this turned out to be the losing side. The baillie of the Forest, John Cranston of that Ilk, was replaced by Lord Home in 1488; James Murray of Touchadam had been currour of Yarrow but lost his office in the same year. Nor is it a coincidence that almost all the stedes in the Yarrow Ward changed hands between 1486 and 1490.

Although this made for a change of occupants, it did not necessarily mean a change of family tenancy. In 1486 the Forest stedes held were, by family: Kerrs – 10, Scotts – 9, Murrays – 9, Pringles – 6. In 1510, the tally was Kerrs – 8, Scotts – 7, Crichtons – 5, Pringles – 5 and Homes – 3.

In team terms it meant that the Kerrs, Scotts and Pringles hung on with a slightly reduced majority; the Murrays dropped a league while the Crichtons and Homes had joined the first division. The final arbiter was James IV who wanted his own supporters in positions of power.

As part of the lease, each stede had to supply two bowmen and a spearman with horse and gear for the king in time of war. This levy made for a potent force of Borderers and may have been the reason why James III had so many men of the Forest on his side at Sauchieburn.

In 1501, a review of the Ettrick Forest stedes raised the rents from £6 Scots to between £20 and £30 Scots but now no rent was paid in kind and the new leases were to be of nine years duration. This was reduced to three or five years in 1506.

The revenue raised from rents alone rose from £700 to £2,670 Scots which would be an immediate help for the exchequer but the total varied through time and circumstance.

The Burgh of Selkirk 1286–1500

In the early medieval period, certain existing settlements were selected and given the status of 'burghs' with trading monopolies over the areas around them. David I established the townships of Berwick and Roxburgh as 'burghs' before he became king. In creating burghs with favoured trading concessions, the king was able to divert some of the profits to the crown by means of rents, taxes and, where applicable, harbour dues.

The principle of burgh foundation was to form a settlement whose inhabitants could buy and sell in markets and fairs within the burgh, creating wealth for the burgesses and taxes for the king. The outsider who wished to trade in the burgh market on an occasional basis had to pay for the privilege with a toll collected by the baillies for onward transmission to the royal Exchequer.

Burgh creation was originally a royal prerogative and of the thirty-one royal burghs founded before 1286, only seven were not associated with royal castles. It is reckoned that one of the seven was Selkirk. This interpretation could be wrong as Selkirk Castle played a noted part in the wars to retain Scottish independence and, as an important pivotal point of the edge of Ettrick Forest, was likely to have remained as a Crown possession.

When was Selkirk established as a royal burgh? The truthful answer is that we don't know for certain but it is most likely to have been in the twelfth century when Peebles and Jedburgh also became royal burghs. This was the period when a great deal of land was lying unused and probably uninhabited. (See Selkirk Common p.393)

In the Selkirk burgh market, trading standards were strict. The baillies, as the king's representatives, supervised the quality of goods sold, especially the staple commodities of bread, meat and ale, and set the prices at which each could be sold. Fleshers could not hold back meat hoping for a better price; bakers were not allowed to buy more flour than they needed in case this caused a shortage; and each brew of ale sold in the market place, had to be tasted and priced by an appointed ale-conner. Goods could not be sold before the market opened or on the way to the market (forestalling) and no goods could be bought for further resale (regrating).

The rules for becoming a burgess were equally strict with certain conditions applied. It was possible to purchase your way into being a burgess but this cost a great deal of money. The best way was to be born into a family who were already burgesses but even then a small sum had to be paid for the privilege.

By tradition, each burgess had to have a piece of ground, known as a 'rood' or 'land', within the burgh boundaries, and burgess privileges depended on occupying, not just owning a burgess rood. The rood was a quarter of an acre and within this was a house fronting on to one of the streets, with a back yard, known in Selkirk as a 'land'.

It is likely that the triangular plan of today's High Street, Kirk Wynd and Back Row, was partly in position in the reign of David I and would not have altered much during the thirteenth and fourteenth centuries. The streets may have extended a little and the market place moved to its present position but otherwise the beginning of the fifteenth century would be a continuation of the previous two. Similarly, the housing would have changed little in structure from that of the previous centuries, except that large timbers were getting scarcer and more dependency would be placed on stone or clay and wattle walls.

Behind the house was a back yard (land/rood) with a shed/byre for cow and pigs or an orchard and garden. As well as this ground, most burgesses had several rigs or strip fields in the burgh lands surrounding the town; these were cultivated to supply food for the burgess and his family. Not simply a town dweller, the average burgess must be looked on as a craftsman/crofter who lived within a trading community.

It must be noted that not every inhabitant of the burgh was a burgess; many would be labourers working in the fields or for a merchant or craftsman burgess.

There had to be some form of enclosure bounding the burgh settlement. Each burgess had the obligation to maintain the part of an outer boundary wall at the end of his 'land'. This seems to have been a 'back dyke', a turf wall made by each burgess to join up with his neighbour's back dyke and form a continuous barrier round the burgh. Though higher than a normal field dyke, it was a barrier to individual thieves rather than a defensive structure to repel reiver bands or English armies, although it could serve as such if the occasion arose. The main purpose of the wall was to prevent landward inhabitants coming into the burgh to sell their goods without paying market tolls to the king via the burgh taxes. There were gates within this dyke on the east, west and south.

As well as personally held land, the community of Selkirk had the use of a common grazing. There is no documentary proof that the huge royal common was ever given exclusively to the people of Selkirk. With the grant of Ettrick Forest to the Douglases on the west and the remainder of Selkirkshire on the east being used by Kelso Abbey, the common lands on the north and south were used by the inhabitants of Selkirk and the neighbouring communities as summer grazing, with timber available for building, fencing and fuel. This land, nominally belonging to the king, seems to have slipped between the medieval documentary cracks as there is no mention of it being granted to anyone. As the burgesses of Selkirk were by far the greatest users of the unclaimed land, the right of possession seems to have overtaken the rights of legality and the area became known as Selkirk Common somewhere in the fourteenth or fifteenth centuries. In fact there were two areas of land claimed by the burgh, the North Common and the South Common, which had to be guarded. This very valuable asset was frequently fought for over the centuries and the long-established Common Riding is a continuation of the days when the burgesses had to ride out to prevent neighbouring lairds from adding to their estates at the expense of the people of Selkirk.

In the circuit court of 1510 there are entries of: 'Cuthbert Brown in Sunderland convicted of oppression made on the community of the burgh of Selkirk in building a house on the common lands of Selkirk' and on the same day several men in Hartwoodburn were convicted of oppression made on the community of Selkirk in pasturing their goods on the common lands of Selkirk.

Almost nothing is known about fourteenth century burgh of Selkirk other than from the English records of building and rebuilding of Selkirk Castle; the burgh gets no mention although it must have been there. The grant of Selkirk Forest to the Douglas family meant that it ceased to be a royal holding although the king retained the burgh of Selkirk as a royal desmesne.

When the Douglases built the castle at Edibertshiels (Auld Wark) the centre of power moved from Selkirk and this would have taken some of the suppliers away from the burgh. Selkirk Castle had been demolished and its timbers removed, leaving nothing to mark its passing except the name the Peelgait (now Castle Street – same thing) and a small piece of land known as 'le pele'.

Despite the loss of importance, subsequent kings of Scots retained Selkirk as a king's or royal burgh even if the interest was mostly military and monetary. David II's charter of 1365 gave the lands of Selkirk to Robert de Dalyell 'except our yearly returns from our burgh'. This was a somewhat forlorn hope as the burgh was desperately poor. In 1368 it was only able to pay 4s:8d as its proportion of a £20,000 indemnity to England.

In the same year, the Chamberlain received £2:14s:4d from the burgh. If this represented the ground rent of the burgh roods which were charged at 5d each, there could have been 130 burgesses in Selkirk, but that is provided that each had only one rood. This is a high figure which would put the population around seven hundred, so it is possible that the sum included other rents, say that of the mill.

There was also the military aspect as to why the king kept a hold on Selkirk. As inhabitants of a royal burgh, the men of Selkirk owed allegiance directly to the king and were required to turn out for forty days' military service in the king's army when called upon. They were 'king's men' who provided a balance against an increasingly powerful nobility.

Nothing worthy of recording seems to have happened in the burgh during early years of the fifteenth century but a raid across the Border by Scots in 1418 was answered by a retaliatory raid by Sir Robert Umfraville, the English Governor of Berwick, who took and burnt the burgh of Selkirk amongst many stedes in the Forest.

In 1424, Selkirk had not been paying their taxes to the king, probably because their houses had been burned and their land wasted during the incursion six years previously. To regularise the situation, the Deputy Chamberlain came down to measure out the land and set the taxes. He decided that the burgh roods 'extended to five times twenty and ten, of which each owed five pence annually to the King' and that he would expect that at the next reckoning.

In the unlikely event that this represented a 110 burgesses and using a factor of three, this would make 330 inhabitants of the burgh; but there must have been people within the burgh who were not burgesses so perhaps the population was around the seven hundred already postu- lated.

Selkirk burgh taxes were a very small but important donation to the king's exchequer. In 1429–30, Baillie George Spardur paid rents of £2:6s:8d with petty customs of 13s:4d. This included rents from the lands of Gelchdene from Martinmas to Whitsunday 2s:6d; Crakwaly 2d; of Pell 6d; of Saussarlande 1d; of Commonwommanlande 1d. No rents were paid for these lands after Pentecost because they had been laid waste during the wars with England.

To demonstrate the difference between burgh and Forest revenues, I have to go to 1477 to compare the £5 from the burgh rents with £1,328:3s:2d collected from the lands of Ettrick Forest. A further comparison with local burghs shows that while Berwick contributed £760, Selkirk only produced £5 and Jedburgh £3.

In 1450, James II, in his feud with the Douglas family, visited Selkirk with a large number of followers at his back. Using Selkirk as a base, he moved through the Douglas lands in Ettrick Forest burning and destroying the corn and orchards. The tower of Craig Douglas was demolished in this year or it may have been 1452, when James returned to quell any uprising after he had murdered the Earl of Douglas with his own hand.

Scotland and England had been at war over the port of Berwick from 1481 to 1484 when it fell to England for the final time. From 1485 to 1488, the Scots and particularly the Borderers, continued to threaten that occupation. With the port of Berwick closed, foreign trade ceased and the effect was that Selkirk was not able to pay any rents to the king's exchequer for some time.

When James IV came to the throne on the death of his father at Sauchieburn in 1488, he followed the time-honoured path of a new incumbent by placing his supporters in the lands of his opponents. As has been noted above, many of the stedes of Ettrick Forest changed hands. In the non-forest lands of Selkirkshire, George Douglas, the son and heir of the Earl of Angus received the lands but not the burgh of Selkirk.

Selkirk received a visit from James IV three months after he had been crowned. The young king was a keen huntsman and could combine the pleasure of the hunt with the administration of the kingdom while he was in Selkirk. On 19 November 1488, the king got twenty half-rose nobles★ in 'Selkrik' and in February 1489 paid five rose nobles★ to 'Gentil Johne the Inglis Fule' while the justice eyre was at Jedburgh. The 15th and 16th of February were spent in Selkirk where the cost was £12. Everything must have been in order as he gave twenty angels★ 'to John Murray of the Forest to buy himself a horse at the king's command'.

In April 1489, 22s was paid to Peter Ker for going with letters for the tax to Selkirk and other places and £36:16s:8d was allowed for the expenses of Lord Drummond's 'children, boys and horses' while on circuit eyres. The king was having a passionate affaire with Lord Drummond's daughter, Margaret, at that time.

In June 1490, the treasurer left fifteen angels★ for the king as he 'raide furth to the Forest Cowrt'. Specifically these were to play cards with the Earl of Bothwell, to offer at first mass, to buy three loaves for alms and to play with the laird of Halket.

There was a justice eyre held in Selkirk in 1491 whose only trace is a payment from the royal exchequer to Lord Drummond for cost made by 'a part of his children, boys and horses' attending the event.

In June 1497, messengers came to Selkirk to warn the men that they had to be prepared to 'rise to the raid'. In August, another letter came warning against the 'incummyng of the Inglismen' but was followed ten days later about the 'scaling of the Inglismen'. This would be when an English army laid siege to Ayton Castle. However, Selkirk had contributed its share of men to the Scots army there. In the Exchequer Rolls, Baillie William Cranston of Selkirk was charged with non-attendance to pay the burgh dues but his excuse was that he was in service of the king at Ayton.

Killings were fairly common in Selkirk during this period. In 1500, Ninian Murray and George Vins killed John Porteus. In the same year, three local assailants killed John Furde on the main street of the town. It was a violent time.

Individual murders were followed by family feuds.

★'Rose nobles and half rose nobles' are gold coins with a rose on the reverse while 'angels' have an angel on the reverse.

I can understand the need for a regular circuit court to come to Selkirk and even James IV coming with his lady friend. What I have never been able to find out is 'Where did they stay?' By using the jigsaw puzzle method of fitting all the evidence of houses and lands together, I was able to make a map of who lived where in Selkirk in the period 1520 to 1545 and there was no large building within the burgh which would have been capable of housing the king and his inamorata, let alone her father and his circuit court twenty years previously.

Ruling out the castle or pele which was long demolished and the land rented at 6d in 1430, I can only surmise that the king's court and the members of the circuit court lodged at the New Wark where the Forest court was held. Nor is it beyond belief that the justice court was held there and the 'Selkirk' of documents referred to the Forest rather than the burgh.

At the circuit court held in Jedburgh in 1502, Adam Turnbull in Hornshole was charged with the treasonable inbringing of Sir John Musgrave, Englishman, who 'wrought immense havoc throughout Ettrick Forest, sweeping the district of its herds and portable goods'. Selkirk was burnt and its inhabitants robbed of goods to the value of 1,000 merks. How many were killed during the raid and what goods were seized is not recorded.

It seems likely that the early records kept in Selkirk were burnt in the flames of Musgrave's raid. So far for the medieval period, I have had to rely on the sparse mentions in exchequer rolls, Forest and circuit court records, *The Calendar of Documents Relating to Scotland*, family histories and other documentary evidence from both sides of the Border. Added to these are some visible remains on the ground and my own interpretations of the possibilities.

This is rather like looking through a keyhole into a darkened room – you can get vague outlines of what is there but no definite shapes and you have to make a reasonable guess on what is there *based on what can be seen*. In fact, archaeology and history is about one per cent definite knowledge and the remainder what we judge to be there on the basis of that one per cent. Added to this is the tendency to thread present-day perceptions into historic realities. This not a good idea.

So it is a pleasure to procede to the next period when the history of Selkirk and Selkirkshire appears in documents, written in the town by people who were witnessing what was happening.

It is not just the great and the good/bad who are worthy of record. The conflicts between monarch and magnates or feuds between great nobles are the main features of recorded history but it is the lives of the 'small people' of the burgh which most interests me. I hope to bring an insight in their lives in the next few chapters.

CHAPTER TWELVE
The Selkirk Papers

T he invention of writing was the earliest and greatest method of information technology; through writing, information in all its forms can be passed through space and time, round the world or through the centuries. Modern IT merely speeds up the processes.

Through writing it is possible to read the important events and minutiae of life in a Border burgh in the later medieval period. In Selkirkshire and more immediately in Selkirk, we are lucky in having two secure sixteenth-century information sources, handwritten in Selkirk with eyewitness accounts of the happenings.

THE BURGH COURT BOOK

Found within the Council offices was the Burgh Court Book of Selkirk, a manuscript of 332 folios written by a series of local priests acting as town clerks and covering the period from 1503 to 1545.

The original manuscript was in poor condition, with damage from damp and severe wear in page corners resulting in the loss of some words and phrases. This had been partly restored with the application of opaque tissue paper on many of the folios and by binding in heavy leather boards. Judging by the technique involved, this was done in Victorian times, probably by Thomas Craig-Brown whose 1886 *History of Selkirkshire* uses many condensed quotations from the Court Book.

The Court Book is actually made up of a number of smaller books and loose pages which have not necessarily been bound in chronological sequence. Variations in the page size confirm this suggestion.

The Court Book was transcribed in full by Dr Margaret Rose on behalf of the members of the Selkirkshire Antiquarian Society and an edited edition of the transcript was prepared by J. Imrie, T.I. Rae and W.D. Ritchie. This was published in two volumes in 1960 and 1969. There is still another volume of the Court Books in the Records Office awaiting transcription and publication.

The editors' comments in the preface are worth quoting.

'*Most of the entries are in the same handwriting, presumably that of sir Ninian Brydin, notary and common clerk of the burgh*★. *This is a cursive hand which is in point of letter-forms and conventions reasonably typical of the period; but careless execution combined with bizarre spelling, even by 16th century standards, raise many problems of decipherment. The language of the record consists partly of rather degenerate Latin for the more formal entries such as court rubrics, amercements, legal instruments and service of heirs, but more often of vernacular Scots with occasional echoes of the vigorous direct speech of the time, for administrative enactments and other less stereotyped proceedings. On occasions, Latin and Scots are amusingly intermingled, as in depositions of witnesses. The standard of record-keeping is low and there are many errors and omissions, particularly in regard to names and dates. Some of the apparent irregularities in dating are obviously due to scribal aberrations, but there are also entries which seem to have been inserted into any convenient blank space.*'

These comments are factual rather than critical. In truth, the 1700 entries in the Burgh Court Book record the daily life in Selkirk in great detail over a period of forty-two years at the beginning of the sixteenth century. Fortunately, the people of Selkirk must have been amongst the most litigious in the country and this provides us with a great deal of information that would otherwise be unknown. The Court Books tend to be disputes on matters of law but not all the entries are petty bickering. There are important *pro bono publico* notices with letters from the king recorded beside warnings about the removal of middens from the public street and market regulations. This is the world cut down to Selkirk-size.

The two published Court Books, 1503–45, are centred on the happenings within the burgh. There is another Burgh Court Book of Selkirk, covering the period 1557–75, whose two hundred very tattered pages were found in a Selkirk baker's loft (see p.493). This is now in the

---

★ This presumption turned out to be wrong.

Scottish Records Office in Edinburgh with a reference B 68/7/1. I will refer to this in the later chapters.

Added to this valuable Court Book resource are a large number of documents rescued from a fire by two Selkirk bakers at the start of the Second World War. These cover the period from 1511 to the late Victorian era. I have known about this collection for forty years and have had the pleasure and privilege of working on it for the last twenty. The story of this collection is worth a section on it own – which I will now do.

THE WALTER MASON PAPERS

At the start of the Second World War there was a general panic throughout Britain that the German Luftwaffe would bomb and burn the whole country to oblivion. With this in mind, a 1940 War Office directive ordered that no quantities of paper or other combustible material should be stored in attics where there was a greater risk of incendiary damage. In Selkirk, the manager of the Commercial Bank knew that there was a lot of paper in the upper storeys of his bank, so he ordered the odd-job man to carry it down and burn it in the back garden. This was before the potential of recycled paper was realised.

Next door to the bank was Mason's Tearoom where the brothers Bruce and Walter Mason worked as bakers. Seeing the smoke, they went to investigate and were aghast to find over four hundred years of Selkirk history going up in flames. They asked permission to go through the mass of paper to pick out items of interest but this was refused owing to the 'confidentiality' of some of them. With a half-crown bribe they persuaded the odd-job man to carry the sack-loads down the stairs slowly, while they rifled through what was already there. This subterfuge saved about half a ton of paper which was only a percentage of what was burned. Literally thousands of documents were stored 'in the bakehoose loft' in flour bags and boxes, tea-boxes and barrels, and remained there for thirty years in almost total secrecy.

I was let into the secret in the late 1950s and spent some years trying to decipher some of the documents in company of Bruce and Walter. Bruce died in 1963 and I became joint keeper of the collection and the secret of its acquisition. Walter Mason was a shy, quiet and gentle man in every sense, whose unassuming nature concealed a vast knowledge.

It became a matter of deduction for us to work out how such a wide range of documents, from pre-Reformation to late Victorian, had come together to be stored in the attics of a Selkirk bank. The early documents and books had been written by the priests and notaries since 1511. After the Reformation, the same men became notaries and clerks to the burgh, and started to dabble in banking and insurance. The banking interest strengthened until the Commercial Bank took over that activity and the building. The town clerks moved to another building, leaving four centuries of accrued paperwork in the attic there. It was part of this that the Mason brothers saved.

At the beginning of his last illness, Walter asked me to take the documents, especially the Protocol Books, for safekeeping. With no immediate family he feared that the documents might be returned to the bonfire from whence they came. He asked only that I 'put them to the best possible use' and opined that I would have a lot of fun with them. He died in January 1988 and I lost a good friend whose intel-lectual stimulus I had enjoyed for many years. Even now, twenty years later, I sometimes find myself thinking, 'I will have to tell Walter that'.

With thousands of documents and handwritten books at my disposal, how would I start? Some were dry and brittle, some were damp and mould-growing; and all were needing care and attention. So I asked Dr John Imrie, who had recently retired as Keeper of the Scottish Records, for his advice. He studied the collection for two days in thoughtful silence and then said that it was of great national impor-tance, most especially the sixteen Protocol Books, which ranged in date from 1511 to 1668. These are the legal notebooks kept by the priests and notaries to record the land transfers, and disputes, marriage contracts, wills and inheritances, letters and commands from the king etc. They were written in medieval Latin and medieval Scots in a form of shorthand, were frayed at the edges by damp or nibbled by mice, and partly burned by English invaders, Scottish reivers and the Commercial Bank manager.

Dr Imrie suggested that the best place would be in the Records Office where they would be kept at a controlled temperature but probably never looked at for many generations. This did not fit in with my instructions to put them 'to the best possible use'. I was resolved that they should stay in Selkirk where they were written and the collection would bear the name of Walter Mason. So I enlisted the help of some friends and formed the Walter Mason Trust, with the sole purpose of conserving and transcribing the papers. This would preserve the unique collection and make them available for study for present and future generations – that was 'the best possible use' to my mind

A short time previously, with a fractured skull by reason of a contretemps with a boy on a bicycle, I had given up working as a fencing contractor and had joined the Ettrick and Lauderdale Museum Service. So I gave some of the collection to the Museum Service, some to the Archives Service and kept a few pieces myself. This is strictly against the recommended practices but I did it for the best possible reason – I wanted to work on the Protocol Books myself. (For the purists, I have now given the whole collection into the keeping of the Museum Service and Archives of Borders Regional Council.)

There were sixteen Protocol Books in various stages of preservation and size. One, which covered the period 1579 to 1587, had 1,842 pages and measured 20cms high when lying on its side. This was going to take some time.

Help was at hand when Teresa Maley came to live in the Borders. She is a Cambridge history graduate specialising in medieval Latin and Anglo-Saxon, with additional medieval Welsh from Bangor – and a trained archivist. Her knowledge of palaeography and Latin exceeded mine, but my reading of Scots and knowledge of local place-names, language and customs, meant that I could make a contribution. Her knowledge of archive preservation and presentation was of immense value as the bulk of the documents were still 'dirty auld bits o paper', according to one viewer.

The first task was to get the documents user-friendly, because to turn over a page in a book might leave you with a scrap of paper with two or three letters between your fingers, and this could destroy the meaning of a sentence. To do this, money was of primary importance but, because the project took the public imagination, around £60,000 was gathered. Tom Valentine, the paper conservator and bookbinder, was given the restoration task which he completed in a remarkably short time and to everybody's satisfaction.

This done, Teresa and I proceeded with the transcription and translation of over five thousand pages which were to shed some new light on the history of Selkirk and the Borders.

For the next two years, we struggled through the often atrocious writing (with pieces missing), puzzled over word contractions (done to save paper), debated the various niceties of the Scots legal system of the sixteenth century and in general had a great time. Working with original sources has an excitement that is not there while merely quoting someone else's work.

In the two years of part-time work, we had transcribed and translated the first four early Protocol Books of sir John Chepman 1511–36/1545–47, sir John Chepman 1536–45, sir John Brydin 1530–37 and a shared Protocol Book of sirs John and Ninian Brydin 1526–36.

A word of explanation. The use of 'sir' is not an indication of a knightly title but rather a priestly one where the local priest acted as a notary for the community, carrying out the duties of the literate few in a largely illiterate society. In his Protocol Book, he recorded land transfers, marriage contracts and wills. The notary also acted as procurator or for the defence in court, and arbiter in times of disagreement, or as clerk to the court or town clerk for the burgh, and recorded on paper anything which might later be required. The notary had priestly training, was able to write, and had some legal training.

One of the most important duties was the delivery of sasine. As Selkirk was a royal or king's burgh, the baillie was the King's representative there. On giving up a burgess rood, symbols of the land and house had to be given to the baillie. This could be sod and stone for the land, or the hasp and staple from the house door. These were given to the new owner or his representative by the baillie, while this and the names of the witnesses were recorded in the notary's protocol book.

When it came to the transcription, we had to agree with the editors of the Selkirk Court Books that the Latin was 'rather degenerate' but we followed their lead in many ways. The Latin sections we translated into English, quoting the original only when it was deemed important, or we weren't quite sure of the meaning. The Scots, we left as it was as an example of Border Scots of the first half of the sixteenth century: but sometimes the Latin was Scoticised or the Scots Latinised.

After going through each book several times, we decided to publish the four books together, as they covered roughly the same period and cross-pollinated each other. Through the offices of Dr Donald Galbraith, then Keeper of the Records of Scotland (and a good friend), the Stair Society heard about our work and came up with an offer we couldn't refuse. The Stair Society had been founded to 'encourage the study and advance the knowledge of the History of Scots Law'.

The offer was: 'can we help to publish the Protocol Books for you?' Indeed they could – and the bargain was sweetened when the Glenfiddich Trust put up the money for our share of the publication.

But neither Teresa nor I are specialists in medieval Scots law, so we asked Professor Bill Gordon and Dr John Durkin of Glasgow and Dr John Imrie of Edinburgh for advice on Scots legal terms and texts of the period. This was willingly given and they picked up some points that we had missed – but I think they were surprised at how much we got right. So the four books were published under the title of *The Selkirk Protocol Books 1511–1547*. The introduction was written by Dr Peter Symms, while the massive task of the index was undertaken by Dr Donald Galbraith. Thankfully!

There is a great deal of social and economic history within the four published books. Wills and lists of goods show the standards of living and trades of the people. Property deals and land transfers appear in numbers and, by adding the information from the Burgh Court Books, it was possible to build up a map of Selkirk for the period 1520–45. This was done on the jig-saw principle of fitting pieces together.

In all the four Protocol Books, there are many transfers of property. These take the form of: '*10th June 1529. James Scot bailie of Selkirk at the request of Robert Chesholm came to his tenement★ lying in the street commonly called 'Fulbrig Myr' between the tenement of Simon Fairle on the south, the tenement of John Vychtman on the north, the yard of Simon Farle on the west*

★A tenement is usually a burgess rood containing a house, outbuildings and yard.

and the king's street on the east, and there, on the ground of the said tenement resigned the tenement in the hands the bailie who gave sasine to John Chesholm first born son of Robert personally present and accepting and to his heirs and assignees, the said John paying yearly 6 shillings after the death of his father to Adam Ker of Shaw, his heirs and assignees and 3 halfpennies in burgh ferme'. Further clauses of condition and a list of four witnesses were added to this entry.

This one entry gives the location of the property lying on the west side of the street leading to Fulbrig Myr; the names of the old and new owner; tells who lived on either side; tells how much the yearly rent was and how much burgh taxes were paid and gives the names of the baillie and four witnesses who attended the transaction.

Multiply this information by about four hundred, the number of times the hundred and fifty burgess roods within the burgh changed hands or were split up, and that is a lot of knowledge. Snippets of information can be drawn from the entries, phrases like 'at the West/East Port', 'the Peelgait' and 'the street that lead to the Well/Cross' can be used to provide the location and a reasonably accurate map of the burgh in the period 1520–1545 emerges.

Added to this are a large number of family relationships, as possession by inheritance usually shows a close kinship to the previous owner and often revealed an intricate network of ownerships, tenancies and sub-tenancies, with a complex structure of rules, customs, practices and traditions. Wealth in the shape of property was important to maintain the status of the family group and its division could lead to disputes. Wills are a great source of information and the burgh ferme gives a measure of the wealth of the individual.

All this adds to the picture of the people of the burgh, and over the last twenty years I have picked up so much information about them that I feel as if I know many of the people personally.

To give a picture of life in Selkirk over the first part of the sixteenth century, I will draw on extracts from the Court Books, the published Protocol Books, and the Protocol Book of sir Ninian Brydin, which has only been published in a condensed form as we ran out of money to tell his fascinating story in detail. Ninian started life as a member of the numerous Brydin family in Selkirk, became a priest and notary in the late 1520s, moved to Edinburgh in middle age and returned to the

Borders in 1560. This book covers one of the most interesting times of Scottish history.

In addition to the above are: the Protocol Book of sir John Chepman and sir John Hall 1542, 1546/7; the Protocol Book of sirs John and William Brydin 1579–87; the Protocol Book of sir William Brydin 1587–92 in two parts – the first was in loose sheets but now bound in a single volume while the original of the second part is lost but a typed transcript of the period 12 April 1591–6 June 1591 is available; the Protocol Book of Henry Blaikie 1592–1613; the Protocol Book of John Kerr 1629–31; the Protocol Book of John Kerr 1630–33 which includes an extract from the Protocol Book of George Wod, notary and town clerk July 1605–December 1614; the Protocol Book of Andrew Andison May 1665–May 1668.

These have been transcribed in draft but a lot more information is held within the conserved pages; it just needs someone with the time and interest to extract it. Taken together, the earlier Protocol Books tell the story of the burgh from 1511 until the time of the Reformation, while those after that are largely concerned with the rural areas, particulary those in the Bowden, St Boswells and Melrose areas where the abbey lands were being divided amongst the neighbouring lairds.

In addition to the Protocol and Court Books, there were also about 13,000 loose documents ranging from the mid sixteenth century to the mid-nineteenth; the bulk of these were from the mid-seventeenth, eighteenth and early nineteenth century period. Taken individually, they are council receipts and bills, letters from kings, nobility and peasants, records of transactions and all the paraphernalia of council; put together they tell the story of life within a Border burgh. Even the paper and parchment was interesting with watermarks showing paper produced by the German papermakers brought into Scotland by James VI in 1592, while some of the parchment had the small holes of warble-fly infestation in the skin of the living sheep. One of the protocol books had a quill pen pushed down the spine of the book.

As most of this information has never been published, I will use some of it in the following chapter and hope that someone else will follow on to use the rest.

CHAPTER THIRTEEN
The Flodden Period

PRE-FLODDEN SELKIRK

In the early years of the sixteenth century Selkirk had a population of around seven hundred. The burgh was almost totally self-sufficient, relying on the produce of the surrounding countryside for food, fuel and the raw material for building and manufacture. Even the wealthiest (a very relative term) of tradesmen and merchants were also crofters with their own rigs and plots of land. The fact that Selkirk was the only town within the vast area of the Ettrick Forest made it a natural market and meeting place. The king's letters were read out at the Merket Cross and his justice eyres may have met within the burgh courtroom. These factors made Selkirk a place of some importance but not a place of much wealth.

If you could have visited Selkirk at the time, you would have found the triangular town plan which still exists in the modern town. The present Back Row, High Street and Kirk Wynd make the triangle and from this the Peelgait, now Castle Street, led to the site of the castle. Haining Loch drained naturally along the south side of the Back Row, giving an additional defense line outside the back walls of the burgess roods; it also made a convenient disposal for waste. Records show that the back walls and ditches received little attention except in time of trouble or danger of invasion.

There were three entrances to the town, the West, East and South Ports, the latter usually known as the Foul Brig Port. This was because of the number of tan pits in the vicinity, and tanning leather with its waste products do not give out a pleasant smell.

The streets were narrow with vennels four feet wide between houses, giving 'harrow and barrow' access to the back yards and buildings. The main public streets, known as 'the king's streets' are likely to have been packed quarry-rubble rather than flagstone.

The houses would have changed from the basically wood/wattle structures previously noted, to thick stone-built walls with thatch and sod roofing. There is evidence to suggest that some had two floors and the name of one, the Sclaithoose, indicates that it was roofed with slates, and this was noteworthy in a thatched town.

Hygiene was notable only by its absence. House and animal waste was collected in 'middens' at the side of, or on the road in front of the houses, before being led out to the fields. The need to empty the middens is a frequent entry in the Court Book.

There were no underground drains, so human and animal waste tended to wash down the ditch on the side of the road surfaces in bad weather. Drinking water came from the few wells in community ownership and at least one in private hands. This source was by no means perfect since most of the water collected had been on the surface further up the brae, and had collected debris/bacteria on the way down. The seepage from the top of the town ran into the Haining Loch, the outlet of which provided drinking water for the lower town further down its course. With stagnant water collected in the wells for drinking water, a dry summer could guarantee a sizable death-rate amongst the old and very young. It is little wonder that the brewing of ale was an important task and subject to many regulations in the Burgh Court Book.

The people of Selkirk had a variety of trades, which they combined with farming the land of their rigs and raising livestock. Their needs of clothing were met by local weavers and tailors; footwear, horse harness, belting etc, by the cordiners who would also supply leather for jacks, the multi-layered thick leather jerkins; which were the poor man's form of armour; tools and weapons were supplied by the blacksmiths, and woodworkers could make doors, furniture and construct houses. The everyday needs of the small community could be met within the area. Food supplies came from the burgess crofts and from the extensive common lands, or could be bought in the weekly market. The Fair days gave the opportunity to sell surplus produce and purchase items which were not produced locally, and had been brought in for the occasion. To all intents and purposes the burgh was largely self-sufficient with its mixture of urban craftsmen and local rural agriculture.

Extracts from the Burgh Court Book

The entries in the Court Book are a record of the everyday life in Selkirk and the 1,700 entries tell much of the functioning of the community in the period 1503 to 1545. The court was a council of the 'best and worthiest of the burgh', presumably men who held a burgess acre, and was presided over by an alderman and two baillies with an 'inquest' of fifteen to twenty burgesses. Their deliberations were noted by the common clerk to the burgh, almost certainly sir William Bryden, priest and notary.

To keep this book in reasonable proportions, I selected some of the more interesting entries to illustrate certain aspects of the history of Selkirk. Some are in a rough version of formal Latin while others have the vigour of spoken sixteenth century Scots. I give examples in italics; many of the quotations have been translated into English for ease of reading but don't expect any standardisation in the spelling of people or places.

19 May 1506. At a court held by the alderman and baillies and eighteen inquisitors, a letter was received from the king (James IV) for their consideration – '*Truist frendis we greit yow weill and foreasmekyll as it is schavine to us (be) Rauff Ker of Primsyd that he beggit and (in)tends to byg for your eis and profeit … ane myll apone his landis of Billisheuch and to draw ane mylne laid to (the samen) fra the water of Aitrek throcht your (commone) betuex Billisheuch and Aitrek, (we pray) yow that ye will for your awyne profeit geff your consent and liscence (to the said) Rauff and his ayris to byg and haif (the said) myll in the place foresaid.*'

Which translates as: 'Truest friends, we greet you well and for as much as it is shown to us by Ralph Ker of Primside that he has built and intends to build for your ease and profit … a mill upon his lands of Billisheuch and to draw a mill-lade to the same from the water of Ettrick through your common between Billisheuch and Ettrick. We pray that you will for your own profit, give your consent and licence to Ralph and his heirs to build and have the said mill in the place mentioned.'

Two points can be taken from this. Evidently the Common was now under the control of the people of Selkirk since permission to dig a mill-lade across the Common had to be requested from the inquest.

Despite this, the Common was still officially the king's land and his wish was granted.

The king was taking a close interest in his town of Selkirk, although his interest may have been as much financial as personal. If the people were earning more money, the taxes could increase – the human condition does not change.

22 October 1509. The inquest decrees that all ale should be sold from Sunday forth by the brewers. It has to be sold at the correct measure with a fine of 8s to the baillies for those who cheated. Bakers have to sell bread in twenty ounces (loaves) and each has to be weighed; failure to do so means a fine of 8s. Non-burgesses was not allowed to bake, brew, buy or sell (presumably in the Fair or market).

Creelmen who sold goods from a basket were a constant source to annoyance to the market regulations as they took trade from the legal stallholders and paid no dues to the town.

28 March 1512. '*This inquest findis that thair sall [be] na crellman gand within the schirefdom for the gret scath and hindranch of the common profet under the payne of dyttecth of oppression. And quha sa sellis bred to crellmen or to ony other that heris gawand ma to the dosoun that ance thai sall be in 8s of unlaw to be payit to the kyrk work without favor.*'

No creelmen, definitely no 'baker's dozen' given, and fines going to the kirk.

20 April 1512. The kirk is getting a steeple. The whole inquest of sixteen men had to swear individually '*be their gret acht* [great oath] *the stepil is maist convenient tae be completit'. And Jok Kene and Jame Chepman thinkis siclyk*'.

In the same entry as this urban planning decision is: '*Jhone Cawers sayis that James Chepmen ordanit to geif stra for his muk to Thome Gluffar quhilk he gat part of the stra. I ask convend ye grant of doin and he sauld haif had ilk ane fuder of muk ane thrauk of stra and twa atour all condutions.*'

This is a broken promise that James Chepman was to give straw to Thomas Gluffar for his muck, and that he was to get a cartload of muck for each thrauk (stack?) of straw and two others as well.

The first decade of the sixteenth century was a time of insecurity within the burgh and regular night watches were set. All burgesses and indwellers were expected to take part in guarding the burgh. That the watch was set for night duty, indicates that the threat was seen to be from sneak thieves rather than from reiver bands or English invasion. The watch was divided in three parts to correspond to the triangular shape of the town and related to the three ports or gates.

However, trouble was brewing along the border line. Henry VIII was crowned king of England in 1509 at the age of seventeen and immediately began to make alliances and wars to bolster England's reputation as a great European power. Despite the Treaty of Perpetual Peace signed at Ayton in 1502, the Borderers on both sides were restive; long years of intermittent but continued raiding had produced a people to whom this was a way of life.

They were products of their time and the 'reivers' came to prominence in places where the authority of law couldn't be enforced. As this happened most frequently in the hill country where ground quality was poor and people went hungry, it is not a coincidence that the most notorious reiver families flourished there.

There were equally wicked ruffians in the families that had risen in status after the fall of the House of Douglas – the Kerrs, Scotts, Humes and Pringles, but they had more men from the flatter lands of the Merse or lower valleys, and should more properly be looked on as robber barons who straddled the law rather than kept it.

Trouble flared up on many occasions and was long remembered. When a noted English reiver, the Bastard Heron, killed Sir Robert Ker, the Scots Warden, on a truce day in 1508, this was a national affront and reputedly used as an excuse for the invasion of 1513. The fact that Robert Ker was vastly unpopular as Warden was not even taken into consideration, but killing a Scots Warden offended national pride and had to be answered eventually.

So it is no surprise that the Selkirk Court Book has entries of instruction to the keepers of the night watch.

5 December 1509. Ordains that night watches were to be kept by men and not boys; they were to walk on the back lands within their watch and not to go to '*potation and drink*' from nine o'clock to cockcrow.

7 October 1510. A watch of eighteen men, neighbours and householders, fully armed as best they might, had to walk each night from nine o'clock until 'lawful' cockcrow. Failure to do so meant a fine of 12 pence.

23 February 1511. A watch of nine well-armed men to walk nightly and to report to Pat Kene, David Broun and Thomas Brydyn *'gif it be tyme to lous'* (go home).

The situation was becoming more fraught in 1513 when an entry dated 25 May, gave a roll call of:

The Community of the Burgesses of Selkirk

James Clerk, James Hogg, Thomas Greenshel, John Burne, John Wolson, Cuthbert Turnbull, John Hastie, George Scott, John Boyle, Thomas Porteous, Robert Ker, Wm Robertson, George Brown, Adam Wilkieson, John Kowper, Thomas Kein, Andrew Strang, Robert Porteous, John Lorimer, Peter Porteous, Egidius Porteous, Wm Turnbull, John Brydyne, Thomas Talzeoure, David Brydyne, Mathew Dryster, Thomas Brydyne, Thomas Watson, Mathew Sewright, Ninian Donaldson, Wm Blake, David Minto, John Hall, George Thompson, Thomas Porteous Wm Watson, John Kein, Walter Hall, John Mows, James Sanderson, Wm Justice, Wm Robertson, John Thomson, Antony Gibson, John Dun, John Lumsden, James Mows, Wm Freer, John Freer, James Brydyne, Mathew Couper, Andrew Laurie, Ninian Donaldson, Ninian Minto, John Sanderson, Andrew Swan, James Scott, Nichol Henderson, Wn Chesame, John Curll, John Forsyth, Patrick Wilkieson, Thomas Legerwood, Solomon Deephope, George Kyll, John Johnstone, Wm Main, Hary Saloman, John Harper, Robert Brown, Nicholas Wilkieson, Laird of Philiphaugh, Allan Forsyth, Patrick Kene, Wm Aitchison, Wm Caidzow, Wm Kene, John Kene, James Kene, Thomas Hall, Thomas Mathoson, Thomas Johnstone, John Farle, Wm Persone, Simon Farle, Allan Dawgless, George Stabill, James Inglisman, Richard Young, James Nithan, John Learmont, John Farle, Robert Todrik, James Watson, John Kune, Patrick Moffat, James Porteous, John Kaidzow, James Helme, John Muthag, Wm Braidfoot, John Scott, James Conchere, Thomas Hall, James Brydyne, John Cant, John Lawson, James Harper, John Kene, John Mospatrick, John Mulros, Stephen Dalglees, James Harper, Richard Chapman, John Brydyne, Wm Couper, John Cornwell, Wm Learmont, Alex Brown, John Smith, James Braidfoot, Roger Murray, John Cavers, Andrew Maturk, John Chapman, James Robertson, Mungo Brown, David Brown, Wm Ker, John Freer, Robert Gillies, Adam Thomson, Thomas Crookshank, Wm Tait, Robert

Chisholm, John Barker, John Lauder, George Chapman, Wm Loremer, Thomas Minto, Stephen Lauder, James Chapman, John Porteous, Thomas Tod, Wm Blake, Robert Brydyne, John Thomson, Robert Benet, Wm Lidderdale, Thomas Henderson, Wm Porteous, Andrew Henderson, John Robertson, John Cowan, Wm Porteous, James Skune.

On the same list are a number of 'Assisters' – Robert Scott, Stephen Lauder, Thomas Johnston, George Scott, David Brown, Thomas Brydyne and John Scott – who also appear on the principal roll.

There are 160 names on this list. They could not have all been burgesses, and must include indwellers who were not, as well as a number of out-dwellers from the neighbouring lands.

The army of sixteenth-century Scotland was a citizen army with all men between sixteen and sixty bound to serve a maximum of forty days in any one year, if called upon. Additionally, they had to provide their own weapons in keeping with their status, and supply their own food for the duration. This gave the usually impoverished Scots kings a large army at little cost.

The system had its disadvantages though. Few men cared to leave their families unprotected and their crops unharvested, and at the end of forty days, the citizen/soldiers could just walk away from a battle to return home, leaving the leaders without an army to lead. This was not the best outlook for the Souters of Selkirk as they were preparing to leave for one of the most iconic battles fought in the Borders.

The Burgh Court Book gives an extensive detailed description of the preparations.

2 August 1513. Finds and ordains all neighbours and indwellers to be armed for war after the tenor of the king's letters produced at the last wapinschawing (muster or weapon-showing), to give their demonstration and show thereof in the Bog before the baillies on Wednesday, St Laurence Day (10 August). '*And that all indwellers for the weal of the town and country, having servant men and children, that they be produced at wapinschawing in best way they can with ane spear, lance and bow. And sae bein he will nocht of cost and free find himself weapons as said is, that his master furnish him thereof of his cost, the said weapons to remain with him after the waypassing of his servant. To be fulfilled under the unlaw of 8s (fine).*

Also finds that the neighbours about the hill lend their horse to bring 5

sledful of turf and who has no horse to come himself and give his pains for casting
and laying of the turf; and that each indweller send on servant betwixt this and
Sunday to the lochend and places about the Bog where need is; and also all
neighbours to cast their heidrooms and fenceplaces as required betwixt this and
the said day – to be completed under pain of 2s (fine) to be poynded and paid
on Saturday at even from the failures. And all places to the east and west end of
the town to be likewise ordered anent the stopping of heidrooms, casting of
souches and barrows making as ever and who so fails to be punished as said is.

    Anent the watch, it is to stand as it is with no boys or children but the
Goodman of the house or a sufficient man in the sight of the bailies.'

    Also that all manner of men come to the kirkyard when a fray happens to
pass with the baillies, under pain of 12 pence (fine).'

This was Selkirk being placed on a war footing at the command of
James IV, king of Scots.

FLODDEN AND THE SELKIRK CONNECTION

There is no happening in the eight hundred years of history of the
burgh of Selkirk which has captured the imagination as much as the
Battle of Flodden.

This battle appears in most Borders Common Riding celebrations
and speeches: the tragedy of a gallant king, his nobles and countrymen
slaughtered while fighting bravely; all the Hawick men killed; all but
one of the Selkirk contingent of seventy killed, and so on. The country
defenceless, and the youths prepared to resist a ruthless invader. It makes
a glorious story as told in Sir Walter Scott's brilliant poetical reconstruction in *Marmion*★.

This poem has been the inspiration of a vast amount of romantic
verse and prose, and the story continues through the Borders in class-
rooms and meeting places. There are many variations on the theme for
every historian, patriotic author, ballad/story-teller and visiting writer,

---

★ Sir William Marmion appears as a knight-errant in Scalacronica p.61 and 62. He was
fighting against the Scots at Norham Castle in the reign of Edward II. This must have
given Scott his introductory lines of the First Canto of *Marmion* – 'Day set on Norham's
castled steep and Tweed's fair river broad and deep'.

to use in some shape or form. I appreciate the colour and vigour of the story but have doubts about many of the 'facts'.

I do not intend to enter into the debate about the actual Battle of Flodden. This is a much written story which usually mirrors the writers' beliefs. In my view, the most balanced account of the Battle can be found in *Border Fury. England and Scotland at War 1296–1568* by John Sadler.

What I will do is collect all the known entries from contemporary documents and some of the earliest versions of the story which have been published, add some comments of my own and leave the rest to personal judgement. The Battle of Flodden is a lethal minefield for a man born in Selkirk but who also likes to have his history authentic.

The generally accepted story is that a contingent of Selkirk men followed their King James IV to Flodden and were all killed while fighting round and protecting their dying king. Only one man, Fletcher, survived and returned to Selkirk with a captured English banner in his blood-stained hand. When asked where were the rest, he was unable to speak, but cast the flag down on the cobbles to signify that they were all dead: a brilliant and moving account which is commemorated at the Casting of the Colours in the Selkirk Market Place after every Common Riding.

In his *History of Selkirkshire*, Thomas Craig-Brown weighs up the evidence of the Selkirk presence at Flodden and the returning warrior, Fletcher. He concludes: 'there is probably no incident in Scottish history so familiar as the part said to have been taken by Selkirk in the fatal fight, and it is regrettable to have to add that there are few stories so much indebted to imagination and so little to facts'.

The Accounts

I will start with the non-contemporary accounts of the battle and its consequences.

The earliest account of Flodden as a disaster was written by John Hodge in 1722 and is preserved in the Advocates Library in Edinburgh. This was written over two hundred years after the battle:

'King James, on the way to Flodden, where he engaged the English army, had from the burgh of Selkirk, eighty well-armed men commanded by the town-clerk, who were all, except the clerk, cut to pieces. The clerk only returned and brought with him one of the English banners and a halbert axe … He created the clerk and his successors knights'.

The next published record within Selkirk was written by the local minister in 1790. The Rev. Robertson increases the number of men to a hundred and states that the standard was taken from the English by a member of the Incorporation of Weavers and that William Brydone, the town clerk at the time, was knighted by James V for his valour.

Sir Walter Scott took up the story and was convinced that William Brydone was knighted on the field, just before the battle commenced.

Contemporary Documents

Evidence from the Court Book and the Protocol Books gives sparse but convincing proof that the burgh of Selkirk was represented at Flodden. The Community Roll Call and the reference to the weapon-showing and the preparation of the town's defences testify to that, but there is only one entry which mentions Flodden.

In the Court Book entry of 29 October 1521. '*That daye Stewyn Clerk tuk preef this day xv daye be Wol Chepman and other part of nychburis of Selkirk that he broucht ane blak hors furtht of Ingland at Flodoun*'.

However Stewyn Clerk does not appear in the Community Roll of Burgesses, so he may not have been a burgess but an indweller. 'James Clerk, stallarius' headed the the Burgess Roll of Selkirk above and Stewyn may be a relative. In the series of Protocol Books, there is only one mention of Flodden.

In the Book of John and Ninian Brydin. '*28 May 1529. The young woman Isabel Murray only daughter and heir of the deceased James Murray in Bouhill who died under the banner of our lord King at Flouden*'.

Definite proof that one 'Flower o the Forest wede awa' on the battlefield. James Murray held one of the stedes of Ettrick Forest; there were others who simply disappeared from their family histories at that period.

The Pringles of Galawater were severely damaged according to the family history. Those who are noted as 'fallen at Flodden' include David Pringle of Galashiels and four of his five sons; William Pringle of Torwoodlee, David Home of Wedderburn, brother-in-law to David Pringle, and George Home, nephew of David.

Also on the list of fallen are John Scott of Haining, John Murray of Philiphaugh, Adam Turnbull of Philiphaugh, William Turnbull, his brother, William Ker of Yair.

The list is by no means complete as only the land-owning aristocracy can be traced through land transfers to the heirs and family traditions.

These are mainly men who held stedes in Ettrick Forest and would have been turned out in the King's service as part of their lease, as did their forefathers under Wallace, Bruce, and later kings of Scots including the king's father, James III.

After the Battle

With the king and most of the nobility dead, the Scots command fell to Lord Home who was much better fitted to the task than the chivalrous James. As a Borderer, he knew the ground and had experience in Border warfare. His first task was to secure the kingdom, and time was not on his side as the Scots citizen army had served twenty-six of their required forty days military commitment. He withdrew from the field to place guards on the fords and hill roads into Scotland.

This left the English in possession of the field and claiming total victory. Less often quoted is the contemporary English historian Halle, who relates how the Scots carried off sixty prisoners, and that many Englishmen had lost their horses and stuff in their tents, the thieves of Tynedale and Teviotdale got the blame, probably correctly.

With Scotland reputedly devastated and its total manpower slain, it would be expected that the English commander would press home his advantage to invade Scotland. He refused to do this on account of the lateness of the season and lack of provisions.

Home had no such qualms, and eleven days after the battle the Bishop of Durham was writing to Wolsey 'fearing that they would have to assent to the truce proposed by Lord Home'. By 22 October, six weeks after the battle, Home was able to guarantee safety to the Merse and had convened the 'heidmen of Tividale, Liddesdale, Eisdale, Ewisdale and Annandale' to organise their own defence.

Henry VIII of England was furious that the Earl of Surrey's reported advantage had not been followed up. But Surrey had handed on the responsibility to Lord Dacre who, two months later, was reluctantly raiding into the Borders with four thousand horsemen and four hundred foot. He was met and defeated at Sclaterford in Roxburghshire. He immediately wrote to his king that he would do no further raiding for fear that the Scots would destroy the English Middle March in his absence.

In February 1514 he was busy at Cocklaw in the Middle March, ransoming prisoners taken by the Scots. By 17 May 1514 he was appealing to the Council of England that: 'the Scottes have, and daily doth distress the King's bordours and subgietts without great hurte is done again to them'.

This does not suggest a country devastated with the flower of its fighting men killed at Flodden. The real disaster of Flodden was that the heads of landed families and their heirs were almost totally annihilated, and these were the men who enforced what order there was in the Borderland. With their demise, there was little security from plundering reivers and raiding bands.

Negative Evidence

In looking at the positive evidence and conclusions, it is right that we also examine the negative evidence.

Of the Selkirk presence at Flodden, nothing is known other than the instance given. There may indeed have been a number killed but I can find no trace of them.

The Battle of Flodden was fought on 9 September, but from 22 August to 15 October, nothing appears in the Burgh Court Book or the Protocol Books. This gap is sometimes taken to mean that, by ignoring it, the battle was blotted out of records and thoughts. This is a strange conclusion as there are similar spaces in other parts of the records, and a book that recorded a dispute about straw for muck would surely have made some mention of a great disaster.

Likewise, if the burgesses of Selkirk had been killed at the battle, there would have been a large number of property transfers given to their heirs and been recorded in either Court Records or Protocol Books. Despite careful scrutiny, I can find none.

I have already explained why the pre-Reformation priests and notaries were styled 'sir' or 'schir', but this knowledge was evidently unknown to John Hodge, the Rev. Robertson and even Sir Walter Scott of Abbotsford, so this led to some misunderstandings and the need to look on a 'sir' as a knight.

The banner and sword in Halliwell's House Museum, long associated with the 'knighted' town clerk, have been dated to the mid-17th century by those who are experts in their particular subjects. The fact that sir William Brydyne, town clerk of Selkirk was a priest, and should have neither a sword nor descendants to pass it down to, is ignored; although it is almost certain that he had both.

The fact that the flag in the Museum has been square with two distinct shuttles, indicate that it is a ceremonial flag to be carried in procession by a Corporation of Weavers. The pennon, a long narrow flag, was the type carried in battle to indicate the position of a leader.

In the time of Sir Walter Scott, the flag in the Museum was considered to be the flag brought home from Flodden, although the irreverent boys of the town referred to it as 'the weavers dish-clout', as it belonged to the Weavers Incorporation. To get round the obvious weaving shuttles, it was suggested that it belonged to Weavers from Macclesfield because the men of Macclesfield are known to have been slaughtered at Flodden. As a consequence of this, Macclesfield has a similar tale of the loss of nearly all their fighting men but with more provable evidence as the brother of Lord Derby took advantage of this, to encroach on the land rights of the remaining burgesses.

Sadly I have to agreed with Craig-Brown that 'few stories are so much indebted to imagination and so little to facts'. Selkirk-born, I would like to be proved wrong but would require contemporary documentation to convince me.

LIFE AFTER FLODDEN

In the Burgh Court Book there is only one reference to Flodden, already quoted, and life seems to have gone on as usual. The records are kept in the same handwriting and names which occurred in previous years appear again within its battered pages. There may be an extra awareness of possible danger but nothing that had not been noted before and with the same restrictions.

25 October 1513. '*This inquest findis the wacht to stand and wak to the number of viii persones at ilk end and wak quhil daye be lycht and that all be sensible men best abolyeit thai may and na boyis.*' This is followed by the usual threats that any who fail to watch shall be fined 8s and any who go to drink fined 20s.

In case of trouble, everybody was to go to the kirkyard to await the baillies' orders. Everybody cast turf to repair their 'yard hedis', failure to do so meant a fine of 40s.

The Treasurer's Accounts of 1515 to 16 remits the taxation due from the burgh of Selkirk to £16 'because at thai war hereit be theivis and pestellence' (impoverished by thieves and plague), so there must have been some deterioration in burgh life.

Despite this, the people of Selkirk were equipped with the necessities of life. On 9 February 1516, William Porteous had from his grandfather and father: '*A cauldron, a muckle pot of 2 gallons, pewter charger or tray, pewter plate, pewter dish, saucer, tin pint, basin, laver, pair of wool combs, brazen chandler, crook, pair of tongs. Window cloth* [curtains]*, pair of plough irons, spit, meat almry, vessel amry, crook, chest, box-bed with pertinents, masking-tub, wryt-stand, a gilfalt, spear, axe, sword, chandler, and a 'quhythalc'. He also had two rigs of land at Lady Shaw, one at Goslawdales and one north of Bawthorne.*'

On 28 April 1517, a tron was set up under the Cross in the Market Place. This was a beam or balance used to weigh heavy goods. Hucksters of flesh, fish, victual, butter, cheese and salt were to be punished. At the end of this entry is a short sentence – '*Also ordains our commons to be ridden next holiday.*'

Trawling through the Court and Protocol Books gives much information about the houses and lands within the burgh, but these tend to be repetitive when looked at in isolation. However, taken collectively, and with not a little deduction, they are a fund of knowledge.

THE MAP OF SELKIRK
1520–45

Ownership or the tenancy of land was an important factor of burgh life. The earliest burgh laws are written on the assumption that only land-holders could become burgesses, and this explains why so many of the entries in the Court and Protocol Books concern property ownership and tenancy.

For the last two decades I have been working intermittently on an early sixteenth-century map of Selkirk as it is noted in the various source books, fitting the information contained in one entry into that of another, and adding those to a third. This explains my previous comment on 'jigsaw history'; it might not give a complete view of the town at that period but it is the best we can do without an eyewitness account.

The map is now as complete as it can be until someone produces further contemporary documents. It covers a white cardboard sheet measuring 1.1m by 80cms with my scarcely legible writing packed tightly on the various burgess plots and houses. So far, I have not been able to devise a method of publishing the map for others to study, debate or question.

What I can do is to give my deductions on the knowledge collected.

Looking at the land plots in Selkirk, I find that the greatest block of houses and lands were owned by the craftsmen, tradesmen and merchants— but only by a short head. They were the usual variety of bakers, fleshers, weavers, smiths and brewers: the workers, tradesmen and crofters expected in a Border burgh of the time, together with a leavening of specialists like tynklers (tin-smiths) and thatchers.

An amazing number of clerics held property within the burgh. It is possible that they moved around from one house to another over the period, and this remains an unknown to factor into the equation. But taking the simple view, the clerics who had property and presumably lived within the bounds of the town were:

sir William Bradfut had one house and plot of land; sir William Brydin had three; sir Richard Brydin had two; there were two sir John Brydins whom I have not been able to separate but between them held four; sir Ninian Brydin had one; sir Andrew Duncan had one; sir David Scott had two; Master John Chepman had five and sir John Chepman (could be the same man) had one; sir William Chepman had one; sir John Kene had two; sir Adam Ker had one; sir John Michelhill had one and sir Simon Shortreid had one.

This is by no means a complete list as several others appear on documents, but not on the property list. In 1539 sir Thomas Skune and sir Stephan Wilkiesone were competing with sir Adam Ker (above), for the right to be chaplain to the Rood Altar in the church. Given that Gilbert Ker was Alderman, it is no surprise that sir Adam Ker was chosen for this prestigious and possibly lucrative post.

Added to this religious congregation were two 'Tenements of the Virgin Mary' and one plot that was held as a 'Shrine of the Holy Cross'.

The third property-owning block were the local land-owners, who found it beneficial to be burgesses of Selkirk with access to the fairs and weekly markets held in the burgh. These were Hector Neutone of Rutherford; Andrew Ker of Primside Loch, a land agent who had four 'lands' within the burgh and numerous rigs outside the boundaries; George Ker and Lancelot Ker of Gaitshaw, probably father and son; William Ker of Shaw; James and Robert Turnbull of Gargunnock, and John Turnbull of Hassendean Bank and Hassendean Loch.

The fourth block of property-owners was composed of burgesses in Edinburgh. Robert Scott, William Lauder, Walter Ker and William Ker were men with Selkirk connections who had settled in Edinburgh for commercial advantage. While the remainder of the family could produce goods in Selkirk, they could not sell in the Edinburgh markets without paying market fees. However, if one of them became a burgess in Edinburgh, the market restrictions did not hold.

There seems to be a regular movement between Selkirk and Edinburgh. The sixteenth-century Edinburgh 'Souters' kept close contact with their family connections at home, and in effect formed a Selkirk 'mafia' in the capital. To illustrate this, I will give one instance.

A Selkirk Entrepreneur?

At some period, probably around 1490, a member of the prominent Selkirk family of Chepman seems to have gone to Edinburgh to seek his fortune. Little is known of his early life. A Walter Chepman witnessed a document dated 2 September 1494 and is described as a notary there, but this is unlikely to be the same one. The other Walter Chepman was a merchant who kept a tavern in the High Street and was a wine-importer. It seems that in the latter capacity he became supplier to the royal household. He must have been in a good way of business because another merchant's imports book shows that he was receiving 'mace [a spice], pepper, saffron and other materials' in or before 1505.

James IV was a scholar as well as a man of action, embracing the new ideas and discoveries that were buzzing about the Continent. He was keen to expand learning and literature in his kingdom, and looked on the new technology of printing as a means of spreading knowledge.

On 15 September 1507 he granted a royal patent to Androw Myllar and Walter Chepman to establish a printing press in Edinburgh with whatever foreign equipment and printers they needed. They were required to produce and sell 'all books that shall be deemed necessary'.

Myllar was a bookseller who had already supplied books to the king and had these printed in Rouen in 1505 and 1506. Chepman provided the money and the commercial expertise. The partnership set up a printing house in the Cowgate and from there their first books were printed in 1508 and, unusually, were in Scots rather than Latin or French. They included the works of two of the most famous poets of medieval Scotland, Robert Henryson and William Dunbar. In Henryson's poem *Orpheus and Eurydice*, the title page incorporates the Tree of Knowledge on which is hung a shield with the initials WC entwined. Androw Myllar's earlier books had a windmill on the front page.

Walter Chepman prospered as a merchant and was acknowledged as the 'King's Printer'. So much so, that he was able to found and endow a chaplaincy at the altar of St John the Evangelist: '*in honour of God, the Blessed Virgin, St John the Apostle and Evangelist and all the saints for the healthful estate and prosperity of the most excellent lord the King of Scotland and of his most serene consort Margaret, Queen of Scotland and of their children; and also for the health of my soul and of Agnes Cockburn, my present wife and of the soul of Mariot Kerkettil my former spouse.*'

Ironically this charter is dated 1st August 1513.

The death of his king and patron did not deter Walter Chepman's rise in status. On 24 October 1514, a year after Flodden, we find that Walter Chepman, Dean of Guild for the City of Edinburgh, was witness at a trial for murder.

He served King James V as he had James IV. For his 'labours in dictating and writing royal letters' in 1526, Chepman was paid £6:13s:4d and £8 for the 'king's new work at Leith' with the same the following year. The Leith works probably were the new harbour planned in the reign of James IV. Evidently the printing press was still running, as Walter Chepman was referred to as the King's Printer in 1526.

In 1527 he was expanding his interests by leasing 'the King's Meadow' in Edinburgh for £13:6s:8d with 'leave to plough the dry ground which was not fit for hay'.

Obviously business was booming as he founded another chaplaincy at the altar of Jesus Christ in St Giles in 1528 and endowed it by giving the rents from a tenement in the Cowgate for living expenses.

In 1536, Walter Chepman was in possession of the Estate of Prestonfield, on the outskirts of Edinburgh.

So far there has been little to suggest a Selkirk connection other than the coincidence of a surname. However, in a loose sheet in the Walter Mason Trust papers there is a document that infers that Walter Chepman kept faith with the people of his birthplace.

'*In September 1544 David Chepman burgess of Edinburgh by virtue of a breve of donation given and sealed by Robert Chepman undoubted patron of the chapel of Blessed John the Evangelist through the late well remembered Walter Chepman, burgess of the burgh of Edinburgh* [founded] *under an invocation of Blessed John the Evangelist situate in the collegiate kirk of St Giles in the same burgh and at the altar of the same chapel and there the said David, by virtue of the breve of donation, gave and sealed through Robert Chepman undoubted patron the same chapel, the discrete man sir Ninian Brydin the chapel present and accepting the same chapel* [now] *in the hands of the said Robert Chepman and as confirmed by the death of the late sir John Keyne last chaplain in possession of the same left vacant with all his holy rents, profits, oblations, death payments and all pertinents* [page torn] *chalices, booths, missals and vestments ... institutes and inducts the said sir Ninian to possession of the benefice of the said chapel.*

Sir Ninian asked instrument done in the said chapel at 10am before sirs John Hountar, John [illegible] *chaplains, George Elwand.*'

Beneath the stiff legal jargon it is seen that sir John Keyne (whose family were in Selkirk) had been given the benefits of Walter Chepman's donation of an altar. When both had died, Robert Chepman (Walter's son) had passed on the benefits to another Selkirk priest, sir Ninian Brydin. Family and local loyalty were as strong in the

Borders as they are now; and Selkirk people look after each other when in strange territories.

THE BURGH SCHOOL

A lot of our knowledge of this period comes from the Burgh Court Book where minutes show that sir William Brydin, the supposed hero of Flodden, was clerk to the burgh and in charge of the common good.

One small entry in the Burgh Court Book for 30 July 1519 under the heading 'Brydin', shows that there was a school in the burgh. This entry gives the cost for '*Thre donattis iis, viii donattis, ix graice bukis xxd, ane qwayr of paper viiid*'. The Donatus was the standard grammar of the period and could be found in any grammar school, but these together with nine grace books and quire of paper suggests a reasonably sized school for a small Border burgh. It is likely that sir William Brydin, was the schoolmaster in addition to his other duties of priest, clerk and notary.

While transcribing the Protocol Books, we noted that all the early clerics of Selkirk wrote in a practically identical hand-writing. This has confused the transcribers of the Burgh Court Books who suggested that they were all the work of sir Ninian Brydin. However, the existing Court Books start in 1503 and if sir Ninian was still working as a notary in 1564 that would be an almost unbelievable life span for a working cleric in the Middle Ages. It is more likely that sir William Brydin taught calligraphy to his pupils and that their writing would imitate his own; thus the writing of John Chepman, John Brydin, John Michelhill and Ninian Brydin are remarkably alike. This made life difficult during transcription, and it was with relief that we found the notaries liked to sign the documents and add their own cartouche, usually with their initials within the design.

It is likely that the school, which lay on the north side of the church, was a seminary for training priests. The five mentioned were all priests of the diocese of Glasgow. A quick skip through the published Protocol Books reveals another fifty priests involved in the thirty-six years covered; most were 'sir', some 'master', some 'chaplain' and others simply 'priest'.

This seems an excessive amount of clergy but they were not all in Selkirk. They travelled about the countryside, acting as notaries over a diverse range of subjects from marriage settlements to apprenticeships and property transfers to wills. Most of the population were unable to write or even sign their own name.

One undated entry in the Burgh Court Book is: '*In wytnenes of the quhilk thing I have twecychit the pen with my hande in presens of sir Niniane Brydin and Jhone Chepman bailey of the burgh for the time and Jhone Jonsone, sir Vylliem Chapman, chapellane, David Jonsone with divers others.*' Evidently the touching of the notary's pen was sufficient to indicate acceptance of the document.

Even quite substantial landowners were unable to sign their name without their hand being guided by the notary. When Janet Scot of Howpaslot required a marriage contract, it had to be read out by sir John Chepman. It was: '*Done at Farnele at* [blank] *am, John Chepman notary public with his own hand*'. When she wanted to sell property, the deed was signed and sealed '*Janet Scot with my hand at the pen. Thomas Makdowell of Makerstoun with my hand at the pen*'. And certified by '*Alexander Young notary public in witness of the above*'.

HEALTH AND HYGIENE

In the Burgh Court Book, the most numerous entries are about changes in land tenure, disputes and debts. In second-equal place are the 'watch and ward' reminders and *pro re publico* decisions on health and hygiene within the burgh.

The burgh of Selkirk was contained within a square kilometre in the sixteenth century and had a variable population of around six or seven hundred. Like any small community in an insanitary age with lack of knowledge of infectious diseases, Selkirk suffered from periodic plagues and infections. In the Court Book, we see a gradual awareness of the causes of plague and how to prevent it from entering the burgh. We cannot tell how successful these measures were as there are no burial records or mortality rates during the epidemics. We can only judge the severity of the outbreak by the number of steps taken to preserve the health of the community.

In the Court Book 1503–1545 there are five entries banning movement of people between infected places and the burgh: town gates were watched to prevent the same, and suspected persons were to be quarantined; two entries for presumed sick people to be quarantined outwith the town; eight entries for the removal of middens: seven orders to prevent pigs roaming the streets and one each of disposal of waste, street drainage and town wells.

THE PLAGUE

Bubonic or pneumonic fever spread to humans by rat fleas and then from human to human with a very high mortality rate. Whether the rate was high in sixteenth-century Selkirk, or whether the already unsanitary conditions in the burgh had given the inhabitants a measure of immunity, is not known.

Health awareness was one of the concerns of James IV's Edinburgh and in January 1513 'Kingis Lettres' were sent to all burghs with suggested methods of preventing the spread of plague. It is not known if Selkirk received one.

In 1515 the tax on the burgh of Selkirk was reduced '*because that thai war heriet be thevis and pestelence*', showing the plague had visited in that year.

In 25 October 1519: '*This inquest ordanes na man to pas to Edinburgh nor to nayn other place that is foull quhill this xv dayis, bot geff it be for ane maid herand and leff askit and optenit of the balyeis under the payne of viiis and vi of ilk man that hes passit and brokyn command of the balyeis as without favour.*'

This is a serious instruction restricting movement to Edinburgh, but if special business had already been arranged they could be given leave to travel by the baillies. Edinburgh, being a national capital, had travellers from the Continent and England and thus more chance of the disease being spread.

On 12 July 1530, the baillies and community had to go to those who had been to Edinburgh or any other place which was infected with the pestilence and command them to stay in their house for eight days.

The pestilence was widespread in Edinburgh and the Lothians in 1530, and the indwellers of Selkirk were forbidden to visit any fairs, near or far, in case they bring the 'seikness' back with them. Failure to obey this order was expulsion from the town for forty days and a fine of eight shillings. The forty days was a standard period of quarantine

However, this edict meant that no trading could be done, so it was amended to require men to swear by their great oaths, whether or not they had been where there was pestilence. Four men were posted at the eastern end of the burgh and required all travellers to swear that they had not been in contact with any infection.

However on 4 October 1530 four Selkirk men were accused of being '*suspekit with this violans pestelence*' and were ordered out of town to go and live in the alders on the bank on the opposite of the Ettrick until they were proven clear of infection. The running water was seen as a barrier against the disease.

On 4 April 1535 two 'giltene breders' (guild brothers) brought infection into the community and forfeited their freedom of the burgh for a year, were fined eight shillings and further endured the judgement of the community to be expelled.

Several more plague visitations are noted in the records including a letter from the king to the Warden of the West March charging all Borderers and others not to go to market with Inglismen for fear of plague.

MIDDENS

In early sixteenth century Selkirk there was no organised disposal of waste. The inhabitants simply piled human and animal waste outside their houses or in the open kirkyard, until it could be collected and spread on the fields as manure. Naturally, some people would collect it periodically as it was a valuable commodity, while others would leave it for a year to mature.

It must be remembered that cows were kept in the byre behind the house and taken out to graze freely on the common land under the supervision of the burgh's cowman. They got milked before they went out and/or after they came in; but this left a twelve-hour gap when they were in their byre, and a lot of cow muck can be voided in that time.

So middens grew up beside houses, or in any convenient open space. Some of the midden sites would be enclosed with a small dyke; others would be open for stray pigs to root and hens to scratch in. In wet weather the rain would soak into the middens and emerge as filthy moisture to run down the open drain on the street.

As most of the water used in the town came from surface collection wells, some of this 'noisome' water found its way into the wells. In a dry summer, the level of water in the wells fell and the bacterial count rose, resulting in an increasing death rate amongst the children: adults and older people were probably more immune having survived their own childhood.

The Kingis Letteris to the provost and baillies of Edinburgh was an order to: '*clenge rewes, windis, closes and gutteris, bayth on baksyd and foresyd … and that na personnis lay middings at portis or entres of oure said burgh*'; and later to '*mak clene before ther durris and closes and clenge awa the filth tharfra*'.

Selkirk took the hint and made it the responsibility of each house-holder to keep the street area immediately in front of his/her house free from waste and sewage, but not everybody complied.

20 October 1520. A baillie court and inquest of fifteen ordained that all middens lying between the wall and the kirk wynd be removed within fifteen days and all stray pigs be confined.

18 December 1522. All middens in the market street to be cleared within fifteen days '*under payne of an unlaw*'. The areas round the market cross had the worst record owing to the amount of market waste generated and it not being the responsibility of any one person.

October 1536. had two entries recording that all the middens be cleared within ten days and another two weeks later, repeating the order with a limit of eight days.

In October 1540, the baillies and officers were instructed to see that all middens were cleared within fifteen days.

Maybe some of the middens were kept quite clean. On 18 March 1538, James Doungell took an act that Jok Mynto had slandered him in the presence of the open court, that he saw him lying with a woman in a midden. No verdict was given in this case.

Drainage must have been a bit of a problem. With open drains running down the side of the street, it must have been a temptation to pour liquid waste out at the front door but at least it would help to flush away the more solid items. This could cause problems.

On 30 October 1526, a dispute between two neighbours came to court who gave the verdict that: '*This inquiest findis that the vatter that standis betuex Jhone Jonsone and Jok Scott it suld pass throu Jok Scott* ['s property] *in the auld guttur quhair it was vont. Alsua we ordand Jhone Jonsone scheild to be set within hymself* [his property] *and the fyltht to pass throu himself* [his property?] *and nocht throu Jok Scott.*'

Obviously there was some bad feeling between the neighbours.

The inhabitants of the southern side of what is now the Back Row solved the problem of waste disposal. In those days, the Haining Loch drained along the hollow south of the Back Row and formed the Easter Pool, roughly where The Bield is now.

This was such a convenient dump that it soon filled up until on 19 March 1531, the baillie court and inquest of sixteen ordained that no man shovel muck into the Easter Pool but give the water free passage as it had before.

Selkirk's Common Land

As seen above, the use of the vast lands shared by Selkirk, neighbouring villages and landowners, was likely to have been given by David I in the first half of the twelfth century. Over centuries of custom and usage, it gradually became known as Selkirk Common despite the fact that others claimed, and used it; but even in the early sixteenth century it was big – 11,200 acres or 4,550 hectares.

There is no evidence that it was ever given to Selkirk by the king of Scots at any period, but in the Burgh Court Book there is an entry for 24 March 1517, after notes that the last tax should be gathered, the night watch be four men and a failure to pay debts, there is an item: '*We ordand yow balyeis to caus certane discret and eldest men in the towne in Pais owk ryd the boundis of the commone and incontinent to discharge thaim occupyis the common quhil tham.*'

Basically, this orders the baillies to get sensible old men to ride the boundaries of the Common and eject those who occupied the common unlawfully. Selkirk had claimed its Common, a decision that would cause endless trouble in the years to come.

This entry appeared many times in the following years.

It is an entry nineteen years later that gives us the boundaries of the claimed South Common. 22 April 1536. *'Pro Re Publica. Rydding of Our Commones.*

'Be tenor of the thre protections laufully proclamet and be verteu of fredome and neu and auld infeftment of oure freedom of Selkyrk, Gilbert Ker, sone and air of Andreu Ker, alderman of Selkyrk, in name of his fader and honorabill men, James Scott, Jhone Mithag, bailyeis of the tyme, with all and sundry burges inhabitouris of our foresaid burgh of Selkyrk passit in fut and hors and raid the soucht sid of our common, all excepand the merches of Quhitmur and Quhitmurhall, all utheres rycht merches, werkis, mesoris, dikis, usit hantit of befor be cognicion of our wel-belovit aigit men undervrytting quhilkis begought and raid merches of Hanyng, Hartvodburn, Norcht Synton, Voster Lillescleif, Freir Schaw, Mydlam, Prestoun, Hors Rig, Quhytlaw Hous, Lynden, Kyrkland, Greenheid and the foresaid weil avyssit landemearis hes founding na wrang dyking within their fredome.'

So the South Common marches seemed fine except that an entry in the Book dated the next day, finds a complaint from the inhabitants of Midlem that their land was from the townheid of Midlem through the common of Selkirk to Cowblanburn and Prieston dykes to their land called the Red Acres and passing the Eastfield of Midlem, and had been recognised as Midlem Common from past memory of man.

On 1 May 1535: *'the North Common was ridden by the worthiest and best men with many others. The bounds were between Parlowbank and the West Mains of the Earl of Angus's lands in the hands of Sheriff Patrick Murray, Carterhaugh and the Duck Pool on the north part and down Yarrow Water until it comes to the back of the Waulk Mill and sometime Corn Mill and the Philophaugh dykes til it comes to the Hareheid field through the meadow called Dymmisdale; over the burn called Philopburn up to the waterfall of the hill called Lamelaw til it comes to the great cairns of the Three Brothers; down the north slope of the hill to the dykes of the Yair. And there they found a fault in the common boundary on the south side of a syke and our land-measurers set up a cairn of stones where the dyke should be made. Whereupon our bailies witnessed this and young William Wood in the name of the Goodman of the Yair promised to remove the dyke and build it where the cairn indicated. Also at Yair Burnfoot, John Watson has built a shiel on our common and has promised to remove it within a year and a day and with tolerance to pray for the King for a year. Also in that place near the Yair, a green [field] with alders in it amongst the stones under the ford of Fairnile and down to the middle of the Tweed to Howdenpots Burn and there a portion of dyke was wrongfully taken by master Thomas Ker of Sonderlandhall. And at the command of the alderman and balyies, he has promised to take it down. Then through Sonderland's dykes, Unis Clois dykes down to the Ettrick and then the lands of Brigheuch on the north side where it comes down to Saint Thomas ford. But our land-measurers find that John Frier has taken a lint field on the south side of the road above the lake and the ballies forbid him to use it any more.'*

The Protocol Book of John Brydin, Ninian Brydin and others 1526 –36 notes a further riding of the north marches carried out by the

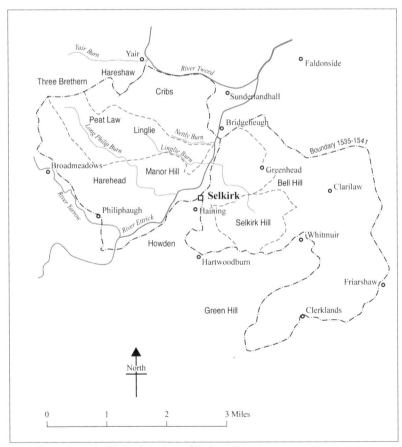

Map information reproduced by kind permission of Dr Symms.

baillies and a number of burgesses on the 25 May 1535. No. 262 in the
Book records that the: *two sheils anent the Yair were knocked down as was a*
new dyke built by 'yonger Voll of Wod' and master Thomas Ker in Sunderland
as well as a portion of the dyke on Tweedsyde and another over the Yair Pots.
They also noted that James Ker of Brigheuch had wrongfully manured and
sowed corn on two rigs below Brigheuch beside the Kirkburn.'

The two rigs were to prove a bone of contention between James
Ker of Brigheuch and the community of Selkirk. When James V
granted the power of electing a provost in a charter dated 2 October
1540 (see below), John Muthag (Mittag) was found able to be provost.

James Ker had '*rave up and tilled the two rigs in 1540*' so the
community summoned him and his accomplices to appear before the
Lords Court in Edinburgh and won the case. While riding to
Edinburgh for the third production of proofs, Provost John Muthag and
Baillie James Kein were ambushed and slain by James Ker, Ralph Ker
and William Renton.

A more detailed description of the North Common occurs in the
Court Book when the Riding was led by Baillie James Scott on 21
September 1541. When Dr Peter Symms was studying the Burgh Court
Book, he produced the map of the Selkirk Common from the infor-
mation therein.

CHAPTER FOURTEEN
The Life and Times of
sir Ninian Brydin

It would be good if we could find a diary of a Selkirk person writing eyewitness accounts of their personal experiences during the first half of the sixteenth century, but no such luck. The nearest we can get to that is the Protocol Book of sir Ninian Brydin which covers the post-Flodden period to the years after the Reformation of 1560. In this time, he witnessed and recorded one of the most interesting periods of Scottish, Borders and Selkirk history.

In this chapter, I intend to use sir Ninian's Protocol Book as a dating ladder of local interest but also mixing in what was happening in the wider world of the Borders and Scotland in the appropriate places.

We know little of Ninian's early life but he first appears as a witness to a land lease in the Burgh Court Book dated 24 May 1524, the other witness being sir William Brydin. Then as 'sir Ninian Brydin', he was witnessing the town's accounts on 17 October 1525. Some time between those dates he had become an ordained priest. Let us assume that he was about twenty years old when he took Holy Orders; then working backwards, his date of birth must have been around 1505.

We have to imagine Ninian growing up in the far-from-safe Selkirk at the beginning of the sixteenth century. We don't know for certain who his parents were because he maintains a strange reticence about them, and this is unusual in a small town where family connections were important. But we can speculate that Ninian was probably the son of sir William Brydin, who was town clerk at that time.

For some reason, the Selkirk pre-Reformation clerics openly acknowledged their daughters but not their sons: these were 'emes', a word which could mean a close blood relation or friend. The Selkirk of the period was a 'Brydin' town. There was often a Brydin as one of the baillies and five of the literate Brydins were priests, notaries, vicars, chaplains or clerks – two Johns, a William, a Richard and eventually Ninian himself.

His Early Life

If Ninian was born around 1505, he would know these were troubled times, and would see the men of the town carrying out nightly duties of watch and ward round the back dykes. To say that Selkirk was a walled town would be a gross exaggeration: the 'walls' were earthen dykes probably about two metres high and with stone buttresses only at the three ports or gateways. Usually nine men were deemed a sufficient nightly guard but this could be doubled or trebled in times of danger.

Ninian would hear the stories of the troubles as when, in 1502, Sir John Musgrave led a party of English into the town and made off with goods to the value of 1,000 merks.

However, Selkirk did not receive quite the same adverse attention which many other Border towns and villages often did. It was further from the border line than Jeddart and the richer Teviotdale. As a king's burgh, it did not suffer the family feuds that were carried from one generation to the next and even the English wardens *might* have hesitated in destroying the king's burgh. Then again, the Court Books show that the burgh had a very vigilant home defence. Selkirk could have been too big and aggressive for small bands of reivers to tackle; too out-of-the-way and poor to make it worth the trouble for a more substantial raid.

He would certainly have seen the Selkirk contingent departing to join the king's army on its way to invade the north of England in 1513 and viewed them returning from Flodden. He would have been ideally placed to record these happenings but, unfortunately he didn't. He would see the effects of recurring plague on the burgh and the steps taken to prevent it.

His First Appearance

Although he had signed as a witness in 1524, Ninian makes his next appearance in the Court Book as 'sir Ninian Brydin' on 17 October 1525, a signature which is just below that of sir William Brydin, the town clerk (scriba de Selkyrk). This might be a coincidence but probably not.

This document was an important legal instrument confirming the burgh court's decision to get all the burgh measures (metlumes) checked to see that they gave the correct weights. The proper measures were to be burned i.e. branded and the others destroyed. Ale was to be priced at twelve pence a gallon if it was good, otherwise at eight pence a gallon; ale conners were to decide the prices. Market regulations were set for wheat, meal, malt, bere and bread. The burgh's accounts were to be checked by the baillies, clerk, priests and the other important people of the town.

A later entry in the Court Book defined the regulated positions of the various stall-holders in the market: the chapmen merchants on the south side of the cross; the cordiners (leatherworkers) on the south side of the tollbooth; wool, skins, cheese and butter about the tron; the meal market where it was before; other foodstuffs east past George Lydderdail's house (now site of Royal Bank), and all to the east of the tollbooth; the market of horse, cattle and sheep in the easter part of the town about the forges. The wood-market to be at Hallewolhill.

In the small burgh, the clergy were in effect the professional class of the community because of their education and social standing. They were expected to stand out in the community, the chaplains to be cleanshaven, to wear a cassock of dark material, a white linen shirt and a round bonnet. The clergy were the writers, the recorders, the teachers, the advisers and the arbiters in disputes as well as being religious leaders. One of their most important services to the community was to act as notary especially in recording and adjudicating in the transfer of land.

So Ninian had joined this upper class of Selkirk society, and for the next two years we find him witnessing land settlements, arguing about rents, collecting proofs and trying to collect a rent which he swore was due on '*aythe be his prestheid*' (his priestly oath).

OUTSIDE SELKIRK
1513–27

Outside the narrow confines of Selkirk and its common, the Borders and Scotland carried on in the usual state of confusion. The thieves and traitors of Liddesdale, Ewesdale, Annandale etc, now freed from any semblance of authority, were rampaging throughout the Borders. Ker of Cessford and Scott of Buccleuch were at feud and numerous other feuds raged within and over the Borders.

James V was crowned king of Scots when he was seventeen months old and the kingdom was ruled jointly by the Regent Albany and the Dowager Queen Margaret. They did not agree, since the Regent pushed the French interest and a French army in Scotland, while the queen, sister to Henry VIII of England, favoured an English alliance. As a marriage of convenience, the queen married Archibald Douglas the sixth Earl of Angus less than a year after Flodden, but it was not successful and divorce followed, complicating the politics of post-Flodden Scotland even further.

A fragile peace was signed between Scotland and England which lasted for nearly ten years, but this had little effect on the Borderers who followed their own ways of life.

In pursuit of the English alliance, the Queen wrote to the Earl of Surrey, chief Warden on the English Border, urging him to bring an army into Scotland to aid her and 'rescue' the young king. Surrey wrote back that he had a large army hovering on the border ready to invade Scotland, and intended to burn Jedburgh and spoil the surrounding countryside – a medieval way on how to win friends and influence people.

In September 1523 Surrey did invade the eastern Border with 10,000 men. He destroyed much of the Merse on his way to Jedburgh, which he captured and demolished on 24 September. Surrey had difficulty destroying the town since the wily indwellers had torn the thatch from the roofs and burned it in the streets before the English got there. So Surrey had to distribute three hundred sixpenny axes to cut down the wooden houses before they could get the fires going properly. Obviously, there were very few stone-built houses within the town.

That same evening, the invaders' horses were stampeded into the English camp and the archers, convinced that they were being attacked by the Scots, shot at and killed many of them. Others were killed by galloping over the steep river bank, some rushed into the burning town and were roasted, while many more were caught and led away by the country people. In writing his account to Wolsey, the Earl blamed 'the devil and six times of spirits and fearful sights'. He went back to

England claiming to have totally destroyed Jedburgh and devastated the Merse and Teviotdale.

In retaliation, the Scottish regent had arranged to gather an army of French and Scots for the invasion of England. The French force arrived in Scotland in mid-October, which was too late for a campaigning season. However, the Scots/French army set off to invade England at the end of October 1523, but when they came to cross the Tweed at Melrose many of the Scots refused to go further as they did not like the way the campaign was being conducted. So the now mainly French army crossed to besiege Wark Castle, while the mainly Scottish Border army waited on the north side of the Tweed at the Abbey of Eccles. On hearing that a large English army was approaching, the Regent quickly withdrew his forces back across the Tweed.

At Eccles, a further dispute arose as the Scottish Borderers were now anxious to give battle, since their homes were being threatened. The Border lairds pointed out to the Regent that the French had yet to fight against the English despite all the time they had been in the country, and that any parts of the Borders left undestroyed by the Earl of Surrey had been more completely 'wasted' by the French. The large French force had eaten much of the food stored for the winter and burned most of the fuel.

It was by mutual consent that the French force left after six weeks in the country. The Regent was so annoyed at the turn of events that he departed for France shortly afterwards, swearing never to return to Scotland.

Meanwhile, the Earl of Angus, Queen Margaret's second husband, had returned from two years exile in England to find that his wife had divorced him to marry a younger and better-looking husband. The queen dowager is said to have had 'a bewildering succession of liaisons', a trait also observed in her brother Henry VIII of England. This created an enmity between Angus and the queen which could have worked in Selkirk's favour since both Angus and the queen had vested interests within the burgh and its surrounding lands.

Angus, as head of a mighty Douglas faction, won the contest for supremacy and a peace was concluded with England on condition that the lawless Borderers were subdued. Angus himself had a surprise raid into Liddesdale, capturing twelve reivers and burning many houses.

Even the church entered into the fray when the Archbishop of Glasgow pronounced what was probably the most lengthy and vituperative curse in history, cursing every aspect of each reiver's life, body, family, home and general existence.

This curse was read in every church in the diocese of Glasgow which included Selkirk. It is likely to have been met with supreme indifference by those at whom it was aimed, for the reivers cared as little for religion as they did for the law of the land. Theirs was a struggle to exist in a very hostile world. They had few virtues other than being noted for always keeping their given word. Any Borderer who broke his sworn word was considered as being completely beyond the pale of civilised Border behaviour. The Bishop of Durham read out the same 'monition of cursing' on the English reivers with equally futile results.

In the year of 1526 the Earl of Angus had not only declared himself as Warden of the East and Middle Marches of Scotland, but also had guardianship of King James V, now a lad of fourteen. Angus brought the king to Jedburgh, which must have been surprisingly quickly rebuilt, to hold a justice eyre. The basic purpose of this court was to hang any reivers careless enough to have allowed themselves to be captured. The famous 'Jeddart Justice' was to hang the prisoner first and ask for evidence afterwards, a quite logical progression when dealing with reivers.

James resented what was virtually captivity as Angus was ruling the kingdom through him. So James sent secret letters to Sir Walter Scott of Branxholm and Buccleuch, begging for rescue from the 'tyranny of Angus'. Sir Walter, recognising the benefits of having the young king in his debt, set up an ambush at Darnick to surprise the royal party on the road back to Edinburgh.

Lord Home and the Kerrs of Cessford and Ferniehirst had escorted Angus and the king to near Darnick and had left their procession when Sir Walter made his move. At first it seemed that Scott, with 600 followers, would win but the Kerr faction returned to the fray and chased them from the field. During the hot pursuit, James Elliot, a Scott retainer, turned and killed the Laird of Cessford with one stroke of his spear. This renewed the Scott/Kerr feud with greater intensity than before.

Sir Walter Scott, known with justification as 'Wicked Wat', was charged with treason and had to retire to France for his own safety; James Elliot was hanged on the same charge.

Ironically, in the protocol book shared by John and Ninian Brydin, in a legal instrument dated 16 March 1526 or 7 the baillies of Selkirk proclaimed letters from the king, warning Archibald, Earl of Angus, James, Earl of Arran and James Hamilton of Finnart not to molest Walter Scott of Branxholm, John Cranstoun of that Ilk, Walter Scott of Synton or their kinsmen or men, under penalty of forfeiture of their estates. The deed finishes '*On the same day, Walter Scot declared to all having an interest that the said lords had attacked him and his kinsmen and that he and his kinsmen on behalf of his excellency the king, had expelled them into their own parts.*' Truth was one of the many casualties in the Borders at this time.

James V eventually escaped from the clutches of Angus and Arran in 1528 and got the chance to put his own ideas into practice. As I have put the affinity between James V and Selkirk in a later chapter, I will concentrate on the upward movement of sir Ninian.

NINIAN: THE FIRST STEPS
1528–39

Meanwhile back in the relative peace of Selkirk, we assume that Ninian was going about his priestly duties. The Burgh Court Book tells that he was witnessing deeds, arranging to collect rents, and that two merks were placed '*in handis and sour keiping of schir Niniane Brydin*' on 28 August 1528. This showed that he was now considered to be a trusted person in the small community.

A Court Book entry of 2 February 1527 shows schir Niniane Brydin was designated as 'chappelaine'. In pre-Reformation Scotland the title of chaplain was often applied to a clergyman who did not have a parochial duty ie the financial benefits of serving one of the altars in the parish church. In the Borders, we find that some of the greater lairds kept a room in their household to serve as a chapel/office where a priest could hold religious services and conduct secular business as required. Thus the laird could claim his own chaplain and the priest his own chapel. It was a mutually beneficial arrangement since the resident priest could record any of the laird's transactions in writing if required and read out any letters sent to him, as few of the lairds were literate.

By now, Ninian was starting to make a name for himself, for we find him witnessing transactions for the more important people of the area. The Court Book entry for 1 July 1529 starts '*In presence of schir Ninian Brydin, notary public*'. Now he had his foot firmly on the ladder.

The notary provided one of the most important offices in the burgh. He was there literally to note ie to put down in writing, any transaction which took place and which might be queried at a later date. Ownership or occupation of land was perhaps the most important facet of burgh life and had to be absolute in its correctness. The slightest doubt or question could cause tension and dispute. The same could be said about the marriage settlements, agreed debts, wills and verbal agreements. The clergy provided literate services in a small community like Selkirk. So the notary was essential to the smooth running of the burgh and his protocol book held the ultimate proof of any transaction. Therefore the notary had to get it right. As a notary public, Ninian would require to have had some legal training and knowledge of the terminology.

A notary's licence to practise came from one of three sources – the Pope, the Holy Roman Emperor or the king. Ninian's came from the Pope through the prebendary of Glasgow and the notary apostolic was not restricted to any area which meant that he was free to move around as he wished.

Now Ninian was able to fulfill all the legal requirements from land transfer to marriage contract. One cunning lawyers' twist was to make a law that no document was legal until the notary had been paid, usually the sum of around four pence.

But Ninian wasn't totally dependent on his legal and priestly earnings, as an entry on 26 February 1531 states that Ninian had a rig 'upone the knowe' and a further Court Book entry of 23 July 1532 orders David Brydin to give Ninian a cow which had been in milk since Candlemas, a calf of that age and a five-year-old cow. This farming endeavour must have been successful since we find him renewing the lease for four years in March 1532. Rigs were about two acres in size, enough land to provide basic foods for the people in what was a mainly crofting community.

On 7 December 1529 he took another public office when an inquest ordained that ale be sold in the burgh at no dearer than 16d a gallon, but allowing those who wished to sell it at 12d a gallon to do so.

The aleconners were duly sworn in on 16 February 1529 and at the end of the list was '*schir Niniane Brydin quhen he may pas*'. We think that this means that Ninian got to try the ale every time he went past. However, the ale could be reduced in price – 12d a gallon for the best and 8d a gallon if the ale-conners thought it was inferior. Occasionally we find that Ninian's writing slopes downwards at the end of each line although this might have no connection whatsoever.

It is not to be assumed that sir Ninian was an over-imbiber; drinking water in the burgh could assume almost lethal propensities, so ale was a necessity of life and, if you have to drink ale, you might as well drink good ale.

He was also given the keeping of the church offerings box which had two keys, one kept by the vicar (sir William), and the other by Simon Fairlie.

In the Burgh Court Book of 14 February 1531 sir William Brydin acts as procurator on behalf of Janet and Elizabeth Portus in an agreement with John Brydin, easter. At the bottom of the entry is '*Ita est Ninianus Brydin*'. Clearly Ninian was standing in for sir William who could not be clerk and pleading counsel at the same time. Fortunately for transcribers, Ninian tended to be somewhat of a graffiti artist and liked to see his own name.

Twelve days later, an entry in one of the previously published Protocol Books has sir William telling the sheriff and inquest that there was nothing to impede or contradict that bargain. This Protocol Book of 1526–1536 had several changes of writing in it. During transcription, we were able to identify sir John Brydin's and sir Ninian's and could classify it as 'the Protocol Book of John and Ninian Brydin & others'.

It is around this period that Ninian's handwriting can definitely be identified and he seems to have shared the legal responsibilities of that Protocol Book until the end of 1536. It is unusual for two notaries to share a Protocol Book, but it may be that Ninian took over the book when sir John started the new one dated 1530–37.

His legal practice was thriving too, for on 28 April 1534 he was taking proofs of a dying oath and '*immediate I, schir N B passit to my chalmer with the said preiffis*'. Now we know that he had a legal chamber in the town.

On 23 May 1534 he was '*schir N B notar and common clerk*' and was writing up the Burgh Court Book. His presumed father, sir William Brydin, comes up in the book as '*vicar of Selkirk*'. From then on, Ninian appears in the Court Book as 'notary', as 'our clerk' or as 'common clerk' and the sentence '*Ita est N Brydin*' is a regular occurrence; sometimes this varied to '*Ita est N Brydin scriba*' to show his clerkly authority.

On 4 March 1536 Ninian was leasing out the market weights and profits for two years, on behalf of the community. This was because of a charter from the king giving Selkirk the right to elect baillies, to hold an annual St Laurence Day Fair and for eight days thereafter, with the right to buy and sell many commodities. This is also noted in other Protocol Books. This important concession from the king is given in detail below.

On 22 November 1538 Ninian was complaining that he had not been paid the fee '*that he and his predecessors gat in all tymes past as use is in all borrowes tounes*.' The community said that they would pay when all the greater bills had been paid. Ninian then gave them a 'shrine' (box) to keep the common seal, charters, instruments, king's letters etc., for safe keeping. However, John Mithag was to mend it and put locks on it for security. This was the same John Mithag who was murdered by the Kers of Brigheuch on 25 July 1541.

On 23 June 1539 sir Ninian was one of the public-spirited citizens who lent the burgh the sum of 5s. The reason for this need for money becomes clear when, later in the year, the king granted a new charter to the burgesses, giving the power to elect a provost annually, exempting the burgh from the jurisdiction of the Sheriff of Selkirkshire, and commuting the burgh dues and petty customs for an annual payment of five pounds.

OUTSIDE SELKIRK – THE PEEL TOWERS

During this time the Borders were in more than their usual turmoil. Buccleuch and Ker raided each other's lands, often with English help, and accused each other of doing so; at other times, large-number raids went into England. The English retaliated, sometimes in advance, burning most of Teviotdale practically every year. The Armstrongs,

Elliots, Nixons, Beatties, Grahams, Bells and Crosiers of Liddesdale and the Debatable Lands raided in every direction.

Liddesdale was not the only Border valley to have its share of villains. At the High Court in Edinburgh in the presence of King James V, William Cockburn of Henderland, Yarrow, was charged with the High Treason of bringing in Englishmen to plunder Archibald Somerville; and for 'Common Theft, common reset of Theft, outputting and inputting thereof'. On 14 May 1530 the verdict was death by beheading.

On 18 May 1530 Adam Scot of Tuschelaw, Ettrick, was convicted of taking blackmail or 'skatt' from the poor tenants of Hopcailzow and Eschiesteil. Also beheaded.

In 1535 the Scottish Parliament passed an Act that every man living in the Borders who possessed a hundred-pound land: '*shall erect a sufficient barmkin* [the walled enclosure round or beside a castle] *upon his heritage and lands, of stone and lime, sixty feet square, an ell* [1m] *thick and six ells high for the reset and defense of himself, his tenants and his goods in troublesome times, with a tower for himself if he thinks it expedient. And all other landed men of smaller rent renew the great peels and strengths as they please for the saving of themselves, their tenants and goods. And that all the said strengths, barmkins and peels be built and completed within two years under pain*' [fine for non-compliance].

This Act was responsible for the construction of most of the peel towers which, in ruins, still dot the upper valleys of the Borders. Until this Act, there were few strongholds in Ettrick Forest but after 1535 the words '*with manor, tower and buildings*' replace '*with manor and buildings*' in documents.

At the same time, more and more of the Forest stedes were being feu-farmed. In this system, the tenant would pay a larger rent together with a grassum (lump sum) when he entered or inherited a property, and in return he had security of tenure and a new status as a landed proprietor. Although the rents were increased when the land was first feued, they could not be raised afterwards. In Ettrick Forest, the new feus often confirmed possession in the hands of those who already held the land in tack, thus stabilising the basic structure of the local community.

But what was not taken into account in feu-farming, was the fact that Scotland was suffering from inflation through the continuing debasement of the coinage, and the longer the possession, the less worth the fixed rent became. This worked well for the men who lived in the Forest but not so well for the Crown.

With security of tenure, the stede-holders could build permanent structures of stone. Although they are called towers or castles, in fact most could be more accurately described as fortified farmhouses. They were pitifully small by modern standards with an internal floor space as little as 4.5m by 3.5m, a vaulted dungeon for storage, an upper floor for living quarters and a garret under the roof for servants' or childrens' sleeping quarters. The more substantial peels had two living floors in the middle rather than one. Despite this, the interiors did not provide much space for the laird and his immediate family. (I have heard a modern proprietor of one of these refurbished towers remark that he would have more room in a council house. A peel tower has three rooms built vertically but enclosed in metre-thick walls.)

It is thought that larger buildings within the barmkin were the actual living quarters and the peel was the place of safety if required.

The peels were strong enough to deter the casual raider or sneak thief, but when a large force appeared, burning their way up the valley, the inhabitants would take their belongings and drive their flocks into hidden fastness in the hills, hoping to be undetected or at least unmolested. Invaders were reluctant to pursue unless in large numbers, fearing an ambush amongst the hills.

If the peel was burned, the stonework took little hurt and a new roof could be quickly replaced. As Wat Tinline recounted after an English raid:

> They cross'd the Liddell at curfew hour
> And burned my little lonely tower,
> The fiend receive their souls therefore
> It had not been burnt this year and more.

This is no poetic license as there are records of towers being taken and burnt twice with one year. As is shown below, the 'town' of Ladhope in Yarrow was burnt twice within five months.

But not all fortifications were made of stone. Bishop Lesley describes how the Borderers: '*construct for themselves towers of a pyramidal form which they call 'pailes' entirely of earth which can neither be burnt nor overthrown without great exertion on the part of the assailants*'. Another account describes strong block-houses made with squared oak baulks, mortised together and covered with turf. These may be the later forms of the motte-and-bailey towers of the Normans, but even Craig-Brown writing in 1886 was not aware of any surviving examples. There could be an easy answer to this, in that wooden buildings eventually rot back into the ground while stone buildings collapse in visible heaps.

It may be that '*the great peels and strengths*' that lesser men were encouraged to re-fortify were hillforts. Several Borders hillforts of Iron or Dark Age construction have produced later medieval finds that would date to this period. Two rectangular buildings of unknown date have been recently noted in a '*place called the Dungyon*' recorded by Lord Dacre in 1513. This report suggests that the Dunion fort was already in permanent occupation before the Act of 1535.

Marion Dalgliesh, Her Goods

The size of a peel tower would suggest that the indwellers were poor, with little material wealth. Deuchar Tower in the Yarrow Valley is one of the smaller towers and now a heap of rubble; its main chamber would be around 7m by 6m maximum.

Marion Dalgliesh was the widow of the owner of Deuchar, and as such was entitled to a terce (third) of his estate. Despite now being married to the laird of Howford in Ettrick, she was reluctant to give possession of Deuchar to her son(?) Adam Dalgliesh so he had to take legal steps to remove her. This included placing a 'stress' chair outside the tower to signify that she was being evicted.

She moved out on 11 August 1540. One would expect that her possessions would be few in number. This is not so. Her goods are listed below; I leave the inventory in the language in which it was written to exercise the mind, and punctuation was not considered necessary for understanding.

'*Item in primis ane clois lokit met almery with gudis contenit in to quhilkis we knaw nocht ane caldron quhilk contenes four gallones ane panne of thre quartes ane less panne ane mekyll pot of fyv quartes ane less pot of thre quartes twa pouder* [pewter] *plaittis twa pouer deiches ane tyne pynt ane chandlair irne speit with ane fut ane girdill with four feit ane veschel almery thre dublairis ane*

ark with certane meill thre f [irlot?] *of estimaciounne ane lytill kyst ane quarter*
of gret quhit ane dry wair with malt in it ane tub with barkit ledder with certane
dry bark and curnes of woll that is all broken extendis to iii quarters ane pair of
auld hoiss Item ane stand bed in the spenss with twa blankattes ane pair of
scheittis twa codes coverit ane [page torn] *ane barnes kyrtill Item ane upp sek*
with bouster uther twa auld pair of scheittis ane covering chalander work thre
auld plaidis ane pair of doubyll blankattis ane uther auld blankat ane kirtill of
blak ane creill full of brokin woll viz half ane stane twa kyrnes ane wyth dry
malt viz thre peks ane uther with mylk ane caissair for cheiss [page torn] *chess*
thre hukis ane spounges ane pound of hardis [page torn] *ane pair of auld cairdis*
ane pokit of ae agit vomanes with certane lynning and auld quhit four ail peiggis
ae sap peig fourtene less tubbis and mair fyv you [yew?] *coigis four chessairis*
with ane ter kyt ane cruyk and ane pair of tangis twa [apes?] *baikbredes half*
ane firlot of salt twa pair of schoune ae doubyll ane neu purss with twa silver
rynges ane gylt twa rubbene beltis twa courchesses ane short curche and ane collair
ane [pokat -scored out] *paitlot of volnoss ane schappinne pair of sleiffes and*
not sevit [ie sewn] *Item ane uther pokat ane spinok of* [volnoss – scored out]
saitting thre courchess iii colleris ane schort courchess with ane snod of vorsat the
thrid pokat ane collar of blak saitting ane lossyn serk ae pair of grene sleiffes viii
ells of lynning ane pair of scheittis twa sleiffis of russat ane auld lossyn serk twa
blak hattes with ane tibpat ae pair of blak houss with rubenes of blak ane kyrtaill
of Ingliss brovn with ane silk laiss ane auld serk ane schort coit with vanes of
velvot ane gown vanet with velvot of crenseid ane jak of plait twa lanss staiffes
ane saddill clath sevin hankes of hardin yarne twa cleves twa auld scheip skynnes
ane purss of the lassis with ane belt of vorsat ane burd with twa formes ane chir
quhilk vas ane stressis of removing twa flaikes to ane boucht ane cok with twa
hennes ane hen with xii burdis ane knokin trouncher of tre / twa quheillis twa
yarne vonnettes ane paire of buttes ane auld tub with bark ane pair of schoune
ane hoiss kayne [comb?] *ane chess burd ane stull with ane roundaill.'*

Although some of the items are kitchen utensils and farmyard stock,
the bulk of the inventory are the possessions of a lady of some wealth
and a considerable wardrobe.

These could not all be stored in a small tower, so this reinforces the
speculation that there was a larger house within the barmkin and that
the peel tower was kept as place of safety in time of need. As an
additional insurance policy, many of the local lairds kept a house within
the burgh of Selkirk.

Gibbie Hately of Gattonside, His Will

On the other hand, the last will and testament of Gibbie Hately of Gattonside Peel, gives an insight to the life and times of a peel–dweller in the more arable lands near Melrose in 1547. This document came to me in an already transcribed form; there may have been some Scots words unknowingly typed as modern English, but I pass them on as received:

'*To Geordie Basten, for the muckle fash he tuke wi my plant land when I couldna attend to it myself and the expensive drive to the mercat o Stirlin for which he couldna be prevailt upon to tak ony thing – na, no sae muckle as the price of a single thousand o plants; to him I leave two ruckles o turves, two winraws o Rab's bog peatis and a lypit-spade and a flaughter-spade for sactin the same.*

To Patie Dickieson for his kindness and attention e'en tho he had gotten a thum[b] cuttit aff at the Elwan Brig by his brither in a duel; for a this he gar'd his menis saw the Cotland barley and the brumseed [broomseed] on the face o the brae, the plantis in the Abbots Meadow and the pickle yaits on the east nuke o the Quarterland and a capfu o linset on the Harper's yard; To him, I leave a yait riddle wi the airne rim, my three best wechts and the brumseed bicker wi the brass lugs, my waster and my fishin tackle.

To Andrew Fisher o the Wast Houses, for helping me when I fell into Hamilton's Burns wi haudin the quachen owre often to my head on the Stears, Thursday fairien. I leave him my hazle staff with the bane head, my best bonnet and hazen and the new shoon that Willie Fair brought me frae Sandy Inglis o Selkirk, made o gude buckis hide and the soles o the same made o the big boar shotten by the Laird o Faldsup; also all my farmin oozlles and snuff-horn, happit wi siller.

To kind Adam Ormistane, the hangman o Embro, for helping my father out o prison the nicht before he was to be hangit for killin ane o the King's deris on the Kaldshiels Muir and the king's forester o the Merouse [Melrose] end o the louch wha was unco keen to mak him his prisoner for killin the beast he had nae right to; to him, I leave my great-grandfather's siller tanker and ane quachen which my great-grandmother receivit frae the Laird Maitland for helping nurice his brother Robert; Also my father's gowd ring in which the emeraud he promisit to Adam Ormistane gif he could slip him out o the window o the prison unseen which he faithful did for the luve he bore my father.

> *To the Laird o Langshaw, I bequeath my braidsword and durk.*
>
> *To the Laird o Hislop, all my hawkis and houndis.*
>
> *To Laird Usher, my brither-in-law of Faftenfield, a hundred merks Scotis and my nobbler and the two auld pricklers which I took frae the lads o the Border when they came ae nicht to harrie me.*
>
> *To my brither-in-law commonly callit Langsword o Fadonside, I leave two hunder merks Scotis.*
>
> *To the Abbot and monchis o Maurose, I leave four hunder merkis Scotis, to pray for my soul and the weel-fare o my sonne Jock.*
>
> *To Jock, I leave a thousand merkis Scotis, ane Cotland and ane Quarter-land, the Abbots' Meadows and the auld Peel which I hope in God he will keep frae a the English loons as his forbears hae weel dune afore him.'*

As usual, wills are full of information. Plants are likely to be kale plants; turves are for roofing; while winraws are rows of peats drying in the sun; yaits are oats; brumseed are broom seeds which are still colourfully growing on the bank behind Gattonside. Andrew Fisher obviously pulled him out of the burn after over-imbibing at a Thursday Fair. Wild boar were still running wild at Fauldshope in Ettrick Forest, where poaching was illegal and carried the death penalty unless you had a gold ring with an emerald in it to buy your way out of prison. Obviously Border reivers were ranging as far as Gattonside despite every effort of king and Wardens.

NINIAN
1536–45

To return to sir Ninian Brydin, the last entry of the joint John and Ninian Protocol Book is dated 2 June 1536 and was enacted in Selkirk. From now on he was striking out on his own with recognition as a priest and notary. The first entry in his book was a precept giving the lands of Haliburton in the sheriffdom of Berwickshire, to Margaret Haliburton as heir of her father Patrick, lord of Haliburton and it was done in the chapel of Haliburton on 10 December 1536.

In the period 1536 to 1546, Ninian's Protocol Book gives an insight into the life within and without the small royal burgh of Selkirk. Most of this is dull – land transactions or debt settlement, though some are interesting because of the various actions or people involved.

Court Book *27 January 1539*. The baillies shall drink one gallon of ale of every man that brewed 16 penny ale. It had to be priced by an aleconner and the bailie had to chalk the price on the door of each hostel which sold it.

Taking a selective sample of the entries in Ninian's book we have:

No. 48 *May 1539* tells of the 'removal' of sheep from Lewinshope in the Yarrow Valley by one Alexander Elliot and his friends.

No. 49–52 *May 1539* is a dispute between the Scotts of Branksholm and the Scotts of Howpasley about the possession of Fawside in Yarrow.

No. 60 *June 1539*. John Hawe, smith, promises not to extend his forge by placing a linen thread round the bounds of his yard to mark its extent.

No. 71 *June 1539*. Gilbert Ker the alderman, and the two baillies of Selkirk appointed a day of weaponshowing, but the community did not come to it and therefore they had let themselves and the burgh down by not obeying the king's letters.

No. 75 *July 1539*. Valuation of the king's sheep. (James V was a major flockmaster in Ettrick Forest with the wool being gathered in Selkirk and sent to Leith for further transmission to the Low Countries. See p.462)

No. 96 *Undated*. Letter from Martin Creichtoun of Cranston Riddell to the Lords of Council, complaining that sir Ninian Brydin would not let him have a copy of the division of lands in Yarrow which were to be shared between himself and Janet Beaton, widow of the late James Creichtoun (and later the third wife of Sir Walter Scott of Buccleuch). As a widow, Janet Beaton was entitled to a terce, however she seems to have kept possession of the total estate.

No. 118 *February 1539*. Precept of Removal (flitting) from the lands of Bolton in the constabulary of Haddington and sheriffdom of Edinburgh.

No. 124 *March 1539*. Slander that Alan Young of Hartwoodburn stole a number of ewes from Margaret Young and ate them. Alan swore on the Holy Bible at time of high mass, that he was innocent of the charge.

No. 133 *April 1540*. Stress stools, creels etc to be put outside the houses of the inhabitants of Lower Bolton as a sign of immediate removal. (This was a legal warning that if the tenants did not vacate the premises voluntarily, they would be forcibly ejected.)

No. 140 *27 May 1540*. The baillie and whole community of Selkirk complain that the Sheriff of Selkirk, Patrick Murray, should not collect the small customs and burgh taxes. (An entry in the Court Book shows that the burgh were already canvassing to have the burgh customs commuted to a yearly sum of five pounds paid directly to the king.)

Nos 141 to 143 *27 May 1540*. These entries tell the story of the battle for the balance and town weights at the tron between the servants of Patrick Murray and the would-be sellers and buyers in the Selkirk Market Place. Whoever controlled the burgh weights received the taxes of the weekly markets.

No. 145 *Undated*. This is a tucked-in copy of a letter of conduct giving leave for an Englishman W.G. of S., to pass and repass through the Middle March, provided that he does nothing harmful to the Queen's realm or leiges. It was signed by Walter Ker of Cessford who was warden of the Middle March.

No. 150 *June 1540*. Agreement for lambs in steelbow.

No. 157 *11 October 1540*. A 1,500 word entry relating how a new charter from the king conferred on the burgh the right to elect a provost and bailies who would also be Sheriffs of Selkirk; the right to have walls, trenches and water ditches round the town; and commuted the burgh's petty customs to £5 annually.

This instrument was enacted in each house within the burgh and sealed by payment of one penny. The entry finishes 'Q Brydin. Glory to God and King James V' (The entry appears in the Court Book in an abbreviated form.) This appears in detail on p.463

No. 168 *January 1540*. Agreement for the price to be paid by John Scot for having slaughtered Walter Downe, flesher burgess of Selkirk. Firstly, John to come to Selkirk parish kirk in linen clothes, to kneel humbly on his knees, offer his sword to James Downe and ask forgiveness. Secondly, to go to all the four head places of pilgrimage in Scotland. Thirdly, to say Mass for Walter in the place where the bones rest. Fourthly, to pay Walter's wife and bairns 20 merks at four terms of the year. Fifthly, to be friendly with all Walter's brothers and kinsfolk.

Paying to keep the widow and bairns would seem to be a more practical option than hanging the killer.

No. 172 *March 1540*. The wand of peace (a legal pardon) delivered to William Elliot as he has now returned to the king's law.

No. 186 *June 1541*. James, Commendator of Kelso Abbey, gives the lands of Cauldshiels to James Lowre for services rendered. A letter from James V warning the Commendator and his friends to keep his hands of the Selkirk Common appears below.

No. 188 *June 1541*. A measure of ale placed in the house of George Michelhill for safe keeping (?). (This was likely to have been the 'Selkirk Stoup', the container used to set the standard measure of ale to be sold within the burgh. Other Border burghs had their own, widely varying measures eg the Hawick Gill and the Jeddart Jug.)

No. 198 *August 1541*. Lands of Sunderland Hall, given to Malcolm, Lord Fleming. They had previously belonged to William Cockburn of Henderland who was 'heidit' in Edinburgh for several acts of treason and crimes against the crown.

No. 199 *August 1541*. Adam Murray, servant of Patrick Murray was threatened by a certain burgess while he was gathering 'shireffis gluffis' (sheriff's gloves) at the St Laurence Day Fair in Selkirk. (The 'sheriff's gloves' was probably a local name for the market rentals; or they could be a sweetener or bribe to the sheriff for his good will – although this might be doing Patrick Murray an injustice.)

No. 221 *April 1542*. Lengthy list of the material delivered for the repair of Newark Castle. This fits in with a loose letter in the Walter Mason Trust collection, from James V to the magistrates of Selkirk asking them to provide fresh supplies for the use of 'our workmen and masons repairing our place or castel of Newark'. (See p.466)

No. 225 *May 1542*. Alexander Hoppringil of Craiglatch causing a disturbance in Selkirk marketplace and letting the blood of sir Peter Syntoun. Alexander hoped that this would not turn to his prejudice.

No. 236 *September 1542*. John Cossair willing to wed Katherine

Mathieson provided he gets a house and croft and his choice of one of four kye. John will give a boll of meal and one of bere and put boards on a kist in return.

No. 256 *February 1543.* Valuation of two horses. One white old blind horse, thirty shillings; a little old nag with the front feet splayed out might be worth ten shillings.

No. 289 (This was a loose sheet bound out of sequence dated January 1547.) Rent of four acres of land in Dirleton set at two rabbits and a load of coal, presumably a horse-load. Rabbits were a rare commodity at that period.

No. 293 *October 1543.* Walter Scott of Branxholme, knight, chosen provost of the burgh of Selkirk by all brother burgesses of the burgh. (Presumably nobody else wanted the job after seeing what happened to John Mithag, who was murdered two years previously.)

No. 339 *No date, loose page inserted.* This is a detailed bill for what seems to be a wedding feast. Included are items of food and clothing, a spousing ring, gloves, a whinger (short sword) and even '*that nicht he was mareit in his purss v shillings*'.

No. 359 *March 1544.* William Elliot gives his bond to bring back George Downe (Englishman) as a safe man from Walter Scott of Branxholme or Perse Elliot, his captors.

No. 384 *Loose page inserted.* John Stevinson promises to pay sir Ninian six shillings and six pence for bed and room for one year, whenever he requires it.

By September 1544, sir Ninian had moved to Edinburgh to receive the benefices of the Chapel of the Blessed John the Evangelist in St Giles and the entries in his book are centred there for the next fifteen years.

OUTWITH THE BURGH

Meanwhile, let us see what was happening in the surrounding Border countryside outside Selkirk and in Scotland as a whole. Things had deteriorated rather than improved.

James V's marriage to two French ladies in succession had annoyed Henry VIII and caused extra tension between the two countries. The

English king was determined that Scotland should embrace the Protestant religion, and there were a considerable number of Scots who wished to do so, although this was probably more for political and territorial gain than religious conviction.

Henry summoned his nephew to a conference at York in September 1541 but James did not attend, thinking, with some justification, that he would be kidnapped. Henry was livid and ordered immediate war. A force of three thousand horsemen under Sir James Bowes came into Teviotdale, but were routed at Hadden Rig by Huntly and Home; six hundred prisoners were taken including the English Warden.

This made the choleric Henry even more furious and he ordered the Earl of Surrey, now the Duke of Norfolk, to gather forty thousand men and burn every castle on the Scottish Borders. Norfolk replied that there were none, as he had burned them all twenty years before. However, he reluctantly did as ordered, crossing the border on 21 October 1542 and burning Teviotdale including Jedburgh once again. He refused to advance towards Edinburgh because of a lack of beer for his troops: beer seemed to be one essential commodity which no English army could march without.

The pillaging ceased when he could no longer find enough food in the devastated countryside and, a week after crossing the border, he returned to Berwick where, presumably, the beer was plentiful. This is not a facetious comment but an indication that beer was regarded as a source of nourishment.

Meanwhile, James had gathered an army near Edinburgh to oppose the invaders and retaliated by raiding the northern counties of England. Many of the Scots nobles would not agree to invade England once they heard the news that Norfolk had withdrawn his troops. James managed to persuade ten thousand men to march with him into England, among whom would have been a number of Selkirk men. In the Burgh Court Book, orders for a muster are recorded on 17th October 1542 '*for the common weill of the gud toun and for thankfull service of our soverane lord his luffin tenentis and legeis*'.

However, they did not get as far as England. The king took ill and remained at Caerlaverock Castle while the army camped at Solway Moss. Here the leaders fell to quarrelling amongst themselves and were surprised by a party of English horse under Lord Dacre, who put the Scots army to flight and captured many noble prisoners. The shame of this defeat completely broke James's spirit and he died a fortnight later, some say of a broken heart but more recent medical thought suggests that it was a form of plague. He left a week-old daughter, 'a very weak child and not likely to live', as his successor to the throne – Mary Queen of Scots had began her troubled reign. The regent was now Mary of Guise who pushed French interests in Scotland.

James V – the Borders / Selkirk Connection

On his maturity, and with the ability to act on his own right, James V seems to have had a particular interest in Ettrick Forest. Like many kings, he was a keen hunter and contemporary records show many entries relating to sporting expeditions into The Forest.

In September 1529 there was a bill for £3 for two ells of Paris-black to be a cloak for the king to ride to hunting in Meggetdale. A few months later, £3 was paid to carry the royal pavilion from Peebles to Meggetdale.

It must have been while hunting in the Forest that James became aware of the devastation caused by the thieves and reivers from Teviotdale and Liddesdale. He tried velvet glove tactics at first. In 1529 he went round the Borders, taking assurance of good behaviour from local lairds and known felons. This did little good as, in November of that year a day-raid from Liddesdale was pursued by the English Warden's men, who rode straight into a Liddesdale ambush and lost twenty men.

James tried more direct methods. In the spring of 1530 he summoned the Border lords to Edinburgh and threw them into prison for failure to keep order. Adam Scott of Tushielaw and William Cockburn of Henderland were tried for various crimes 'and heidit' with their heads displayed on the Tolbooth of Edinburgh.

On 2 July 1530, James rode out of Edinburgh with eight thousand men to hunt in Meggetdale and much of Ettrick Forest. From there, the king with his retinue went to Caerlanrig in Teviotdale where he met up with, and hanged, Johnie Armstrong of Gilnockie. This provided the Borders with another great ballad, but the event was officially recorded as 'John Armestrange, alias Black Jok and Thomas his brother convicted of common theft and reset – hanged'.

This act might not have earned the king many friends in Liddesdale, Upper Teviotdale and the upper parts of Ettrick Forest but did make him friends in the area around Selkirk which had suffered from the depredations of the reivers.

James married Madelaine, the daughter of Francis I of France, on 1 January 1537, but she died in July of the same year having spent a mere two months in Scotland. Less than a year later James had acquired another French bride, Mary of Guise, and a second dowry into the bargain. They had two sons but both died in infancy before 1541.

With the French connection, James was allied to the Catholic cause, whereas Henry VIII of England, James's uncle, was trying to persuade him to cast his lot with the Protestant religion. This did not make for easy relations between the two already disturbed countries and the Borders took the brunt.

James V was an interesting character who is sometimes ignored by being between his charismatic father James IV, who died spectacularly on the field at Flodden, and his beautiful but unfortunate daughter, Mary, Queen of Scots.

James V was as much a Renaisance man as his father. The Palace of Linlithgow and Stirling Castle are evidence of his interest in architecture. Like his father, James V was anxious to take his place as one of the foremost kings in Europe and, like his father, was frequently short of funds to develop his aims. However, James V was a much more successful fund-raiser than his predecessor.

Amongst other accomplishments, James was a skilful diplomat manipulating the religious politics of Europe for his own ends. At this period, the Catholic Church owned about half of the most fertile land in Scotland and thus was ripe for take-over. The Scottish Catholic Church had become a lucrative dumping ground for illegitimate royal offspring. Five of James's under-age bastard sons★ held revenues from the wealthiest abbeys and priories in Scotland, in total producing

---

★ He had nine bastard sons, proving that infertility was not the impediment to producing a legitimate male heir for the throne. It is ironic that one of the sons, James, prior of St Andrews, was a figurehead of the Protestant revolution of 1560.

around £40,000 for the royal exchequer, a sum greater than the revenue from the rest of the kingdom. Successive popes were prepared to turn a blind eye to this legalised robbery to keep Scotland within the sphere of the Catholic Church, and as a counterbalance to Henry's Protestant England. Through six new taxes levied from 1533 onwards, James managed to fill the exchequer box that accompanied him in his travels between royal palaces.

As a king, James V's influence on Selkirk and Selkirkshire was second only to that of David I.

The tenure of the Forest stedes changing to feu from the original tack, meant more security for the inhabitants, and the Act of 1535 encouraged them to build permanent peel towers in stone. It is not entirely a coincidence that this combination enriched the exchequer as well, with the large initial entrance fees, the 'grassum', and the greater rents to be paid.

But the change from short-term tack to long-term feu did not always benefit the inhabitants. In the Protocol Book of sir John Brydin 1530–37, we find on 29 March 1536 that master Thomas Cranston was given the feu of Elburne (Helmburn) for the new rental of £22 at 11 o'clock. This was followed by '*The same day, master Thomas warned all the inhabitants of the tack of Elburne to remove themselves and their goods from the place and lands of Elburne between this* [day] *and Whitsunday.*

After having had a go at the reivers with little lasting success, and placing the Ettrick Forest on a more economic footing, James turned his attention to the burgh of Selkirk itself. At this time, Selkirk was a small and poor community, largely self-sufficient, with most of its requirements grown, raised or made locally. A settlement of around six or seven hundred population, it was the only sizable community in the area and, as such, became the shire-town and focal centre. Local trade and agriculture were enough to sustain the inhabitants but the standard of living must have been low. Taxation records shows that the burgh contributed £65 Scots to the exchequer for the years between 1521 and 1539, but a special effort had been made when £105:0s:8d was found in 1536, to cover the cost of the charter giving Royal Burgh status.

Included in this charter was the privilege of having a Fair. This was not simply a gift as it might seem, nor was it just a bigger version of the weekly market held in the burgh. A Fair drew in traders and customers from a wide area, giving people the opportunity to buy from a larger range of products; and a Fair in a royal burgh meant that none of the neighbouring towns could hold a market during the eight days of the Fair. This resulted in an influx of people coming into the town and, for the magistrates, a highly profitable income boost from stall rents.

It also meant an increase in the customs dues paid into the royal exchequer. As can be seen in the king's grant below, this must have gone some way to compensate for the '*great damage of his Majesty in the matter of customs*'.

From the Great Seal Register iii No. 15,55
Given at St Andrews, 4 March 1535

'*Whereas the charters of the old foundation of the burgh of Selkirk and its liberties granted by the King's progenitors have for the most part been destroyed through assaults of war, pestilence, fire and others whereby the usages of trade have ceased among her burgesses to the great harm of them and of the commonweal and to the prejudice and great damage of his Majesty in the matter of customs, the King has infeft of new, to the burgesses and community [of] the burgh of Selkirk in free burgh with the commons and possessions belonging to the same with the power of electing bailies, of holding a fair annually on St Laurence day and during the octaves thereof with court-house, prison, power of holding burgh courts and with the liberty to buy and sell wine, wax, ale, spices, broad and narrow woollen and linen and other merchandise whatsoever, and of having bakers, brewers, vendors of fish and flesh as freely and in the same manner as any other burgh within the kingdom: To hold of the Crown in fee and heritage and free burgage for ever, for the payment of the burgh fermes and other duties, use and wont as in times past.*'

This charter appears in a slightly condensed form in the Protocol Book of sir John Brydin 1530–37. On 22 March, before the whole community, the sasine was given to the bailies, James Scott and John Mithag and accepted by John Chepman, John Brown, Alexander Gledstains, burgesses for themselves, other burgesses, the whole community and others living in the said burgh. This was done at the mercat cross and repeated in the North and South Commons before a long list of witnesses.

Wishing to take full benefit from the new possession, the Council had the St Laurence Day Fair proclaimed by criers with handbells at the mercat crosses of the burgh towns of Hawick, Jedburgh, Kelso, Peebles, Melrose, Haddington, Lauder, Lanark and Linlithgow '*in all goodly haste*'. This was done to refill the burgh's resources because a king's charter does not come cheaply. For the expenses incurred in the procurement of the charter, the burgh taxed its existing inhabitants and added the entrance fees of twenty-six new burgesses to make up the sum of £105:0s:8d, of which £57:8s:4d was given to sir William Chepman for his labours, seals and writings of the infeftment of the said burgh.

James Scott and John Mithag were appointed bailies for the time being and John Chepman was given the task of keeping the charter, seal and precepts of the king in 'our common box'. The council further ordered that all the documents should be copied faithfully and put in the sure keeping of three faithful men. This duplication was to lessen the chances of the destruction of valuable documents as had happened previously.

With even limited power comes responsibility. Both the annual Fair and the weekly market had to be well policed by the magistrates, as there were those who would take the advantage to buy or sell without paying the market customs, defrauding both the burgh and the king. In the Protocol Book of John and Ninian Brydin 1526–36, we find that, on 12 October 1535 '*William Vilsone, Thomas Goven, David Jonsone, Robert Hauden, William Winterhoup and their accomplices came on Thursday to the mercat place with a view to waylaying both openly and secretly the burgesses of the said burgh and they gave signals and used tricks and devices to let men selling goods know that they should slip away secretly with their goods for sale to inns, so that all defrauded the customs and the weill of the burgh to the hindrance of all indwellers of the town.*'

Thereafter followed five court cases discharging and recharging the villains. One legal eagle quibbled that the letter from the king did not mention the '*market*' constituted in the burgh of Selkirk (it was the Fair) and '*why all Scots men should not have licence to buy and sell their goods*'. Eventually the case was settled with only William Vilsone, burgess, being disbarred from selling in the market.

These six entries show that tax-evaders, slippery lawyers and dicey justice are not just modern inventions.

Realising that cultivated land could produce more in food and revenues than the Forest pastures, James gave the burgh the right to clear and plough a thousand acres of the Common lands, which could be cultivated or leased for rent. Logically, and from later records, these would be the Linglie, Smedheugh and South Common farms which are still in possession of the Selkirk Common Good Fund to this day.

From the Great Seal Register. iii No. 1773

At Stirling, 20 June 1536.

We, for the good, true and thankful service done and to be done to us by our beloved baillies, burgesses and community of our burgh of Selkirk and for certain other causes, grant licence to them and their successors to clear, break and till 1000 acres yearly of the common lands of our said burgh in what part that they please, for policy, strengthening and building the same for our good and that of our lieges protection and defence against our old enemies of England and others; and will and grant that they shall not be called or accused nor incur any danger or harm through this in their persons, lands and goods, notwithstanding any of our acts or statutes made or to be made to the contrary – with power for them to occupy the said lands with their own goods or to rent them to tenants as they think most expedient for the benefit of our said burgh with free exit and entry. Given under our signet and signed by our hand.

James R

This favour was repaid on 20 July 1535 when Selkirk contributed £9:5s:6d as its proportion of a £6,000 tax to pay the expenses of an embassy to France to negotiate the king's marriage. It happened to be money well-spent as James eventually married two French ladies and secured two substantial dowries thereby.

Two months later, Selkirk was further privileged with another Fair.

From the Great Seal Register. iii No. 1773

At Kirkcaldy, 2 September 1536.

We, understanding that our burgh of Selkirk and the inhabitants thereof [have] continually since the field of Flodden, been oppressed, herried and over-run by thieves and traitors whereby the 'hant of merchandice' [literally the practice of trading] has ceased amongst them a long time past, and [they] were herried therethrough, and we were defrauded of our customs and duties – therefore and with other reasonable causes moving us, of our kingly power, free motive and royal authority, [we] grant to them and their successors [the right to have] *a Fair Day beginning at the Feast of the Conception of Our Lady* [8 September] *next to come and by the octaves of the same perpetually in time to come.*

  Subscribed with our hand etc James R.

James V – The Wool Merchant

This seeming generosity was not given without some ulterior motive. Dr Peter Symms in his paper 'Some Aspects of the Sheep Farming Activities of James V' puts forward an interesting and probably correct theory that James was protecting his interest in the wool clip from his Ettrick Forest stedes.

  Sir Ralph Sadler, Henry VIII's ambassador, had clyped to his master that James had ten thousand sheep grazing in Ettrick Forest. Henry wrote to James that being a flockmaster was not commensurate with a king's estate. James denied that he had any sheep although admitted that there might be some grazing on royal land.

  In fact the Treasurer's accounts show that in 1535-6 his wool crop was being collected at Selkirk. From figures given, Dr Symms was able to work out that this clip would be around 12,760 pounds of wool being stored and processed in the burgh before being packed for onward transmission. This obviously created some employment in Selkirk.

From the Lord High Treasurer's Accounts of Scotland.

Wages, food and drink for the shearers and carriage of the wool to the store in Selkirk	£19:18s:0d
A lock for the storage loft in Selkirk	1s:6d
Canvas for making wool packs	£17:5s:0d
Pack thread	8s:1d
Carriage of the canvas to Selkirk	2s:0d
Weighing wool at the Selkirk tron	2s:0d
Packing and porterage in Selkirk	£3:1s:8d
Carriage of 35 packs to Edinburgh	£10:10s:0d
Marking fee	£1:2s:0d
Candles	4d

Porterage at the tron in Edinburgh	12s:7d
Wages and food for the packers	£3:4s:8d
Carriage of the wool to Leith for shipment	£1:18s:0d

	£58:14:6d

As James was making a profit of around £1,333 Scots per year from his sheep and cattle, he was in no mind to heed his uncle's advice.

More Royal favours were to come to Selkirk in 1540.

From the Protocol Book of sir Ninian Brydin, is an entry 'pro re publica'.

'In the name of God Amen by this present public instrument dated 11 October 1540, in presence of me notary public and witnesses underwritten in the Head Court of the Burgh of Selkirk held in the Court House of the same, after the feast of St. Michael, by John Mithag, John Bridin then bailies of the same and by reason of the same charter and practice of the bailies and community of Selkirk and their successors given and granted by our supreme lord king under the great seal at St. Andrews the 2 October 1540 by which charter, practice and authority read out, made public and declared in common tongue by me notary public underwritten in the same court an election was held of provost and bailies of the said burgh, as was the use in former times by the discretion of worthy burgesses of the said burgh, and an inquest of the same and the said persons after they were elected by the inquest were sworn outside, inside and on entering the court house [illegible] John Mithag [was elected?] provost and James Scot and James Keyne bailies [illegible] within the burgh and freedom and bounds of the same following the tenor of the said charter and practice of the bailies and community of the said burgh granted as foresaid by our supreme lord king named and elected which election is by right and as use is in the burgh, the worthy man William Haw sheriff in that part by letters of our supreme lord king under his signet specially constituted to the within written produced the said letters of which tenor follows in this form "James be the graice of god king of scottis To our lovittis William Haw Jhonne Brown Villiam Burne our schireffis in that part coniunctlie and soveraly specialie constitut gretting forsameikill as it is humely menit and schawn to ws be our lovittis burgess inhabitairis and commonite of our burgh of Selkirk that we for diverss racionabill causs and consideraciones moving ws hes gevin and grantit licence faculte and fredome to the saidis inhabitairis burgess and

comonite and thairis successouris to cheiss and haw ane provest and baillies
within our said burgh to minister iustice to thaim and all utheris dwelland within
the fredome of the samyn and to that effect hess maid and constitut thaim and
thairis successouris ouris schireffis in Selkirk within our said burgh liberte and
fredome of the samynne for evir in tyme cumyng as the infeftment gevin to thaim
thairupone proporttis quhairin our shireff principaill of Selkirk his deputtis and
officiaris ar dischairgit of all calling atteiching summoning and persewing of the
saidis burgesses inhabitairis and commonite and thairis successouris before our
said schireff principaill his deputtis and at the instance of all personis and of all
trubling inquietaciounne and perturbacionne of thaim and thairis successouris
thaim and thairis landis and gudes for quhatsumevir causs accionnes concerning
thaim in tyme to cum and of thairis officies and iurisdictiones in that part and
the saidis burgess inhabitairis and comonite exemit thairfra for evir as saidis Our
will is heirfor and we chairgis yow straitly and commandis that incontinent thir
ouris lettres sen ye pass and in our nayme and autorite tak and resave the aythes
of the saidis provest and bailies of our said burgh now chossin or to be chossine
be the saidis burgesses inhabitairis and comonite for leill iust trew administra-
ciounne to be maid be thaim and thairis successouris within the samynne to the
inhabitairis thairof in all tyme cumyng conforme to the said infeftment for the
causses abone vrytting according to iustice as ye wil anschir to ws thairupone the
quhilk to do we commit to you coniunctlie and soverary our full power be thir
our lettres delivering thaim be you [illegible] *execut and indorsat agane to the*
berar gevin under our signet at edinburght the vii day of october and of our regnne
the xxviii yeiris.'

The original document was in Latin and was given a translation
into 'the common tongue' so that everyone could understand it.
Similarly, the first part of the Protocol Book entry was in Latin, which
we transcribed into English, and the second part, giving the 'common
tongue', we quote at length above as an example of the written
medieval Scots of the Borders.

After that, William Burn, as sheriff in the king's name, gave the new
provost and bailies one penny each and then went through the burgh
to give one penny to each householder.

At the bottom of this document is 'Q Brydin Glory to God and
King James V'.

On looking at Ninian's 'common tongue' translation, I find it quite
understandable, having Borders Scots as my mother tongue. In fact,

there is much in common between Ninian's speech patterns of the 1540s and the language I grew up with in the 1940s. In the Ettrick Valley of my youth, everybody spoke in Border Scots except for the minister, the teacher and one or two of the better-off farmers who had been sent to public schools to get the Scotticisms eradicated from their speech (as well as get an education presumably). One had to speak 'proper' in those days to get anywhere in life.

In present-day Border Scots, 'thaim' and 'thair' are still the recognised pronunciation of them and their, but 'thir' with a short 'i', is these or there; 'be' is by and the 'it' or 'et' endings are still the spoken forms of 'ed'; and there are many other similarities. Some things have dropped out of speech, notably the 'is' and 'es' ending – 'landis' becomes lands: it would be interesting to know whether sixteenth-century Borderers pronounced the 'i' and 'e' but some things have to remain a mystery. All languages have words which are not pronounced as they are spelt, or have the same spelling but a different pronunciation eg plough, rough, through and though.

Realising that this is very much a minority interest, I have tried to curb my enthusiasm and have translated many of the documents into modern English, except when I come across a particularly fine specimen of the rich Border tongue which was common to king, noble and peasant.

However, after looking at a considerable number of original documents, I was able to discern a difference between the Border Scots of the Selkirk Protocol Books and the Scots of the king's letters. As there was no standardisation of Scots in the shape of a dictionary of the written word, I can only think the difference lay in accent, and the Selkirk clerics wrote down their 'common tongue' from their own phonetic pronunciations.

James V also took an interest in what was happening around Selkirk and wrote letters to various people in the area. These would be dictated to, and written by a scribe, but signed by the king himself. These are not recorded in the Register of the Great Seal as they were sealed by the king's personal signet. Two such letters relating to Selkirk have survived. One relates to intrusions into the Selkirk Common by the officers of Kelso Abbey and the other is requiring supplies to restoring the king's Castle of Newark.

Letter from James V to the Baillie of Kelso Abbey. 31 August 1542

Rex

    Baillie of the Regality of Kelso and your deputies. It is our will and we charge that ye, bie yourself, your kin, servants and (?) portioners. Nor nane others that ye may let make onie invasion, skaith, harm or displeasure to our burgh of Selkirk or inhabitants thereof bounds and freedoms of the same in onie ways in time coming bie eating and destruction of corn sown or other ways but bie order and process of law discharging you thereof notwithstanding onie other of our private writings to the contrary. Because we have ordanit and command … to albait (?) on your most force in that time of trouble as you be requiret … be you fair and (?) again to the burgh. Given at Edinburgh the last day of August and of our reign xxix years.

    James Rex

Letter to the Provost and Baillies of Selkirk. 31 May 1542

Rex

    Provost and baillies of our burgh of Selkirk we grete you weill. Forsamekle as we have put certane masonis and various to the bigging of our castell and place of Newerk. And necessary is that thai be supportit by yow with met, drink and sic various stuff as thai myster. Oure will is heirfor and we charge yow that ye caus the nychbouris and inhabitaris of our said burgh, baik and brew guid breid and ail with fische, fleshe and various necessaries and sell the samyn of competent price to our said werkmen upon expensis sua that thai want it not quhill attending of our said werk. As ye will do ws plesser and ansuer to us thereupon. Subscrivit with our hand and under oure signet at Sanctandrews the last day of Maii and of our reign the 29 year.

    James Rex

Although this request is dated 31 May 1542, the king had already made sure that the necessary supplies were on site at Newark Castle.

Entry No. 222 in the Protocol Book of sir Ninian Brydin.

On the first day of April 1542, Sir Andrew Duncan, Chamberlain to the King's Grace in the forest of Ettrick delivered to Alexander Hoppringil in Trinlinyknowes the following timber and materials for the reconstruction of the king's castle of Newark:

Item in primis six planks of sawn ash timber 16 feet long.

*Item two planks of ash standard joists 40 feet long with a brace of ash closed at
    the head, 12 feet long.*

*Item in the hall of the castle, five iron windows, each window 5 feet long and 4
    foot broad.*

Item delivered within the castle [page torn] *planks of ash.*

Item a number of fir planks [illegible] *a plank. Item a number of planks of fir,
    17 feet long.*

*Item 10 oak boards, 2 pieces of ash, 14 window frames. Item more or less 54
    boards*

Item a meat board with 3 forms. Item two old broken joists.

Item 21 new black bands for the doors (not hung). Item 8 crooks to [page torn].

Item 48 bands trimmed for windows with part of [page torn].

Item 8 white bands for portcullis doors with white nails.

Item 20 through[?]*-rings for great and small windows and doors.*

Item 4 great catches for portcullis doors with staples and other gear.

Item 12 small catches for windows. Item two new locks with keys.

Item all this neu vork is noth put upone [?]

Item within the house nine hung doors. Item 12 hung doors, double and single.

Item diverse pieces of old timber.

Item 4 roof lofts with joists and boards closely made.

Item 12 estland [Scandinavian] *boards within the kitchen.*

Item a great iron bar [to be fitted to] *the lower iron bar* [of the gate?]

The royal arms on the west side of the tower are likely to date from this
period.

An intriguing report written in the reign of James V by Robert
Seton, commonly designed 'of Mexico', noted that gold could be found
in several places within Selkirkshire: the Glengaber burn, the
Mountbenger burn, Douglas Craig and the Linglie burn were those
noted. It is reckoned that the very rare Scottish gold coin called a 'hat-
piece' of James V, was struck from gold found at Glengaber.

This exploration was followed up by Earl Morton in 1575 who
contracted a Fleming called Petersonn to look for gold at Glengaber.
He must have been successful because he is known to have sold gold at
6s:8d per ounce to the earl. A little later, an 'ingenious gentleman' called
Bulmer was claiming that he got 'the greatest gold, the like to it no

other place before in Scotland'.

In more recent times, enough gold has been washed from the Glengaber burn to make a ring for the Master of Napier, and a post-war owner of the café at St Mary's Loch managed to pan a small quantity in the mid twentieth century. I have also seen a small amount in a matchbox that a somewhat eccentric haulage contractor from Selkirk had managed to pan out with the aid of a handle-less frying pan.

On the subject of coins: the changing design on the Scottish coinage led to each coin being given its own name: the hat-piece when the king wore a hat; a rose noble when the coin had a rose on the reverse; a 'lion' where the lion of Scotland appeared on the coin and a 'unicorn' when that mythical beast was depicted. So when a small billon coin with the infant head of Mary, Queen of Scots, was struck in 1544, it was known as a 'bawbie' or baby. In time the term 'bawbee' became used for the smallest Scottish coin. There have been attempts to pass the term as a derivation of 'bas billon' (base metal) but I have never managed to get a contemporary reference to the coin known as a bawbee before 1544 whereas there were billon coins before and after that date.

CHAPTER FIFTEEN
The Rough Wooing

—————

After the death of the king following the disaster of Solway Moss, the kingdom was now ruled by quarreling regents and it would have been easy for English forces to take the southern part of Scotland up to and including the capital. However, Henry VIII decided to try a new and cheaper plan to annexe Scotland and was determined to marry his son Prince Edward to the infant queen. The Scots lords were mainly against the idea and removed the young queen to Stirling Castle for safety.

Henry, a man of quick temper when his wishes were thwarted, was even more furious than before and ordered the Earl of Hertford to obliterate Scotland, putting man, woman and child to the sword. All buildings were to be destroyed and even the animals were to be killed. This time became known as the Rough Wooing as English armies tried to force the Scots to agree to the marriage.

After Edinburghshire, Leith, Dunbar, the Lothians and Fife had been torched, the Borders were next to suffer. Between August 1543 and December 1544 the force commanded by Sir Ralph Evers and Sir Brian Latoun devastated the Borders area. They reported 192 towns, towers, stedes, barmkins, parish churches, bastle-houses burned or destroyed; 403 Scots slain and 816 taken prisoner; 10,386 cattle, 12,492 sheep, 1,296 horses and an enormous quantity of corn and gear carried off or destroyed.

In charge of the devastation of Selkirkshire was Sir Thomas Wharton, one of the victors at Solway Moss and a veteran of many Border encounters. In the months after the battle, Wharton had been sounding out the riding families of the Scottish West and Middle Marches. By a combination of threats and bribes, he persuaded the most aggressive of them to work in England's interest as well as their own.

They were literally being paid to pursue their personal vendettas – which they would be doing anyway; this was the way of the Borders. By playing on the feuds which were endemic in Border society, Wharton was able to enlist most of the Liddesdale families to the English cause.

In the voluminous 'Hamilton Papers', a collection by the Dukes of Hamilton, the letters between the various protagonists, friends and foes allow us to follow the campaign of ethnic cleansing in the Scottish Borders. It seems that everybody had spies in each other's camps, paying bribes and making promises to induce the main players to change sides; added to this were Bosnian-style massacres and burnings. It makes interesting but not inspiring reading.

Amongst the reported wheelings and dealings are details of individual raids which were dispatched to London at frequent intervals. I have picked out those dealing with raids into Selkirkshire. In doing so, it must be noted that Scottish Borderers from Liddesdale took a major part in the raids; whether they were the main instigators acting on their own initiative, or under orders, is not known although the end results would probably have been the same. Most of the depredations were carried out in the lands of the Scott families who held most of Upper Teviotdale and the Ettrick and Yarrow Valleys.

Details of the raiding were reported to Henry VIII as they happened. It must have pleased the king to realise that he was getting good value for the money expended on the Armstrongs and other Border families who were doing the work for him. These were hit-and-run raids in limited force and the families came from both sides of the Border. On 8 October 1543, 30 Scottish Nixons, 30 English Nixons and some Elliots and Liddells burnt Rowcastle, a mile from Jedburgh, took three prisoners, ten horses, thirty cattle and hurt many people at the fight at the barmkin. The next day, the rivers being in flood, they returned home.

(In using the following figures, I have Anglicised the text and modernised the spelling of place-names. 'Oxen, nolte and kene' are noted as cattle and the 'towns' burnt were basically farms steadings.)

9 September 1543. By the Armstrongs at Wharton's command – At Ettrick, a town of lords of Buccleuch (robbed) of his own goods, 30 cattle, 200 sheep and 1 horse.

15 September 1543. By the Armstrongs – At Helmburn, the young Lord Cranston's land – 40 cattle, 6 horses, all the goods from 6 houses.

16 September 1543. By the Armstrongs – The towns of Kirkhope with the gates of the tower burnt. Baillielees and Shaws, 400 cattle, 1200 sheep, all the horses and goods from the said towns.

21 September 1543. By the Armstrongs – 160 men took Midgehope and Thirlstane, 200 cattle, 20 horses, 5 prisoners, all the goods from the said towns.

21 September 1543. By William Foster – 19 men took Eldinhope, a town of the lord Buccleuch's, 40 cattle and some goods.

9 October 1543. By the Grahams – The towns of Deloraine and Bellendean burnt, 7 prisoners brought away, 1 slain, 100 cattle.

31 October 1543. By Edward Storey and eleven others at Wharton's command, set fire in the market town of Selkirk where 'the watchmen being more in numbers than in readiness', beat the Englishmen from the town and put out the fire. And after they were chased from the town, the raiders burnt 8 great corn stacks standing on the backsides of the houses there; and in their home-coming they burnt a grange of the Lord Buccleuch's with five onsets called Huntlie, two mills on the side of Ettrick with many cattle and much corn in the stores and houses there. They had gunpowder for their better purpose and came home 'without hurt albeit they were very sorely chased by the Scotsmen'.

November 1543. By John Armstrong and other Scotsmen – The town of Howpaslot spoiled and the keys of the gate brought to Mr Wharton, 16 cattle taken and all the goods, 6 prisoners taken and 4 hurt to death.

7 November 1543. By Anthony Armstrong, John Foster etc – The town of Borthwickshiels fired and spoiled; 4 prisoners, 60 cattle, 10 horses, all the goods.

7 November 1543. By the Armstrongs of Liddesdale – the town of Annelshop burnt, 80 cattle, 200 sheep, 4 prisoners, 1 horse, much goods.

8 November 1543. By Robert Foster with others – the town of Whitehillbrae burnt; 4 prisoners, 40 cattle, 10 horses, all the goods and some hurt.

13 November 1543. By the Grahams, Fosters and others – three towns

of Essenside (Ale Water) with all the corn burnt, 1 prisoner, 30 horses, 30 cattle.

20 November 1543. By the Armstrongs – 200 men took and burnt the towns of Over and Nether Kirkhope and then Branxholm. Took 4 horses, 40 cattle and many goods. These belonged to Mr Michael Scott (of Aikwood), chief councillor to the Lord Buccleuch

8 December 15 43. By Robyn Foster and 80 others, Scots and English – the town of Singlie burnt, 1,400 sheep, 2 prisoners, 2 slain. Of the flock, 1,300 were driven over the Border, 100 were given to the Scotsmen and another 40 to a Scotsman whose horse was killed at the burning of the town.

19 February 1544. By the Armstrongs – the town of Ladhope belonging to the lord of Howpaslot, burnt; 40 cattle, 4 horses, 4 prisoners with goods.

There was a gap of five months in the reporting, if not in the actual raiding. Reiving was not an all-year occupation – the normal riding time was from August to February. There is a reason for this, as sir Robert Carey, a later Warden of the English East March would write in his memoirs: '*Border thieves will never lightly steal hard before Lammas (1st August) for fear of the assises but once that is passed, they will return to their former trade and unless in such years as they cannot ride upon the wastes by reason of snows and storms, the last months are their chief time of stealing for then the nights are longest, their horses hard at meat and will ride best, cattle* [will be] *strong and drive furthest; after Candlemass* [2 February] *the nights grow shorter, all cattle grow weaker and, oats growing dearer, they feed their horses worse and quickly turn them to grass*'.

In other words, go raiding when horses and cattle are well-fed and strong, and the nights are dark but not too dark. There is also the more practical reason that, after February, breeding stock would be unable to be driven at any speed without incurring great loss, but after August, the lambs/calves/foals would be able to keep up with their mothers. An even more practical reason is that the reivers remained at home to look after their own stock through the lambing/calfing/foaling period.

The Armstrongs must have extended the season as Lord Wharton was reporting that on:

17 July 1544. The Armstrongs ran a foray to the town of Ladhope, the
    Lord of Howpaslot's, burnt the town and brought away 1 cow, 1
    horse, many goods, 4 prisoners and burnt much wool in the town.

27 August 1544. The West and Middle Marches [men of England] with
    certain Scots invaded West Teviotdale, the Lord of Buccleuch's land
    – burnt divers towns and stedes and burnt the the barmkin of Lord
    Buccleuch's tower at Branxham and brought away 600 cattle, 600
    sheep, certain horses, 200 goats and as much goods as they could
    carry; have taken 30 prisoners and slain 8 Scots.

13 October 1544. Sir Ralph Evers reports – The Tynedale and
    Redesdale [men] with the Crosiers took the Abbot of Glasgow's
    town [Ashkirk] and took 30 horse, 40 cattle, 6 prisoners and killed
    divers Scots.

23 October 1544. Lord Evers raided Harehead [Yarrow] and took 30
    cattle and 3 or 4 horses.

17 October 1544. Certain Armstrongs of Liddesdale spoiled the town
    of Langhope [Ale Water] and brought away all the goods and 4
    prisoners.

        There is information to be gleaned from the brief and brutal
    accounts of the raids.

Ladhope had been burnt on the 17 February 1544 and again on 17 July.
The first raid took forty cattle and four horses, while the second only
produced one horse and one cow. Either the law of diminishing returns
was in operation, or the inhabitants of Ladhope were becoming more
skilled in evasion tactics. Despite this short period between the raids,
'much wool' was burnt, meaning that a large flock of sheep had
survived the first raid, had been clipped during the summer and the
wool stored for despatch.

    It is likely that the Armstrongs et al, kept some back as 'finders fees',
but the numbers of declared animals taken gives credence to the theory
that the Ettrick Forest stedes were almost as productive as the present-
day farms. The unknown factor is the number of animals hidden in the
hills and forest to avoid being stolen.

    Singlie had 1,400 sheep taken and Shaws/Baillielees lost 1,200.
Even if no sheep had been hidden away from the raiders, these figures
still denote very healthy sheep farms. The farm of Annelshope had 80

cattle, 200 sheep and a horse lifted on 7 November 1543: now, in 2009, it is stocked with 30 cows, 800 sheep and 4 horses.

In assessing the animals stolen, we would have to take into account the fact that a herd of cattle could be driven by men on horseback while a flock of sheep moving more slowly had to be herded by men on foot. This is one reason why every Border raiding party had a number of horsemen and some footmen.

The Battle of Ancrum Moor

King Henry was so pleased with the devastation caused by Sir Ralph Evers and Sir Brian Latoun that he gave them 'in absentia' tenure of the lands they had destroyed. This was a mistake on the king's part as some of the land in this premature grant belonged to the Earl of Angus who, at that time, was uncertain of his allegiance.

Evers and Latoun offered to extend their campaign into the Lothians on the same terms and provided they received more troops. Henry despatched 3,000 mercenaries and a further 2,000 men from the Borders, of whom about 700 were 'assured Scots'.

As well as the threats, Henry was trying bribery to attain his aims. The wily Wharton was meeting with Sir Walter Scott of Buccleuch whose lands had been receiving special attention. Wharton was trying to persuade Buccleuch to transfer his allegiance to England, but Buccleuch left the meeting without giving a definite answer.

Meanwhile Evers and Latoun left Berwick, hoping to surprise the meagre Scots army at Melrose, but it had retreated to Galashiels on the other side of the river. At Melrose, the invaders destroyed some property, including the Abbey where they desecrated the tombs of Angus's Douglas ancestors. This was to be another serious mistake, the results of which saw Angus joining the Scots army. While the English retreated southwards along the old Roman road of Dere Street, the Scots were reinforced by three hundred horsemen from Fife and the men of Teviotdale and Selkirk under Sir Walter Scott of Buccleuch.

Using the well-known stratagem of appearing to flee, the Scots drew the invaders into an ambush where they were slaughtered in numbers on Ancrum moor. Seeing this, the assured Scots in the English ranks ripped the red cross of England from their tunics and turned on their former comrades. It was reckoned that eight hundred invaders were killed, including Evers and Latoun, 1,000 captured for ransom and all the booty taken in their previous raids was recovered, but it must be admitted that these numbers were probably massaged. This was a rare Scots victory against superior numbers. The battle was fought on 17 February 1545.

Henry was livid. Having lost two of his most able commanders, he commissioned Hertford to head another avenging raid into Scotland.

Hertford marched into the Borders at the head of an army of foreign mercenaries whom he judged better suited to his purpose than the English Borderers who would not willingly burn their neighbours' property. The invasion started in September 1545 and this time it concentrated on the arable lands of The Merse, the bread-basket of the Borders. The towns and abbeys of Kelso, Melrose, Jedburgh and Dryburgh were taken and slighted. In the countryside, each village and building was levelled to the ground and all the abundant corn crop was burnt to deprive surviving Scots of food for the next twelve months. Although this force was within a few miles of Selkirk, it did not consider that the town was worth burning again.

Hertford reported to his king that he had: '*burnt and destroyed suche a deal of corne, as well in townes and lying in the fieldes, as also hidde in woodes and caves, that the Scottes seye themselves that they were never so brent, scourged and punished in no journey, and that they received not half so moche losse and detryment by the last journey that was made to Edinburghe as they have don by this. Surely this country is very fayre and so good a corne countrey and such plenty of the same as we have not seen the more plenteous in England; And undoubtedly there is brent a wonderful deale of corne for by reason that the year hath been so forward, they had done moche of their harvest and made up their corn in stackes about theyr houses or had it lying in shocks in the fields' and none at all left unshorn, the burning thereof can be no little ympoverishment to them, besides the burnying and spoil of their houses; as when the journey is ended, we shall make your majesty a full declaration of the whole.*'

The tally of destruction was 7 monastries and friars houses, 16 castles and towers, 243 villages, 13 mills, 3 hospitals, and waste laid to all the country on Tweed, Teviot, Jed and the neighbouring district. At the finish of his report, he adds '*we wolde lytell have thought to have found so fayre a country in Scotland*'.

However, Hertford found that he had done his work only too well and found himself against an enemy whom he could not beat – hunger. Having destroyed all the food in the district, there was none for his own troops and he had to retreat from the devastated Borders, leaving the survivors to rebuild their lives as best they could.

Henry VIII of England died on 28 January 1547, still urging that the war against the Scots should be continued until they agreed to accept the marriage of Edward and Mary.

In 1547 Hertford, now Duke of Somerset and Protector of England, tried a third campaign against the Scots to secure the marriage. At Pinkiecleuch, the numerically superior Scots were soundly defeated by the professional English army who had more cavalry and some warships lying off the coast. Hertford went on to occupy Edinburgh, but was unable to hold it. On his way homewards, he accepted the oath of fealty from most of the landed families.

Blackmail

There were two kinds of 'mail' or rent paid in the sixteenth-century Borders. In general terms, mail was the rent or tribute paid to a superior for a farm or house. Whitemail was the legal rent for a property, and was paid to the king or owner. The other, 'blackmail', was the illegal protection money paid to the nearest band of thugs to prevent your property being ransacked, robbed and burnt. The derivation of the word is supposed to be that this protection money was usually paid in cattle and the cattle of the Borders were small and black. The word is one of the few that the Border reivers introduced into the English language.

Through custom and usage, it was often easier to pay the money/cattle than to fight to protect your own property. Soon the collection of this insurance money became a matter of course – especially if it was asked for politely.

In the Haddington Papers, there is a letter from William Scott of Buccleuch to Alexander MacDouall of Makerston. It is in Scots but here transcribed into English.

'Right worshipful sir, I commend me to you. For as much as you shall

> *know that last night, I was at Kelso. I sent Will Scott of Harden, Adam Scott of Burnfoot and Clemmet Crosier* to your house, who spoke to your wife and they assured me that you were not at home yourself; and so I rode past and did you no harm at that time. I desire you now to send me your gray horse or if the gray is not in place, send me the brown. And if you do not, it shall teach me never to do you any favours in the future and I shall do you great harm, twice the worth of the horse as I live. And take this for a warning and nothing else, but God keep you. Wm Scott (younger of Buccleuch).'*
>
> It is not known whether this broad hint was successful or not.

NINIAN – THE EDINBURGH YEARS,
1546

While the Rough Wooing was devastating the Borders, sir Ninian Brydin was in the relative safety of Edinburgh where he was using the contacts he had previously made. Most of them had Borders connections:

No. 394 Undated 1546. Marion Haliburton of Dirleton gives a nineteen-year lease of a half of her father's tenement in Edinburgh to Katherine Levinstoun and Robert Haliburton. This lease was signed in the townhouse of Lord Home.

No. 395 July 1546. John Downe, merchant and seaman in Leith gives his share of the ship and profits of its voyage to his mother and sister. James Barton and Watte Barton had a quarter share each. (The Downe family were merchants and fleshers in Selkirk. Walter Downe had been slaughtered in Selkirk in January 1540/41; the Bartons were from a family of noted Scottish seafarers.)

No. 396 A note from John Downe lists the debts he owes including what seems to be harbour dues in Musselburgh.

---

* Three well-known reivers and landed ruffians.

No. 397 August 1546. Master R. Richardson, vicar of Eckford summoned to the aisle of St John the Evangelist in St Giles Kirk to be censured.

No. 398 August 1546. Sir Walter Scott of Branxholm and Janet Ker of Bedrule intends to marry. Janet Ker to attend the Chapel of St Mungo in Lilliesleaf to receive the agreed marriage settlement in money or goods.

No. 399 August 1546. The gist is that Janet Ker was not happy with the settlement and wanted to back out. (Janet Ker of Ferniehirst was the widow of Turnbull of Bedrule. She eventually became the second wife of Sir Walter Scott of Branxholm.)

From two years from 18 August 1546 to 29 July 1548, there are no entries in Ninian's protocol book. We have no evidence of his whereabouts from any other source known at present.

IN THE COUNTRYSIDE

Of the surrounding country, much is known. This was the period of the second phase of the Rough Wooing when the English/Protestant headquarters were at Haddington and the French/Catholic one at Stirling and Edinburgh. There were Scots on both sides but mainly on the French one. Basically the French and the English were using Scotland to fight their war. Mercenary troops were poured into the country, Spanish, Irish and Welsh as well as Scots, English and French.

The English/Protestant party had seized the Castle of St Andrews in May 1546 and held out there until it fell to a French force in July 1547. The nobles were put into a French prison and the others, including John Knox, sent to the galleys.

The Church was doing everything it could to keep Scotland Catholic and using its priests to encourage anti-English feeling. So when the Scots army gathered in the hills above Pinkiecleuch just outside Musselburgh in September 1547, there were a large number of priests in their midst to encourage their side. There was the usual factionalism in the Scots ranks with the clergy urging bloodshed and slaughter, 'Death to the Godless' etc, while the men who would be doing the fighting were recommending caution and delay.

Despite the fact that it was known that the English were on the point of starvation, the clergy won. The conclusion was that the English were victorious, killing thousands of Scots including many of the belligerent priests★ and capturing fifteen hundred prisoners.

The battle was not such a disaster for Borderers from both sides. As usual, each nation's combatants wore stitched-on flags to indicate their allegiance: the Cross of St George for England and St Andrews Cross for Scotland. These were useful aides, easily detached and substituted as desired. During the battle, those thus marked were seen to have stopped fighting and were speaking to their acquaintances in the other army. On being observed, they ran at each other and struck a few blows ' by assent and appointment'.

By 1548 the conflict had become a war of attrition. The French and the English tried to grind each other down while the Scots, divided as ever, split into three parties, one pro-Catholic and two Protestant parties; or four if you count the Borderers who fought on their own account anyway.

With the removal of the young queen to France in July 1548, the odds changed. A treaty between the Scots and French for the marriage of Mary to the young dauphin was signed and, in return, a French-paid garrison of 6,000 troops was to be quartered in Scotland. The Earl of Arran's agreement to this brought him the Dukedom of Chatelherault.

Meanwhile, England was not having it too good. There were rebellions in Cornwall and in East Anglia and some political manoeuvring got Hertford removed from office. The English garrisons were removed from most of Scotland and a virtual peace was made.

This peace did not extend to the Borders where family feuds continued to exercise minds and bodies. The Scott/Kerr debate blazed again when Lord Grey and a party of English made a raid into the Borders with specific instructions to attack the property of Sir Walter

---

★The Protocol Book of sir John Chepman published by the Walter Mason Trust, ends with the final entry dated 13 August 1547. This may just be a pure happenstance but a later Selkirk Council minute mentions 'Bartholmelew Robertson of Selkirk chaplain was killed at the field of Pynkiecleugh'. The record notes him as son of the late James Robertson who was an indweller in the burgh of Selkirk.

Scott of Buccleuch. By agreement, the Kerrs assisted and guided the raiders to burn Hawick on 8 October 1548. Eleven days later, they reported that they had: '*destroyed the whole towns and steadings pertaining to the said Walter, his kin, friends and servants upon the waters of Yarrow and Ettrick lying within the Forest and burnt the said Walter's mother, the Dowager Lady Buccleuch*★ *within the tower of Catslack in Yarrow. And likewise had burnt the Castle of Newark*★★ *with all its contents, killing four of his servants and a woman within the same. Also burnt and harried the town of Selkirk where the said Walter was provost.*'

NINIAN – THE LATER EDINBURGH YEARS
1548–59

It may be purely co-incidence, but the first entry in Ninian's book for two years appears on the same month as Mary, Queen of Scots, sailed for France. The entries in this book show that Ninian was now engaged in a wider range of litigations, ranging between everyday disputes and those of the Church and trade guilds.

No. 400 29 July 1548. Sir Alexander Alesone, vicar pensioner of the parish kirk of Auldhamstockis in the diocese of St Andrews hands over the rectorship to sir Thomas Dausone.

No. 402 October 1548. Gavin Tait worried that the wooden tenement sold to him by his cousin David Tait might catch fire. Agreement signed in David's booth in Edinburgh.

No. 403 May 1548. A discrete young man in a voice of lamentation declared and alleged that he was the son of the deceased venerable master John Villemsone provost of Seton Collegiate Church. Sir Gilbert Anderson was moved by pity and gave twenty shillings to

---

★ The unfortunate lady was herself a Ker of Cessford, and aunt or great aunt of the leader of the Ker faction destroying the valley. However, the fact that she was mother of Buccleuch was enough to render all claims of kinship invalid.

★★ Buccleuch had been made 'Captain and Keeper of her Majesty's castle of Newark in the Lordship of Ettrick Forest' in 1543. This was deemed sufficient excuse for the Kers to burn the castle.

the youth who promised, in the presence of witnesses, never to ask
for anything in the future.

No. 407 Undated. George Gibson, sometime master baker to James V,
makes provision for prayers to be said for himself and his wife, for
his elder son slain at Pynkecleucht and his younger son slain in
'Albony', for James V and his ancestors and many others – these
prayers to be said at the altar of St Hubert, patron saint of bakers in
St Giles Kirk in Edinburgh. A long list of conditions and individu-
alised payments follows and penalties for non-compliance.

No. 411 July 1551. An entry signed 'at my chamber' in Edinburgh ie sir
Ninian's.

About this period, Ninian seems to be doing the legal business of the
bakers and leatherworkers guilds in Edinburgh and handling some
apostolic appointments of the monastery of Holy Rood. He returned
to the Borders for a short time in July 1552.

No. 432 Loose sheet bound in. Undated but around 1552–4. This is a
list of the books presumably in the library of sir Ninian.
These include:

THE PSALMS OF DAVID
THE LIFE OF ST NINIAN IN TEN PARTS
THE LIFE OF ST BRIGID
THE BOOK OF TEN SERMONS ETC.

This shows that Ninian was keeping up with the religious thought of the
time and his library was up to date. It would be interesting to know if
these books were handwritten copies or were some of the new-fangled
printed ones. It would be even more interesting to know if any Walter
Chepman books (see p.423) appeared on Ninian's library shelves.

Also tucked in around here was a poem in Ninian's writing. We do
not know whether he wrote it himself or copied it from a now-
unknown source. However, his poem on 'Wisdom' bears noting.

Quha wauld be reycht haf ee to honour ay
For reyches followis honour evir mair

And honor to vysdome is the air
And vysdome cummis of sciens and lair
And sciens cummes only throu godis graice
Conquest throu gud lyf an halyness

The deliveraunce of ye vysman
The visman teyches as ze may heir
Ane gud teychment quhe vil it leir
To think one thir four nicht and day
And in zour levand to hauld thaim ay
The dreidfu deid yat ze man dae
The strait jugsment that nayne flee
The paynes of hel wythout end
The joyis of hevin yat ar unkend.

The reverse of this poem has the fragments of another, this time in Latin. This has no cheerful hopes since every second line seems to be welcoming death. Written down the side is a list of priests, some known Selkirk ones but with others now untraceable. 'Schir N.B.' appears in the list.

No. 435 October 1554. Janet Dunbar and John Glendinning agreed to support their son and brother Simon Glendinning year about and to put money in safekeeping at the Blackfriars Kirk to guard him against future poverty. (Women kept being known by their maiden names long after marriage.)

No. 439 July 1556. Alexander Bishop pays part of his debt with all his crops of corn, wheat, bere, peas and oats, a cow, ten sheep, two horses, six oxen and all the plenishings in his steading.

No. 442 November 1556. George Gibson (the baker to James V) came to St Giles to receive money from Alexander Wardlaw of Kilbarton but Alexander did not appear.

No. 445 January 1557. Conditions of cordiner's apprentice in Edinburgh. James Harkas to teach Edward Neilson all the skills of the shoemakers' trade; Edward to remain in the work except for twenty days at harvest time.

No. 446 July 1557. George Home in Broxmouth desires to pay his rent to the earl of Argyl. This was to be paid in corn.

No. 449–451 July 1557. Three entries concerning a pitched battle over peas on the Borrowe Mur (Edinburgh). William Symsome says that he found Margaret Marjoribanks picking his peas; she claimed that they were her peas and came with various men with swords, sticks, lances, crossbows and guns to make her point.

No. 460 March 1558. George Home in Broxmouth insists that the earl of Argyl collects his rent in victuals within three days. The earl's agent said that he would collect them as soon as he could get a ship.

No. 462 9 May 1558. George Home of Broxmouth insists that the victuals be collected within three days before the English or French lay waste to them and said that he would not be responsible if such a thing happened.

No. 463 23 May 1558. George Home of Broxmouth said that if the Earl of Argyl or his factor did not collect the victuals within three days, they would be laid waste and burned by the English or sold or eaten by the French; and it would not be his fault if this happened. (At this time, the fort at Eyemouth was garrisoned by the French, besieged by the English and skirmished around by the Scots.)

No. 466 August 1558. Isabel Brady sets out to prove that Mathew Windygaits and his kin are thieves, resetters and breakers of booths (burglars).

No. 469 December 1558. This is an inserted copy of the legacy of the late Thomas Leithman of Bowden which was extracted from the Melrose Abbey records by sir William Philp sacristan and John Forrus, monk of Melrose.

During the two years of 1558 and 59, Ninian must have either been keeping quiet or have had little business which merited inclusion in his Protocol Book. The last entry we can definitely date which has an Edinburgh connection is that of 8 July 1559. It is the simple payment of a rent but is done at the house of George Gibson in Edinburgh and has at the bottom '*Ita est Ninianus Briden notarius ad premissam*'.

The years 1558 and 59 must have been a time of uncertainty for Ninian, no matter on which side of the religious divide his true loyalties lay. He was a Catholic priest and notary, with an amount of responsible church business. On the other hand, he had connections with the

Edinburgh guilds especially the bakers and leatherworkers who were notably pro-Reformation. His landowner clients were split in their religious beliefs, if they had any.

By this time, Henry VIII had died of syphilis, traces of which he had passed on to his three surviving children. Edward VI had died of tuberculosis and had been followed on the throne in 1553 by Mary, known to the world as 'Bloody Mary', through trying to please her husband, Philip of Spain, a fervent enemy of Protestantism. Mary's reign lasted five years before she succumbed to her inherited disease. She was followed on the English throne by her half-sister Elizabeth.

Elizabeth was a different kettle of fish – strong-willed, clever, resourceful and cunning; she had already seen much of the worst of human nature when she ascended the throne at the age of twenty-five. She saw the crisis in Scotland and set about to exploit it for the benefit of her own realm: judicious bribes, promises and threats divided the already critically split Scots.

THE REFORMATION

Scotland had been a Catholic country for five hundred years with nominal subservience to Rome, but by the mid sixteenth century, time and distance had loosened the ties. The Scottish monasteries were property-owning businesses, more intent on material benefit than spiritual leadership, and the Crown was the greatest beneficiary. When James V proposed to have his bastard sons installed as abbots of Melrose, Charterhouse and Kelso, and priors of St Andrews, Pittenweem and Coldingham, the Pope dared not risk refusing as it could have driven Scotland into the Protestant arms of Henry VIII's England. This gave the finances and control to the Crown, rather than the Pope in far-away Rome.

Within the affluent monasteries, the numbers of monks were declining because fewer men were being admitted to holy orders. As the number grew less, the portions which each monk enjoyed grew larger – the fewer divisions of the cake, the bigger the slices. Melrose had only sixteen monks in 1555.

Reports of 'lewdness' regularly winged their way to Rome, and abbots were expected to have one or more concubines as a matter of course. Archbishop Hamilton, himself a church reformer, was prescribed a ten-week course of 'moderate and carefully regulated incontinence' on medical grounds. There were also accounts of how immoral nuns didn't bother to live within nunnery precincts, and were too illiterate to write their own names.

In the country parishes, a law to legitimise offspring found that two Scotsmen in every six hundred were priests, while two newly legit-imised children in every seven had been fathered by a priest. Even if these reports are much inflated, as they probably were, this still shows a religious society ripe for reform.

The Reformation had been a crisis waiting to happen for some time. It was sparked off in Scotland when John Knox came back from Geneva and preached a sermon 'vehement against the idolatory of Rome' in Perth on 11 May 1559. Eleven days later there was a riot there, with the town's churches and religious establishments plundered and destroyed. By the beginning of July, many of the towns of central Scotland had suffered a similar fate and on the seventh of the month, John Knox had been installed as the first Protestant minister of Edinburgh.

The Lords of the Congregation, the pro-Reformation grouping, were a fair cross-section of Scottish society: lords, lairds, burgesses and a good number of former priests mixed together and, for once, presented an almost united front. By now, lawyers and merchants were gradually having more influence in the running of the country. The speed of their success had taken many of the Reformers by surprise and they were simply unprepared to run a national church. It would be another twenty years before the religion of Scotland could truly be called Presbyterian.

Mary of Guise was deposed as Regent in October 1559 and died in June the following year. A provisional Protestant government was set up with military and financial aid from England, although Francis and Mary were still to be recognised as the king and queen of Scots. The arrival of an English fleet in the Forth in January 1559 and an English army two months later, may have gone some way in influencing the waverers. This was an unusual English fleet and army, for now they were being seen as friends by many of the town-dwelling population.

Sir Ninian's star seems to have risen in the last major phase of Catholicism in Scotland, when wealth was coming from the merchant classes rather than the landed nobility. The land-owning Catholic Church had been severely taxed by James V and had lost some of its influence in the government of the country; but it was not the totally corrupt organisation so often depicted by the Reformers. In the Borders, parish churches were still the centres of the community; the schools were taught by the local priests as part of their duties; hospitals were run by the Church and many still paid to have masses said for their souls. Most Borderers were quite happy with the status quo as far as religion went.

There was opposition to the Francophile policies of Mary of Guise and the government, as these were seen as diversionary tactics to draw English troops from France. So Protestantism became a suitable rallying cause to oppose Scotland's alliance with Roman-Catholic France. With French and English forces and their supporters using the Borders as a battleground, this was not a good time to be around.

In 1560, the Treaty of Edinburgh was concluded with the English, and the French commissioners and all foreign troops were to leave Scotland. This left the Scots free to do what they did best – quarrel amongst themselves. There were Catholics for the Reformation but against England, and Protestants who were for England but against reform.

The chief proponents of reform were those who had their eyes on the wide Catholic Church lands and livings. It is no coincidence that Protestantism was strongest in the flatter and more fertile lands of the Lothians, Fife, Angus and Ayrshire, where the richest abbeys were situated. A decidedly dodgy parliament met in March 1560 and declared that Protestantism would be the religion of choice with the abolition of the Mass and the substitution of the Protestant Confession of Faith. This was not universally accepted and places like the Borders retained their allegiance to the old religion.

A further complication was added when Mary decided to return to Scotland in August 1560. She was a beautiful nineteen-year-old widow, formerly Queen of France, the Queen of Scots who had been brought up in France and was a devout Catholic. This could have caused immediate divisions but Mary kept the status quo, maintaining her own Catholic faith in private while allowing the Protestants to worship as they pleased. Like her forebears, she kept an international court, encouraging music, plays and poetry, and providing a meeting place where Catholic and Protestant nobility could meet in brilliant surroundings. In fact, Mary was continuing the traditions laid down by the previous five Stuart Kings of Scots.

In all, it was a very civilised Reformation that trod lightly on the Catholic clerics who still enjoyed two-thirds of their old incomes for the remainder of their lives. There was no blood-letting on any scale, but the priests were forbidden to presevere with their former duties, especially that of saying Mass. Only one man is known to have sought and suffered death as a Catholic martyr. Of the four principal bishops, one left the country while the other three became Protestants. In the monasteries, the monks continued to draw their portions, and lay abbots or commendators kept most of the land but now in their own hands rather than that of the Church. Although the plethora of jobs which the Catholic Church provided had disappeared, many priests carried on as before, except that they now sang from a different hymn book. Some priests became full-time notaries and writers (lawyers); many became Protestant ministers: some were teachers while others held on to their calling as Catholic priests. To see how this affected one priest, we have to turn back to Ninian's Protocol Book.

SIR NINIAN BRYDIN – BACK IN THE BORDERS, 1560–64

We cannot say why Ninian decided to return to the Borders. Perhaps it had something to do with the fact that Edinburgh now had a Reformation Minister in St Giles instead of a priestly hierarchy; perhaps the arrival of an English fleet and army to back up the new religion influenced his decision; or maybe he just wanted to get back to the Borders again.

Whatever the reason, we find that Ninian was back by the 6th of January 1559 with an entry giving the use of a piece of land in Bowden as a marriage settlement *with the consent of the lord abbot of Kelso* and was enacted *in the chapel of St Katherine in Bowden*.

For the next year, we find that the transactions in Ninian's book, centre round the Bowden area. The following years have entries for lands at Bowden, Midlem, Maxpoffle, Holydean, Kippilaw, Eildon and Lessudden, and most was being transferred to the Ker family. The obvious connection is the breaking up of the landholdings of Kelso and Melrose Abbeys, where Ker of Cessford was the main beneficiary.

Ninian seems to have been dividing his time between the Bowden area and Selkirk. On 5 February 1561 he was transacting business in a house in the Fulbrig Raw in Selkirk.

Nos. 491 & 496 23 December 1561. An interesting item on witchcraft in Selkirk. Mungo Cruickshanks takes a legal oath that he had not cheated Christine Loremur twenty-seven years before. Thinking she had been worsted in a bargain, Christine 'in her wodness' (madness), had wrapped a dead mole in a bob (roll) of birch bark and had thrown it into his booth. For the last twenty-seven years he, Mungo, had been ready to answer the judgment of men and now was ready to answer to God.

About this period in his life, we would surmise that Ninian had come down on the side of the Reformation. His main clients were amongst the reformers and we read in entry No. 504 that one of the witnesses was 'Joke Brydin, sone to schir N.B.', probably the same 'Johne Brydin, scolar' who witnesses No. 508. Ninian was now confident enough to recognise his son officially.

A loose page amongst the Walter Mason Trust papers gives a further clue to Ninian's family. This is a written statement from John Brydin, son and heir of the late John Brydin, burgess of Selkirk, saying that his father owed some money to his 'eme' (uncle) sir Ninian and that he personally owed Ninian certain sums for his, John's, own costs, travels, food and clothing in his youth. John promises to pay his 'eme schir Niniane Bridin' in his need if he asks it; otherwise to give Ninian's daughter 20 merks as a dowry when she comes of age. He also promises to be kind and true with help and good counsel to Ninian's lass and lad both, without fraud or guile.

This is a time of religious confusion in Selkirk and the surrounding countryside. The Scotts of Buccleuch and others favoured the queen's/Catholic/French side while the Kers of Cessford/Faldonside were generally pro-Reformation.

Interestingly, entry No. 508 mentions 'Schir Johne Brydin, vicar of Selkirk' and is dated 25 August 1561. A month later, on 25 September 1561, entry No. 510 is witnessed by 'William Leirmonth, minister in Selkirk for the time' but this was a temporary post of short duration.

The above would suggest that Selkirk could be one of the first burghs to accept the new religion, but this might not be the case. The Kerrs of Cavers were receiving the 'fruits of the vicarage' in 1563 and 1566. In 1574, Thomas Cranston was presented to the vicarage, to be followed by Alexander Douglas in 1577. Other than the temporary William Leirmonth, the first Protestant minister to be inducted in Selkirk was Michael Cranston in 1580.

Ninian's book shows that the chapels named after saints, were still active eg the chapel of St Mungo in Lilliesleaf (No. 530) but the Master of Hamilton was selling a quarter of the timber of the cloister of Melrose Abbey to Isobel Ker, Lady of Cessford. (No. 528).

No. 534 March 1562. Written offer to Joke Brydin (the son of sir Ninian?) from Thomas Hendry offering him marriage to one [two scored out] of his youngest daughters. Joke was to get meat, clothing, bed and board and be taught a skilled trade so that he could live honestly. Joke had to pay 6 shillings yearly and give Thomas the use of his half husbandland.

Around this period, there was a great deal of land changing hands in the areas of Midlem, Lilliesleaf, Bowden, Kippelaw and Melrose. These were the lands which had been 'freed' from the abbeys by the local landowners. We are only guessing there as the abbeys are seldom mentioned, but how else would so much former abbey lands come into private ownership? Ninian was getting his share of the transactions.

However, the monks of Melrose did not give up their rents and dues without a fight. Nos. 549 and 550 on the last day of June 1564 show they were still demanding their legal rights and No. 551 shows that the laird of Hermiston was still paying his dues to Glasgow.

If the monks were not giving up their rights easily, neither were the people of Selkirk. In a public instrument dated 5 September 1562, the provost, baillies and community of the burgh rode the lands of the South Common 'to serche and se gef the merches thereof wer kepit undfylist *be ane or ony personis agiacent thereto*' and discovered that the lands of Quhitlaw (Whitlaw) and the common had been '*revin furth, telit and sawn with aittes*' by Robert Kerr, brother to Andrew Kerr in Faldonside. On appearing before them, the said Robert confessed that he had no right or title to the said land as it was common land. He was ordered to remove his corn immediately and desist from similar action in future.

The last entry, No. 551 in Ninian, Protocol Book, was witnessed by John Rutherfurd, 'doctor to the bairns' in Selkirk. He was not a medical doctor but a teacher, thus giving a convincing proof that the church school had survived the Reformation. John Rutherford was the maternal great-grandfather of Sir Walter Scott of Abbotsford.

This last entry in the book dated 13 November 1564, gives a half quarter of land and the steading at Elibank to James Stewart, brother german to the lord of Traquair.

What happened to sir Ninian afterwards we do not know but he certainly lived in exciting times.

CHAPTER SIXTEEN
Reformation to Union

In Craig-Brown's *History of Selkirkshire*, he mourns the fact that '*By a most unfortunate and regrettable loss of the burgh archives from 1545 to 1635, we are left in ignorance of the attitude of the burgesses when John Knox brought about the Reformation.*' This is no longer the case. The Protocol Books of John and William Brydin 1579–87, a number of loose sheets of William Brydin 1587–92 and that of Henry Blaikie 1592–1613, cover the period up to and past the Union of the Crowns in 1603. In more complicated circumstances, another Selkirk Burgh Court Book covering the period 1557–75 turned up.

When Bruce Mason died in 1963, his attic in a council house in Thornfield was totally crammed with his various collections. Mrs Mason was anxious to get these cleared away, so Walter Mason asked me to help. Amongst an assortment of Roman pottery, Chinese snuff mulls and French glass paperweights, were books of all periods. Amongst the books we found around two hundred pages from a Burgh Court book which dated from 1557 to 1575. Walter took them away to work on.

About 1970, Dr John Imrie came to Selkirk to give classes on Scottish handwriting.

In the talk after one class, Walter produced the battered pages and Dr Imrie took them away for conservation and transcription. John was the ultimate scholar, needing to have his work absolutely correct before releasing it, so it was a long process. The last time I spoke to him, he said that the transcription was nearly finished and he would send me a copy. However he died shortly afterwards. I did notice that the original is now in the Scottish Records Office with reference B 68/7/1. This is the best place for them, even if I did find a note in Walter's writing that: 'It should be noted that although Register House has the care of these records, they remain the property of the burgh and are available for research work by students of Scottish history on request at any time.' Fortunately for my purposes, some of Walter's transcriptions have survived and I use them below.

In general terms, the Protocol Books are mainly given over to land transactions and marriage settlements, while the Court Books tell what is happening within the town.

SELECTED ITEMS FROM THE
BURGH COURT BOOK, 1557–75

The entries given below are those which Walter Mason picked out as being of special interest: some are taken for a particular word or phrase, others for an incident, or to fit Selkirk into a particular time in Scottish history. I do not intend to give each entry in full and the many 'great tulzies' and property transfers within the burgh are ignored. The next few documents have not been published before but, as Walter's writing is often less decipherable than that of the original writers, I may have made some mis-readings.

April 1561. The Copy of the Cordiners' Subscripture and Licence.

> '*The inquest above written with the advice of the Provost and Baillies above written has licenced the craftsmen* [?] *themselves in manner underwritten that gif any unfreemen works within this burgh that are not worthy or knows not the misteries of the said craft and causes other craftsmen to be liket and desperate through them and their orders and gif ony of their servants will not work conforming to their feeing and conditions or gif ony fee ane* [of the] *others servant, they being bound or gif ony of the said craufft fights or tulzies with ane another, that the said craftsmen shall order, punish and correct the trespassers for their faults concerning their* [misdemeanours?] *among themselves and if they do in the contrary or is disobedient that they sall call the said disobeyor before the provost and Baillies for the time who shall judge and punish them for the said trespass*'.

In effect this is an indication that the Shoemakers or Cordiners had formed themselves into a craft guild long before they received their Seal of Cause in 1609.

July 1561. Salt. '*The which day the Baillies and council being informed that the salters most unhonestly deceive both the burgh and the landward in measuring their salt with Lothian measures whiles they ought to measure the same both without and within the burgh with the town's measures.*

Therefore Cornelius Inglis, Thomas Inglis, Robert Elliot, Robert Mitchelhill, all salters within the burgh are fined each of them 6 merks and ordained to sell no salt within the burgh or landward but with the town's measures under the pain of £20 without mitigation and ordains this order to be published at the mercat cross.'

With a number of animals being killed in the late autumn to conserve the fodder to over-winter the breeding stock, the use of salt was the main method of preserving meat at this period. So it was essential that a plentiful supply should be available at the cheapest price. Obviously the Lothian measures were smaller than the town ones.

Four salters within the burgh might seem excessive but they have to supply the surrounding countryside as well. There are some 'Salt Roads' within the Borders but I have not heard of one leading to Selkirk.

October 1563. The kirk and kirkyard are being abused by swine and other bestial uses so it is to be let out.

3 December 1563. The queen's Great Justice General is to hold a Justicaire hastily and the town does not have a tollbooth so Alexander Gledstaine will give up part of his tenement for an annual rent of forty shillings. (It was to be ten years later that the burgh got round to building a new tollbooth.)

1567. Andrew Elliot flouts the queen's authority in court.

1567. The Town of Selkirk and other Border towns has *to* '*prepair and have in reddines bakin breid, browin aill, hors meit, mannis meit and uther neidfuull ludgeings and provision for 6th November*'. This was for a raid against the thieves of Liddesdale.

January 1569. James Scott complains that he had the customs of the market for 1568 but 'the pest' came and the market was closed for 20 weeks and he was hurt thereby. Council forgives him for the £20 Scots owed.

December 1569. The council has ordered nine footmen and one horseman to ride to the king's army. Each footman who is well-armed to have five shillings daily. Each burgess to pay a tax of three shillings.

November 1571. Tax of 4 pence per boll of oats grown on the Common, to be paid as compensation to remain at home from the Sovereign Lords Army at Leith on October 1571. (This was a time when Selkirk supported the queen's party and had to pay for the privilege.)

24 October 1571. The inquest ordains all men having bairns of age to receive teachment and nurture that they put them to John Scott and he to teach them as it will please the bairns watchet (watched/overlooked) and to pay him according to the auld act and he to have his meat about with the bairns.

John Scott was a 'Reader and Exhorter' of the Reformed Religion in Selkirk 1568 and obviously had turned to education by 1571.

February 1572. The treasurer to pay John Watson, common minstrel, the sum of £3:10s being on his account of all bygones to this day.

Buccleuch's Pension

In the summer of 1569, Selkirk seems to have been a sink of iniquity as the Court Book entry for the 16 July records that: '*The inquest aforesaid finds that the provost and baillies does not their duties concerning theire office in suffering ane multitude of hoormongers, hoors and their common oppressers to remain within the toon in respect that they were delated and ordains the said provost to put them out of the toon according to their duty and if they suffer them to remain unpunished the said provost and baillies are in default thereof.*'

However, this problem was resolved at the next election as the Court Book records in November 1569, that after a discussion on the 'lyttis' (nominations), '*all in one voice finds Walter Scott of Branxholm, Knight is to be provost and Andrew Hallowell, John Bryden of Wool and Mungo Johnstone to be baillies.*'

Sir Walter had married Lady Margaret Douglas when he was under sixteen and was around nineteen when he became provost of Selkirk. Despite his youth, he was a strong supporter of the party of Mary, Queen of Scots, who in 1569 had been a prisoner of Elizabeth of England for a year; but her supporters had not given up hopes of seeing her on the throne again and were plotting accordingly. The Roman Catholics, despite being a minority in Scotland, had many powerful friends who were willing to rise in her defence. Amongst these were Lord Home, Scott of Buccleuch and Kerr of Ferniehurst.

In the later part of 1569 a rebellion against Elizabeth had broken out in the north of England. It was uncoordinated and too quickly commenced but the leaders, the Earls of Northumberland and Westmoreland, were too committed to draw back. That rising fizzled out and the leaders had to seek refuge in Liddesdale of all places.

Meanwhile the queen's party in Scotland gathered their forces and marched into England as far as Newcastle. In 1570, Queen Elizabeth retaliated by sending the Earl of Sussex to destroy the Borders; which he did by overthrowing more than five hundred towns, villages, towers and houses. Sir Walter Scott burnt his own tower at Branxholm rather than let the English boast of having destroyed it.

This did not daunt the young Sir Walter who continued to fight in the queen's cause before he was eventually taken prisoner and was warded in Doune Castle in Menteith. Realising that his devastated lands were producing no revenue, and his wife and children were destitute, he looked to his friends for help.

The Selkirk Court Book minute of January 1571 reads (in translation): '*The which day, the Baillies of the said Burgh sitting in inquest in the Tolbooth thereof and the Council and Community thereof being there convenit having consideration of the many freedoms given and gratitudes and pleasures done to them by ane nobil man Sir Walter Scott of Branxholm, Knight, their provost, at mony times bygane in defence of them and their said Burgh, checking thieves and traitors and also in many other friendly acts at different times bygane and being of guid mind and will and thankfulness towards him, therefore we the said Baillies, Council and Community of the said Burgh, them and their successors gives, grants, disposes and assigns to the said Sir Walter Scott yearly in all time coming during his lifetime ane yearly pension of ane hundred pounds money of the realm to be takit up and payit by them at Whitsunday and ane time in Winter each portion from the Common Good of the said Burgh. The said Baillies Council and Community of this Burgh binds and obliges them and their successors faithfully to consent and pay the said Sir Walter yearly at the times aforesaid during his lifetime, the first term and the payment thereof to be and begin at the feast of the Whitsunday last bypast before the date hereof and further they shall find certain honest men, Burgesses of the said Burgh, twa, three or four to assist collecting and secondly cautioners and sovereigntors in the common book of the said Burgh for yearly payment at the times foresaid of the said pension to Sir Walter during his lifetime to the contentment and pleasure of the said Walter and whenever the said cautioners or any of them be deceased or the said Sir Walter or any of them be altered that the said Baillies and Council find new cautioners accepted as brothers of the Burgesses, freemen of the Burgh in place of the others for yearly payment of the pension to Sir Walter to his contentment and pleasure at the terms above written during his lifetime as said is. The Baillies and Council and Community are content and consent that this act and gift and obligation be enterit in the Common Book of the said Burgh.'*

Minuted on 24 May 1572 is a letter from Sir Walter, still a prisoner in Doune Castle, asking that his pension be given to Thomas Wilson on his signature. However, Baillie Mitchelhill reminded the Council that the Common Good was not able to meet the sum without an extra tax on the community, but the burgesses agreed to the extra tax and it was minuted '*That every man pay an extra tax of 3 pence on every bowl of aitts (oats) sown upon the Common Land and the extra sum be payit to the Treasurer and his collector howsoever he requirit herewith and every Burgess to appear upon Wednesday next which is the 28th day of May instantly bringing with him their annual mailles with all bygones owing*'.

In July 1572, Sir Walter was released to return home to put his affairs in order but this was to be of short duration as he died on 17 April 1574. After his debts were paid, his remaining estate amounted to £1395:12s Scots or £116 sterling, so the Selkirk pension must have been very welcome.

This is the first and only time that the burgh of Selkirk paid a pension to the family of Buccleuch.

Fornication – Always a Favourite Subject

From the Burgh Court Book January 1572. James Kerr was charged with '*lying in fornication with Janette Chisholm and the said James was bounden and obliget him never to have 'melling'* [intimacy] *with her except he make completely and solemnly the holybond of matrimony with her*'.

The same day John Watson was accused of deflowering Christian

Dawson of her virginity by leaving her with child. This was left to John and Christian's father to sort out.

There was also the restitution of conjugal rights. In an undated entry: David Stoddard would not suffer his wife Margaret Scott to remain within the house but '*the said David declared that he had never deported or put her forth from his house and likewise was ready to receive her and use her as wife to his power in all agreement*'.

23 May 1573. Thomas Kerr of Kippilaw said that sir John Brydin was not competent to sit in inquest as he took sacrament in the old religion. Sir John replied that he had been in office as master and clerk of the Sheriff Court for twenty-eight years.

Thomas Kerr changed his attack and said that Adam Ewart should not sit in court in that he had one bairn by his wife and one by another woman. The baillies said that Adam might sit in court as he had made repentance in the kirk and had taken communion at different times since.

Presumably Adam had been charged with the more serious crime of 'manifest adultery' rather than that of fornication. For manifest adultery the offenders were forced to stand in sackcloth, bareheaded and barefoot at the kirk door, and then on the stool of repentence in front of the congregation every Sunday for up to six months. Few resisted this punishment as, by the statutes of 1563 and 1581, anyone refusing to submit could be put to death by the legal authorities.

Gambling

This entry is undated but is worth quoting in full. '*The which day the hail community has ordanit that nane young men or others indwellers such as honest mens bairns or servants that has the credit of others men's guds play at cards or dice but for aill in time coming whether within the burgh or without under the pain of remaining in the tollbooth in irons or in the stoke* [stocks] *aye and until he funds sovereignts that he shall not remain within the toon for ane year thereafter except that gif gentlemen require ane honest man in their own house or other place for the gentlemens pleasure*'.

This seems to say that it was all right to play for ale if you were young or a peasant but gentlemen could play as they wished in their own houses.

12 July 1573. Contract for a New Tollbooth. Contractors are James Murray, burgess and William Moody in Darnwick. The tollbooth walls to be three feet thick, side walls 14 feet high, the length of the side walls 10 feet, with three gables, two of them, three and a half feet thick and the other, three feet thick. Three walls, the house to be within these walls beneath 15 feet of board and (?) above. Four hewn doors under, and two above, with three hewn windows.

The price of the tollbooth to be £50 with condition that they work only to one o'clock on Saturday and rest to the end of the week. Also the Baillies to lay in all necessaries as lime, clay, stones, water barrels and (?) with scaffolding and other necessaries laid within 40 feet of the said house.

22 July, 1573. The council appoint two joiners to work the timber required.

19 August 1573. Tax on the whole community for an army to ride against the thieves and traitors on the Borders of the realm. Also the council shall elect so many men to ride on the said raid.

16 March 1574. The council ordains that every man shall till and sow their corn on the common land between this day and 24th April. Whoever fails to do so shall lose his freedom of the burgh and his land.

2 June 1574. A rent of 9 merks was accepted for the Common Bog land provided that '*shooting, playing at the football with other siclike games be usit as it was before*'.

September 1574. All burghs within the realm to be taxed by the Lord Sovereign's decree in order to put a ship and a bark (barque) '*for resisting certain conspiring Englishmen who trouble burgesses and merchants who travel by sea.*'

24 November 1574. Pest. Two men to be placed at each port to stop the pest from entering the burgh. They were to challenge any footmen coming into the town. The gates were to be opened in the morning and closed at 6 o'clock at night. Nobody allowed to receive strangers by night or day without the baillies' permission. No men to pass to Edinburgh without the baillies' testimonial and any person who does to be kept out of the town for seven weeks.

June? 1575. Forgeries.

'*The which day compeared Robert Fletcher and persuit Thomas Wilson allegand that he was persuit in the last court by John Chisholm in*

> *Fairmeadows for the sum of xlii shillings delivered by him to the said John,*
> *in Hardheads and Mauchlin* [Mechelin, the Belgian town notorious
> as a place of origin for counterfeit coins] *placks for oats after the procla-*
> *mation and that he was determined to receive the former and to pay good*
> *money therefore and the said Robert refusit the former from Thomas Wilson*
> *who instantly had persuit the said Thomas for relief thereof.*
>
> *Compeirit the said persons personally in Court and the said Thomas*
> *confessit the said deliverance thereof and denied the former to be the same*
> *false Hardheads and Placks and therefore the said John Chisholm's oath be*
> *given gif they be the same false Hardheads and Placks.'*

Hardheads and placks are small Scottish billon coins worth twopence
and one penny respectively at this period. Being thin base metal with a
wash of silver, they were easy to forge, making a good profit for the
forger. Robert Jacke, a merchant of Dundee, was hanged and quartered
for having hardheads forged in Flanders and then bringing them into
Scotland. Importing false coins into the country must have been
considered a more severe offence as the many forgers within Scotland
were merely hanged.

New Minister at Ashkirk, 19 January 1579. *'The which day in presence of*
> *me notary public and witnesses underwritten, Mr Thomas Cranstoun,*
> *minister of the God's word having in his hands ane collation and ane insti-*
> *tution of the pasturage and vicarage of the parish kirk of Ashkirk, lying*
> *within the Divinity of Glasgow and Sherrifdom of Roxburgh* [delivered?]
> *be Patrick Gaittis*[?] *Minister of Dunce and commissioner within the*
> *Sherrifdom of Roxburgh to James Scott, reader at Ashkirk requiring him*
> *after the syght of the said collation to pass with the said Thomas to the said*
> *Parishkirk of Ashkirk and there place him on the pulpit and deliver the*
> *Book of God in his hands and to give him full and actual possession and*
> *institution of the said pasturage and vicarage manse, glebe and kirklands of*
> *the same during his lifetime according to his promising made thereupon as*
> *the same and under the subscription and signed of the date of the said*
> *subscrition on the date the 18th day of January the year of God 1579.'*

(He only lasted three years as Ashkirk minister, during which
time complaints were made about his slackness and Romish
tendencies.)

3rd August 1580. Tree bark.

Agreement between David Fairlie and Walter Chisholm in Haining on behalf of named others.

'*That is to say the said David Failie and Walter Chisholm themselves and taking the burden on them for the said persons of their own free will and confession and grants that they have sold and disposit all and sundry the bark there of the wood callit Hislieside coft by them from Robert Scott of Aikwood thereby baith aik bark, byrk bark, sautch bark, and aller bark to the said George, Andrew and William Thomson to be peilit be them in manner following. The said David Fairlie and Walter Chisholm faithfully bound and obliged them, their heirs and servants that they shall not cut nane of the said wood only aik bark, aller or sautch wood frae lands lay bare yearly to the 11th day of April suffand* [except?] *thirty tress allanerlie for the which thirty trees the said David and Walter has faithfully bound and obliges them and the foresaid four themselves and taking the binding on them for the said parties to satisfy the said George, Andrew and William for the bark of the said trees at their own specification and shall allow so muckle of the forest and sums underwritten to be paid be them to the said David and Walter aforesaid. And likewise the said David and Walter has faithfully bound and obliged them and the foresaid for themselves and taking on the burden for the others that they shall hold but ane cutter and ane snedder in the wood and they shall cut one day and leave ane ither day uncuttit on the oak and for the which the said George, Andrew and William has faithfully bundden and obliged them and the aforesaid to refund, content and pay to the said David Fairlie and Walter Chisholm and the rest of his marrows above specified the sum of seven score merks at the feast of Lunnas to cum 1581 years in haill and compleat payment.*

And likewise the said George and Andrew has faithfully bunden not to cut any buggar stakes in the wood and gif they cut ony, they shall satisfy the said David and they bind themselves not to take away any of the said Walter's woods.'

This agreement seems extremely long-winded but both the timber in the trees and the bark were a valuable and diminishing resource, the bark especially so as it was used in tanning leather. In the eighteenth century the Souters (cordiners, shoemakers) of Selkirk would have to travel as far afield as Langhom to get oak bark.

The phrase 'buggar stakes' is not a vulgar expression but the lower part of the bougar or rafter which reached to the ground in old houses.

26 May 1591. Drink and bribery. A shortened translation:

> *Thomas Ker, writer in Selkirk promises his brothers James in Whitmuir and John in Whitmuirhall that, from the feast of Whitsunday 1592, he will not drink in any place in Selkirk or other places where he has to pay silver or money except in his own house where he is allowed 3 chopins (3 Scots halfpints = 2.55 litres) per day. Also any drink in his work service with his master where he shall get his food and drink for nothing. If Thomas bides by the contract he will get the gray russet breeks which James was presently wearing and the white fustian doublet which John was presently wearing.*

This bribed abstinence must have been successful as John became a notary in Selkirk with his own Protocol Book 1629–33.

Arranged Marriages

During the sixteenth century it seemed to be quite the thing for parents to arrange marriages for their children. It all depended on the marriage settlement and how much land the bride or groom brought with them into the family.

From the Protocol Book of sir John Chepman, 3 February 1531: '*Margaret Lundy spouse of David Hoppringill of Smailholm (and Galashiels) asserts that the said David had a marriage contract of George Brown of Colstone … and the said Margaret requests that he take in marriage either Janet or Margaret Hoppringill, her daughters as pleases the said David.*'

From the Protocol Book of John and William Brydin, 14 October 1580: '*Marriage agreement made between James Scharpe in Langnewtoun and his son James Scharpe on the one part and John Hodge in Standhill and his daughter Elizabeth on the other, narrating that the said James [younger] and Elizabeth will complete holy matrimony in face of kirk between this and Whitsunday 1586 but if one of them dies before the marriage takes place, if James [elder] has other sons, one of them will marry a daughter of the said John, according to the laws of the Holy Kirk. James Scharpe has given to the said James [younger] and his future spouse Elizabeth and the heirs begotten between them all his husbandland with onset, croft and toft and pertinents lying in the town and territory of Langnewtoun, reserving to the said James elder and his spouse Katherine Haswell liferents of the same.'*

CHAPTER SEVENTEEN
Galashiels

———————

The medieval history of Galashiels lacks the detail of Selkirk and is basically contained in the Privy Council, Great Seal and Exchequer Roll records. We can learn about the noble families who lived there and owned the land but of the lower orders, almost nothing. So we rely on the records of the Hoppringle/Pringle family for the fifteenth and sixteenth centuries and the succeeding Scott family as Lairds of Gala for the seventeenth and eighteenth centuries, for the early history of the town. The late eighteenth and early nineteenth century saw the initial establishment of a textile industry which would spread its offshoots throughout the neighbouring towns; and the production of tweed created prosperity in the Borders for the next century and a half.

It has been shown that the area now covered by the modern town of Galashiels had been occupied in antiquity but it is only in 1337 that the name 'Galuschel' appears in records. The name is Anglian meaning the shiels or houses beside the Gala Water. As it is the centre of a number of other Anglian names – Blindlee, Mossilee, Easter and Wester Langlee with Langlee Mains – there is a quite distinct possibility that it was the focal point of an Anglian schir which would put its dating to seventh or eighth century.

The name 'Gorgum', now known as Gala Hill, has been dubiously identified as Gorkhelm, which was a stronghold of Wallace during the Wars of Independence. This owes more to Victorian imagination than historical certainty.

On surer recorded ground, when the good Sir James Douglas received the lands of Ettrick Forest from Robert I and leased the tacks of the forest stedes of Galashiels and Mossilee to the Hoppringles, he retained part of the land for his own use when hunting in the forest.

After the disaster of Halidon Hill in 1337, the Scots tried to redress the balance by besieging Edinburgh, then in English hands. English forces moved to relieve the siege but were beaten back, retreating as far as the Tweed. On evidence from the Scalacronica, which is a contemporary account, the pursuing Scots 'loged themself at Galuschel'.

According to legend, a party of English marauders were foraging in the lower Gala Water area where they found some plum trees. Stopping to savour the fruit, they were surprised by a band of local men and massacred at a place near Netherdale now called 'the Englishman's Syke'. This is a good story that might just be true, but the commemorative stone was taken from the Gala Water and erected in situ in 1931.

In 1416, Archibald, the fourth Earl of Douglas, settled a land dispute between Melrose Abbey and Haig of Bemersyde and recorded it '*vndre oure Sealle at Gallowschel on th xvij day of the moneth of decemb. the yhere of g[ra]ce Mīcccc and the xvj*' [1416]. This could have been signed and sealed at a small stone-built hunting lodge which stood on the site of the Parish School and was described as a 'two-chambered building with stone walls six feet thick'. This may be the site of 'Nether Galashiels' which is mentioned in the 1599 charter. However, a more probable site was on the knowe just above the Englishman's Syke, where the Sanderson Hospital stands. In the 1599 charter 'Easter Galashiels' is noted, and I would venture a guess that it stood on this ideal site. In 1416 it is likely to have been a wooden structure and surrounding settlement like the one at Auld Wark in Yarrow.

The fourth earl was known as the Tyneman (or Loser) for being on the wrong side in every major battle in which he fought. His shield-bearer in his final battle at Verneuil was Robert Hoppringle of Galashiels and Mossilee.

On the fall of the House of Douglas in 1455, the Hoppringles lost no time in acquiring the lands as tenants of the king, and their lands comprised most of the Gala and Caddon Waters. For the historian, this was a benefit as the Exchequer Rolls from 1467 onwards show that the area around Galashiels was well populated. I have given the proposition that this area was the artillery arsenal of Scotland (see p.349).

Around 1460 a second Robert Hoppringle, son of the shield-bearer, first leased and then feued the forest stede of Galashiels. He married a wealthy heiress, Elspeth Dishington, daughter of Sir William Dishington of Ardross, and used her dowry to erect a stone-built house on the present site of Old Gala House, in 1457. There is said to have been a carved inscription above the door:

> Elspeth Dishington builted me.
> In syn lye not;
> The things thou canst not get
> Desyre not.

A worthy thought, although I am not quite sure of its intention, but it did acknowledge that Elspeth's dowry made it possible to build the tower. This was recorded as still standing in 1544, but no trace of it can be seen in the later towers and halls of Old Gala House.

Not content with the tower, Robert Hoppringle built a bridge over the Tweed near the foot of Gala Water. This consisted of three piers standing in the river, the middle pier having a chamber in which the bridge-keeper and his family lived. This middle pier also held two wooden drawbridges that could be let down or raised by the keeper. On the same pier was another stone with the coat of arms of Robert Hoppringle, now calling himself Pringill, and a verse recording that:

> I, Robert Pringill of Pilmure Steid
> Gave a hundred nobles of the goud sae reid
> To big my brig upon the Tweed

Known as Pringill's Brig, the piers were still standing in 1743 and Sir Walter Scott writes that he saw the bases while he was out 'burning the water for salmon' (spearing fish by torchlight) after he came to Abbotsford. He also used the bridge in his book *The Monastery*.

The location and purpose of this bridge has been queried and learned opinion declares that it was to allow pilgrims easy access along the 'Girthgate' to and from Melrose Abbey.

I am suspicious that this is a story made to suit a theory. In the first place the Girthgate is not actually a pathway linking places of pilgrimage; in fact it is not even a road as its route wanders along hilltops and hillfaces and does not pass any known pilgrim sites. On the other hand, Dere Street the Roman road, known later as Malcolm's Road, has a string of pilgrim places along its path, viz Cheildhelles Chapel, Channelkirk and Soutra Aisle.

In defining 'girth', much has been placed on the riding aspect of a horse girth but the same word can mean a place of sanctuary or an enclosing boundary. Looking at the land enclosed by the Girthgate, it could have been an Anglian schir or estate which never survived into written record.

On the 1st of June 1503 a large gathering of the great and good from both sides of the Border met at Galloschelis to witness the handing over of the lands of Ettrick Forest and the tower of Newark to the attorneys of Princess Margaret of England as part of her settlement of £2,000 per annum when she married James IV, king of Scots. Leaving aside the honorific titles and designations, it is worth quoting this document at length: '*holding in their hands a certain precept of sasine, sealed according to custom with the green seal of the Chancery of our said most excellent lord the King of Scots, did come in the presence of the noble and circum-spect squire John Murray of Fawlohyll, Sheriff of Selkirk and from the same desired and humbly sought sasine and possession of all and whole the lordships of the Forest of Ettick together with the Forest of Ettrick itself, with its pertinents in the Sheriffdom of Selkirk with the tower, fortalice or manor of Newark within the said Forest. After the reading of which precept, the said Sheriff by the power and in virtue of his office, personally went to the said Forest and Lordship of Ettrick and there upon upon the soil of the same, gave real and substantial sasine and possession of the same, with the tower and manor of Newark by the tradi-tional ceremony of earth and stone. And these acts were done upon the soil of the foresaid lordship near the shiel★ and manor of Galloschelis at the second hour after noon or thereabouts, year, month and day aforesaid in the presence of honourable and noble men and gentlemen Walter Scot of Bukcleuch, David Hoppringle of Smalehame, Nicholas Ridley of Willemontswyke, Edward Par,*

★ In the original Latin document, this was 'tugurium' which is properly translated as a shiel or cottage, but it is unlikely that a meeting of this size and importance would be held in or near a small cottage. The most likely place would be at the tower built by Robert Pringill (formerly Hoppringill) and Elspeth Dishington, which was still there in 1544. The use of the plural 'schelis' implies that there would have been a settlement beside the tower but its size remains unknown.

esquire of England, William Ker, Master James Murleye [Murray?] *rector of Wilton, William Hoppringle, sir Thomas Fyndyne, rector of Wyle, Henry Brown, Englishman. Master John Murray, notary. Under the red-wax seal of the foresaid Sheriff of Selkirk.*

Thirty years later, Margaret Tudor, now dowager queen of Scots, gave the income of the lands to Henry Stewart, Lord Methven, her third husband but this did not mean that the Pringles were ousted from possession of the land.

6 January 1535. From the Great Seal. '*James by the grace of God, king of Scots to his sheriff and baillies of Selkirk … because on the advice of our queen of Scots, liferentrix of the said lands and our controllers of the rolls, we give and grant and demit in heritable feu ferme to our … cousin … Henry of Methven all the lands of Gallowayschellis and Mosele with pertinents and pendicles as is fully contained in his charter made thereon … and command you to give sasine of the said lands to Henry lord of Methven without delay.*' This was done on the lands of the same by Gilbert Scott to John Scott, attorney of Henry lord of Methven before witnesses on the lands of the same.

In 1510 the David Pringle who witnessed the document of sasine to Margaret Tudor, pledged himself and his followers to join the Earl of Angus to clear Ettrick Forest and Teviotdale of all Liddesdale and Eskdale men with their wives and bairns. The family history tells that four of his five sons were killed at Flodden, leaving succession to the youngest son John.

16 December 1527. '*On the which day, David Hoppringill of Galloschellis denied that he held David Spotsvod by gift of his deceased father but by gift of my first-born John Hoppringill and apparent heir; the said John held the said David by gift of the deceased and afterwards the said young man splendidly and honourably had victuals and clothing from me because my son did not have a place in his own right and straightaway at your request, I shall deliver the said David with the approval of my son and I now make demand on the said sir Ninian Spotsvod for his expenses in times past.*'

This is a complicated story where an orphaned David Spotsvod was brought up by David and John Hoppringill, but now that he was of an age to inherit and contract a marriage settlement, his tutor sir Ninian Spotsvod wanted him back.

It was not uncommon for a landed family to place their sons to be brought up by another family in similar circumstances.

17 July 1529. David Hoppringill of Galloschelis and lord of the lands of Smailham Crags appoints Margaret Lundy★ his spouse and James (John?) Hoppringill his first born son as his executors with his moveable goods to be given to his four daughters, viz Agnes, Christian, Janet and Margaret.

Already quoted on p.501. 1531. Margaret Lundy spouse of David Hoppringill of Smaillem asserts that the said David has a marriage contract of George Brown of Colstone … and the said Margaret requests that he take in marriage either Janet or Margaret Hoppringill as pleases the said David.

10th February 1536 'Margaret Lundy relict of the deceased David Hoppringill of Smallam'.

John Pringle of Galashiels, son of the deceased David, was present at the Battle of Pinkie in 1547 and was an assiduous attender on the Warden of the Middle Marches in his attempts to keep peace in the Borders.

In his will dated 13 March 1564, he left '*his saul to the protectioun and mercy of all mighty God and his bodie to be burit as hes bene of his predecessors within the kirk of Melros*'. His two eldest sons predeceased him and he was succeeded by his youngest son, Andrew, then a minor.

Andrew Pringle was served heir in 1573, several years after his father's death. Before coming into his inheritance, he had been one of the Border landowners who formed an alliance against the king's enemies, notably the Laird of Ferniehirst in 1561. This places him firmly on the side of the Reformation.

Andrew left tangible remains of his life in the oldest part of Old Gala House. The north-east wing of the present building was originally a free-standing tower-house which can be dated to 1583 if the armorial panel of Andrew Pringle and his wife Mariota Borthwick is correct. Measuring 44ft by 22ft externally, with walls 4ft thick, the tower is two floors high with two rooms in each floor. The original doorway on the ground floor faced south-west.

Andrew Pringle died on the 28th of February 1585 and was buried in the family burial-place in a chapel of Melrose Abbey.

Andrew was succeeded by his youngest son James, who was only

★ Margaret Lundy was his second wife.

nineteen when he inherited the estates. The Pringles of Galashiels, through beneficial marriages, and the constructive use of the Wardenship of the Tweed Ward of Ettrick Forest, had acquired extensive properties throughout the area.

But rather than engage in the rough and tumble of Border life, James Pringle turned to the glamorous politics of the court of James VI. Much about court, he was living in a style beyond his means, despite his lands and obvious wealth. As a young and handsome man, he became a great favourite with James VI who conferred a knighthood upon him.

While spending more at court than his estates supplied in rental, James Pringle sought to remedy the deficit. This was a time when there was rapid monetary devaluation in Scotland, with trade replacing land possession as a wealth producer. Consequently, many landowners were looking for ways to expand the commercial potential of their estates. One method by which this could be done was by the foundation of Burghs of Barony on the estate, a scheme which seemed to have no losers. This requires some explanation.

The Burgh of Barony

The royal burgh was a privileged community of merchants and tradesmen, to whom the king had given the use of common lands, a measure of self-rule in the burgh laws with the right to hold a weekly market and an annual Fair. The importance of this monopoly market can be illustrated by the example in the reign of William the Lion, 1165–1214. The inhabitants of the Abbot's village of Kelso were allowed to buy fuel and corn from those carting it, and sell food from their booths; however this concession was cancelled on Roxburgh Fair days when the king's burgesses took precedent over all others. A similar situation occurred in Selkirkshire when the royal burgh of Selkirk had a market or Fair day, only Selkirk burgesses were allow to sell or buy. Indwellers without the freedom of the burgh and out-dwellers had to pay for the privilege. This income boost went into burgh funds, with a cut sent to the royal exchequer.

The 'burgh of barony' was rather like the royal burgh, with the crown giving the landowner the right to erect a burgh on his own

barony, but he had to pay for the privilege. For the landowner, the establishment of a burgh increased his prestige and boosted his income from
increasingly valuable market and ground rentals, as more people came
to live within the new burgh. For the crown, the creation of burghs of
barony, with additional trade and increasing wealth, also meant a boost
to the tax revenues due to the exchequer. No losers – with the possible
exception of existing royal burghs who saw competition from these
modern upstarts.

Sir James Pringle was granted a charter making Galashiels a burgh
of barony on 17 December 1599, conferring the usual privileges of
holding a baron's court under the baron's baillie (a court of law under
the jurisdiction of his officer, the baillie), holding a weekly market on a
Wednesday and a yearly Fair on St Peter's Day, called Midsummer Day.
A further charter under the Great Seal ratified the grant on 2 October
1617 but this time with two Fairs, on 24 June and 29 September, added.

In the Great Seal charter, the lands of Sir James Pringle are
enumerated: Nether and Easter Mains of Galashiels, Bolesyde,
Galashiels, Mossilee, together with the corn and waulk mills and salmon
and other fishings upon the Tweed, both sides of the water betwixt the
bridge of Melrose and the lands of Sunderland where Ettrick runs into
the Tweed; and also all the lands of Craigleich (Newhall) with the
pendicle called Knows in Ettrick Forest; the lands of Pilmuir and
Blackchester with the pendicles called Moorhouse, Harkerland, Little
Laurence Land and Scotscroft in Lauderdale; the lands of Halcroft and
the dominical lands of Smailholm in Roxburghshire and the gift of the
patronage of the vicar of the Kirk of Lindean; all lands to be erected
into a barony to be called the Barony of Galashiels.

With such wide lands and the commercial advantages of having a
burgh of barony on his lands, it might be thought that Sir James would
have no financial difficulties, but this was not so. Being in favour at the
court meant increased expenditure and he was spending beyond his
income to impress others. He had to have a residence commensurate
with his position, so he built on a large addition to his father's 1583
tower. This was 70ft by 25ft and was three floors high, with each floor
subdivided into three rooms.

Inserted over the fireplace in one of the lower rooms was a large
fireplace-lintel measuring 9ft 5in in length by 1ft 8in high. In this are

two panels, one has a shield with five shells on a saltire and the initials, I P for James Pringle, and the other, a shield which has three mullets on a chevron and a pelican feeding her young, with the initials I K for Jean Kerr of Linton. There is a date of 1611 in a sunk panel, and the initials AP and MB at the junction of the panels which represent the parents of Sir James.

That lintel stone has a story of its own. When the Scotts of Gala moved from Old Gala House to a Victorian ' new-build' mansion in the early 1880s, the builder took the carved stone from Old Gala House for placement in the new house. Probably because of its size and weight, it was placed 'in the back room of the keeper's house in the policies'.

However, the Victorian New Gala House succumbed to dry rot and woodworm, and was knocked down a hundred years after its construction. Fortunately the lintel was saved, but for a while nobody knew where it was but during the refurbishment of Old Gala House in 1988 by the then Ettrick and Lauderdale District Council, it was found under some tractor parts at Hollybush Farm. With a great deal of difficulty, it was pushed, pulled and sweated up the stairs at Old Gala House and installed in the Painted Ceiling Room there.

The rooms of the new building were entered by means of a large square stair-tower on the south-west centre. Adding to his own profligate extravagances, he had four sons and four daughters who had to be maintained and set up/dowered to their own high expectations. Soon Sir James was taking bonds on property for the heavy sums mentioned frequently in court records. Of the fifty years of possession of the properties, the last twenty years of his life were spent in poverty with his lands so burdened with debt that he had to sell most of it.

Nor was he was greatly helped by his family connections, with assorted Pringles being called up before the Privy Council for discharging pistolets at each other and robbing each others' tenants etc. The reivers were still active throughout the Borders and as head of the Pringle family and with friends at Court, Sir James was expected to smooth out any trouble in which they were involved.

Perhaps the strangest court case was an implication against his wife. This was heard during the trial of Agnes Sampson, a wise woman of Keith, for conspiring to cause the king's death by witchcraft, sorcery etc in 1590.

The thirty-ninth charge is: '*That sche* [Agnes Sampson] *haiffing done pleasour to the gudewyfe of Gallowscheles for the quhilk she did not satisfe her sa sone als the said Agnes desyret, thairfore sche said to the said gudewyfe that 'sche sould repent it' and within a few houris thairafter the said gudwyfe tuik ane wodnes* [madness] *and her toung schot out of her heid and swalled like ane pot; quairfore sche sent to her the thing sche desyret and peyit her to come to her and sche baid the serviand "Ga away hame for the gudewyfe was weill"'.*

With another fifty-two charges against her, Agnes was convicted and sentenced to death. It is not recorded if the Gudewyfe suffered further from witches or witch-finders.

Before his death in 1635, Sir James Pringle, the last of the Pringles of Galashiels, conveyed the lands and barony of Galashiels to James Scott, the son of Hugh Scott of Deuchar, and Jean Pringle, his eldest daughter. This was ratified in 1633 under the Great Seal. Included in the properties conferred was '*Togider with the advocatione, donatione and richt of patronage of the vicarage of the Kirk of the Lyndane*'.

The Kirk of Lindean / Boleside / Galashiels

'Lindean is almost certainly the site of the abbey of Selkirk founded by Earl David about 1119 and transferred to Kelso before 1128'. *Inventory of Selkirkshire* No. 3.

This site served as a church for the inhabitants of the local communities within Selkirkshire Abbey lands for four and a half centuries until the Reformation, when this parish included the small but growing village of Galashiels.

In 1591 it was reported to the Privy Council by the minister, deacons and elders of Lindean that the Kirk there 'was decayed and falling down and that by common consent was very incommodious: that the River Tweed separated the kirk from the most populous part of the parish and that the kirk should be transported from where it stands and a new Kirk be built at the west end of the toun of Boldsyde. The new Kirk to be forty feet long and the walls sixteen feet high: that this should retain the name the Kirk of Lindean and keep the benefits of the vicarage, glebe and lands of the old kirk. The burial place should remain at the site of the old Kirk, which would have a dyke built round it, and the parish should provide a coble to bring the dead over to the burial ground.'

There was no opposition to the plan even from William Kerr, Vicar of Lindean and the plan was 'endit, perfyted and accomplished'. The Kirk of Boldsyde was to prove of short duration. Thanks in part to the establishment as a burgh of barony, Galashiels was increasing in population and prestige, and it made sense that worship was centred within the town. In 1617, a new Parish Kirk was built at the east end of the burgh. This was eventually demolished in 1813 by which time Galashiels had outgrown its name as 'the cottages on the Gala Water' and was a thriving community, using the fast-flowing Gala Water to become a major textile town.

The known history of Galashiels in the sixteenth century is poorly known when compared with that of Selkirk. As county town and royal burgh, Selkirk was a privileged community, with surviving written records from the early sixteenth century. Galashiels did not have such a detailed history, but by 1600 it would probably have the same number of people living in it as Selkirk. Unfortunately, we have no way of knowing this, but later events in Selkirk suggest that the people of that royal burgh were becoming somewhat restive at the rapid development of Galashiels.

As a burgh of barony, Galashiels required the essential symbols of burgh authority: a town cross from which to read royal and baronial proclamations; and a tolbooth which could serve as council chamber, a collection place for paying market dues and a prison when needed. Fair regulations banned 'all Egyptians, randy-beggars and cutters of purses from being present and no one could be molested for old debt or new debt, old feud or new feud'.

In collecting information from sources as different as the Protocol Books and spare documents in the Walter Mason papers, the Criminal Trial Records and the Great Seal, I found some which do not fit comfortably anywhere else, so I note them as individual items.

19 February 1526. William Wilsone in Galoschelis took some ewes from a house near the market place in Selkirk.

6 December 1529. Mention of an oratory or chapel of Galloshellis but
the Parish Church was at Lyndene (Lindean). The oratory chapel is
likely to have been a small room in the Dishington building of 1460.

5 April 1532. A deed handing over lands 'Done at the hall of
Galloschelles'.

17 June 1535. The Baillies of Selkirk warn non-burgesses and indwellers
without the freedom of the burgh that they are not to sell goods
within the burgh *especially warning the indwellers of the town of
Galloschellis*. Even as early as this, the growing population of
Galashiels was beginning to be a threat to the monopoly trading
rights of the Selkirk burgesses.

During the Rough Wooing, while the English forces were devastating
the Borders, the Regent Arran was using Galashiels as a gathering point,
sending heralds to summon the neighbouring lairds to meet him there
in all possible haste. Enough gathered to win the Battle of Ancrum
Moor which was fought on 17 February 1545

1561. Waulk Mill in Galashiels. John Scott in Deloraine complains that
he gave cloth to John Haldane in Gallowshiels to be waulkit but
received a different cloth back. To waulk is to full, or make cloth
thick and felted by a process of soaking, beating and shrinking. This
must have produced a superior type of cloth because the reivers of
Liddesdale would steal it in preference to any other.

> *Thair is ane callet Clement's Hob,*
> *Fra ilk puir wife reiffes the wob.*

If John Scott took the trouble to send his cloth from Deloraine in the
Ettrick Valley, sixteen miles from Galashiels, the process must have been
special.

In a 1582 document in the Walter Mason Trust collection there is
the mention of thirteen mills in the lower Gala Water, three of these
being waulk mills. This presumes a concentration of people in the area,
and that weaving was an important business in the area. It would be
around three hundred years later before water power was used to drive
textile looms in the town.

CHAPTER EIGHTEEN
Mayhem to Murder, 1568–1603

In the last part of the sixteenth century the Borders took a pace back from the mainstream politics of Scotland and England. For the first time in generations, there were no English armies marching through the area with a view to total conquest, and no major Scottish retribution raids into the north of England. As far as both countries were concerned, the lands and people on both sides of the Border were something that they would have preferred to ignore – as long as everybody else did the same.

This did not make for a peaceful Borders.

In England, Elizabeth was deemed illegitimate by half of her lieges, and Mary, Queen of Scots the rightful Queen of England. But Mary, being Scots by blood and French by upbringing, as well as being formerly queen of France, was a Catholic. This did not suit the other half of the English population who were Protestant by religion and in possession of the former Catholic Church lands.

In international relations, Elizabeth was skating on thin ice, seeking to support the Protestants in the Low Countries and Normandy while not offending the Catholic kings of Spain and France or the ever-lowering Pope in Rome. Ireland was permanently in revolt in one part or another.

Her problems were increased when Mary, Queen of Scots, sought refuge in England after fleeing from her own Protestant lords in 1568. First a guest and then a prisoner, Mary was to prove a disrupting influence in English affairs. A beautiful, serial plotter, she was the perfect 'Princess in the Tower' as a focal point for revolting subjects. After many years' resistance, Elizabeth had her rival executed in 1587 and blamed her secretary Davidson for the 'error'. It is a wonder that it took her so long.

Relations between Elizabeth and Philip of Spain broke down when she sent aid to the Dutch Protestant rebels in Spanish Netherlands in 1585. In 1588 Philip sent an Armada to bring England back into the Catholic Church, to prevent English help from reaching the Dutch and to stop English privateers' attacks on Spanish shipping in the West Indies. Although it was principally severe storms off the west coast of Scotland that defeated the Armada, the defeat of a large naval force brought England international repute.

Elizabeth's policy on the Borders was to maintain a large number of 'information-gatherers', paying good money to any Scottish Borderers who would pursue their own feuds against fellow Scots. Fighting like with like, she employed the most able English ruffians as Wardens of the Marches to keep her own Borderers in check.

She also paid a renumeration to James VI of Scotland, and sent frequent letters of advice on his conduct and the behaviour of his Borderers. In her later years, Elizabeth was hinting that James would be her successor to the English throne, so he kept a calm sough, received and usually ignored her advice; and waited.

In the Scotland of the 1560s the divisions were largely religious, the Reformers against the supporters of the Old Religion. Traditionally, innovation appears and spreads through the more fertile/heavily populated low lands while the higher land retains its own language, customs and usages far longer. So is it with religion, with the Reformers dominating the towns of central Scotland, Ayrshire and the east coast while the Highlands and most of the Borders remained Roman Catholic. Mary's flight into England in 1568 did not end the civil war in Scotland, which dragged on until the mid 1570s.

The Regent Morton had been active in keeping the Borders under control for nearly a decade, and the Privy Council of Scotland noted that what harm or inconvenience there was, was due to ignorance of the laws and the 'lovable' customs thereof.

The English solution to secure a peaceable Border was to systematically waste the Scottish side of the March. This happened in 1570 when a large-scale English invasion under the Earl of Sussex prevented any raiding by the Scots. A later solution put forward to the English Crown, was to build a large wall across northern England from sea to sea to keep the Scots and Catholics out. The frugal Elizabeth did not consider this an option.

Thanks to the efforts of Morton and Sussex, the 1570s were relatively trouble-free except on the Borders where violence could break out at any slight offence given or taken and family feuds continued without much external interference.

In July 1586 Elizabeth's chief minister, William Cecil, personally negotiated the terms for an Anglo-Scottish Treaty, signed at Berwick. Although nothing was put on paper, there was a tacit understanding that James was next in line for the English throne and he was given an English renumeration, for which he frequently had to ask. For the two countries to sign a permanent alliance for offence and defence was not unusual but this time it held.

Despite the execution of Mary, Queen of Scots in 1587, James had his eye firmly on the main chance. He had never known his mother, and disliked violence. So the future prospect of the English throne, together with a present pension, weighed heavier than a war on a principle, a war which he could not win anyway. So he waited – and took action against the Borderers who could quite easily upset the balance of peace with ill-considered raiding or killing.

On the Borderline

Despite the fact that the two countries were at peace and had pacified their own Borders as far as they could, their plans were not very successful and this was to prove the most turbulent period of Borders history. There was a certain amount of cynicism as both governments deplored the bloody unrest, but were equally prepared to use the restless Borderers for their own ends. Each side of the border line held a large mobile force of fighting men who could be called into service if war broke out, or even if it didn't. Encouraging the Borderers by bribery or coercion to continue with their bloody feuds produced a comforting buffer zone between the old enemies.

But this buffer zone was further split by geology, early settlement and language. The East and Middle Marches of both countries were on rivers which drained to the North Sea. These were the lands of Bernicia or Northumbria in Dark Age times and their inhabitants spoke Anglian or Early English. The West Marches of both were in what was formerly an Early-Welsh-speaking Strathclyde whose lands drained into the

Solway. So even within each country, there were divisions.

To formalise the divisions in 1248, six knights from England and six from Scotland met to draw up the laws 'according to the ancient and approved custom of the March such matters as required to be redressed'. The following year a meeting of twelve knights from each side produced the first written Border Laws that were intended to cover cross-Border crimes. For the next three centuries, these were amended, changed and altered to make a vague and complicated series of March Laws, which could be open to wide interpretation.

To make them workable, the border line was divided into three with a Warden in each. The six Wardens, three from each nation, with an additional Keeper appointed for Liddesdale, were in nominal charge of their respective areas, charged to keep the peace, defend the lieges, and capture, hang, drown or kill by any means, those who broke the laws.

As defenders of their respective national boundaries, the Wardens had to co-operate with their opposite numbers. To do this, 'Days of Truce' were arranged at several places along the Border, where complaints were heard and villains charged for trans-Border offences. Violence, and the settling of old or new scores, was forbidden on truce days, but with large gatherings of mutually hostile Borderers on hand the Leges Marchiarum (an eighteenth-century title) were occasionally broken and when this happened the Peace Treaty of 1586 was sorely tested.

The one problem that made the duties of the Wardens particularly difficult was that the Scottish and English Borderers were of the same race, and when they were not actually at feud, killing or robbing each other, they got on very well together. This had not been taken into account by the lawmakers in Edinburgh and London. Even at the present time, and in most cases, a Borderer is a Borderer first and Scottish or English second.

So Borderers from both sides could meet on an international level at race meetings, football matches, Fairs, feasts and inns. That they often planned murder and mayhem against mutual enemies was quite probable, and nationality did not come into the equation. That was accepted as their way of life and often death.

The result of this social intercourse was intermarriage, which both governments tried to prevent by passing laws forbidding their subjects to marry across the Border unless by special licence. As with most laws handed down by government decree, this was consistently ignored. Intermarriage made for some peculiar decisions as far as loyalty was concerned. Was it loyalty to family name or family relations, despite the name, or to the Warden of the March, or to king, law or country, with the last coming a long way behind.

The records of the Privy Council and Pitcairn's *Criminal Trials in Scotland 1488–1624* (published 1833) are full of the deeds and misdeeds of the people of the Borders. I 'waled with judicious care' to find two reports to represent the sixteenth-century Borders: one is a little known family feud and the other a well-known ballad/exploit which could have changed the history of Britain.

December 1568: The Sack of Torwoodlie

Although far from the hot-bed of evil which was Liddesdale, the lower Gala and Caddon Waters had their own homegrown ruffians, of whom George Hoppringle of Torwoodlie was by no means the worst. In 1534 he helped to burn the church in Selkirk; he brought in and consorted with Englishmen in 1547, the same year as he fought against them at the Battle of Pinkie; he was absent from the king's army at Gladsmuir in 1548 and was part of the Kerrs' slaughter of Sir Walter Scott of Branxholme on the High Street in Edinburgh in 1552. These are his recorded crimes but there would be many more. In 1564 the Privy Council directed 'the Guidman of Torwodlie' to return to serving the Wardens against the thieves of Liddesdale but the Border lairds '*abstracted their presence, making no service but in a lightly manner*'. George Hoppringle did not live to regret his decision.

In pursuance of an old feud, the Elliots, with a little help from their friends, descended on Torwoodlie in 1568. Pitcairn's *Criminal Trials* describes the '*detestabill enormities daalie comittit be thame upon peciabill subjectis*' scene although I have rendered it into English.

'*For as much as the said John Ellote of Copschaw, Robert Ellote, called Martin's Hob and John Airmstrange called the Laird's Jock, with their accomplices from the clans of Airmstranges, Ellotes, Batiesons, Grahames and remnant clans dwelling on the English and Scottish Borders, all common thieves, outlaws and broken men to the number of three hundred or thereby, armed for war with jacks, spears, steel-bonnets, lancestaffs and pistolets expressly forbidden to be borne, worn, used or shot with by diverse Acts of Parliament and Secret Council, in the month of December 1568, came forward in hostile manner on horse and foot, to the place of Torwoodlie and there, under silence and cloud of night with fore-hammers and beams knocked down the doors of the said place and by force and violence entered the same; and took the late George Hoppringle from his bed and led him away as captive and prisoner with them to Scaddoness in Yarrow within the Sherrifdom of Selkirk and most cruelly and unmercifully murdered and slew the late George; committing not only cruel and abominable murder and slaughter but also the usurption of our sovereign Lord's authority upon them in taking the said late George captive without power or commission, he being our sovereign Lord's free liege. And at the same time, John Ellote and his accomplices broke chests, coffers and locked doors within the said place and thefteously stole, concealed, reset and took away from the said place of Torwoodlie and stables seventeen horses worth over £100 each which belonged to the said late George; £1000 in gold from his purse; 3 silver pieces weighing 80 ounces each; two dozen silver spoons weighing 2 ounces each; together with the whole bedding, table linen, clothing, arms, contents and furnishings within the place, worth the sum of 5,000 merks and had transported them away with them and disposed of it at their pleasure'.*

On the way home with their booty, the reivers were 'set upon by certain of the country', at Scaddoness in the Yarrow Valley, but beat them off and captured eighty of the rescuers to eventually be ransomed – Elliot Reivers Inc did well out of that raid.

Unfortunately, George Hoppringle was killed during the melee.

Two years later in 1570 the Elliots and Hoppringles were summoned to the Law Court in Edinburgh, to resolve their differences but they met on the High Street and had the people of the town not 'redd them, there would have been great slaughter'. No further attempt was made to settle the feud, until in 1607, John Ellote of Copshaw was called to trial. He wisely did not appear and was denounced rebel with his moveable goods forfeited for the slaughter of George Hoppringle. William Ellote of Falnash had gone surety for his appearance and was fined 500 merks. It is more than probable that John slipped William the money for his hip pocket. After thirty-nine years, it was a good bargain, although John seems to have come to a sticky and anonymous end later.

Kinmont Willie

Willie Armstrong of Morton Rigg on the Border, more commonly known as Kinmont Willie, was a reiver in the semi-infamous ranks, who would have gone almost un-noticed in history except for a few mentions in Pitcairn's *Criminal Trials*, none of which were in his favour. By dint of getting illegally captured on a truce day, and equally illegally rescued, he became famed in song and story. That the ballad is only founded on fact and is a piece of Scottish propaganda, does not prevent it from being a 'ripping good yarn'.

In 1596 a truce day was arranged at Kershopfoot near the Border between Thomas Salkeld, the deputy Warden of the English West March and Scott of Haining, the deputy Keeper of Liddesdale. This was held on 17 March and among the attenders was Kinmont Willie, who was safe from molestation on a truce day.

The day passed without incident, but on his way home Willie was pursued and captured by a number of English riders, who had given in to the temptation to settle old scores and had crossed the frontier line to make the arrest. There is no doubt that the arrest was fully justified for past crimes, even although it broke the Border Laws, but, as in most Border history, there are two accounts of the episode.

Willie was taken to Carlisle Castle to be hanged (Scots version) or placed on parole before being ransomed (more likely). Lord Scrope, the Warden of the March, returned home to find an embarrassing situation that could have been rectified by giving Kinmont Willie an apology, a good feast and a fresh horse to get him home. However, Lord Scrope seems to have enjoyed the situation of having an old opponent where he could see him, so Willie was kept in Carlisle for a few more days. The excuse was that Willie was being detained until he gave security for better behaviour and recompense for damages lately done on the English Border.

Meanwhile the Keeper of Liddesdale, Sir Walter Scott of Buccleuch, showing an unusual restraint, was writing to Scrope, Salkeld and eventually to Sir Robert Bowes, the English ambassador at James VI's court. Letters passed back and forward going further up the political ladder each time. Bowes wrote to Scrope insisting that Kinmont Willie be released before things got out of hand; but by now personal pride and 'face' was involved, with the situation not helped by personal animosity between Scrope and Buccleuch.

Buccleuch had taken the imprisonment as a personal insult and an affront to his status as a lawkeeper on the Scottish side of the Border, ignoring the fact that he was perhaps the greatest lawbreaker on the Marches. He set about gathering a commando force to release Kinmont from durance vile.

Using a Saturday at Langhom Races as cover, he met with Auld Wat o Harden, Gilbert Eliott of Stobs and the infamous Carleton brothers, Thomas and Lance, who were English West March officers, to plan the assault. It is here that the complexity of cross-Border marriages shows to best effect. Thomas Carleton had been Scrope's deputy and Constable of Carlisle Castle but, through the Grahams, was closely related by marriage to Kinmont Willie Armstrong.

So far, the ballad remains reasonably true to the known facts but departs from reality when the raiding party is given as forty Scotts and one Elliot. They went with ladders, crowbars and forehammers to break into the Castle and retrieve Kinmont Willie, and trumpets to warn people to avoid them while they did so.

Buccleuch was to note later that only eight Scotts were in the raiders, including Auld Wat o Harden, and the rest were Armstrongs including Kinmont's four sons, Grahams from both sides of the Border, Elliots, Irvines, Bells and several English Borderers who joined through family loyalties or hatred for the Wardens.

In Buccleuch's account, eighty men rode to Carlisle but he had taken the precaution of arranging two ambushes to cover their retreat if required. It added to the cosmopolitan force that one of these consisted of Irvines and the other of Johnstones.

It is difficult to know what happened next. The ballad version gives Buccleuch first up the ladders and silencing the only watchman. Then, contrary to all notions of nightime operations:

> "Now sound out, trumpets!" quo Bucceluch;
> "Let's waken Lord Scrope right merrily!"
> Then loud the warden's trumpet blew –
> O wha dare meddle wi me?

The assailants then set about with crowbars and hammers and 'garr'd the bars bang merrilie' until they came to the inner prison and then the lower prison. There, Kinmont was hoisted on to the shoulders of Red Rowan, the strongest man in Teviotdale. On horse, the raiders crossed the Eden Water although it was running full, bank to bank, but the pursuing Lord Scrope and his thousand followers refused to follow.

It makes a good story but one which doesn't quite fit in with reported facts.

The original account of the raid was found in Archbishop Spottiswoode's papers. Spottiswoode lived from 1565 to 1639, so that account is likely to be first or second-hand knowledge. When Sir Walter Scott published the ballad version, he notes that it was 'preserved by tradition on the West Borders, but much mangled by reciters; so that some conjectural emendations have been absolutely necessary to render it intelligible'. Sir Walter had a strong family pride and I would suspect that the forty Scotts and one related Elliot could have been one of the emendations.

When the ladders were found to be too short, the postern wall 'had to be opened a little' which could not have been done quietly. The idea that eighty Scots could get into the castle and start banging away merrily while Lord Scrope, Thomas Salkeld and the garrison did nothing, is less than believable.

Kinmont Willie is likely to have known that a rescue bid was to be made when one of the Grahams delivered Buccleuch's ring and a message to him. Scrope maintained that Kinmont had given his parole and was in a house within the castle ground; this is consistent with Border custom of the time and as a parolee, he would not have either been chained or kept in a dungeon.

The most likely senario is that Kinmont Willie, free within the castle precincts, was visited by his wife who was Andrew Graham's sister and knew about the rescue attempt. Obviously Buccleuch had inside knowledge and accomplices. A quick strike and withdrawal was planned for and accomplished. If the Warden's trumpet blew at all, it was to signal for a speedy retreat and, despite the ballad, there was no pursuit. It is not beyond the realms of possibility that Lord Scrope and Salkeld had knowledge of the attempt, staying out of the way in order to clear up an embarrassing situation.

Whatever the truth, the story echoed round the Borders and Lord Scrope was called to explain. He blamed everyone but himself – Buccleuch, the Carletons, the Grahams and even the bad sportsmanship of Kinmont himself, who gave his parole and the assurance that he would not try to escape, and then went back on his word.

Elizabeth was livid at this lese-majestie, demanding Buccleuch's head as castle-breaking scoundrel and a popish plotter: or at least that he submit himself to her justice. Sharp letters were exchanged between the monarchs and government, and Elizabeth threatened to have James's pension stopped.

Meanwhile James, who was probably chorkling quietly away to himself, did not hesitate to use the fearsome reputation of the Borderers when it suited him. On 17 December 1596, certain ministers of the Kirk incited a riot on behalf of the independence of the Kirk, insulted the king and made him leave Edinburgh for his own safety. On his return, he let it be known that, in addition to his own bodyguard, he was accompanied by a large number of Borderers. A contemporary writer records that 'There was ane grate rumour and word among the tounes-men, that the King's Majesty sould send in Will Kinmonde, the common thieffe and so many southland men as sould spulyie the toun of Edinburgh.' This quickly quelled the riot as the rioters scuttled to the safety of their own homes. Buccleuch was believed to be in command of the Borderers on this occasion.

Following the Kinmont Willie rescue, raiding across the Border increased with Scrope taking revenge for his loss of face on the Scottish West March, while Buccleuch and Kerr of Cessford pulverised Tynedale.

Both kingdoms were still divided on religious lines with potential or actual Roman Catholic rebellions against the Protestant rulers. The ageing Elizabeth and the aspiring James both recognised this and decided that co-operation was the only choice on the table, yet neither could afford to be seen to be selling out their own subjects.

Thanks to Buccleuch's raid on Carlisle and his later descent on Tynedale, there was a strong probability of war breaking out between the nations. On weighing up the options, everybody came to their senses and, in the autumn of 1597, Buccleuch handed himself over to England where he charmed his captors. He was returned to Scotland in

February 1598, while his son took his place as a hostage. Buccleuch then spent a year in France to allow things to cool down, before coming back to Scotland.

On his return, he was a different man; the reckless Borderer had become more of a diplomat, with the realisation that the pen was indeed mightier than the sword, as well as less dangerous and much more lucrative.

As Keeper of Liddesdale, he set about discharging his duties with great diligence. James VI gave him a wide remit in a letter of indemnity approved by the Lords of the Privy Council '*There occurred to our memory our most dear cousin, Walter Scott of Buccleuch, a man of energy, prompt in council and action, powerful in fortune, force arms and following, to whom we found and esteemed that enterprise worthy to be intrusted on account of his by past, famous and honourable services done to us and the Commonwealth, and on account of his great fidelity in times by past in executing with honour and dignity the affairs which we entrusted to him, and that to the great help and welfare of all loyal and dutiful subjects.*'

At this time, most of the inhabitants of Liddesdale had been justifiably 'put to the horn' ie outlawed, for many misdemeanours. This meant that they would be killed or dispossessed without any recourse to law, and their land could be claimed by the killer. So it was no surprise that Buccleuch had to resort to severe measures to accomplish his purpose: '*In consequence of the lack of prisons and to prevent the importunate intercession of certain good persons, the most part of these desperate men were hanged immediately on their apprehension; dispensing with the ordinary forms of justice, as they are well known; and even boasted of their crimes.*'

The proceedings against the Scottish Borderers took several years of intensified bloodshed, during which many were put to death by hanging, drowning or by the sword and spear, before any semblance of law and order could be discerned.

By 1603, Sir Walter Scott of Buccleuch was well established as the Keeper of Liddesdale, most of which he kept for himself, and much of which is still in possession of the Buccleuch Estates.

On the English side of the Border, the same rules were applied and each parish had to keep a sleuth-hound to track malefactors through the mosses. Many Scottish and English Borderers were banished to Ireland, where they caused trouble by dispossessing the native Irish and extending the religious wars of their homelands to that troubled province.

Although both nations had attempted to control border raiding, their methods could only be partly effective as long as the nations were separate. The frontier was used as a convenient bolthole for the fleeing villains of both countries. That started to close when Sir Robert Carey stumbled into James VI's bedroom in the late evening of 26 March 1603, to hail him as James I of England.

Sir Robert Carey was Warden of the English Middle March, a doughty fighter, a skilled planner and an opportunist with an eye on the main chance. In the winter of 1603 he was attending court in London. Knowing that he might need a rapid return to Scotland, he had arranged a relay of good horses to be posted at regular intervals along the road from London to Edinburgh. Carey knew that it would stand in his favour if he were the first to tell James the news that he had been waiting for all his adult life.

At the English court, Elizabeth, now seventy years old, was ill – 'No Robin, I am not well' according to Carey's memoir of the meeting. She died in the early morning of 24 March. On the Queen's death, Carey's sister, Philadelphia, who was one of the ladies in waiting, cut the coronation ring from her finger. She rushed down to where her brother was waiting, already mounted, with the token that would prove the reliability of Carey's news when he got to Scotland. He reached Doncaster on the first night and Northumberland on the second. He expected to be in Edinburgh before darkness on the third day, but his horse threw him near Norham and kicked him on the head as it scrambled to its feet. So it was late evening of the third day before he arrived at Holyrood Palace with the news. It had taken him sixty hours to ride the four hundred miles between the capitals.

Carey's memoir records that he said: 'I had brought him a blue ring by a fair lady'. James took it and replied 'It is enough; I know by this you are a true messenger.'

Despite all the trouble that he had taken to be first with the news, Carey was severely reprimanded when the official news was brought by the English authorities two days later.

On 6 April 1603 the new king of Scotland and England was at Berwick, being acclaimed by the cheering populace, the discharging of guns, a sermon from the Bishop of Durham and a purse of £2,000 from the English authorities.

There he pointed out that the Borders were now the centre of the combined countries, and should be called the Middle Shires of the realm, North and South Britain, but the Borderers were to have one last fling before this idea became reality.

Bibliography

My greatest source of information is from the ground of the Borders, which is an education in itself, but it is almost impossible to list the number of books and individual papers I have read, without doubling the size of 'Selkirkshire, Part One'.

The following is a list of the main books I have used, quoted from and queried; these would be of interest to those who wish to make a further study of the multi-cultured Borders.

Bain J. *Calendar of Documents of Scotland*, 1881
Bain J. (Ed.) *The Hamilton Papers,* 1890
Barrow, G.W. *The Kingdom of the Scots*, 1973
    Kingship and Unity. Scotland 1000–1306, 1981
Bede, *Ecclesiastical History of the English People*, Penguin 1955
Breeze, D. The *Northern Frontiers of Roman Britain*, 1982
Byers, J. *Liddesdale*, 1952
Carver, Martin, *Portmahomack*, 2008
Cowie, T. (Ed.) *The Manor Valley*, 2000
Curle, J. A. *Roman Frontier Post and its People,* 1911
Davies, N. *The Isles,* 1999
Dickson, C. & Dickson, J. *Plants and People in Ancient Scotland*, 2000
Dixon, P. Puir *Labourers and Busy Husbandmen*, nd
Duncan, A.A.M. *Scotland – The Making of a Kingdom,* 1975
Elliot, G.F.S. *The Border Elliots*,1897
Exchequer Rolls of Scotland, The, 1895
Fraser, G.M. *The Steel Bonnets*, 1971
Frere, S. *Brittania, A History of Roman Britain*, 1987
Gilbert, John N. (Ed.) *The Flower of the Forest*, 1985
    Hunting and Hunting Reserves in Medieval Scotland, 1979

Haldane, A.R.B. *The Drove Roads of Scotland*, 1960

Hall, R. *The History of Galashiels*, 1898

Hanson, W.S. *Agricola*, 1987

Harding, D.W. *The Iron Age in Northern Britain*, 2004

Henig, Martin, *A Corpus of Roman Gemstones from British Sites*, 1978
    Religion in Roman Britain, 1984

Higham, N.J. *The Kingdom of Northumbria*, AD 350–1100, 1993

Holmes, N. *Scottish Coins*, 1998

Hunter, F. *Beyond the edge of the empire – Caledonians, Picts and Romans*,
    2007

Imrie, J. (Ed.) *The Burgh Court Book of Selkirk*, 1960 and 1969

Jamieson, J. *The Scottish Dictionary*, 1808

Jones, Jean, *James Hutton in The Scottish Enlightenment*, 1986

Keppie, L. *Scotland's Roman Remains*, 1986

Liber S. Marie de Dryburgh, *The Bannatyne Club*, 1847

Liber S. Marie de Melros, *The Bannatyne Club*, 1837

Liber S. Marie de Calchou, *The Bannatyne Club*, 1846

Lynch, Michael, *Scotland – A New History*, 1991

McNeill, P & Nicholson, R. *An Historical Atlas of Scotland c.400–c.1600*,
    1975

Maley, T. & Elliot, W. *Selkirk Protocol Books*, 1993
    Protocol Book of Robert Wedderop, 1993
    Protocol Book of Sir Ninian Brydin, 1995

Mason, W.D. *The Selkirk Burgh Court Book, 1557–1575*

Masson, D. (Ed.) *Register of the Privy Council of Scotland*, 1884

Maxwell, G.S. *The Romans in Scotland*, 1989

Miket, R. & Burgess, C. *Between and Beyond the Walls*, 1984

Moffat, A. *Arthur and the Lost Kingdoms*, 1999
    The Borders, 2002
    Before Scotland, 2005

Morris, J. *The Age of Arthur*, 1973

Nicolaisen, W.F.H. *Scottish Place-names*, 1976

Omand, Donald (Ed.) *The Borders Book*, 1995

Oram, Richard, *David, I: The King who made Scotland*, 2004

Playfair, J. *Biographical Account of the late Dr James Hutton*, 1970

Pitcairn, R. *Criminal Trials in Scotland, 1488–1624*, 1833

Proceedings of the Society of Antiquaries of Scotland. (Many)

Rackham, Oliver, *The Illustrated History of the Countryside*, 1994

Raine, J. *The Inventory of the Priory of Coldingham* [in] *1374*, 1841

RCAHMS, *Peeblesshire*, 1967

RCAHMS, *Roxburghshire*, 1956

RCAHMS, *Selkirkshire*, 1957

Roy, W. *The Military Antiquities of the Romans in Britain*, 1793

Russel, James, *Reminiscences of Yarrow*, 1894

Sadler, J. *Border Fury*, 2006

Scott, W. *The Minstrelsy of the Scottish Border*, 1802

Smout, T.C. (Ed.) *People and Woods in Scotland*, 2003
    A History of the Scottish People, 1970

Stewart, B.H.I.H. *The Scottish Coinage*, 1967

Symms, Dr Peter, unpublished PhD thesis

Thomas, C. *Christianity In Roman Britain To* AD *500*, 1981

Waddington, C. & Passmore, D. *Ancient Northumberland*, 2004

Watson, W.J. *The Celtic Placenames of Scotland*, 1993

Watson, Fiona, *Under The Hammer*, 1998

Whyte, I. D. *Scotland Before The Industrial Revolution*, 1995

Wickham-Jones, C.R. *Scotland's First Settlers*, 1994

Winterbottom, M. *Gildas, The Ruin of Britain*, 1978

Wooliscroft, D.J. & Hoffman, B. *Rome's First Frontier: The Flavian Occupation of Northern Scotland*, 2006

Yeoman, Peter, *Medieval Scotland*, 1995

Index

Mountbenger

Dryhope

Cappercleuch

Megget Water

St Mary's Loch

Crosslee

Tushielaw

Little Yarrow

Ettrick Water

Glenkerry

North